The American Occupation of the Philippines 1898-1912

Preface

> Pardon, gentles all,
> The flat unraised spirit that hath dared
> On this unworthy scaffold to bring forth
> So great an object.
>
> *Henry V.*

To have gone out to the other side of the world with an army of invasion, and had a part, however small, in the subjugation of a strange people, and then to see a new government set up, and, as an official of that government, watch it work out through a number of years, is an unusual and interesting experience, especially to a lawyer. What seem to me the most valuable things I learned in the course of that experience are herein submitted to my fellow-countrymen, in connection with a narrative covering the whole of the American occupation of the Philippines to date.

This book is an attempt, by one whose intimate acquaintance with two remotely separated peoples will be denied in no quarter, to interpret each to the other. How intelligent that acquaintance is, is of course altogether another matter, which the reader will determine for himself.

The task here undertaken is to make audible to a great free nation the voice of a weaker subject people who passionately and rightly long to be also free, but whose longings have been systematically denied for the last fourteen years, sometimes ignorantly, sometimes viciously, and always cruelly, on the wholly erroneous idea that where the *end* is benevolent, it justifies the *means*, regardless of the means necessary to the end.

At a time when all our military and fiscal experts agree that having the Philippines on our hands is a grave strategic and economic mistake, fraught with peril to the nation's prestige in the early stages of our next great war, we are keeping the Filipinos in industrial bondage through unrighteous Congressional legislation for which special interests in America are responsible, in bald repudiation of the Open Door policy, and against their helpless but universal protest, a wholly unprotected and easy prey to the first first-class Power with which we become involved in war. Yet all the while the very highest considerations of national honor require us to choose between making the Filipino people free and independent without unnecessary delay, as they of right ought to be, or else imperilling the perpetuity of our own institutions by the creation and maintenance of a great standing army, sufficient properly to guard overseas possessions.

A cheerful blindness to the inevitable worthy of Mark Tapley himself, the stale Micawberism that "something is bound to turn up," and a Mrs. Jellyby philanthropy hopelessly callous to domestic duties, expenses, and distresses, have hitherto successfully united to prevent the one simple and supreme need of the situation—a frank, formal, and definite declaration, by *the law-making power* of the government, of the nation's purpose in the premises. What is needed is a formal legislative announcement that the governing of a remote and alien people is to have no permanent place in the purposes of our national life, and that we do *bona fide* intend, just as soon as a stable government, republican in form, can be established by the people of the Philippine Islands, to turn over, upon terms which shall be reasonable and just, the government and control of the islands to the people thereof.

The essentials of the problem, being at least as immutable as human nature and geography, will not change much with time. And whenever the American people are ready to abandon the strange gods whose guidance has necessitated a new definition of Liberty consistent with taxation without representation and unanimous protest by the governed, they will at once set about to secure to a people who have proven themselves brave and self-sacrificing in war, and gentle, generous, and tractable in peace, the right to pursue happiness in *their own* way, in lieu of somebody else's way, as the spirit of our Constitution, and the teachings of our God, Who is also theirs, alike demand.

After seven years spent at the storm-centre of so-called "Expansion," the first of the seven as a volunteer officer in Cuba during and after the Spanish War, the next two in a like capacity in the Philippines, and the remainder as a United States judge in the last-named country, the writer was finally invalided home in 1905, sustained in spirit, at parting, by cordial farewells, oral and written, personal and official, but convinced that foreign kindness will not cure the desire of a people, once awakened, for what used to be known as Freedom before we freed Cuba and then subjugated the Philippines; and that to permanently eradicate sedition from the Philippine Islands, the American courts there must be given jurisdiction over thought as well as over overt act, and must learn the method of drawing an indictment against a whole people.

Seven other years of interested observation from the Western Hemisphere end of the line have confirmed and fortified the convictions above set forth.

If we give the Filipinos this independence they so ardently desire and ever clamor for until made to shut up, "the holy cause," as their brilliant young representative in the American House of Representatives, Mr. Quezon, always calls it, will *not* be at once spoiled, as the American hemp and other special interests so contemptuously insist, by the gentleman named, and his compatriot, Señor Osmeña, the Speaker of the Philippine Assembly, and the rest of the leaders of the patriot cause, in a general mutual throat-cutting incidental to a scramble for the offices. This sort of contention is merely the hiss of the same old serpent of tyranny which has always beset the pathway of man's struggle for free institutions.

When first the talk in America, after the battle of Manila Bay, about keeping the Philippines, reached the islands, one of the Filipino leaders wrote to another during the negotiations between their commanding general and our own looking to preservation of the peace until the results of the Paris Peace Conference which settled the fate of the islands should be known, in effect, thus: "The Filipinos will not be fit for independence in ten, twenty, or a hundred years if it be left to American colonial office-holders drawing good salaries to determine the question." Is there not some human nature in that remark? Suppose, reader, you were in the enjoyment of a salary of five, ten, or twenty thousand dollars a year as a government official in the Philippines, how precipitately would you hasten to recommend yourself out of office, and evict yourself into this cold Western world with which you had meantime lost all touch?

The Filipinos can run a far better government than the Cubans. In 1898, when Admiral Dewey read in the papers that we were going to give Cuba independence, he wired home from Manila:

These people are far superior in their intelligence, and more capable of self-government than the people of Cuba, and I am familiar with both races.

After a year in Cuba and nearly six in the Philippines, two as an officer of the army that subjugated the Filipinos, and the remainder as a judge over them, I cordially concur in the opinion of Admiral Dewey, but with this addition, viz., that the people of those islands, whatever of conscious political unity they may have lacked in 1898, were welded into absolute oneness as a people by their original struggle for independence against us, and will remain forever so welded by their incurable aspirations for a national life of their own under a republic framed in imitation of ours. Furthermore, the one great difference between Cuba and the Philippines is that the latter country has no race cancer forever menacing its peace, and sapping its self-reliance. The Philippine people are absolutely one people, as to race, color, and previous condition. Again, American sugar and tobacco interests will never permit the competitive Philippine sugar and tobacco industries to grow as Nature and Nature's God intended; and the American importers of Manila hemp—which is to the Philippines what cotton is to the South—have, through special Congressional legislation still standing on our statute books—to the shame of the nation—so depressed the hemp industry of the islands that the market price it brings to-day is just one half what it brought ten years ago.

If three strong and able Americans, familiar with insular conditions and still young enough to undertake the task, were told by a President of the United States, by authority of Congress, "Go out there and set up a stable native government by July 4, 1921,1 and then come away," they could and would do it; and that government would be a success; and one of the greatest moral victories in the annals of free government would have been written by the gentlemen concerned upon the pages of their country's history.

We ought to give the Filipinos their independence, even if we have to guarantee it to them. But, by neutralization treaties with the other great Powers similar to those which safeguard the integrity and independence of Switzerland to-day, whereby the other Powers would agree not to seize the islands after we give them their independence, the Philippines can be made as permanently neutral territory in Asiatic politics as Switzerland is to-day in European politics.

JAMES H. BLOUNT.

1406 G Street, N. W.,
WASHINGTON, D. C.,
July 4, 1912.

P.S.—The preparation of this book has entailed examination of a vast mass of official documents, as will appear from the foot-note citations to the page and volume from which quotations have been made. The object has been to place all material statements of fact beyond question. For the purpose of this research work, Mr. Herbert Putnam, Librarian of Congress, was kind enough to extend me the privileges of the national library, and it would be most ungracious to fail to acknowledge the obligation I am under, in this regard, to one whom the country is indeed fortunate in having at the head of that great institution. I should also make acknowledgment of the obligation I am under to Mr. W. W. Bishop, the able superintendent of the reading-room, for aid rendered whenever asked, and to my life-long friends, John and Hugh Morrison, the most valuable men, to the general public, except the two gentlemen above named, on the whole great roll of employees of the Library of Congress.

J. H. B.

₁The date contemplated by the pending Philippine Independence Bill, introduced in the House of Representatives in March, 1912, by Hon. W. A. Jones, Chairman of the Committee on Insular Affairs.

Chapter I. Mr. Pratt's Serenade

Had I but served my God with half the zeal
I served my king, he would not in mine age
Have left me naked to mine enemies.

King Henry VIII., Act III., Sc. 2.

Any narrative covering our acquisition of the Philippine Islands must, of course, centre in the outset about Admiral Dewey, and the destruction by him of the Spanish fleet in Manila Bay on Sunday morning, May 1, 1898. But as the Admiral had brought Aguinaldo down from Hong Kong to Manila after the battle, and landed him on May 19th to start an auxiliary insurrection, which insurrection kept the Spaniards bottled up in Manila on the land side for three and a half months while Dewey did the same by sea, until ten thousand American troops arrived, and easily completed the reduction and capture of the beleaguered and famished city on August 13th, it is necessary to a clear understanding of the *de facto* alliance between the Americans and Aguinaldo thus created, to know who brought the Admiral and Aguinaldo together and how, and why.

The United States declared war against Spain, April 21, 1898, to free Cuba, and at once arranged an understanding with the Cuban revolutionists looking to co-operation between their forces and ours to that end. For some years prior to this, political conditions in the Philippines had been quite similar to those in Cuba, so that when, two days after war broke out, the Honorable Spencer Pratt, Consul-General of the United States at Singapore, in the British Straits Settlements, found Aguinaldo, who had headed the last organized outbreak against Spain in the Philippines, temporarily sojourning as a political refugee at Singapore, in the Filipino colony there, he naturally sought to arrange for his co-operating with us against Spain, as Gomez and Garcia were doing in Cuba. Thereby hangs the story of "Mr. Pratt's Serenade." However, before we listen to the band whose strains spoke the gratitude of the Filipinos to Mr. Pratt for having introduced Aguinaldo to Dewey, let us learn somewhat of Aguinaldo's antecedents, as related to the purposes of the introduction.

The first low rumbling of official thunder premonitory to the war with Spain was heard in Mr. McKinley's annual message to Congress of December, 1897,₁ wherein he said, among other things:

The most important problem with which this government is now called upon to deal pertaining to its foreign relations concerns its duty toward Spain and the Cuban insurrection.

In that very month of December, 1897, Aguinaldo was heading a formidable insurrection against Spanish tyranny in the Philippines, and the Filipinos and their revolutionary committees everywhere were watching with eager interest the course of "The Great North American Republic," as they were wont to term our government.

The Report of the First Philippine Commission sent out to the Islands by President McKinley in February, 1899, of which President Schurman of Cornell University was Chairman, contains a succinct memorandum concerning the Filipino revolutionary movement of 1896–7, which had been begun by Aguinaldo in 1896, and had culminated in what is known as the Treaty of Biac-na-Bato,2 signed December 14, 1897. This treaty had promised certain reforms, such as representation in the Spanish Cortez, sending the Friars away, etc., and had also promised the leaders $400,000 if Aguinaldo and his Cabinet would leave the country and go to Hong Kong. "No definite time was fixed," says President Schurman (vol. I., p. 171), "during which these men were to remain away from the Philippines; and if the promises made by Spain were not fulfilled, they had the right to return." Of course, "the promises made by Spain" were *not* fulfilled. Spain thought she had bought Aguinaldo and his crowd off. "Two hundred thousand dollars," says Prof. Schurman, "was paid to Aguinaldo when he arrived in Hong Kong." But instead of using this money in riotous living, the little group of exiles began to take notice of the struggles of their brothers in wretchedness in Cuba, and the ever-increasing probability of intervention by the United States in that unhappy Spanish colony, which, of course, would be*their* opportunity to strike for Independence. They had only been in Hong Kong about two months when the *Maine* blew up February 15, 1898, Then they knew there would be "something doing." Hong Kong being the cross-roads of the Far East and the gateway to Asia, and being only sixty hours across the choppy China Sea from Manila, was the best place in that part of the world to brew another insurrection against Spain. But Singapore is also a good place for a branch office for such an enterprise, being on the main-travelled route between the Philippines and Spain by way of the Suez Canal, about four or five days out of Hong Kong by a good liner, and but little farther from Manila, as the crow flies, than Hong Kong itself. Owing to political unrest in the Philippines in 1896–7–8, there was quite a colony of Filipino political refugees living at Singapore during that period. Aguinaldo had gone over from Hong Kong to Singapore in the latter half of April, 1898, arriving there, it so chanced, the day we declared war against Spain, April 21st. He was immediately sought out by Mr. Pratt, who had learned of his presence in the community through an Englishman of Singapore, a former resident of Manila, a Mr. Bray, who seems to have been a kind of striker for the Filipino general. Aguinaldo had come *incognito*. Out of Mr. Pratt's interview with the insurgent chief thus obtained, and its results, grew the episode which is the subject of this chapter.

A word just here, preliminary to this interview, concerning the personal equation of Aguinaldo, would seem to be advisable.

While I personally chased him and his outfit a good deal in the latter part of 1899, in the northern advance of a column of General Lawton's Division from San Isidro across the Rio Grande de Pampanga, over the boggy passes of the Caraballa Mountains to the China Sea, and up the Luzon West Coast road, we never did catch him, and I never personally met him but once, and that was after he was captured in 1901. He was as insignificant looking physically as a Japanese diplomat. But his presence suggested, equally with that of his wonderful racial cousins who represent the great empire of the Mikado abroad, both a high order of intelligence and baffling reserve. And Major-General J. Franklin Bell, recently Chief of Staff, United States Army, who was a Major on General Merritt's staff in 1898, having charge of the "Office of Military Information," in a confidential report prepared for his chief dated August 29, 1898, "sizing up" the various insurgent leaders, in view of the then apparent probability of trouble with them, gives these notes on Aguinaldo, the head and front of the revolution: "Aguinaldo: Honest, sincere, and * * * a natural leader of men."3

Any one acquainted with General Bell knows that he knows what he is talking about when he speaks of "a natural leader of men," for he is one himself. Our ablest men in the early days were the first to cease considering the little brown soldiers a joke, and their government an *opera-bouffe* affair. General Bell also says in the same report that he, Aguinaldo, is undoubtedly endowed in a wonderful degree with "the power of creating among the people confidence in himself." He was, indeed, the very incarnation of "the legitimate aspirations of" his people, to use one of the favorite phrases of his early state papers, and the faithful interpreter thereof. That was the secret of his power, that and a most remarkable talent for surrounding himself with an atmosphere of impenetrable reserve. This last used to make our young army officers suspect him of being what they called a "four-flusher," which being interpreted means a man who is partially successful in making people think him far more important than he really is. But we have seen General Bell's estimate. And the day Aguinaldo took the oath of allegiance to the United States, in 1901, General MacArthur, then commanding the American forces in the Philippines, signalized the event by liberating 1000 Filipino prisoners of war. General Funston, the man who captured him in 1901, says in *Scribner's Magazine* for November, 1911, "He is a man of many excellent qualities and * * * far and away the best Filipino I was ever brought in contact with."

Aguinaldo was born in 1869. To-day, 1912, he is farming about twenty miles out of Manila in his native province of Cavite; has always scrupulously observed his oath of allegiance aforesaid; occasionally comes to town and plays chess with Governor-General Forbes; and in all respects has played for the last ten years with really fine dignity the rôle of Chieftain of a Lost Cause on which his all had been staked. He was a school-teacher at Cavite at one time, but is not a college graduate, and so far as mere book education is concerned, he is not a highly educated man. Whether or not he can give the principal parts of the principal irregular Greek verbs I do not know, but his place in the history of his country, and in the annals of wars for independence, cannot, and for the honor of human nature should not, be a small one. Dr. Rizal, the Filipino patriot whose picture we print on the Philippine postage stamps, and who was shot for sedition by the Spaniards before our time out there, was what Colonel Roosevelt would jocularly call "one of these darned literary fellows." He was a sort of "Sweetness and Light" proposition, who only *wrote* about "The Rights of Man," and finally *let* the Spaniards shoot him—stuck his head in the lion's mouth, so to speak. Aguinaldo was a born leader of men, who knew how to put the fear of God into the hearts of the ancient oppressors of his people. Mr. Pratt's own story of how he earned his serenade is preserved to future ages in the published records of the State Department.4 We will now attempt to summarize, not so eloquently as Mr. Pratt, but more briefly, the manner of its earning, the serenade itself, and its resultant effects both upon the personal fortunes of Mr. Pratt and upon Filipino confidence in American official assurances.

It was on the evening of Saturday, April 23, 1898, that Mr. Pratt was confidentially informed of Aguinaldo's arrival at Singapore, *incognito*. "Being aware," says Mr. Pratt, "of the great prestige of General Aguinaldo with the insurgents, and that no one, either at home or abroad, could exert over them the same influence and control that he could, I determined at once to see him." Accordingly, he did see him the following Sunday morning, the 24th.

At this interview, it was arranged that if Admiral Dewey, then at Hong Kong with his squadron awaiting orders, should so desire, Aguinaldo should proceed to Hong Kong to arrange for co-operation of the insurgents at Manila with our naval forces in the prospective operations against the Spaniards.

Accordingly, that Sunday, Mr. Pratt telegraphed Dewey through our consul at Hong Kong:

Aguinaldo, insurgent leader, here. Will come Hong Kong arrange with Commodore for general co-operation insurgents Manila if desired. Telegraph.

Admiral Dewey (then Commodore) replied:

Tell Aguinaldo come soon as possible.

This message was received late Sunday night, April 24th, and was at once communicated to Aguinaldo. Mr. Pratt then did considerable bustling around for the benefit of his new-found ally, whom, with his aide-de-camp and private secretary, all under assumed names he "succeeded in getting off," to use his phrase, by the British steamer *Malacca*, which left Singapore for Hong Kong, April 26th. In the letter reporting all this to the State Department, Mr. Pratt adds that he trusts this action "in arranging for his [Aguinaldo's] direct co-operation with the commander of our forces" will meet with the Government's approval. A little later Mr. Pratt sends the State Department a copy of the *Singapore Free Press* of May 4, 1898, containing an impressive account of the above transaction and the negotiations leading up to it. This account describes the political conditions among the population of the Philippine archipelago, "which," it goes on to say, "merely awaits the signal from General Aguinaldo to rise *en masse*." Speaking of Pratt's interview with Aguinaldo, it says:

General Aguinaldo's policy embraces the independence of the Philippines. * * * American protection would be desirable temporarily, on the same lines as that which might be instituted hereafter in Cuba.

Mr. Pratt also forwards a proclamation gotten up by the Filipino insurgent leaders at Hong Kong and sent over to the Philippines in advance of Admiral Dewey's coming, calling upon the Filipinos not to heed any appeals of the Spaniards to oppose the Americans, but to rally to the support of the latter. This manifesto of the Filipinos is headed, prominently—for all we know it may have had a heading as big as a Hearst newspaper box-car type announcement of the latest violation of the Seventh Commandment—: "America's Allies."

It begins thus:

Compatriots: Divine Providence is about to place independence within our reach. * * * The Americans, not from mercenary motives, but for the sake of humanity and the lamentations of so many persecuted people, have considered it opportune * * * etc. [Here follows a reference to Cuba.] At the present moment an American squadron is preparing to sail for the Philippines. * * * The Americans will attack by sea and prevent any reinforcements coming from Spain; * * * we insurgents must attack by land. Probably you will have more than sufficient arms, because the Americans have arms and will find means to assist us. *There where you see the American flag flying, assemble in numbers; they are our redeemers!*5

For twelve days after his letter to the State Department enclosing the above proclamation, Mr. Pratt, so far as the record discloses, contemplated his *coup d'état* in silent satisfaction. Since its successful pulling off, Admiral Dewey had smashed the Spanish fleet, and Aguinaldo had started his auxiliary insurrection. The former was patting the latter on the back, as it were, and saying, "Go it little man." But nobody was patting Pratt on the back, yet. Therefore, on June 2d, Mr. Pratt writes the State Department, purring for patting thus:

Considering the enthusiastic manner General Aguinaldo has been received by the natives and the confidence with which he already appears to have inspired Admiral Dewey, it will be admitted, I think, that I did not over-rate his importance and *that I have materially assisted* the cause of the United States in the Philippines in securing his co-operation.6

A glow of conscious superiority, in value to the Government, over his consular colleague and neighbor, Mr. Wildman, at Hong Kong, next suffuses Mr. Pratt's diction, being manifested thus:

Why this co-operation should not have been secured to us during the months General Aguinaldo remained awaiting events in Hong Kong, and that he was allowed to leave there without having been approached in the interest of our Government, I cannot understand.

Considering that in his letter accepting the nomination for the Vice-Presidency two years after this Mr. Roosevelt compared Aguinaldo and his people to that squalid old Apache medicine man, Sitting Bull, and his band of dirty paint-streaked cut-throats, Mr. Pratt's next Pickwickian sigh of complacent, if neglected, worth is particularly interesting:

No *close observer* of what had transpired in the Philippines during the past four years could have failed to recognize that General Aguinaldo enjoyed above all others the confidence of the Filipino insurgents and the respect alike of Spaniards and foreigners in the islands, all of whom vouched for his high sense of justice and honor.

In other words, knowing the proverbial ingratitude of republics, Mr. Pratt is determined to impress upon his Government and on the discerning historian of the future that he was "the original Aguinaldo man." A week later (June 9th) Mr. Pratt writes the Department enclosing copies of the Singapore papers of that date, giving an account of a generous outburst of Filipino enthusiasm at Singapore in honor of America, Admiral Dewey, and, last, if not least, Mr. Pratt. He encloses duplicate copies of these newspaper notices "for the press, should you consider their publication desirable." His letter begins:

I have the honor to report that this afternoon, on the occasion of the receipt of the news of General Aguinaldo's recent successes near Manila, I was waited upon by the Philippine residents in Singapore and presented an address.
* * *

He then proceeds with further details of the event, without self-laudation. The Singapore papers which he encloses, however, not handicapped by the inexorable modesty of official correspondence, give a glowing account of the presentation of the "address," and of the serenade and toasts which followed. Says one of them, the *Straits Times:*

The United States consulate at Singapore was yesterday afternoon in an unusual state of bustle. That bustle extended itself to Raffles Hotel, of which the consulate forms an outlying part. From a period shortly prior to 5 o'clock, afternoon, the natives of the Philippines resident in Singapore began to assemble at the consulate. Their object was to present an address to Hon. Spencer Pratt, United States Consul-General, and, partly, to serenade him, for which purpose some twenty-five or thirty of the Filipinos came equipped with musical instruments.

First there was music by the band. Then followed the formal reading and presentation of the address by a Dr. Santos, representing the Filipino community of Singapore. The address pledged the "eternal gratitude" of the Filipino people to Admiral Dewey and the honored addressee, alluded to the glories of independence, and to how Aguinaldo had been enabled by the arrangement so happily effected with Admiral Dewey by Consul Pratt to arouse 8,000,000 of Filipinos to take up arms "in defence of those principles of justice and liberty of which your country is the foremost champion" and trusted "that the United States * * * will efficaciously second the programme arranged between you, sir, and General Aguinaldo in this port of Singapore, and secure to us our independence under the protection of the United States."

Mr. Pratt arose and "proceeded speaking in French," says the newspaper—it does not say Alabama French, but that is doubtless what it was—"to state his belief that the Filipinos would prove and were now proving themselves fit for self-government." The gentleman from Alabama then went on to review the mighty events and developments of the preceding six weeks, Dewey's victory of May 1st,

the brilliant achievements of your own distinguished leader, General Emilio Aguinaldo, *co-operating on land with the Americans at sea*, etc. You have just reason to be proud of what has been and is being accomplished by General Aguinaldo and your fellow-countrymen under his command. When, six weeks ago, I learned that General Aguinaldo had arrived *incognito* in Singapore, I immediately *sought him out*. An hour's interview convinced me that he was *the man for the occasion*; and, having communicated with Admiral Dewey, I accordingly arranged for him to join the latter, which he did at Cavite. The rest you know.

Says the newspaper clipping which has preserved the Pratt oration: "At the conclusion of Mr. Pratt's speech refreshments were served, and as the Filipinos, *being Christians, drink alcohol*,7 there was no difficulty in arranging as to refreshments."

Then followed a general drinking of toasts to America, Dewey, Pratt, and Aguinaldo. Then the band played. Then the meeting broke up. Then the Honorable Spencer Pratt, Consul-General of the United States, retired to the seclusion of his apartments in Raffles Hotel, and, under the soothing swish of his *plunkah*, forgot the accursed heat of that stepping-off place, Singapore, and dreamed of future greatness.

A few days later the even tenor of Mr. Pratt's meditations was disturbed by a letter from the State Department saying, in effect, that it was all right to get Aguinaldo's assistance "*if* in so doing he was not induced to form hopes which it might not be practicable to gratify."8 But it did*not* tell him to tell the Filipinos so. For Aguinaldo was keeping the Spaniards bottled up in the old walled city of Manila on short and ever shortening rations, and American troops were on the way to join him, and the shorter the food supply grew in Manila the readier the garrison would be to surrender when they did arrive, and the fewer American soldiers' lives would have to be sacrificed in the final capture of the town. Every day of Aguinaldo's service under the Dewey-Pratt arrangement was worth an American life, perhaps many. It was too valuable to repudiate, just yet. July 20th, the State Department wrote Mr. Pratt a letter acknowledging receipt of his of June 9th "enclosing printed copies of a report from the *Straits Times* of the same day, entitled 'Mr. Spencer Pratt's Serenade,' with a view to its communication to the press," and not only not felicitating him *on* his serenade, but making him sorry he had ever *had* a serenade. It said, among other things:

"The extract now communicated by you from the *Straits Times* of the 9th of June has occasioned *a feeling of disquietude and a doubt as to whether some of your acts may not have borne a significance and produced an impression which this government would feel compelled to regret*."9 Hapless Pratt! "Feel compelled to regret" is State Department for "You are liable to be fired."

The letter of reprimand proceeds:

"The address * * * discloses an understanding on their part that * * * the ultimate object of our action is * * * the independence of the Philippines * * *. Your address does not repel this implication * * *".

The letter then scores Pratt for having called Aguinaldo "the man for the occasion," and for having said that the "arrangement" between Aguinaldo and Dewey had "resulted so happily," and after a few further animadversions, concludes with this great blow to the reading public of Alabama:

"For these reasons the Department has not caused the article to be given to the press lest it might seem thereby to lend a sanction to views the expression of which it had not authorized."

"The Department" was very scrupulous about even the appearance, at the American end of the line, of "lending a sanction" to Pratt's arrangement with Aguinaldo, while all the time it was knowingly permitting the latter to daily risk his own life and the lives of his countrymen on the faith of that very "arrangement," and it was so permitting this to be done because the "arrangement" was daily operating to reduce the number of American lives which it would be necessary to sacrifice in the final taking of Manila. The day the letter of reprimand was written our troop-ships were on the ocean, speeding toward the Philippines. And Aguinaldo and his people were fighting the Spaniards with the pent-up feeling of centuries impelling their little steel-jacketed messengers of death, thinking of "Cuba Libre," and dreaming of a Star of Philippine Independence risen in the Far East.

Such are the circumstances from which the Filipino people derived their first impressions concerning the faith and honor of a strange people they had never theretofore seen, who succeeded the Spaniards as their overlords. Mr. Pratt was subsequently quietly separated from the consular service, and doubtless lived to regret that he had ever unloosed the fountains of his Alabama French on the Filipino colony of Singapore.

1*Congressional Record*, December 6, 1897, p. 3.

2Split Rock.

3*Senate Document 62*, p. 381.

4See pages 341 *et seq.*, *Senate Document 62*, part 1, 55th Cong., 3d Sess., 1898–9.

5*Senate Document 62*, p. 346.

6*Ib.*, 349.

7The natives in and about Singapore are Mohammedans, forbidden by their religion to use alcoholic beverages.

8*Senate Document 62*, p. 354.

9*Senate Document 62*, p. 356.

Chapter II. Dewey and Aguinaldo

Armaments that thunderstrike the walls
Of rock-built cities, bidding nations quake
And monarchs tremble in their capitals.

Childe Harold.

The battle of Manila Bay was fought May 1, 1898. Until the thunder of Dewey's guns reverberated around the world, there was perhaps no part of it the American people knew less about than the Philippine Islands.

We have all heard much of what happened after the battle, but comparatively few, probably, have ever had a glimpse at our great sailor while he was there in Hong Kong harbor, getting ready to go to sea to destroy the Spanish armada. Such a glimpse is modestly afforded by the Admiral in his testimony before the Senate Committee in 1902.1

Asked by the Committee when he first heard from Aguinaldo and his people in 1898, Admiral Dewey said2:

I should think about a month before leaving Hong Kong, that is, about the first of April, when it became pretty certain that there was to be war with Spain, I heard that there were a number of Filipinos in the city of Hong Kong who were anxious to accompany the squadron to Manila in case we went over. I saw these men two or three times myself. They seemed to be all very young earnest boys. I did not attach much importance to what they said or to themselves. Finally, before we left Hong Kong for Mirs Bay3 I received a telegram from Consul-General Pratt at Singapore saying that Aguinaldo was there and anxious to see me. I said to him "All right; tell him to come on," but I attached so little importance to Aguinaldo that I did not wait for him. He did not arrive, and we sailed from Mirs Bay without any Filipinos.

From his testimony before the Committee it is clear that Admiral Dewey's first impressions of the Filipinos, like those of most Americans after him, were not very favorable, that is to say, he did not in the outset take them very seriously. It will be interesting to consider these impressions, and then to compare them with those he gathered on better acquaintance from observing their early struggles for independence. The more intimate acquaintance, as has been the case with all his fellow countrymen since, caused him to revise his first verdict. Answering a question put by Senator Carmack concerning what transpired between him and the Philippine Revolutionists at Hong Kong before he sailed in search of the Spanish fleet, the Admiral said4:

They were bothering me. I was getting my squadron ready for battle, and these little men were coming on board my ship at Hong Kong and taking a good deal of my time, and I did not attach the slightest importance to anything they could do, and they did nothing; that is, none of them went with me when I went to Mirs Bay. There had been a good deal of talk, but when the time came they did not go. *One of them didn't go because he didn't have any tooth-brush.*

SENATOR BURROWS : "Did he give that as his reason?"

ADMIRAL DEWEY : "Yes, he said 'I have no tooth-brush.'"

They used to come aboard my ship and take my time, and finally I would not see them at all, but turned them over to my staff.

Now the lack of a tooth-brush is hardly a valid excuse for not going into battle, however great a convenience it may be in campaign. But the absence of orders from your commanding officer stands on a very different footing. Aguinaldo had not yet arrived. Three hundred years of Spanish misgovernment and cruelty is not conducive to aversion to fictitious excuses by the lowly in the presence of supreme authority. The answer was amusingly uncandid, but disproved neither patriotism nor intelligence.

Aguinaldo arrived at Hong Kong from Singapore a day or so after Admiral Dewey had sailed for Manila. Of the battle of May 1st, no detailed mention is essential here. Every schoolboy is familiar with it. It will remain, as long as the republic lasts, a part of the heritage of the nation. But the true glory of that battle, to my mind, rests, not upon the circumstance that we have the Philippines, but upon the tremendous fact that before it occurred the attitude of our State Department toward an American citizen sojourning in distant lands and becoming involved in difficulties there had long been, "Why didn't he stay at home? Let him stew in his own juice"; whereas, since then, to be an American has been more like it was in the days of St. Paul to be a Roman citizen.

May 16th, our consul at Hong Kong, Mr. Wildman, succeeded in getting the insurgent leader and his staff off for Manila on board the U. S. S.*McCulloch* by authority of Admiral Dewey. Like his colleague over at Singapore, Consul Wildman was bent on the rôle of Warwick. Admiral Dewey was quite busy there in Manila Bay the first two or three weeks after the battle, but yielding to the letters of Wildman, who meantime had constituted himself a kind of fiscal agent at Hong Kong for the prospective revolution in the matter of the purchase of guns and otherwise, the Admiral told the commanding officer of the *McCulloch* that on his next trip to Hong Kong he might bring down a dozen or so of the Filipinos there. The frame of mind they were in on reaching Manila, as a result of the assurances of Pratt and Wildman, is well illustrated by a letter the latter wrote Aguinaldo a little later (June 25th) which is undoubtedly in keeping with what he had been telling him earlier:

Do not forget that the United States undertook this war for the sole purpose of relieving the Cubans from the cruelties under which they were suffering, and not for the love of conquest or the hope of gain. *They are actuated by precisely the same feelings for the Filipinos.*5

And at the time, they were.

"Every American citizen who came in contact with the Filipinos at the inception of the Spanish War, or at any time within a few months after hostilities began," said General Anderson in an interview published in the *Chicago Record* of February 24, 1900, "probably told those he talked with * * * that we intended to free them from Spanish oppression. The general expression, was 'We intend to whip the Spaniards and set you free.'"

The *McCulloch* arrived in Manila Bay with Aguinaldo and his outfit, May 19th. Let Admiral Dewey tell what happened then6:

Aguinaldo came to see me. I said, "Well now, go ashore there; we have got our forces at the arsenal at Cavite, go ashore and start your army." He came back in the course of a few hours and said, "I want to leave here; I want to go to Japan." I said, "Don't give it up, Don Emilio." *I wanted his help, you know.* He did not sleep ashore that night; he slept on board the ship. The next morning he went on shore, *still inside my lines*, and began recruiting men.

Enterprises of great pith and moment have often turned awry and lost the name of action for lack of a word spoken in season by a stout heart. Admiral Dewey spoke the word, and Aguinaldo, his protégé, did the rest. "Then he began operations toward Manila, and he did wonderfully well. He whipped the Spaniards battle after battle * * *."7 In fact, the desperate bravery of those little brown men after they got warmed up reminds one of the Japs at the walls of Peking, in the advance of the Allied Armies to the relief of the foreign legations during the Boxer troubles of 1900. Admiral Dewey told the Senate Committee in 1902 that Aguinaldo actually wanted to put one of the old smooth-bore Spanish guns he found at Cavite *on a barge* and have him (Dewey) *tow it* up in front of Manila so he could attack the city with it. "I said, 'Oh no, no; we can do nothing until our troops come.'"

Otherwise he was constantly advising and encouraging him. Why? Let the Admiral answer: "I knew that what he was doing—driving the Spaniards in—was *saving our troops*."7 In other words they were daily dying that American soldiers might live, on the faith of the reasons for which we had declared war, and trusting, because of the words of our consuls and the acts of our admiral, in the sentiment subsequently so nobly expressed by Mr. McKinley in his instructions to the Paris peace Commissioners:

The United States in making peace should follow the same high rule of conduct which guided it in facing war.8

"I did not know what the action of our Government would be," said the Admiral to the Committee,9 adding that he simply used his best judgment on the spot at the time; presumably supposing that his Government would do the decent thing by these people who considered us their liberators. "They looked on us as their liberators," said he.10 "Up to the time the army came he (Aguinaldo) did everything I requested. He was most obedient; whatever I told him to do he did. I saw him almost daily.11 I had not much to do with him after the army came."12

That was no ordinary occasion, that midsummer session of the Senate Committee in 1902. It was a case of the powerful of the earth discussing a question of ethics, even as they do in Boston. The nation had been intoxicated in 1898 with the pride of power—power revealed to it by the Spanish War; and in a spirit thus mellowed had taken the Philippines as a sort of political foreign mission, forgetting the injunction of the Fathers to keep Church and State separate, but not forgetting the possible profits of trade with the saved. A long war with the prospective saved had followed, developing many barbarities avenged in kind, and the breezes from the South Seas were suggesting the aroma of shambles. "How did we get into all this mess, anyhow?" said the people. "Let us pause, and consider." Hear the still small voice of a nation's conscience mingling with demagogic nonsense perpetrated by potent, grave, and reverend Senators:

Admiral Dewey: "I do not think it makes any difference what my opinion is on these things."

Senator Patterson: "There is no man whose opinion goes farther with the country than yours does, Admiral, and therefore I think you ought to be very prudent in expressing your views."

Senator Beveridge (Acting Chairman): "The Chairman will not permit any member to lecture Admiral Dewey on his prudence or imprudence."

This of course would read well to "Mary of the Vine-clad Cottage" out in Indiana, whose four-year-old boy was named George Dewey—, or to her counterpart up in Vermont who might name her next boy after the brilliant and distinguished Acting Chairman, in token of her choice for the Presidency.

Senator Patterson: "I was not lecturing him."

Senator Beveridge: "Yes; you said he ought to be prudent."

Senator Patterson: "And I think it was well enough to suggest those things."13

Thawed into theorizing by these indubitably genuine evidences of a nation's high regard, the man of action tried to help the nation out. He said he had used the Filipinos as the Federal troops used the negroes in the Civil War. Senator Patterson struck this suggestion amidships and sunk it with the remark that the negroes were expecting freedom. Admiral Dewey had said "The Filipinos were slaves too" and considered him their liberator.14 But he never did elaborate on the new definition of freedom which had followed in the wake of his ships to Manila, viz., that Freedom does not necessarily mean freedom from alien domination, but only a change of masters deemed by the new master beneficial to the "slave."

Apropos of why he accepted Aguinaldo's help, the Admiral also said:

I was waiting for troops to arrive, and I felt sure the Filipinos could not take Manila, and I thought that *the closer they invested the city the easier it would be when our troops arrived to march in*. The Filipinos were our friends, assisting us; they were doing our work.15

Asked as to how big a force Aguinaldo had under arms then and afterwards, the Admiral said maybe 25,000, adding, by way of illustration of the pluck, vim, and patriotism of his valuable new-made friends, "They could have had any number of *men*; it was just a question of *arming*them. *They could have had the whole population.*"16 Eleven months after that, when we captured the first insurgent capital, Malolos, General MacArthur, the ablest and one of the bravest generals we ever set to slaughtering Filipinos, said to a newspaper man just after a bloody and of course victorious fight: "When I first started in against these rebels, I believed that Aguinaldo's troops represented only a faction." "*I did not like,*" said this veteran of three wars, who was always "on the job" in action out there as elsewhere, "*I did not like to believe that the whole*population of Luzon * * * was opposed to us * * * but after having come thus far, and having been brought much in contact with both*insurrectos* and *amigos, I have been reluctantly compelled to believe that the Filipino masses are loyal to Aguinaldo and the government which he heads*".17

Is it at all unlikely that Admiral Dewey did in fact say of his protégés, the Filipinos, to an American visiting Manila in January, 1899, three or four weeks before the war broke out, "Rather than make a war of conquest upon the Filipino people, I would up anchor and sail out of the harbor."18

If Dewey and MacArthur were right, then, about the situation around Manila in 1898, it was a case of an entire people united in an aspiration, and looking to us for its fulfilment.

When the American troops reached the Philippines and perfected their battle formations about Manila, and the order to advance was given, they did "march in," to use Admiral Dewey's expression above quoted. But they did not let the Filipinos have a finger in the pie. The conquest and retention of the islands had then been determined upon. The Admiral's reasons for saddling his protégé with a series of bloody battles and a long and arduous campaign are certainly stated with the proverbial frankness of the sailorman: "I wanted his help, you know." But what was Aguinaldo to get out of the transaction, from the Dewey point of view?

"They wanted to get rid of the Spaniards. I do not think they looked much beyond that,"19 said the Admiral to the Senate Committee. Let us see whether they did or not. Aguinaldo had been shipped by the Honorable E. Spencer Pratt, Consul-General of the United States at Singapore, from that point to Hong

Kong on April 26th, consigned to his fellow Warwick, the Honorable Rounseville Wildman, Consul-General of the United States at the last-named place, and had been received in due course by the consignee. May 5th, at Hong Kong, the Filipino Revolutionary Committee had a meeting, the minutes of which we subsequently came into possession of, along with other captured insurgent papers. The following is an extract from those minutes:

Once the President [Aguinaldo] is in the Philippines with his prestige, he will be able to arouse the masses to combat the demands of the United States, if they should colonize that country, and will drive them, the Filipinos, if circumstances render it necessary, to a Titanic struggle for their independence, even if later they should succumb to the weight of the yoke of a new oppressor. If Washington proposes to carry out the fundamental principles of its Constitution, *it is most improbable that an attempt will be made to colonize the Philippines or annex them. It is probable then that independence will be guaranteed.*20

The truth is that instead of leaving everything to the chance of our continuing in the same unselfish frame of mind we were really in when the Spanish-American War started, Aguinaldo and his people, not sure but what in the wind-up they might even be thrown back upon the tender mercies of Spain, played their cards boldly and consistently from the beginning with a view of organizing a *de facto* government and getting it recognized by the Powers as such at the very earliest practicable moment. They believed that the Lord helps those who help themselves. They had anticipated our change of heart and already had it discounted before we were aware of it ourselves. They were already acting on the idea that eternal vigilance is the price of liberty while public opinion in the United States concerning them was in a chrysalis state, and trying to develop a new definition of Liberty which should comport with the subjugation of distant island subjects by a continental commonwealth on the other side of the world based on representative government. The prospective subjects did not believe that a legislature ten thousand miles away in which they had no vote would ever give them a square deal about tariff and other laws dictated by special interests. They had had three hundred years of just that very sort of thing under Spain and instinctively dreaded continuance of it. That their instincts did not deceive them, our later study of Congressional legislation will show. The Filipinos had greatly pondered their future in their hearts during the last twelve months of Spain's colonial empire, watching her Cuban embarrassments with eager eye.

Having seen the frame of mind in which they approached the contract implied in Admiral Dewey's cheery words, "Well now, go ashore there and start your army," what were the facts of recent history within the knowledge of both parties at the time? What had been the screams of the American eagle, if any, concerning his moral leadership of the family of unfeathered bipeds?

President McKinley's annual message to Congress of December, 1897,21 calling attention to conditions in Cuba as intolerable, had declared that if we should intervene to put a stop to them, we certainly would not make it the occasion of a land-grab. The other nations said: "We are from Missouri." But Mr. McKinley said, "forcible annexation" was not to be thought of by us. "That by *our* code of morality would be criminal," etc. So the world said, "We shall see what we shall see." Then had come the war message of April 11, 1898,22 reiterating the declaration of the Cuban message of December previous, that "forcible annexation by *our* code of morality would be criminal aggression." In other words we announced to the overcrowded monarchies of the old world, whose land-lust is ever tempted by the broad acres of South America, and ever cooled by the virile menace of the Monroe doctrine, that we not only were against the *principle* of land-grabbing, but would not indulge in the *practice*. Immediately upon the conclusion of the reading of the war message, Senator Stewart was recognized, and said, among other things: "Under the law of nations, intervention for conquest is condemned, and is opposed to the universal sentiment of mankind. It is unjust, it is robbery, to intervene for conquest." Then Mr. Lodge stood up, "in the Senate House a Senator," and said:

We are there [meaning in this present Cuban situation] because we represent the spirit of liberty and the spirit of the new time, and Spain is over against us because she is mediæval, cruel, dying. We have grasped no man's territory, we have taken no man's property, we have invaded no man's rights. *We do not ask their lands.*23

These speeches went forth to the world almost like a part of the message itself. And Admiral Dewey, like every other American, in his early dealings with Aguinaldo, after war broke out, must have assumed a mental attitude in harmony with these announcements. But the world said, "All this is merely what you Americans yourselves call 'hot air.' We repeat, 'We are from Missouri.'" Then we said: "Oh very well, we will show you." So in the declaration of war against Spain we inserted the following:

Fourth: That the United States hereby disclaims any disposition or intention to exercise sovereignty, jurisdiction, or control over said island except for the pacification thereof, and asserts its determination when that is accomplished, to leave the government and control of the island to its people.

This meant, "It is true we do love the Almighty Dollar very dearly, oh, Sisters of the Family of Nations, but there are some axiomatic principles of human liberty that we love better, and one of them is the 'unalienable right' of every people to pursue happiness in their own way, free from alien domination." All these things were well known to both the contracting parties when Admiral Dewey set Aguinaldo ashore at Cavite, May 20, 1898, and got him to start his insurrection "under the protection of our guns," as he expressed it.24 Accordingly, when the insurgent leader went ashore, the declaration of war was his major premise, the assurances of our consuls and the acts of our Admiral pursuant thereto were his minor premise, and Independence was his conclusion. Trusting to the faith and honor of the American people, he took his life in his hands, left the panoplied safety of our mighty squadron, and plunged, single-handed, into the struggle for Freedom.

What was the state of the public mind on shore, and how was it prepared to receive his assurances of American aid? Consider the following picture in the light of its sombre sequel.

Just as the war broke out, Consul Williams had left Manila and gone over to Hong Kong, where he joined Admiral Dewey, and accompanied him back to Manila, and was thus privileged to be present at the battle of Manila Bay, May 1st. Under date of May 12th, from his consular headquarters aboard the U. S. S. *Baltimore*, he reports25 going ashore at Cavite and being received with enthusiastic greetings by vast crowds of Filipinos. "They crowded around me," says Brother Williams, "hats off, shouting '*Viva los Americanos*,' thronged about me by hundreds to shake either hand, even several at a time, men, women, and children, striving to get even a finger to shake. So I moved *half a mile*, shaking continuously with both hands."

Tut! tut! says the casual reader. What did the Government at Washington know of all these goings on, that it should be charged later with having violated as binding a moral obligation as ever a nation assumed? It is true that the news of the Williams ovation, as in the case of the Pratt serenade, reached Washington only by the slow channels of the mail. But Washington did in fact receive the said news by due course of mail. When it came, however, Washington was nursing visions of savages in blankets smoking the pipe of peace with the agents of the Great White Father in the White House—*i.e.*, thought, or hoped, the Filipinos were savages—and remained as deaf to the sounds of the Williams ovation as it had been to the strains of the Pratt serenade.

However, hardly had Admiral Dewey taken his binoculars from the gig that carried Aguinaldo ashore to raise his auxiliary insurrection, when he called his Flag Secretary, or the equivalent, and dictated the following cablegram to the Secretary of the Navy:

Aguinaldo, the rebel commander-in-chief, was brought down by the *McCulloch*. Organizing forces near Cavite, and *may render assistance that will be valuable*.26

This sounds a little more serious than "earnest boys" alleging the lack of a toothbrush as an excuse for declining mortal combat, does it not?*How* valuable did this assistance prove? Admiral Dewey had to wait three and one half months for the army to arrive, and this is how the commanding general of the American forces describes conditions as he found them in the latter part of August:

For three and one half months Admiral Dewey with his squadron and the insurgents on land had kept Manila tightly bottled. All commerce had been interdicted, internal trade paralyzed, and food supplies were nearly exhausted.27

And, he might have added, the taking of the city was thus made perfectly easy. Otherwise, as Aguinaldo put it in one of his letters to General Otis, we would not have taken a city, but only *the ruins* of a city. Admiral Dewey said to the Senate Committee in 1902: "They [the Spaniards] surrendered on August 13th, and they had not gotten a thing in after the 1st of May."28

In the early part of the next year, 1899, President McKinley sent out a kind of olive-branch commission, of which President Schurman of Cornell University was Chairman. The olive branch got withered in the sulphur of exploding gun-powder, so the Commission contented itself with making a report. And this is what they said concerning what followed the Dewey-Aguinaldo *entente*:

Shortly afterwards, the Filipinos began to attack the Spanish. Their number was rapidly augmented by the militia who had been given arms by Spain, all of whom revolted and joined the insurgents. Great Filipino successes followed, many Spaniards were taken prisoners, and while the Spanish troops now remained quietly in Manila, the Filipino forces made themselves masters of *the entire island* [of Luzon] except that city.29

Of conditions in July, sixty days after Admiral Dewey had on May 20th said to Aguinaldo in effect, "Go it, little man, we need you in our business," Mr. Wildman, our Consul at Hong Kong, writing to the State Department, said, in defending himself for his share in the business of getting Aguinaldo's help under promises, both express and implied, which were subsequently repudiated, that after he, Wildman, put the insurgent chief aboard the *McCulloch*, May 16th, bound for Manila to co-operate by land with our navy: "He * * * organized a government * * * and from that day to this he has been uninterruptedly successful in the field and dignified and just as the head of his government,"30 a statement which Admiral Dewey subsequently endorsed.31

We have seen the preliminaries of this "government" started under the auspices of our Admiral and under what he himself called "the protection of our guns" (*ante*). Let us note its progress. If you turn the leaves of the contemporaneous official reports, you see quite a moving picture show, and the action is rapid. On May 24th, still "under the protection of our guns," Aguinaldo proclaimed his revolutionary government and summoned the people to his standard for the purpose of driving the Spaniards out forever. The situation was an exact counterpart of the cotemporary Cuban one as regards identity of purpose between "liberator" and "oppressed." His proclamation promised a constitutional convention to be called later (and which *was* duly called later) to elect a President and Cabinet, in whose favor he would resign the emergency authority now assumed; referred to the United States as "undoubtedly disinterested" and as considering the Filipinos "capable of governing for ourselves our unfortunate country"; and formally announced the temporary assumption of supreme authority as dictator. Copies of these proclamations were duly furnished Admiral Dewey. The latter was too busy looking after the men behind his guns and watching the progress of his plucky little ally to study Spanish, so he forwarded them to the Navy Department without comment—"without reading them," said he to the Senate Committee in 1902.32 When his attention was called to them before the Committee by one of the members reading them, his comment was, "Nothing about independence there, is there?"33 It seems to me it did not take an international lawyer to see *a good deal* "there," about independence. In a proclamation published at Tarlac in the latter part of 1899, which appears to have been a sort of swan-song of the Philippine Republic, Aguinaldo had said, in effect, "Certainly Admiral Dewey did not bring me from Hong Kong to Manila to fight the Spaniards for the benefit of American Trade Expansion," and in this proclamation he claimed that Admiral Dewey promised him independence. It is true, that in a letter to Senator Lodge, which that distinguished gentleman read on the floor of the Senate on January 31, 1900, Admiral Dewey denounced this last statement as false. It is also true that those Americans are few and far between who will take Aguinaldo's word in preference to Admiral Dewey's. Certainly the writer is not one of them. But Aguinaldo is no Spanish scholar, being more of a leader of men than a master of language, and what sort of an interpreter acted between him and the Admiral does not appear. Certainly he never did get anything in writing from Admiral Dewey. But after the latter brought him to Manila, set him to fighting the common enemy, and helped him with guns and otherwise in quickly organizing an army for the purpose, the Admiral was at least put on inquiry as to just what Aguinaldo supposed he *was* fighting for. What did the Admiral probably suppose? He told the Senate Committee that the idea that they wanted independence "never entered his head." The roar of mighty guns seems to have made it difficult for him to hear the prattlings of what Aguinaldo's proclamations of the time called "the legitimate aspirations of a people." The milk in the cocoanut is this: How could it ever occur to a great naval commander, such as Admiral Dewey, familiar with the four quarters of the globe, that a coterie of politicians at home would be so foolish as to buy a vast straggly archipelago of jungle-covered islands in the South Seas which had been a nuisance to every government that ever owned them? But let us turn from the Senate Committee's studies of 1902 to the progress of the infant republic of 1898 at Cavite.

The same day the above proclamations of May 24th were issued, we find Consul Williams, now become a sort of amphibious civilian aide to Dewey, having his consular headquarters afloat, on the U. S. S. *Baltimore*, of the squadron, writing the State Department, describing the great successes of the insurgents, his various conferences with Aguinaldo and the other leaders, and his own activities in arranging the execution of a power of attorney whereby Aguinaldo released to certain parties in Hong Kong $400,000 then on deposit to his credit in a Hong Kong bank, for the purpose of enabling them to pay for 3000 stand of arms bought there and expected to arrive at Cavite on the morrow, and for other needed expenses of the revolutionary movement. He says, in part: "Officers have visited me during the darkness of the night to inform *the fleet and me* of their operations, and to report increase of strength. When General Merritt arrives he will find large auxiliary land forces adapted to his service and used to the climate."34 Throughout this period Admiral Dewey reports various cordial conferences with Aguinaldo, though he is not so literary as to vivify his accounts with allusions to the weather. In one despatch he states that he has "refrained from assisting him * * * with the forces under my command"35—explaining to him that "the squadron could not act until the arrival of the United States troops."

Six days after the issuance of the Dictatorship proclamations above mentioned, viz., on May 30th, Admiral Dewey cables the Navy Department36:

Aguinaldo, revolutionary leader, visited *Olympia* yesterday. He expects to make general attack May 31st.

He did not succeed entirely, but there was hard fighting, and the cordon around the doomed Spaniards in Manila and its suburbs was drawn ever closer and closer.

The remarkable feat of Aguinaldo's raising a right formidable fighting force in twelve days after his little "Return from Elba," which force kept growing like a snowball, is difficult, for one who does not know the Filipinos, and the conditions then, to credit. It is explained by the fact that Admiral Dewey let him have the captured guns in the Cavite arsenal, that Cavite was a populous hotbed of insurrection, and that many native regiments, or parts of regiments, quite suited to be the nucleus of an army, having lots of veteran non-commissioned officers, deserted the Spaniards and went over to the insurgents, their countrymen, as soon as Aguinaldo arrived.

On June 6th, we have another bulletin sent to the Navy Department by Admiral Dewey, transmitting with perceptible satisfaction further information as to the progress of his indefatigable protégé:

Insurgents have been engaged actively within the province of Cavite during the last week; they have had several small victories, taking prisoners about 1800 men, 50 officers; Spanish troops, not native.37

Along about this period Aguinaldo happens to get hold of a belated copy of the *London Times* of May 5, 1898. It contains considerable speculation on the future of the Philippines which casts a shadow over the soul of the president of the incipient republic. Having read President McKinley's immortal State papers about the moral obliquity of "forcible annexation," he is moved to write direct to the source of those noble sentiments. The letter is dated June 10, 1898. It is addressed, with a quaintness now pathetic, "To the President of the Republic of the Great North American Nation." It greets the addressee with "the most tender effusion of" the writer's soul, expresses his "deep and sincere gratitude," in the name of his people, "for the efficient and *disinterested* protection which you have decided to give it to shake off the yoke of the cruel and corrupt Spanish domination, as you are doing to the equally unfortunate Cuba" and then proceeds to tell of "the great sorrow which all of us Filipinos felt on reading in the *Times* the astounding statement that you, sir, will retain these islands," etc. He proceeds:

The Philippine people * * * have seen in your nation, ever since your fleet destroyed in a moment the Spanish fleet which was here * * * *the angel who is the harbinger of their liberty*; and they *rose like a single wave* * * * as soon as I trod these shores; and captured in ten days nearly the whole garrison of this Province of Cavite *in whose port I have my government—by the consent of the Admiral of your triumphant fleet*.38

The writer closes his letter with an impassioned protest against the occurrence of what is suggested in the *Times*, and speaks of his fellow-countrymen as "a people which trusts blindly in you not to abandon it to the tyranny of Spain, but to leave it free and independent," and adds his "fervent prayers for the ever-increasing prosperity of your powerful nation."39

But the signer of the foregoing letter did not spend all his time *praying* for us, as may be observed in this bulletin from Admiral Dewey concerning the way he was lambasting the common enemy, sent the Navy Department, June 12th:

Insurgents continue hostilities and have practically surrounded Manila. They have taken 2500 Spanish prisoners, whom they treat most humanely. They do not intend to attack city proper until the arrival of United States troops thither; I have advised.40

Four days later Washington chided the hapless Pratt at Singapore about having talked to Aguinaldo of "direct co-operation" with Admiral Dewey, saying: "To obtain the unconditional personal assistance of General Aguinaldo in the expedition to Manila was proper, if in so doing he was not induced to form hopes which it might not be practicable to gratify."41 This communication goes on to advise Mr. Pratt that the Department cannot approve anything he may have said to Aguinaldo on behalf of the United States which would concede that in accepting his co-operation we would owe him anything. Yet it did not tell Admiral Dewey to quit coaching him, because *the service he was rendering was too valuable*. There is no communication to Admiral Dewey about "hopes which it might not be practicable to gratify" in the official archives of those times. There was Admiral Dewey coaching Aguinaldo and telling him to wait for the main attack until General Merritt should arrive with our troops. Why? Because he expected Merritt to co-operate with Aguinaldo, and of course Aguinaldo expected exactly what Dewey expected.

In reviewing the history of those times the writer has not been so careless as to have overlooked Senator Lodge's elaborate speech in the Senate on March 7, 1900, wherein attention is called to the circumstance that a few days after Aguinaldo landed at Cavite, the Navy Department cabled cautioning Dewey to have no alliance with him that might complicate us, and that the Admiral answered he had made no alliance and would make none. But if actions speak louder than words, the Senator's point does not rise above the dignity of a technicality.

The same day the State Department reprimanded Pratt, as above indicated, viz., June 16th, Consul Williams at Manila wrote them a glowing communication42 about how "active and almost uniformly successful" Aguinaldo was continuing to be. But no resultant enthusiasm is of record. Two days later, on June 18th, Aguinaldo issued his first formal Declaration of Independence. The infant republic was now less than a month old, but it already had a fine set of teeth. The Spaniards had seen them. The proclamation was of course addressed to the Filipino people, and called on them to rally to the cause, but he was also driving at recognition by the Powers. It read in part: "In the face of the whole world I have proclaimed that the aspiration of my whole life, the final object of all my wishes and efforts, is your independence, because I have the inner conviction that it is also your constant longing."43 Many Americans insist that this is mere "hot air" and that the average Filipino peasant does not think much more than his plough animal, the scoffer himself being stupidly unaware that this has been precisely the argument of tyranny in all ages. But the pride a people will have in seeing the best educated and most able men of their own race in charge of their affairs seems to me too obvious to need elaboration. It was always accepted by us as axiomatic until we took the Philippines. It is a cruel species of wickedness for an American to tell his countrymen that the Filipino people *do not want* independence, for some of them may believe it.

The Declaration of Independence of June 18th is known to students of Philippine political archæology as the Proclamation establishing the "dictatorial" government. The principal thing it did was to supplement the absolute dictatorship proclaimed May 24th by provisions for organizing in detail. It also declared independence. A more elaborate Declaration followed on June 23d, known as the proclamation establishing the "revolutionary" government. This made provision for a Congress, a Cabinet, and courts. Of course it was only a paper government the day the ink dried on it. But we will follow it through its teething, and adolescence, to the attainment of its majority at an inauguration where the president was driven to the place of the taking of the oath of office in a coach and four, through a short and very self-respecting heyday, and a longer peripatetic existence, to final dissolution. The document of June 23d reminds us of a fact which in reading it at this late date we are apt to forget, viz., that the Filipinos did not know at what moment their powerful ally, the American squadron, might up anchor and sail away to the high seas, to meet another Spanish fleet; thus leaving them to the tender mercies of the Spaniards, possibly forever. So they were losing no time. In fact, they had set to work from the very beginning with a determination to try and secure recognition from the Powers at the earliest moment. In appealing to the public opinion of the world with a view of paving the way to recognition by the Powers—which recognition would mean getting arms for war with Spain or any other power without the inconveniences of filibustering—Aguinaldo says on behalf of his people in the proclamation of June 23d, above mentioned, that they "now no longer limit themselves to asking for assimilation with the political constitution of Spain, but ask for a complete separation (and) strive for independence, completely assured that the time has come when they can and ought to govern themselves."

Mr. Frank D. Millet, who reached Manila soon enough (in July) to see the ripples of this proclamation, describes the effect on the people. While Mr. Millet is one of the best men that anybody ever knew, a proposition as to which I am quite sure the President of the United States and many people great and small in many lands would affirm my judgment,[44] still, he writes from a frankly White Man's Burden or land-grabbing standpoint—is in harmony with his environment. At page 50 of his book,[45] he reproduces the proclamation last above quoted from, and adds the following satirical comment: "This flowery production was widely circulated and had a great effect on the imagination of the people, who, in the elation of their present success in investing the town and *in their belief that the United States was beginning a campaign in the Philippines to free them from Spanish oppression* (italics mine) shortly came to think that they were already a nation."

Copies of these June proclamations also, as in the case of those of May 24th, were duly forwarded by Aguinaldo to Admiral Dewey[46] and by him forwarded to Washington without comment. In his letter transmitting them to Dewey, Aguinaldo announces that his government has *"taken possession of the various provinces of the archipelago."* Just exactly how many provinces he had control of on June 23d will be examined later. *The very same day the proclamation of June 23d declaring independence was issued*, Admiral Dewey cabled the Navy Department[47]: "Aguinaldo has acted independently of the squadron, but *has kept me advised of his progress which has been wonderful.* I have allowed him to take from the arsenal such Spanish arms and ammunition as he needed." After adding that "Aguinaldo expects to capture Manila without any assistance," the Admiral, evidently divining the temptation that was then luring the political St. Anthonies at Washington, volunteers this timely suggestion:

In my opinion these people are superior in intelligence and more capable of self-government than the natives of Cuba, and I am familiar with both races.[47]

That there may be no doubt about the motive behind that suggestion, it may be noted here that the Admiral told the Senate Committee in 1902: "*I wrote that because I saw in the newspapers that Congress contemplated giving the Cubans independence.*"[48]

But this is not all. On August 13th, the day after the Peace Protocol was signed, Mr. McKinley wired Admiral Dewey asking about "the desirability of the several islands," the "coal *and mineral* deposits," and in reply on August 29th, the Admiral wrote:

In a telegram sent the Department on June 23d, I expressed the opinion that "these people are far superior in their intelligence and more capable of self-government than the natives of Cuba, and I am familiar with both races." *Further intercourse with them has confirmed me in this opinion.*49

As a result of one year's stay in Cuba, and six in the Philippines—two in the army that subjugated the Filipinos and four as a judge over them—I heartily concur in the above opinion of Admiral Dewey, but with this addition: Whatever of solidarity for governmental purposes the Filipinos may have lacked at the date of the Admiral's communications, they were certainly welded into conscious political unity, *as one people*, in their war for independence against us.

In the 1609 or Douay (pronounce Dewey) version of the Bible, the Latin Vulgate, Luke's version of the Lord's Prayer only says "Lead us not into temptation," while Matthew adds "but deliver us from evil." The Dewey suggestions to the Washington Government in 1898 remind a regretful nation of both the evangelical versions mentioned, for the first seems to say what Luke says, and the second seems to add what Matthew adds.

There is not an American who has known the Filipinos since the beginning of the American occupation who doubts for a moment that but for our intervention a Republic would have been established out there under the lead of Aguinaldo, Mabini, and their associates, which would have compared well with the republican governments between the United States and Cape Horn. The writer doubts very much if President Taft is of a contrary opinion. The real issue is, now that we have them, should we keep them in spite of the tariff iniquities which the Trusts perpetrate on them through Congress, until they have received the best possible tuition we can give them, or be content to give them their independence when they are already at least as fit for it as the Republics to the South of us, guaranteeing them independence by international agreement like that which protects Belgium and Switzerland?

Now why did Admiral Dewey repeat to his home government and emphasize on August 29th a suggestion so extremely pertinent to the capacity of the Filipinos for self-government which he had already made in lucid language on June 23d previous? The answer is not far to seek. General Anderson had arrived between the two dates, with the first American troops that reached the islands after the naval battle of May 1st, and brought the Admiral the first intimation, which came somewhat as a surprise of course, that there was serious talk in the United States of retaining the Philippines. "I was the first to tell Admiral Dewey," says General Anderson in the *North American Review* for February, 1900, "that there was any disposition on the part of the American people to hold the Philippines if they were captured." He adds: "Whether Admiral Dewey and Consuls Pratt, Wildman, and Williams did or did not give Aguinaldo assurances that a Filipino government would be recognized, the Filipinos certainly thought so, judging from their acts rather than from their words. Admiral Dewey gave them arms and ammunition, as I did subsequently at his request."

General Anderson might have added that whenever the Admiral captured prisoners from the Spaniards he would promptly turn them over to the Filipinos—1300 at one clip in the month of June at Olongapo.50 These 1300 were men a German man-of-war prevented the Filipinos from taking until Aguinaldo reported the matter to Admiral Dewey, whereupon, he promptly sent Captain Coghlan with the *Raleigh* and another of his ships to the scene of the trouble, and Captain Coghlan said to the German " Hoch der Kaiser " etc. or words to that effect, and made him go about his business and let our ally alone. Then Captain Coghlan took the 1300 prisoners himself and turned them over to Aguinaldo by direction of Admiral Dewey. The motive for, as well as the test of, an alliance, is that the other fellow can bring into the partnership something you lack. The navy had no way to keep prisoners of war. There can be no doubt that if Admiral Dewey's original notions about meeting the problems presented by his great victory of May 1, 1898, had been followed, we never would have had any trouble with the Filipinos; nor can there be any doubt that he made them his allies and used them as such. They were very obedient allies at that, until they saw the Washington Government was going to repudiate the "alliance," and withhold from them what they had a right to consider the object and meaning of the alliance, if it meant anything.

The truth is, as Secretary of War Taft said in 1905, before the National Geographic Society in Washington, "We blundered into colonization."[51] As we have seen, Admiral Dewey repeatedly expressed the opinion, in the summer of 1898, that the Filipinos were far superior in intelligence to the Cubans and more capable of self-government. He of course saw quite clearly then, when he was sending home those commendations of Filipino fitness for self-government, just as we have all come to realize since, that a coaling station would be; the main thing we should need in that part of the world in time of war; that Manila, being quite away from the mainland of Asia, could never supersede Hong Kong as the gateway to the markets of Asia, since neither shippers nor the carrying trade of the world will ever see their way to unload cargo at Manila by way of rehearsal before unloading on the mainland; and that the taking of the islands was a dubious step from a financial standpoint, and a still more dubious one from the strategic standpoint of defending them by land, in the event of war with Japan, Germany, or any other first-class power. At this late date, when the passions and controversies of that period have long since subsided, is it not perfectly clear that after he destroyed the Spanish fleet, Admiral Dewey not only dealt with the Filipinos, until the army came out, substantially as Admiral Sampson and General Shafter did with the Cubans, but also that he did all he properly could to save President McKinley from the one great blunder of our history, the taking of the Philippine Islands?

---

[1] Hearings on Philippine affairs, *Senate Document 331*, part 3, 57th Cong., 1st Sess., 1901–2, proceedings of June 26–8, 1902.

[2] *S. D. 331*, pt. 3, p. 2927.

[3] The *Senate Document* has it backwards "left Mirs Bay for Hong Kong," clearly an error.

[4] *S. D. 331*, pt. 3, p. 2932.

[5] *Cong. Record*, April 17, 1900, p. 4287.

[6] *S. D. 331*, pt. 3, p. 2928.

[7] *Ib.*

[8] *S. D. 148*, 56th Cong., 2d Sess., 1901, p. 6.

[9] *S. D. 331*, pt. 3, p. 2937.

[10] *S. D. 331*, pt. 3, p. 2934.

[11] *Ib.*, p. 2967.

[12] See pp. 2928 and 2956, *S. D. 331*, part 3.

[13] *S. D. 331*, pt.3, p. 2965.

[14] *S. D. 331*, pt. 3, p. 2939.

[15] *Ib.*, p. 2936.

[16] *Ib.*, p. 2940.

17See letter of H. Irving Hancock, American war correspondent in the field, dated Manila, May 3, 1899, published *New York Criterion*, June 17, 1899. This Hancock interview with General MacArthur was quoted in debate on the floor of the Senate on April 17, 1900 (see *Cong. Rec.* of that date), and was corroborated by General MacArthur himself as substantially correct in that officer's testimony before the Senate in 1902, *S. D. 331*, pt. 2, 57th Congress, 1st Session, p. 1942, in answer to questions put by Senator Culberson.

18Rev. Clay Macaulay, who afterwards made that statement in a letter to the *Boston Transcript*.

19*S. D. 331*, pt. 3, p. 2939.

20*S. D. 208*, part 2, 56th Congress, 1st Sess., pp. 7, 8.

21*Cong. Record*, December, 1897.

22See *Cong. Record*, April 11, 1898, pp. 3699 *et seq.*

23*Cong. Record*, April 13, 1898, pp. 3701 *et seq.*

24*Navy Dept. Report*, 1898, Appendix, p. 103.

25*S. D. 62*, p. 327.

26*Navy Dept. Report*, 1898, App., p. 100. Dispatch May 20, 1898.

27*War Dept. Report*, 1899, vol. i, pt. 4, p. 13.

28*S. D. 331*, pt. 3, p. 2930.

29*Report Schurman Commission*, vol. i., p. 172.

30*S. D. 62*, p. 337.

31*S. D. 331*, pt. 3, 1902, p. 2951.

32*S. D. 331*, p. 2955.

33*Ib.*, p. 2954.

34*S. D. 62*, pp. 328–9.

35*Navy Dept. Report*, 1898, Appendix, p. 103.

36*Ib.*, p. 102.

37*Navy Dept. Report*, 1898, Appendix, p. 102.

38*S. D. 62*, p. 362.

39*Ib.*, pp. 360–1.

40*Navy Dept. Report*, 1898, Appendix, p. 106.

41*S. D. 62*, p. 354.

42*S. D. 62*, p. 329.

43*Ib.*, p. 432.

44Alas, that rare man, Frank Millet, perished in the *Titanic* disaster of April, 1912, since the above was written.

45*Expedition to the Philippines.*

46*Navy Dept. Report*, 1898, Appendix, p. 111.

47See p. 2934, *S. D. 331*, pt. 3, 57th Cong., 1st Sess.

48See p. 2934, *S. D. 331*, pt. 3, 57th Cong., 1st Sess.

49*S. D. 62*, p. 383.

50See Admiral Dewey's testimony before the Senate Committee of 1902, *S. D. 331*, pp. 2942, 2957.

51See *National Geographic Magazine*, August, 1905.

Chapter III. Anderson and Aguinaldo

Well, honor is the subject of my story.

Julius Cæsar, Act. I, Sc. 2.

The destruction of the Spanish fleet in Manila Bay on May 1, 1898, ten days after the outbreak of the war with Spain, having necessitated sending troops to the Philippines to complete the reduction of the Spanish power in that quarter, Major-General Wesley Merritt was on May 16th selected to organize and command such an expedition.

"The First Expedition," as it was always distinguished, by the officers and men of the Eighth Army Corps, there having been many subsequent expeditions sent out before our war with the Filipinos was over, was itself subdivided into a number of different expeditions, troops being hurried to Manila as fast as they could be assembled and properly equipped in sufficient numbers. The first batch that were whipped into shape left San Francisco under command of Brigadier-General Thomas M. Anderson, on May 25th, and arrived off Manila, June 30th. General Merritt did not arrive until July 25th. It was General Anderson, therefore, who broke the ice of the American occupation of the Philippines.

In his annual message to Congress of December, following,[1] summing up the War with Spain and its results, Mr. McKinley gives a brief account of the First Expedition. After recounting Admiral Dewey's victory of May 1st previous, he states that "on the seventh day of May the Government was advised officially of the victory at Manila, and at once inquired of the commander of the fleet what troops would be required." President McKinley does not give the Admiral's answer, though he does state that it was received on the 15th day of May. The Admiral's answer appears, however, in the *Report of the Navy Department* for 1898, Appendix, page 98. It was: "In my best judgment, a well-equipped force of 5000 men." But the President's message does state that he at once sent a "total force consisting of 641 officers and 15,058 enlisted men."

The difference of view-point of the Admiral and the President is clear from the language of both. In recommending 5000 troops, the Admiral had said they would be necessary "to retain possession [of Manila] and thus control Philippine Islands." This counted, of course, on the friendship of the people, as in Cuba. "I had in view simply taking possession of the city." said Admiral Dewey to the Senate Committee in 1902.[2]

The purpose of the President in sending three times as many troops as were needed for the purpose Admiral Dewey had in mind is indicated in his account of what happened. After describing the taking of Manila by our troops on August 13th, the presidential message says:

By this *the conquest of the Philippine Islands*, virtually accomplished when the Spanish capacity for resistance was destroyed by Admiral Dewey's victory of May 1st, *was formally sealed*.[3]

Admiral Dewey contemplated that we should merely remain masters of the situation out where he was until the end of the war. President McKinley set about to effect "the conquest of the Philippine Islands." The naval victory of Manila Bay having made it certain that at the conclusion of our war against a decadent monarchy we would at last have an adequate coaling station and naval base in the Far East, the sending of troops to the Philippines, in appropriate prosecution of the war, to reduce and capture Manila, the capital and chief port, raised the question at once "And then what?"

The genesis of the idea of taking over the archipelago is traceable to within a few days after the destruction of the Spanish fleet.

Within a few days after the official news of the battle of Manila Bay reached Washington, the Treasury Department set a man to work making a "Report on Financial and Industrial Conditions of the Philippine Islands."[4] The Interior Department also awoke, about the same time to possibilities of an El Dorado in the new overseas conquest. "In May, 1898," says Secretary of the Interior, C. N. Bliss, in a letter intended for the Peace Commissioners who met at Paris that fall, "by arrangement between the Secretary of War with this Department"—Mr. Bliss's grammar is bad, but his meaning is plain—"a geologist of the United States Geological Survey accompanied the military expedition to the Philippines for the purpose of procuring information touching the geological *and mineral* resources of said islands."[5] This report, which accompanies the Bliss letter, reads like a mining stock prospectus. That summer an Assistant Secretary of the Treasury, presumably echoing the sentiments of the Administration, came out in one of the great magazines of the period, the *Century*, with an article in which he said: "We see with sudden clearness that some of the most revered of our political maxims have outlived their force. * * * A new mainspring * * * has become the directing force * * * the mainspring of commercialism."[6] Of course, the writer did not mention that Manila is an out-of-the-way place, so far as regards the main-travelled routes across the Pacific Ocean, and also forgot that, as has been suggested once before, the carrying trade of the world, and the shippers on which it depends, in the contest of the nations for the markets of Asia, would never take to the practice of unloading at Manila by way of rehearsal, before finally discharging cargo on the mainland of Asia, where the name of the Ultimate Consumer is legion. Nevertheless "Expansion"—of Trade, mainly—was the slogan of the hour, and any one who did not catch the contagion of exuberant allusion to "Our New Possessions" was considered crusty and out of date. People who referred back to the political maxims of Washington's Farewell Address, and the cognate set represented by the Monroe Doctrine, were regarded merely as not knowing a good thing when they saw it. So on rode the country, on the crest of the wave of war. When President McKinley sent the troops to the Philippines, their job was to hurry up and effect what his subsequent message to Congress describing their work called "the conquest of the Philippine Islands." That is, they were to effect a *constructive* conquest of the archipelago before Spain should sue for peace. It never seemed to occur to anybody at home that the Filipinos would object. If the country had, through some divine interposition, gotten it into its head that the Filipinos were quite a decent lot and really did object very bitterly, it would have risen in its wrath and smitten down any suggestion of forcing a government on them against their will. But nobody knew anything about them. They were a wholly new proposition.

General Anderson was of course furnished with a copy of the President's instructions to his chief, General Merritt. They are quite long, and go into details about a number of administrative matters that would necessarily come up after the city should surrender, such as the raising of revenue, the military commander's duty under the law of nations with regard to the seizure of transportation lines by land or sea, the protection of places of worship from desecration or destruction, and the like. The only portion of them that is essential to a clear understanding of subsequent events is now submitted: They are dated Executive Mansion, May 18, 1898, and read in part[7]:

PRESIDENT McKINLEY'S INSTRUCTIONS TO GENERAL MERRITT

The destruction of the Spanish fleet at Manila, followed by the taking of the naval station at Cavite, the paroling of the garrisons, and acquisition of control of the bay, have rendered it necessary, in the further prosecution of the measures adopted by this Government for the purpose of bringing about an honorable and durable peace with Spain, to send an army of occupation to the Philippines for *the twofold purpose* of completing the reduction of the Spanish power in that quarter, and of *giving order and security* to the islands while in the possession of the United States.

For the command of this expedition I have designated Major-General Wesley Merritt, and it now becomes my duty to give instructions as to the manner in which the movements shall be conducted.

The first effect of the military occupation of the enemy's territory is the severance of the former political relations of the inhabitants and the establishment of a new political power. Under this changed condition of things the inhabitants, so long as they perform their duties, are entitled to security in their persons and property and in all their private rights and relations. It is my desire that the people of the Philippines should be acquainted with the purpose of the United States to discharge to the fullest extent its obligations in this regard. It will therefore be the duty of the commander of the expedition, *immediately upon his arrival* in the islands, to publish a proclamation declaring that we come not to make war upon the people of the Philippines nor upon any party or *faction* among them, but to protect them in their homes, in their employments, and in their personal and religious rights. All persons who, either by active aid or by honest submission, co-operate with the United States in its efforts to give effect to this beneficent purpose will receive the reward of its support and protection. Our occupation should be as free from severity as possible. Though *the powers of the military occupant are absolute and supreme and operate immediately upon the political condition of the inhabitants*, the municipal laws of the conquered territory, such as affect private rights of persons and property and provide for the punishment of crime, are to be considered as continuing in force, so far as they are compatible with the new order of things, until they are suspended or superseded by the occupying belligerents; and in practice they are not usually abrogated, but are allowed to remain in force and to be administered by the ordinary tribunals substantially as they were before the occupation. This enlightened practice is, so far as possible, to be adhered to on the present occasion. * * * The freedom of the people to pursue their accustomed occupations will be abridged only when it may be necessary to do so.

While the rule of conduct of the American commander-in-chief will be such as has just been defined, it will be his duty to adopt measures of a different kind if, unfortunately, the course of the people should render such measures indispensable to the maintenance of law and order. He will then possess the power to replace or expel the native officials in part or altogether, to substitute new courts of his own constitution for those that now exist, or to create such supplementary tribunals as may be necessary. In the exercise of these high powers the commander must be guided by his judgment and experience and a high sense of justice.

While this document declares the purpose of our government to be a "two fold purpose," viz., first, to make an appropriate move in the game of war, and, second, to police the Islands "while in the possession of the United States," it is wholly free from inherent evidence of any intention out of harmony with the policy as to Cuba. In fact when the city of Santiago de Cuba surrendered to our forces in July thereafter, and it became necessary to issue instructions for the guidance of the military commander there, exactly the same instructions were given him,8*verbatim et literatim*. But in respect of the Cuban instructions there was never any concealment practised or necessary because the Cubans had been assured by the Teller amendment to the resolutions declaring war against Spain that we had no ulterior designs on their country, and that, as soon as peace and public order were restored, we intended "to leave the government and control of the island to its people." The Cuban instructions were therefore frankly and promptly published in General Orders No. 101 by the War Department, July 18, 1898, five days after they were received from the President, and were then translated into Spanish and spread broadcast over Santiago province without unnecessary delay. I remember poring over a Spanish copy of General Orders 101, at Santiago de Cuba, shortly after the fall of that city, which copy was one of many already posted about that city by direction of General Wood. The words "the powers of the military occupant are *absolute and supreme and operate immediately upon the political condition of the inhabitants*" never disturbed the Cuban leaders in the least, because they were read in the light of the disclaimer contained in the declaration of war. On the other hand, the proclamation which the military commander in the Philippines was enjoined by his instructions to publish "immediately upon his arrival in the islands," which arrival occurred July 25th, was not so published until after we had taken Manila, August 13th, and then it copied only the glittering generalities of the instructions themselves, such as the part assuring the people that we had not come to make war on them and that vested rights would be respected, but it carefully omitted the words about the powers of the military occupant being absolute and supreme, because when the army arrived it found a native government that had already issued its declaration of independence, was making wonderful progress against the common enemy, and was able to put up a right good fight against us also, in case we should deny them independence.9

General Anderson arrived in Manila Bay, June 30, 1898, with about 2500 men, and when General Merritt arrived, July 25th, we had about 10,000 all told, while the Filipinos had half again that many, and there were 12,000 Spanish soldiers in Manila. General Anderson had not been long camped on the bayshore, under cover of the Navy's guns and in the neighborhood of Aguinaldo's headquarters, before he understood the whole situation clearly and wrote the War Department as follows:

Since reading the President's instructions to General Merritt, I think I should state to you that the establishment of a provisional government on our part will probably bring us in conflict with insurgents.

This letter is dated July 18, 1898.10

When General Anderson arrived in the islands on June 30th, the Washington Government was still wrestling with the angel of its announced creed about "Forcible Annexation" being "criminal aggression," and Mr. McKinley had to get both that angel's shoulders on the mat and put him out of business before he could get his own consent to giving any instructions to his generals which might sanction their killing people for objecting to forcible annexation. Hence his early anxiety to avoid a rupture with the Filipino leaders. The first stage of this wrestling coincides in point of time with General Anderson's tenure as the ranking military officer commanding our forces in the Philippines, which was from June 30th until the date of General Merritt's arrival, July 25th. As already made plain, the President's instructions for the guidance of the military commander were entirely free from any land-grabbing suggestion. On the other hand, when General Anderson left San Francisco for Manila, May 25th, there was already talk in the United States about retaining the Islands, if they were captured, for he so informed Admiral Dewey in the first interview they had after the transports which brought his command cast anchor near our squadron in Manila Bay on the last day of June. "I was the first to tell Admiral Dewey," says he, in the *North American Review* for February, 1900, "that there was any disposition on the part of the American people to hold the Philippines, if they were captured. The current opinion was setting that way when the expeditionary force left San Francisco, but this the Admiral had no reason to surmise."

Relegated by the circumstances to his own discretion as to how he should act until Washington knew its mind, General Anderson's attitude in the outset represented a "peace-at-any-price" policy, suffused with benevolent pride at championing the cause of the oppressed, but secretly knowing from the beginning that it might become necessary later to slaughter said "oppressed," should they seriously object to a change of masters.

"On July 1st," says General Anderson, in the *North American Review* article above quoted, "I called on Aguinaldo with Admiral Dewey." Of the Admiral's dealings with the insurgent chief prior to this time, the General says in this same article:

"Whether Admiral Dewey and Consuls Pratt, Wildman, and Williams did or did not give Aguinaldo assurances that a Filipino government would be recognized, the Filipinos certainly thought so, probably inferring this from their acts rather than from their statements." This last quoted passage was read to Admiral Dewey by a member of the Senate Committee in 1902, along with other parts of the magazine article cited, and he was asked to comment on the same. He said:

"These are General Anderson's statements. They are very interesting, indeed; I am here to make my own statements."

He had stated that he never did specifically promise Aguinaldo independence, and the questioner was trying to show that his *acts* had amounted to assurances and therefore had committed the Government to giving the Filipinos their independence. Then Senator Patterson began another question, and had gotten as far as "I want to know whether your views—" when out came this, as of a sailor-man clearing decks for action:

"I do not like your questions a bit. I did not like them yesterday and I do not like them to-day." So the Admiral's feelings were respected and the question was not pressed. There is no doubt at all that in the Philippines in the summer of 1898 the army turned the back of its hand to Aguinaldo as soon as it got there and baldly repudiated what the navy had done in the way of befriending the Filipinos. But both had acted under the authority of the Commander-in-Chief of the Army and Navy—the President. The Admiral's sensitiveness on the subject *ought* to have been respected. And it was.

By the time Admiral Dewey and General Anderson decided to call on "Don Emilio," the day after the General's arrival, the unexpected intimations which the latter brought, as to the Washington programme for the Philippine revolutionists being different from that as to Cuba, had begun to get in its work on the former. Not being a politician, the gallant Admiral was there ready and able to carry out any orders his government might send him, whenever the politicians should decide what they wanted to do. But in the absence of orders, he began to trim his sails a bit, so as to be prepared for whatever might be the policy. Accordingly, before he and the General started out to pay their call on "Don Emilio Aguinaldo y Famy, President of the Revolutionary Government of the Philippines and General in Chief of its Army"—as he had styled himself in his proclamation of June 23d,—the Admiral said, "Do not take your sword or put on your uniform, but just put on your blouse. Do not go with any ceremony." And says he, in telling this, "We went in that way."11 The reason of thus avoiding too much ceremony toward our "ally" claiming to represent an existing government which had lately declared its independence, is explained by an expression of the Admiral's concerning said Declaration of Independence itself: "That was my idea, not taking it seriously." At that same hearing the Admiral explained with much genuine feeling that from the day of the naval battle of May 1st until the arrival of the army "these great questions" were coming up constantly and he simply met them as they arose by acting on his best judgment on the spot at the time.

But what a terrible mistake it was not to take that Declaration of Independence of June 23d, seriously, backed as it was by an army of 15,000 men flushed with victory, and under the absolute control of the author of the Declaration! Of course the Declaration had been published to the army. Could its author have checked them by repudiating it even if he had wanted to? As Aguinaldo himself expressed what would happen in such a contingency, "They would fail to recognize me as *the interpreter of their aspirations* and would punish me as a traitor, replacing me by another more careful of his own honor and dignity."12

This Dewey-Anderson call on Aguinaldo was on July 1st. Admiral Dewey now began to foresee that the Washington programme was going to put him in an awkward position. So he began to take Aguinaldo more seriously. On July 4th, he wired Washington: "Aguinaldo proclaimed himself President of the Revolutionary Republic on July 1st."13 It was on July 7th that Admiral Dewey captured 1300 armed Spanish prisoners, the garrison of Isla la Grande, off Olongapo, and turned them over to the forces of the Aguinaldo government because he had no way to keep them.14 Was not that taking that government a bit seriously? How wholly unauthorized by the facts was this of "not taking it seriously," on the part of "The Liberator of the Filipinos,"15 the immortal victor of Manila Bay, who two months before had taught the nation the magnitude of its power for good, in a cause as righteous as the crusades of old, and more sensible!

But to return to General Anderson's account in the *North American Review* of his call, with Admiral Dewey, on the insurgent chief: "He asked me at once whether the 'United States of the North' either had, or would recognize his government. I am not quite sure as to the form of the question, whether it was 'had' or 'would'? *In either form it was embarrassing.*" General Anderson then tells of Aguinaldo's returning his call: "A few days thereafter he made an official call, coming with cabinet, staff, and band. He asked if we, the North Americans, as he called us, intended to hold the Philippines as dependencies. I said I could not answer that, but that in 122 years we had established no colonies. He then made this remarkable statement: '*I have studied attentively the Constitution of the United States, and I find in it no authority for colonies, and I have no fear.*'" General Anderson adds: "It may seem that my answer was evasive, but I was at the time trying to contract with the Filipinos for horses, fuel, and forage."

While this history must not lapse into an almanac, it may not be amiss to follow these early stages of this matter through a few more successive dates, because the history of that period was all indelibly branded into Filipino memory shortly afterward with the red-hot iron of war.

July 4th, General Anderson writes the Filipino candidate for Independence inviting him to "co-operate with us in military operations against the Spanish forces."16 This was written not to arrange any *plan* of co-operation but in order to get room about Cavite as a military base without a row. In his *North American Review* article General Anderson says that on that same day, the Fourth of July, Aguinaldo was invited to witness a parade and review "in honor of our national holiday." "He did not come," says the article, "because he was not invited as President but as General Aguinaldo." An odd situation, was it not? Here was a man claiming to be President of a newly established republic based on the principles set forth in our Declaration of Independence, which republic had just issued a like Declaration, and he was invited to come and hear *our* declaration read, and declined *because we would not recognize his right to assert the same truths.* On subsequent anniversaries of the day in the Philippines it was deemed wise simply to prohibit the reading of our Declaration before gatherings of the Filipino people. It saved discussion.

July 6th, General Anderson writes telling Aguinaldo that he is expecting more troops soon and therefore "*I would like to have your excellency's advice and co-operation.*"17

July 9th, General Anderson writes the War Department that Aguinaldo tells him he has about 15,000 fighting men, 11,000 armed with guns, and some 4000 prisoners,18 and adds: "When we first landed he seemed very suspicious, and not at all friendly but I have now come to a better understanding with him and he is much more friendly and seems *willing to co-operate*."

July 13th, we find Admiral Dewey also still in a co-operative mood. On that day he cables the Navy Department of the capture of the 1,300 prisoners on July 7th, mentioned above, which capture was made, it appears, because Aguinaldo complained to him that a German war-ship was interfering with his operations,19 the prisoners being at once turned over to Aguinaldo, as stated above.

July 18th, is the date of the letter to the War Department in which General Anderson states that the establishment of a provisional government by us will probably mean a conflict with the insurgents. This was equivalent to saying that they will probably be ready to fight whenever we assert the "absolute and supreme" authority that the President's instructions had directed to be asserted by the army as soon as it should arrive in the Philippines. Yet in the fall of 1899, President McKinley said he "never dreamed" that Aguinaldo's "little band" would oppose our rule to the extent of war against it. It would have been more accurate if the martyred Christian gentleman who used those words had said he "always hoped" they would not, instead of "never dreamed" they would. This letter of July 18th, informs the Department:

Aguinaldo has declared himself dictator and self-appointed president. He has declared martial law and promulgated a minute method of procedure under it.

July 19th, General Anderson sends Major (now Major-General) J. F. Bell, to Aguinaldo, and asks of him a number of favors, such as any soldier may properly ask of an ally, for example, permission to see his military maps, etc., and that Aguinaldo "place at his [Bell's] disposal any *information you may have* on the above subjects, and also give him [Bell] a letter or pass addressed to your subordinates which will*authorize them to furnish him any information they can* * * * and to facilitate his passage along the lines, upon a reconnaissance around Manila, on which I propose to send him."20 All of which Aguinaldo did.

Military training is very keen on honor. Talk about what the French call *foi d'officier*,—the "word of an officer"! Did ever a letter from one soldier to another more completely commit the faith and honor of his government, to recognition of the existence of an alliance? "In 122 years we have established no colonies," he had told Aguinaldo. "It looks like we are about to go into the colonizing business," he had, in effect, said to Admiral Dewey, about the same time.

July 21st, General Anderson writes the Adjutant-General of the army as follows:

Since I last wrote, Aguinaldo has put in operation an elaborate system of military government. * * * It may seem strange that I have made no formal protest against his proclamation as dictator, his declaration of martial law, etc. I wrote such a protest but did not publish it at Admiral Dewey's request.21

When he wrote this letter, General Anderson was evidently beginning to have some compunctions about the trouble he now saw ahead. He was a veteran of the Civil War, whose gallantry had then been proven on many a field against an enemy compared with whom these people would be a picnic. But things did not look to the grim old hero like there was going to be a square deal. So he put this in the letter:

I submit, with all deference, that we have heretofore underrated the natives. They are *not* ignorant savage tribes, but have a civilization of their own, and although insignificant in appearance are fierce fighters and for a tropical people they are industrious. A small detail of natives will do more work than a regiment of volunteers.

Of course, this slam at "volunteers" *was* a bit rough. But the battle-scarred veteran's sense of fair play was getting on his nerves. He foresaw the coming conflict, and though he did not shirk it, he did not relish it. He understood the "game," and it seemed to him the cards were stacked, to meet the necessity of demonstrating that forcible annexation, instead of being criminal aggression, was merely Trade Expansion, and that his government was right then irrevocably committing itself, without any knowledge of, or acquaintance with, the Filipinos, to the assumption that they were incapable of running a government of their own.

The next day, July 22d, General Anderson wrote Aguinaldo a letter advising him that he was without orders as yet concerning the question of recognizing his government. But that this letter was neither a protest nor in the nature of a protest, is evident from its text:

I observe that Your Excellency has announced yourself dictator and proclaimed martial law. As I am here simply in a military capacity, I have no authority to recognize such an assumption. *I have no orders from my government on the subject.*[22]

Yet General Anderson's letter to the Adjutant-General of the army of July 18th[23] uses the words "since reading the President's instructions to General Merritt," etc., showing that he had a copy of them; and those instructions order and direct (see *ante*) that as soon as the commanding general of the American troops arrives he is to let the Filipinos know that "the powers of the military occupant are *absolute and supreme and immediately operate* upon the political condition of the inhabitants." A charitable view of the matter would be that, technically, those were Merritt's orders, not Anderson's. But the whole scheme was to conceal the intention to assume supreme authority and keep Aguinaldo quiet "until," as General Merritt afterwards expressed it in his report, "I should be in possession of the city of Manila, * * * as I would not until then be in a position to * * * enforce my authority, in the event that his [Aguinaldo's] pretensions should clash with my designs."[24]

The same day that General Anderson wrote Aguinaldo his *billet doux* about the dictatorship, viz., July 22d, he cabled Washington a much franker and more serious message; which read: "Aguinaldo declares dictatorship and martial law over all islands. THE PEOPLE EXPECT INDEPENDENCE. " The very next day, July 23d, he wrote Aguinaldo asking his assistance in getting five hundred horses, and fifty oxen and ox-carts, and manifesting considerable impatience that he had not already complied with a similar request previously made "*as it was to fight in the cause of your people.*"[25] The following day, July 24th, replying to General Anderson's letter of the 22d wherein General Anderson had advised him that he was as yet without orders concerning the question of recognizing his government, Aguinaldo wrote:

It is true that my government has not been acknowledged by any of the foreign powers, but we expected that the great North American nation, which had struggled first for its independence, and afterwards for the abolition of slavery, *and is now actually struggling for the independence of Cuba*, would look upon it with greater benevolence than any other nation.[26]

That cablegram of July 22d, above quoted, in which the commanding general of our forces in the Philippines advises the Washington government, "The people expect independence," is the hardest thing in the published archives of our government covering that momentous period for those who love the memory of Mr. McKinley to get around.27 After the war with the Filipinos broke out Mr. McKinley said repeatedly in public speeches, "I never dreamed they would turn against us." You do not find the Anderson cablegram of July 22d in the published report of the War Department covering the period under consideration. General Anderson addressed it to the Secretary of War and signed it, and, probably for lack of army cable facilities, got Admiral Dewey to send it to the Secretary of the Navy for transmission to the Secretary of War.28 Certain it must be that at some Cabinet meeting on or after July 22, 1898, either the Secretary of the Navy or the Secretary of War read in the hearing of the President and the rest of his advisers that message from General Anderson, " THE PEOPLE EXPECT INDEPENDENCE." The object here is *not* to inveigh against Mr. McKinley. It is to show that, as Gibbon told us long ago, in speaking of the discontent of far distant possessions and the lack of hold of the possessor on the affections of the inhabitants thereof, "the cry of remote distress is ever faintly heard." The average American to-day, if told the Filipinos want independence, will give the statement about the same consideration Mr. McKinley did then, and if told that the desire among them for a government *of* their people *by their* people *for* their people has not been diminished since the late war by tariff taxation without representation, and the steady development of race prejudice between the dominant alien race and the subject one, he will begin to realize by personal experience how faintly the uttered longings of a whole people may fall on distant ears.

We saw above that in a letter written July 21st, the day before the telegram about the "people expect independence," which letter must have reached Washington within thirty days, General Anderson not only notified Washington all about Aguinaldo's government and its pretensions, but stated that at the request of Admiral Dewey he had made no protest against it.29 Yet straight on through the period of General Merritt's sojourn in the Islands, which began July 25th, and terminated August 29th, we find no protest ordered by Washington, and we further find the purpose of the President as announced in the instructions to Merritt, "The powers of the military occupant are *absolute and supreme*" throughout the Islands, not only *not* communicated to the Filipino people, but deliberately suppressed from the proclamation published by General Merritt pursuant to those instructions.30

Comments and conclusions are usually impertinent and unwelcome save as mere addenda to *facts*, but in the light of the facts derivable from our own official records, is it any wonder that General Anderson, a gallant veteran of the Civil War, and perhaps the most conspicuous figure of the early fighting in the Philippines, delivered an address some time after he came back home before the Oregon Commandery of the Loyal Legion of the United States31 on the subject, "Should republics have colonies?" and answered the question emphatically "No!"

1*Congressional Record*, December 5, 1898.

2See p. 2938, *S. D. 331* (1902).

3*Congressional Record*, December 5, 1898, p. 5.

4*Senate Document 169*, 55th Cong., 3d Sess. (1898).

5*Ib.*

6Hon. Frank A. Vanderlip, August, 1898 *Century Magazine*.

7See p. 85, *S. D. 208*, 1900.

8See General Orders No. 101, series 1898, Adjutant-General's Office, Washington, July 18, 1898, a copy of which accompanied the President's message to Congress of December, 1898, and may be seen at p. 783, *House Document No. 1*, 55th Cong., 3d Sess., 1898–9.

9For a copy of this proclamation, see p. 86, *S. D. 208*, 56th Cong., 1st Sess.

10*S. D. 208*, p. 8.

11*S. D. 331*, p. 2976, Hearings before Senate Committee, 1902.

12*S. D. 208*, 56th Cong., 1st Sess., 1900, p. 16.

13*Correspondence, War with Spain,* vol. ii., p. 720.

14For Admiral Dewey's cable report of this, see *Navy Dept. Report*, 1898, Appendix, p. 110. For particulars, given by him subsequently, see *S. D. 331*, 1902, p. 2942.

15*S. D. 331*, pt. 3, 1902, p. 2942, and thereabouts.

16*S. D. 208*, 56th Cong., 1st Sess., 1900, p. 4.

17*S. D. 208*, p. 4.

18Anderson only had about 2500 troops then.

19See *Navy Dept. Report*, 1898, Appendix, p. 110; *S. D. 331*, 1902, p. 2942.

20*Senate Document 208*, 1900, p. 8.

21*Ib.*, pp. 12–13.

22*S. D. 208*, 1900, p. 9.

23*Ib.*, p. 8.

24See page 40 of General Merritt's Report, *War Dept. Report*, 1898, vol. i., part 2.

25*S. D. 208*, 1900, 56th Cong., 1st Sess., p. 11.

26*Ib.*, p. 10.

27The writer is certainly one of these, and while calling in question the wisdom and righteousness of our Philippine policy, he cannot refrain from avowing just here a feeling of individual obligation to Mr. Root for his exquisite tribute to the *personal* equation of Mr. McKinley, delivered at the National Republican Convention of 1904, which was, in part, as follows: "How wise and skilful he was. How modest and self-effacing. How deep his insight into the human heart. *How swift the intuitions of his sympathy. How compelling the charm of his gracious presence.* He was so unselfish, so genuine a lover of his kind. And he was the kindest and tenderest friend who ever grasped another's hand. Alas, that his virtues did plead in vain against his cruel fate."

28See *Navy Dept. Report*, 1898, Appendix, p. 117.

29*S. D. 208*, 1900, p. 13.

30For the Merritt proclamation, see *S. D. 208*, p. 86.

31In 1906.

Chapter IV. Merritt and Aguinaldo

There are no tricks in plain and simple faith.

Julius Cæsar, Act IV., Sc. 2.

Major-General Wesley Merritt's account of the operations of the troops under his command in the First Expedition to the Philippines may be found in volume i., part 2, *War Department Report* for 1898. He left San Francisco accompanied by his staff, June 29, 1898, arrived at Cavite, Manila Bay, July 25th, received the surrender of the city of Manila August 13th, and sailed thence August 30th, in obedience to orders from Washington to proceed without unnecessary delay to Paris, France, for conference with the Peace Commissioners. According to General Merritt's report, about the time he arrived Aguinaldo had some 12,000 men under arms, with plenty of ammunition, and a number of field-pieces. The late lamented Frank D. Millet has preserved for us, in his *Expedition to the Philippines*, some valuable and intimate studies of this army of Filipino besiegers whom our troops found busily at work when they arrived in the Islands:

It was an interesting sight at Camp Dewey to see the insurgents strolling to and from the front. Pretty much all day long they were coming and going, never in military formation, but singly, and in small groups, perfectly clean and tidy in dress, often accompanied by their wives and children, and all chatting as merrily as if they were going off on a pigeon shoot. The men who sold fish and vegetables in camp in the morning would be seen every day or two dressed in holiday garments, with rifle and cartridge boxes, strolling off to take their turn at the Spaniards.

The reader will readily understand that there were many times as many volunteers as guns. Mr. Millet continues:

When they had been at the front twenty-four hours they were relieved and returned home for a rest. They generally passed their rifles and equipments on to another man and thus a limited number of weapons served to arm a great many besiegers. They had no distinctive uniform, the only badge of service being a red and blue cockade with a white triangle bearing the Malay symbol of the sun and three stars, and sometimes a red and blue band pinned diagonally across the lower part of the left sleeve. * * * Many of them * * * had belonged to the native volunteer force. * * * The recruits were soon hammered into shape by the veterans of the rank and file. * * * Their men were perfectly obedient to orders * * * and they made the most devoted soldiers. There was no visible Commissary or Quartermaster's Departments, but the insurgent force was always supplied with food and ammunition and there was no lack of transportation. The food issued at the front was mostly rice*brought up in carromatas to within a few hundred yards of the trenches, when it was cooked by the women.* * * * Each man had a double handful of rice, sometimes enriched by a small proportion of meat and fish, which was served him in a square of plantain leaf. Thus he was unencumbered with a plate or knife or fork and threw away his primitive but excellent dish when he had "licked the platter clean." It was noticeable that the insurgents carried no water bottles nor haversacks, and no equipments indeed, but cartridge boxes. They did not seem to be worried by thirst like our men.

"Although insignificant in appearance, they are fierce fighters," wrote General Anderson to the Adjutant-General of the army in July.1

General Merritt states in his report that Aguinaldo had "proclaimed an independent government, republican in form, with himself as President, and at the time of my arrival in the Islands the entire edifice of executive and legislative departments had been accomplished, at least *on paper*."2 Of course at that time we were still officially declining to take Filipino aspirations for independence seriously, and preferred to treat Aguinaldo's government as purely a matter of stationery. As a matter of fact, an exhaustive examination of the official documents of that period, made with a view of ascertaining just how much of that Aguinaldo government of 1898 was stationery fiction and how much was stable fact, has absolutely surprised one man who was out there from 1899 to 1905 (the writer), and I have no doubt will be interesting, as mere matter of political necrology, to any American who was there "in the days of the empire" as the "ninety-niners" called it.

Early in the spring of 1899, Mr. McKinley sent out the Commission of which President Schurman of Cornell University was Chairman, to try to stop the war. They bent themselves to the task in a spirit as kindly as that in which we know Mr. McKinley himself would have acted. They failed because the war was already on and the Filipinos were bent on fighting for independence to the bitter end. But they learned a good deal about the facts of the earlier situation. Speaking of these in their report to the President3 with especial reference to the period beginning with Aguinaldo's landing at Cavite in May, after describing how the Filipino successes in battle with the Spaniards finally resulted in all of them being driven into Manila, where they remained hemmed in, they say:

While the Spanish troops now remained quietly in Manila, the Filipino forces made themselves *masters of the entire island except that city*.

"For three and one half months," says General Otis in describing the facts of this same situation a year later, "the insurgents on land had kept Manila tightly bottled [meaning while Admiral Dewey had been blockading the place by water] * * * and food supplies were exhausted."4"We had Manila and Cavite. The rest of the island was held *not* by the Spanish but by the Filipinos," said General Anderson, in the *North American Review* for February, 1900. "It is a fact that they were in possession, they had gotten pretty much the whole thing except Manila," said Admiral Dewey to the Senate Committee in 1902.5

General Merritt took Manila August 13th, and sailed away for Paris August 31st, and only a week after that General Otis wired Washington (under date of September 7th) from Manila: "Insurgents have captured all Spanish garrisons in island [of Luzon] and control affairs outside of Cavite and this city."6

The recruiting by Aguinaldo of an army of 40,000 men with guns within one hundred days after his little "Return from Elba"—"15,000 fighting men, 11,000 of them armed with guns," in fifty days,7 which number had swelled to nearly 40,000 men with guns in another fifty days (by August 29th)8—is no more remarkable than his progress in organizing his government and making its grip on the whole island of Luzon effective in a short space of time.

As all Americans who know the Filipinos know how fond they are of what government offices call "paper work," and how their *escribientes*9can work like bees in drafting documents, it might be easy to ignore Aguinaldo's various proclamations, already hereinbefore noticed in Chapter II., as representing merely "a government on paper," were there no other proof. But among the insurgent captured papers we found long afterward, there is a document containing the minutes of a convention of the *insurrecto* presidentes from all the pueblos of fifteen different provinces, on August 6, 1898, which throws a flood of light on the subject now under consideration.10 This convention was held at Bacoor, then Aguinaldo's headquarters, a little town on the bay shore between Manila and Cavite. The minutes of the convention recite that its members had been previously chosen as presidentes of their respective pueblos in the manner prescribed by previous decrees issued by Aguinaldo (already noticed), and that thereafter they had taken the oath of office before Aguinaldo as President of the government, etc. They then declare that the Filipino people whom they speak for are "not ambitious for power, nor honors, nor riches, aside from the rational aspirations for a free and independent life," and "proclaim solemnly, in the face of the whole world, the Independence of the Philippines." They also re-affirm allegiance to Aguinaldo as President of the government and request him to seek recognition of it at the hands of the Powers, "because," says the paper, "to no one is it permitted to * * * stifle the legitimate aspirations of a people"—as if Europe cared a rap what *we* did to them except in the way of regret that *it* did not have a finger in the pie. However, they were not only apprehensive, on the one hand, lest we might be tempted to take their country away from Spain for ourselves, but also, on the other hand, lest we might in the wind-up decide to leave them to Spain at the end of the war. That this last was not an idle fear is shown by the fact that during the deliberations of the Paris Peace Commission, Judge Gray urged, in behalf of his contention against taking the islands at all, that if Dewey had sunk the Spanish fleet off Cadiz, instead of in Manila Bay, and the Carlists had incidentally helped us about that time, we would have been under no resulting obligation "to stay by them at the conclusion of the war."11 When the presidentes in convention assembled as aforesaid got through with theirWHEREASES and RESOLUTIONS they presented them to His Excellency the President of the Republic, Aguinaldo, who then issued a proclamation which recited, among other things: "In these provinces [the fifteen represented in the convention] complete order and perfect tranquillity reign, administered by the authorities elected"12 according to his previous decrees as Dictator, which decrees have already been placed before the reader. The proclamation claims that the new government has 9,000 prisoners of war and 30,000 combatants. The former claim no one having any acquaintance with those times and conditions will question for a moment. As to the 30,000 combatants, if he had 11,000 men armed with guns on July 9th and 40,000 on August 29th, why not 30,000 on August 6th? Of course, men without guns, bolo men, do not count for much in a serious connection like this now being considered. In November, 1899, at San José, in Nueva Ecija province, I heard General Lawton tell Colonel Jack Hayes to disarm and turn loose 175 bolo men the colonel had just captured and was lining up on the public square as we rode into the town. But we are considering how much of a government the Filipinos had in 1898, because the answer is pertinent to what sort of a government they could run if permitted *now* or at any time in the future; and, physical force being the ultimate basis of stability in all government, when we come to estimate how much of an army they had when their government was claiming recognition as a legitimate living thing, we must remember that "It was just a question of arming them. They could have had the whole population."13

Now the great significant fact about this Bacoor convention of presidentes of August 6th—a week before Manila surrendered to our forces—is that in it more than half the population of the island of Luzon was represented. The total population of the Philippines is about 7,600,000,14and, of these, one-half, or 3,800,00015 live on Luzon. The other islands may be said to dangle from Luzon like the tail of a kite. Taking the tables of the American census of the Philippines of 1903 (vol. ii., p. 123), as a basis on which to judge what Aguinaldo's claims of August 6th amounted to if true, the population of the provinces thus duly incorporated into the new government and in working order on that date, was, in round numbers, about as follows: South of Manila:—Cavite, 135,000; Batangas, 260,000; Laguna, 150,000; Tayabas, 150,000; North of Manila:—Bulacan, 225,000; Pampamga, 225,000; Nueva Ecija, 135,000; Tarlac, 135,000; Pangasinan, 400,000; Union, 140,000; Bataan, 45,000; Zambales, 105,000. This represents a total of more than 2,000,000 of people.

But Aguinaldo's claims of August 6th are not the only evidence as to the political status of the provinces of Luzon in August, 1898. Toward the end of that month, Maj. J. F. Bell, Chief of General Merritt's Bureau of Military Information, made a report on the situation as it stood August 29th, the report being made after most careful investigation, and intended as a summary of the then situation according to the most reliable information obtainable, in order that General Merritt might know, as far as practicable, what he would be "up against" in the event of trouble with the insurgents.16

This report not only corroborates Aguinaldo's claims of August 6th, but it also concedes to the Aguinaldo people eight other important provinces—four south of the Pasig River with a total population of about 630,000,[17] the only four of southern Luzon not included in Aguinaldo's claim of August 6th, thus conceding him practically all of Luzon south of the Pasig; and it furthermore concedes him four great provinces of northern Luzon with a total population of nearly 600,000.[18] General Bell states that these last are "still in the possession of the Spanish," but practically certain to be with the insurgents in the very near future. "Insurgents have been dispatched to attack the Spanish in these provinces," says the Bell report.

In this same report Major Bell said: "There is not a particle of doubt but what Aguinaldo and his leaders will resist any attempt *of any government* to reorganize a colonial government here."[19] When the insurgent government was finally dislodged from its last capital and Aguinaldo became a fugitive hotly pursued by our troops, he started for the mountains of northern Luzon, passing through provinces he had never visited before. The diary of one of his staff officers, Major Villa, in describing a brief stop they made in a town *en route* (Aringay, in Union province) says: "After the honorable President had urged them [the townspeople] to be patriotic, we continued the march."[20] They certainly did "continue the march." The Maccabebe scouts, of which the writer commanded a company at the time, took the town a few hours later, Aguinaldo's rear-guard retiring after a brief resistance, following which we found, among the dead in the trenches, a major other than Villa. Certainly, to read this little extract from the diary of Aguinaldo's retreat is to feel the pulse of northern Luzon as to its loyalty to the revolution at that time, and is corroborative of these claims of Aguinaldo made in August, 1898, supplemented, as we have seen them, by General Bell's appraisal.

As to the political conditions which prevailed in southern Luzon, particularly in the Camarines, in August and the fall of 1898, information derived from one who was there then would seem appropriate here. Major Blanton Winship, Judge Advocate's Corps, U. S. A., Major Archibald W. Butt, the late lamented military aide to President Taft, and the writer, lived together in Manila, in 1900, at the house of a Spanish physician, a Dr. Lopez, who had been a "prisoner" at Nueva Caceres, a town situated in one of the provinces of southern Luzon (Camarines) in the fall of 1898. Dr. Lopez had a large family. They had also been "prisoners" down there. No evil befell them at the hands of their "captors." They had the freedom of the town they were in. They had good reason to be pretty well scared as to what the insurgents might do to them. But they were never maltreated. The main impression we got from Dr. Lopez and his family was that the political grip of the Aguinaldo government on southern Luzon was complete during the time they were "prisoners" there. If anybody doubts the absoluteness of the grip of the Revolutionary government on the situation in the provinces which were represented at the Bacoor convention of August 6, 1898, above mentioned, when the Filipino Declaration of Independence was signed and proclaimed, let him ask any American who had a part in putting down the Philippine insurrection what a presidente, an *insurrecto* presidente, in a Filipino town, was in 1899 and 1900. He was "the whole thing." Even to-day the presidente of a pueblo is as absolute boss of his town as Charles F. Murphy is of Tammany Hall. And a *town* or *pueblo* in the Philippines is more than an area covered by more or less contiguous buildings and grounds. It is more like a township in Massachusetts. So that when you account governmentally for the pueblos of a given province, you account for every square foot of that province and for every man in it. For several years before our war with Spain, nearly every Filipino of any education and spirit in the archipelago belonged to the secret revolutionary society known as the Katipunan. This had its organization in every town when Dewey sank the Spanish fleet and landed Aguinaldo at Cavite. The rest may be imagined.

By September, 1898, Aguinaldo was absolute master of the whole of Luzon. Before the Treaty of Paris was signed (December 10, 1898), in fact while Judge Gray of the Peace Commission was cabling President McKinley that not to leave the government of the Philippines to the people thereof "would be to make a mockery of instructions," Aguinaldo had become equally absolute master of the situation throughout the rest of the archipelago outside of Manila.

Toward the end of July, 1898, our Manila Consul, Mr. Williams, who was one of our consular triumvirate of would-be Warwicks, or "original Aguinaldo men," of 1898, used to have nice talks with Aguinaldo about the lion and the lamb lying down together without the lion eating the lamb, and in one instance, at least, he goes so far as to represent Aguinaldo as willing to some such arrangement—*e. g.*, annexation, or some vague scheme of dependence. But whenever we hear from Aguinaldo over his own signature, we hear him saying whatever means in Tagalo "Timeo Danaos et dona ferentes." For instance, at page 15, of *Senate Document 208*, he writes Williams, under date of August 1st, with fine courtesy:

I congratulate you with all sincerity on the acuteness and ingenuity which you have displayed in painting in an admirable manner the benefits which, *especially for me and my leaders*, and in general for all my compatriots, would be secured by the union of these islands with the United States of America. Ah! that picture, so happy and so finished * * * This is not saying that I am not of your opinion * * * You say all this and yet more will result from annexing ourselves to your people * * * You are my friend and the friend of the Filipinos and have said it. But why should we say it? Will my people believe it? * * * I have done what they desire, establishing a government * * * not only because it was my duty, but also because had I acted in any other manner they would fail to recognize me as *the interpreter of their aspirations*, and would punish me as a traitor, replacing me by another *more careful of his own honor and dignity.*

Now that we know what was in the Filipino mind when General Merritt arrived in the Philippines, let us see what was in the American military mind out there at the same time. Says General Merritt: "General Aguinaldo did not visit me on my arrival nor offer his services as a subordinate leader." We trust the reason of this at once suggests itself from what has preceded, including General Anderson's dealings with the insurgent chief. The latter wanted some understanding as to what *the intentions of our government were*, and what was to be the programme afterward, should he and his countrymen assist in the little fighting that now remained necessary to complete the taking of Manila. *Those intentions were precisely what Merritt was determined to conceal.* "As my instructions from the President fully contemplated the occupation of *the Islands* by the American land forces, and stated that 'the powers of the military occupant are absolute and supreme and immediately operate upon the political condition of the inhabitants,' I did not consider it wise to hold any direct communication with the insurgent leader until I should be in possession of the city of Manila."[21]

On one occasion General Merritt passed through the village of Bacoor where Aguinaldo had his headquarters, but, says Mr. Millet[22] in mentioning this, "They never met." After the taking of the city, General Merritt remembered that with some 13,000 Spanish prisoners to guard, and a city of 300,000 people, all but a sprinkling of whom were in sympathy with the insurgent cause, on his hands, and an army of at least 14,000 insurgents—probably far more than that—clamoring without the gates of that city, and only 10,000 men of his own with whom to handle such a situation, frankness was out of the question, in view of his orders from the President.[23] Therefore, on the day after the city surrendered, General Merritt issued a proclamation, copying[24] *verbatim* from Mr. McKinley's instructions (*ante*) such innocuous milk-and-water passages as the one which assured the people that our government "has not come to wage war upon them * * * but to protect them in their homes, in their employments, and in their personal and religious rights; all persons who, by active aid or honest submission, co-operate with the United States * * * will receive the reward of its support and protection." But he carefully omitted the words quoted above about the powers of the military occupant being absolute and supreme, "lest his [Aguinaldo's] pretensions," to use General Merritt's expression, "should clash with my designs." "For these reasons," says General Merritt (p. 40), "the preparations for the attack on the city were * * * conducted without reference to the situation of the insurgent forces."

Here General Merritt is speaking frankly but not accurately. He means he made his preparations without any more reference to the situation of the insurgent forces than he could help. As a matter of fact, their situation bothered him a good deal. They were in the way. For instance, there was a whole brigade of them at one point between our people and Manila. "This," says General Merritt (p. 41), "was overcome by instructions to General Greene to *arrange if possible* with the insurgent brigade commander in his immediate vicinity to move to the right and allow the American forces unobstructed control of the roads in their immediate front. No objection was made," etc. That reads very well—that about "arrange if possible," "no objection was made," etc.,—does it not? Nothing there through which "the lustre and the moral strength" of the motives that prompted the Spanish war might be "dimmed by ulterior designs which might tempt us,"25 is there? It was stated above that General Merritt was speaking frankly in this report. He was. He probably did not know how General Greene carried out the order to "arrange if possible with the insurgent brigadier-commander." But it so happened that there was a newspaper correspondent along with General Greene who has since told us. This gentleman was Mr. Frank D. Millet, from whom we have already above quoted, the correspondent of the *London Times* and of *Harper's Weekly*. General Greene had known him years before in the campaigns of the Turco-Russian war. Mr. Millet had been a war correspondent in those campaigns also, and General Greene was there taking observations. So that in the operations against Manila, Mr. Millet, being an old friend of General Greene's, known to be a handy man to have around in a close place, was acting as a civilian volunteer aide to the general.26 Here is Mr. Millet's account of what happened, taken from his book, *The Expedition to the Philippines*:

On the afternoon of the 28th [of July, 1898], General Greene received a verbal message from General Merritt suggesting that he *juggle the insurgents out of part of their lines*, always on his own responsibility, and without committing in any way the commanding general to any recognition of the native leaders or opening up the prospect of an alliance. This General Greene accomplished very cleverly.

Mr. Millet then goes on to tell how General Greene persuaded one of Aguinaldo's generals (Noriel) to evacuate certain trenches so he (Greene) could occupy them, "with a condition attached that General Greene must give a written receipt for the entrenchments." This condition, Mr. Millet says, was imposed by "the astute leader" (Aguinaldo). General Greene's "cleverness" consisted in purposely failing and omitting to give the receipt, which Mr. Millet says "looked very much like a bargain concluded over a signature, and was a little more formal than General Greene thought advisable." The key to this sorry business may be found in the first paragraph of General Merritt's instructions to all his generals at the time:

No rupture with insurgents. This is imperative. *Can ask* insurgent generals or Aguinaldo for *permission* to occupy trenches, but if refused not to use force.27

"I am quite unable to explain," says Mr. Millet (p. 61), "why we did not in the very beginning make them understand that we were masters of the situation, and that they must come strictly under our authority."

The obvious reason was that a war of conquest to subjugate a remote people struggling to be free from the yoke of alien domination was sure to be more or less unpopular with many of the sovereign voters of a republic, and more or less dangerous therefore, like all unpopular wars, to the tenure of office of the party in power. So that in entering upon a war for conquest, a republic *must* "play politics," using the military arm of the government for the twofold purpose of crushing opposition and proving that there is none.

The maxim which makes all fair in war often covers a multitude of sins. But let us turn for a moment from strategy to principle, and see what two other distinguished American war correspondents were thinking and saying about the same time. Writing to *Harper's Weekly* from Cavite, under date of July 16th, concerning the work of the Filipinos during the eight weeks before that, Mr. O. K. Davis said: "The insurgents have driven them [the Spaniards] back over twenty miles of country practically impassable for our men. * * * Aguinaldo has saved our troops a lot of desperately hard campaigning * * *. The insurgent works extend clear around Manila, and the Spaniards are completely hemmed in. There is no hope for them but surrender." Writing to the same paper under date of August 6th, Mr. John F. Bass says: "We forget that they drove the Spaniards from Cavite to their present intrenched position, thus saving us a long-continued fight through the jungle." This gentleman did not tackle the question of inventing a new definition of liberty consistent with alien domination. He simply says: "Give them their liberty and guarantee it to them." In the face of such plucky patriotism as he had witnessed, political casuistry about "capacity for self-government" would have hung its head. Yet Mr. Bass was by no means a novice. He had served with the British army in Egypt in 1895, through the Armenian massacres of 1896, and in the Cretan rebellion and Greek War of 1897. His sentiments were simply precisely what those of the average American not under military orders would have been at the time. After the fall of Manila he wrote (August 17th): "I am inclined to think that the insurgents intend to fight *us* if we stay and *Spain* if we go."

There were 8500 American troops in the taking of the city of Manila, on August 13, 1898. The Filipinos were ignored by them, although they afterwards claimed to have helped. As a matter of fact, the Spanish officers in command were very anxious to surrender and get back to Spain. The Filipinos had already made them "long for peace," to use a famous expression of General J. F. Bell. The garrison only put up a very slight resistance, "to save their face," as the Chinese say, *i. e.*, to save themselves from being court-martialed under some quixotic article of the Spanish army regulations. The assault was begun about 9.30 A.M. , and early that afternoon the Spanish flag had been lowered from the flag-staff in the main square and the Stars and Stripes run up in its stead, amid the convulsive sobs of dark-eyed señoritas and the muttered curses of melodramatic Spanish cavaliers. Thanks to the Filipinos' three and one half months' work, the performance only cost us five men killed out of the 8500. The list of wounded totalled 43. Our antecedent loss in the trenches prior to the day of the assault had been fourteen killed and sixty wounded. So the job was completed, so far as the records show, at a cost of less than a score of American lives.28

As Aguinaldo's troops surged forward in the wake of the American advance they were stopped by orders from the American commander, and prevented from following the retreating Spaniards into Manila. They were not even allowed what is known to the modern small boy as "a look-in." They were not permitted to come into the city to *see* the surrender. President McKinley's message to Congress of December, 1898, describes "the last scene of the war" as having been "enacted at Manila its starting place."29 It says: "On August 13th, after a brief assault upon the works by the land forces, in which the squadron assisted, the capital surrendered unconditionally." In this connection, by way of explaining Aguinaldo's treatment at the hands of our generals from the beginning, the message says, "Divided victory was not permissible." "It was fitting that whatever was to be done * * * should be accomplished by the strong arm of the United States alone." But what takes much of the virtue out of the "strong arm" proposition is that Generals

Merritt and Anderson were carrying out President McKinley's orders all the time they were juggling Aguinaldo out of his positions before Manila, and giving him evasive answers, until the city could be taken by the said "strong arm" *alone*. For, as the message puts it, in speaking of the taking of the city, "By this the conquest of the Philippine Islands * * * was formally sealed."

When General Merritt left Manila on August 30th, he proceeded to Paris to appear before the Peace Commission there. His views doubtless had great weight with them on the momentous questions they had to decide. But his views were wholly erroneous, and that they were so is not surprising. As above stated, he did not even meet Aguinaldo, purposely holding himself aloof from him and his leaders. He never did know how deeply they were incensed at being shut out of Manila when the city surrendered. In his report prepared aboard the steamship *China*, en route for Paris, he says: "Doubtless much dissatisfaction is felt by the rank and file of the insurgents, but * * * I am of the opinion that the leaders will be *able to prevent* serious disturbances," etc. (p. 40). If General Merritt had caught the temper of the trenches he would have known better, but he saw nothing of the fighting prior to the final scene, nor did he take the field in person on the day of the combined assault on the city, August 13th, and therefore missed the supreme opportunity to understand how the Filipinos felt. Says General Anderson in his report:

I understood from the general commanding that he would be personally present on the day of battle. * * * On the morning of the 13th, General Babcock came to my headquarters and informed me that the major-general commanding would remain on a despatch boat.30

Indeed, so reduced was Manila, by reason of the long siege conducted by the insurgents, that the assault of August 13th, not only was, but was expected to be, little more than a sham battle. Says Lieutenant-Colonel Pope, chief quartermaster, "On the evening of August 12th an order was sent me to report with two battalions of the Second Oregon Volunteers, under Colonel Summers the next day on the *Kwong Hoi* to the commanding general on the *Newport*, as an escort on his entrance into Manila. At the hour named, I reported etc."31 As soon as Spanish "honor" was satisfied, up went the white flag and General Merritt was duly escorted ashore and into the city, where he received the surrender of the Spanish general.

In the Civil War, General Merritt had received six successive promotions for gallantry, at Gettysburg, Yellow Tavern, Five Forks, etc., and had been with Sheridan at Winchester. So the way he "commanded" the assault on Manila is proof only of the obligations we then owed the Filipinos. They had left very little to be done.

In his account of General Merritt's original personal disembarkation at Cavite, Mr. Frank Millet acquaints his readers with a Philippine custom we afterwards grew quite familiar with and found quite useful, of keeping your shoes dry in landing from a rowboat on a beach by riding astride the shoulders of some husky native boatman. The boatmen make it a point of special pride not to let their passengers get their feet wet. Mr. Millet tells us that a general in uniform looks neither dignified nor picturesque under such circumstances, and that therefore he will not elaborate on the picture, but that it is suggestive "more of the hilarious than of the heroic." Presumably when General Merritt went ashore on August 13th, from the despatch boat from which he had been watching the assault on Manila, to receive the surrender of the Spanish general, he followed the same custom of the country he had used on the occasion of his original disembarkation. So that in the taking of Manila, we were probably literally, as well as ethically, like General Mahone of Virginia as he is pictured in a familiar *post-bellum* negro story, according to which the general met a negro on a steep part of the road to heaven, told him that St. Peter would only admit mounted parties, mounted the negro with the latter's consent, rode on his back the rest of the toilsome journey to the heavenly gate, dismounted, knocked, and was cordially welcomed by the saint at the sacred portal thus: "Why how d' ye do, General Mahone; jess tie yoh hoss and come in."

---

[1] *S. D. 208*, 1900, p. 13.

[2] *Ib.*, p. 40.

[3] *Report First Philippine Commission*, vol. i., p. 172.

[4] *War Dept. Report*, 1899, vol. i., pt. 4. Otis report, p. 13.

[5] *S. D. 331*, 1902, p. 2941.

[6] *Correspondence Relating to the War with Spain*, vol. ii., p. 788.

[7] May 19th–July 9th; see General Anderson's report to the Adjutant-General of the army of July 9, 1898, *S. D. 208*, p. 6.

[8] See Major J. F. Bell's report to Merritt of August 29, 1898, *S. D. 62*, p. 379.

[9] Clerks.

[10] See *S. D. 208*, pp. 101–2.

[11] *Senate Document 148*, 56th Cong., 2d Sess., 1901, p. 34.

[12] *S. D. 208*, p. 99.

[13] Admiral Dewey to Senate Committee, 1902, *S. D. 331*, 1902, p. 2940.

[14] 7,635,426. See *Philippine Census of 1903*, vol. ii., p. 15.

[15] 3,798,507. See *Philippine Census of 1903*, vol. ii., p. 125.

[16] See *Senate Document 62*, 1898, p. 379.

[17] Albay, Camarines Norte, Camarines Sur, and Sorsogon.

[18] Ilocos Norte, Ilocos Sur, Isabela, Cagayan.

[19] *S. D. 62*, p. 380.

[20] Diary of Major Simeon Villa, p. 1898, *Senate Document 331*, pt. 3, 56th Congress, 1st Session, 1902.

[21] See Merritt's Report for 1898, *War Dept. Report*, 1898, vol. i., pt. 2, p. 40.

[22] *Expedition to the Philippines*, p. 61.

[23] "With 10,000 men, we would have had to guard 13,300 Spanish prisoners, and to fight 14,000 Filipinos," says General Anderson, *North American Review* for February, 1900.

[24] *Senate Document 208*, p. 86.

[25] Mr. McKinley's instructions to the Peace Commissioners, *Senate Document 148*, 56th Cong., 2d Sess., 1901, p. 6.

[26] See General Greene's Report, *W. D. R.*, 1898, vol. i., pt. 2, p. 72, where Mr. Millet's conduct in the assault on the city receives special mention.

[27] *War Dept. Report*, 1898, vol. i., pt. 2, p. 73.

[28] See *War Dept. Report*, 1898, vol. i., pt. 2, p. 58.

[29] *Congressional Record*, December 5, 1898, p. 5.

30 *War Dept. Report*, 1898, vol. i., pt. 2, p. 57.

31 *Ib.*, vol. i., pt. 4, p. 190.

Chapter V. Otis and Aguinaldo

Where people and leaders are agreed,
What can the archon do?

Athenian Maxims.

Major-general Elwell S. Otis and staff arrived at Manila August 21, 1898.1 He relieved General Merritt and succeeded to the command of the American troops in the Philippines, August 29th. Archbishop Chapelle, who was papal delegate to the Philippines in 1900, once said to the writer at Manila, in that year, that General Otis was "of about the right mental calibre to command a one-company post in Arizona." The impatience manifested in the remark was due to differences between him and the commanding-general about the Friar question. The remark itself was of course intended, and understood, as hyperbole. But the selection of General Otis to handle the Philippine situation *was* a serious mistake. He was past sixty when he took command. He continued in command from August 29, 1898, to May 5, 1900, a period of some twenty months. The insurrection was held in abeyance for some five months after he took hold, the leaders hoping against hope that the Treaty of Paris would leave their country to them as it did Cuba to the Cubans; and during all that time General Otis was apparently unable to see that war would be inevitable in the event the decision at Paris was adverse to Filipino hopes. A member of General Otis's staff once told me in speaking of the insurrection period that his chief pooh-poohed the likelihood of an outbreak right along up to the very day before the outbreak of February 4, 1899,
occurred. *Before* the insurrection came he *would* not see it, and *after* it came he—literally—*did not* see it; that is to say, during fifteen months of fighting he commanded the Eighth Army Corps from a desk in Manila and never once took the field. His Civil War record was all right, but he was now getting well along in years. He was also a graduate of the Harvard Law School of the Class of 1861, rather prided himself on being "a pretty fair jack-leg lawyer," and had a most absorbing passion for the details of administrative work. They used to say that the only occasion on which General Otis ever went out of Manila the whole time he was there was when he went up the railroad once to Angeles to see that a proper valuation was put on a then recently deceased Quartermaster's Department mule. When he left the Islands he remarked to a newspaper man that he had had but one "day off" since he had been there. Unswerving devotion to a desk in time of war, on the part of the commanding general of the army in the field, seemed to him an appropriate subject for just pride. This showed his limitations. He was a man wholly unable to see the essentials of an important situation, or to take in the whole horizon. He was known to the Eighth Corps, his command, as a sort of "Fussy Grandpa," his personality and general management of things always suggesting the picture of a painfully near-sighted be-spectacled old gentleman busily nosing over papers you had submitted, and finding fault to show he knew a thing or two. However, he had many eminently respectable traits, and did the best he knew how, though wholly devoid of that noble serenity of vision which used to enable Mr. Lincoln, amid the darkest and most tremendous of his problems, to say with a smile to Horace Greeley: "Don't shoot the organist, he's doing the best he can."

Before General Otis relieved General Merritt, the latter had written Aguinaldo politely requesting him to move his troops beyond certain specified lines about the city,2 and Aguinaldo had replied August 27th, agreeing to do so, but asking that the Americans promise to restore to him the positions thus vacated in the event under the treaty the United States should leave the Philippines to Spain.3 August 31st, Otis notified Aguinaldo, then still at Bacoor, his first capital, that General Merritt had been unexpectedly called away, and that he, Otis, being unacquainted with the situation must take time before answering the Aguinaldo letter to Merritt of the 27th. On September 8th, he did answer, in a preposterously long communication of about 3000 words, which says, among other things: "I have not been instructed as to what policy the United States intends to pursue in regard to its legitimate holdings here"; and therefore declines to promise anything about restoring the insurgent positions in the event we should leave the Islands to Spain under the treaty. Commenting on this in the *North American Review* for February, 1900, General Anderson says: "I believe we came to the parting of the ways when we refused this request." General Anderson was right. General Merritt had on August 21st sent Aguinaldo a memorandum by the hand of Major J. Franklin Bell which promised: "Care will be taken to leave him [Aguinaldo] *in as good condition as he was found by the forces of the government.*"4 In the rôle of political henchman for President McKinley, which General Otis seems to have conceived it his duty to play from the very beginning in the Philippines, it thus appears that he was not troubled about keeping unsullied the faith and honor of the government as pledged by his predecessor. His 3000-word letter to Aguinaldo of September 8th ignores Merritt's promise as coolly as if it had never been made. His only concern appears to have been to leave the government free to throw the Filipinos overboard if it should wish to. He peevishly implies later on that Aguinaldo's requests in this regard were merely a cloak for designs against us (p. 40). But his real reason is given in a sort of stage "aside"—a letter to the Adjutant-General of the army dated September 12, 1898, wherein he explains: "Should I promise them that in case of the return of the city to Spain, upon United States evacuation, their forces would be placed by us in positions which they now occupy, I thoroughly believe that they would evacuate at once. But, of course, under the international obligations resting upon us * * * no such promise can be given."5 In the sacred name of National Honor what of the Merritt promise? You only have to turn a few pages in the *War Department Report* for 1899 from the Merritt promise to the Otis repudiation of it. Yes, General Anderson was right. It was when General Otis practically repudiated in writing the written promise of his predecessor, General Merritt, that we "came to the parting of the ways" in our relations with the Filipinos. Let no American suppose for a moment that the author of this volume is engaged in the ungracious, and frequently deservedly thankless task of mere muck-raking. He never met General Otis but once, and then for a very brief official interview of an agreeable nature. He is only attempting to make a small contribution to the righting of a great wrong unwittingly done by a great, free, and generous people to another people then struggling to be free—a wrong which he doubts not will one day be righted, whether he lives to see it so righted or not. General Otis's letter to the Adjutant-General of the army of September 12th, above quoted, shows that he was holding himself in readiness to carry out in the Philippines any political programme the Administration might determine upon, which would mean that he would afterwards come home and tell how entirely righteous that programme had been. Had the Administration hearkened back to Admiral Dewey's suggestion that the Filipinos were far superior to the Cubans, and decided to set before General Otis in the Philippines the same task it had set before General Wood in Cuba, we would have heard nothing about Filipino "incapacity for self-government." General Otis would have taken his cue from the President, his commander-in chief, and said: "I cordially concur in the opinion of Admiral Dewey." Then he would have gone to work in a spirit of generous rivalry to do in the Philippines just what Wood did in Cuba. And the task would have been easier. Had the Administration taken the view urged by Judge Gray, as a member of the Paris Peace Commission, that "if we had captured Cadiz and the Carlists had helped us [we] would not owe duty to stay by them at the conclusion of the war,"6 and therefore we were not bound to see the Filipinos through their struggle, General Otis would have adopted that view with equal loyalty and in the presidential campaign of 1900, he would have furnished the Administration with arguments to justify that course. This would have been an easy task, also, for two of Spain's fleets had been destroyed by us, leaving her but one to guard her home coast cities, and making the sending of reinforcements to the besieged and demoralized garrison of Manila impossible. The native army she relied on throughout the archipelago had gone over bodily to the patriot cause, and there was no hope of successful resistance to it. But General Otis did not have the boundless prestige of Admiral Dewey and so volunteered no advice. As soon as the Administration chose its course, he set to work to prove the correctness of it. From him, of course, came all the McKinley Administration's original arguments against doing for the Filipinos as we did in the case of Cuba. He was the only legitimate source the American people could look to at that time to help them in their dilemma. They were standing with reluctant feet where democracy and its antithesis meet, and Otis was their sole guide. But the guide was of the kind who wait until you point and ask "Is that the right direction?" and then answer "Yes." Four days after General Otis sent his above quoted letter of September 12th, to Adjutant-General Corbin, Mr. McKinley signed his instructions to the Paris Peace Commissioners, directing them to insist on the cession of Luzon at least, the instructions being full of eloquent but specious argument about the necessity of establishing a guardianship over people of whom we then knew nothing. From that day forward General Otis bent himself to the task of showing the righteousness of that course. "I will let nothing go that will hurt the Administration," was his favorite expression to the newspaper correspondents when they used to complain about his press censorship. Hypocrisy is defined to be "a false assumption of piety or virtue." The false assumption of piety or virtue which has handicapped the American occupation of the Philippines from the beginning, and which will always handicap it, until we throw off the mask and honestly set to work to give the Filipinos a square deal on the question of whether they can or cannot run a decent government of their own if permitted, is traceable back to the Otis letter to the Adjutant-General of September 12, 1898, ignoring General Merritt's promise to leave Aguinaldo "in as good condition as he was found by the forces of the government" in case we should, under the terms of the treaty of peace, leave the Islands to Spain.

General Otis's letter of September 8th to Aguinaldo is apparently intended to convince him that he ought to consider everything the Americans had done up to date as exactly the correct thing, according to the standards of up-to-date, philanthropic, liberty-loving nations which pity double-dealing as mediæval; and that he should cheer up, and feel grateful and happy, instead of sulking, Achilles-like, in his tents; and furthermore—which was the crux—that he must move said tents. General Otis does not forget "that the revolutionary forces under your command have made many sacrifices in the interest of *civil liberty* (observe, he does not call it independence) and for the welfare of your people"; admits that they have "endured great hardships, and have rendered aid"; and avers, as a reason for Aguinaldo's evacuating that part of the environs of Manila occupied by his troops: "It [the war with Spain] was undertaken by the United States for humanity's sake * * * not for * * * aggrandizement or for any national profit." After stating, as above indicated, that he does not yet know what the policy of the United States is to be "in regard to its legitimate holdings here," General Otis proceeds to declare that in any event he will not be a party to any joint occupation of any part of the city, bay, and harbor of Manila—the territory covered by the Peace Protocol of August 13th—and that Aguinaldo must effect the evacuation demanded in the letter of General Merritt "before Tuesday the 15th" (of September), *i.e.*, within a week. Aguinaldo finally withdrew his troops, after much useless parleying and much waste of ink.

There was some of the parleying and ink, however, that was not wholly wasted. But to properly appreciate it as illustrative of the fortitude and tact which the early Filipino leaders seem to have combined in a remarkable degree, some prefatory data are essential.

Aguinaldo's capital was then at Bacoor, one of the small coast villages you pass through in going by land from Manila to Cavite. From Manila over to Cavite by water is about seven miles, and by land about three or four times that. The coast line from Manila to Cavite makes a loop, so that a straight line over the water from Manila to Cavite subtends a curve, near the Cavite end of which lies Bacoor. Thus, Bacoor, being at the mercy of the big guns at Cavite, and also easily accessible by a land force from Manila, to say nothing of Dewey's mighty armada riding at anchor in the offing, was a good place to move away from. There it lay, right in the lion's jaws, should the lion happen to get hungry. Aguinaldo had reflected on all this, and had determined to get himself a capital away from "the city, bay, and harbor of Manila," that is to say, to take his head out of the lion's jaws. General Otis's demand of September 8th that he move his troops out of the suburbs of Manila determined him to move his capital as well. He moved it to a place called Malolos, in Bulacan province. Bulacan lies over on the north shore of Manila Bay, opposite Cavite province on the south shore. Malolos is situated some distance inland, out of sight and range of a fleet's guns, and about twenty-odd miles by railroad northwest of Manila. Malolos was also desirable because it was in the heart of an insurgent province having a population of nearly a quarter of a million people, a province which, by reason of being on the north side of the bay, was sure to be in touch, strategically and politically, with all Luzon north of the Pasig River, just as Cavite province, the birthplace of Aguinaldo, and also of the revolutionary government, had been with all Luzon south of the Pasig. Should the worst come to the worst—and as has already been indicated, the insurgents played a sweepstake game from the beginning for independence, with only war as the limit—northern Luzon had more inaccessible mountains from which to conduct such a struggle for an indefinite period than southern Luzon. But while the Otis demand of September 8th decided the matter of the change of capital, Aguinaldo could not afford to tell his troops that he was moving them from the environs of Manila because made to. He was going to accept war cheerfully when it should become necessary to fight for independence, but he still had some hopes of the Paris Peace Conference deciding to do with the Philippines as with Cuba, and wished to await patiently the outcome of that conference. Besides, he was getting in shipments of guns all the time, as fast as the revenues of his government would permit, and thus his ability to protract an ultimate war for independence was constantly enlarging by accretion. The Hong Kong conference of the Filipino revolutionary leaders held in the city named on May 4, 1898, at which Aguinaldo presided, and which mapped out a programme covering every possible contingency, has already been mentioned. Its minutes say:

If Washington proposes to carry out the fundamental principles of its Constitution, it is most improbable that an attempt will be made to colonize the Philippines or annex them.7

On the other hand, the minutes of this same meeting as we saw recognized that America might be tempted into entering upon a career of colonization, once she should get a foothold in the islands. The programme of Aguinaldo and his people was thus, from the beginning, not to precipitate hostilities until it should become clear that, in the matter of land-grabbing, the gleam of hope held out by the American programme for Cuba was illusive. According to the minutes of the meeting alluded to, such a contingency would, of course, "drive them, the Filipinos * * * to a struggle for their independence, even if they should succumb to the weight of the yoke," etc. Such a struggle, as all the world knows, did ultimately ensue. That part of the parleying following Otis's demand of September 8th (that Aguinaldo move his troops) which was *not* useless was this: In order to "save their face," with the rank and file of their army, the Filipino Commissioners asked General Otis "if I [Otis,] would express in writing a simple *request* to Aguinaldo to withdraw to the lines which I designated—something which he could show to the troops."8 So, on September 13th, General Otis wrote such a "request," and Aguinaldo moved his troops as demanded, but no farther than demanded. He wanted to be in the best position possible in case the United States should finally leave the Philippines to Spain, and always so insisted. Long afterward General Otis insinuated in his report that this insistence, which was uniformly pressed until after the Treaty was signed, was mere dishonest pretence, to cloak warlike intentions against the United States. Yet, as we have seen above, one of our Peace Commissioners at Paris, Judge Gray, just about the same time, was taking that contingency quite as seriously as did Aguinaldo. And early in May, 1898, our Secretary of the Navy, Mr. Long, had cabled Admiral Dewey "not to have political alliances with the insurgents * * * that would incur liability to maintain their cause in the future."9 Before moving his troops pursuant to the Otis demand of September 8th, the Otis "request" was duly published to the insurgent army, and as the insurgents withdrew, the American troops presented arms in most friendly fashion. "They certainly made a brave show," says Mr. Millet (*Expedition to the Philippines*, p. 255), "for they were neatly uniformed, had excellent rifles, marched well, and looked very soldierly and intelligent." "The withdrawal," says General Otis (p. 10), "was effected adroitly, as the insurgents marched out in excellent spirits, cheering the American forces." Absolute master of all Luzon outside Manila at this time, with complete machinery of government in each province for all matters of justice, taxes, and police, an army of some 30,000 men at his beck, and his whole people a unit at his back, Aguinaldo formally inaugurated his permanent government—permanent as opposed to the previous provisional government—with a Constitution, Congress, and Cabinet, patterned after our own,10 just as the South American republics had done before him when *they* were freed from Spain, at Malolos, the new capital, on September 15, 1898. *The next day, September 16th, at Washington, President McKinley delivered to his Peace Commissioners, then getting ready to start for the Paris Peace Conference, their letter of instructions, directing them to insist on the cession by Spain to the United States of the island of Luzon "at least."*11 In other words, the day after the little Filipino republic, gay with banners and glad with music, started forth on its journey, Mr. McKinley signed its death-warrant. The political student of 1912 may say just here, "Oh, I read all that in the papers at the time, or at least it was all ventilated in the Presidential campaign of 1900." Mr. McKinley's instructions to the Paris Peace Commission were not made public until after the Presidential election of 1900. To be specific, they were first printed and given out to the public in 1901, in *Senate Document 148*, having been extracted from the jealous custody of the Executive by a Senate resolution. It was not until then that the veil was lifted. By that time, no American who was not transcendental enough to have lost his love for the old maxim, "Right or wrong, my country," cared to hear the details of the story. The Filipinos and "our boys" had been diligently engaged in killing each other for a couple of years, and the American people said, "A truce to scolding; let us finish this war, now we are in it."

But to return from the death-warrant of the Philippine republic signed by Mr. McKinley on September 16th, to its christening, or inauguration, the day before. Mr. Millet gives an intensely interesting account of the inaugural ceremonies of September 15th, which as Manila correspondent of the *London Times* and *Harper's Weekly* he had the good fortune to witness. Says he:

The date was at last * * * fixed for September 15th. A few days before Aguinaldo had made a triumphant entry into Malolos in a carriage drawn by white horses, and there had been a general celebration of his arrival, with speeches, a gala dinner, open air concerts, and a military parade. Mr. Higgins (an Englishman), the manager of the Railway, kindly offered to take me up to Malolos to witness the ceremony of the inauguration of the new government. * * * The only other passenger was to be Aguinaldo's secretary * * * a small boyish-looking young man. * * *12

It seems there had been a strike of the native employees of the railway up the road.

Mr. Higgins calmly remarked to the secretary that, in his opinion, if the affairs of the Filipino government were managed in the future as they were at present, the proposed republic would be nothing but a cheap farce. The secretary timidly asked what there was to complain about.

Then came a tirade from Higgins, ending with, "I am going to lay this * * * before Aguinaldo to-day, and I shall expect you to arrange an interview for my friend and myself." Then, turning to the astonished Millet, he said in English: "It does these chaps good to be talked to straight from the shoulder. Since they came to Malolos, the earth isn't big enough to hold them."

This scene on the train is, decidedly, as Thomas Carlyle would say, "of real interest to universal history." Mr. Millet's Government was a lion about to eat a lamb, but the head of his nation, Mr. McKinley, clothed with absolute authority in the premises for the nonce, was balking at the diet. Now, Mr. Millet rather admired the British boldness, just as a Northern man likes to hear a Southerner talk straight from the shoulder to a "darkey." As soon as the era of good feeling was over, our people quit treating the Filipinos as Perry did the Japanese in 1854, and began calling them "niggers." In fact the commanding general found it necessary a little later to put a stop to this pernicious practice among the soldiers by issuing a General Order prohibiting it. But Mr. Millet's admiration would have been somewhat toned down had he known what we found out later. The real secret of Higgins's personal arrogance was this. The Filipino government needed his railroad in its business. During the war which followed, the insurgents long controlled a large part of this railway, from Manila to Dagupan, which was the only railway in the Philippines. The railway properties suffered much damage incident to the war, and—just how willingly is beside the question—the company rendered material aid to the insurgent cause. So much did they render, that when Higgins had the assurance later to want our Government to pay the damages his properties had suffered at the hands of the insurgents, our government at Manila promptly turned his claim down. Subsequently the London office of his company actually inveigled the British Foreign Office into making representation to our State Department about the matter—obviously a very grave step, in international law. The claim was promptly turned down by Washington also, and, happily, that "closed the incident."13

Having exploded Mr. Millet's bubble, let us resume the thread of his story:

We reached the station [at Malolos] in about an hour and a half. * * * The town numbers perhaps thirty or forty thousand people. * * * From the first humble *nipa* shack to the great square where the convent stands, thousands of insurgent flags fluttered from every window and every post. * * * Every man had an insurgent tri-color cockade in his hat.

Then follows a detailed account of being introduced, after some ceremony, to Aguinaldo, who is described as "a small individual, in full evening black suit, and flowing black tie." Higgins made his complaint about the strikers, and Aguinaldo said, "I will attend to this matter of the strikers," and then changed the topic, asking if the visitors did not wish to attend the opening of the Congress—which they did.

From Mr. Millet's account, it is evident that, like Admiral Dewey and most of the Americans who first dealt with the Filipinos except Generals Anderson, MacArthur, and J. F. Bell, he failed to take the Filipinos as seriously as the facts demanded. At that time the Japanese had not yet taught the world that national aspirations are not necessarily to be treated with contumely because a people are small of stature and not white of skin. Consul Wildman at Hong Kong at first wrote the State Department quite peevishly that Aguinaldo seemed much more concerned about the kind of cane he should wear than about the figure he might make in history. Wildman did not then know, apparently, that canes, with all Spanish-Filipino colonial officialdom, were badges of official rank, like shoulder-straps are with us. The reader will also remember the toothbrush incident hereinbefore reproduced, told by Admiral Dewey to the Senate Committee, in 1902. That incident, naturally enough, amused the Committee not a little. But we who know the Filipino know it was merely an awkward and embarrassed answer due to diffidence, and made on the spur of the moment to cloak some real reason which if disclosed would not seem so childish.

Misunderstanding is the principal cause of hate in this world. When you understand people, hatred disappears in a way strikingly analogous to the disappearance of darkness on the arrival of light. The more you know of the educated patriotic Filipino, the more certain you become that the government we destroyed in 1898 would have worked quite as well as most any of the republics now in operation between the Rio Grande and Patagonia. The masses of the people down there, the peons, are probably quite as ignorant and docile as the Filipino *tao* (peasant), and I question if the educated men of Latin America, the class of men who, after all, control in every country, could, after meeting and knowing the corresponding class in the Philippines, get their own consent to declare the latter their inferiors either in intelligence, character, or patriotism.

But to return to the inauguration. Mr. Millet saw the inaugural ceremonies in the church, and heard Aguinaldo's address to the Congress. Of the audience he says "few among them would have escaped notice in a crowd for they were exceptionally alert, keen, and intelligent in appearance." Of this same Congress and government, Mr. John Barrett, who was American Minister to Siam about that time, and is now (1912) head of the Bureau of American Republics at Washington—an institution organized and run for the purpose of persuading Latin-America that we do *not* belong to the Imperial International Society for the Partition of the Earth and that we are *not* in the business of gobbling up little countries on pretext of "policing" them—said in an address before the Shanghai Chamber of Commerce on January 12, 1899:

He [Aguinaldo] has organized a government which has practically been administering the affairs of that great island [Luzon] since the American occupation of Manila, which is certainly better than the former administration; he has a properly constituted Cabinet and Congress, the members of which compare favorably with Japanese statesmen.

The present Philippine Assembly had not had its first meeting when I left the Islands in the spring of 1905. It was organized in 1907. In the summer of 1911, I had the pleasure of renewing an old and very cordial acquaintance with Dr. Heiser, Director of Public Health of the Philippine Islands, who is one of the most considerable men connected with our government out there, and is also thoroughly in sympathy with its indefinite continuance in its present form. The Doctor is a broad-gauged man likely to be worth to any government, in matters of Public Health, whatever such government could reasonably afford to pay in the way of salary, and is doubtless well-paid by the Philippine Insular Government. He can hardly be blamed, therefore, for being in sympathy with its indefinite continuance in its present form. Doctor Heiser is a man of too much genuine dignity to be very much addicted to slang, but when I asked him about the Philippine Assembly, I think he said it was "a cracker-jack." At any rate, I have never heard any legislative body spoken of in more genuinely complimentary terms than those in which he described the Philippine Assembly. I learned from him incidentally that their "capacity for self-government" is so crude, however, as yet, that the members have not yet learned to read newspapers while a colleague whose seat is next to theirs is addressing the house and trying to get the attention of his fellows, nor do they keep up such a buzz of conversation that the man who has the floor cannot hear himself talk. They listen to the programme of the public business.

Some five years ago in an article written for the *North American Review* concerning the Philippine problem, the author of the present volume said, among other things: "During nearly four years of service on the bench in the Philippines the writer heard as much genuine, impassioned, and effective eloquence from Filipino lawyers, saw exhibited in the trial of causes as much industrious preparation, and zealous, loyal advocacy of the rights of clients, as any ordinary *nisi prius* judge at home is likely to meet with in the same length of time."14 Any country that has plenty of good lawyers and plenty of good soldiers, backed by plenty of good farmers, is capable of self-government. As President Schurman of Cornell University, who headed the first Philippine Commission, the one that went out in 1899, said in closing his Founder's Day Address at that institution on January 11, 1902: "Any decent kind of government of Filipinos by Filipinos is better than the best possible government of Filipinos by Americans." The

Malolos government which Mr. Millet saw inaugurated on September 15, 1898, would probably have filled this bill. Had the Filipino people then possessed the consciousness of racial and political unity *as a* people which was developed by their subsequent long struggle against us for independence, and which has been steadily developing more and more under the mild sway of a*quasi*-freedom whose princely prodigality in spreading education is marred only by its declared programme that no living beneficiary thereof may hope to see the independence of his country, and that the present generation must resign itself to tariff schedules "fixed" at Washington, there is no reasonable doubt that the original Malolos government of 1898 would have been a very "decent kind of government."

All through the last four months of 1898, the two hostile armies faced each other in a mood which it needed but a spark to ignite, awaiting the outcome of the peace negotiations arranged for in September, commenced in October, and concluded in December. While they are thus engaged about Manila, let us turn to a happier picture, the situation in the provinces under the Aguinaldo government.

---

[1] See his Report, *War Dept. Report*, 1899, vol. i., pt. 4, p. 3.

[2] On August 20th. *War Dept. Report*, 1899, vol. i., pt. 4, p. 345.

[3] *Ib.*, p. 5.

[4] *War Dept. Report*, 1899, vol. 1., pt. 4, pp. 346–7.

[5] *Ib.* p. 335.

[6] *Senate Document 148*, 56th Cong., 2d Sess., p. 34.

[7] *S. D. 208*, pt. ii., pp. 7, 8.

[8] Otis's *Report*, p. 10.

[9] *Navy Dept. Report*, 1898, Appendix, p. 101.

[10] To say nothing of the "chariot and four, and a band of a hundred pieces, and everything in the grandest style," of which Admiral Dewey told the Senate Committee in 1902 (*S. D. 331*, 1902, p. 2972).

[11] See p. 7, *S. D. 148*, 56th Cong., 2d Sess.

[12] *Expedition to the Philippines*, p. 255.

[13] "Putting the road and accessories into the same state as they were on February 4, 1899," was the language in which Mr. Higgins formulated his demand in a letter to General Otis on Jan. 25, 1900. See *War Dept. Record*, 1900, vol. i., pt. 4, p. 516.

[14] *North American Review*, January 18, 1907, p. 140.

Chapter VI. The Wilcox-Sargent Trip

A smiling, peaceful, and plenteous land
As yet unblighted by the scourge of war;
Where happiness and hospitality walk hand in hand
And new-born Freedom bows to Law.

ANONYMOUS.

In the last chapter, we saw Aguinaldo's republic formally established at Malolos, September 15th, claiming jurisdiction over all Luzon. InChapter IV., entitled "Merritt and Aguinaldo," we saw the political condition of southern Luzon in August, 1898, and the following months, and verified the correctness of Aguinaldo's claims as to complete mastery there then. Let us now examine the state of affairs in northern Luzon in the fall of 1898.

In *Senate Document 196*, 56th Congress, 1st Session, dated February 26, 1900, transmitted by Secretary of the Navy Long, in response to a Senate resolution, may be found a report of a tour of observation through the half of Luzon Island which lies north of Manila and the Pasig River, made between October 8 and November 20, 1898,—note the dates, for the Paris Peace Conference began October 1st and ended December 10th,—by Paymaster W. B. Wilcox and Naval Cadet L. R. Sargent. This report was submitted by them to Admiral Dewey under date of November 23, 1898, and by him forwarded to the Navy Department for its information, with the comment that it "in my opinion contains the most complete and reliable information obtainable in regard to the present state of the northern part of Luzon Island." The Admiral's endorsement was not sent to the Senate along with the report. It appears in a book afterwards published by Paymaster Wilcox in 1901, entitled *Through Luzon on Highways and Byways*. The book is merely an elaboration of the report, and reproduces most of the report, if not all of it, *verbatim*. The book of Paymaster Wilcox may be treated as, practically, official, for historical purposes. The preface recites that in October, 1898, American control was effective only in Manila and Cavite, that the insurgents, under Aguinaldo, who had proclaimed himself President of the whole Archipelago, immediately after Dewey's victory, were in supposedly complete possession of every part of the Island outside of these two cities, that their lines were so close to the outposts of our army that their people could at times converse with our soldiers, and that General Otis's authority did not extend much beyond a three-mile radius from the centre of Manila, while Admiral Dewey held and operated the navy-yard at Cavite. "Even the country between Manila and Cavite was in the hands of Aguinaldo, so much so that our officers had been refused permission to land at any intermediate point by water, and were prohibited from traversing the distance by road." Wilcox and Sargent procured leave of absence from Admiral Dewey to make their trip. They went first to Malolos, but failed to get anything in the way of safe-conduct from Aguinaldo. He is described, however, as of "great force of character * * * and he dominates all around him with a power that seems peculiar to himself." Wilcox had seen him before at Cavite. "He adroitly read between the lines that the Government of the United States did not then, nor would it at any future time, recognize his authority," says the writer.

Our travellers left Manila, October 8, 1898, on the Manila-Dagupan Railway, for a place called Bayambang, which is the capital of Pangasinan province, about one hundred miles north of Manila. In Pangasinan "the people were all very respectful and polite and offered the hospitality of their homes." From Bayambang they struck off from the railroad and proceeded eastward comfortably and unmolested a day's journey, to a town in the adjoining province of Nueva Ecija (Rosales) where they received a cordial reception at the hands of the Presidente (Mayor)—Aguinaldo's Presidente of course, not the Presidente left over from the Spanish régime. "At this time all the local government of the different towns was in the hands of Aguinaldo's adherents," says the descriptive itinerary we are following. The tourists were provided at Rosales by order of Aguinaldo with a military escort, "which was continued by relays all the way to Aparri" (the northernmost town of Luzon, at the mouth of the Cagayan River). Paymaster Wilcox says he carried five hundred Mexican dollars in his saddle-bags, but used only a trifling portion of this amount, "for in every town my entertainment was given without pay." They went from Rosales to Humingan, in Nueva Ecija. At Humingan they were again entertained by the Presidente at dinner, with music following, and comfortably housed. The Presidente made many inquiries about "the War with Spain and their own future." Their future, as revealed by the raised curtain of a year later, was that their country was being overrun by Lawton's Division of the Eighth Army Corps, the author of this volume having passed through this same town of Humingan in November, 1899, as an officer of the scouts used to develop fire for General Lawton's column. They journeyed eastward through the province of Nueva Ecija from Humingan to a little village (Puncan) in the foothills of the mountains they planned to cross. Of this place and the hospitality there, our traveller remarks: "I shall never forget the welcome of the local official" the Presidente. Thence they proceeded a few more stages and parasangs, northward over the Caranglan pass, into Nueva Vizcaya province, the watershed of north central Luzon, and thence down the valley of the Cagayan River via Iligan and Tuguegarao to Aparri, being always hospitably entertained in every town through which they passed by the Presidente or Mayor of the town, the local representative of the Philippine republic. In the *New York Independent* of September 14, 1899, Cadet Sargent, in an article about this trip, gives the words of the new Filipino national Hymn, which he describes as sung with great enthusiasm everywhere he and Wilcox were entertained in the various towns. I desire to preserve a sample verse of it here. The music it is set to is much like the *Marseillaise*—quite as stirring:

Del sueño de tres siglos
Hermanos Despertad!
Gritando "Fuera España!
Viva La Libertad!"

which, being interpreted, means:

From the sleep of three centuries
Brothers, awake!
Crying "Out with Spain!
Live Liberty!"

Had another Sargent and another Wilcox made a similar trip through the provinces of southern Luzon about this same time, under similar friendly auspices, before we turned friendship to hate and fear and misery, in the name of Benevolent Assimilation, they would, we now know, have found similar conditions.

Some suspicions were aroused on one or two occasions, but once the local authorities became convinced that the trip was being made by consent of "The Illustrious Presidente" (Aguinaldo—"El Egregio Presidente" is the Spanish of it) all was sunshine again. The Mayor of each town—the Presidente—would receive from the escort coming with them from the last town they had stopped at, a letter from the Mayor, or Presidente, of said last town; the old escort would return to *their* town, and a new one would be provided to give them safe-conduct to the next town. This was no new-fangled scheme of Aguinaldo's. It was an ancient custom of the Spanish Government, and was an ideal nucleus of administration for the new government. Curiously enough, the army knew practically nothing of this trip in the days of the early fighting. All that country was to us a *terra incognita*, until overrun by Captain Bacthelor, with a part of the 25th Infantry in the fall of 1899, the following year. So was the rest of the archipelago a like *terra incognita*, until likewise slowly conquered by hard fighting. That is why we so utterly failed to understand what a wonderfully complete "going concern" Aguinaldo's government had become throughout the Philippine archipelago before the Treaty of Paris was signed. Descending from the watershed of north central Luzon in the province of Nueva Viscaya already mentioned, our travellers reached the town of Carig, in the foothills which fringe that side of the watershed. There they were met by Simeon Villa, military commander of Isabela province, the man who was chief of staff to Aguinaldo afterwards, and was captured by General Funston along with Aguinaldo in the spring of 1901. Villa's immediate superior was Colonel Tirona, at Aparri, the colonel commanding all the insurgent forces of the Cagayan valley. Villa was accompanied by his aide, Lieutenant Ventura Guzman. The latter is an old acquaintance of the author of the present volume, who tried him afterwards, in 1901, for playing a minor part in the murder of an officer of the Spanish army committed under Villa's orders just prior to, or about the time of, the Wilcox-Sargent visit. He was found guilty, and sentenced, but later liberated under President Roosevelt's amnesty of 1902. He *was* guilty, but the deceased, so the people in the Cagayan valley used to say, in being tortured to death, got only the same sort of medicine he had often administered thereabouts. At any rate, that was the broad theory of the amnesty in wiping out all these old cases. Villa was a Tagal and had come up from Manila with the expedition commanded by Colonel Tirona, which expedition was fitted out with guns furnished Aguinaldo by Admiral Dewey, or, if not furnished, permitted to be furnished. But Guzman was a member of one of the wealthiest and most influential native families of that province (Isabela). General Otis's reports are full of the most inexcusable blunders about how "the Tagals" took possession of the various provinces and *made* the people do this or that. Villa's relations with Guzman were just about those of a New Yorker or a Bostonian sent up to Vermont in the days of the American Revolution to help organize the resistance there, in conjunction with one of the local leaders of the patriot cause in the Green Mountain State. Both were members of the Katipunan, the Filipino Revolutionary Secret Society, an organization patterned after Masonry, membership in which was always treated by the Spaniards as sedition, and usually visited with capital punishment. Nearly every Filipino of any spirit belonged to it on May 1, 1898, the date of the naval battle of Manila Bay. It is the all-pervading completeness of this organization at that time—it could give old Tammany Hall cards and spades—which explains the astonishing rapidity of Aguinaldo's political success, *i.e.*, the astonishing rapidity with which the Malolos Government acquired control of Luzon between May and October, 1898. Their cabalistic watchword was "Paisano" (fellow-countryman), their battle cry "Independence." In the fall of 1898, at the time of this Wilcox-Sargent trip through Luzon, the Filipinos really "had tasted the sweets of Independence," to use the phrase of the people of Iloilo in declining *on that ground* to surrender to General Miller in December thereafter and electing the arbitrament of war. The writer is perhaps as familiar with the history of that Cagayan valley as almost any other American. It is true there were cruelties practised by the Filipinos on the Spaniards. But they were ebullitions of revenge for three centuries of tyranny. They do not prove unfitness for self-government. I for one prefer to follow the example set by the Roosevelt amnesty of 1902, and draw the veil over all those matters. With the Spaniards it was a case of *Sauve qui peut*. With the Filipinos, it was a case, as old man Dimas Guzman, father to this Lieutenant Ventura we have just met, used to put it, of *Me las vais a pagar*, which, liberally interpreted, means, "The bad quarter of an hour has arrived for the Spaniards. The day of reckoning has come." I sentenced both Dimas and Ventura to life imprisonment for being accessory to the murder of the Spanish officer above named, Lieutenant Piera. Villa officiated as archfiend of the gruesome occasion. I am quite sure I would have hung Villa without any compunction at that time, if I could have gotten hold of him. I tried to get hold of him, but Governor Taft's Attorney-General, Mr. Wilfley, wrote me that Villa was somewhere over on the mainland of Asia on British territory, and extradition would involve application to the London Foreign Office. The intimation was that we had trouble enough of our own without borrowing any from feuds that had existed under our predecessors in sovereignty. I have understood that Villa is now practising medicine in Manila. More than one officer of the American army that I know, afterwards did things to the Filipinos almost as cruel as Villa did to that unhappy Spanish officer, Lieutenant Piera. On the whole, I think President Roosevelt acted wisely and humanely in wiping the slate. We had new problems to deal with, and were not bound to handicap ourselves with the old ones left over from the Spanish régime.

It appears that Villa became a little suspicious of the travellers. He detained them at Carig seven days. Finally there came a telegram from his chief at Aparri, Colonel Tirona, to our two travellers, which read:

"I salute you affectionately, and authorize Villa to accompany you to Iligan." At Iligan, the capital of Isabela province, the travellers were lavishly entertained. They were given a grand *baile* (ball) and *fiesta* (feast), a kind of dinner-dance, we would call it. To the light Messrs. Sargent and Wilcox throw on the then universal acknowledgment of the authority of the Aguinaldo government, and the perfect tranquillity and public order maintained under it, in the Cagayan valley, I may add that as judge of that district in 1901–2 there came before me a number of cases in the trial of which the fact would be brought out of this or that difference among the local authorities having been referred to the Malolos Government for settlement. *And they always waited until they heard from it.* The doubting Thomas will attribute this to the partiality of the Filipinos to procrastination in general. I know it was due to the hearty co-operation of the people with, and their loyalty to, the then existing government, and to their pride in it. Mr. Sargent tells a characteristic story of Villa, whose vengeful feeling toward the Spaniards showed on all occasions. The former Spanish governor of the province was of course a prisoner in Villa's custody. Villa had the ex-governor brought in, for the travellers to see him, and remarked, in his presence to them, "This is the man who robbed this province of $25,000 during the last year of his office." From Iligan our travellers proceeded to Aparri, cordially received everywhere, and finding the country in fact, as Aguinaldo always claimed in his proclamations of that period seeking recognition of his government by the Powers, in a state of profound peace and tranquillity—free from brigandage and the like. At Aparri the visitors were cordially welcomed by Colonel Tirona, and much fêted. While they were there, Tirona transferred his authority to a civil régime. Says Paymaster Wilcox:

The steamer *Saturnus*, which had left the harbor the day before our arrival, brought news from Hong Kong papers that the Senators from the United States at the Congress at Paris favored the independence of the islands with an American protectorate. Colonel Tirona considered the information of sufficient reliability to justify him in regarding Philippine Independence as assured, and warfare in the Islands at an end.

He then goes on to describe the inauguration of civil government in Cagayan province. I hope all this will not weary the American reader. It was vividly interesting to me when I read it for the first time thirteen years afterward, in 1911, because it was such unexpected information, so surprising. It will be equally interesting to all other Americans who participated in putting down the subsequent insurrection and in setting up the Taft civil government in that same valley three years later. I was in that town, for a similar purpose, with Governor Taft in 1901, after a bloody war which almost certainly would not have occurred had the Paris Peace Commission known the conditions then existing, just like this, all over Luzon and the Visayan Islands. Of course the Southern Islands were a little slower. But as Luzon goes, so go the rest. The rest of the archipelago is but the tail to the Luzon kite. Luzon contains 4,000,000 of the 8,000,000 people out there, and Manila is to the Filipino people what Paris is to the French and to France. Luzon is about the size of Ohio, and the other six islands that really matter,[1] are in size mere little Connecticuts and Rhode Islands, and in population mere Arizonas or New Mexicos. Describing the ceremonies of the inauguration of civil government in Cagayan, the Wilcox-Sargent report to Admiral Dewey says:

The Presidentes of all the towns in the province were present at the ceremony. * * * Colonel Tirona made a short speech. * * * He then handed the staff of office to the man who had been elected "Jefe Provincial" [Governor of the Province]. This officer also made a speech in which he thanked the military forces * * * and assured them that the work they had begun would be perpetuated by the people, where *every man, woman, and child stood ready to take up arms to defend their newly won liberty and to resist with the last drop of their blood the attempt of any nation whatever to bring them back to their former state of dependence.* He then knelt, placed his hand on an open Bible, and took the oath of office.[2]

Does not such language in an official report made by officers of the navy to Admiral Dewey in November, 1898, show an undercurrent of deep feeling at the position the Administration had put Admiral Dewey in with Aguinaldo, when it decided to take the Philippines, and accordingly sent out an army whose generals ignored his protégé?

The speech of the provincial governor was followed, says the Wilcox-Sargent report (same page) by speeches from "the other officers who constitute the provincial government, the heads of the three departments—justice, police, and internal revenue. Every town in this province has the same organization." Article III. of Aguinaldo's decree of June 18th, previous, providing an organic law or constitution for his provisional government (see Chapter II., *ante*) had provided precisely the organization which Wilcox and Sargent thus saw working at Aparri and throughout the Cagayan valley in October, 1898. The importance of all this to the question of how the Filipinos feel toward us to-day, in this year of grace, 1912, and to the element of righteousness there is in that feeling, is too obvious to need comment. Americans interested in business in the Philippines come back to this country from time to time and give out interviews in the papers declaring that the Filipinos do not want independence. What they really mean is that it makes no difference whether they want it or not, they are not going to get it. And it is precisely these Americans, and their business associates in the United States, who have gotten through Congress the legislation which enables them to give the Filipino just half of what he got ten years ago for his hemp, and other like legislation, and the Filipinos know it. The gulf in the Philippines between the dominant and the subject race will continue to widen as the years go by, so long as indirect taxation without representation continues to be perpetrated at Washington for the benefit of special interests having a powerful lobby. If the American people themselves are groaning under this very sort of thing, and apparently unable to help themselves, what is the *a priori* probability as to our voteless and therefore defenceless little brown brother. Like the sheep before the shearer, he is dumb. But to return to our travellers and their journey.

A Norwegian steamer came into port [meaning the harbor of Aparri] that afternoon, and this seemed our only hope. She was chartered by two Chinamen * * *. At first they refused us permission to embark, and declined to put in at any port on the west coast. No sooner was this related to Colonel Tirona than he sent notice that the ship could not clear without taking us and making a landing where we desired. This argument was convincing.

Colonel Tirona provided them with a letter addressed to Colonel Tiño at Vigan, the chief town of the west coast of Luzon and the capital of the province of Ilocos Sur, which province fronts the China Sea. Messrs. Wilcox and Sargent proceeded aboard the Norwegian steamer from Aparri westward, doubling the northwest corner of Luzon, and steaming thence due south to the nearest port. Vigan was the Filipino military headquarters of the western half of northern Luzon, just as Aparri was at the same time of the eastern half. On the west coast the travellers were treated always courteously, but with considerable suspicion. The explanation is easy. That region is in closer touch with Manila, and with what is going on and may be learned at the capital, than is the Cagayan valley which our tourists had just left. They bade the commanding officer at Vigan good-bye, November 13, 1898. Passing south through Namacpacan (which the command I was with took a year or so later), they came to San Fernando de Union, some twenty miles farther south along the coast road. Here they met Colonel Tiño and presented their letter from Tirona. He gave them a dinner, of course. How a Filipino does love to entertain, and make you enjoy yourself! Talk about your "true Southern hospitality"! You get it there. "Speeches were made, and great things promised by the Philippine republic in the near future" says Mr. Wilcox. After the dinner and speech-making came the inevitable dance. After that Colonel Tiño started them off on their journey southward toward Manila duly provided with carriages. Passing Aringay on November 18, 1898[3] our travellers finally reached Dagupan, the northern terminus of the Manila-Dagupan Railway, and there took a train for Manila, 120 miles away.

In his report covering the fall of 1898, General Otis always scoldingly says of the Filipinos that in all the parleyings of his commissioners with Aguinaldo's commissioners before the outbreak, the latter never did know what they really wanted. The truth was they believed the Americans were going to do with them exactly as every other white race they knew of had done with every other brown race they knew of, but they did not tell General Otis so. Mr. Wilcox, a more friendly witness of that same period states their position thus at page twenty of the report to Admiral Dewey: "They desire the protection of the United States at sea, but fear any interference on land." "On one point they seemed united, viz., that whatever our government may have done for them, it had not gained the right to annex them," adding, in relation to the physical preparations to make good this contention, in the event of war, "The Philippine Government has an organized force in every province we visited."

The whole tone of the Wilcox-Sargent report and the subsequent Wilcox book is an implied reiteration, after intimate, extended, and friendly contact with the people of all Luzon north of the Pasig River, of Admiral Dewey's telegram sent to the Navy Department, June 23, 1898: "The people are far superior in intelligence and capacity for self-government to the people of Cuba and I am familiar with both races." In fact Messrs. Wilcox and Sargent do not raise the question of "capacity for self-government" at all, any more than Commodore Perry did when similarly welcomed in 1854 by the Japanese.

---

[1] The six main Visayan Islands. Mohammedan Mindanao is always dealt with in this book as a separate and distinct problem.

[2] *Senate Document 196*, 56th Cong., 1st. Sess., p. 14.

[3] Here the author's commanding officer, Major Batson, was shot a year and a day later while directing with his usual clear-headed intrepidity the fire of a part of his battalion to protect the crossing of the rest of it over the Aringay River, we being at the time in hot pursuit of Aguinaldo, whose rear-guard made a stand in the trenches on the other side of the river.

Chapter VII. The Treaty of Paris

No man can serve two masters.

MATTHEW vi., 24.

Confine the Empire within those limits which nature seems to have fixed as its natural bulwarks and boundaries.

AUGUSTUS CÆSAR'S WILL.

This is a tale of three cities, Paris, Washington, and Manila.

Article III. of the Peace Protocol signed at Washington, August 12, 1898, provided:

The United States will occupy and hold the city, bay, and harbor of Manila, pending the conclusion of a Treaty of Peace which shall determine the control, disposition, and government of the Philippines.[1]

The "Papers relating to the Treaty with Spain" including the telegraphic correspondence between President McKinley and our Peace Commissioners pending the negotiations, were sent to the Senate, January 30, 1899, just one week before the final vote on the treaty, but the injunction of secrecy was not removed until January 31, 1901—*after* the presidential election of 1900. They then were published as *Senate Document 148*, 56th Congress, 2d Session. It was not until then that the veil was lifted. The instructions to the Peace Commissioners were dated September 16, 1898. The Commissioners were: William R. Day, of Ohio, Republican, just previously Secretary of State, now (1912) Associate Justice of the Supreme Court of the United States; Whitelaw Reid, Republican, then editor of the *New York Tribune*, now Ambassador to Great Britain, and three members of the United States Senate, Cushman K. Davis, of Minnesota, William P. Frye, of Maine, Republicans, and George Gray, of Delaware, Democrat. Senator Davis died in 1900, and Senator Frye in 1911. Senator Gray has been, since 1899, and is now, United States Circuit Judge for the 3d Judicial District. Among other things, the President's instructions to the Commissioners said:

It is my earnest wish that *the United States in making peace should follow the same high rule of conduct which guided it in facing war.* * * **The lustre and the moral strength* attaching to a cause which can be confidently rested upon the considerate judgment of the world *should not under any illusion of the hour be dimmed by ulterior designs which might tempt us* * * * *into an adventurous departure on untried paths.*

By elaborate rhetorical gradations, the instructions finally get down to this:

Incidental to our tenure in the Philippines is the commercial opportunity. * * * The United States cannot accept less than the cession in full right and sovereignty of the island of Luzon.

Though already noticed, we venture, in this connection, again to recall that in the month previous (August, 1898) a gentleman high in the councils of the Administration2 declared in one of the great reviews of the period: "We see with sudden clearness that some of the most revered of our political maxims have outlived their force." Among these "revered maxims" thus suddenly fossilized by his *ipse dixit*, Mr. Vanderlip exuberantly includes the teachings of "Washington's Farewell Address and the later crystallization of its main thought by President Monroe"—the Monroe Doctrine, adding that in lieu of these "A new mainspring * * * has become the directing force * * * the mainspring of commercialism."

As permanent chairman of the Philadelphia convention which renominated Mr. McKinley for the Presidency thereafter, in 1900, Senator Lodge, speaking of the issues raised by the Treaty of Paris, said: "We make no hypocritical pretence of being interested in the Philippines solely on account of others. We believe in Trade Expansion."

"Philanthropy and five per cent. go hand in hand," said Mr. Vanderlip's Chief, Secretary of the Treasury Lyman J. Gage, about the same time. Such was the temper of the times when the treaty was made.

The first meeting with the Spanish Commissioners took place at Paris, October 1st. The opening event of the meeting, the initial move of the Spaniards, is extremely interesting in the light of subsequent events, especially in connection with the Iloilo Fiasco, hereinafter described (Chapter IX.).

"Spanish communication represents," says Judge Day's cablegram to the President,3 "that *status quo* has been altered and continues to be altered to the prejudice of Spain by Tagalo rebels, whom it describes as *an auxiliary force* to the regular American troops."

Even diplomacy, in a conciliatory communication limited to the obvious, called the Filipinos our allies.

The Spanish initial move was more immediately prompted by the fact that in point of absolute astronomical time Manila, though captured when it was morning of August 13th *there*, was captured when it was evening of August 12th, at Washington, and the protocol was signed at Washington in the evening of August 12th. While this point was material, because we had captured $900,000 in cash in the Spanish treasury at Manila and much other property, the title to which, under the laws of war between civilized nations, depended on just *what time* it was captured, the matter was finally swallowed up and lost sight of in the agreement to give Spain a lump $20,000,000 for the archipelago. But the initial move had other aspects. In the event we should take the Philippines off her hands, Spain was going to insist that we should get back from the Filipinos, our "allies," and restore to her all the Spaniards they captured after August 12th. She knew that in all probability if we bought the Islands we would be buying an insurrection, and she was "taking care of her own" at our expense.

The next feature of the proceedings entitled to attention in a bird's-eye view like this, concerns the question whether we should take only Luzon, or the whole archipelago. President McKinley cabled Admiral Dewey on August 13th, the day after the protocol was signed, asking as to "the desirability of the several islands," "coal *and other mineral deposits*," and "in a naval and commercial sense which (of the several islands) would be most advantageous."[4] Admiral Dewey had replied, of course, that Luzon was "the most desirable," but volunteered no advice. He *did* state, "No coal of good quality can be procured in the Philippine Islands," which is still true. Allusion is made to this telegram in the proceedings, but no copy of it is there set forth. On October 4th, our Commissioners wired President McKinley suggesting that he cable out to the Admiral and ask him "whether it would be better * * * to retain Luzon * * * or the whole group." Mr. McKinley answered that he had asked Admiral Dewey before General Merritt left Manila to give the latter his views in writing "on general question of Philippines," and that "his report is in your hands in response to both questions." But the commission replied that Admiral Dewey had sent only a copy of a report of General Francis V. Greene's and nothing else. There is no record of any further advice or opinion from Admiral Dewey on the point except that in General Otis's Report (p. 67) we get glimpses of a telegram that has never yet, apparently, been published, sent by Dewey to Washington early in December, 1898, suggesting that we "interfere as little as possible in the internal affairs of the Islands." No; Admiral Dewey must be acquitted of having ever counselled the McKinley Administration to buy the Philippines.

On October 7th the Commission telegraphed Washington that General Merritt attaches much weight to the opinion of the Belgian Consul at Manila, M. André, and that "Consul says United States must take all or nothing"; that "if southern islands remained with Spain they would be in constant revolt, and United States would have a second Cuba"; that "Spanish government would not improve," and "would still protect monks in their extortion."

To this advice there was absolutely no answer. It *was* a case of "all or nothing," and it had already become a case of "all" when on September 16th previous Mr. McKinley signed his original instructions to the Commission stating "The United States cannot accept less than Luzon."

The Commission's telegram of October 7th goes on to quote from the Belgian Consul's opinion that "Present rebellion represents only one half of one per cent. of the inhabitants." The Consul was not before them in person. They were quoting from a memorandum submitted by him to General Merritt at Merritt's request, made at Manila and dated August 29th, the day General Merritt sailed away from Manila bound for Paris via the Suez Canal. He had brought the memorandum along with him. From the previous chapters the reader will, of course, understand that Americans and Europeans at Manila in August, 1898, were paying very little attention to Aguinaldo and his claims as to the extent of his authority in the provinces. It is therefore not surprising that M. André's memorandum of August 29th should have made the foolish statement, "Present rebellion represents only one half of one per cent. of inhabitants." But it is eternally regrettable that his statement on this point had any weight with the Commissioners, for it was, or by that time at least (October 7th) had become, just about 99½ per cent. wide of the mark. As a matter of fact, by October 7th it would have been more accurate to have said, in lieu of the above, "Present rebellion represents practically whole people." You see, we started an insurrection in May, in October it had become a full grown affair, and in December we bought it. The telegram of October 7th also quoted General Merritt as saying, "Insurgents would be victorious unless Spaniards did better in future than in past," and as considering it "feasible for United States to take Luzon and perhaps some adjacent islands and hold them as England does her colonies." These are about the only two sound suggestions General Merritt made to that Commission. In the next breath they quote him as saying, "Natives could not resist 5000 troops." The fact that they did resist more than 120,000 troops, that it took more than that, all told, to put down the insurrection, is sufficient to show how much General Merritt's advice was worth. He was right on two points, as indicated. Both Spanish fleets had been destroyed and Spain had but one left to protect her home coast cities. The death knell of her once proud colonial empire had sounded. Decrepit as she was, she could not possibly have sent any reinforcements to the Philippines. Besides the Filipinos would have "eaten them up." General Merritt's suggestion to "hold them as England does her colonies" was also sensible. In fact that was the only thoroughly honest thing to have done, if we were going to take them at all. England never acts the hypocrite with her colonies. *She makes them behave.* She does not let native people preach sedition in native newspapers, because of "sentimental bosh" about freedom of the press, until the whole country becomes a smouldering hot-bed of sedition. She *has* blown offending natives from the cannon's mouth, when deemed necessary to cure them and their country of the desire for independence. If we are going to have colonies at all, we ought to govern them with the upright downright ruthless honesty of the British. *It is more merciful in the long run.* But we ought not to have colonies at all. For if there is one thing this republic stands for, above all other things, it is the righteousness of aversion to a foreign yoke.

In their telegram of October 7th,5 the Peace Commissioners, now squarely confronted with the question of forcible annexation, begin to let the Administration down easy. They say:

General Anderson in correspondence with Aguinaldo in June and July seemed to treat him and his forces as allies and native authorities, *but subsequently changed his tone*. Merritt and Dewey both kept clear of any *compromising* communications.

A despatch sent by Judge Day certainly comes from high authority. The word "compromising" is therefore important. To say that Admiral Dewey did not treat Aguinaldo as an ally is to raise a mere technical point. But Aguinaldo never did get anything from him in writing. What he got consisted more of deeds than words. And actions speak louder than words. We *had* an alliance with Aguinaldo, a most "compromising" alliance and afterwards repudiated it. Admiral Dewey made it and General Merritt repudiated it. Dewey did, without the President's knowledge, exactly what the President and the American people would have had him do at the time. And Merritt did exactly what the President ordered him to do. But between the making of the alliance, and the repudiation of it, the President and the American people changed their minds. I say the American people, because they afterwards ratified all that Mr. McKinley did. You see the bitterness that lies away down in the secret recesses of the hearts of the Filipino people to-day has its source at this point. They had "a gentleman's agreement," as it were, with us, not in writing, made at a time when the thought of a colony had never entered our minds. They fought in a common cause with us on the faith of that agreement—drove the Spaniards into Manila in numerous victorious engagements involving much loss of life, on their part, keeping the Dons thereafter bottled up in Manila on the land side while their "ally" Admiral Dewey was doing the same on the sea side. The said Dons were living on horses and rats, and famine was imminent when our troops arrived and began to finish the work of taking the beleaguered city. And then, having changed our minds and decided to annex the islands, we repudiated our "gentleman's agreement," on the idea that the end justified the means. And the end, as it has turned out, did not even justify the means, seeing that the islands have proved a heavy financial liability instead of a profitable asset. Judge Day's telegram to Secretary Hay of October 12th (p. 27) contains this curious and surprising passage as to Cuba:

Senator Gray in favor of accepting sovereignty unconditionally * * * that we may thereby avoid future complications with Cubans, claiming sovereignty while we are in process of pacifying island * * * We desire instructions on this point.

The future of Cuba, however, trembled in the balance but for a moment. Before "the shell-burred cables" had had time to quit vibrating with the question thus propounded, there came back this splendidly clean-cut answer from the President:

We must carry out the spirit and letter of the resolution of Congress [declaring war].

In characterizing Judge Gray's position, above indicated, as "surprising," no reflection upon him is intended. On the contrary, such a position, assumed by a man of such conceded intellectual probity, is illuminating as to the attitude subsequently taken concerning the Philippines by the Democratic Senators who voted for the treaty. This attitude is stated by Senator Lodge, in his *History of the War with Spain*, with all the incisive forcefulness to which the country has so long been accustomed in the public utterances of that distinguished man, and, seeing that no promise had been made, as in the case of Cuba, Senator Lodge's statement of the position of those who voted for the treaty should forever set at rest the stale injustice, still occasionally repeated, that Mr. Bryan, "played politics" in 1898–9 in urging his friends in the Senate to vote for its ratification. Says Senator Lodge (*History of the War with Spain*, p. 231):

The friends of ratification took the very simple ground that the treaty committed the United States to no policy, but left them free to do exactly as seemed best with all the islands; that the American people could be safely entrusted with this grave responsibility, and that patriotism and common sense alike demanded the end of the war and the re-establishment of peace, which could only be effected by the adoption of the treaty.

October 14th, Washington wires the commission that Admiral Dewey has just cabled:

It is important that the disposition of the Philippine Islands should be decided as soon as possible. * * * General anarchy prevails without the limits of the city and bay of Manila. Natives appear unable to govern.

In this cablegram the Admiral most unfortunately repeated as true some wild rumors then currently accepted by the Europeans and Americans at Manila which of course were impossible of verification. I say "unfortunately" with some earnestness, because it does not appear on the face of his message that they *were* mere rumors. And, that they were wholly erroneous, in point of fact, has already been cleared up in previous chapters, wherein the real state of peace, order and tranquillity which prevailed throughout Luzon at that time has been, it is believed, put beyond all doubt. But what manna in the wilderness to the

McKinley Administration, now that it was bent on taking the islands, was that Dewey message of October 14th, "The natives appear unable to govern"!

On October 17th, Mr. Day wires Mr. Hay that the Peace Commissioners feel the importance of preserving, so far as possible, the condition of things existing at the time of signing the protocol, to prevent any change in the *status quo*. He says:

Might not our government * * * take more active and positive measures than heretofore for preservation of order and protection of life and property in Philippine Islands?

How could we, when Aguinaldo and his people were in the saddle all over Luzon, had taken the *status quo* between their teeth and run away with it, and were prepared to fight if bidden to halt and dismount; and, which is more, were preserving order perfectly themselves?

On October 19th, Mr. Hay repeated by wire to Mr. Day a cablegram from General Otis which said: "Do not anticipate trouble with insurgents * * * Affairs progressing favorably."

General Otis was making a desperate effort to humor Mr. McKinley's "consent-of-the-governed" theory and programme. But it was a situation, not a theory, which confronted him.

The date of the high-water mark of the Paris peace negotiations is October 25th. On that day, Mr. Day wired Mr. Hay:

Differences of opinion among commissioners concerning Philippine Islands are set forth in statements transmitted (by cable also) herewith. On these we request early consideration and explicit instructions. Liable now to be confronted with this question in joint commission almost immediately.

Messrs. Davis, Frye, and Reid, sent a joint signed statement. They urged taking over the whole archipelago, saying that, as their instructions provided for the retention at least of Luzon, "we do not consider the question of remaining in the Philippine Islands as at all now properly before us." They also urged that as Spain governed and defended the islands from Manila, we became, with the destruction of her fleet and the surrender of her army, "as complete masters of the whole group as she had been, with nothing needed to complete the conquest save to proceed with the *ample* forces we had at hand to take *unopposed* possession." The vice of this proposition, from the strategic as well as the ethical point of view, is of course clear enough *now*.

Spain's government was already tottering in the Philippines when the Spanish-American war broke out. To be "as complete masters as she had been" was like becoming the recipient of a quit-claim deed. Also, ours was not a case of taking "unopposed possession." An adverse claimant, relying on immemorial prescription, was in full possession; all the tenants on the land had attorned to him, and he and they were ready to defend their claim against all comers with their lives. They reminded one of the recurrent small farmer whom some great timber or other corporation seeks to oust, patrolling his land lines rifle in hand, on the lookout for the corporation's agent and the sheriff with the dispossessory warrant.

Messrs. Davis, Frye, and Reid go on to say:

Military and naval witnesses agree that it would be practically as easy to hold and defend the whole as a part.

Hardly any one can fail to read with interest the following accurate and vivid picture which they give of the physical strategic unity of the Philippine Islands:

There is hardly a single island in the group from which you cannot shoot across to one or more of the others—scarcely another archipelago in the world in which the islands are crowded so closely together and so interdependent.

This explains also why the Filipino people are *a people*. Whenever the American people understand that, they will give them their independence, unless they get an idea that government *of* their people *by* their people *for* their people would be distasteful to them.

In the memorandum of their views telegraphed to Washington on October 25th, Messrs. Davis, Frye, and Reid also say:

Public opinion in Europe, *including that of Rome*, expects us to retain whole of Philippine Islands.

Archbishop Chapelle was in Paris at the time of these negotiations. He afterwards told the writer in Manila that he got that $20,000,000 put in the Treaty of Paris. The Church preferred that our title should be a title by purchase rather than a title by conquest, and Mr. McKinley was vigorously urging the latter. Between the legal effects of the two, there is a world of difference. The Church outgeneralled the President—checkmated him with a bishop. Look at that part of the treaty which affects church property:

Article VIII. The * * * cession * * * cannot in any respect impair the property or rights * * * of * * * ecclesiastical * * * bodies.

The Church of Rome, or at least some of the ecclesiastical bodies pertaining to it in the Philippines, owned the cream of the agricultural estates. By the treaty they have not lost a dollar. It might have been otherwise, had not Mr. McKinley's original claim of title by conquest been overcome at Paris.

Judge Day's memorandum of his own views, telegraphed on October 25th along with those of his colleagues, stated that he was unable to agree that we should peremptorily demand the entire Philippine group; that

In the spirit of our instructions, and bearing in mind the often declared disinterestedness of purpose and freedom from designs of conquest with which the war was undertaken, *we should be consistent* in demands in making peace * * * with due regard to our responsibility because of *the conduct of our military and naval authorities in dealing with the insurgents*.

Again, he says:

We cannot leave the insurgents either to form a government [he of course did not know what a complete government they had already formed] or to battle against a foe which * * * might readily overcome them.

He also was of course unaware how thoroughly anxious the Spaniards then in the Philippines were to get away, and how completely they were at the mercy of the new Philippine Republic and its forces. "On all hands" says Judge Day, "it is agreed that the inhabitants of the islands are unfit for self-government." Of course we knew absolutely nothing worth mentioning about the Filipinos at that time. Judge Day then proposes, for the reasons indicated, to accept Luzon and some adjacent islands, as being of "strategic advantage," and to leave Spain the rest, with a "treaty stipulation for non-alienation without the consent of the United States." It seems to me that Judge Day's scheme was the least desirable of all.

Senator Gray's memorandum of the same date is a red-hot argument against taking over any part of the archipelago. He begins thus:

The undersigned cannot agree that it is wise to take Philippine Islands in whole or in part. To do so would be to reverse accepted continental policy of the country, declared and acted upon through our history. * * * It will make necessary * * * immense sums for fortifications and harbors * * * Climate and social conditions demoralizing to character of American youth * * *. On whole, instead of indemnity, injury * * *. Cannot agree that any obligation incurred to insurgents * * *. If we had captured Cadiz and Carlists had helped us, would not be our duty to stay by them at the conclusion of war * * *. No place for * * * government of subject people in American system * * *. Even conceding all benefits claimed for annexation, we thereby abandon * * * the moral grandeur and strength to be gained by keeping our word to nations of the world * * * for doubtful material advantages and *shameful stepping down from high moral position boastfully assumed.* * * * Now that we have achieved all and more than our object, *let us simply keep our word* * * *. *Above all let us not make a mockery of the* [President's] *instructions,* where, after stating that we took up arms only in obedience to the dictates of humanity * * * and that we had no designs of aggrandizement and no ambition for conquest, the President * * * eloquently says: "It is my earnest wish that the United States in making peace should follow the same high rule of conduct which guided it in facing war."

The next day, October 26th, came this laconic answer:

The cession must be of the whole archipelago or none. The latter is wholly inadmissible and the former must be required.

Probably the one thing about the Paris Peace negotiations that is sure to interest the average American most at this late date is the matter of how we came to pay that twenty millions. It was this way. On October 27th, the Commission wired Washington:

Last night Spanish ambassador called upon Mr. Reid.

It seems they talked long and earnestly far into the night, trying to find a way which would prevent the conference from resulting in sudden disruption, and consequent resumption of the war. Mr. Reid made plain the inflexible determination of the American people not to assume the Cuban debt. The Ambassador said: "Montero Rios6 *could not return to Madrid* now if known to have accepted entire Cuban indebtedness," and asked delay to see "if some concessions elsewhere might not be found which would save Spanish Commissioners from utter repudiation at home." There is no doubt that the talk we are now considering was a "heart-to-heart" affair, probably quite informal. Yet it is one of the most important talks that have occurred between any two men in this world in the last fifty years. Mr. Reid finally threw out a hint to the effect that as the preponderance of American public sentiment seemed rather inclined to retain the Philippines, "It was possible," he said, "but not probable that out of these conditions the Spanish Commissioners might find something *either in territory or debt*7 which might *seem to their people at least like a concession.*!"8

It was the leaven of this hint that leavened the whole loaf. There was doubtless much informal parleying after that, but finally, the American Commissioners, having become satisfied that Spanish honor would not be offended by an offer having the substance, if not the form, of charity, and being very tired of Spain's sparring for wind in the hope of a European coalition against us should war be resumed, submitted the following proposal:

The Government of the United States is unable to modify the proposal heretofore made for the cession of the entire archipelago of the Philippine Islands, but the American Commissioners are authorized to offer to Spain, in case the cession should be agreed to, the sum of $20,000,000.

This alluring offer was accompanied with the stern announcement that

Upon the acceptance * * * of the proposals herein made * * * *but not otherwise*, it will be possible * * * to proceed to the consideration * * * of other matters.

Also, our Commissioners wired Washington:

If the Spanish Commissioners refuse our proposition * * * nothing remains except to close the negotiations.

This was very American and very final. Washington answered: "Your proposed action approved."

November 29th, Mr. Day wired Mr. Hay:

Spanish Commissioners at to-day's conference presented a definite and final acceptance of our last proposition.

And that is how that twenty millions found its way into the treaty—not forgetting the prayers and other contemporaneous activities of Archbishop Chapelle.

After the tremendous eight weeks' tension had relaxed, and before the final reduction to writing of all the details, we see this dear little telegram, from Secretary of State Hay, himself a writer of note, come bravely paddling into port, where it was cordially received by both sides, taken in out of the wet, and put under the shelter of the treaty:

Mr. Hay to Mr. Day: In renewing conventional arrangements do not lose sight of copyright agreement.

And here is the last act of the drama:

Mr. Day to Mr. Hay, Paris, December 10, 1898: Treaty signed at 8.50 this evening.

---

[1] *Senate Document 62*, pt. 1, 55th Cong., 3d Sess., 1898–9, p. 283.

[2] Hon. Frank A. Vanderlip, then Assistant Secretary of the Treasury, now (1912) President of the National City Bank, New York, in the *Century Magazine*, August, 1898.

[3] *S. D. 148*, p. 15.

[4] *Navy Department Report* for 1898, Appendix, p. 122.

5*Senate Document 148*, p. 19.

6Chairman of the Spanish Commission.

7Meaning evidently payment of some of Spain's debts with money she could probably get from us for the asking, as a matter of sympathy for the fellow who is "down and out."

8Mr. McKinley had before that sent word significantly that he was not unmindful of the distressing financial embarrassments of Spain.

Chapter VIII. The Benevolent Assimilation Proclamation

Prometheus stole the heavenly fire from the altar of Jupiter to benefit mankind, and Jupiter thereupon punished both Prometheus and the rest of mankind by creating and giving to them the woman Pandora, a supposed blessing but a real curse. Pandora brought along a box of blessings, and when she opened it, everything flew out and away but Hope.

Tales from Æschylus.

The ever-memorable Benevolent Assimilation Proclamation, the Pandora box of Philippine woes, was signed December 21, 1898, and its contents were let loose in the Philippines on January 1, 1899.

Let us consider for a moment the total misapprehension of conditions in the islands under which Mr. McKinley drafted and signed that famous document—a misapprehension due to General Otis's curious blindness to the great vital fact of the situation, viz., that the Filipinos were bent on independence from the first, and preparing to fight for it to the last. Take the following Otis utterance, for example, concerning a date when practically everybody in the Eighth Army Corps, and every newspaper correspondent in the Philippines, recognized that war would be certain in the event the Paris Peace negotiations should result, as common rumor then said they would result, in our taking over the islands:

My own confidence at this time in a satisfactory solution of the difficulties which confronted us may be gathered from a despatch sent to Washington on December 7th, wherein I stated that conditions were improving, and that there were signs of revolutionary disintegration.1

There can be no doubt that, at the date of that despatch, General Otis had been given to understand that under the Treaty of Paris we were going to keep the islands *if* the treaty should be ratified, and also that the *if* might give the Administration trouble, should trouble arise with the Filipinos before the *if* was disposed of at home. As heretofore intimated, in addition to his preference for legal and administrative work to the work of his profession, in the Philippines General Otis constituted himself from the beginning a political henchman. Ample evidence will be introduced later on to show beyond all doubt that all through the early difficulties, when the American people should have been frankly dealt with and given the facts, General Otis would, in the exercise of his military powers as press censor, always say to the war correspondents, "I will let nothing go that will hurt the Administration."

Let us see what the real facts of the Philippine situation were at the date of the Treaty of Paris, December 10th, or, which is the same thing, when General Otis sent his despatch of December 7th. When the Treaty of Paris was signed, General Otis was in possession of Manila and Cavite, with less than 20,000 men under his command, and Aguinaldo was in possession of practically all the rest of the archipelago, with between 35,000 and 40,000 men under his command, armed with guns, and the whole Filipino population were in sympathy with the army of their country. We have already seen the conditions in the various provinces at that time and also the inauguration of the native central government. Let us now examine the military figures.

Ten thousand American soldiers were on hand when Manila was captured, August 13th, and 5000 more had arrived under command of Major-General Elwell S. Otis a week or so after the fall of the city.[2] They had 13,000 Spanish soldiers to guard. In addition to this, by the terms of the capitulation, the city (population say 300,000), its inhabitants, its churches and educational establishments, and its private property of all descriptions had been placed "under the special safeguard of the faith and honor of the American army."[3] Some 4500 to 5000 more troops began to swarm out of San Francisco bound for Manila in the latter part of October, 1898, the last of them reaching Manila December 11th, the day after the Treaty of Paris was signed. After that there were no further additions to General Otis's command prior to the outbreak of war with the Filipinos, February 4, 1899.[3] Of these (approximately) 20,000 men, only 1500 to 2000 were regulars, having the Krag-Jorgensen smokeless gun. The rest were State volunteers, armed with the antiquated Springfield rifles, the same the 71st New York and the 2d Massachusetts had been permitted to carry into the Santiago campaign the summer before. Aguinaldo's people were equipped entirely with Mausers captured from the Spaniards, and other rifles, bought in Hong Kong mostly, using smokeless ammunition. Major (now Major-General) J. F. Bell, who is, in the judgment of many, one of the best all-round soldiers in the American army to-day, was in charge of the "Division of Military Information" at Manila both before and after the taking of the city. General Bell has done many fine things, in the way of reckless bravery in battle at the critical moment and of bold reconnoitring in campaign, and what he fails to find out about an enemy, or a prospective enemy, is not apt to be ascertainable. In a report bearing date August 29, 1898,[4] prepared in anticipation of possible trouble with the Filipinos, he estimated the number of men under arms that Aguinaldo had at between 35,000 and 40,000. This estimate is based by General Bell in his report on the number of guns out in the hands of the Filipinos, which he figures thus:

Captured from Spanish militia	12,500
From Cavite arsenal	2,500
From Jackson & Evans (American merchants trading with Hong Kong)	2,000
From Spanish (captured in battle)	8,000
In hands of Filipinos previous to May 1, 1898	15,000
Total	40,000

From this number General Bell deducts several thousands as having been recaptured by the Spaniards, or bought in. I at once hear some former comrade-in-arms of the Philippine insurrection say: "Oh, no. They couldn't have had as many as 40,000 guns, or near that." I thought the same thing when I first read General Bell's report on the matter. But he removes the doubt thus: "They are being continually sent away to other provinces."

We did not understand Aguinaldo's movements then. All his troops were not around Manila. From what I learned from General Lawton and his staff in 1899, my belief is that Aguinaldo had perhaps 30,000 men with guns around Manila, and out along the railroad, at the time of the outbreak of February 4th. It is idle, of course, at this late date, to claim that the Filipinos were not bent on independence from the first. The matured plans of their leaders, formulated at Hong Kong May 4, 1898, before they ever started the insurrection, preserved in the captured minutes of the meeting already noticed,5 provide the programme to be adopted in the event we should be tempted to keep the islands. In that event, they were prepared against surprise, or any necessity for making new plans, and were agreed to accept war as inevitable. From the first, they made ready for it.

Governmentally and strategically, the Philippine Islands, except Mohammedan Mindanao, which is a separate and distinct problem, may be described very simply and sufficiently as consisting of the great island of Luzon, on which Manila is situated, and the Visayan group.6 We are already familiar with the conditions in Luzon in December, 1898. You hear a great deal about the Philippine archipelago consisting of a thousand and one islands, but there are only eight that are, broadly speaking, worth considering here. The moment a jagged submarine ledge peeps out of the water it becomes an island. And even before that it may wreck a ship. But we are talking about islands that need to be charted on the sea of world politics. The Visayan Islands that really count at all in a great problem such as that we are now considering, are but six in number: Panay, capital Iloilo; Cebu, capital Cebu; Bohol, Negros, Samar, and Leyte.7 Iloilo is some three hundred and odd miles south of Manila, and, besides being the capital of Panay, is the chief port of the Visayas and the second city of the archipelago, Cebu being the third. Under the Spaniards, as now under us, a vessel might clear from either of these places for any part of the world. As we saw in the chapter preceding this, as early as November 18th, Admiral Dewey had cabled Washington that the entire island of Panay was in possession of insurgents, except Iloilo. By the end of December, all the Spanish garrisons in the Visayan Islands had surrendered to the insurgents. (*Otis's Report*, p. 61.) Iloilo did not surrender to the insurgents until the day before Christmas. But let us not anticipate.

December 13th, General Otis received a petition for protection signed by the business men and firms of Iloilo (p. 54), sent of course with the approval of the general commanding the imperilled Spanish garrison. December 14th, he wired Washington for instructions as to what action he should take on this petition, saying, among other things, "Spanish authorities are still holding out, but *will receive* American troops"; and adding one of his inevitable notes of optimism as to the tameness of Filipino aspirations (at Iloilo) for independence: "Insurgents reported favorable to American annexation."

General Otis knew the Spanish troops were hard pressed by the insurgents down at Iloilo, and eagerly awaited a reply. President McKinley was then away from Washington, on a southern trip, to Atlanta and Macon, Georgia, and other points, and nobody at home was giving any thought to the Filipinos, while they were knocking successively at the gates of the various Visayan capitals, and receiving the surrender of their Spanish defenders. It was getting toward the yuletide season. President McKinley was engaged, quite seasonably, in putting the finishing touches to the great work of his life, which was welding the North and the South together forever by wise and kindly manipulation of the countless opportunities to do so presented by the latest war. It was a season of general peace and rejoicing in a thrice-blessed land, and nobody in the United States was looking for trouble with the Filipinos. With our people it was a case of ignorance being bliss, so far as the Philippine Islands and their inhabitants were concerned. In his *Autobiography of Seventy Years*, Senator Hoar tells of an interview with President McKinley concerning his (the Senator's) attitude toward the Treaty of Paris, early in December, 1898.8 "He greeted me with the delightful and affectionate cordiality which I always found in him. He took me by the hand, and said: 'How are you feeling this winter, Mr. Senator?' I was determined there should be no misunderstanding. I replied at once: 'Pretty pugnacious, I confess, Mr. President.' The tears came into his eyes and he said, grasping my hand again: 'I shall always love you whatever you do.'"

It behooves this nation, and all nations, to consider those tears. They explain all the subsequent history of the Philippines to date. Mr. McKinley had proved himself a gallant soldier in his youth, and he knew something of the horrors of war. He was also one of the most amiable gentlemen that ever lived. But it is no disrespect to his memory to say that while Mr. McKinley was a good man, Senator Hoar was his superior in moral fibre, and he knew it, and he knew the country knew it. He knew that Senator Hoar was going to fight the ratification of the treaty to the last ditch, speaking for the Rights of Man and such old "worn out formulæ," and that his only defence before the bar of history would have to rest on "Trade Expansion," alias the "Almighty Dollar." Those tears were harbingers of the coming strife in the Philippines. They were shed for such lives as that strife might cost. They were an assumption of responsibility for such shedding of blood as the treaty might entail. The President returned to Washington from his southern trip on December 21st, and on December 23d (p. 55) cabled General Otis the following reply to his request of December 14th for instructions:

Send necessary troops to Iloilo, to *preserve the peace* and protect life and property. *It is most important that there should be no conflict with the insurgents. Be conciliatory but firm.*

Senator Hoar had put Mr. McKinley on notice that he was going to present the ethics of the case in the debate on the treaty. Congress had gone home for the holidays, and after it re-assembled in January the treaty would come up. The vote was sure to be close, and a too vigorous manifestation of belief on the part of the Filipinos that this nation was *not* closing the war with Spain animated by "the same high rule of conduct which guided it in facing war" (Mr. McKinley's instructions to the Peace Commissioners) might defeat the ratification of the treaty. Indeed, the final vote of February 6th, was so close that the Administration had but one vote to spare. The final vote was fifty-seven to twenty-seven—just one over the necessary two-thirds. The smoke of a battle to subjugate the Filipinos might "dim the lustre and the moral strength," as Mr. McKinley had expressed it in his instructions to the Peace Commissioners, of a war to free the Cubans. Therefore there must be no trouble, at least until after the ratification of the treaty. President McKinley had invented in the case of Cuba a very catchy phrase, "Forcible annexation would be criminal aggression," and every time anybody now quoted it on him it tended to take the wind out of his sails. So benevolently eager was that truly kind-hearted and Christian gentleman to avoid the appearance of "criminal aggression" that he evidently got to thinking about that telegram of December 23d in which he had authorized General Otis to send troops to the relief of the beleaguered Spanish garrison at Iloilo, and also about the message from Admiral Dewey received November 18th previous, to the effect that the entire island of Panay except Iloilo was then already in the hands of the insurgents. The result was that he decided not to let his conciliatory proclamation of December 21st await the slow process of the mails, and therefore, though it consisted of something like one thousand words, he had it cabled out to General Otis in full on December 27th. It is now here reproduced in full because it precipitated the war in the Philippines, and is the key to all our subsequent dealings with them[9]:

THE BENEVOLENT ASSIMILATION PROCLAMATION

EXECUTIVE MANSION, WASHINGTON, December 21, 1898.

The destruction of the Spanish fleet in the harbor of Manila by the United States naval squadron commanded by Rear-Admiral Dewey, followed by the reduction of the city and the surrender of the Spanish forces, practically effected the conquest of the Philippine Islands and the suspension of Spanish sovereignty therein. With the signature of the treaty of peace between the United States and Spain by their respective plenipotentiaries at Paris on the 10th instant, and as a result of the victories of American arms, *the future control, disposition, and government of the Philippine Islands are ceded to the United States*. In the fulfilment of the *rights of sovereignty* thus acquired and the responsible obligations of government thus assumed, the actual occupation and administration of the entire group of the Philippine Islands becomes immediately necessary, and the *military government* heretofore maintained by the United States in the city, harbor, and bay of Manila *is to be extended* with all possible despatch *to the whole of the ceded territory*. In performing this duty the military commander of the United States is enjoined to make known to the inhabitants of the Philippine Islands that in *succeeding to the sovereignty of Spain*, in severing the former political relations, and in establishing a new political power, the authority of the United States is to be exerted for the securing of the persons and property of the people of the islands and for the confirmation of all their private rights and relations. It will be the duty of the commander of the forces of occupation to announce and proclaim in the most public manner that *we come* not as invaders or conquerors, but as friends, *to protect* the natives in their homes, in their employments, and in their personal and religious rights. All persons who, either by active aid or by honest submission, co-operate with the Government of the United States to give effect to these beneficent purposes will receive the reward of its support and *protection*. All others will be brought within the lawful rule we have assumed, with firmness if need be, but without severity, so far as possible. Within the absolute domain of *military authority*, which necessarily is and *must remain supreme* in the ceded territory until the legislation of the United States shall otherwise provide, the municipal laws of the territory in respect to private rights and property and the repression of crime are to be considered as continuing in force, and to be administered by the ordinary tribunals, so far as practicable. The operations of civil and municipal government are to be performed by such officers as may accept *the supremacy of the United States* by taking the oath of allegiance, or by officers chosen, as far as practicable, from the inhabitants of the islands. While the control of all the public property and the revenues of the state passes with the cession, and while the use and management of all public means of transportation are necessarily reserved to the authority of the United States, private property, whether belonging to individuals or corporations, is to be respected except for cause duly established. The taxes and duties heretofore payable by the inhabitants to the late government become payable to the authorities of the United States unless it be seen fit to substitute for them other reasonable rates or modes of contribution to the expenses of government, whether general or local. If private property be taken for military use, it shall be paid for when possible in cash, at a fair valuation, and when payment in cash is not practicable, receipts are to be given. All ports and places in the Philippine Islands in the actual possession of the land and naval forces of the United States will be opened to the commerce of all friendly nations. All goods and wares not prohibited for military reasons by due announcement of the military authority will be admitted upon payment of such duties and other charges as shall be in force at the time of their importation. Finally, it should be the earnest wish and paramount aim of the military administration to win the confidence, respect, and affection of the inhabitants of the Philippines by assuring them in every possible way that full measure of individual rights and liberties which is the heritage of free peoples, and by proving to them that the mission of the United States is one of

BENEVOLENT ASSIMILATION

substituting the mild sway of justice and right for arbitrary rule. In the fulfilment of this high mission, supporting the temperate administration of affairs for the greatest good of the governed, there must be sedulously maintained the strong arm of authority, to repress disturbance and to overcome all obstacles to the bestowal of the blessings of good and stable government upon the people of the Philippine Islands under the free flag of the United States.

WILLIAM MCKINLEY.

The words used in the foregoing proclamation which were regarded by the Filipinos as "fighting words," *i. e.*, as making certain the long anticipated probability of a war for independence, are those which appear in italics. The rest of the proclamation counted for nothing with them. They had been used to the hollow rhetoric and flowery promises of equally eloquent Spanish proclamations all their lives, they and their fathers before them.

In suing to President McKinley for peace on July 22d, previous, the Prime Minister of Spain had justified all the atrocities committed and permitted by his government in Cuba during the thirty years' struggle for independence there which preceded the Spanish-American War by saying that what Spain had done had been prompted only by a "desire to spare the great island from the dangers of premature independence."[10]

Clearly, from the Filipino point of view, the United States was now determined "to spare them from the dangers of premature independence," using such force as might be necessary for the accomplishment of that pious purpose.

The truth is that, Prometheus-like, we stole the sacred fire from the altar of Freedom whereupon the flames of the Spanish War were kindled, and gave it to the Filipinos, justifying the means by the end; and "the links of the lame Lemnian" have been festering in our flesh ever since. The Benevolent Assimilation Proclamation was a kind of Pandora Box, supposed to contain all the blessings of Liberty, but when the lid was taken off, woes innumerable befell the intended beneficiaries, and left them only the Hope of Freedom—from us. Verily there is nothing new under the sun. It is written: "Thou shalt not steal" anything—not even "sacred fire." There is no such thing as nimble morality. The lesson of the old Greek poet fits our case. So also, indeed, do those of the modern sage, Maeterlinck, for the Filipinos could have found their own Bluebird for happiness. The record of our experience in the Philippines is full of reminders, which will multiply as the years go by, that, after all, every people have an "unalienable right" to pursue happiness *in their own way* as opposed to *somebody else's way*. That is the law of God, as God gives me to see the right. Conceived during the Christmas holiday season and in the spirit of that blessed season and presented to the Filipino people on New Year's Day, received by them practically as a declaration of war and baptized in the blood of thousands of them in the battle of February 4th thereafter, the manner of the reception of this famous document, the initial reversal and subsequent evolution of its policies, and all the lights and shadows of Benevolent Assimilation will be traced in the chapters which follow.

---

[1] Otis's *Report for 1899*, p. 43.

[2] *War Dept. Report*, 1899, vol. i, pt. 4, p. 3.

[3] *Ib.*, pt. 2, p. 75.

[4] *Senate Document 62*, p. 379.

[5] Published at page 7 of *Senate Document 208*, pt. 2, 56th Congress, 1st Session (1900).

[6] Called in Spanish "Visayas," or Bisayas. Visayas is an adjective derived from the name of the Bay of Biscay, "b" and "v" being interchangeable in Spanish.

[7] For a fuller description of the archipelago, see Chapter XII.

[8] Vol. ii., p. 315.

9This proclamation has been printed many times, in various government publications, *e.g., War Department Report*, 1899, vol. i., pt. 4, pp. 355–6; *Senate Document 208*, 56th Congress, 1st Session (1900), pp. 82–3, etc.

10*Senate Document 62*, pt. 1, 55th Congress, 3d Session, p. 272.

Chapter IX. The Iloilo Fiasco

The King of France with forty thousand men
Marched up the hill and then marched down again.

Old English Ballad.

We have already seen how busily Aguinaldo occupied himself during the protracted peace negotiations at Paris in getting his government and people ready for the struggle for independence which he early and shrewdly guessed would be ultimately forthcoming. General Otis was in no position to preserve the *status quo*. The *status quo* was a worm in hot ashes that would not stay still. The revolution was a snow-ball that *would* roll. The day after Christmas, General Otis at last sent an expedition under General Marcus P. Miller to the relief of Iloilo, but when it arrived, December 28th, the Spaniards had already turned the town over to the insurgent authorities, and sailed away. When General Miller arrived, being under imperative orders from Washington to be conciliatory, and under no circumstances to have a clash with the insurgents, the Administration's most earnest solicitude being to avoid a clash, at least until the treaty of peace with Spain should be ratified by the United States Senate, he courteously *asked permission* to land, several times, being refused each time. With a request of this sort sent ashore January 1, 1899, he transmitted a copy of the proclamation set forth in the preceding chapter. The insurgent reply defiantly forbade him to land. Therefore he did not land—because Washington was pulling the strings—until after the treaty was ratified. "So here we are at Iloilo, an exploded bluff," wrote war correspondent J. F. Bass to his paper, *Harper's Weekly.*

By the time the treaty was ratified the battle of Manila of February 4th had occurred, and the pusillanimity of self-doubting diplomacy had given way to the red honesty of war.1

As was noticed in the chapter preceding this, by the end of December, 1898, all military stations outside Luzon, with the exception of Zamboanga, in the extreme south of the great Mohammedan island of Mindanao near Borneo, had been turned over by the Spaniards to the insurgents. When General Miller, commanding the expedition to Iloilo, arrived in the harbor of that city with his teeming troop-ships and naval escorts on December 28th, an aide of the Filipino commanding general came aboard the boat he was on and "desired to know," says General Miller's report,2 "if we had anything against them—were we going to interfere with them." General Miller then sent some of his own aides ashore with a letter to the insurgent authorities, explaining the peaceful nature of his errand. They at once asked if our people had brought down any instructions from Aguinaldo. Answering in the negative, General Miller's aides handed them his olive-branch letter. They read it and said they could do nothing without orders from Aguinaldo "in cases affecting their Federal Government." The grim veteran commanding the American troops smoked on this for a day or so, and then asked a delegation of insurgents that were visiting his ship by his invitation—they would not let him land, you see—whether if he landed they would meet him with armed resistance. The Malay reverence for the relation of host and guest resulted in an evasive reply. They could not answer. But after they went back to the city they did answer. And this is what they wrote:

Upon the return of your commissioners last night, we * * * discussed the situation and attitude of this region of Bisayas in regard to its relations and dependence upon the central government of Luzon (the Aguinaldo government, of course); and * * * I have the honor to notify you that, in conjunction with the people, the army, and the committee, we insist upon our pretension *not to consent * * * to any foreign interference without express orders from the central government of Luzon * * * with which we are one in ideas, as we have been until now in sacrifices.* * * * If you insist * * * upon disembarking your forces, this is our final attitude. *May God forgive you, etc.*"

Iloilo, December 30, 1898.3

This letter is recited in General Miller's report to be from "President Lopez, of the Federal Government of Visayas." General Miller then wrote Otis begging permission to attack on the ground that upon the success of the expedition he was in charge of "depends the future speedy yielding of insurrectionary movements in the islands." War correspondent Bass, who was on the ground at the time, also wrote his paper: "The effect on the natives will be incalculable all over the islands." But General Otis was trying to help Mr. McKinley nurse the treaty through the Senate on the idea that there weren't going to be any "insurrectionary movements in the islands," that all dark and misguided conspiracies of selfishly ambitious leaders looking to such impious ends would fade before the sunlight of Benevolent Assimilation.

Cautioning Otis against any clash at Iloilo, Mr. McKinley wired January 9th: "Conflict would be most unfortunate, considering the present. * * * Time given the insurgents cannot injure us, and must weaken and discourage them. They will see our benevolent purpose, etc."4

The Iloilo fiasco did indeed furnish to the insurgent cause aid and comfort at the psychologic moment when it most needed encouragement to bring things to a head. It presented a spectacle of vacillation and seeming cowardice which heartened the timid among the insurgents and started among them a general eagerness for war which had been lacking before. In one of his bulletins5 to Otis, General Miller tells of two boats' crews of the 51st Iowa landing on January 5th, and being met by a force of armed natives who "asked them their business and warned them off," whereupon they heeded the warning and returned to their transport. This regiment had then been cooped up on their transport continuously since leaving San Francisco November 3d, previous, sixty-three days. They were kept lying off Iloilo until January 29th, and then brought back to Manila and landed, after eighty-nine days aboard ship, all idea of taking Iloilo before the Senate should act having been abandoned.

The Benevolent Assimilation Proclamation was received by cable in cipher, at Manila, December 29th, and as soon as it had been written out in long hand General Otis hurried a copy down to General Miller at Iloilo by a ship sailing that day, so that General Miller might "understand the position and policy of our government." But he forgot to tell Miller to conceal the policy for the present.6 So the latter, on January 1st, not only sent a copy of it to the "President of the Federal Government of Visayas," Mr. Lopez,7 but *in the note of transmittal* he "asked," says his report, "that they *permit* the entry of my troops."8 What a fatal mistake! Here was a proclamation representing all the "majesty, dominion, and power" of the American Government, signed by the President of the United States, in terms asserting immediate, absolute, and supreme authority, and the natives were "asked" if they would "permit" its enforcement. General Miller's report says that he also had the proclamation "translated into Spanish and distributed to the people."9 "The people laugh at it," he says. "The insurgents call us cowards and are fortifying at the point of the peninsula, and are mounting old smooth-bore guns left by the Spaniards. They are intrenching everywhere, are bent on having one fight, and are confident of victory. *The longer we wait before the attack the harder it will be to put down the insurrection.*" This is especially interesting in the light of President McKinley's justification of the wisdom of temporizing—on the idea that delay would weaken the insurgents and could not hurt us. "*Let no one convince you,*" writes Miller to Otis on January 5th, "that peaceful means can settle the difficulty here."

The appeal to Otis to permit commencement of operations was without avail. Otis was the Manila agent of the Aldrich Old Guard in the Senate, in charge of the pending treaty. He would simply send the disgusted Miller messages not to be hasty, assuring him that the firing of a shot at Iloilo would mean the precipitation of general conflict about Manila and all over the place, and that this would be "most disappointing to the President of the United States, who continually urges extreme caution and no conflict."10

The Administration was counting senatorial noses at the time, and that its anxiety was justified is apparent from the fact already noted, that on the final vote whereby the treaty was ratified it had but one vote to spare. So General Miller sat sunning himself on the deck of his transport, and watching the insurgents working like ants at their fortifications, and vainly wishing his 2500 men could get ashore at least long enough to stretch themselves a bit. John F. Bass, correspondent for *Harper's Weekly*, left Iloilo, returned to Manila, and wrote his paper on January 23d: "I returned to Manila well knowing that there was nothing more to be done in Iloilo until the Senate voted on the Treaty of Peace."

On the eighth day after General Miller had asked permission of the Iloilo village Hampdens to enforce the orders of the President of the United States, the "Federal Government of the Visayas," through its President, Señor Lopez, finally deigned to notice Mr. McKinley's proclamation. It said under date of January 9th:

General: We have the high honor of having received your message, dated January 1st, of this year, enclosing letter of President McKinley. You say in one clause of your message: "As indicated in the President's cablegram, under these conditions the inhabitants of the island of Panay ought to obey the political authority of the United States, and they will incur a grave responsibility if, after deliberating, they decide to resist said authority." So the council of state of this region of Visayas are, at this present moment, between the authority of the United States, that you try to impose on us, and the authority of the central government of Malolos.

Then follows this remarkable statement of the case for the Filipinos:

The supposed authority of the United States began with the Treaty of Paris, on the 10th December, 1898. *The authority of the Central Government of Malolos is founded in the sacred and natural bonds of blood, language, uses, customs, ideas, (and) sacrifices.*11

General Otis was fond of throwing cold water on any particularly eloquent Filipino *insurrecto* document he had occasion to put in his reports by saying that Mabini was "the brains of" the Malolos Government—meaning the only brains it had12—and that he probably wrote such document, whatever it might be. But here is a piece of real eloquence, originating away down in the Visayan Islands, as far away from Malolos as Colonel Stark and his "Green Mountain Boys" were from Washington and Hamilton in 1776 and after. What then is the explanation of composition so forceful in its impassioned simplicity, and in the light of subsequent events, so pathetic? There is but one explanation. It came from the heart. It was the cry of the Soul of Humanity seeking its natural affiliations. It was the language of what Aguinaldo's early state papers always used to call the "legitimate aspirations of" his people—legitimate aspirations which we later strangled. The reason of the writer's earnestness is that a few months later he helped do some of the strangling. Thirteen years afterwards, a thorough acquaintance with the Filipino side of the matter, derived from an examination of the information which has been gradually accumulated and published by our government during that time, causes him to say, "Father forgive me, for I knew not what I did." The 35,000 volunteers of 1899 knew nothing about the Filipinos or their side of the case. We were like the deputy sheriff who goes out with a warrant duly issued to arrest a man charged with unlawful breach of the peace. It is not his business to inquire whether the man is guilty or not. If the man resists arrest, he takes the consequences.

On the second day after the above defiance of the President of the United States was served up to General Miller, that gallant officer having dutifully swallowed it, sent an officer ashore on a diplomatic mission. The name and rank of this military ambassador were Acting Assistant Surgeon Henry DuR. Phelan, who clearly appears to have been a man of keen insight and considerable ability. His written report to General Miller of what transpired is a document of permanent interest and importance to the annals of men's struggles for free institutions.13 It states that at the meeting the spokesman of the Filipinos, Attorney Raimundo Melliza, began by saying that "all the Americans owned was Manila." That was unquestionably true, so our ambassador, it seems, did not gainsay it. Dr. Phelan suggested that the Americans had sacrificed lives and money in destroying the power of Spain. The spokesman, Attorney Melliza, replied that *"they also* had made great sacrifice in lives, *and that they had a right to their country* which they had fought for, and that we are here now to take from them what they had won by fighting;*that they had been our allies, and we had used them as such."* Dr. Phelan's report goes on to say: "I replied that military occupation was a necessity for a time, * * * and that as soon as order was assured it would be withdrawn * * *. *They smiled at this."* Well they might. Fourteen years have elapsed since then, and the law-making power of the United States has never yet declared whether the American occupation of the Philippine Islands is to be temporary, like our occupation of Cuba was, or permanent, like the British occupation of Egypt is. True, Dr. Phelan said "military" occupation, but the smile was provoked by the suggestion of *temporariness*. After the committee smiled, they remarked:

We have fought for independence and feel that we have the power of governing and need no assistance. *We are showing it now. You might inquire of the foreigners if it is not so.*

Dr. Phelan's report proceeds:

They stated that their orders were not to allow us to disembark, and that they were powerless to allow us to come in without express orders from their government.

In regard to the Treaty of Paris, the spokesman, Lawyer Melliza, said:

International law forbids a nation to make a contract in regard to taking the liberties of its colonies.

Lawyer Melliza was wrong. If he had said "the law of righteousness," instead of "international law," his proposition, thus amended, would have been incontrovertible. On September 19, 1911, one of the great newspapers of this country, the *Denver Post*, sent out to the members of the Congress of the United States, and to "The Fourth Estate" also, the newspaper editors, a circular letter proposing that we sell the Philippine Islands to Japan. A member of the United States Senate sent this answer:

I do not favor your proposition. Selling the Islands means selling the inhabitants. The question of traffic in human beings, whether by wholesale or retail, was forever settled by the Civil War.

About the same time a leading daily paper of Georgia had an editorial on the *Denver Post's* proposition, the most conspicuous feature of which was that *Japan was too poor to pay us well*, should we contemplate selling the Filipinos to her, so it was no use to discuss the matter at length.

No; Lawyer Melliza's proposition has no standing in international law *yet*. But it has with what Mr. Lincoln's First Inaugural called "the better angels of our nature," if we stop to reflect.

Another interesting feature of the Phelan report to General Miller is the following:

I asked Lawyer Melliza if Aguinaldo said we could occupy the city would they agree to it. He replied most emphatically that they would.

At that time, in January, 1899, while the debate on the treaty was in progress in the United States Senate, there was hardly a province in that archipelago where you would not have encountered the same inflexible adherence to the Aguinaldo government.

Dr. Phelan's report closes thus:

At the conclusion of the meeting it was said that as this question *involved the integrity of the entire republic*, it could not be further discussed here, but must be referred to the Malolos Government.

There is one other statement made by the spokesman of the Filipinos, at their meeting with Dr. Phelan, which arrested and gripped my attention. That it may interest the reader as it did me, it will need but a word or so as preface. In the fall of that same year, 1899, when my regiment, the 29th Infantry, U. S. Volunteers, reached the Islands, it was supposed that the insurrection had about played out, *i.e.*, that it had been "beaten to a frazzle," because the Filipinos no longer offered to do battle in force in the open. Yet all that fall, and all through 1900 and after, a most obstinate guerrilla warfare was kept up. Anywhere in the archipelago you were liable to be fired on from ambush. At first we could not understand this. Later we found out it was the result of an order of Aguinaldo's, faithfully carried out, not to assemble in large commands, but to conduct a systematic guerrilla warfare indefinitely. We learned this by capturing a copy of the order, which was quite elaborate. Dr. Phelan's report says:

I told him [Melliza] that the city was in our power, and that we could destroy it at any time * * *. Lawyer Melliza replied that he cared nothing about the city; that we could destroy it if we wished * * *. "*We will withdraw to the mountains and repeat the North American Indian warfare. You must not forget that.*"

Later, they did.

On January 15th, General Otis wrote General Miller[14] again cautioning him against any clash at Iloilo, and saying of conditions at Manila and Malolos: "The revolutionary government is *very anxious* for peaceful relations."

Three days later Senator Bacon saw the situation with clearer vision from the other side of the world than General Otis could see it under his nose, and said on the floor of the Senate on January 18th concerning the conditions at Manila and Malolos:

While there is no declaration of war, while there is no avowal of hostile intent, with two such armies fronting each other with such divers intents and resolves, it will take but a spark to ignite the magazines which is to explode.15

The spark was ignited on February 4, 1899, by a sentinel of the Nebraska regiment firing on some Filipino soldiers who disregarded his challenge to halt, and killing one of them. War once on, General Miller was directed on February 10th, after he had lain in Iloilo harbor for forty-four days, to take the city. So at last he gave written notice to the insurgents in Iloilo demanding the surrender of the city and garrison "before sunset Saturday, the 11th instant" and requesting them to give warning to all non-combatants.16 Thereupon the insurgents set fire to the city and departed.

---

1 The "self-doubting" lay in the doubt of the Administration as to whether its programme of conquest would or would not be ratified by the Senate. The "pusillanimity" lay, wholly unbeknown to Washington of course, in the estimate of us it produced among the Filipinos.

2 *War Department Report*, 1899, vol. i., pt. 4, p. 62.

3 *War Department Report*, 1899, vol. i., pt. 4, p. 64.

4 *War Dept. Report*, 1899, vol. i., pt. 4, p. 79.

5 *Ib.*, p. 67.

6 "I sent you the President's proclamation, not for publication, but for your information," wrote Otis to Miller after the latter had let the cat out of the bag. *Senate Document 208*, p. 58.

7 *Senate Document 208*, 56th Cong., 1st Sess., p. 54.

8 *War Dept. Report*, 1899, vol. i., pt. 4, p. 66.

9 *Ibid.*

10 *War Dept. Report*, 1899, vol. i., pt. 4, p. 59.

11 *Senate Document 208*, 56th Cong., 1st Sess. (1900), pp. 54–5.

12 Colonel Enoch H. Crowder, General Otis's Judge Advocate, was "the brains of" the Otis government. But the difference between General Otis and Aguinaldo was that Aguinaldo always had the good sense to follow Mabini's advice, while Otis did not always follow Crowder's.

13 *Senate Document 208*, p. 56.

14 *S. D. 208*, p. 58.

15 See *Congressional Record*, January 18, 1899, p. 734.

16 *Senate Document 208*, p. 59.

Chapter X. Otis and Aguinaldo (*Continued*)

A word spoken in due season, how good is it!

PROVERBS xv., 23.

In the last chapter we saw the début of the Benevolent Assimilation programme at Iloilo. We are now to observe it at Manila. General Otis says in his report for 1899[1]:

After fully considering the President's proclamation and the temper of the Tagalos with whom I was daily discussing political problems and the friendly intentions of the United States Government toward them, I concluded that there were certain words and expressions therein, such as "sovereignty," "right of cession," and those which directed immediate occupation, etc., * * * which might be advantageously used by the Tagalo war party to incite widespread hostilities among the natives. * * * It was my opinion, therefore, that I would be justified in so amending the paper that the beneficent object of the United States Government would be clearly brought within the comprehension of the people.

Accordingly, he published a proclamation as indicated, on January 4th, at Manila. In a less formal communication concerning this proclamation, viz., a letter to General Miller at Iloilo, General Otis comes to the point more quickly thus:

After some deliberation we put out one of our own which it was believed would suit the temper of the people.[2]

The only thing in the Otis proclamation specifically directed toward soothing "the temper of the people" was a hint that the United States would, under the government it was going to impose, "appoint the representative men now forming the controlling element of the Filipinos to civil positions of responsibility and trust" (p. 69). And this, far from soothing Filipino temper, was interpreted as an offer of a bribe if they would desert the cause of their country. The *bona fides* of the offer they did not doubt for a moment. In fact it caught a number of the more timid prominent men, especially the elderly ones of the ultraconservative element preferring submission to strife. But the younger and bolder spirits were faithful, many of them unto death, and all of them unto many battles and much "hiking."[3]

General Otis's report goes on to tell how, about the middle of January, after he had published his sugar-coated edition of the presidential proclamation at Manila, it then at last occurred to him that General Miller might have published the original text of it in full at Iloilo, and, "fearing that," says he, "I again despatched Lieut. Col. Potter to Iloilo"—evidently post-haste. But it appears that when the breathless Potter arrived, the lid was already off. The horse had left the stable and the door was open, as we saw in the preceding chapter. However, as the Otis report indicates in this connection (p. 67), copies of the original McKinley proclamation, as published in full at Iloilo by General Miller, were of course promptly forwarded by the insurgents at Iloilo to the insurgent government at Malolos. So all that General Otis got for his pains was detection in the attempt to conceal the *crucial words* asserting American sovereignty in plain English. He tells us himself that as soon as the Malolos people discovered the trick, "it [the proclamation] became"—in the light of the Otis doctoring—"the object of venomous attack." His report was of course written long after all these matters occurred, but its language shows a total failure on the part of its author, even then, to understand the cause of the bitterness he denominates "venom." This bitterness grew naturally out of what seemed to the Filipinos an evident purpose of the United States to take and keep the Islands and an accompanying unwillingness to acknowledge that purpose, as shown by the conspicuous discrepancies between the original text of the proclamation as published at Iloilo by General Miller, on January 1st, and the modified version of it given out by General Otis at Manila on January 4th. "The ablest of the insurgent newspapers," says he (p. 69), "which was now issued at Malolos and edited by the uncompromising Luna * * * attacked the policy * * * as declared in the proclamation, and its assumption of sovereignty * * * with all the vigor of which he was capable." The nature of Editor Luna's philippics is not described by General Otis in detail, the only specific notion we get of them being from General Otis's echo of their tone, which, he tells us, was to the effect that "everything tended simply to a change of masters." But in another part of the Otis *Report* (p. 163) we find an epistle written about that time by one partisan of the revolution to another, whose key-note, given in the following extracts, was doubtless in harmony with the Luna editorials:

We shall not have them (Filipinos enough to conduct a decent government) in 10, 20, or a 100 years, because the Yankees will never acknowledge the aptitude of an "inferior" race to govern the country. Do not dream that when American sovereignty is implanted in the country the American office-holders will give up. Never! If * * * it depends upon them to say whether the Filipinos have sufficient men for the government of the country * * * they will never say it.

Is not the American who pretends that he would have done anything but just what the Filipinos did, had he been in their place, *i.e.*, fought to the last ditch for the independence of his country, the rankest sort of a hypocrite? General Otis was a soldier, and his views may have been honestly colored by his environment. But how at this late date can any fair-minded man read the above extracts illustrative of the temper in which the Filipinos went to war with us without acknowledging the righteousness of the motives which impelled them?

Aguinaldo promptly met General Otis's proclamation of January 4th by a counter-proclamation put out the very next day, in which he indignantly protested against the United States assuming *sovereignty* over the Islands. "Even the women," says General Otis (p. 70), "in a document numerously signed by them, gave me to understand that after the men were all killed off they were prepared to shed their patriotic blood for the liberty and independence of their country." General Otis actually intended this last as a sly touch of humor. But when we recollect Mr. Millet's description (Chapter IV. *ante*) of the women coming to the trenches and cooking rice for the men while the Filipinos were slowly drawing their cordon ever closer about the doomed Spanish garrison of Manila in July and August previous, fighting their way over the ground between them and the besieged main body of their ancient enemies inch by inch, while Admiral Dewey blockaded them by sea, General Otis's sly touch of humor loses some of its slyness. "The insurgent army also," he says (p. 70), "was especially affected * * * and only awaited an opportunity to demonstrate its invincibility in war with the United States troops * * * whom it had commenced to insult and charge with cowardice."

The benighted condition of the insurgents in this regard was directly traceable to the Iloilo fiasco. It was that, principally, which made the insurgents so foolishly over-confident and the subsequent slaughter of them so tremendous. Further on in his report General Otis says, with perceptible petulance, in summing up his case against the Filipinos:

The pretext that the United States was about to substitute itself for Spain * * * was resorted to and had its effect on the ignorant masses.

Speaking of his own modified version of the Benevolent Assimilation Proclamation, General Otis says (p. 76):

No sooner was it published than it brought out a virtual declaration of war from, in this instance at least, the wretchedly advised President Aguinaldo, who, on January 5th, issued the following

—giving the reply proclamation in full. No man can read the Otis report itself without feeling that if he, the reader, had been playing Aguinaldo's hand he would have played it exactly as Aguinaldo did. To General Otis the government at Malolos—"their Malolos arrangement," he used to call it—seemed quite an impudent little *opera-bouffe* affair, "a tin-horn government," as Senator Spooner suggested in the same debate on the treaty, in which he called his rugged and fiery friend from South Carolina, Senator Tillman, "the Senator from Aguinaldo," and immediately thereafter, with that engaging frankness that always so endeared him to his colleagues on both sides of the Chamber, removed the sting from the jest by admitting that neither he (Spooner), nor Tillman, nor anybody else in the United States, knew anything about Aguinaldo or his government. But in the calmer retrospect of many years after, we have seen, through the official documents which have become available in the interval, that said government was in complete and effective control of practically the whole archipelago, and had the moral support of the whole population at a time when our troops controlled absolutely nothing but the two towns of Manila and Cavite. Therefore, when we read in the Aguinaldo proclamation such phrases as, "In view of this, I summoned a council of my generals and asked the advice of my cabinet, and in conformity with the opinion of both bodies I" did so and so; "My government cannot remain indifferent to" this or that act of the Americans assuming sovereignty over the islands; "Thus it is that my government is disposed to open hostilities if" etc.; they do not sound to us so irritatingly bombastic as they did to General Otis, distributed under his nose as the proclamation containing them at once was, by thousands, throughout a city of which he was nominally in possession, but nine-tenths of whose 300,000 inhabitants he was obliged to believe in sympathy with the insurgents.

"My government," says the Aguinaldo proclamation, "rules the whole of Luzon, the Visayan Islands, and a part of Mindanao." Except as to Mindanao, which cut absolutely no figure in the insurrection until well toward the end of the guerrilla part of it, we have already examined this claim and found by careful analysis that it was absolutely true by the end of December, 1898.

After a rapid review of how he had been aided and encouraged in starting the revolution against the Spaniards by Admiral Dewey, and then given the cold shoulder by the army when it came, Aguinaldo's manifesto says:

It was also taken for granted that the American forces would necessarily sympathize with the revolution which they had managed to encourage, and which had saved them much blood and great hardships; and, above all, we entertained absolute confidence in the history and traditions of a people which fought for its independence and for the abolition of slavery, and which *posed as the champion and liberator of oppressed peoples. We felt ourselves under the safeguard of a free people.*

That this statement also was authorized by the facts is evident from the minutes of the Hong Kong meeting of May 4th, already noticed, presided over by Aguinaldo, and called to formulate the programme for the insurrection he was about to sail for the Philippines to inaugurate, in which, after much discussion among the revolutionary leaders it was agreed that while they must be prepared for all possible contingencies, yet,

if Washington proposes to carry out the fundamental principles of its constitution, it is most improbable that an attempt will be made to colonize the Filipinos or annex them.4

In short, the Aguinaldo proclamation of January 5th suggests with a briefness which Filipino familiarity with the great mass of facts already laid before the reader in the preceding chapters made appropriate, all the causes for which the Malolos Government was ready, if need be, to declare war, and winds up by boldly serving General Otis with notice that if the Americans try to take Iloilo and the Visayan Islands "my government is disposed to open hostilities."

On January 9th President McKinley cabled out to General Otis asking if it would help matters to send a commission out to explain to the Filipinos our benevolent intentions. This idea thus suggested materialized, a few weeks later, in the Schurman Commission, of which more anon. The next day, January 10th, General Otis answered endorsing the sending of "commissioners of tact and discretion," and adding:4

Great difficulty is that leaders cannot control ignorant classes.5

As a matter of fact the leaders were leading. They were not *arguing* with the tide. They were merely *riding the crest* of it. Actually, General Otis would have stopped "The Six Hundred Marseillaise Who Knew How to Die"—the ones whose march to Paris, according to Thomas Carlyle, inspired the composition of the French national air, "The Marseillaise"—and tried to parley with the head of the column on the idea of getting them to abandon their enterprise and disperse to their several homes. He also says, in the cablegram under consideration:

If peace kept for several days more immediate danger will have passed.

In other words, he was holding off the calf as best he could pending the ratification of the treaty. From the text itself, however, of General Otis's report, it is clear enough, that even he was getting anxious to give the Filipinos a drubbing as soon as the treaty should be safely passed. Referring to a message from the President enjoining avoidance of a clash with the Filipinos he says (p. 80):

The injunction of his Excellency the President of the United States to exert ourselves to preserve the peace had an excellent effect upon the command. Officers and men * * * *were* restless under the restraints * * * imposed, and * * * eager to avenge the insults received. *Now* they submit very quietly to the taunts and aggressive demonstrations of the insurgent army who continue to throng the streets of the business portion of the city.

See the lamb kick the lion viciously in the face, and observe the lion as he first lifts his eyes heavenward and says meekly: "Thy will be done. This is Benevolent Assimilation"; and then turns them Senate-ward and murmurs: "I cannot stand this much longer, kind sirs. Say when!" The way war correspondent John F. Bass puts the situation about this time in a letter to his paper, *Harper's Weekly*, was this:

Jimmie Green6 bites his lip, hangs on to himself, and finds comfort in the idea that his time will come.

After Aguinaldo's ultimatum of January 5th about fighting if we took Iloilo, General Otis refrained from taking Iloilo, and continued to communicate with the insurgent chieftain, appointing commissioners to meet commissioners appointed by him. These held divers and sundry sessions, whose only result was to kill time, or at least to mark time, while the Administration was getting the treaty through the Senate. The object of these meetings is thus set forth in the military order of January 9, 1899, appointing the Otis portion of the Joint High Parleying Board:

To meet a commission of like number appointed by General Aguinaldo, and to confer with regard to the situation of affairs and to arrive at a mutual understanding of the intent, purposes, aim, and desires of the Filipino people and the people of the United States, that peace and harmonious relations between these respective peoples may be continued.7

The minutes of the first meeting of this board, prepared by the Spanish-speaking clerk or recorder, recite the above declared purpose *verbatim*, in all its verbosity, and then go on to say that our side asked

That the commissioners appointed by General Aguinaldo give their opinion as to what *were* the purposes, aspirations, aims, and desires of the people of the archipelago.

The next paragraph is almost Pickwickian in its unconscious terseness:

To this request the commissioners appointed by General Aguinaldo made response that in their opinion the aspirations, purposes, and desires of the Philippine people might be summed up in *two words* "Absolute Independence."

Of course even General Otis does not reproduce this laconic answer as part of his petulant summing up of how little the Filipinos knew, before the outbreak of February 4th, as to what they really wanted. He merely alludes to it as being of record elsewhere. It is one of the various pieces of jetsam and flotsam that have floated from the sea of those great events to the shores of government publications since. The minutes of these meetings may be found among the hearings before the Senate Committee of 1902.8

General Otis's report complains that Aguinaldo's commissioners did not know what they wanted, "could not give any satisfactory explanation" of the "measure of protection" they wanted, they having declared that they would greatly prefer the United States to establish a protectorate over them to keep them from being annexed by some other power. But he fails to state, which is a fact shown by the minutes of the meeting of January 14 (p. 2721), that the Filipino commissioners did say that this was a question which would only be reached between their government and ours when the latter should agree to officially recognize the former. To quote their exact language, which is rather clumsily translated, they said: "The aspiration of the Filipino people is the independence with the restrictions resulting from the conditions which its government may agree with the American, *when the latter agree to officially recognize the former*."

It is perfectly clear from the voluminous minutes of the proceedings that the Filipinos were only seeking *some declaration of the purpose of our government* which would satisfy their people that the programme was something more than a mere change of masters. "They begged," says General Otis (p. 82), "for *some tangible concession* from the United States Government—one *which they could present to the people* and which might serve to allay excitement." General Otis of course had no authority to bind the government and so could make no promise. But the day this Otis-Aguinaldo parleying board had its second meeting, January 11th, and probably with no more knowledge of its existence than the reader has of what is going on in the Fiji Islands at the moment he reads these lines, Senator Bacon introduced in the United States Senate some resolutions which were precisely the medicine the case required and precisely the thing the Filipinos were pleading for. These resolutions concluded thus:

That the United States hereby disclaim any disposition or intention to exercise sovereignty, jurisdiction, or control over said islands except for the pacification thereof, and assert their determination when an independent government shall have been duly erected therein entitled to recognition as such, to transfer to said government, upon terms which shall be reasonable and just, all rights secured under the cession by Spain, and to thereupon leave the government and control of the islands to their people.

They were a twin brother to the Teller Cuban resolution which was incorporated into the resolution declaring war against Spain, being *verbatim* the same, except with the necessary changes of name, of "islands" for "island," etc.

On January 18th, while the futile parleying board aforesaid was still futilely parleying at Manila, Senator Bacon made an argument in the Senate in support of his resolution, whose far-sighted statesmanship, considered in relation to the analogies of its historic setting, most strikingly reminds us of Burke's great speech on conciliation with America delivered under similar circumstances nearly a century and a quarter earlier. After alluding to the naturalness of the apprehension of the Filipinos "that it is the purpose of the United States Government to maintain permanent dominion over them,"9 Senator Bacon urged:

The fundamental requirement in these resolutions is that the Government of the United States will not undertake to exercise *permanent dominion* over the Philippine Islands. The resolutions are intentionally made broad, so that *those who agree on that fundamental proposition may stand upon them* even though they may differ materially as to a great many other things relative to the future course of the government in connection with the Philippine Islands.

Senator Bacon then quoted the following from some remarks Senator Foraker had previously made in the course of the great debate on the treaty:

I do not understand anybody to be proposing to take the Philippine Islands with the idea and view of permanently holding them. * * * The President of the United States does not, I know, and no Senator in this chamber has made any such statement;

and added:

If the views expressed by the learned Senator from Ohio in his speech * * * are those upon which we are to act, there is very little difference between us; and there will be no future contention between us * * * if we can have an authoritative expression from THE LAW-MAKING POWER of the United States in a joint resolution that such is the purpose of the future.10

Says the Holy Scripture: "A word spoken in season, how good is it!" Had the Bacon resolutions passed the United States Senate in January, 1899, we never would have had any war with the Filipinos.11 They would have presented at the psychologic moment the very thing the best and bravest of the Filipino leaders were then pleading with General Otis for, something "tangible," something "which they could present to their people and which would allay excitement," by allaying the universal fear that we were going to do with them exactly as all other white men they had ever heard of had done with all other brown men they had ever heard of under like circumstances, viz., keep them under permanent dominion with a view of profit.

In his letter accepting the nomination for the Presidency in 1900, Mr. McKinley sought to show the Filipinos to have been the aggressors in the war by a reference to the fact that the outbreak occurred *while the Bacon resolution was under discussion* in the Senate. This hardly came with good grace from an Administration whose friends in the Senate had all along opposed not only the Bacon resolution but also all other resolutions frankly declaratory of the purpose of our government. The supreme need of the hour then was, and the supreme need of every hour of every day we have been in the Philippines since has been, "an authoritative expression from the law-making power of the United States"—not mere surmises of a President, confessedly devoid of binding force, but an *authoritative expression from the law-making power*, declaratory of the purpose of our government with regard to the Philippine Islands. Secretary of War Taft visited Manila in 1907 to be present at the opening of the Philippine Assembly. In view of the universal longing which he knew existed for some definite authoritative declaration as to whether our government intends to keep the Islands permanently or not, he said:

I cannot speak with authority * * *. The policy to be pursued with respect to them is, therefore, ultimately for Congress to determine. * * * I have no authority to speak for Congress in respect to the ultimate disposition of the Islands.12

This bitter disappointment of the public expectation and hope of something definite, certainly did not lessen the belief of the Filipinos that we have no notion of ever giving them their independence. Had the Senate known what the Filipino commissioners were so earnestly asking of the Otis commissioners in January, 1899, the Bacon resolution would probably have passed. In fact it is demonstrable almost mathematically that, had the Administration's friends in the Senate allowed that resolution to come to a vote before the outbreak of February 4th, instead of filibustering against it until after that event, it would have passed. As stated in the foot-note, the roll-call on the final vote on it, which was not taken until February 14th, showed a tie—29 to 29, the Vice-President of the United States casting the deciding vote which defeated it. Much dealing with real life and real death has blunted my artistic sensibilities to thrills from the mere pantomime of the stage. But as here was a vote where, had a single Senator who voted No voted Aye, some 300,000,000 of dollars, over a thousand lives of American soldiers killed in battle, some 16,000 lives of Filipino soldiers killed in battle, and possibly 100,000 Filipino lives snuffed out through famine, pestilence, and other ills consequent on the war, would have been saved, I can not refrain from reproducing the vote—perhaps the most uniquely momentous single roll-call in the parliamentary history of Christendom13:

Ayes

- Bacon
- Bate
- Berry
- Caffery
- Chilton
- Clay
- Cockrell
- Faulkner
- Gorman
- Gray
- Hale
- Harris
- Heitfield
- Hoar
- Jones of Arkansas
- Jones of Nevada
- Lindsay
- McLaurin
- Martin
- Money
- Murphy
- Perkins
- Pettigrew
- Pettus
- Quay
- Rawlins
- Smith
- Tillman
- Turner

Nays

- Allison
- Burrows
- Carter
- Chandler
- Deboe
- Fairbanks
- Frye
- Gear
- Hanna
- Hawley
- Kyle
- Lodge
- McBride
- McEnery
- McMillan
- Mantle
- Morgan
- Nelson
- Penrose
- Platt of Connecticut
- Platt of New York
- Pritchard
- Ross
- Shoup
- Simon
- Stewart
- Teller
- Warren
- Wolcott

In January, 1899, the out-and-out land-grabbers had not yet made bold to show their hand, the friends of the treaty confining themselves to the alleged shame of doing as we had done with Cuba, on account of the supposed semi-barbarous condition of "the various tribes out there," leaving the possibility of profit to quietly suggest *itself* amid the noisy exhortations of altruism. It was not until after the milk of human kindness had been spilled in war that Senator Lodge said at the Philadelphia National Republican Convention of 1900:

We make no hypocritical pretence of being interested in the Philippines solely on account of others. We believe in Trade Expansion.

Speaking (p. 82) of the meetings of what for lack of a better term I have above called the Otis-Aguinaldo Joint High Parleying Board, General Otis says in his report:

Finally, the conferences became the object of insurgent suspicion, * * * and * * * amusement.

The Filipino newspapers called attention to the fact that large reinforcements of American troops were on the way to Manila, and very plausibly inferred that the parleying was for delay only. By January 26th the politeness of both the American and the Filipino commissioners had been worn to a frazzle, and they adjourned, each recognizing that the differences between them could ultimately be settled only on the field of battle, in the event of the ratification of the treaty.

January 27th, General Otis cabled to Washington a letter from Aguinaldo, of which he says in his report: "I was surprised * * * because of the boldness with which he therein indicated his purpose to continue his assumptions and establish their correctness by the arbitrament of war" (p. 84). General Otis was "surprised" to the last. Aguinaldo's letter is not at all surprising, though extremely interesting. It sends General Otis a proclamation issued January 21st, announcing the publication of a constitution modelled substantially after that of the United States, even beginning with the familiar words about "securing the blessings of liberty, promoting the general welfare," etc., and concludes with an expression of confident hope that the United States will recognize his government, and a bold implication of determination to fight if it does not. On the evening of February 4th an insurgent soldier approaching an American picket failed to halt or answer when challenged, and was shot and killed. Nearly six months of nervous tension thereupon pressed for liberation in a general engagement which continued throughout the night and until toward sundown of the next day, thus finally unleashing the dogs of war. In the *Washington Post* of February 6, 1899, Senator Bacon is quoted as saying:

I will cheerfully vote all the money that may be necessary to carry on the war in the Philippines, but I still maintain that we could have avoided a conflict with those people had the Senate adopted my resolution, or a similar resolution *announcing our honest intentions with regard to the Philippines.*

Said the *New York Criterion* of February 11, 1899:

Whether we like it or not, we must go on slaughtering the natives in the English fashion, and taking what muddy glory lies in this wholesale killing until they have learned to respect our arms. *The more difficult task of getting them to respect our intentions will follow.*

The *Washington Post* of February 6, 1899, may not have quoted Senator Bacon with exactitude. But what the Senator *did* say on the floor of the Senate *is* important, historically. Under date of February 22, 1912, Senator Bacon writes me, in answer to an inquiry:

I enclose a speech made by me upon the subject in the Senate February 27, 1899, and upon pages 6, 7, and 8 of which you will find a statement of my position, and the reasons given by me therefor. Of course you cannot go at length into that question in your narration of the events of that day, but my position was that, while I did not approve of the war, and did not approve of the enslavement of the Filipinos, and while if I had my way I would immediately set them free, at the same time, as war was then flagrant, and there were then some twenty odd thousand American troops in the Philippine Islands, we must either support them or leave them to defeat and death. I do not know how far you can use anything then said by me, but if you make allusion to the fact that I was willing to supply money and troops to carry on the war in the Philippines, I would be glad for it to be accompanied by a very brief statement of the ground upon which I based such action.

The above makes it unnecessary to quote at length from the speech referred to, which may be found at pp. 2456 *et seq* of the *Congressional Record* for February 27, 1899. However, there is one passage in the speech to which I especially say Amen, and invite all whose creed of patriotism is not too sublimated for such a common feeling to join me in so doing. Senator Bacon will now state the creed:

The oft-repeated expression "our country, right or wrong" has a vital principle in it, and upon that principle I stand.

The Senator immediately follows his creed with these commentaries:

In this annexation of the Philippine Islands through the ratification of the treaty, and in waging war to subjugate the Filipinos, I think the country, acting through constitutional authorities, is wrong. But it is not for me to say because the country has been committed to a policy that I do not favor and have opposed, in consequence of which there is war, that I will not support the government.

Under the civilizing influence of Krag-Jorgensen rifles and the moral uplift of high explosive projectiles, what our soldiers used to call, with questionable piety, "the fear of God," was finally put into the hearts of the Filipinos, after much carnage by wholesale in battle formation and later by retail in a species of guerrilla warfare as irritating as it was obstinate. But they have never yet learned to respect our intentions, because under the guidance of three successive Presidents we have studiously refrained from any authoritative declaration as to what those intentions are. We are loth to hark back to the only right course, a course similar to our action in Cuba, because of the expense we have been to in the Philippines. But we also know that the islands are and are likely to continue, a costly burden, a nuisance, and a distinct strategic disadvantage in the event of war; and that Mr. Cleveland was right when he said:

The government of remote and alien people should have no permanent place in the purposes of our national life.

The mistaken policy which involved us in a war to subjugate the Filipinos, following our war to free the Cubans, will never stand atoned for before the bar of history, nor can the Filipinos ever in reason be expected to respect our intentions, until the law-making power of the government shall have authoritatively declared what those intentions are—*i. e.*, what we intend ultimately to do with the islands. Senator Bacon's resolutions of 1899 were, are, and always will be the last word on the first act needed to rectify the original Philippine blunder, "announcing" as they would, to use the language attributed to their distinguished author by the *Washington Post* of February 6, 1899, above-quoted, "our honest intentions with regard to the Philippines." So eager is the exploiter to exploit the islands, and so apprehensive is the Filipino that the exploiter will have more influence at Washington than himself and therefore be able ultimately to bring about a practical industrial slavery, that common honesty demands such a declaration. To doctor present Filipino discontent with Benevolent Uncertainty is a mere makeshift. The remedy the situation needs is simple, but as yet untried—Frankness. The chief of the causes of the present discontent among the Filipinos with American rule is precisely the same old serpent that precipitated the war thirteen years ago, to wit, lack of a frank and honest declaration of our purpose. The trouble then lay, and still lies, and, in the absence of some such declaration as that proposed by the Bacon resolution, will always lie in what seemed then, and still seems, to the Filipinos "an evident purpose to keep the islands and an accompanying unwillingness to acknowledge that purpose." Some may object that one Congress cannot bind another. The same argument would have killed the Teller amendment to the declaration of war with Spain avowing our purpose as to Cuba. Such an argument assumes that this nation has no sense of honor, and that it should cling for a while longer to the stale Micawberism that the Islands may yet pay, before it decides whether it will do right or not, and signalizes such decision by formal announcement through Congress. To men capable of such an assumption as the one just indicated, this book is not addressed. Three successive Presidents, Messrs. McKinley, Roosevelt, and Taft, have with earnest asseveration of benevolent intention tried without success all these years to win the affections of the Filipino people, and to make them feel that "our flag had not lost its gift of benediction in its world-wide journey to their shores," as Mr. McKinley used to say. But the corner-stone of the policy was laid before we knew anything about how the land lay, and on the assumption, made practically without any knowledge whatever on the subject, that the Filipino people were incapable of self-government. The corner-stone of our Philippine policy has been from the beginning precisely that urged by Spain for not freeing Cuba, viz., "to spare the people from the dangers of premature independence." The three Presidents named above have always been willing to imply independence, but never to promise it. And the unwillingness to declare a purpose ultimately to give the Filipinos their independence has always been due to the desire to catch the vote of those who are determined they shall never have it. In this inexorable and unchangeable political necessity lies the essential contemptibleness of republican imperialism, and the secret of why the Filipinos, notwithstanding our good intentions, do not like us, and never will under the present policy. How can you blame them?

Yet the more you know of the Filipinos, the better you like them. Self-sacrificing, brave, and faithful unto death in war, they are gentle, generous, and tractable in peace. Moreover, respect for constituted authority, as such, is innate in practically every Filipino, which I am not sure can be predicated concerning each and every citizen of my beloved native land. And we can win the grateful and lasting affection of the whole seven or eight millions of them any day we wish to. How? Have done with vague, vote-catching Presidential *obiter*, and through your Congress declare your purpose!

1*War Department Report*, 1899, vol. i., pt. 4, p. 66.

2*Senate Document 208*, 56th Cong., 1st Sess., 1900, p. 58, letter to General Miller.

3A campaign synonym for forced marching. It has no known etymology, but to the initiated it suggests torrential downpouring of rain and bedraggled mud-spattered columns of troops.

4*Senate Document 208*, pt. 2, p. 7.

5*Otis Report*, p. 80.

6The American "Tommy Atkins."

7*Otis Report*, 1899 *War Dept. Rpt.*, 1899, vol. i., pt. 4, p. 81.

8See *Senate Document 331*, 1902, p. 2709 *et seq*.

9*Congressional Record*, January 11, 1899, p. 735.

10*Ib.*, January 18, 1899, p. 733.

11The vote on the Bacon resolution was a tie, 29 to 29, and the Vice-President of the United States then cast the deciding vote against it. *Cong. Rec.*, Feby. 14, 1899, p. 1845.

12See *Present-Day Problems*, by Wm. H. Taft, p. 9; Dodd, Mead, & Co., N. Y., 1908.

13*Congressional Record*, February 14, 1899, p. 1846 (55th Cong., 3d Sess.).

Chapter XI. Otis and the War

Am I the boss, or am I a tool,
Am I Governor-General or a hobo—hobo;
Now I'd like to know who's the boss of the show,
Is it me, or Emilio Aguinaldo?

Army Song of the Philippines under Otis.

"The thing is on," said General Hughes, Provost Marshal of Manila, to General Otis, at Malacañan palace, on the night of February 4, 1899, about half past eight o'clock, as soon as the firing started.1 He was talking about something which every American in Manila except General Otis had for months frankly recognized as inevitable—the war.

On the day of the outbreak of February 4th, General Otis had under his command 838 officers and 20,032 enlisted men, say in round numbers a total of 21,000. Of these some 15,500 were State volunteers mostly from the Western States, and the rest were regulars. All the volunteers and 1650 of the regulars were, or were about to become, entitled to their discharge, and their right was perfected by the exchange of ratifications of the treaty of peace with Spain on April 11, 1899. The total force which he was thus entitled to command for any considerable period consisted of less than 4000. Of the 21,000 men on hand as aforesaid, on February 4th, deducting those at Cavite and Iloilo, the sick and wounded, those serving in civil departments, and in the staff organizations, the effective fighting force was 14,000, and of these 3000 constituted the Provost Guard in the great and hostile city of Manila.2 Thus there were only 11,000 men, including those entitled to discharge, available to engage the insurgent army, "which," says Secretary of War Root, "was two or three times that number, well armed and equipped, and included many of the native troops formerly comprised in the Spanish army."

Such was the predicament into which General Otis's supremely zealous efforts to help the Administration get the treaty through the Senate by withholding from the American people the knowledge of facts which might have put them on notice that they were paying $20,000,000 for a $200,000,000 insurrection, had brought us. This is not a tale of woe. It is a tale of the disgust—good-humored, because stoical—which finally found expression at the time in the army song that heads this chapter, disgust at unnecessary sacrifice of American life which could so easily have been prevented had General Otis only revealed the real situation in time to have had plenty of troops on hand. It is a requiem over those brave men of the Eighth Army Corps from Pennsylvania, Tennessee, and the Western States that bore the brunt of the early fighting, whose lives were needlessly sacrificed in 1899 as the result of an unpreparedness for war due to anxiety not to embarrass Mr. McKinley in his efforts to get the treaty through the Senate, an unpreparedness which remained long unremedied thereafter in order to conceal from the people of the United States the unanimity of the desire of the Filipinos for Independence.

It is quite true that none of our people then in the Islands realized this unanimity in all its pathos at the outset, but it soon became clear to everybody except the commanding general. It naturally dawned on him last of all, because he did not visit the most reliable sources of information, to wit, the battlefields during the fighting, and therefore did not see how tenaciously the Filipinos fought for the independence of their country. Moreover, General Otis tried to think till the last along lines in harmony with the original theory of Benevolent Assimilation. Hence Mr. Root's nonsense of 1899 and 1900 about "the patient and unconsenting millions" dominated by "the Tagalo tribe," which nonsense was immensely serviceable in a campaign for the presidency wherein antidotes for sympathy with a people struggling to be free were of supreme practical political value. General Otis actually had Mr. McKinley believing as late as December, 1899, at least, that the opposition to a change of masters in lieu of Freedom was confined to a little coterie of self-seeking politicians who were in the business for what they could get out of it, and that the great majority would prefer him, Otis, to Aguinaldo, as governor-general. It *is* difficult on first blush to accept this statement as dispassionately correct, but there is no escape from the record. Mr. McKinley said in his annual message to Congress in December, 1899, in reviewing the direction he gave to the Paris peace negotiations which ended in the purchase of the islands, and the war with the Filipinos which had followed, and had then been raging since February 4th previous, "I had every reason to believe, and *still believe* that the transfer of sovereignty was in accordance with the wishes and aspirations of the great mass of the Filipino people."

Yet every American soldier who served in the Philippines at the time knows that Aguinaldo held the whole people in the hollow of his hand, because he was their recognized leader, the incarnation of their aspirations.3

During the presidential campaign of 1900, while the war with the Filipinos was still raging, partisan rancour bitterly called in question the sincerity of President McKinley's statement in his annual message to Congress of December, 1899, that he then still believed "the transfer of sovereignty was in accord with the wishes and aspirations of the great mass of the Filipino people," on the ground that he must by the time he made that statement have understood how grossly—however honestly—General Otis had misled him as to the unanimity and tenacity of the Filipino purpose. But it is only necessary to read Admiral Dewey's testimony before the Senate Committee of 1902 to understand Mr. McKinley's allusion in this same message to Congress of 1899 to "the sinister ambition of a few leaders," and this, once understood, explains the other statement of the message. Admiral Dewey came home in the fall of 1899 and undoubtedly filled Mr. McKinley with the estimate of Aguinaldo which makes such painful reading in the Admiral's testimony of 1902 before the Senate Committee, where he abused Aguinaldo like a pick-pocket, so to speak, saying his original motive was principally loot.4 In the fall of 1899 Aguinaldo had issued a proclamation claiming that Admiral Dewey originally promised him independence, and Admiral Dewey had bitterly denounced this as a falsehood, so that the Admiral always cherished a very real resentment against the insurgent chief thereafter. His estimate of the Filipino leader as being in the insurrection merely for what he could get out of it was wholly erroneous, and has long since been exploded, all our generals of the early fighting and all Americans who have known him since being unanimous that Aguinaldo was and is a sincere patriot; but it undoubtedly explains Mr. McKinley's still clinging, in 1899, to the notion derived from General Otis that the insurrection did not have the moral and material backing of the whole Filipino people. The Filipino leaders were familiar with the spirit of our institutions. The men who controlled their counsels were high-minded, educated, patriotic men. "For myself and the officers and men under my command," wrote General Merritt to Aguinaldo in August, 1898, just after the fall of Manila, "I can say that we have conceived a high respect for the abilities and qualities of the Filipinos, and if called upon by the Government to express an opinion, it will be to that effect."5

The leaders believed that the American people did not fully understand the identity of the Philippine situation with that in Cuba, and that if they had, the treaty would not have been ratified. They also knew the supreme futility of trying to get the facts before the American people by peaceful means. And it was really with the abandon of genuine patriotism that they plunged their country into war. We did not know it then, but we do know it now. It would be simply wooden-headed to affirm that they ever expected to succeed in a war with us. Of course some of the *jeunesse dorée*, as General Bell calls them in one of his early reports,6 grew very aggressive and insulting toward the last. But the thinking men went into the war for independence in a spirit of "decent respect to the opinions of mankind," to correct the impression General Otis had communicated to Mr. McKinley, and through him to our people, in the hope that the more lives they sacrificed in such a war (they risked—and many of them lost—their own also), the nearer they would come to refuting the idea that they did not know what they wanted. It was the only way they had to appeal to Cæsar, *i.e.*, to the great heart of the American people. As the war grew more and more unpopular in the United States, the impression was more and more nursed here at home that the people did not really want independence, but were being coerced; and that they were like dumb driven cattle. The striking similarity of these suggestions to those by which tyranny has always met the struggles of men to be free, did not seem to occur to the American public. They were accepted as authoritative, being convenient also as an antidote to sympathy. General Otis had suppressed such words as "sovereignty," "protection," and the like from his original sugar-coated edition of the Benevolent Assimilation Proclamation, offering an elaborate cock-and-bull explanation of why he did so. The Filipino answer to this took the form of a very clever newspaper cartoon, representing an American in a carromata—a kind of two-wheeled buggy—with a Filipino between the shafts pulling it; which cartoon of course, never reached the United States. The Filipinos had never heard the story on General Mahone about "tie yoh hoss an' come in,"7 but they had heard of the jinrickshaws of Japan, and they had read in Holy Writ and elsewhere of conquered people becoming hewers of wood and drawers of water to invading conquerors.

And they are *not* without a sense of humor. It is a common mistake with many Americans—for quite a few among us suffer intellectually from over-sophistication—to suppose we monopolize all the sense of humor there is, and that that alone is proof of a due sense of proportion. At any rate, the Filipinos, with all due respect to General Otis's good intentions, understood that "sovereignty" and "protection" meant alien domination, so there was nothing in the Otis notion that for them those words had a "*peculiar* meaning which might be advantageously used by the Tagalo war party to incite," etc.8

Having now gotten into a war on the theory that only a small fraction of the Filipino people were opposed to a new and unknown yoke in lieu of the old one, General Otis still continued to try to square his theory with the facts. For many months he sat at his desk in Manila cheerily waging war with an inadequate force, and retaining in the service and on the firing line after their terms of enlistment expired, under pretence that they consented to it willingly, a lot of fellows from Pennsylvania, Tennessee, and the Western States, who had volunteered for the war with Spain, with intent to kill Spaniards in order to free Cubans, and not with intent to kill Filipinos for also wanting to be free. Seeing nothing of the fighting himself, he of course failed to get a correct estimate of the tenacity of the Filipino purpose. No purpose is here entertained to suggest that any of those early volunteers went around preaching mutiny, or feeling mutinous. They did not originally like the Filipinos especially; furthermore, they liked the Philippines less than they did the Filipinos, and they had a vague notion that some one had blundered. But it was not theirs to ask the reason why. Besides, the orders from Washington being not to clash with the Filipinos at least until the treaty was ratified, the Filipino soldiers and subaltern officers had been calling them cowards for some time with impunity. So that as soon as the treaty was safely "put over," they were very glad to let off steam by killing a few hundred of them. But their hearts were not in the fight, in the sense of clear and profound conviction of the righteousness of the war. However, war is war, and they were soldiers, and "orders is orders," as Tommy Atkins says. So let us turn to an honester, if grimmer, side of the picture.

The first battle of the war began about 8:30 o'clock on the night of February 4th, and lasted all through that night and until about 5 o'clock in the afternoon of the next day. Our casualties numbered about 250 killed and wounded. The insurgent loss was estimated at 3000. "Those of the insurgents will never be known," says General Otis.9 "We buried 700 of them."10 There was fighting pretty much all around Manila, for the insurgents had the city almost hemmed in. An arc of a circle, broken in places possibly, but several miles long, drawn about the city, would probably suggest the general idea of the enemy's lines. They had been allowed to dig trenches without interference while the debate in the Senate on the treaty was in progress, pursuant to the temporary "peace-at-any-price" programme. The arc was broken into smithereens by 5P.M. of February 5th. When the morning of February 6th came Col. James F. Smith, commanding the First Californias, was *non est inventus*, and so was a large part of his regiment. "No one seemed to know definitely his location," says the Otis *Report*.11 As a matter of fact he had taken two battalions of his regiment and waded clean through the enemy's lines, and had to be sent for to come back to form again with the line of battle needed to protect the city. So the Californias probably carried off the pick of the laurels of the first day's fighting. General Anderson, commanding the First Division of the Eighth Corps, threw them some very handsome well earned bouquets in his report, stating also that their colonel had shown "the very best qualities of a volunteer officer"—why he limited it to "volunteer" does not appear, but is inferable from the well-known disposition of all regulars to consider all volunteers "rookies"12—and recommended that he be made a brigadier general, which shortly afterward was done.13

It would be invidious to follow the various phases of the subsequent early fighting, and single out one or more States14 and tell of the hard earned and well deserved honors they won, because space forbids a proper tribute to the heroism of all of them. As for the regulars,15 they were the same they were at

Santiago de Cuba, the same they always are anywhere you put them. When a newspaper man would come around a regular regiment during the fighting before Santiago he would be told that they had no news to give him, "We ain't heroes, we're regulars," they would say. After the outbreak of February 4th, all our people did well, acted nobly, "Angels could no more." Neither could devils, as shown by the losses inflicted on the enemy.

There was more fighting outside Manila during the next two or three days, and when that was done the somewhat shattered insurgent legions had recoiled to the distantly visible foot-hills, convinced that their notion they could take Manila was very foolish and very rash.

At the town of Caloocan, some three or four miles out to the north of Manila, were located the shops and round houses of the Manila and Dagupan Railway, which runs from Manila in a northwesterly direction about 120 miles to Dagupan, and was then the only railroad in the archipelago. It was fed by a vast rich farming country, the great plain of central Luzon. Naturally, the central plain which fed the railroad that traversed it and kept its teeming myriads of small farmers in touch with the great outside world was to be sooner or later, the theatre of war. To seize transportation is instinctively the first tactical move of a military man. Lieutenant-General Luna, commander-in-chief, next to Aguinaldo, of the revolutionary forces, the man whom later Aguinaldo had shot, was just then at Caloocan with 4000 men. So it fell to General MacArthur, commanding the Second Division of the Eighth Corps, to move on Caloocan, which he did on February 10th.

John F. Bass, correspondent for *Harper's Weekly*, writing from Manila a short time after this, describes this movement. It was our first move away from the city of Manila. With a few masterly strokes of the pen, which I regret there is not space to reproduce here in full, Mr. Bass gives a vivid picture of the various engagements, and of "a background of burning villages, smoke, fire, shot, and shell, the ceaseless tramp of tired and often bleeding feet," etc. "Heroism," he says, "became a matter of course and death an incident." Finally his story pauses for a moment thus: "The natural comment is that all this is merely war—the *business* of the soldier. True, nor do I think Jimmie Green [Mr. Bass's name for our "Tommy Atkins"] is troubled with heroics. He accepts the situation without excitement or hysterics. *He has little feeling in this matter for his heart is not in this fight.*" Here brother Bass's moralizing ceases abruptly, and the contagious excitement of the hour catches him, just as it always does the average man under such circumstances:

From La Loma church you may get the full view of our long line crossing the open field, evenly, steadily, irresistibly, like an inrolling wave on the beach * * *. Watch the regiments go forward, and form under fire, and move on and on, and you will exclaim: "Magnificent," and you will gulp a little and feel proud *without exactly knowing why*. Then gradually the *power* of that line will force itself upon you, and you will feel that you must follow, that wherever that line goes you must go also. By and by you will be sorry, but for the present the might of an American regiment has got possession of you.

Anybody who has ever been with an American regiment in action knows exactly how the man who wrote that felt. The American who has never had the experience Mr. Bass describes above has missed one way of realizing the majesty of the power of the republic whereof he is privileged to be a citizen. For if there is one national trait which more than any other explains the greatness of our country, it is the instinct for organization, the fondness for self-multiplication to the nth power by intelligent co-operation with one's fellows to a common end. Especially is the experience in question inspiring where the example of the field officers is particularly appropriate to the occasion. Take for instance the following, concerning the conduct of Major J. Franklin Bell in this advance on Caloocan, from the report of Major Kobbe, Commanding the Artillery:

As the right cleared the head of the ravine, I could see Maj. J. F. Bell * * * leading a company of Montana troops in front of the right * * * advancing, firing, toward intrenchments * * *. He was on a black horse to the last * * * leading and cheering the men. His work was most gallant and * * * especially cheering to me.16

No mere scribe can magnify General Bell's matchless efficiency in action, but it is certainly inspiring to contemplate. There are no "fuss and feathers" about him. Yet his power, proven on many a field in the Philippines, to kindle martial ardor by example, suggests the ubiquitous "Helmet of Navarre" of Lord Macaulay's poem.

A little later correspondent Bass develops what he meant by "by and by you will be sorry." You see it is not comfortable business, this of hustling about among the dead and dying. In the excitement, you are so liable to step on the face of some poor devil you knew well, maybe a once warm friend. In this connection Mr. Bass says: "There is this difference between the manner in which American and Filipino soldiers die. The American falls in a heap and dies hard; the Filipino stretches himself out, and when dead is always found in some easy attitude, generally with his head on his arms. They die the way a wild animal dies—in just such a position as one finds a deer or an antelope which one has shot in the woods."

So far as the writer is advised and believes, nobody who knows John F. Bass ever suspected him of being a quitter. He must have been reading the *London Standard*, which said about that time: "It *is* a little startling to find the liberators of Cuba engaged in suppressing a youthful republic which claims the sacred right of self-government." Bass had written his newspaper in August previous, after observing how pluckily the Filipinos had fought and licked the Spaniards: "Give them their independence and guarantee it to them." The overwhelming sentiment of the Eighth Army Corps when we took the Philippines was against taking them; and those who had kept informed knew that the Senate had ratified the treaty by a majority only one more than enough to squeeze it through, the vote having been 57 to 27, at least 56 being thus indispensable to make the necessary constitutional two-thirds of the 84 votes cast; and that Wall Street and the White Man's Burden or land-grabbing contingent—"Philanthropy and Five per cent," as Secretary of the Treasury Lyman J. Gage put it at the time—were responsible for these shambles Mr. Bass describes.

At this juncture some soft-headed gentleman asks: "What is this man who writes this book driving at? Is he trying to show that the American soldiers in the Philippines in February, 1899, all wanted to quit as soon as the war broke out?" Not at all. In the first place it hardly lay in American soldier nature to want to quit when Aguinaldo was telling us "if you don't take your flag down and out of these islands at once and promptly get out yourselves along with it, I will proceed to kick *you* out and throw *it* out." And in the next place, in the war with the Filipinos, as in all other wars, fuel was added to the flame as soon as the war broke out. Among the Americans, charges soon came into general circulation and acceptance that the Filipinos had planned (but been frustrated in) a plot looking to a general massacre of all foreigners in Manila. This alleged plot was supposed to have been scheduled to be carried out on a certain night shortly after February 15, 1899. Among the Filipinos, on the other hand, counter-charges soon followed, and met with general credence, that the Americans made a practise of killing prisoners taken in battle, including the wounded. Neither charge was ever proven, but both served the purpose, at the psychologic moment, of possessing each side with the desire to kill, which is the business of war. Let us glance briefly at these recriminations.

Between pages 1916 and 1917 of *Senate Document 331*, part 217 may be found a photo-lithograph of the celebrated alleged order of the Filipino Revolutionary Government of February 15, 1899, to massacre all foreign residents of Manila. In his report for 1899[18] General Otis himself describes this order as one "which for barbarous intent is unequalled in these modern times in civilized warfare," and speaks of it as "issued by the Malolos Government through the responsible officer who had raised and organized the hostile inhabitants within the city." After Aguinaldo was captured in 1901, according to an account given by General MacArthur to the Senate Committee in 1902, of a conversation with the insurgent leader, the latter was shown a copy of this document purporting to have been signed by General Luna, one of his generals. He disclaimed having in any way sanctioned it, in fact disclaimed any prior knowledge of it whatsoever,[19] a disclaimer which General MacArthur appears to have accepted as true, frankly and entirely. At page 1890 of the same volume, Captain J. R. M. Taylor, 14th U. S. Infantry, a gallant soldier and an accomplished scholar, who was in charge in 1901 of the captured insurgent records at Manila, states that he was "informed" that the document was originally "signed by Sandico, then Secretary of the Interior" of the revolutionary government. Captain Taylor made an attempt to run the matter down, but obtained no evidence convincing to him. A like investigation by General MacArthur in 1901 had a like result.[20]

On the other hand, Major Wm. H. Bishop, of the 20th Kansas, was credited in a soldier's letter written home, which first came to light in this country, with killing unarmed prisoners during the advance on Caloocan. The charges originated with a private of that regiment. Major Bishop denied the charges.[21] An investigation followed, in the course of which somebody made an innuendo, or charge—it is not important which—that other officers used their influence to prevent a full ventilation of the matter, specifically, General Funston, then Colonel of the 20th Kansas, and Major Metcalf, of the same regiment. These last two also made a most vigorous general denial, and nothing whatever was established against them. The whole matter was finally disposed of by being forwarded to the War Department at Washington by General Otis on July 13, 1899, some six months after the occurrences alleged, with the remark that he (General Otis) "doubted the wisdom of a court-martial" of the soldier who had made the charge against Major Bishop, "as it would give the insurgent authorities a knowledge of what was taking place, and they would assert positively that our troops practised inhumanities, whether the charges could be proven or not" and that they would use the incident "as an excuse to defend their own barbarities."[22] The last endorsement on the papers preceding General Otis's final endorsement was one by Colonel Crowder, now (1912) Judge Advocate General of the United States Army, in which he said: "I am not convinced from a careful reading of this report, that Private Brenner has made a false charge against Captain Bishop"; adding that "considerations of public policy, sufficiently grave to silence every other demand, require that no further action be taken in this case."[23] The "considerations of public policy" were of course those indicated in General Otis's final endorsement on the papers, already quoted. They were compellingly controlling, in my judgment, independently of the merits. Washing one's soiled linen in public is never advisable, and placing a weapon in your enemy's hand in time of war is at least equally unwise. Some shreds of this once much mooted matter doubtless still linger in the public memory. It has been thus briefly ventilated here solely to trace the genesis of the bitterness of that war, and of numerous later barbarities avenged in kind. The bitterness thus early begun grew as the war went on, until every time a hapless Filipino peasant soldier speaking only two or three words of Spanish would falsely explain, when captured, that he was a non-combatant, an *amigo* (friend), it usually at once filled the captor with vivid recollections of slain comrades, and of rumored or sometimes proven mutilation of their bodies after death, and these reflections would at once fill him with a yearning desire to blow the top of the *amigo's* head off, whether he yielded to the desire or not. Of no instance where he did so yield am I aware. But I do know that the invariable statement of all Filipinos unarmed and un-uniformed when captured, to the effect that they were *amigos*, became to the American soldier not remotely dissimilar to the waving of a red rag at a bull. Of course this was also due, largely, to the guerrilla practice of hiding guns when hard-pressed and actually plunging at once into some make-believe agricultural pursuit. As for Major Bishop, it is inconceivable to me that he gave any order to kill unarmed prisoners. Even admitting for the sake of the argument that he is a fiend, he is not a fool. As a matter of fact, he was a brave soldier, as all the reports show, and is a reputable lawyer, having many warm friends whose opinion of any man would command respect anywhere. The truth of the whole matter probably is that just before going into battle, when our troops were in an ugly temper by reason of the rumors of barbarities alleged to have been perpetrated by the enemy, or contemplated by him, the word was passed along the line to "Take no more prisoners than we have to," and that that thought originated with some irresponsible private soldier of the line inflamed by stories of mutilation of our dead or of maltreatment of our wounded. Such a "word," so passed from man to man, can, in the heat of conflict, very soon evolve into something having for practical purposes all the force and effect of an order.

Through the foregoing, and like causes, including the "water cure," later invented to persuade *amigos* to discover the whereabouts of hidden insurgent guns or give information as to the movements of the enemy,24 our war with the Filipinos became, before it was over, a rather "dark and bloody" affair, accentuated as it was, from time to time, by occasional Filipino success in surprising detachments from ambush, or by taking them unawares and off their guard in their quarters, and eliminating them, the most notable instance of the first being the crumpling of a large command of the 15th Infantry by General Juan Cailles, in southern Luzon, and the most indelibly remembered and important example of the second being the massacre of the 9th Infantry people at Balangiga, in Samar, in the fall of 1901. Certainly more than one American in that long-drawn-out war did things unworthy of any civilized man, things he would have believed it impossible, before he went out there, ever to come to. Personally, I have heard, so far as I now recollect, of comparatively few barbarities perpetrated by Filipinos on captured American soldiers. Barbarities on their side seemed to have been reserved for those of their own race whom they found disloyal to the cause of their country. Personally I have never seen the water-cure administered. But I once went on a confidential mission by direction of General MacArthur, in the course of which I reported first, on arriving in the neighborhood of the contemplated destination, to a general officer of the regular army who is still such to-day.25 That night the general was good enough to extend the usual courtesy of a cot to sleep on, in the headquarters building. Toward dusk I went to dine with a certain lieutenant, also of the regular army.26 As we approached the lieutenant's quarters a sergeant came up with a prisoner, and asked instructions as to what to do with him. The lieutenant said: "Take him out and find out what he knows. *Do you understand*, Sergeant?" The sergeant saluted, answered in the affirmative, and moved away with his prisoner. We went in to the lieutenant's quarters, and while at dinner heard groans outside. I said "What is that, Jones?"27 Jones said: "That's the water-cure he's giving that *hombre*.28 Want to see it?" I replied that I certainly did not. Returning that night to the general's headquarters, after breakfast the next morning I met my friend Jones coming out of the general's office. I said: "What's the matter, what are you doing here," he having mentioned the evening before an expedition planned for the morrow. He said: "Well, I've just had a talk with the general to see if I could get my resignation from the army accepted?" "Why?" said I. "Well," was the reply, "that ——" (designating the prisoner of the night before by a double barrelled epithet) "died on me last night." Just how the matter was hushed up I have never known, but Jones was never punished. More than one general officer of the United States Army in the Philippines during our war with the Filipinos at least winked at the water-cure as a means of getting information, and quite a number of subalterns made a custom of applying it for that purpose. It was practically the only way you could get them to betray their countrymen. Did I report the incident to General MacArthur? Certainly not. It was the business of the general commanding the district. The water-cure, though very painful, was seldom fatal, and when not fatal was almost never permanently damaging, and it was about the only way to shake the loyalty of the average Filipino and make him give information as to hidden insurgent guns, guerrilla bands, etc. It was a part of Benevolent Assimilation.

Let us now return to the early battlefields about Manila which we left, initially, to analyze the extreme bitterness of the feeling between the combatants that very early began to develop.

We left war correspondent John F. Bass among the dead and dying on one of these fields, supposedly musing on the White Man's Burden, or Land-Grabbing, or Trust-for-Civilization theory, or whatever it was that moved the fifty-seven senators whose votes had ratified the treaty by a majority of just one more than the constitutionally necessary two-thirds.

The reason the writer lays so much stress on Mr. Bass's letters to *Harper's Weekly* on the early fighting in the Philippines, is because his remarks come direct from the battlefield, and are, as it were, *res gestæ*. They were made *dum fervet opus*, to use a law Latin phrase which in plain English means "while the iron is hot." They reflect more or less accurately the feelings of the men whose deeds he was recording. He, and O. K. Davis, now Washington correspondent of the *New York Times*, and John T. McCutcheon, of Chicago, the now famous cartoonist (who was with Dewey in the battle of Manila Bay), and Robert Collins, now London correspondent of the Associated Press, and "Dick" Little of the *Chicago Tribune,*— a little man about six feet three,—and lots of other good men and true, were all through that fighting, and we will later come to an issue of personal veracity between them and General Otis which culminated in the retirement from office of Secretary of War Alger, and ought to have resulted in the recall of General Otis, but did not, because to have acknowledged what a blunderer General Otis had been and to have relieved him from command, as he should have been relieved, would have been to "swap horses crossing a stream," as Mr. Lincoln used to put it in declining to change generals during a given campaign. The object here is to bring out the truth of history as to how the men who bore the brunt of the early fighting felt about it. Testimony as to what the officers and men of the army said would be of no value, because a complaining soldier's complaints are too often only a proof of "cold feet."29

These newspaper men, not under military orders, were daily risking their lives voluntarily, just to keep the American public informed, and the American public were kept in darkness and only vouchsafed bulletins giving them the progressive lists of their dead and wounded, and this last only on demand made upon Secretary Alger by the people of Minnesota, the Dakotas, etc., through their senators. The War Department did not want the people to know, did not want to admit itself, how plucky, vigorous, and patriotic the resistance was. The period of the fighting done by the State Volunteers from February until fall, when public opinion finally forced the Administration to send General Otis an adequate force, is slurred by Secretary of War Root in his report for 1899. I do not mean that it was slurred intentionally. But the Philippines were a long way off, and Mr. Root and Mr. McKinley naturally relied for their information on their commanding general on the spot. There were gallant deeds done in the Philippines by those Western fellows of the State regiments which volunteered for the war with Spain, that would have made the little fighting around Santiago look like—well, to borrow from "Chimmie" Fadden's fertile vocabulary, "like 30 cents." But General Otis was not in a position to get the thrill of such things from his office window, so very few of them were given much prominence by him in his despatches to the Adjutant-General of the army. This was wise enough from a political standpoint, seeing that a presidential campaign was to ensue in 1900 predicated on the proposition that American sovereignty was "in accord with the wishes and aspirations of the great mass of the Filipinos," to use the words of the President's message to Congress of December, 1899.

Caloocan was taken by General MacArthur on February 10th. The natural line of advance thereafter was of course up the railroad, because the insurgents held it, and needed it as much as we would. Throughout February there were engagements too numerous to mention. The navy also entertained the enemy whenever he came too near the shores of Manila Bay. One incident in particular is worthy of note, and worthy of the best traditions of the navy. I refer to the conduct of Assistant Engineer Emory Winship off Malabon, March 4, 1899. Malabon is five miles north of Manila, on the bay, not far from Caloocan. On the day named, a landing party of 125 men from the U. S. S. *Bennington* went ashore near Malabon to make photographs, in aid of navy gunnery, of certain entrenchments and buildings that had been struck by shells from the *Monadnock*. They foolishly failed to throw out scouts ahead of their column, and were suddenly greeted with a withering fire from a whole regiment of insurgents who had seen them first and lain in wait for them. They retired with considerably more haste than they had gone forth. The insurgents advanced, firing, at double quick, toward the comparative handful of Americans, and would undoubtedly have killed the last man jack of them, but Engineer Winship, who had been left in charge of the tug that brought the landing party shoreward, to keep up steam, saw the situation and promptly met it. He unlimbered a 37*mm*. Hotchkiss revolving machine gun which stood in the bow of the tug, and opened up with accurate aim on the advancing regiment of Filipinos. Naturally he at once became a more important target than the retreating body. Nevertheless, he kept pumping lead into that long howling murderous advancing brown line until, when within two hundred yards of where the tug lay, the line recoiled and retreated, and the landing party got safely back to the ship. It was, literally, a case of saving the lives of more than a hundred men, by fearless promptness and dogged tenacity in the intelligent and skilful performance of duty. The awnings of the tug were torn in shreds by the enemy's rain of bullets, and her woodwork was much peppered. Winship was hit five times, and still carries the bullets in his body, having been retired on account of disability resulting therefrom, after being promoted in recognition of his work.

Soon after March 25th, General MacArthur, commanding the Second Division of the Eighth Army Corps, advanced from Caloocan up the railroad to Malolos, the insurgent capital, some twenty miles away. Malolos was taken March 31st. Our February killed were six officers and seventy-one enlisted men, total seventy-seven, and a total of 378 wounded. By the end of March the list swelled to twelve officers and 127 enlisted men killed, total 139, and a total of 881 wounded, making our total casualties, as reported April 1st, 1020. Also 15% of the command, or about 2500, were on sick report on that date from heat prostrations and the like.30 For these and other reasons, farther advance up the railroad was halted for a while.

Meantime, General Lawton, with his staff, consisting of Colonel Edwards, Major Starr, and Captains King and Sewall, "the big four" they were called, had come out from New York City by way of the Suez Canal, bringing most welcome reinforcements, the 4th and 17th Infantry. These people arrived between the 10th and the 22d of March. What happened soon after, as a result of their arrival, must now become for a brief moment, a part of the panorama, the lay of the land General Lawton first swept over being first indicated.

Luzon is practically bisected, east and west, by the Pasig River and a lake out of which it flows almost due west into Manila Bay, Manila being at the mouth of the river. Under the Spaniards, all Luzon north of the Pasig had been one military district and all Luzon south of the Pasig another. The Eighth Army Corps always spoke of northern Luzon as "the north line," and of southern Luzon as "the south line." The lake above mentioned is called the Laguna de Bay. It is nearly as big as Manila Bay, which last is called twenty odd miles wide by thirty long. On the map, the Laguna de Bay roughly resembles a half-moon, the man in which looks north, the western horn being near Manila, and the eastern near the Pacific coast of

Luzon. General Otis had learned that at a place called Santa Cruz, toward the eastern end of the Laguna de Bay, there were a lot of steam launches and a Spanish gun-boat, which, if captured, would prove invaluable for river fighting and transportation of supplies along the Rio Grande de Pampanga and the other streams that watered the great central plain through which the railroad ran and which would have to be occupied later. So as soon as possible after General Lawton arrived and the necessary men could be spared, he was sent with 1500 troops to seize and bring back the boats in question. Of course the country he should overrun would have to be overrun again, because there were not troops enough to spare to garrison and hold it. But for the present, the launches would help. This expedition was successful, leaving the head of the lake nearest Manila on April 9th, and returning April 17th. It met with some good hard fighting on the way, sweeping everything before it of course, inflicting considerable loss, and suffering some. General Lawton's report mentions, among other officers whose conspicuous gallantry and efficiency in action attracted his attention, Colonel Clarence R. Edwards, now Chief of the Bureau of Insular Affairs of the War Department, of whose conduct in the capture of Santa Cruz on the morning of April 10th, he says: "No line of battle could have been more courageously or intelligently led."31 The resistance was pretty real to Colonel Edwards then, *i.e.*, the Benevolent Assimilation was quite strenuous, and it continued to be so until his great commander was shot through the breast in the forefront of battle in the hour of victory in December thereafter, and the colonel came home with the general's body. Since then the colonel has soldiered no more, but has remained on duty at Washington, the birthplace of the original theory that the Filipinos welcomed our rule, charged with the duty of yearning over the erring Filipino who thinks he can govern himself but is mistaken, and also with the still more difficult task of trying to live up to the original theory as far as circumstances will permit. As a matter of fact, the Filipinos would probably have gotten along much better than the Cubans if we had let General Lawton do there what he and General Wood were set to work doing in Cuba shortly after Santiago fell. Public opinion is a very dangerous thing to trifle with, and when, in September, 1899, there was a story going the rounds of the American newspapers that Lawton, the hero of El Caney, the man who had reflected more glory on American arms in striking the shackles of Spain from Cuba than any other one soldier in the army, had called the war in the Philippines "this accursed war," the War Department got busy over the cable to General Otis and obtained from him a denial that General Lawton had made such a remark. But the public knew its Lawton and what he had done in Cuba, and had a suspicion there might be some truth in the rumor. So the War Department cabled out saying "Newspapers say Lawton's denial insufficient," and then repeating the words attributed to him. So General Otis sent another denial that filled the bill.32 Of course General Lawton made no such remark. He was too good a soldier. It would have demoralized his whole command. But I served under him in both hemispheres, and I will always believe that he had a certain amount of regret at having to fight the Filipinos to keep them from having independence, when they were a so much likelier lot, take it all in all, than the Cubans we saw about Santiago. Moreover, I believe that had it not been then too late to ask him, he would have subscribed to the opinion Admiral Dewey had cabled home the previous summer: "These people are far superior in their intelligence and more capable of self-government than the natives of Cuba, and I am familiar with both races."

After the expedition down the lake, General Lawton went on "The North Line." So let us now turn thither also. For wherever Lawton was, there was fighting.

In the latter half of April, General MacArthur advanced north along the railroad, and took Calumpit, where the railroad crosses the Rio Grande, on April 28th. This was the place where under cover of "the accurate concentrated fire of the guns of the Utah Light Artillery commanded by Major Young"33 a few Kansas men with ropes tied to their bodies swam the river in the face of a heavy fire from the enemy, fastened the ropes to some boats on the enemy's side, and were pulled back in the boats, by their comrades, to the side they had come from; the Kansans then crossing the river under the lead of the gallant Funston, and driving the enemy from his trenches. The desperate bravery of the performance, like so many other things General Funston did in the Philippines, was so superb that one forgets how contrary it was to all known rules of the game of war. If it was Providence that saved Funston and his Kansans from annihilation, certainly Providence was ably assisted on that occasion by Major Young and his Utah Battery.34

Shortly after this General MacArthur entered San Fernando, the second insurgent capital, which is forty miles or so up the railroad from Manila.

During the month of May General Lawton kept the insurgents busy to the east of the railroad, between it and the Pacific coast range, taking San Isidro, whither the third insurgent capital was moved after Malolos fell, on May 17th. Here he made his headquarters for a time, as did General MacArthur at San Fernando.

It had been supposed that practically the whole body of the insurgent army was concentrated in the country to the north of Manila, but this proved a mistake. They now began to threaten Manila from the country south of the Pasig. Says General Otis:

The enemy had become again boldly demonstrative at the South and it became necessary to throw him back once more.35

General Lawton was directed to concentrate his troops in the country about San Isidro, turn them over to the command of some one else, and come to Manila to organize for a campaign on the south line. The *details* of this expedition belong to a military history, which this is not. The expedition left its initial point of concentration near Manila on June 9th. Its great event was the battle of Zapote River on June 13th. Along this river in 1896 the insurgents had gained a great victory over the Spaniards. They had trenches on the farther side of the river which they deemed impregnable. General Lawton attacked them in these intrenchments June 13th. At three o'clock that afternoon he wired General Otis at Manila giving him an idea of the battle and stating that the enemy was fighting in strong force and with determination. At 3:30 o'clock he wired:

We are having a beautiful battle. Hurry up ammunition; we will need it;

and at 4 o'clock:

We have the bridge. It has cost us dearly. Battle not yet over. It is a battle however.36

It was in this battle of Zapote River that Lieutenant William L. Kenly, of the regular artillery, did what was perhaps the finest single bit of soldier work of the whole war,37 in recognition of which his conduct in the battle was characterized as "magnificent" by so thorough a soldier as General Lawton, who recommended him to be brevetted for distinguished gallantry in the presence of the enemy, with this remark:

As General Ovenshine says, speaking of Lieutenant Kenly and his battery, "This is probably *the first time in history* that a battery has been advanced and *fought without cover within thirty yards of* strongly manned trenches."38

For what he did on that occasion, Kenly ought to have had a medal of honor, which, except life insurance and a good education, is the finest legacy any government can enable a soldier to bequeath to his children. If the war had been backed by the sentiment of the whole country, as the Spanish War was, he would have gotten it. As it was, the only thing he ever got for it, so far as the writer is advised, was to have his name spelt wrong in an account of the incident in the only book wherein there has yet been attempted a record of the many deeds of splendid daring that marked the only war into which this nation ever blundered.39

While there were divers and sundry movements of our troops hither and thither, and much sacrifice of life, after General Lawton's Zapote River campaign in June, no substantial progress was made in conquering and occupying the Islands until the fall following the Zapote River campaign above mentioned, when the twenty-five regiments of volunteers were organized and sent out. All that was done until then, after the capture of San Fernando, may be summed up broadly, by saying that we protected Manila and held the railroad, as far as we had fought our way up it. It is true that the city of Iloilo had been occupied on February 11th, the city of Cebu shortly afterward, the island of Negros, an oasis of comparative quiet in a great desert of hostility, a little later; also that a small Spanish garrison at the little port of Jolo in the Mohammedan country near Borneo had also been relieved by a small American force on the 19th of May. But these irresolute movements accomplished nothing except to deprive our force at the front of about 4000 men and to awaken the Visayan Islands to active and thorough organization against us.

Preparatory to an understanding of the fall campaign, in which patchwork and piecemeal warfare was superseded by the real thing, it will now be necessary to consider the political—or let us call it, the politico-military—aspect of the first half year of the war.

General Otis's folly had led him to advise Washington as early as November, 1898, that he could get along with 25,000 troops,40 and the Otis under-estimate of the resistance we would meet if we took the Islands had undoubtedly influenced Mr. McKinley in deciding to take them. Twenty-five thousand troops was only 5000 more than General Otis had with him at the time he made the recommendation, and signified that he was not expecting trouble. The Treaty of Paris was signed on December 10, 1898, and on December 16th, President McKinley's Secretary of War informed Congress that 25,000 troops would be enough for the Philippines.41 When the treaty was ratified February 6, 1899, the war in the Philippines had already broken out. On March 2, 1899, two days before the 55th Congress expired, in fact on the very day that Congress appropriated the $20,000,000 to pay Spain for the Islands, an act was passed authorizing the President to enlist 35,000 volunteers to put down the insurrection in the Islands. The term of enlistment of these volunteers was to expire June 30, 1901. As the New Thought people would say "Hold the Thought!" June 30, 1901, is the end of our government's fiscal year. That date, the date of expiration of the enlistment of the volunteer army raised under the act of March 2, 1899, is a convenient key to the whole history of the American occupation of the Philippines since the outbreak of our war with the Filipinos, February 4, 1899, including the titanic efforts of the McKinley Administration in the latter half of 1899 and the first half of 1900 to retrieve the Otis blunders; the premature resumption by Judge Taft, during and in aid of Mr. McKinley's campaign for the Presidency in 1900, of the original McKinley Benevolent Assimilation programme, on the theory, already wholly exploded by a long and bitter war, that the great majority of the people welcomed American rule and had only been coerced into opposing us; and the premature setting up of the Civil Government on July 4, 1901. No candid mind seeking only the truth of history can fail to see that when President McKinley sent the Taft Commission to the Philippines in the spring of 1900, part of their problem was to facilitate Mr. McKinley in avoiding later on any further call for volunteers to take the place of those whose terms would expire June 30, 1901. The amount of force that has been needed to saddle our government firmly on the Filipino people is the only honest test by which to examine the claim that it is unto them as Castoria unto children. In February, 1899, the dogs of war being already let loose, President McKinley had resumed his now wholly impossible Benevolent Assimilation programme, by sending out the Schurman Commission, which was the prototype of the Taft Commission, to yearningly explain our intentions to the insurgents, and to make clear to them how unqualifiedly benevolent those intentions were. The scheme was like trying to put salt on a bird's tail after you have flushed him. This commission was headed by President Schurman, of Cornell University. It arrived in March, armed with instructions as benevolent in their rhetoric as any the Filipinos had ever read in the days of our predecessors in sovereignty, the Spaniards. And the commission were of course duly astounded that their publication had no effect. The Filipinos in Manila tore them down as soon as they were put up. The instructions clothed the commission with authority to yield every point in issue except the only one in dispute—Independence. On this alone they were firm. But so were the people who had already submitted the issue to the arbitrament of war. Of course the Schurman Commission, therefore, accomplished nothing. It held frequent communication with the enemy in the field and came near an open rupture with General Otis, who was nominally a member of it. But even that unwise man knew war when he saw it, and knew the futility of trying to mix peace with war. War being hell, the sooner 'tis over the better for all concerned. After Professor Schurman had been quite optimistically explaining our intentions for about three months, under the tragically mistaken notion Mr. McKinley had originally derived from General Otis that the insurrection had been brought about by "the sinister ambition of a few leaders,"42 General Otis wired Washington, on June 4th, "Negotiations and conferences with insurgent leaders cost soldiers' lives and prolong our difficulties,"43 adding with regard to the Schurman Commission: "Ostensibly it will be supported * * * here, and to the outside world gentle peace shall prevail," but intimating that he would be very much gratified if the Department would allow him to handle the enemy, and stop Dr. Schurman from having their leaders come in under flags of truce to parley. After that Dr. Schurman's activities seem to have been confined to the less mischievous business of gathering statistics. His mistake was simply the one he had brought with him, derived from President McKinley. He came back home, however, thoroughly satisfied that the Filipinos did of a verity want the independence they were fighting for, and quite as sure that republics should not have colonies as General Anderson's experience had previously made him. It has long been known throughout the length and breadth of the United States that Dr. Schurman is in favor of Philippine independence.

On June 26th, just thirteen days after the Zapote River fight had stopped the insurgents on the south line from threatening almost the very gates of the city of Manila itself, General Otis had another attack of optimism. On that date he wired Washington: "Insurgent cause may collapse at any time."44 Finally, the war correspondents at Manila, wearied with the military press censorship whereby General Otis had so long kept the situation from the people at home, with his eternal "situation-well-in-hand" telegrams, got together, inspired no doubt by the example of the Roosevelt round robin that had rescued the Fifth Army Corps from Cuba after the fighting down there, and prepared a round robin of their own—a protest against further misrepresentation of the facts. This they of course knew General Otis would not let them cable home. However, they asked his permission to do so, the committee appointed to beard the lion in his den being O. K. Davis, John T. McCutcheon, Robert Collins, and John F. Bass. General Otis threatened to "put them off the island." This did not bother them in the least. General Otis told the War Department afterwards that he did not punish them because they were "courting martyrdom," or words to that effect. As a matter of fact, they were merely determined that the American people should know the facts. That of "putting them off the island" was just a fussy phrase of "Mother" Otis, long familiar to them. They were under his jurisdiction. But they were Americans, and reputable gentlemen, and he knew he was responsible for their right treatment. After General Otis had duly put the expected veto on the proposed cablegram of protest, the newspaper men sent their protest over to Hong Kong by mail, and had it cabled to the United States from there. It was published in the newspapers of this country July 17, 1899.

A copy of it may be found in any public library which keeps the bound copies of the great magazines, in the *Review of Reviews* for August, 1899, pp. 137–8. It read as follows:

The undersigned, being all staff correspondents of American newspapers stationed in Manila, unite in the following statement:

We believe that, owing to official despatches from Manila made public in Washington, the people of the United States have not received a correct impression of the situation in the Philippines, but that those despatches have presented an ultra-optimistic view that is not shared by the general officers in the field.

We believe the despatches incorrectly represent the existing conditions among the Filipinos in respect to internal dissension and demoralization resulting from the American campaign and to the brigand character of their army.

We believe the despatches err in the declaration that "the situation is well in hand," and in the assumption that the insurrection can be speedily ended without a greatly increased force.

We think the tenacity of the Filipino purpose has been under-estimated, and that the statements are unfounded that volunteers are willing to engage in further service.

The censorship has compelled us to participate in this misrepresentation by excising or altering uncontroverted statements of facts on the plea that "they would alarm the people at home," or "have the people of the United States by the ears."

The men of the pen had been so long under military rule and had seen so much of courts-martial that their document savored of military jurisprudence. After making the above charges, it set forth what it called "specifications." These were:

Prohibition of hospital reports; suppression of full reports of field operations in the event of failure; numbers of heat prostrations in the field; systematic minimization of naval operations; and suppression of complete reports of the situation.

The paper was signed by John T. McCutcheon and Harry Armstrong, representing the Chicago *Record*; O. K. Davis and P. G. MacDonnell, representing the New York *Sun*; Robert M. Collins, John P. Dunning, and L. Jones, representing the Associated Press; John F. Bass and William Dinwiddie, representing the New York *Herald*; E. D. Skeene, representing the Scripps-McRae Association; and Richard Little, representing the Chicago *Tribune*. Mr. Collins, the Associated Press representative, wrote his people an account of this whole episode, which was also given wide publicity. After describing the committee's interview with the General down to a certain point, he says:

But when General Otis came down to the frank admission that it was his purpose to keep the knowledge of conditions here from the public at home, and when the censor had repeatedly told us, in ruling out plain statements of undisputed facts, "My instructions are to let nothing go that can hurt the Administration," we concluded that protest was justifiable.

Collins had written what he considered a conservative review of the situation in June, saying reinforcements were needed. Of the suppression of this he says:

The censor's comment (I made a note of it) was: "Of course we all know that we are in a terrible mess out here, but we don't want the people to get excited about it. If you fellows will only keep quiet now we will pull through *in time*45 without any fuss at home!"

Mr. Collins's letter proceeds: "When I went to see him [Otis] he repeated the same old story about the insurrection going to pieces."

As to the charge of suppressing the real condition of our sick in the hospitals, Mr. Collins says that General Otis remarked that the "hospitals were full of perfectly well men who were shirking and should be turned out." On June 2, 1899, according to General Otis's report (p. 121), sixty per cent. of one of the State volunteer regiments were in hospital sick or wounded and there were in its ranks an average of but eight men to a company fit for duty. The report of the regimental surgeon stating this was forwarded by General Otis to Washington with the comment that there were few cases of serious illness; that the then "present station of these troops"—the place where the fighting was hottest, San Fernando—"is considered by the Filipinos as a health resort," and that "when orders to take passage to the United States are issued, both the Montana and South Dakota troops will recover *with astonishing rapidity.*"46

This round robin of course produced a profound sensation in the United States. It was just what the American public had long suspected was the case. Shortly afterward Secretary of War Alger resigned. Coming as it did on the heels of the scandal about "embalmed beef" having been furnished to the army in Cuba, it made him too much of a load for the Administration to carry. He was succeeded by Mr. Root, an eminent member of the New York Bar, whose masterful mind soon saw the essentials of the situation and proceeded to get a volunteer army recruited, equipped, and sent to the Philippines without further unnecessary delay.

1See General Hughes's testimony before Senate Committee, 1902, *Senate Document 331*, p. 508.

2See *Annual Report of the Secretary of War to the President for 1899*, pp. 7 *et seq.*

3This is no mere attempt at rhetorical decoration. Said General MacArthur to the Senate Committee in 1902 concerning Aguinaldo: "He was the incarnation of the feelings of the Filipinos." *Senate Document 331*, 1902, p. 1926.

4*Senate Document 331*, 1902, pp. 2927 *et seq.*

5*Senate Document 208*, 56th Cong., 1st Sess., p. 23.

6*Senate Document 62*, 55th Cong., 3d Sess., 1898–9, p. 383.

7See end of Chapter IV. *ante.*

8*Otis Report for 1899*, p. 66.

9*Report*, p. 99.

10*Ib.*, p. 100.

11*Ib.*, p. 150.

12Raw recruits.

13*War Department Report*, 1899, vol. i., pt. 4, p. 375.

14There were thirteen States represented by at least one organization. These were the First Californias, Second Oregons, First Colorados, First Nebraskas, Tenth Pennsylvanias, Major Young's Utah Battery, the First Idahos, Thirteenth Minnesotas, the North Dakota Artillery, the Twentieth Kansas, and the Tennessees, Montanas, and Wyomings.

15The regular regiments represented were the 14th, 8th, and 23d Infantry and 4th Cavalry. There were also some batteries of the Third Regular Artillery, and a number of Engineers, Hospital Corps, and Signal Corps people.

16*War Dept. Report*, 1899, vol. i., pt. 4, p. 440.

17Hearings on affairs in Philippine Islands, 1902.

18*War Department Report*, 1899, vol. i., pt. 4, p. 109.

19*Senate Document 331*, p. 1890.

20*Senate Document 331*, pp. 1890 *et seq*.

21*Ib.*, p. 1436.

22*Senate Document 331*, p. 1448.

23*Ib.*, pt. 2, p. 1447.

24The "water cure" (a cure for reticence) consisted in placing a bamboo reed in the victim's mouth and pouring water down his throat thus painfully distending his stomach and crowding all his viscera. Allowed to void this after a time, he would, under threat of repetition, give the desired information.

25Since the above was written, the officer in question has joined the Great Majority. It was that fearless, faithful, and kindly man, General Fred. D. Grant, who died in April, 1912.

26The lieutenant is no longer in the army, but he resigned voluntarily long after the incident related in the text, and for reasons wholly foreign to said incident.

27Of course my host's name was not Jones, but Jones will do.

28Spanish for man.

29A Philippine campaign expression for losing one's nerve and wanting to quit.

30Otis's *Report*, p. 133.

31*War Dept. Report*, 1899, vol. i., pt. 5, p. 35. In this handsome commendation General Lawton also included Maj. Charles G. Starr, one of the best all-round soldiers I ever knew.

32See *Correspondence Relating to the War with Spain*, vol. ii., pp. 1068 *et seq*.

33Otis's *Report*, p. 115.

34An interesting account of this experience is given by General Funston himself in the October, 1911, number of *Scribner's Magazine*, in an article entitled "From Malolos to San Fernando."

35Otis's *Report*, p. 136.

36*War Dept. Report*, 1899, vol. i., pt. 4, p. 138.

37Except, of course, the capture of Aguinaldo by General Funston nearly two years later.

38See General Lawton's Report on the Zapote River fight, *War Department Report*, 1900, vol. i., pt. 5, p. 282.

39See Harper's *History of the War in the Philippines*, p. 214, where the name of the gentleman is spelled "Kanly."

40*Correspondence Relating to the War with Spain*, Otis Despatches of November 27th, vol. ii., p. 846.

41*House Document 85*, 55th Cong., 3d Sess.

42The words quoted are from President McKinley's message to Congress of December, 1899.

43*Correspondence Relating to the War with Spain*, vol. ii., p. 1002.

44*Correspondence Relating to the War with Spain*, vol. ii., p. 1020.

45Meaning, of course, in time not to embarrass President McKinley's prospective candidacy for re-election in 1900, in a campaign in which all knew the acquisition of the Philippines was sure to be the paramount issue.

46*War Dept. Report*, 1899, vol. i., part 4, p. 122.

Chapter XII. Otis and the War (*Continued*)

And now, a man of head being at the centre of it, the whole matter gets vital.—Carlyle's*French Revolution.*

There can surely be little doubt in any quarter that Mr. Root is, in intellectual endowment and equipment at least, one of the greatest, if he is not *the* greatest, of living American statesmen. Mankind will always yield due acclaim to men who, in great emergencies, see the essentials of a given situation, and at once proceed to get the thing done that ought to be done. Whether the war in the Philippines was regrettable or not, it had become, by midsummer of 1899, supremely important, from any rational and patriotic standpoint, to end it as soon as possible.

Mr. Root had not been in office as Secretary of War very long before fleets of troop-ships, carrying some twenty-five well-equipped volunteer regiments,1 were swarming out of New York harbor bound for Manila by way of the Suez Canal, and out of the Golden Gate for the same destination *via* Honolulu. Nor was there any confusion as in the Cuban helter-skelter. Everything went as if by clockwork. Moreover, along with the new and ample force, went a clear, masterly, comprehensive plan of campaign, prepared, not by General Otis at Manila, but in the War Department at Washington, by officers already familiar with the islands.

It was the purpose of this government at last to demonstrate conclusively to the Filipino people that the representative of the United States at Manila was "the boss of the show," and that Aguinaldo was *not*—a demonstration then sorely needed by the exigencies of American prestige. The purpose can readily be appreciated, but to understand the plan of campaign, and the method of its execution, somewhat of the geography of Luzon must now be considered. Before we approach the shores of Luzon and the city of Manila, however, let us consider from a distance, in a bird's-eye view, as it were, the relation of Luzon to the rest of the archipelago, so as to know, in a comprehensive way, what we are "going out for to see." We may as well pause at this point, long enough to learn all we will ever need to know, for the purposes of the scope of this narrative, concerning the general geography of the Philippine archipelago, and the governmental problems it presents. (*See folding map at end of volume.*)

It is a common saying that Paris is France. In the same sense Manila *is* the Philippines. In fact, the latter expression is more accurate than the former, for Manila, besides being the capital city of the country, *and* its chief port, is a city of over 200,000 people, while no one of the two or three cities next to it in rank in population had more than 20,000.2 By parity of reasoning it may be said that Luzon *was* the Philippines, so far as the problem which confronted us when we went there was concerned, relatively both to the original conception in 1898 of the struggle for independence, its birth in 1899, its life, and its slow, lingering obstinate death in 1900–1902, in which last year the insurrection was finally correctly stated to be practically ended. To know just how and why this was true, is necessary to a clear understanding of that struggle, including not only its genesis and its exodus, but also its gospels, its acts, its revelations, and the multitudinous subsequent commentaries thereon.

The total land area of the Philippine archipelago, according to the American Census of 1903, is 115,000 square miles.[3] The area of Luzon, the principal island, on which Manila is situated, is 41,000 square miles, and that of Mindanao, the only other large island, is 36,000.[4] Between these two large islands, Luzon on the north, and Mindanao on the south, there are a number of smaller ones, but acquaintance with only six of these is essential to a clear understanding of the American occupation. Many Americans, too busy to have paid much attention to the Philippine Islands, which are, and must ever remain, a thing wholly apart from American life, have a vague notion that there are several thousand of them. This is true, in a way. American energy has made, for the first time in their history, an actual count of them, "including everything which at high tide appeared as a separate island."[5] The work was done for our Census of 1903 by Mr. George R. Putnam, now head of the Lighthouse Board of the United States. Mr. Putnam, counted 3141 of them.[6] Of these, of course, many—many hundred perhaps—are merely rocks fit only for a resting place for birds. 2775, have an area of less than a square mile each, 262 have an area of between 1 and 10 square miles, 73 between 10 and 100 square miles, and 20 between 100 and 1000 square miles. This accounts for, and may dismiss at once from consideration 3130—all but 11. Most of these 3130 that are large enough to demand even so much as a single word here are poorly adapted to human habitation, being in most instances, without good harbors or other landing places, and usually covered either with dense jungle or inhospitable mountains, or both. Their total area is only about 8500 square miles, of the 115,500 square miles of land in the archipelago. None of them have ever had any political significance, either in Spain's time, or our own, and therefore, the whole 3130 may at once be eliminated from consideration, leaving 11 only requiring any special notice at all—the 11 largest islands. Of these, Luzon and Mindanao have already been mentioned. The remaining 9, with their respective areas and populations, are:

Island	*Area*[7] *in Square Miles*	*Population*[8]
Panay	4,611	743,646
Negros	4,881	560,776
Cebu	1,762	592,247
Bohol	1,411	243,148
Samar	5,031	222,690
Leyte	2,722[9]	357,641
Mindoro	3,851	28,361
Masbate	1,236	29,451
Paragua	4,027[10]	10,918
Total	29,532	2,788,878

The political or governmental problem being now reduced from 3141 islands to eleven, the last three of the nine contained in the above table may also be eliminated as follows: (*See map at end of volume.*)

Paragua, the long narrow island seen at the extreme lower left of any map of the archipelago, extending northeast southwest at an angle of about 45°, is practically worthless, being fit for nothing much except a penal colony, for which purpose it is in fact now used.

Masbate—easily located on the map at a glance, because the twelfth parallel of north latitude intersects the 124th meridian of longitude east of Greenwich in its southeast corner—though noted for cattle and other quadrupeds, is not essential to a clear understanding of the human problem in its broader governmental aspects.

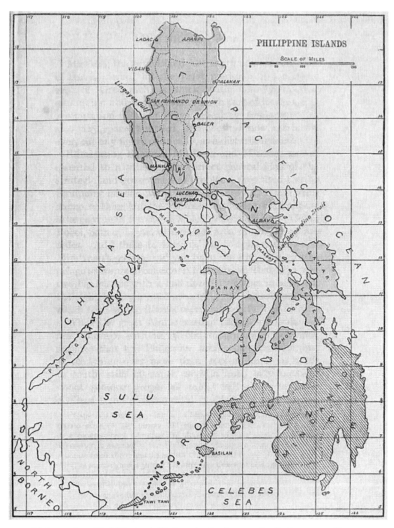

Bird's-eye view of the Philippine Archipelago, showing the preponderating importance of Luzon.

For greater details, see folding map at end of volume.

Mindoro, the large island just south of the main bulk of Luzon, pierced by the 121st meridian of longitude east of Greenwich, is thick with densely wooded mountains and jungle over a large part of its area, has a reputation of being very unhealthy (malarious), is also very sparsely settled, and does not now, nor has it ever, cut any figure politically, as a disturbing factor.11

Eliminating Paragua, Masbate, and Mindoro as not essential to a substantially correct general idea of the strategic and governmental problems presented by the Philippine Islands, we have left, besides Luzon and Mindanao, nothing but the half-dozen islands which appear in large type in the above table: Panay, Negros, Cebu, Bohol, Samar, Leyte, with a total area of 20,500 square miles. Add these to Luzon's 41,000 square miles and Mindanao's 36,000, and you have the Philippine archipelago as we are to consider it in this book, that is to say, two big islands with a half dozen little ones in between, the eight having a total area of 97,500 square miles, of which the two big islands represent nearly four-fifths.

While the great Mohammedan island of Mindanao, near Borneo, with its 36,000 square miles12 of area, requires that the Philippine archipelago be described as stretching over more than 1000 miles from north to south, still, inasmuch as Mindanao only contains about 500,000 people all told,13 half of them semi-civilized,14 the governmental problem it presents has no more to do with the main problem of whether, if ever, we are to grant independence to the 7,000,000 Christians of the other islands, than the questions that have to be passed on by our Commissioner of Indian Affairs have to do with the tariff.

Mindanao's 36,000 square miles constitute nearly a third of the total area of the Philippine archipelago, and more than that fraction of the 97,500 square miles of territory to a consideration of which our attention is reduced by the process of elimination above indicated. Turning over Mindanao to those crudely Mohammedan, semi-civilized Moros would indeed be "like granting self-government to an Apache reservation under some local chief," as Mr. Roosevelt, in the campaign of 1900, ignorantly declared it would be to grant self-government to Luzon under Aguinaldo.15 Furthermore, the Moros, so far as they can think, would prefer to owe allegiance to, and be entitled to recognition as subjects of, some great nation.16 Again, because, the Filipinos have no moral right to control the Moros, and could not if they would, the latter being fierce fighters and bitterly opposed to the thought of possible ultimate domination by the Filipinos, the most uncompromising advocate of the consent-of-the-governed principle has not a leg to stand on with regard to Mohammedan Mindanao. Hence I affirm that as to it, we have a distinct and separate problem, which cannot be solved in the lifetime of anybody now living. But it is a problem which need not in the least delay the advent of independence for the other fourteen-fifteenths of the inhabitants of the archipelago17—all Christians living on islands north of Mindanao. It is true that there are some Christian Filipinos on Mindanao, but in policing the Moros, our government would of course protect them from the Moros. If they did not like our government, they could move to such parts of the island as we might permit to be incorporated in an ultimate Philippine republic. Inasmuch as the 300,000 or so Moros of the Mohammedan island of Mindanao and the adjacent islets called Jolo (the "Sulu Archipelago," so called, "reigned over" by the Sultan of comic opera fame) originally presented, as they will always present, a distinct and separate problem, and never did have anything more to do with the Philippine insurrection against us than their cousins and co-religionists over in nearby Borneo, the task which confronted Mr. Root in the fall of 1899, to wit, the suppression of the Philippine insurrection, meant, practically, the subjugation of one big island, Luzon, containing half the population and one-third the total area of the archipelago, and six neighboring smaller ones, the Visayan Islands.

And now let us concentrate our attention upon Luzon as Mr. Root no doubt did, with infinite pains, in the fall of 1899. Of the 7,600,000 people of the Philippines18 almost exactly one-half, *i.e.*, 3,800,000,19 live on Luzon, and these are practically all civilized.20 It so happens that the State of our Union which is nearer the size of Luzon than any other is the one which furnished the first American Civil Governor for the Philippine Islands, Governor Taft. President Taft's native State of Ohio is 41,061 square miles in area, and Luzon is 40,969.21 Roughly speaking, Luzon may also be said to be about the size of Cuba,22 though it is about twice as thickly populated as the latter, Cuba, having something over 2,000,000 people to Luzon's nearly 4,000,000.23

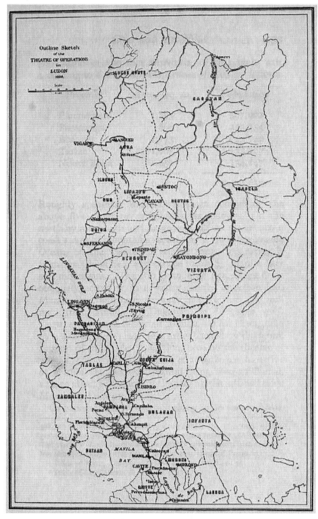

Outline sketch of the theatre of operations in Luzon, 1899.

By all Americans in the Philippines since our occupation, the island of Luzon is always contemplated as consisting of two parts, to wit, northern Luzon, or that part north of Manila, and southern Luzon, the part south of Manila. The great central plain of Luzon, lying just north of Manila, is nearly as large as the republic of Salvador, or the State of New Jersey, *i.e.*, in the neighborhood of 7000 square miles area[24]—and, like Salvador, it contains a population of something over 1,000,000 inhabitants. The area and population of the five provinces of this plain are, according to the *Philippine Census of 1903*, as follows:

Province	*Area*[25] (sq. m.)	*Population*[26]
Pangasinan	1,193	397,902
Pampanga	868	223,754
Bulacan	1,173	223,742
Tarlac	1,205	135,107
Nueva Ecija	1,950	134,147
	6,389	1,114,652

Roughly speaking, the central plain comprising the above five provinces is bounded as follows: On the north by mountains and Lingayen Gulf, on the east by a coast range of mountains separating it from the Pacific Ocean, on the west by a similar range separating it from the China Sea, and on the south by Manila Bay and mountains. The Rio Grande de Pampanga flows obliquely across it in a southwesterly direction into Manila Bay, and near its western edge runs the railroad from Manila to Dagupan on Lingayen gulf. Dagupan is 120 miles from Manila. This plain, held by a well-equipped insurgent army backed by the moral support of the whole population, became the theatre of war as soon as the volunteers of 1899 began to arrive at Manila, the insurgent capital being then at Tarlac, a place about two-thirds of the way up the railroad from Manila to Dagupan.

Of course the first essential thing to do was to break the backbone of the insurgent army, and scatter it, and the next thing to do was to capture Aguinaldo, the head and front of the whole business, the incarnation of the aspirations of the Filipino people. The operations to this end commenced in October, and involved three movements of three separate forces:

(1) A column under General Lawton, proceeding up the Rio Grande and along the northeastern borders of the plain, and bending around westward along its northern boundary toward the gulf of Lingayen, garrisoning the towns en route, and occupying the mountain passes on the northeast which give exit over the divide into the great valleys beyond.

(2) An expedition under General Wheaton, some 2500 in all, proceeding by transports to the gulf of Lingayen, the chief port of which, Dagupan, was the northern terminus of the railroad; the objective being to land on the shore of that gulf at the northwest corner of the plain, occupy the great coast road which runs from that point to the northern extremity of the island, and also to proceed eastward and effect a junction with the Lawton column.

(3) A third column under General MacArthur, proceeding up the railroad to the capture of Tarlac, the third insurgent capital, and thence still up the railroad to its end at Dagupan, driving the enemy's forces before it toward the line held by the first two columns.

On October 12th, General Lawton moved up the Rio Grande from a place called Aryat, a few miles up stream from where the railroad crosses the river at Calumpit, driving the insurgents before him to the northward and westward. His command was made up mainly from the 3d Cavalry and the 22d Infantry, together with several hundred scouts, American and Maccabebee. On the 20th San Isidro was again captured. That was the place Lawton had evacuated in May previous. Arriving in the Islands with Colonel E. E. Hardin's regiment, the 29th U. S. Volunteer Infantry, on November 3, 1899, the writer was immediately detailed to the Maccabebee scouts, to take the place of Lieutenant Boutelle, of the regular artillery, a young West Pointer from Oregon, who had been killed a day or two previous, and reported to Major C. G. Starr, General Lawton's Adjutant-General in the field (whom he had known at Santiago de Cuba the previous year) at San Isidro on or about November 8th. Major Starr said: "We took this town last spring," stating how much our loss had been in so doing, "but, partly as a result of the Schurman Commission parleying with the insurgents General Otis had us fall back. We have just had to take it again." General Lawton garrisoned San Isidro this time once for all, and pressed on north, capturing the successive towns en route. Meantime, General Young's cavalry, and the Maccabebee scouts under Major Batson, a lieutenant of the regular army, and a medal-of-honor graduate of the Santiago campaign, were operating to the west of the general line of advance, striking insurgent detachments wherever found and driving them toward the line of the railroad. By November 13th, Lawton's advance had turned to the westward, according to the concerted plan of campaign above described, garrisoning, as fast as they were taken, such of the towns of the country over which he swept as there were troops to spare for. We knew that Aguinaldo had been at Tarlac when the advance began, and every officer and enlisted man of the command was on the *qui vive* to catch him. By November 18th, General Lawton's forces held a line of posts extending up the eastern side of the plain, and curving around across the northern end to within a few miles of the gulf of Lingayen.

On November 6th, General Wheaton set sail from Manila for Lingayen Gulf, with 2500 men of the 13th Regular and 33d Volunteer Infantry, and a platoon of the 6th Artillery, convoyed by the ships of the navy, and next day the expedition was successfully landed at San Fabian, "with effective assistance from the naval convoy against spirited resistance," says Secretary of War Root, in his annual report for 1899. The navy's assistance on that occasion was indeed "effective," but such passing mention hardly covers the case. In the first place, they selected the landing point, their patrols being already familiar with the coasts. As soon as the transports were sighted, about eleven o'clock on the morning of November 7th, Commander Knox, the senior officer present, who commanded the *Princeton*, and Commander Moore, of the *Helena*, went out to meet and confer with General Wheaton. This done, the landing was effected under protection of the navy's guns. Besides the naval vessels above named, there were also present the *Bennington* under Commander Arnold, the *Manila* under Lieutenant-Commander Nazro, and two captured Spanish gun-boats small enough to get close in shore, the *Callao*, and the *Samar*. The troops were disembarked in two columns of small boats towed by launches. Lieutenant-Commander Tappan in charge of the *Callao*, and Ensign Mustin, commanding the *Samar*, were especially commended in the despatches of Admiral Watson, commander-in-chief of the Asiatic squadron. Both bombarded the insurgent trenches at close range during the landing, and Mustin actually steamed in between the insurgents and the head of the column of troop-boats, so as to intercept and receive the brunt of their fire himself, and, selecting a point about seventy-five yards from the enemy's trenches whence he could effectually pepper them, ran his ship aground so she would stick, and commenced rapid firing at point blank range, driving the enemy from his trenches, and enabling Colonel Hare of the 33d, and those who followed, to land without being subjected to further fire while on the water.27

On the 11th of November, Colonel Hare with the 33d Volunteer Infantry and one Gatling gun under Captain Charles R. Howland of the 28th Volunteer Infantry, a lieutenant of the regular army, and a member of General Wheaton's staff, proceeded southeastward to San Jacinto, and attacked and routed some 1200 to 1600 intrenched insurgents, Major John A. Logan being among our killed. The enemy left eighty-one dead in the trenches, and suffered a total loss estimated at three hundred. While space does not permit dwelling on the details of engagements, it may be remarked here, once for all, that the 33d Volunteer Infantry, Colonel Luther R. Hare commanding, made more reputation than any other of the twenty-five regiments of the volunteer army of 1899, except, possibly, Colonel J. Franklin Bell's regiment, the 36th. This is no reflection on the rest. These two were lucky enough to have more opportunities. In meeting his opportunities, however, Colonel Hare, like Colonel Bell, proved himself a superb soldier; his field-officers, especially Major March,28 were particularly indefatigable; and his men were mostly Texans, accustomed to handling a rifle with effect. Space also forbids following Captain Howland and his Gatling gun into the engagement of November 11th, but from the uniformity with which General Wheaton's official reports commend his young aide's bravery and efficiency on numerous occasions in 1899–1900, it may be safely assumed that those qualities were behind that Gatling gun at San Jacinto. There was a vicious rumor started after the San Jacinto fight and given wide circulation in the United States, that Major Logan was shot in the back by his own men. I saw a major surgeon a few days later who had been an eye-witness to his death. He said an insurgent sharpshooter shot Major Logan from a tree, and that the said sharpshooter was promptly thereafter dropped from his perch full of 33d Infantry bullets. Says General Wheaton's despatch of November 12th: "Major Logan fell while gallantly leading his battalion."29

On November 5th, General MacArthur, with a strong column, composed mainly of the 9th, 17th, and 36th Regiments of Infantry, two troops of the 4th Cavalry, two platoons of the 1st Artillery, and a detachment of scouts, advanced up the railroad from Angeles, in execution of his part of the programme.30 Angeles is some distance up the railroad from Calumpit, where the railroad crosses the Rio Grande.31 General MacArthur's column encountered and overwhelmed the enemy at every point, entering Tarlac on November 12th, and effecting a junction with General Wheaton at Dagupan, the northern terminus of the Manila-Dagupan Railroad, 120 miles from Manila, on November 20th.

After General Lawton had finished his part of the round-up, he had a final conference with General Young on November 18th at Pozorubio, which is near the northeastern border of the plain, bade him good-bye, and soon afterward went south to dispose of a body of insurgents who were giving trouble near Manila. It was in this last expedition that he lost his life at San Mateo about twelve miles out of Manila on December 19, 1899.

The first of the two purposes of the great Wheaton-Lawton-MacArthur northern advance, viz., the dispersion of the insurgent army of northern Luzon had been duly accomplished. The other purpose had failed of realization. Aguinaldo had not been captured. He escaped through our lines.

Such is in brief the story of the destruction of the Aguinaldo government in 1899 by General Otis, or rather by Mr. Root. But the trouble about it was that it would not stay destroyed. It "played possum" for a while, the honorable President retiring to permanent headquarters in the mountains "with his government concealed about his person," as Senator Lodge put it later in a summary of the case for the Administration, before the Senate, in the spring of 1900. If the distinguished and accomplished senator from Massachusetts, in adding at that time to the gaiety of nations, had had access to a certain diary kept by one of Aguinaldo's personal staff throughout that period, subsequently submitted, in 1902, to the Senate Committee of that year, he could have swelled the innocuous merriment with such cheery entries as "Here we tightened our belts and went to bed on the ground"—the time alluded to being midnight after a hard day's march without food, the place, some chilly mountain top up which the "Honorable Presidente" and party had that day been guided by the ever-present and ever-willing *paisano* (fellow countryman) of the immediate neighborhood—whatever the neighborhood—to facilitate them in eluding General Young's hard riding cavalry and scouts. The writer has no quarrel with Senator Lodge's witticism above quoted, having derived on reading it, in full measure, the suggestive amusement it was intended to afford. It is true that about all then left of the "Honorable Presidente's" government, for the nonce, was in fact concealed about his person. It was of a nature easily portable. It needed neither bull trains, pack ponies, nor coolies to carry it. It consisted solely of the loyal support of the whole people, who looked to him as the incarnation of their aspirations. Said General MacArthur to the Senate Committee in 1902 concerning Aguinaldo: "He was the incarnation of the feelings of the Filipinos." "Senator Culberson: 'And represented the Filipino people?' General MacArthur: 'I think so; yes'."32 We of the 8th Army Corps did not know what a complete structure the Philippine republic of 1898–9 was until, having shot it to pieces, we had abundant leisure to examine the ruins. To admit, in the same breath, participation in that war and profound regret that it ever had occurred, is not an incriminating admission. In this case as in any other where you have done another a wrong, by thrashing him or otherwise, under a mistake of fact, the first step toward righting the wrong is to frankly acknowledge it. As soon as Aguinaldo's flight and wanderings terminated in the finding of permanent headquarters, he began sending messages to his various generals all over Luzon and the other islands, and wherever those orders were not intercepted they were delivered and loyally obeyed. This kept up until General Funston captured him in 1901. One traitor among all those teeming millions might have betrayed his whereabouts, but none appeared. The obstinate character and long continuance of the warfare in northern Luzon after the great round-up which terminated with the final junction of the Lawton, Wheaton, and MacArthur columns near Dagupan, as elsewhere later throughout the archipelago, was at first very surprising to our generals. It had been supposed that to disperse the insurgent army would end the insurrection. As events turned out, it only made the resistance more effective. So long as the insurgents kept together in large bodies they could not hide. And as they were poor marksmen, while the men behind our guns, like most other young Americans, knew something about shooting, the ratio of their casualties to ours was about 16 to 1.33 When General MacArthur began his advance on Tarlac, General Lawton his great march up the valley of the Rio Grande, and General Wheaton his closing in from Dagupan, Aguinaldo with his cabinet, generals, and headquarters troops abandoned Tarlac, their capital, and went up the railroad to Bayambang. Here they held a council of war, which General MacArthur describes in his report for 1900 (from information obtained later on) as follows:

At a council of war held at Bayambang, Pangasinan, about November 12, 1899, which was attended by General Aguinaldo and many of the Filipino military leaders, a resolution was adopted to the effect that the insurgent forces were incapable of further resistance in the field, and as a consequence it was decided to disband the army, the generals and the men to return to their own provinces, with a view to organizing the people for general resistance by means of guerrilla warfare.34

This had been the plan from the beginning, the council of war simply determining that the time to put the plan into effect had arrived. Accordingly, the uniformed insurgent battalions and regiments broke up into small bands which maintained a most persistent guerrilla warfare for years thereafter. During those years they seldom wore uniforms, disappearing and hiding their guns when hotly pursued, and reappearing as non-combatant peasants interrupted in agricultural pursuits, with invariable protestations of friendship.

Hence all such came to be known as *amigos* (friends), and the word *amigo*, or friend, became a bitter by-word, meaning to all American soldiers throughout the archipelago an enemy falsely claiming to be a friend. *And every Filipino was an "amigo."*

Still, the volunteers had arrived in time to enable Mr. Root to make a very nice showing to Congress, and through it to the people, in his annual report to the President for 1899, dated November 29th. This report is full of cheerful chirps from General Otis to the effect that the resistance was practically ended, and the substance of the information it conveyed duly found its way into the President's message of December of that year and through it to the general public. One of the Otis despatches said: "Claim to government by insurgents can be made no longer."35 This message went on to state that nothing was now left but "banditti," and that the people are all friendly to our troops. Thus misled, Mr. Root repeated to the President and through him to Congress and the country the following nonsense:

It is gratifying to know that as our troops got away from the immediate vicinity of Manila they found the natives of the country exceedingly friendly * * *. This was doubtless due in some measure to the fact that the Pampangos, who inhabit the provinces of Pampanga and Tarlac, and the Pangasinanes, who inhabit Pangasinan, as well as the other more northerly tribes, are unfriendly to the Tagalogs, and had simply submitted to the military domination of that tribe, from which they were glad to be relieved.

In characterizing this as nonsense no disrespect is intended to Mr. Root. He did not know any better. He was relying on General Otis. But it is sorely difficult to convey in written words what utter nonsense those expressions about "the Pampangos" and "the Pangasinanes" are to any one who was in that northern advance in the fall of 1899. Imagine a British cabinet minister making a report to Parliament in 1776 couched in the following words, to wit:

The Massachusetts-ites, who inhabit Massachusetts, and the Virginia-ites who inhabit Virginia, as well as most of the other inhabitants are unfriendly to the New York-ites, and have simply submitted to the military domination of the last named,

and you have a faint idea of the accuracy of Mr. Root's report. It is quite true that the Tagalos were the prime movers in the insurrection against us, as they had been in all previous insurrections against Spain. But the "Tagalo tribe" was no more alone among the Filipino people in their wishes and views than the "unterrified" Tammany tribe who inhabit the wilds of Manhattan Island, at the mouth of the Hudson River, are alone in their views among our people.

On page 70 of this report, Secretary Root reproduces a telegram from General Otis dated November 18, 1899, stating that on the road from San Nicolas to San Manuel, a day or so previous, General Lawton was "cordially received by the inhabitants." He announces in the same telegram the drowning of Captain Luna, a volunteer officer from New Mexico, who was one of General Lawton's aides, and had been a captain in Colonel Roosevelt's regiment of Rough Riders before Santiago. The writer happens to have been on that ride with General Lawton from San Nicolas to San Manuel, and was within a dozen feet of Captain Luna when the angry current of the Agno River caught him and his pony in its grip and swept both out of sight forever, along with divers troopers of the 4th Cavalry, horses and riders writhing to their death in one awful, tangled, struggling mass. He can never forget the magnificent dash back into the wide, ugly, swollen stream made by Captain Edward L. King of General Lawton's staff, as he spurred his horse in, followed by several troopers who had responded to his call for mounted volunteers to accompany him in an effort to save the lives of the men who went down. Their generous work proved futile. But it was inspired partly by common dread of what they knew would happen to any half-drowned soldier who might be washed ashore far away from the column and captured. If an army was ever "in enemy's country" it was then and there. When we reached San Manuel that night, Captains King and Sewall, the two surviving personal aides of General Lawton's staff, and the writer, stopped, along with the general, in a little *nipa* shack on the roadside. General Lawton, was in an upper room busy with couriers and the like, but downstairs King, Sewall, and myself set to work to *buscar*36 something to eat. I got hold of an *hombre* (literally, a man; colloquially a native peasant man), who went to work with apparent alacrity, and managed to provide three ravenously hungry young men with a good meal of chicken, eggs, and rice. After supper, being new in the country, the writer remarked to the general on the alacrity of the *hombre*. I had brought out from the United States the notions there current about the nature of the resistance. General Lawton said, with a humorous twinkle in those fine eyes of his: "Humph! If you expected to be killed the next minute if you didn't find a chicken, *you'd* probably find one too." It is true that in the course of the campaign General Young sent a telegram to General Otis at Manila characterizing his reception at the hands of the natives as friendly. This was prompted by our column being met as it would come into a town by the town band. It did not take long to see through this, and other like hypocrisy entirely justifiable in war, though such tactics deceived us for a little while at first into thinking the people were genuine *amigos* (friends). General Otis, not being near the scene, remained under our original brief illusion. Let us return, however, from Mr. Root's "patient and unconsenting millions dominated by the Tagalo tribe," of 1899, to the facts, and follow the course of events succeeding Lawton's junction with Wheaton and MacArthur and his farewell to Young.

General Young, with his cavalry, and the Maccabebee scouts, continued in pursuit of Aguinaldo through the passes of the mountains, the latter having managed to run the gauntlet of our lines successfully by a very close shave. How narrowly he escaped is illustrated by the fact that after a fight we had at the Aringay River on November 19th, in which Major Batson was wounded while gallantly directing the crossing of the river, we remained that night in the town of Aringay, and at the very time we were "hustling for chow" in Aringay, Aguinaldo was in the village of Naguilian an hour or so distant, as was authoritatively ascertained long afterward from a captured diary of one of his staff officers.37

General Young proceeded up the coast road, in hot haste, taking one town, San Fernando de Union, after a brief engagement led by the general in person—imagine a brigadier-general leading a charge at the head of thirty-seven men!—but Aguinaldo had turned off to the right and taken to the mountains. General Lawton wired General Otis about that time, in effect, in announcing Aguinaldo's escape through our lines and his own tireless brigade-commander's bold dash in pursuit of him with an inadequate force of cavalry hampered by lack of horseshoes and nails for the same, "If Young does not catch Aguinaldo, he will at least make him very unhappy." The Young column garrisoned the towns along the route over which it went, occupying all the western part of Northern Luzon, hereafter described, and also later on rescued Lieutenant Gilmore of the navy, Mr. Albert Sonnichsen, previously an enlisted man and since a writer of some note, and other American prisoners who had been in the hands of the insurgents for many months. General Young finally made his headquarters at Vigan, in the province of Ilocos Sur, a fine town in a fine country. The Ilocanos are called "the Yankees of the Philippines," on account of their energy and industry. Vigan is on the China sea coast of Luzon (the west coast), about one hundred miles up the old Spanish coast road, or "King's Highway" (Camino Real), from Lingayen Gulf (where the hundred-and-twenty mile railroad from Manila to Dagupan ends) and about eighty miles from the extreme northern end of the island of Luzon.38

As subsequent policies and their effect on one's attitude toward a great historic panorama do not interfere in the least with a proper appreciation of the bravery and efficiency of the army of one's country, it is with much regret that this narrative cannot properly chronicle in detail what the War Department reports record of the stirring deeds of General Young, and the officers and men of his command, Colonels Hare and Howze, Captains Chase and Dodd, and the rest,39 performed during the long course of the work now under consideration. One incident, however, is appropriate in this connection, not only to a collection of *genre* pictures of the war itself, but also to a place among the lights and shadows of the general picture of the American occupation. On December 2, 1899, Major March of the 33d Infantry had his famous fight at Tila pass, in which young Gregorio del Pilar, one of the ablest and bravest of the insurgent generals, was killed. The locality mentioned is a wild pass in the mountains of the west coast of Luzon, that overlook the China Sea, some 4500 feet above sea level. It was strongly fortified, and was believed by the insurgents to be impregnable. The trail winds up the mountains in a sharp zigzag, and was commanded by stone barricades loop-holed for infantry fire. The advance of our people was checked at first by a heavy fire from these barricades. The approach being precipitous, it looked for a while as if the position would indeed be impregnable, and the idea of taking it by a frontal attack was abandoned. But a hill to the left front of the barricade was seized by some of our sharpshooters—those Texans of the 33d were indeed*sharpshooters*—and after that, under cover of their fire, our troops managed to get in a fire simultaneously both on the flank and rear of the occupants of the barricades, climbing the precipitous slope up the mountain side by means of twigs and the like, and finally killing some fifty-two of the enemy, General Pilar among the number. After the fight was over, Lieutenant Quinlan, heretofore mentioned, moved by certain indignities in the nature of looting perpetrated upon the remains of General Pilar, buried them with such military honors as could be hastily provided, after first taking from a pocket of the dead general's uniform a souvenir in the shape of an unfinished poem written in Spanish by him the night before, addressed to his sweetheart; and, the burial finished, the American officer placed on the rude headstone left to mark the spot this generous inscription:

General Gregorio Pilar, killed at the battle of Tila Pass, December 2d, 1899, commanding Aguinaldo's rearguard. *An officer and a gentleman.*(Signed) D. P. Quinlan, 2d Lieutenant, 11th Cavalry.

The brief incident over, Quinlan hurried on, rejoined the column, and resumed the work of Benevolent Assimilation and the war against Home Rule with all the dauntless ardor of his impetuous Irish nature. Whatever the ultimate analysis of the ethics of this scene—Quinlan at the grave of Pilar—clearly the Second Lieutenant Quinlan of 1899 would hardly have agreed with the vice-presidential candidate of 1900, Colonel Roosevelt, that granting self-government to the Filipinos would be like granting self-government to an Apache reservation under some local chief.

The territory occupied and finally "pacified" by General Young, with the effective assistance of the officers heretofore mentioned, and many other good men and true, was ultimately organized into a military district, which was called the First District of the Department of Northern Luzon. As territory was fought over, occupied, and finally reduced to submission, that territory would be organized into a military district by the commanding general or colonel of the invading column, under the direction of the division commander. The military "Division of the Philippines," which was succeeded by the Civil Government of the Philippines under Governor Taft in 1901, of course covered all the territory ceded by the Treaty of Paris. It was divided into four "Departments," the Department of Northern Luzon, the Department of Southern Luzon, the Department of the Visayas,40 and the Department of Mindanao and Jolo. General Young commanded the First District of the Department of Northern Luzon—which included the three west coast provinces north of Lingayen Gulf, and the three adjacent mountain provinces—from the time he led his brigade into that region in pursuit of Aguinaldo until shortly before Governor Taft's inauguration in the summer of 1901. Many were the combats, great and small, of General Young's brigade, in compassing the task of crushing the resistance in that part of Luzon into which he led the first American troops in the winter of 1899–1900. The resistance was obstinate, desperate, and long drawn out, but when he finally reported the territory under his command "pacified," it *was* pacified. A soldier's task had been performed in a soldierly manner. The work had been done thoroughly. General Young gave the Ilocano country a lesson it never forgot, before politics had time to interfere. We have never had any trouble in that region from that day to this.

Before the army of occupation had had time to do in southern Luzon what General Young did in northern Luzon and thereby secure like permanent results in that region, a "peace-at-any-price" policy was inaugurated to meet the exigencies of Mr. McKinley's campaign for the Presidency in 1900. Our last martyred President clung all through that campaign to his original assumption that Benevolent Assimilation would work, and that the single burning need of the hour was to make clear to the Filipinos what our intentions were—as if powder and lead did not spell denial of independence plain enough, as if that were not the sole issue, and as if that issue had not been submitted, with deadly finality, to the stern arbitrament of war. However, neither Lord Roberts in India, nor Lord Kitchener in Egypt ever more effectively convinced the people of those countries that his flag must be respected as an emblem of sovereignty, than General Young did the Ilocanos. Take the month of April, 1900 for instance. Several days after the expiration of said month (on May 5th) General Otis was relieved and went home. During the month of April, General Young killed five hundred insurgents in his district.41 But this did not prevent General Otis, arriving as he did in the United States in the month of June, when the national political conventions meet, from "repeating the same old story about the insurrection going to pieces"42— *only*, not "going" now, but "gone." Nor did it, and like sputterings of insurrection all over the place, prevent Judge Taft—the "Mark Tapley of this Philippine business" as he humorously told the Senate Committee of 1902 he had been called—from cabling home, during the presidential campaign of 1900, a series of superlatively optimistic bulletins,43 based on the testimony of Filipinos who had abandoned the cause of their country as soon as patriotism meant personal peril, all such testimony being eagerly accepted, as testimony of the kind one wants and needs badly usually is, in total disregard of information directly to the contrary furnished by General MacArthur and other distinguished soldiers who had been then on the ground for two years.

The area and population of the territory occupied by General Young, the "First District of the Department of Northern Luzon," was, according to the Census of 1903, as follows:

Province	*Area* (sq. m.)44	*Population*45
Ilocos Norte	1,330	178,995
Ilocos Sur	471	187,411
Union	634	137,839
Abra	1,171	51,860
Lepanto-Bontoc46	2,005	72,750
Benguet	822	22,745
	6,433	651,600

As this narrative purposes so to present the geography of the Philippine Islands as to facilitate an easy remembrance of *the essentials only* of the governmental problem there presented, we will hereafter speak of the First District as containing, roughly, 6500 square miles, and 650,000 people. Whenever, if ever, a Philippine republic is set up, these six provinces are very likely, for geographical and other reasons, to become one of the original states comprising that republic, just as the states of Mexico are made up of groups of provinces.47

The rest of the story of the northern campaign of 1899–1900 immediately following Aguinaldo's escape into the mountains through General Young's and General Lawton's lines, being a necessary part of the American occupation of the Philippines, may also serve as a text for further acquainting the reader with the geography of Luzon. War is the best possible teacher of geography, and it may be well to communicate in broken doses, as we received them, the lessons on the subject which the 8th Army Corps learned in 1899 and the subsequent years so thoroughly that we could all pronounce with astonishing glibness, the most unpronounceable names imaginable.

When the great Wheaton-Lawton-MacArthur "Round-up" reached the mountains on the northeast of the great central plain, in the latter part of November 1899, Captain Joseph B. Batchelor, with one battalion of the 24th (negro) Infantry, and some scouts under Lieutenant Castner, a very intrepid and tireless officer, boldly cut loose from the column of which he was a part, and, pressing on over the Caranglan pass, overran the province of Nueva Vizcaya, which is part of the watershed of north central Luzon, proceeding from Bayombong, the capital of Nueva Vizcaya, down the valley of the Magat River, by the same route Messrs. Wilcox and Sargent of the navy had made their pleasant junket in the fall of 1898 as described in Chapter VI (*ante*). Following this route Captain Batchelor finally came into Isabela province, where the Magat empties into the Cagayan River, reaching Iligan, the capital of Isabela, ninety miles northeast of Bayombong, about December 8th. From Iligan Batchelor went on, promptly overcoming all resistance offered, down the great Cagayan valley, some 110 miles due north, to the sea at Aparri, the northernmost town of Luzon and of the archipelago, where he met two vessels of our navy, the *Newark* and the *Helena*, under Captain McCalla, and found, to his inexpressible (but partially and rather fervently expressed) chagrin, that the insurgents who had fled before him, and also the garrison at Aparri, had already surrendered to the navy. The territory thus covered by Batchelor's bold, brilliant, and memorable march over two hundred miles of hostile country from the mountains of central Luzon down the Cagayan valley to the northern end of the island, at Aparri,48 consisted of the three provinces of Cagayan, Isabela, and Nueva Vizcaya. The area and population of these three, according to the census tables of 1903, are as follows:

Province	*Area* (sq. m.)49	*Population*50
Cagayan	5,052	156,239
Isabela	5,018	76,431
Nueva Vizcaya	1,950	62,541
Total	12,020	295,211

The troops of Captain Batchelor's command were later on relieved by the 16th Infantry, commanded by Colonel Hood, under whom the above group of three provinces finally became the "Second District of the Department of Northern Luzon." As part of the plan to provide the reader with a fair general idea of

Luzon conveniently portable in memory, he is requested to note, at this point, that hereinafter the Cagayan valley, with its three provinces,51 will be alluded to as a district containing 12,000 square miles and 300,000 people. As was remarked concerning the original military district commanded by General Young, to wit, the First District, so of Colonel Hood's district, the Second—that is to say, as the Ilocano country may some day become the state of Ilocos, so, for like geographical and other governmental reasons, the three provinces of the Cagayan valley may some day become the state of Cagayan in the possible Philippine republic of the future.

Having now followed the "far-flung battle line" of the volunteers of '99 and their comrades in arms, the regulars, from Manila northward across the rice paddies of central Luzon and over the mountains to the northern extremity of the island, let us return to the central plain, for reasons which will be stated in so doing. Between the China Sea and the coast range which forms the western boundary of the central plain of Luzon, there is a long strip of territory—a west wing of the plain, as it were—about 125 miles long, with an average width of not more than twenty miles, stretching from Manila Bay to Lingayen Gulf. This is divided, for governmental purposes into two provinces, Bataan on the south, whose southern extremity lay on Admiral Dewey's port side as he entered Manila Bay the night before the naval battle of May 1, 1898, and Zambales on the north. The area and population of this territory are as follows:

Province	Area (sq. m.)	Population
Bataan	537	46,787
Zambales	2,125	104,549
	2,662	151,336

Also, between the Pacific Ocean and the coast range which forms the eastern boundary of the plain is a longer, narrower, and very sparsely populated strip, or east wing, divided also into two provinces, Principe on the north and Infanta on the south, each supposed to contain about fifteen thousand people. Principe and Infanta are wholly unimportant, except that, to avoid confusion, we must account for all the provinces visible on the maps of Luzon. These two provinces never gave any trouble and no one ever bothered about them.52 In the mountains of Zambales and Bataan, however, as in most of the other provinces of the archipelago, the struggle was long kept up, just as the Boers kept up their war for independence against Great Britain about the same time, by guerrilla warfare.

The central plain with five provinces has already been fully described. If to this plain you add its two wings, above mentioned, you have the nine provinces of central Luzon you see on the map. And if to them you add the six provinces of the Ilocos country and the three of the Cagayan valley, you have clearly before you the political make-up of northern Luzon—eighteen provinces in all. When central Luzon was arranged by districts under the military occupation, it was divided into three parts, the Third, Fourth, and Fifth districts of the Department of Northern Luzon, the Third District being under General Jacob H. Smith of Samar fame,53 the Fourth under General Funston, and the Fifth under General Grant. The Sixth and last district of northern Luzon was made up of the city of Manila and adjacent territory.

General Smith's district, the Third, comprised the provinces of

Province   Area (sq. m.) Population

Province	Area (sq. m.)	Population
Zambales	2,125	104,549
Pangasinan	1,193	397,902
Tarlac	1,205	135,107
	4,523	637,558

Pangasinan with its near 400,000 people is the largest, in point of population, of the twenty-five provinces of Luzon, and the third largest of the archipelago.

General Funston's district, the Fourth, comprised the provinces of

Province	Area (sq. m.)	Population
Nueva Ecija	2,169	134,147
Principe[54]	331	15,853
	2,500	150,000

General Grant's district, the Fifth, comprised the provinces of

Province	Area (sq. m.)	Population
Bataan	537	46,787
Pampanga	868	223,754
Bulacan	1,173	223,742
	2,578	494,283
	2,500	150,000
Totals, 4th and 5th Districts:	5,078	644,283

It will be seen from the foregoing that the Third District was nearly equal in area to the Fourth and Fifth added together, and that the same was true as to its population figure.

Just as the six provinces of the Ilocano country, first occupied by General Young and organized as "The First District of the Department of Northern Luzon," should some day evolve into a State of Ilocos, and the three provinces of the Cagayan valley, occupied by Colonel Hood as the Second District, into an ultimate State of Cagayan, so the provinces of General Smith's old district, the Third, should finally become a State of Pangasinan.[55] This Third District may be conveniently recollected as accounting for, roughly speaking, 4500 square miles of territory and 625,000 people. The total combined area of General Funston's old district, the Fourth,56 and the adjacent one, the Fifth, General Grant's district, is—roughly—5000 square miles, and its total population 650,000. No reason is apparent why these two districts, the Fourth and Fifth, should not ultimately evolve into a State of Pampanga. The five original military districts,57 which in 1900 constituted all of the Department of Northern Luzon except the city of Manila and vicinity, might make four ultimate states, with names, areas, and populations as follows:

State	Area (sq. m.)	Population
Ilocos	6,500	650,000
Cagayan	12,000	300,000
Pangasinan	4,500	625,000
Pampanga	5,000	650,000
	28,000	2,225,000

It may surprise the reader after all the blood and thunder to which his attention has hereinabove been subjected, apropos of northern Luzon and the winter of 1899–1900, to know that the insurgents were still bearding the lion in his den, *i. e.*, General Otis in Manila, by operating in very considerable force in the village-dotted country within cannon-shot of the road from Manila to Cavite in January, 1900. Nevertheless such was the case.

On the 4th of January, 1900, General J. C. Bates was assigned to the command of the First Division of the Eighth Army Corps, General Lawton's old division, and an active campaign was commenced in southern Luzon. The plan adopted was that General Wheaton with a strong force should engage and hold the enemy in the neighborhood of Cavite, while General Schwan, starting at the western horn of the half moon to which the great lake called Laguna de Bay has already been likened, should move rapidly down the west shore of the lake, and around its south shore to Santa Cruz near its eastern end, or horn, garrisoning the towns en route, as taken, instead of leaving them to be re-occupied by the insurgents. Santa Cruz is the same place where General Lawton had "touched second base," as it were, with a flying column in April, 1899.

This plan was duly carried out. The Schwan column started from San Pedro Macati, the initial rendezvous, a few miles out of Manila, on January 4, 1900, now garrisoning the towns en route, instead of leaving them to be fought over and captured again as heretofore. The first stiff fight we had in that campaign was at Biñan, on January 6, 1900, one of the places General Lawton's expedition had taken when he fought his way over the same country the year before. O. K. Davis and John T. McCutcheon, who were in that fight and campaign—in fact one of them had the ice-cold nerve to photograph the Biñan fight while it was going on, as I learned when we all went down to the creek near the town, after we took it, to freshen up—can testify that we did not then hear any nonsense about a "Tagal" insurrection, such as Secretary of War Root's *Report for 1899*, published shortly before, is full of, and that on the contrary the whole country was as much a unit against us and as loyal to the Aguinaldo government as northern Luzon had been. And inasmuch as I am doing some "testifying" along here myself, and assuming to brush aside without the slightest hesitation, as wholly erroneous, information conveyed to the American public at the time in the state papers of President McKinley and Secretary of War Root, it is only due the reader, whose attention is being seriously asked, that "the witness" should "qualify" as to the opportunities he may have had, if any, to know whereof he speaks, concerning the character of the opposition. To that end, the following document, which General Schwan was kind enough to send me afterwards, is submitted as sent:

EXTRACT COPY.

Headquarters   Detachment   Macabebe   Scouts.
The Adjutant General, Schwan's Expeditionary Brigade:

Sir: I have the honor to submit the following report of the operations of the Detachment of Macabebe Scouts, under my command, while forming a part of your Brigade.

The Detachment, consisting of five (5) officers and one hundred and forty (140) men, was divided into two companies, commanded by 1st Lt. J. Lee Hall, 33rd Inf., and 1st Lt. Blount, 29th Inf., left San Pedro Macati the afternoon of Jan. 4th, 1900 * * *.

I wish to invite your attention, especially, to the good work done in the fight at Biñan by Lieut. Blount, 29th Inf., who led the line by at least twenty-five yards * * *.

Very   Respectfully,
WM. C. GEIGER , 1st Lt. 14th Inf., Com'd'g Det.

I hereby certify that the above is a true copy of extracts from the report of the operations of the Detachment of Macabebe Scouts forming part of an Expeditionary Brigade under my command, in the months of January and February, 1900.

THEO.   SCHWAN ,
Brig.   General,   U.   S.   Vols.
Aug. 16, 1900.

The activities of Generals Bates and Wheaton, and the Schwan Expedition of January-February, 1900, extended the American occupation, so far as there were troops enough immediately available to go around, over the lake-shore portions and the principal towns of the two great provinces of southern Luzon bordering on the Laguna de Bay, viz., Cavite and Laguna; and over parts of the two adjacent provinces of Batangas and Tayabas.

Batangas bounds Cavite on the south, and is itself bounded on the south by the sea, where a fairly good port offered a fine gateway for smuggling arms into the interior from abroad. Tayabas province adjoins Laguna on the southeast. Cavite province has always been, since the opening of the Suez Canal, about 1869, and the agitations for political reform in Spain which culminated in the Spanish republic of 1873, quickened the thought of Spain's East Indies, the home of insurrection, the breeding place of political agitation. Aguinaldo himself was born within its limits in 1869. Laguna province comprehends most of the country lying between the southern and eastern lake-shore of the Laguna de Bay and the mountains which skirt that body of water in the blue distance, all parts of it being thus in easy and safe touch by water transportation by night with Cavite, the home and headquarters of insurgency.

Just as northern Luzon had been gradually organized into military districts as conquered, so was southern Luzon. The territory, over-run, as above described, by Generals Bates, Wheaton, and Schwan, was divided into two districts.58 Colonel Hare commanded the First District, Cavite province and vicinity. General Hall commanded the Second District, Batangas, Laguna, and Tayabas. The area and population of these four provinces, according to the Census of 1903, were as follows:

Province	Area (sq. m.)	Population
Cavite	619	134,779
Batangas	1,201	257,715
Laguna	629	148,606
Tayabas	5,993	153,065
	8,442	694,165

For convenience of subsequent allusion, this group of provinces may be treated as representing roughly 8500 square miles of territory and 700,000 people. These four provinces group themselves together naturally from a military standpoint. As physical force is the final basis of all government, these four provinces constitute a logical administrative governmental unit, as shown by the action of our military authorities in their extension of the American occupation. It would seem therefore that if there should ever be a Philippine republic, they would probably constitute one of its states—the State, let us say, of Cavite.

The rest of southern Luzon below that part above described consists of a peninsula which, owing to its odd formation, is easy to remember. The mainland of Luzon, that is to-say, that part of the island which our narrative has already covered, remotely suggests, in shape, the State of Illinois. At least it resembles Illinois more than it does any other State of our Union, in that its length runs north and south, and its average length and width are nearer that of Illinois than any other. At the southeast corner of this mainland, the observer of the map will see, jutting off to the southeast from the mainland, the peninsula in question. It is about a hundred and fifty miles long, with an average width of possibly thirty miles—a minimum width of, say, ten miles, and a maximum of fifty,—and is separated from Samar by the narrow, swift, and treacherous San Bernardino Strait, which connects the Pacific Ocean with the China Sea. This peninsula is frequently called "the Hemp Peninsula." The importance of controlling the hemp ports prompted General Otis to send General Bates with an expedition to those ports on February 15, 1900.59 This expedition did little more than occupy those ports. The great interior continued under insurgent control some time afterward. The report of the Secretary of War, Mr. Root, for 1900, goes on to describe an engagement, or two, sustained by the Bates Expedition shortly after it landed, and concludes, with a complacency almost Otis-like, by stating that shortly thereafter "the normal conditions of industry and trade relations with Manila were resumed by the inhabitants." Of course Mr. Root believed this, and so did Mr. McKinley. More the pity, as we shall later see. General Otis was now getting anxious to go home, and hastened to "occupy" and organize the rest of the archipelago, on paper, at least, the hemp peninsula becoming, on March 20, 1900, the Third District of the Department of Southern Luzon,

Brigadier-General James M. Bell commanding. The provinces comprised in this district, with their areas and populations as given by the Census of 1903, were as follows:

Province	Area (sq. m.)	Population
Camarines[60]	3,279	239,405
Albay	1,783	240,326
Sorsogon	755	120,495
	5,817	600,226

For convenience of subsequent allusion, these three provinces of the hemp peninsula which constituted the Third Military District of the Military Department of Southern Luzon in 1900, may be regarded as comprising, roughly, 6000 square miles of territory and 600,000 people. If the Philippine republic of the future which is the dream of the Filipino people, prove other than an idle dream, the hemp peninsula will probably some day constitute a state of that republic, an appropriate and probable name for which would be the State of Camarines.

The Fourth District of southern Luzon—there were but four—was occupied by the 29th U. S. Volunteer Infantry, commanded by Colonel E. E. Hardin, one of the best executive officers General Otis had in his whole command. The Fourth District comprised a lot of islands unnecessary to be considered at length in this bird's-eye view of the panorama, but necessary to be mentioned in outlining the military occupation. The 29th, like the other twenty-four volunteer regiments, settled down with equanimity to the business of policing a hostile country, sang with zest, like the rest of the twenty-five volunteer regiments, that old familiar song, "Damn, Damn, Damn the Filipino," etc., and waited with the uniquely admirable stoicism of the American soldier for the season of their home-going to roll round, which, under the Act of Congress,[61] would be the spring of the following year.

In volume i., part 5, *War Department Report*, 1899, at pages 5 *et seq.*, may be found a journal illustrating the nature of the "police" work done by the volunteers of 1899, in 1900, and at pages 5 *et seq.* of the same report for 1900 (volume i., part 4) may be found a similar diary carried up to June 30, 1901. Throughout the period covered by those reports, scarcely a day passed without what the military folk coolly call "contacts" with the enemy.

The Visayan Islands were in course of time duly organized, as Luzon had previously been, departmentally and by military districts. The Visayan Islands became the Department of Visayas, divided into districts commanded either by regimental commanders having a regiment or more with them, or by general officers. For a long time no attempt to make military occupation effective in these various islands, save in the coast towns, was attempted. However, the indicated disposition of troops completed, technically at least, the American occupation of the Visayan Islands.

Pursuant to the plan followed, as we have hitherto followed the army in our narrative, first throughout northern Luzon and later through southern Luzon, some data are now in order concerning the Visayan Islands.

As already made clear, there are but six of the Visayan Islands with which any one interested in the Philippines merely as a student of world politics or of history need bother. The area and population of these are as follows:62

Island	Area (sq. m.)	Population
Panay	4,611	743,646
Negros	4,881	460,776
Cebu	1,762	592,247
Leyte	2,722	356,641
Samar	5,031	222,090
Bohol	1,441	243,148

Whenever, if ever, an independent republic is established in the Philippines, the six islands above mentioned could and should constitute self-governing commonwealths similar to the several States of the American Union. The rest of the islands lying between Luzon and Mindanao could easily be disposed of governmentally by being attached to the jurisdiction of one of the said six islands.

Mindanao and the adjacent islets called Jolo were organized as the Department of Mindanao and Jolo, under General Kobbe, with the 31st Volunteer Infantry, Colonel Pettit's regiment, the 40th Volunteer Infantry, Colonel Godwin's regiment, and the 23rd Regular Infantry. Thus the archipelago was completely accounted for, for the time being, just as all the territory of the United States was long accounted for by our military authorities at home, with the Department of the East, headquarters Governor's Island, New York; the Department of the Lakes, headquarters Chicago; the Department of the Gulf, headquarters Atlanta, etc. In this state of the case, General Otis re-embraced his early pet delusion— if it was a delusion, which charity and the probabilities suggest it should be called—about the insurrection having gone to pieces; and decided to come home. Possibly, also, he was homesick. General Otis was a very positive character, a strong man. But even strong men get homesick after long exile. When you hear the call of the homeland after long residence "east of Suez," you must answer the call, duty not forbidding. General Otis had stood by his ink wells and the Administration with unswerving devotion for twenty months, and was entitled to come back home and tell the public all about the fighting in the Philippines, and how entirely over it was, and how wholly right Mr. McKinley was in his theory that the visible opposition to our rule and the seeming desire to be free and independent did not represent the wishes of the Filipino people at all, but only the "sinister ambitions of a few unscrupulous Tagalo leaders." Accordingly on May 5, 1900, he was relieved at his own request, and departed for the United States. He was succeeded in command by a very different type of man, Major-General Arthur MacArthur, upon whom now devolved the problem of holding down the situation and of actually getting it stably "well in hand" by June 30, 1901, the date of expiration of the term of enlistment of the twenty-five volunteer regiments organized under the Act of March 2, 1899.

---

[1] Strictly speaking, only twenty-three regiments were sent out from the United States. Under the Act of March 2, 1899, providing the volunteer army of 35,000 men for the Philippines, twenty-four regiments of infantry and one of cavalry were organized. The

infantry regiments were numbered Twenty-six to Forty-nine, both inclusive, the numbering taking up where the numbering of the regular infantry regiments then ended, with the Twenty-fifth. The cavalry regiment was called the Eleventh Cavalry, the regular cavalry regimental enumeration ending at that time with the Tenth. The Eleventh Cavalry and the Thirty-sixth Infantry were organized, officered, and largely recruited from men of the State Volunteers sent out in '98, who, in consideration of liberal inducements offered by the Government, consented to remain.

2 The population of the city of Manila according to the *Philippine Census of 1903*, vol. ii., p. 16; was 219,928. The three next largest towns are: Laoag, in the province of Ilocos Norte, about 270 miles north of Manila, near the northwest corner of Luzon, population 19,699; Iloilo, capital of the island of Panay and chief city and port of the Visayan Islands, some 300 miles south of Manila, population 19,054; and Cebu, capital and chief port of the island of Cebu, a day's voyage from Iloilo, population 18,330. See *Philippine Census of 1903*, vol. ii., p. 38.

3 115,026 is the exact figure. See *Philippine Census*, vol. i., p. 57.

4 The exact figure for Luzon is 40,969, and that for Mindanao, 36,292. *Ib.*

5 *Philippine Census*, vol. i., p. 56.

6 *Ibid.*

7 Table of Areas, *Census*, 1903, vol. i., p. 263.

8 Table of Populations, *ib.*, vol. ii., p. 126.

9 Total of these six in large type 20,418 square miles, say roughly 20,500.

10 Total of these last three in smaller type 9114 square miles.

11 There is a large sugar estate on Mindoro, supposed to contain over 60,000 acres or, say, ninety odd square miles, which in 1911 figured in a congressional investigation of certain charges against Professor Worcester, a member of the Philippine Commission, but this is wholly separate from the original problem of public order.

12 The exact figure is 36,292. *Philippine Census*, vol. i., p. 263.

13 499,634, *Philippine Census*, vol. ii., p. 126.

14 The semi-civilized Moros of Mindanao live mostly in the interior, and have a crude form of Mohammedanism. The civilized Christian Filipinos of Mindanao live mostly on the littoral.

15 This was said in no mere speech. Speeches are often misquoted. It was a letter signed by the foremost man of this age, Mr. Roosevelt, written September 15, 1900, accepting the nomination for the Vice-Presidency. (See *Proceedings of the Republican National Committee*, 1900, p. 86.) Yet it represented then one of the many current misapprehensions about the Filipinos which moved this great nation to destroy a young republic set up in a spirit of intelligent and generous emulation of our own.

16 One of the sultans, or head-men, was believed in 1899, to have tried on his return from a pilgrimage to Mecca made before we took the Philippines, by some dickering at Singapore or near there in the Straits Settlements, to sell out for a consideration to Great Britain, so as to be under the protection and in the pay of British North Borneo.

17 The fraction used is based on 500,000 (the population of Mindanao), being that fraction of 7,500,000 (which last is, roughly speaking, the total population of the archipelago). The census figures being 499,634 and 7,635,426 respectively, as heretofore stated.

18 7,635,426. *Philippine Census*, vol. ii., p. 15.

19 3,798,507. *Philippine Census*, vol. ii., p. 125.

20 223,506 is the total of the uncivilized tribes still extant in Luzon, *Philippine Census*, vol. ii., p. 125, but they live in the mountains and you might live in the Philippines a long lifetime without ever seeing a sample of them, unless you happen to be an energetic ethnologist fond of mountain climbing.

21 *Philippine Census of 1903*, vol. i., p. 57.

22 The area of Cuba is about 44,000 square miles.

23 Except Ohio, the States of Pennsylvania and Tennessee are nearer the size of Luzon than any others of the Union, the former containing about 45,000 square miles and the latter about 42,000.

24 This comparison does not pretend to be mathematically exact. New Jersey's area is nearer 8000 than 7000 square miles. For further illustration by comparison, it may be noted in this connection that the area of Massachusetts is over 8000 square miles (8315) and that of Vermont between 9000 and 10,000 (9565). As Costa Rica has only 368,780 inhabitants (*Statesman's Year Book*), the province of Pangasinan alone contains more people than the republic of Costa Rica. The average of intelligence and industry of the masses in both is doubtless about the same, with the probabilities in favor of Pangasinan.

25 Table of Areas, *Philippine Census of 1903*, vol. i., p. 58.

26 Table of Populations, *ib.*, vol. ii., p. 123.

27 In alluding, in complimentary terms, to this officer's gallant conduct on that occasion, Harper's *History of the War in the Philippines* spells the name "Hustin," as it had previously misspelled the name of the star actor among the younger officers who participated in the Zapote River fight "Kanly." "Such is fame." The gentleman's right name is Mustin. He is now a lieutenant-commander, well known in the navy to-day, as the inventor of the "Mustin gun-sight."

28 There is a notable unanimity, among the men in the army of about Major March's age and rank, in the opinion that he is a man of very extraordinary ability. This unanimity is so generous and genuine that I deem it a duty as well as a pleasure to emphasize it here.

29 See Otis's *Report* covering September 1, 1899, to May 5, 1900, *War Dept. Report*, 1900, vol. i., pt. 4, p. 261.

30 The 12th, part of the 25th, and the 32d Infantry being used to guard the railroad and for other purposes.

31 Calumpit will be remembered as the place where in the previous spring Colonel Funston and his Kansans performed the daring and successful manœuvre of crossing the Bagbag River under fire.

32 *Senate Document 331*, pt. 2 (1902), p. 1926.

33 This ratio is no jest. It is a statistical fact, figured out from one of the War Department Reports.

34 *War Department Report*, 1900, vol. i., pt. 5, p. 59.

35 *Report of Secretary of War*, 1899, p. 12.

36 Campaign Spanish for "look for." Generals Lawton and Young had cut loose from their base of supplies and their command was trusting for subsistence to living upon the country.

37 See translation of diary of Major Simeon Villa, *Senate Document 331*, pt. 3, 57th Cong., 1st Sess. (1902), p. 1988. It was in this Aringay fight that one of the narrowest escapes from death in battle ever officially authenticated occurred. Lieutenant Dennis P. Quinlan, now a captain of the 5th U. S. Cavalry, was struck just over the heart by an insurgent bullet (probably more or less spent) while crossing the river in the face of a hot fire, the bullet being deflected by a plug of tobacco carried in the breast pocket of the regulation campaign blue shirt he was wearing, which pocket, any one acquainted with that shirt will remember, is at the left breast just over the heart (*War Department Report*, 1900, vol. i., pt. 6, pp. 166, 279). He was knocked over, but soon recovered and went on. The flesh of the left breast over the heart was bruised black and blue. He was recommended for a medal of honor on account of the incident (*War Department Report*, 1900, vol. i., pt. 7, p. 136).

38 If these figures are not exact, they are approximately correct. We always called it three hundred miles from Manila to the northern end of Luzon via Vigan and the lighthouse at Cape Bojeador.

39 For instance, there was what used to be known to the 8th Corps as "Col. Jim Parker's night attack at Vigan," which occurred early in December, 1899, soon after that place was occupied, the insurgents coming into the town in large numbers, at night

under command of General Tiñio, through a tunnel so it was said, and being driven out only after desperate close quarters' fighting from about two o'clock in the morning until after broad daylight, leaving the streets and plaza of Vigan much cumbered with their dead. Again, later on, there was the sudden order, swiftly executed, in obedience to which Lieutenant Grayson V. Heidt with a part of a troop of the 3d Cavalry, rode from Laoag to Batac to the rescue of a besieged garrison at the latter place, arriving in time to prevent a small Custer massacre, the garrison having gotten short of ammunition, and having just managed to telegraph for reinforcements a few moments before the enemy cut the telegraph wire. Then, there was Lieutenant Hannay, of the 22d Infantry, who being at the front, received an order from General Lawton to come back to build a bridge. The order made him sick, the surgeon reported him sick, the messenger returned with that message, and then Hannay promptly got well, and stayed at the front. And so on, *ad infinitum*.

40 The Visayan Islands—the half-dozen islands between Luzon and Mindanao already mentioned, as the only ones worth mentioning for our purposes, together with the various smaller islands, islets, and rocks "visible at high water."

41 "During April, in the First District, comprising the provinces of Ilocos Norte, Ilocos Sur, Union, Abra, Lepanto, Benguet, and Bontoc, Brigadier General S. B. M. Young, commanding, the insurgents manifested considerable activity and endeavored to take the offensive against the scattered detachments in the district. The insurgents were in every instance defeated, and lost more than 500 men killed." *War Dept. Report* 1900, vol. i., pt. 5, p. 196.

42 The language quoted is that employed by Robert Collins, Associated Press Correspondent, in connection with the Round Robin incident of nine months previous, described in the concluding part of the chapter preceding this.

43 Hereinafter more fully set forth.

44 For the Table of Areas, see *Philippine Census*, vol. i., p. 58.

45 For the Table of Populations, see *Philippine Census*, vol. ii., p. 123.

46 Under the Spaniards, these were two provinces. They were combined by us.

47 A province in Latin countries corresponds more nearly to what we call a county than to anything else familiar to our system of political divisions.

48 For the details of this march, see *War Department Report*, 1900, vol. i., pt. 4, p. 309. Captain Batchelor had neither orders nor permission to do what he did. When he cut loose from the command he belonged to, he took very long chances on finding subsistence for his men in the unknown country he had set out to conquer, to say nothing of the highly probable chances of annihilation of his whole command. When an officer commanding troops does this in time of war, he does so at his peril, and signal success is his only salvation.

49 Area tables, *Philippine Census*, vol. i., p. 58.

50 Population tables, *Philippine Census*, vol. ii., p. 123.

51 Though Nueva Vizcaya is not *in* the Cagayan valley, but on a plateau of the great divide, still, its streams all flow into the Cagayan valley, and that term will be used in this book, as it is colloquially in the Philippines, to include not only the Cagayan valley proper, but also the adjoining tributary province of Nueva Vizcaya.

52 The only thing of interest to the American people that ever happened over there was the capture of Lieutenant Gilmore of the Navy, and his men, at Baler, on the Pacific coast, in Principe, a capture which, it will be recollected, was followed by long captivity, and ultimately terminated in rescue. The interested student will see these two provinces on the American maps of the islands, but they were each attached by the Taft government for administration purposes to another province, and do not appear in the American census list of provinces. Therefore, they cut no figure in the census totals, either of area or population.

53 The officer on whom public attention in the United States was later focussed by an alleged order, charged to have been issued by him in a campaign in Samar to "kill everything over ten years old." This alleged order was called by the American newspapers of the period "Jake Smith's Kill and Burn Order."

54The figures as to Principe are mere arbitrary guesses, the exact figures used being fixed on merely to get convenient round numbers, there being no statistics as to Principe.

55Of course the Filipinos should be consulted as to what provinces should constitute each state, but I am simply sketching a tentative governmental scheme based upon the way our army perfected its original grip on public order and the general administrative situation.

56All along here we, of course, deal in round numbers only.

57See *War Department Report*, 1900, vol. i., part 5, pp. 45 *et seq.* The city of Manila and vicinity constituted the Sixth District of the Department of Northern Luzon.

58*War Dept. Report*, 1900, vol. i., part 5, pp. 47–8.

59*War Dept. Report*, 1900, vol. i., part 1, p. 9.

60The Spanish word *camarin* means a warehouse. The province of Camarines was originally two provinces, and is still referred to as two, though governmentally but one.

61Of March 2, 1899. Under it the term of enlistment of the volunteers was to expire June 30, 1901.

62Table of Areas, *Philippine Census of 1903*, vol. i., p. 263. Table of Population, *ib.*, vol. ii., pp. 123 *et seq.*

Chapter XIII. MacArthur and the War

Damn, damn, damn the Filipino,
Pock-marked khakiac ladrone;[1]
Underneath the starry flag
Civilize him with a Krag,
And return us to our own beloved home.

Army Song of the Philippines under MacArthur.[2]

Some one has said, "Let me write the songs of a people and I care not who makes their laws." Give me the campaign songs of a war, and I will so write the history of that war that he who runs may read, and, reading, *know* the truth. The volunteers of 1899 had, most of them, been in the Spanish War of '98. That struggle had been so brief that, to borrow a phrase of the principal beneficiary of it, Colonel Roosevelt, there had not been "war enough to go 'round." The Philippine insurrection had already broken out when the Spanish War volunteers returned from Cuba in the first half of 1899. Few of them knew exactly where the Philippines were on the map. They simply knew that we had bought the islands, that disturbances of public order were in progress there, and that the Government desired to suppress them. The President had called for volunteers. That was enough. When they reached the islands, instead of finding a lot of outlaws, brigands, etc., such as that pestiferous, ill-conditioned outfit of horse-thieves and cane-field burning patriots we volunteers of '98 had to comb out of the eastern end of Cuba under General Wood in the winter of 1898–9, they found Manila, on their arrival, practically almost a besieged city. They knew that the erroneous impression they had brought with them was the result of misrepresentation. Who was responsible for that misrepresentation they did not attempt to analyze. They simply set to work with American energy to put down the insurrection. Nobody questioned the unanimity of the opposition. There it was, a *fact*—denied at home, but a fact. In the course of the fight against the organized insurgent army they lost a great many of their comrades, and in that way the unanimity of the resistance was quite forcibly impressed upon them. By kindred psychologic processes equally free from mystery, their determination to overcome the resistance early became very set—a state of mind which boded no good to the Filipinos. The army song given at the beginning of Chapter XI (*ante*), in which General Otis is made to sing, after the fashion of some of the characters in *Pinafore*, that pensive query to himself

Am I the boss, or am I a tool?

the first stanza of which closes

Now I'd like to know who's the boss of the show,
Is it me or Emilio Aguinaldo?

was a point of departure, in the matter of information, which served to acquaint them with all that had gone before. They resented the loss of prestige to American arms and desired to restore that prestige. While engaged in so doing, they became aware, during the Presidential year 1900, that the campaign of that year in the United States was based largely upon the pretence that the majority of the Filipinos welcomed our rule. Naturally, their experience led them to a very general and very cordial detestation of this pretence. For one thing, it was an unfair belittling of the actual military service they were rendering. People hate a lie whether they are able to trace its devious windings to its source or sources, or to analyze all its causes, or calculate all its possible effects, or not. The real rock-bottom falsehood, not as fully understood then as it became later, consisted in the impression sought to be produced at home, in order to get votes, that the great body of the Filipino people were not really in sympathy with their country's struggle for freedom, and would be really glad tamely to accept the alien domination so benevolently offered by a superior people, but were being coerced into fighting through intimidation by a few selfish leaders acting for their own selfish ends. While our fighting generals in the field,—General MacArthur, for instance, whose interview with a newspaper man just after the fall of Malolos, in March, 1899, subsequently verified by him before the Senate Committee of 1902, has already been noticed—at first believed that it was only a faction that we had to contend with, they soon discovered that the whole people were loyal to Aguinaldo and the cause he represented. But, while the point as to how unanimous the resistance was remained a disputed matter for some little time among those of our people who did not have to "go up against it," the most curious fact of that whole historic situation, to my mind, is the absolute identity of the disputed suggestion with that which had previously been used in like cases in all ages by the powerful against people struggling to be free, and the cotemporaneous absence of any notation of the coincidence by any conspicuous spectator of the drama, to say nothing of us smaller fry who bore the brunt of the war or any portion of it.

Those men of '99 in the Philippines realized in 1900, vaguely it may be, but actually, that they were waging a war of conquest after the manner of the British as sung by Kipling, but under the hypocritical pretence that they were doing missionary work to improve the Filipino. They did not know whether the Filipinos could or could not run a decent government if permitted. It was too early to form any judgment. And even then there was no unanimous feeling that they could not. Brigadier-General Charles King, the famous novelist, who was in the fighting out there during the first half of 1899, was quoted in the *Catholic Citizen*, of Milwaukee, Wisconsin, in June, 1899, as having said in an interview given at Milwaukee:

There is no reason in the world why the people should not have the self-government which they so passionately desire, so far as their ability to carry it on goes.

The real reason why the war was being waged was stated with the honesty which heated public discussion always brings forth, by Hon. Charles Denby, a member of the Schurman Commission of 1899, in an article which appeared in the *Forum* for February, 1899, entitled "Why the Treaty Should be Ratified:"3

The cold, hard, practical question alone remains: "Will the possession of the islands benefit us as a nation?" If it will not, set them free to-morrow.

But in the same magazine, the *Forum*, for June, 1900, in other words to the very same audience, in an article whose title is a protest, "Do we Owe the Filipinos Independence?" we find this same distinguished diplomat sagaciously deferring to that not inconsiderable element of the American public which is opposed to wars for conquest, with the rank hypocrisy which must ever characterize a republic warring for gain against the ideals that made it great, thus:

A little time ought to be conceded to the Administration to ascertain what the wish of the people [meaning the people of the Philippine Islands] really is;4

adding some of the stale but ever-welcome salve originally invented by General Otis for use by Mr. McKinley on the public conscience of America, about the war having been "fomented by professional politicians," and not having the moral support of the whole people. "A majority of the Filipinos are friendly to us," he says. Even as early as January 4, 1900, in the New York *Independent*, we find Mr. Denby abandoning all his previous honesty of 1899 about "the cold, hard, practical question," and rubbing his hands with invisible soap to the tune of the following hypocrisy:

Let us find out how many of the people want independence, and how many are willing to remain loyal to our government. It is believed a large majority [etc.].5

The same article even assumed an air of injured innocence and urged that as soon as the insurgent army laid down its arms6 "the intentions of our government will be made known by Congress." That was just thirteen years ago, and "the intentions of our government" have never yet been "made known by Congress," despite the fact that the omission has all these years been like a buzzing insect, lighting intermittently on the sores of race prejudice and political difference in the Philippines, to say nothing of the circumstance that such omission leaves everybody guessing, including ourselves. The omission has been due to the fact that both the McKinley Administration which committed the original blunder of taking the islands, and the succeeding Administrations which have been the legatees of that blunder, have always needed in their Philippine business the support both of those whose votes are caught by the Denby honesty of 1899 and those whose votes are caught by the Denby hypocrisy of 1900.

War is a great silencer of hypocrisy. In the presence of real sorrow and genuine anger, it slinks away and is seen no more until more piping times. The lists of casualties had been duly bulletined to the United States from time to time between February, 1899, and June, 1900, so that by the date last named it had become "good politics" to throw off the mask. Hence, at the Republican National Convention held in Philadelphia June 19–21, 1900, we find that astute past-master of the science of government by parties, Senator Lodge, boldly throwing off the mask thus:

We make no hypocritical pretense of being interested in the Philippines solely on account of others. We believe in trade expansion.

Now the words of a United States Senator are much listened to by an army in the field. When a war breaks out, it is usually your Senator who gets your commission for you originally, and has you promoted and made captain, colonel, or general, as the case may be, if you do anything to deserve it, or lifted from the ranks to a commission, if you do anything to deserve it, or sees that something fitting is done if you die in any specially decent way. An army in the field thinks a United States Senator is about one of the biggest institutions going—which, seriously, is not far from the truth, with all due respect to the blasé pessimists of the press gallery. Consider then how wholly uninspiring, as a sentiment to die by and kill by, the above senatorial utterance was to the men in the field in the Philippines, who did not even then believe the islands would pay. The "cold, hard, practical" fact was, if the Senator was to be believed, that we were fighting for what is generically called "Wall Street;" that it was primarily a Wall Street war: an expedition fitted out to kill enough Filipinos to make the survivors good future customers—"Ultimate Consumers"—and only incidentally a war to make people follow your way of being happy in lieu of their own. Yet we had most of us, but shortly previously to that, gone trooping headlong to Cuba, in the wake of the most inspiring single personality of this age—Senator Lodge's friend, Colonel Roosevelt—some of our American thoraxes inflated with sentiments thus nobly expressed by the same distinguished Senator in his speech on the resolution which declared war against Spain:

"We are there" (meaning in the then Cuban situation), Senator Lodge had said in the Senate, in the matchless outburst of eloquence with which he set the keynote to the war with Spain—

We are there because we represent the spirit of liberty and the new time. * * * We have grasped no man's territory, we have taken no man's property, we have invaded no man's rights. *We do not ask their lands.*7

What difference, however, did it make to men under military orders, and that far away from home, where American public opinion could not and never can affect any given situation in time to help it, whether they were serving God or the devil? Everything disappeared but the primal fighting instinct. So the slaughter proceeded right merrily, at a ratio of about sixteen to one, and many a Filipino died with the word "Independence" on his lips,8 while many an obscure American life went out, fighting under the Denby-Lodge dollar-mark flag of pseudo-trade expansion. Can you imagine a more thankless job? Do you wonder at the song that heads the chapter? Still, war is war, once you are in it. All through 1900 the volunteers of 1899 kept on, cheerfully doing their country's work, not in the least hampered by whys or wherefores, so far as the quality of their work went. They knew that the Filipinos were not heathen, and they were not perfectly clear that they themselves were doing the Lord's work, unless "putting the fear of God into the heart of the *insurrecto*"—one of their campaign expressions—was the Lord's work. However, if any of them gave any special thought to the ethics of the situation, this did not in the least affect their efficiency in action, nor their determination to lick the Filipino into submission. When the brief organized resistance of the insurgent armies in the field (February to November, 1899) underwent its transition to the far more formidable guerrilla tactics, they realized that they were "up against" a long and tedious task, in which would be no special glamour, as there had been in Cuba, because the war was not much more popular at home than it was with them. The rank net hypocrisy of the whole situation, as they viewed it, is expressed in the song which heads this chapter. It is an answer to the Taft nonsense of 1900 about "the people long for peace and are willing to accept government under United States."9 That is why the Caribao Society do not sing it to Mr. Taft when he attends their annual banquet, notwithstanding that it is the star song of their repertoire.10This statement of Judge Taft's, as well as other like statements of his which followed it during the presidential campaign of 1900, would have been perfectly harmless in home politics. It was made in the same spirit of optimism in which a Taft man will tell you to-day, "The people are willing to see the Taft Administration endorsed." But at that time in the Philippines there was no possible way to prove or disprove the statement to the satisfaction of anybody at home—or elsewhere, for that matter. And, under the circumstances, it was at once a libel on Filipino patriotism and an ungracious belittling of the work of the American army. It was a libel on Filipino patriotism because it denied the loyal (even if ill-advised) unanimity of the Filipino people in their struggle for independence, and was a statement made recklessly, without knowledge, in aid of a presidential candidate in the United States. That it was highly inaccurate was well known to some 70,000 American soldiers then in the field, who were daily getting *insurrecto* lead pumped into them, and also well known to their gallant commander, General MacArthur, who told Judge Taft just that thing. That it was an ungracious belittling of the work of the army is certainly obvious enough, and it was so considered by the army, and its commanding general aforesaid, who practically told Judge Taft just that thing. But Mr. Root, then Secretary of War, was as much interested in Mr. McKinley's re-election as Judge Taft was. So he spread the Taft cablegrams broadcast throughout the United States during the presidential campaign, and pigeonholed the MacArthur messages and reports on the situation in the dusty and innocuous desuetude of the War Department archives. Four years later at the Republican National Convention of 1904, Mr. Root told the naked truth, thus:

When the last national convention met, over 70,000 soldiers from more than 500 stations held a still vigorous enemy in check.11

The foregoing is all a record made and unalterable. It is a fair sample of the initial stages of one more of the experiments in colonization by a republic which are scattered through history and teach but one lesson. All the gentlemen concerned were personally men of high type. But look at the net result of their work. The impression it produced in the United States, at a tremendously critical period in the country's history, when the men at the helm of state were bending every energy to railroad the republic into a career of overseas conquest, and using the army for that purpose, can be called by a short and ugly word. The splendor of Mr. Root's intellect is positively alluring, but he is a dangerous man to republican institutions. Mr. Taft's part in that conspiracy for the suppression of the facts of the Philippine situation in 1900 was really due to kindliness of heart, regret at the war, and earnest hope that it would soon end. Mr. Denby's part was that of the out-and-out imperialist who has frank doubts in his own mind as to whether it is axiomatic, after all, that the form of government bequeathed us by our fathers is the best form of government yet devised. But the conspiracy was really a sin against the progress of the world, because it deceived the American people as to the genuineness and unanimity of the desire of the Filipino people to imitate the example set by us in 1776, which has since served as a beacon-light of hope to so many people in so many lands in their several struggles to be free.

By the spring of 1900, when General MacArthur relieved General Otis, the volunteers of 1899 had gotten thoroughly warmed up to the work of showing the Filipinos who was in fact "the boss of the show," and by June, 1900, when Judge Taft arrived, they had gotten still warmer12; and in General Otis's successor they had a commander who understood his men thoroughly, and was determined to carry out honestly, with firmness, and without playing, as his predecessor had done, the rôle of political henchman, the purpose for which the army he commanded had been sent to the Islands to accomplish. In this state of the case, the Taft Commission came out.

This would seem rather an odd point at which to terminate a chapter on "MacArthur and the War," seeing that General MacArthur continued to command the American forces in the Philippines and to direct their strenuous field operations until July, 1901, more than a year later, when he was relieved by General Chaffee, on whom thereafter devolved the subsequent conduct of the war. But we must follow the inexorable thread of chronological order, and so yield the centre of the stage from June, 1900, on, to Mr.

Taft, else the resultant net confusion of ideas about the American occupation of the Philippines might remain as great as that which this narrative is an attempt in some degree to correct.

All through the official correspondence of 1899 and 1900 between the Adjutant-General of the Army, General Corbin, and General Otis at Manila, one sees Mr. McKinley's sensitiveness to public opinion. "In view of the impatience of the people" you will do thus and so, is a typical sample of this feature of that correspondence.13 Troubled, possibly, with misgivings, as to whether, after all, in view of the vigorous and undeniably obstinate struggle for independence the Filipinos were putting up, it would not have been wiser to have done with them as we had done in the case of Cuba, and troubled, beyond the peradventure of a doubt, about the effect of the possible Philippine situation on the fortunes of his party and himself in the approaching campaign for the presidency, Mr. McKinley sent Mr. Taft out, in the spring preceding the election of 1900, to help General MacArthur run the war. We must now, therefore, turn our attention to Mr. Taft, not forgetting General MacArthur in so doing.

1Copper-colored thief.

2Sung to the tune of "Tramp, tramp, tramp, the boys are marching."

3See *Forum*, vol. xxvi., p. 647.

4See *Forum*, vol. xxix., p. 403.

5These quotations are not taken from a scrap-book. Many readers forget that the bound volumes of all the great magazines are permanently available in the great libraries of the country.

6Hostilities had not yet broken out when the article now being considered appeared on January 4th, and did not break out until thirty days later, to wit, on February 4th.

7*Congressional Record*, April 13, 1898, p. 3701.

8In the early days of the fighting they used to hurrah a good deal, and shout " Viva la Independencia " (Live Independence).

9See Judge Taft's cablegram to Secretary of War Root of August 21, 1900, *War Department Report*, vol. i., pt. 1, p. 80.

10The Caribao Society is an organization composed mainly of officers of the regular army, but to which any one who served as an officer, volunteer or regular, in the Philippine Insurrection, is eligible. Their principal function, like that of the famous Gridiron Club, is to give an annual dinner.

11*Addresses at Republican National Convention* (1904), p. 62, published by Isaac H. Blanchard & Co., New York, 1904. The Republican National Convention of 1900 met June 19th, just sixteen days after the Taft Commission arrived at Manila.

12General MacArthur relieved General Otis May 5, 1900, and the Taft Commission arrived at Manila June 3d thereafter.

13*Correspondence Relating to the War with Spain*, vol. ii., p. 1051.

Chapter XIV. The Taft Commission

The papers 'id it 'andsome,
But you bet the army knows.

Kipling, *Ballad of the Boer War.*

The essentials of the situation which confronted the Taft Commission on its arrival in the islands in June, 1900, and the mental attitude in which they approached that situation, may now be briefly summarized, with entire confidence that such summary will commend itself as fairly accurate to the impartial judgment both of the historian of the future and of any candid contemporary mind.

It is not necessary to "vex the dull ear" of a mighty people much engrossed with their own affairs, by repetition of any further details concerning the original *de facto* alliance between Admiral Dewey and Aguinaldo. Suffice it to remind a people whose saving grace is a love of fair play, that, after the battle of Manila Bay, when Admiral Dewey brought Aguinaldo down from Hong Kong to Cavite, both the Admiral and his Filipino allies were keenly cognizant of the national purpose set forth in the declaration of war against Spain, and that the Filipinos could not have been expected to make any substantial distinction between the casual remarks of a victorious admiral on the quarter-deck of his flagship in May, remarks concurrent and consistent with actual treatment of the Filipinos as allies, and the imperious commands of a general ashore in December thereafter, acting under specific orders pursuant to the Treaty of Paris. The one great fact of the situation, "as huge as high Olympus," they *did* grasp, *viz.*, that both were representatives of America on the ground at the time of their respective utterances, and that one in December in effect repudiated without a word of explanation what the other had done from May to August. They had helped us to take the city of Manila in August, and, to use the current phrase of the passing hour, coined in this period of awakening of the national conscience to a proper attitude toward double-dealing in general, they felt that they had been "given the double cross." In other words they believed that the American Government had been guilty of a duplicity rankly Machiavellian. And that was the cause of the war.

We have seen in the chapters on "The Benevolent Assimilation Proclamation" and "The Iloilo Fiasco" that, in the Philippines at any rate, no matter how mellifluously pacific it may have sounded at home—no matter how soothing to the troubled doubts of the national conscience—the Benevolent Assimilation Proclamation of December 21, 1898, was recognized both by the Eighth Army Corps and by Aguinaldo's people as a call to arms—a signal to the former to get ready for the work of "civilizing with a Krag"; a signal to the latter to gird up their loins for the fight to the death for government of their people, by their people, for their people; and that the yearning benevolence of said proclamation was calculated strikingly to remind the Filipinos of Spain's previous traditional yearnings for the welfare of Cuba, indignantly cut short by us—yearnings "to spare the great island from the danger of premature independence"[1] which that decadent monarchy could not even help repeating in the swan-song wherein she sued to President McKinley for peace. We did not realize the absoluteness of the analogy then. It is all clear enough now. We can now understand how and why Mr. McKinley's programme of Annexation and Benevolent Assimilation of 1898–9, blindly earnest as was his belief that it would make the Filipino people at once cheerfully forego the "legitimate aspirations" to which we ourselves had originally given a momentum so generous that nothing but bullets could then possibly have stopped it, was in fact received by them in a manner compared with which Canada's response in 1911 to Speaker Champ Clark's equally benevolent suggestion of United States willingness to accord to Canada *also*, gradual Benevolent Assimilation and Ultimate Annexation, was one great sisterly sob of sheer joy as at the finding of a long lost brother. From the arrival of the American troops on June 30, 1898, until the outbreak of February 4, 1899, there had been two armies camped not far from each other, one born of the idea of independence and bent upon it, the other at first groping in the dark without instructions, and finally instructed to deny independence. There was never any faltering or evasion on the part of Aguinaldo and his people. They knew what they wanted and said so on all occasions. At all times and in all places they made it clear, by proclamation, by letter, by conversation, and otherwise, that independence was the one thing to which, whether they were fit for it or not, they had pledged "their lives, their fortunes, and their sacred honor."

We have seen how easily the war itself could have been averted by the Bacon Resolution of January, 1899, or some similar resolution frankly declaring the purpose of our government; how here was Senator Bacon at this end of the line pleading with his colleagues to be frank, and to make a declaration in keeping with "the high purpose" for which we had gone to war with Spain, instead of holding on to the Philippines on the idea that they might prove a second Klondike, while justifying such retention by arbitrarily assuming, without any knowledge whatever on the subject, that the Filipinos were incapable of self-government; how, there, at the other end of the line, at Manila, Aguinaldo's Commissioners, familiar with our Constitution and the history and traditions of our government, were making, substantially, though in more diplomatic language, precisely the same plea, and imploring General Otis's Commissioners to give them some assurance which would quiet the apprehensions of their people, and calm the fear that the original assurance, "We are going to lick the Spaniards and set you free," was now about to be ignored because the islands might be profitable to the United States.

We have seen the war itself, as far as it had progressed by June, 1900, one of the bitterest wars in history, punctuated by frequent barbarities avenged in kind, and how, if the Taft Commission had not come out with McKinley spectacles on, they would have seen the picture of a bleeding, prostrate, and deeply hostile people, still bent on fighting to the last ditch, not only animated by a feeling against annexation by us similar to that the Canadians would have to-day if we should also try the Benevolent Assimilation game on them—first with proclamations breathing benevolence and then with cannon belching grape-shot—but further animated by the instinctive as well as inherited knowledge common to all colored peoples, whether red, yellow brown, or black, that wheresoever white men and colored live in the same country together, *there the white man will rule*. Understand, this was before Judge Taft had had a chance to assure them, with the kindly Taft smile and the hearty Taft hand-shake, that their benevolent new masters were going to reverse the verdict of the ages, and treat them with a fraternal love wholly free from race prejudice. If Judge Taft could only have arrived in January, 1899, and told them that the Bacon Resolution really represented the spirit of the attitude of the American people toward them, then the finely commanding bearing of Mr. Taft, and the noble genuineness of his desire to see peace on earth and goodwill toward men, might even have prevented the war. But this is merely what *might* have been. What actually *was*, when he *did* arrive, in June, 1900, was that the milk of human kindness had long since been spilled, and his task was to gather it up and put it back in the pail. When I, a Southern man who have taken part in the only two wars this nation has had in my lifetime, reflect that in this year of grace, 1912, Mr. Underwood's otherwise matchless availability as the candidate of his party for President is questioned on the idea that it might be a tactical blunder, because of "the late war," which broke out before either Mr. Underwood or myself were born, I cannot share the Taft optimism as to the rapidity with which the scars of "the late war" in the Philippines will heal, and as to the affectionate gratitude toward the United States with which the McKinley-Taft programme of Benevolent Assimilation will presently be regarded by the people of the Philippine Islands.

We have seen the futile efforts of the Schurman Commission of 1899, sent out that spring, in deference to American public opinion, with definite instructions to try and patch up a peace, by talking to the leading spirits of a war for independence, *now in full swing*, about the desirability of benevolent leading-strings. "They [meaning the Schurman Commission] had come," says Mr. McKinley, in his annual message to Congress of December 5, 1899,[2] "with the hope of co-operating with Admiral Dewey and General Otis in establishing peace and order." They came, they saw, they went, recognizing the futility of the errand on which they had been sent. And now came the Taft Commission a year later, on precisely the same errand, after the Filipinos had sunk all their original petty differences and jealousies in a very reasonable instinctive common fear of economic exploitation, and a very unreasonable but, to them, very real common fear of race elimination, amounting to terror, and been welded into absolute oneness—if that were somewhat lacking before—in the fierce crucible of sixteen months of bloody fighting against a foreign foe for the independence of their common country. President McKinley's message to Congress of December, 1899, is full of the old insufferable drivel, so grossly, though unwittingly, ungenerous to our army then in the field in the Philippines, about the triviality of the resistance we were "up against." The message in one place blandly speaks of "the peaceable and loyal majority who ask nothing better than to accept our authority," in another of "the sinister ambitions of a few selfish Filipinos." Thus was outlined, in the message announcing the purpose to send out the Taft Commission, the view that no real fundamental resistance existed in the islands. Basing contemplated action on this sort of stuff, the presidential message outlines the presidential purpose as follows—this in December, 1899, mind you:

There is no reason why steps should not be taken from time to time to inaugurate governments *essentially popular in their form* as fast as territory is held and controlled by our troops.

Then follows the genesis of the idea which resulted in the Taft Commission:

To this end I am considering the advisability of the return [to the islands] of the commission [the Schurman Commission] or such of the members thereof as can be secured.

In Cuba, General Wood began the work of reconstruction at Havana with a central government and the best men he could get hold of, and acted through them, letting his plans and purposes percolate *downward* to the masses of the people. Not so in the Philippines. Reconstruction there was to begin by establishing municipal governments, to be later followed by provincial governments, and finally by a central one; in other words, by placing the waters of self-government at the bottom of the social fabric among the most ignorant people, and letting them percolate *up*, according to some mysterious law of gravitation apparently deemed applicable to political physics. Of course, these poor people simply always took their cue from their leaders, knowing nothing themselves that could affect the success of this project except that we were their enemies and that they might get knocked in the head if they did not play the game. "I have believed," says Mr. McKinley, in his message to Congress of December, 1899, "that reconstruction should not begin by the establishment of one central civil government for all the islands, with its seat at Manila, but rather that the work should be commenced by *building up from the bottom*." Whereat, the young giant America bowed, in puzzled hope, and worldly-wise old Europe smiled, in silent but amused contempt.

If at the time he formulated this scheme for their government Mr. McKinley had known anything about the Philippines, or the Filipinos, he would have known that what he so suavely called "building from the bottom" was like trying to make water run up hill, *i.e.*, like starting out to have ideas percolate upward, so that through "the masses" the more intelligent people might be redeemed. The "nigger in the woodpile" lay in the words "essentially popular in form." Of course no government by us "essentially popular" was possible at the time. But a government "popular in form" would sound well to the American people, and, if they could be kept quiet until after the presidential election of 1900, maybe the supposed misunderstanding on the part of the Filipinos of the benevolence of our intentions might be corrected by kindness. Accordingly, the following spring, cotemporaneously with General Otis's final departure from Manila to the United States, in which free country he might say the war was over as much as he pleased without being molested with round-robins by Bob Collins, O. K. Davis, John McCutcheon, and the rest of those banes of his insular career, who so pestiferously insisted that the American public ought to know the facts, the Taft Commission was sent out, to "aid" General MacArthur, as the Schurman Commission had "aided" General Otis.3

It would seem fairly beyond any reasonable doubt that the official information the Taft Commission were given by President McKinley concerning the state of public order they would find in the islands on arrival was in keeping with the information solemnly imparted to Congress by him in December thereafter, which was as follows: "By the spring of this year (1900) the effective opposition of *the dissatisfied Tagals*"—always the same minimization of the task of the army as a sop to the American conscience—"was virtually ended." Then follows a glowing picture of how the Filipinos are going to love us after we rescue them from the hated Tagal, but with this circumspect reservation: "He would be rash who, with the teachings of contemporary history, would fix a limit" as to how long it will take to produce such a state of affairs. Looking at that mighty panorama of events from the dispassionate standpoint now possible, it seems to me that Mr. McKinley's whole Philippine policy of 1899–1900 was animated by the belief that the more the Philippine situation should resemble the really identical Cuban one in the estimation of the American people, the more likely his Philippine policy was to be repudiated at the polls in the fall of 1900. The Taft Commission left Washington for Manila in the spring of 1900, after their final conference with the President who had appointed them and was a candidate for re-election in the coming fall, as completely committed as circumstances can commit any man or set of men to the programme of occupation which was to follow the subjugation of the inhabitants, and to the proposition of present incapacity for self-government, its corner-stone; to say nothing of the embarrassment felt at Washington by reason of having stumbled into a bloody war with people whom we honestly wanted to help, had never seen, and had nothing but the kindliest feelings for. While the serene and capacious intellect of William H. Taft was still pursuing the even tenor of its way in the halls of justice (as United States Circuit Judge for the 8th Circuit), the Philippine programme was formulated at Washington. Judge Taft went to Manila to make the best of a situation which he had not created, to write the lines of the *Deus ex machina* for a Tragedy of Errors up to that point composed wholly by others. It has been frequently stated and generally believed that when Mr. McKinley sent for him and proposed the Philippine mission, Judge Taft replied, substantially: "Mr. President, I am not the man for the place. *I don't want the Philippines.*" To which Mr. McKinley is supposed to have replied: "You *are* the man for the place, Judge. I had rather *have* a man out there who doesn't want them." The point of the original story lay in what Mr. McKinley said. The point of the repetition of it here lies in what Mr. Taft said, the inference therefrom being that he did not think the true interests of his country "wanted" them, and that had he been called into President McKinley's council sooner he would have so advised; an inference warranted by his subsequent admission that "we blundered into colonization."4

It is utterly fatal to clear thinking on this great subject, which concerns the liberties of a whole people, to treat Judge Taft's reports as Commissioner to, and later Governor of, the Philippines as in the nature of a judicial decision on the capacity of the Filipinos for self-government. When he consented to go out there, he went, not to review the findings of the Paris Peace Commission, but at the urgent solicitation of an Administration whose fortunes were irrevocably committed to those findings, including the express finding that they were unfit for self-government, and the implied one that we must remain to improve the condition of the inhabitants. He was thus not a judge come out to decide on the fitness of the people for self-government, but an advocate to make the best possible case for their unfitness, and its corollary, the necessity to remain indefinitely, just as England has remained in Egypt. The war itself convinced the whole army of the United States that Aguinaldo would have been the "Boss of the Show" had Dewey sailed away from Manila after sinking the Spanish fleet. The war satisfied us all that Aguinaldo would have been a small edition of Porfirio Diaz, and that the Filipino republic-that-might-have-been would have been, very decidedly, "a going concern," although Aguinaldo probably would have been able to say with a degree of accuracy, as Diaz might have said in Mexico for so many years, "The Republic? *I* am the Republic." The war demonstrated to the army, to a Q. E. D., that the Filipinos are "capable of self-government," unless the kind which happens to suit the genius of the American people is the only kind of government on earth that is respectable, and the one panacea for all the ills of government among men without regard to their temperament or historical antecedents. The educated patriotic Filipinos can control the masses of the people in their several districts as completely as a captain ever controlled a company.5 While the municipal officials of the McKinley-Taft municipal kindergarten were stumbling along with the strange new town government system imported from America, and atoning to their benignant masters for mistakes by writing them letters about how benignant they—the teachers—were, they—the pupils,—according to the contemporaneous description by the commanding general of the United States forces in the islands, were running a superbly efficient municipal system throughout the whole archipelago, "simultaneously and in the same sphere as the American governments, and in many instances through the same personnel,"6 in aid of the insurrection. General MacArthur humorously adds that the town officials "acted openly in behalf of the Americans and secretly in behalf of the insurgents, and, *with considerable apparent solicitude for the interest of both*." In short, the war at once demonstrated their "capacity for self-government" and made granting it to them for the time being unthinkable. For the war was fought not on the issue of the *capacity*, but on the issue of the *granting*. The Treaty of Paris settled the "capacity" part. The army in 1898, 1899, and 1900 can hardly be said to have had any much more decided opinion on the *capacity* branch of the subject, than Perry did about the Japanese in 1854. The Paris Peace Commission having solemnly decided the "capacity part" adversely to the Filipinos and the war having followed, thereafter Mr. Taft went out to make out the best case possible in support of the action of the Peace Commission and, *ex vi termini*, in support of everything made necessary by the fact of the purchase. Unless some one goes out to present to the American people the other side of the case, they will never arrive at a just verdict.

Committed, *a priori*, to the task of squaring the McKinley Administration with its course as to Cuba, the only course possible for the Taft Commission was to set up a benevolent government based upon the incompetency of the governed, which, being a standing affront to the intelligence of the people, earns their hatred, however it may crave their love. By the very bitterness of the opposition it permits yet disregards, it binds itself ever more irrevocably to remain a benevolent engenderer of malevolence. Government and governed thus get wider apart as the years go by, and, the *raison d'être* of the former being the mental deficiencies of the latter, it must, in self-defence, assert those deficiencies the more offensively, the more vehemently they are denied. What hope therefore can there be that the light that shone upon Saul on the road to Damascus will ever break upon the President? What hope that he will ever re-attune his ears to the voice of the Declaration of Independence, calling down from where the Signers (we hope without untoward exception) have gone, crying: "William, William, why persecutest thou me? it is hard for thee to kick against the right of a people to pursue happiness in *their own way*"? The difference between the President and the writer is that both went out to scoff and the latter remained—much longer—to pray.

The Taft Commission arrived at Manila on June 3, 1900, loaded to the guards with kindly belief in the stale falsehood wherewith General Otis, ably assisted by his press censor, had been systematically soothing Mr. McKinley's and the general American conscience during the whole twenty months he had commanded the Eighth Army Corps,7 viz., that the insurrection was due solely to "the sinister ambitions of a few selfish leaders," and did *not* represent the wishes of the whole people. It is true that the insurrection originally started under Admiral Dewey's auspices and under the initial protection of his puissant guns was headed by a group of men most of whom, including Aguinaldo, were Tagalos. But all Filipinos look alike, the whole seven or eight millions of them. They differ from one another not one whit more than one Japanese differs from another. And they all feel alike on most things,8 because they all have the same customs, tastes, and habits of thought. Said Governor Taft to the Senate Committee in 1902:

While it is true that there are a number of Christian "tribes," so-called,—I do not know the number, possibly eight or ten, or twelve,—that speak different languages, there is a homogeneity in the people in appearance, in habits, and in many avenues of thought. To begin with, *they are Catholics.*"9

Certainly this should forever crucify the stale slander, still ignorantly repeated in the United States at intervals, which seeks to make the American people think the great body of the Filipino people are still in a tribal state, ethnologically.10 A Tagalo leader is about as much a "tribal" leader as is a Tammany "brave" of Irish antecedents. In fact there is much in common between the two. Both are clannish. Both have a genius for organization that is simply superb. Both are irrepressible about Home Rule. Countless generations ago the Filipinos were lifted by the Spanish priests out of the tribal state, and the educated people all speak Spanish. But the original tribal dialects, which the Spanish priests patiently mastered and finally reduced for them to a written language, still survive in the several localities of their origin. So that every Filipino of a well-to-do family is brought up speaking two languages, Spanish, and the local dialect of his native place, which is the only language known to the poorer natives of the same neighborhood. Surely even the valor of ignorance can see that we are presumptuously seeking to reverse the order of God and nature in assuming that an alien race can lead a people out of the wilderness better than could a government by the leading men of their own race to whom the less favored look with an ardent pride that would be a guarantee of loyal and inspiring co-operation. You can beat a balking horse to death but you *cannot* make him wag his tail, or otherwise indicate contentment or a disposition to cordial co-operation which will make for progress. Mr. Bryan has visited the Philippines, and his evidence is simply cumulative of mine, as mine, based on six years' acquaintance with the Filipinos, is simply cumulative of Admiral Dewey's testimony of 1898, so often cited hereinbefore, and of the opinion of Hon. George Curry, a Republican member of Congress from New Mexico who served eight years in the Philippines, and believes they can safely be given their independence by 1921. Mr. Bryan says:

So far as their own internal affairs are concerned, they do not need to be subject to any alien government.

He further says:

There is a wide difference, it is true, between the general intelligence of the educated Filipino and the laborer on the street and in the field, but this is not a barrier to self-government. Intelligence controls in every government, except where it is suppressed by military force. Nine tenths of the Japanese have no part in the law-making. In Mexico, the gap between the educated classes and the peons is fully as great as, if not greater than, the gap between the extremes of Filipino society. Those who question the capacity of the Filipinos for self-government forget that *patriotism raises up persons fitted for the work that needs to be done.*"11

It is because I believe that in the Philippines we are doing ourselves an injustice and keeping back the progress of the world by depreciating and scoffing at the value of patriotism as a factor in self-government and in the maintenance of free institutions, that I have written this book. There is no more patriotic people in the world than the Filipino people. I base this opinion upon an intimate knowledge of them, and in the light of considerable observation throughout most of Europe, and in Asia from the Golden Horn to the mouth of the Yang-tse. Woe to the nonsense, sometimes ignorant, sometimes vicious, wherewith we are regaled from time to time by Americans who go to Manila, smoke a cigar or two in some American club there, and then come back home and depreciate the Filipino people without at least correcting Col. Roosevelt's wholly uninformed and cruel random assertions of 1900 about the Filipinos being a "jumble of savage tribes," and about Aguinaldo being "the Osceola of the Filipinos," or their "Sitting Bull!" It is wonderfully inspiring to turn from such stale slander to Mr. Bryan's above statement of the case for our Oriental subjects, a statement framed in his own infinitely sympathetic and inimitable way, which says for me just what I had long wanted to express, but could not, so well. And in the midst of the recurring slander that the Filipino people are "a heterogeneous lot," it is refreshing to find in a preface to the American Census of the Philippines of 1903, by the Director thereof, a passage where, in comparing the tables of that census with those of the Twelfth Census of the United States, he says:

"Those of the Philippine Census are somewhat simpler, the differences being due mainly to *the more homogeneous character of the population of the Philippine Islands.*"12

When we consider the above in the light of the past and present operation of our own immigration laws, it is not flattering, but it may and should tend to awaken some realization of the manifold nature and blinding effects of current misapprehensions in the United States concerning the inhabitants of the Philippines. One Filipino does not differ from another any more than one American does from another American—in fact they differ less, considering immigration. The Filipino people are not rendered a heterogeneous lot by having three different languages, Ilocano, Tagalo, and Visayan,13 which are respectively the languages spoken in the northern, the central, and the southern part of their country, any more than the people of Switzerland are rendered heterogeneous by the circumstance that in northern Switzerland you find German spoken for the most part, while farther south you find French, and near the southernmost extremities some Italian. At this late date no credible person acquainted with the facts will be so poor in spirit as to deny that the motives of the men who originally started the insurrection were patriotic. Nor will any one who served under General Otis's command in the Philippines deny that that eminent desk soldier continued to cling to his early theory that it was a purely Tagalo insurrection long after the deadly unanimity of the opposition had seeped, with all-pervading thoroughness, into the general mind of the army of occupation. The white flag or rag of truce, *alias* treachery, used to be hoisted to put us off our guard in pretence of welcome to our columns approaching their towns and barrios. Such use of such a flag, followed by treachery, the ultimate weapon of the weak, had been in turn followed, with relentless impartiality in countless instances, by due unloosening of the vials of American wrath, until every *nipa* shack14 in the Philippine Islands that remained unburned had had its lesson, written in the blood of its occupants or their kin, to the tune of the Krag-Jorgensen or the Gatling. Yet General Otis's reports are always bland, and always convey the idea of an insurrection exclusively Tagalo.

In the summer of 1900, the newly arrived civilians, the Taft Commission, had no special interest in the soldiers who, for better, for worse, were "doing their country's work," as Kipling calls his own country's countless wars against its refractory subjects in the far East; and no especial sympathy with that work. Two years later we find President Roosevelt, in connection with the general amnesty of July 4, 1902, congratulating his "bowld lads," as Mr. Dooley would call them—meaning General Chaffee and the Eighth Army Corps—on a total of "two thousand combats, great and small" up to that time, but you never find in any of Governor Taft's Philippine state papers any more affirmative recognition of continued resistance to American rule than some mild allusion to "small but hard knocks" being administered here and there by the army. From the beginning there was a systematic belittling, on the part of the Taft Commission, of the work of the army, incidentally to belittling the reality and unanimity of the opposition which was daily calling it forth.15 This was not vicious. It was essentially benevolent. It was part of the initial fermentation of their preconceived theory. But the trouble about their theory was that it was only a theory. It would not square with the facts. They were trying to square the subjugation of the Philippines with the freeing of Cuba, a task quite as soluble as the squaring of a circle. They hoped, with all the kindly benevolence of Mr. McKinley himself, that the opposition to our rule was not as great as some people seemed to think. They had come out to the islands earnestly wishing to find conditions not as bad as they had been asserted to be. And the wish became father to the thought and the thought soon found expression in words—cablegrams to the United States presenting an optimistic view as to the prospects of necessity for further shedding of blood in the interest of Benevolent Assimilation, alias Trade Expansion. Some flippant person will say, "That is a polite way of charging insincerity." This book is not addressed to flippant persons. It is a serious attempt to deal with a problem involving the liberties of a whole people, and will be, as far as the writer can make it, straightforward, dignified, and candid. Judge Taft's fearful mistake of 1900–1901 in the matter of his premature planting of the civil government—a mistake because based on the idea that "the great majority of the people" welcomed American rule, and a fearful mistake because fraught with so much subsequent sacrifice of life due to too early withdrawal of the police protection of the army—was not the first instance in American history where an ordinarily level-headed public man has, with egregious folly, mistaken the mood and temper of a whole people. The key to his mistake lay in the fact that, coming into a strange country in the midst of a war, he ignored the advice of the commanding general of the army of his country concerning the military situation, and took the advice of a few native Tories, or Copperheads, of wealth, who had never really been in sympathy with the insurrection and who, flocking about him as soon as he arrived, told him what he so longed to be told, viz., that the war did not represent the wishes of the people but was kept up by "a conspiracy of assassination" of all who did not contribute to it either in service or money. He thereupon decided that the men who told him this really represented the voice of the people, and that the men in the field who had then been keeping up the struggle for independence for sixteen months, in season and out of season, were simply "a Mafia on a very large scale." Consequently the Taft Commission had been in the islands less than three months when Secretary of War Root at Washington was giving the widest possible publicity to cablegrams from them, such as that dated August 21, 1900, mentioned in the preceding chapter, conveying the glad tidings that "large number of people long for peace and are willing to accept government under United States"16; and by November next thereafter, the "large number" had grown to "a great majority," and the "willing" to "entirely willing." The November statement was:

A great majority of the people long for peace and are *entirely* willing to accept the establishment of a government under the supremacy of the United States.17

Yet, as we saw in the preceding chapter, the real situation in the Philippines at this very time was described four years later at the Republican National Convention of 1904 by Mr. Root thus:

When the last national convention met, over 70,000 American soldiers from more than 500 stations held a still vigorous enemy in check.

Between the date of their arrival in the Islands on June 3d, and the date of this August 21st telegram, the Taft Commission did little junketing, but remained in Manila imbibing the welcome views of the "Tories" or "Copperheads," and seeking very little information from the army. But it so happens that the Adjutant-General at Manila used to keep a record of the daily engagements during that period, which record was later published in the annual *War Department Report*,18 and it shows a total of about five hundred killings (of Filipinos) between June 3d, and August 21st, to say nothing of probably many times that number hit but not killed, and therefore able to get away. (You could not include any Filipino in your returns of your killings except dead you had actually counted.) It also happens that on June 4th, the day after Judge Taft's arrival, General MacArthur, in response to an order from Washington sent some time previous at the instance of Congress, had all the Filipino casualties our military records showed up to that time (*i. e.*, during the sixteen months from the day of the outbreak, February 4, 1899, to June 3, 1900), tabulated and totalled, and the total Filipino killed accordingly reported by cablegram to the War Department on June 4, 1900, was 10,780.19

Ten thousand in sixteen months is 625 per month. So that by the time Judge Taft arrived, the Filipinos had been sufficiently beaten into submission to decrease the death-rate due to the Independence Bug from something over six hundred per month to about two hundred per month. Judge Taft called this enthusiasm. I call it exhaustion. Whereupon, exclaims a Boston Anti-Imperialist, "Why don't you issue Mr. Taft a certificate as a member of the Ananias Club at once, and be done with it?" My answer is that I do not believe the Taft Commission in 1900 either knew these figures or wanted to know them. They came out preaching a Gospel of Hope to the exclusion of all else, a species of mental healing. They said, soothingly to Dame Filipina, "Be not afraid; you are well; you are well"—of the desire for independence she had conceived, when what that lady needed was the surgical operation indispensable for the removal of a still-born child.

The will of the American people is ascertainable, and quadrennially announced, through certain prescribed methods. And (nearly) everybody takes the result good-humoredly, God bless our country, whatever the result. But just how Mr. Taft and his colleagues could assume to speak for the "great majority" of the Filipino people at the tremendous juncture in their destinies now under consideration during the Presidential election of 1900, does not clearly appear, except that in their first report they say:

Many witnesses were examined as to the form of government best adapted to these islands and *satisfactory to the people*,20

a statement which obviously takes for granted the only point involved in the war, viz., whether *any kind* of alien government would be "satisfactory to the people." And in their various other communications to Washington they describe themselves, with no small degree of benevolent satisfaction, as enthusiastically received by natives not under arms at the moment of such reception. As a matter of fact, a carpet-bag governor of Georgia might just as well have reported to Andrew Johnson an enthusiastic reception at the hands of the people whose homes had lately been put to the torch, and their kith and kin to the sword, while the whole fair face of nature from Atlanta to the sea lay bruised and bleeding under the iron heel of Sherman's army. Let no advocate of Indefinite Tutelage whet his scalping-knife for me because of the use of that word "carpet-bag." It was as free from ill-will as the explosion incident to flash-light photography. We are trying to develop a picture of those times. Two at least of the Commission, Messrs. Taft and Wright, were the kind of men who in all the personal relations of life, meet the ultimate test of human confidence and friendship—you would make either, if he would consent to act, executor of your will, or testamentary guardian of your child. But they came out with the preconceived notion that kindness would win the people over, whereas what those people wanted was not foreign kindness but home rule, not silken political swaddling clothes, but freedom. And as the acquisition of the Philippines has placed us under the necessity of getting up a new definition of freedom, one consistent with tariff taxation without representation—through legislation by a Congress on the other side of the world in which "our new possessions" have no vote—it should be added that one of the things Freedom meant with us before 1898, was freedom to frame the laws—tariff and other—which largely determine the selling price of crops and the purchase price of the necessities of life, freedom to see the intelligent and educated men of your own race in charge of your common destiny, freedom to have a flag as an emblem of your common interests, in a word, just Freedom. And that was what the war was about. They wanted to be free and independent. Whether they were fit for such freedom is wholly foreign to the reality and unanimity of their desire for it. General Otis used to be very fond of taking the wind out of the sails of their commissioners and other officials before the outbreak by saying that their people had not the slightest notion of what the word independence meant. It is true that they knew nothing about it by experience, but equally true that whatever it was, they wanted it. Of the ten thousand men we had already killed when Judge Taft arrived, there can be no question, as already heretofore suggested, that many of them may have been hit just as they were hurrahing for independence, in other words, died with the word "Independence" on their lips. When men have been thus fighting against overwhelming odds for some sixteen months for government *of their* people *by* their people *for* their people—however inarticulate the emotions of the rank and file on going into battle—it is idle to claim that they do not know what they want, whether the great majority of the rank and file can read and write or not. But pursuant to the idea that kindness would cure the desire for independence, Judge Taft ignored, in the outset, all advice from the military department, because that was not the kindness department, accepting as truly representative of the temper of the whole people the views of a few ultra-conservatives of large means who had always been part and parcel of the Spanish Administration.

On the other hand, General MacArthur and the whole Eighth Army Corps had seen a great insurrection drag on from month to month and from one year to another, under General Otis, when short shrift would have been made of it in the outset, and far less life sacrificed, if Mr. McKinley had not needed, in aid of his Philippine policy, the support of both of those who believed it was right *and* of those who believed it would pay. The one central thought which had seemed to animate General Otis from the beginning, a thought which we have already traced through all its humiliating manifestations, was that he must neither do or permit anything that might hurt the Administration. When the "impatience of the people" at home, which figures so prominently in the correspondence already cited between the Adjutant General of the army, General Corbin, and General Otis at Manila, had begun to cast its shadows on the presidential year, 1900, the master mind of Mr. Root had interrupted the fatal Otis treatment of the insurrection, indicated by General Otis's long failure to call for volunteers, his stupid stream of "situation well in hand" and "insurrection about to collapse" telegrams, and his utterly unpardonable persistence in calling it a purely "Tagalo insurrection," by sending him a competent force, and a plan of campaign, and directing him to carry out the plan. General Otis did this, because he was told to, and then began again to sing the same old song. MacArthur, Wheaton, Lawton, Bates, Young, Funston, and the rest of the fighting generals, had submitted to all the Otis follies without a murmur, because insubordination degrades an army into a rabble. But they[21] believed the army was there to put down that insurrection, not to have a symposium with its leaders on the rights of man. They had taken up "The White Man's Burden," after the manner of Lords Kitchener and Roberts, and they had no qualms. Above all, they wanted *peace*, no matter how much fighting it took to get it. Mindful of the attempts of the Schurman Commission of the year before to mix peace with war, and of the immense encouragement thus given the insurgents, they had not looked forward with enthusiasm to the coming of the Taft Commission, and to the highly probable renewal of negotiations with the insurgent leaders in the field, pursuant to a presidential policy of patching up a peace at any price, suggested by the exigencies of political expediency, to give the government a semblance of having more or less of the consent of the governed. That the anticipations of the military authorities in this regard did not receive a pleasant disappointment, has already been suggested by the nature of the views adopted by the commission soon after its arrival.

The military view of the situation, as it stood when Judge Taft and his colleagues arrived at Manila in June, 1900, is set forth in the annual report of the commanding general, General MacArthur, rendered shortly thereafter; rendered, not in aid of any political candidate at home, nor of a sudden, but at the usual and customary annual season for the making of such reports; and rendered by a soldier of no mean experience and ability, who was a man of great kindliness of heart as well, to the war department of his government, to acquaint it with the facts of a military situation he had been dealing with for two years prior to the arrival of the Taft Commission. General MacArthur's views, as expressed in his report, must now be contrasted with the Taft view, not to show that MacArthur is a bigger man than Taft, nor for any other idle or petty purpose, but because, if, in 1900, General MacArthur was right, and Judge Taft was wrong, about the unanimity of the whole Filipino people against us, then the institution of the Civil

Government of the Philippines on July 4, 1901, was premature; and, therefore, by reason of the withdrawal of the strong arm of the military at a critical period of public order, it was not calculated to give adequate protection to the lives and property of those who were willing to abandon the struggle for independence and submit to our rule. And if, as we shall see later, it did in fact grossly fail to afford such adequate protection for life and property, it was derelict in the most sacred duty enjoined upon it by Mr. McKinley's instructions to the Taft Commission. But first let me introduce you to General MacArthur.

General MacArthur is not only a soldier of a high order of ability, but a statesman as well. Moreover, he was a thoroughgoing "expansionist." He believed in keeping the Philippines permanently, just as England does her colonies. But he was perfectly honest about it. He recognized the fact that they were against our rule. But he did not attach any more weight to that circumstance than Lord Kitchener would have done. Also, he had come out to the islands with the first expedition, in 1898, had been in the field continuously for fifteen months prior to assuming supreme military command, and knew the Filipinos thoroughly. As soon as he took command, on May 5, 1900, of the 70,000 troops then in the Islands, he set himself with patience and firmness to the great task of ending the insurrection, which at that time promised to continue indefinitely, the far more formidable guerrilla warfare that had followed the brief period of serried resistance having now settled down to a chronic stage, aided and abetted by the whole population. I have said General MacArthur was a "thoroughgoing" expansionist. This needs a slight qualification. At first he appears to have had a few qualms. Shortly after the outbreak of the war with the Filipinos, when he took the first insurgent capital Malolos, in March, 1899, he had said at Malolos, as we have seen, to a newspaper man who accompanied the expedition:

When I first started in against these rebels, I believed that Aguinaldo's troops represented only a faction. I did not believe that the whole population of Luzon was opposed to us; but I have been *reluctantly* compelled to believe that the Filipinos are loyal to Aguinaldo and the government which he represents.22

General MacArthur's reports concerning the war in the Philippines during the period of his command are succinct and luminous. He makes it perfectly clear that the original resistance offered by the insurgent armies in the field after the arrival of the overwhelmingly ample reinforcements sent out from this country in the fall of 1899, was little more than a mere flash in the pan, compared with the well-planned scheme of resistance which followed the dispersion of those armies to the several provinces which had furnished them to the cause, and Aguinaldo's simultaneous flight into the mountains "with his government concealed about his person," as Senator Lodge exultantly described that incident in his speech of April, 1900, in defence of the Administration's Philippine policy. Speaking of this period, General MacArthur says:

It has since been ascertained that the expediency of adopting guerrilla warfare from the inception of hostilities was seriously discussed by the native leaders, and advocated with much emphasis as the system best adapted to the peculiar conditions of the struggle. It was finally determined, however, that a concentrated field army, conducting regular operations, would, in the event of success, attract the favorable attention of the world, and be accepted as a practical demonstration of capacity for organization and self-government. The disbandment of the field army, therefore, having been a subject of contemplation from the start, the actual event, in pursuance of the deliberate action of the council of war in Bayambang about November 12, 1899 (already hereinbefore noticed), *was not regarded by Filipinos in the light of a calamity, but simply as a transition from one form of action to another*; a change which by many was regarded as a positive advantage, and was relied upon to accomplish more effectively the end in view. The Filipino idea behind the dissolution of their field army was not at the time of the occurrence well understood in the American camp. As a consequence, misleading conclusions were reached to the effect that the insurrection itself had been destroyed, and that it only remained to sweep up the fag ends of the rebel army by a system of police administration not likely to be either onerous or dangerous.23

In his report covering the period from May 5th, to October 1, 1900, General MacArthur says of the policy of resistance above outlined:

The country affords great advantages for the practical development of such a policy. The practice of discarding the uniform enables the insurgents to appear and disappear almost at their convenience. At one time they are in the ranks as soldiers, and immediately thereafter are within the American lines in the attitude of peaceful natives, absorbed in *a dense mass of sympathetic people*.24

In this same connection the report includes a copy of the original order of the insurgent government which was the corner stone of the guerrilla policy, and states that "systemized regulations" for its effective prosecution throughout the archipelago had been compiled and published by the Filipino junta, or revolutionary committee at Madrid, and distributed among the insurgent forces. The report also appends a copy of the "Army Regulations" under which the insurgent forces were to conduct the guerrilla warfare. It also describes in detail the system of warfare prescribed under these regulations, and states that as a result of the measures which he, General MacArthur, took to combat that warfare "the 53 stations of American troops occupied in the archipelago on November 1, 1899, had on September 1, 1900, expanded to 413," and that during this period, the casualties to our troops were 268 killed, 750 wounded, 55 captured, and to the insurgents, so far as our records showed, 3227 killed, 694 wounded, and 2864 captured. Says he:

The extensive distribution of troops has strained the soldiers of the army to the full limit of endurance. Each little command has had to provide its own service of security and information by never ceasing patrols, explorations, escorts, outposts, and regular guards. An idea seems to have been established in the public mind [he meant the public mind at home, of course] that the field work of the army is in the nature of police, in regulating a few bands of guerrillas, and involving none of the vicissitudes of war. [Here he is meeting the Otis theory, then being industriously circulated in the United States.] *Such a narrow statement of the case is unfair to the service.* In all things requiring endurance, fortitude, and patient diligence, the guerrilla period has been pre-eminent. It is difficult for the non-professional observer [he means Judge Taft] to understand that apparently desultory work, such as has prevailed in the Philippines during the past ten months,25 has demanded *more of discipline and as much of valor* as was required during the period of regular operations against the concentrated field forces of the insurrection. It is, therefore, a great privilege to speak warmly in respect of the importance of the service rendered day by day, with unremitting vigilance, by the splendid men who," etc.26

It was not until July 4, 1902, that President Roosevelt officially declared, by his amnesty proclamation of that date that the insurrection in the Philippines was at last ended. It was by no means beaten to a frazzle, as we shall later see. But of course, knowing the impatience of a large portion of the American people with a situation about which there was a wide-spread notion that much remained undisclosed, Mr. Roosevelt would have issued such a proclamation earlier, had the facts seemed to him to so authorize. General MacArthur's relentless "never ceasing patrols, explorations," etc., continued straight on through the presidential campaign of 1900 side by side in point of time with the roseate Taft cablegrams of the same period, and long thereafter—how long will be later indicated. Says General MacArthur, in his report for 1901:

It had been suggested that some of the Filipino leaders were willing to submit the issue to the judgment of the American people, which was soon to be expressed at the polls, and to abide by the result of the presidential election of November, 1900.27 But subsequent events demonstrated that the hope of ending the war without further effusion of blood was not well founded, and that as a matter of fact the Filipinos were *organizing for further desperate resistance* by means of a general banding of the people in support of the guerrillas in the field.28

General MacArthur then goes on to tell how, as part of this programme, the insurgent authorities,

announced a primal and inflexible principle, to the effect that every native, without any exception, residing within the limits of the archipelago, owed active allegiance to the insurgent cause. This jurisdiction was enjoined under severe penalties, which were systematically enforced.

This is what Judge Taft afterwards described as "a conspiracy of murder, a Mafia on a very large scale",29 the characterization being made in support of his theory that "the great majority of the people" with whom we were then at war would welcome our rule if allowed to follow their real preferences, and that they were being cruelly coerced to fight for the independence of their country. General MacArthur's view, however, did not support this theory. His report deals with this branch of the subject thus:

The cohesion of Filipino society in behalf of insurgent interests is most emphatically illustrated by the fact that assassination, which was extensively employed, was generally accepted as a legitimate expression of insurgent governmental authority. *The individuals marked for death would not appeal to American protection, although condemned exclusively on account of supposed pro-Americanism.*

Later on, when we came to understand the Filipinos better, this summary method of dealing with the faint-hearted lost much of its initial horrifying force, and the failure of such to appeal to us for protection lost much of its strangeness. In the first place, nobody loves a traitor. Even those to whom he claims to have betrayed his countrymen do not trust him implicitly. Again, Latin countries never assume that before a man is punished for alleged crime he has been confronted with the witnesses against him. Such testimony is, under their jurisprudence, frequently received in his absence. The legal department of General MacArthur's office once got hold of a captured insurgent paper subscribed with the autograph of Juan Cailles, one of their best generals. It directed that a named Filipino residing in a certain town garrisoned by American troops be executed—we of course, would call it "assassinated"—at a certain hour on a certain day in a public street of the town, and that the soldier or soldiers performing the "execution" should declare to the bystanders, if any, in so doing, that it was done because the man was a traitor, a friend of the Americans. We kept this paper, intending to hang Juan whenever he should be captured. He held out a long time, and finally surrendered unconditionally—but he proved such an elegant fellow, game as a pebble, courteous as Chesterfield, and immensely popular with his people, that it was decided he could be of more service as a live governor of a province than he could as a dead general,30 so he was appointed a provincial governor by Governor Taft, and made a splendid official.

Another reason why Filipinos suspected, during the insurrection, by the more obstinate and stout-hearted of their compatriots who held out longer in the struggle for independence, of weakening toward the cause of their country, in other words, suspected of what might be called "Copperhead" or "Tory" tendencies, would not appeal to us for protection, is strikingly presented in General MacArthur's report for 1901. He says they naturally had "grave doubt as to the wisdom" of siding with us, "as the United States had made no formal announcement of an inflexible purpose to hold the archipelago and afford protection to pro-Americans."31

The one great thing that has crippled progress in the Philippines from the beginning of the American occupation down to date is the uncertainty as to what our policy for the future is to be, the lack of some, "formal announcement of an inflexible purpose." And of course I mean, as General MacArthur meant, by "*formal*" announcement, an authoritative declaration by *the law-making power* of the government. If Congress should formally declare that it is the purpose of this government to hold the Philippines permanently, American and other capital would at once go there in abundance and the place would "blossom like a rose." If, on the other hand, Congress should formally declare that it is the purpose of this government to give the Filipinos their independence as soon as a stable native government can be set up, thus holding out to the present generation the prospect of living to see the independence of their country, the place would also quickly blossom as aforesaid, through the generous ardor of native love of country. In either event, everybody out there would know where he is "at." At present all is uncertainty, both with the resident members of the dominant alien race, and with those over whom we are ruling.

It took over 120,000 American troops, first and last, to put down the struggle of the Filipinos for independence.32 The war began February 4, 1899, and the last public official announcement that it was ended was on July 4, 1902.33 Of course this does not imply that every province was at all times during that period a theatre of actual war. Putting down the insurrection was something like putting out a fire in a field of dry grass. At first the trouble was general. Gradually it diminished toward the end. But for a while, no sooner was it quenched in one province than it would break out in another. How the Filipinos were able to prolong the struggle as long as they did against such apparently overwhelming odds is most interestingly explained by General MacArthur in his report for 1900. After describing the method he followed of establishing native municipal governments in territory as conquered, he says, with a patient stateliness that is almost humorous:

The institution of municipal government under American auspices, of course, carried the idea of exclusive fidelity to the sovereign power of the United States. All the necessary moral obligations to that end were readily assumed by municipal bodies, and all outward forms of loyalty and decorum carefully preserved. But precisely at this point the psychologic conditions referred to above [meaning the unity against us],34 began to work with great energy, in assistance of insurgent field operations. For this purpose most of the towns secretly organized complete insurgent municipal governments, to proceed *simultaneously and in the same sphere as the American governments and* in many instances *through the same personnel*—that is to say, the presidentes and town officials acted openly in behalf of the Americans and secretly in behalf of the insurgents, and, paradoxical as it may seem, with considerable apparent solicitude for the interests of both. In all matters touching the peace of the town, the regulation of markets, the primitive work possible on roads, streets, and bridges, and the institution of schools, their open activity was commendable; at the same time they were exacting and collecting contributions and supplies and recruiting men for the Filipino forces, and sending all obtainable military information to the Filipino leaders. Wherever, throughout the archipelago, there is a group of the insurgent army, it is a fact beyond dispute, that all contiguous towns contribute to the maintenance thereof. In other words, the towns, regardless of the fact of American occupation and town organization, are the actual bases for all insurgent military activities; and not only so in the sense of furnishing supplies for the so-called flying columns of guerrillas, but as affording secure places of refuge. Indeed, it is now the most important maxim of Filipino tactics to disband when closely pressed and seek safety in the nearest *barrio*; a manœuvre quickly accomplished by reason of the assistance of the people and the ease with which the Filipino soldier is transformed into the appearance of a peaceful native.35

To contrast a cold, hard military fact involving the lives of American soldiers with a lot of political nonsense intended for consumption in the United States during a presidential election, the next paragraph is particularly interesting in the light of the cotemporaneous Taft view:36

The success of this unique system of war depends upon almost complete unity of action of the entire native population. That such unity is a fact is too obvious to admit of discussion. Intimidation has undoubtedly accomplished much to this end, but fear as the only motive is hardly sufficient to account for the *united and apparently spontaneous action of several millions of people*.37 One traitor in each town would effectually destroy such a complex organization.

Then follows this bit of grim humor:

It is more probable that the adhesive principle comes from ethnological homogeneity which induces men to respond for a time to the appeals of consanguineous leadership—

in other words, to stick to *their own kith and kin*. He had in a previous paragraph used that very expression thus: "The people seem to be actuated by the idea that in politics or war men are never nearer right then when going with their own kith and kin."

In all the foregoing, General MacArthur was not simply trying to score a point against Judge Taft, though his resentment of the effort of the Taft Commission of 1900 to mix politics with war in the presidential year was quite as decided, and quite as well known in the islands at the time, as was General Otis's similar attitude toward the Schurman Commission of the previous year.38 He is simply laying before the War Department, as a soldier, the familiar facts of a situation which he had been dealing with for two years past, as well known to the 70,000 officers and men under his command as to himself. And as the details into which he goes are simply prefatory to an account of the remedy he applied to the situation, that remedy must now claim our attention. The remedy General MacArthur finally applied was a proclamation, explaining to the Filipino people—"to all classes throughout the archipelago," it read, and especially to the leaders in the field, many of whose captured comrades-in-arms he had now become thoroughly acquainted with—the severities sanctioned by the laws of civilized nations under such circumstances, and the reasons therefor; and, further, serving them with notice that thenceforward he proposed to enforce those laws with full rigor.39

The eminent lawyers of the Taft Commission were too busy about that time acquainting themselves with the situation through natives not in arms, to attach much importance to General MacArthur's proclamation, but the Eighth Army Corps always believed that that proclamation, and the army's work under it, was the main factor in making the civil government at all possible by the date it was set up, July 4, 1901. The issuance of this document was not only a wise military move, but a subtle stroke of statesmanship as well. It assumed that the Filipino people were a *civilized people*, an assumption never indulged by Spain during the whole of her rule, but always freely admitted by General MacArthur in all his dealings with their leading men to be a fact. It therefore appealed to their *amour propre*, and to the *noblesse oblige* of many of the most obstinate and trusted fighting leaders. The writer was, at the date of the proclamation under consideration, on duty at General MacArthur's headquarters, as assistant to Colonel Crowder, his judge advocate, now Judge Advocate General of the United States Army, and prepared the first rough, tentative suggestions for the final draft of it, accompanying such suggestions with a memorandum showing the course taken by Wellington in France in 1815, and by Bismarck's generals at the close of the Franco-Prussian War, as well as that followed under General Order No. 100,

1863, for the government of the armies of the United States in the field. Having then entertained the opinion that that proclamation, though drastic, was wise and right under the facts of the situation which confronted us, and having nowise changed that opinion since, it may be well for the writer of this book to explain his reasons for that opinion. This must be done wholly without reference to "the authorities," for neither at the bar of public opinion, nor at the bar of final judgment, do "the authorities" count for much. In so doing, however, we must start with the *assumption* that it was a case of American military occupation of hostile territory, notwithstanding that Judge Taft began soon after his arrival in the islands in the June previous to the December now referred to, to cable home impressions which, if correct, amounted to a denial that the great body of the people were hostile. Military occupation is a fact which admits of no debate, and the necessity of making your country's flag respected is always fully and keenly recognized as the one supreme consideration by every good American except one who, obsessed with the idea that kindness will cure the desire of a people for independence, proceeds to act on that idea in the midst of a war for independence.

Under the laws of war the commanding general of the occupying force owes protection, both of life and property, to all persons residing within the territory occupied. The object of General MacArthur's proclamation was to put a stop to such "executions," or assassinations, as that perpetrated by Juan Cailles, mentioned above, and to separate the insurgents in the field from their main reliance, the towns. The latter end of a bloody war is no time for a discussion of the causes of the war between victor and vanquished. Nor is it any time to believe the representative of the enemy who tells you that most of him is really in sympathy with you and merely coerced. Your duty is to stop the war. You and your enemy having had a difference, and having referred it to the arbitrament of war, which is, unfortunately, at present the only human jurisdiction having power to enforce decisions concerning such differences, if you win, and your enemy refuses to abide the decision, he is simply, as it were in contempt of court, and, in the scheme of things, as at present ordered, deserves punishment as an enemy to the general peace. To state the ethics of the matter juridically, "there should be an end of litigation"—somewhere.

I do not believe in the doctrine that might makes right, and I cherish the high hope that this human family of ours will survive to see war superseded, as the ultimate arbiter, by something more like heaven and less like hell. But in the Philippines in 1900 it was a situation, not a theory, that confronted us, and, as far as my consciously fallible thinking apparatus lights the way which then lay before us, that way led to a shrine whereon was written "A life for a life." This is no mere academic discussion. With me it is a tremendously practical one. In the gravest possible acceptation of the term it is AWE -fully so. If I am wrong, every execution I approved by memorandum review furnished Colonel Crowder and General MacArthur, of military commission findings out there was wrong, and so were a number of the executions I ordered as a judge appointed by Governor Taft under a government which, though nominally a civil government, was no more "civil" in so far as that term implies absence of necessity for the presence of military force, than other governments immediately following conquest usually are. The propriety of the imposition of capital punishment by the constituted authorities of a nation as part of a set policy to make its sovereignty respected, is wholly independent of whether you call your colonial government a civil or a military one. So that in justifying General MacArthur I am also justifying Governor Taft, and as it was on the recommendation of the former that the latter appointed me to the Bench, we are certainly all three in the same boat in the matter of the capital punishments under consideration. And while the company you were in on earth in a given transaction, however distinguished that company, is not going to help you with the Recording Angel,40 still, it is some comfort to know that wiser and abler men than yourself approved a course of imposing capital punishments to which you were a party, such punishments having been inflicted as part of a policy whose subsequent evolution revealed it to you as fundamentally wrong. And this reflection is quite relevant in the present connection to the question whether the government of

Benevolent Assimilation we have maintained over the Filipinos for the last fourteen years is one which was originally imposed by force against their will, or whether it was ever welcomed by them or any considerable fraction of them.

That the MacArthur proclamation of December 20, 1900, concerning the laws of war, was at the time a military necessity, is as perfectly clear to me now as it was then. And yet it may well give the thoughtful and patriotic American pause. It is sometimes difficult to understand why men are so often entirely willing to go on fighting and dying in a cause they must know to be hopeless. The famous passage of Edmund Burke's speech on "Conciliation with America,"

If I were an American, as I am an Englishman, so long as foreign troops remained on my native soil, I never would lay down my arms, no, never, never, never!

sounds well to us, but from the standpoint of a conqueror, there is a good deal of wind-jamming to it, after all. It was the language of a man who knew nothing of the horrors of war by actual experience, or of what hell it slowly becomes to everybody concerned after most of the high officials of the vanquished government have been captured and are sleeping on dry, warm beds, eating good wholesome food, and smoking good cigars, in comfortable custody, while the vanquished army, no longer strong enough to come out in the open and fight, is relegated to ambuscades and other tactics equally akin to the methods of the assassin. The law of nations in this regard is an expression of the views of successive generations of civilized and enlightened men of all nations *whose profession* was war—men familiar with the horrors inevitably incident to it and anxious to mitigate them as far as possible. That law represents the common consensus of Christendom resulting from that experience. It recognizes that after resistance becomes utterly hopeless, it becomes a crime against society and the general peace, and this is wholly independent of the merits or demerits of the questions involved in the war. In other words, the greatest good of the greatest number cries aloud that the war must stop. The cold, hard fact is that the great majority of the men who hold out longest are, usually, either single men having no one dependent on them, or nothing to lose, or both, or else they are men more or less indifferent to the ties of family affection, and callous to the suffering fruitlessly entailed upon innocent noncombatants by the various and sundry horrors of war, such as decimation of the plough animals of the country due to their running at large without caretakers or forage; resultant untilled fields and scant food; pestilence and famine consequent upon insufficient nourishment; arson, robbery, rape, and murder inevitably committed in such times by sorry scamps and ruffians claiming to be patriots but yielding no allegiance to any responsible head; and so on, *ad infinitum.*

General MacArthur's proclamation of December 20, 1900, served notice on the leaders of a hopeless cause that assassinations, such as that ordered by Juan Cailles, above mentioned, must stop; that the universal practice of the townfolk, of sending money, supplies, and information concerning our movements to the enemy in the field, must stop; that participating in hostilities intermittently, in citizen garb, followed by return to home and avocation when too hard pressed, must stop; in short that *the war must stop.* Yet the proclamation explained in so firm and kindly a way why the penalties it promised were only reasonable under the circumstances, that "as an educational document the effect was immediate and far-reaching,"[41] to quote from an opinion expressed by its author in the body of it, an opinion entirely consistent with modesty and fully justified by the facts. General MacArthur also goes on to say of his unrelenting and rigid enforcement of the terms of this proclamation that the results "preclude all possibility of doubt * * * that the effective pacification of the archipelago *commenced* December 20, 1900"—its date. It is a part of the history of those times, familiar to all who are familiar with them, that the Taft Civil Commission thought its assurances of the benevolent intentions of our government were what made the civil government possible by midsummer, 1901. But whatever the Filipinos may think of us at present, now that they understand us better, certainly in 1900–01, in view of the events of the preceding two or three years, which formed the basis of the only acquaintance they then had with us, and in view of the fact that their experience for the preceding two or three hundred years had made force the only effective governmental argument with them, and governmental promises a mere mockery, and in view of the fact that the "never-ceasing patrols, explorations, escorts, outposts," etc., of General MacArthur's 70,000 men were relentlessly kept up during the six months immediately following the proclamation and in aid of it, it at once becomes obvious how infinitesimal a fraction of the final partial pacification which made the civil government possible, the Taft assurances to the Filipinos as to our intentions must have been. These matters are of prime importance to any honest effort toward a clear understanding of present conditions, because far and away the greatest wrong which we, in our genuinely benevolent misinformation, have done the Filipinos, not even excepting the tariff legislation perpetrated upon them by Congress, lies in the insufferably hypocritical pretence that they ever consented to our rule, or that they consent to it now—a pretence conceived in 1898 by Trade Expansion, to beguile a nation the breath of whose own life is political liberty based on consent of the governed, into a career of conquest, but not even countenanced since by those who believe the Government should go into the politico-missionary business, after the manner of Spain in the sixteenth century.

Having now exhaustively examined the differences of opinion between Judge Taft and General MacArthur, when the former set to work, in the summer of 1900, to get a civil government started by the date of expiration of the term of enlistment of the volunteer army (June 30, 1901), let us follow the facts of the situation up to the date last named, or, which is practically the same thing, up to the inauguration of Judge Taft as Civil Governor of the islands on July 4, 1901, pausing, in passing, for such reflections as may force themselves upon us as pertinent to the Philippine problem of to-day.

On September 19, 1900, General MacArthur wired Secretary of War Root—General Corbin, the Adjutant-General of the Army, to be exact, but it is the same thing—describing what he calls "considerable activity" throughout Luzon, ominously stating that General Young (up in the Ilocano country, into which we followed him and his cavalry in Chapter XII, *ante*) "has called so emphatically for more force," that he, MacArthur, feels grave concern; adding that Luzon north of the Pasig is "very much disturbed," and that south of the Pasig the same conditions prevail.42

October 26th, General MacArthur cables outlining a plan for a great campaign on comprehensive lines, stating that "Full development of this scheme requires about four months and all troops now in the islands," and deprecating any move on Mr. Root's part to reduce his force of 70,000 men by starting any of the volunteers homeward before it should be absolutely necessary.43 October 28th, General MacArthur wires, "Shall push everything with great vigor," adding "Expect to have everything in full operation November 15th."44 November 5th, as if to reassure General MacArthur that he and the General understand each other and that the Taft cotemporaneous nonsense is not going to be allowed to interfere with more serious business, Secretary Root, through the Adjutant-General, sends this cable message:

Secretary of War directs no instructions from here be allowed interfere or impede progress your military operations which he expects you force to successful conclusion.45

So that while the American people were being pacified with the Taft cablegrams to Secretary Root that the Filipino people wanted peace, General MacArthur, under Mr. Root's direction, was simultaneously proceeding to *make* them want it with the customary argument used to settle irreconcilable differences between nations—powder and lead. Mr. Root was all the time in constant communication with both, but he gave out only the Taft optimism to the public, and withheld the actual facts within his knowledge. December 25th, General MacArthur wires Secretary Root, "Expectations based on result of election have not been realized." "Progress," he says, is "very slow."[46]

And now I come to one of the most important things that all my researches into the official records of our government concerning the Philippine Islands have developed. On December 28, 1900, General MacArthur reports by cable the contents of some important insurgent papers captured in Cavite Province about that time. The Filipinos have a great way of reducing to writing, or making minutes of, whatever occurs at any important conference. This habit they did not abandon in the field. The papers in question belonged to General Trias, the Lieutenant-General commanding all the insurgent armies in the field, and, next to Aguinaldo, the highest official connected with the revolutionary government. One of these papers, according to General MacArthur's despatch of December 28th, purported to be the minutes of a certain meeting had October 11th previous, between General Trias and the Japanese Consul at Manila. As to whether or not the paper was really authentic, General MacArthur says: "I accept it as such without hesitation." Communicating the contents of the paper he says:

Consul advised that Trias visit Japan. Filipinos represented that concessions which they might be forced to make to Washington would be more agreeable if made to Japan, *which as a nation of kindred blood would not be likely to assert superiority.* Consul said Japan desired coaling station, freedom to trade and build railways.[47]

I consider these negotiations of the Japanese Government with the Philippine insurgents important to be related here because they have never been generally known, for the good reason, of course, that the President of the United States cannot take the public into his confidence about such grave and delicate matters when they occur. The incident is not "ancient history" relatively to present-day problems, for the following reasons:

(1) Because it is credibly reported and currently believed in the United States that in Japan, during the cruise of our battleship fleet around the world in 1907, one of the reception committee of Japanese officers who welcomed our officers was recognized by one of the latter as having been, not a great while before that, a servant aboard an American battleship.

(2) Because of the following incident, related to me, in 1911, without the slightest injunction of secrecy, by the Director of Public Health of the Philippine Islands, then on a visit to the United States. Shortly before the Director's said visit home, while he was out in one of the provinces, there was brought to his attention a Filipino with a broken arm. There was a Japanese doctor in the town, at least a Japanese who had a sign out as a doctor. The Director carried the sufferer to the "doctor," not being a surgeon himself. The "doctor" turned out to be a civil engineer, who had been making maps and plans of fortifications. The plans were found in his possession.

(3) Because from one of the islands through which the northern line of the Treaty of Paris runs, situated only a pleasant morning's journey in a launch due north of Aparri, the northernmost town of Luzon, you can see, on a clear day, with a good field-glass, the southern end of Formosa, some 60 or 70 miles away. *Japan can land an army on American soil at Aparri any time she wants to, overnight*—an army several times that of the total American force now in the Philippines,[48] or likely ever to be there. From Aparri it is 70 miles up the river to Tueguegarao, 40 more to Iligan, and 90 more, all fairly good marching, to Bayombong, in Nueva Viscaya (total distance, Aparri to Bayombong, 200 miles) the province which lies in the heart of the watershed of Central Luzon. I know what I am talking about, because that region was the first judicial district I presided over, and many a hard journey I have had over

it, circuit riding, on a scrubby pony. Part of it I have been through in the company of President Taft. It thus appears that from Aparri to Bayombong there would be but a week or ten days of unresisted marching to reach the watershed region, Nueva Viscaya. The Japanese soldier's ration is mainly rice, so that he can carry more days' travel rations than almost any other soldier in the world. Never fear about their making the journey inside of a week or ten days, once they start. To descend from the watershed aforesaid, over the Caranglan Pass, and down the valley of the Rio Grande de Pampanga to Manila, another three or four days would be all that would be needed. It would be a Japanese picnic. Fortifying Corregidor Island, at the entrance to Manila Bay, which is about all the serious scheme of defence against a foreign foe we have out there, is quite like the reliance of the Spaniards on Morro Castle, at the mouth of the harbor of Santiago de Cuba, against our landing at Guantanamo. Our garrison in the Philippines, all told, is but a handful. Aparri is an absolutely unfortified seaport, at which the Japanese could land an army overnight from the southern end of Formosa. There are no military fortifications whatsoever to stay the advance of an invading army from Aparri down the Cagayan Valley, and thence over the watershed of Nueva Viscaya Province, through the Caranglan Pass, and down the valley of the Pampanga River to Manila. So that to-day Japan can take Manila inside of two weeks any time she wants to. That is why I object to the President's "jollying" the situation along as best he can, without taking the American people into his confidence. Any army officer at our War College will inform any member of the House or Senate on inquiry, that Japan can take the Philippines any time she wants to. President Taft and the Mikado may keep on exchanging the most cordial cablegrams imaginable, but the map-making goes on just the same. And, earnest and sincere as both the President and the Emperor undoubtedly are in their desire to preserve the general peace, who is going to restrain Hobson and Hearst, and several of Japan's public men equally distinguished and equally inflammatory? Heads of nations cannot restrain gusts of popular passion. The Pacific Coast is not so friendly to Japan as the rest of our country, and as between Japan and the Pacific Coast, we are pretty apt to stand by the latter without inquiring with meticulous nicety into any differences that may arise.

The reason I said in the chapter before this one that Mr. Root is a dangerous man to Republican institutions was because he is of the type who are constantly finding situations which they consider it best for the people not to know about. After the McKinley election of 1900 was safely "put over," Mr. Root, as Secretary of War, let Judge Taft go ahead and ride his dove-of-peace hobby-horse in the Philippines, duly repeating to the American people all the cheery Taft cluckings to said horse, at a time when the real situation is indicated by such grim correspondence as the following cablegram dated January 29, 1901:

Wood, Havana: Secretary of War is desirous to know if you can give your consent to the immediate withdrawal Tenth Infantry from Cuba.*Imperative that we have immediate use of every available company we can lay our hands on for service in the Philippines.* (Signed) Corbin.49

But let us turn from this sorry spectacle of Mr. Root pulling the wool over the eyes of his countrymen to make them believe the Filipinos were not quite so unconsenting as they seemed to be, and again look at the sheer splendor of American military ability to get anything done the Government wants done. I refer to the capture of Aguinaldo.

One of the most eminent lawyers in this country once said to me, "I would not let that man Funston enter my house." I tried to enlighten him, but as I happened to be a guest in his house at the time, which entitled him to exemption from light if he insisted—which he did—General Funston and he have continued to miss what might have been a real pleasure to them both. The following is, as briefly as I can dispose of it, the story of the capture of Aguinaldo on March 23, 1901.

Ever since Aguinaldo had escaped through our lines in November, 1899, his capture had been the one great consummation most devoutly wished. It has already been shown how busy with the war the army was all the time Judge Taft was gayly jogging away astride of his peace hobby about the insurrection being really quite regretted and over. However, in the favorite remark with which he used to wave the insurrection into thin air, to the effect that it was now merely "a Mafia on a large scale," there was one element of truth. The general feeling of the people, both educated and uneducated, was such as to countenance the attitude of the leaders that pro-American tendencies were treason. Any leader who surrendered of course was thereafter an object of at least some suspicion to his fellow-countrymen, however assiduous his subsequent double-dealing. As long as Aguinaldo remained out, this state of affairs was sure to continue indefinitely, possibly for years to come. If captured, *he* would probably himself give up the struggle, and use his influence with the rest to do likewise. Therefore, in the spring of 1901, each and every one of General MacArthur's 70,000 men was, and had been since 1899, on the *qui vive* to make his own personal fortunes secure for life, and gain lasting military distinction, by taking any sort of chances to capture Aguinaldo. On February 8, 1901, an officer of General Funston's district, the Fourth, in central Luzon, intercepted a messenger bearing despatches from Aguinaldo to one of his generals of that region, directing the general (Lacuna) to send some reinforcements to him, Aguinaldo. General Funston's headquarters were then at San Fernando, in the province of Pampanga—organized as a "civil" government province by act of the Taft Commission just five days later.50 Through these despatches and their bearer, General Funston ascertained the hiding-place of the insurgent chieftain to be at a place called Palanan, in the mountains of Isabela Province, in northeastern Luzon, near the Pacific Coast. Early in the war we had availed ourselves of a certain tribe, or clan, known as the Maccabebes, who look nowise different from all other Filipinos, but who had, under the Spanish government, by reason of long-standing feuds with their more rebellious neighbors, come to be absolutely loyal to the Spanish authorities. When we came they had transferred that loyalty to us, and had now become a recognized and valuable part of our military force. So it occurred to General Funston; "Why not personate the reinforcements called for, the American officers to command the expedition assuming the rôle of captured American prisoners?" The plan was submitted to General MacArthur and adopted. A picked company of Maccabebes was selected, consisting of about eighty men, and General Funston decided to go himself, taking with him on the perilous expedition four young officers of proven mettle: Captain Harry W. Newton, 34th Infantry, U. S. Volunteers, now a captain of the Coast Artillery; Captain R. T. Hazzard, 11th Volunteer Cavalry; Lieutenant O. P. M. Hazzard, his brother, of the same regiment, the latter now an officer of the regular army, and Lieutenant Mitchell, "my efficient aid."51 March 6, 1901, the U.S.S. *Vicksburg* slipped quietly out of Manila Bay, bearing the participants in the desperate enterprise— as desperate an undertaking as the heart and brain of a soldier ever carried to a successful conclusion. General Thomas H. Barry wrote Secretary of War Root, after they left, telling of their departure, and stating that he did not much expect ever to see them again. The chances were ten to one that the eighty men would meet five or ten times their number, and, as they were to masquerade as troops of the enemy, they could not complain, under the recognized laws of war as to spies, at being summarily shot if captured alive. And the whole Filipino people were a secret service ready to warn Aguinaldo, should the carefully concocted ruse be discovered anywhere along the journey. They went down to the southern end of Luzon, and through the San Bernardino Straits into the Pacific Ocean, and thence up the east coast of Luzon to Casiguran Bay, about 100 miles south of Palanan, landing at Casiguran Bay, March 14th. The "little Macks," as General Funston calls the Maccabebes, were made to discard their dapper American uniforms after they got aboard the ship, and don instead a lot of nondescript clothing gathered by the military authorities at Manila before the *Vicksburg* sailed, so as to resemble the average insurgent command. Not a man of them had been told of the nature of the expedition before sailing. This was not for fear of treachery, but lest some one of the faithful "Macks" should get his tongue loosed by hospitality before departing. Also, their Krag-Jorgensen regulation rifles were taken from them, and a miscellaneous assortment of old Springfields, Mausers, etc., given them instead, to complete the deception. An exinsurgent officer, well known to Aguinaldo, but now in General Funston's employ, was to play the rôle of commanding officer of the "reinforcements." To read General Funston's account of this expedition is a more convincing rebuttal of the contemporaneous Taft denials of Filipino hostility and of the unanimity of the feeling of the people against us, than a thousand quotations from official documents could ever be. It was necessary to land more than 100 miles south of Aguinaldo's hiding-place, lest the smoke of the approaching vessel should be sighted from a distance, and some peasant or lookout give the alarm. Accordingly, they landed at Casiguran Bay by night, with the ship's lights screened, the *Vicksburg* at once departing out of sight of land, and agreeing to meet them off Palanan, their destination, on March 25th, eleven days later. From the beginning they vigilantly and consummately played the rôle planned, the "Macks" having been drilled on the way up, each and all, in the story they were to tell at the first village near Casiguran Bay, and everywhere thereafter, to the effect that they had come across country, and en route had met ten American soldiers out map-making, and had killed two, wounded three, and captured five. They were to point to General Funston and the four other Americans in corroboration of their story. Speaking of himself and his four fellow "prisoners," General Funston says, "We were a pretty scrubby looking lot of privates." The villagers received the patriot forces, thus flushed with triumph, in an appropriate manner, and supplied them with rations and guides for the rest of their 100-mile journey to the headquarters of the "dictator." General Funston is even at pains to say for the village officials that they were very humane and courteous to himself and the other four American "prisoners." They reached Palanan Bay, eight miles from Palanan, on March 22d. Here Hilario Tal Placido, the ex-insurgent officer whose rôle in the present thrilling drama was that of "commanding officer" of the expedition, sent a note to Aguinaldo, stating that he had halted his command for a rest at the beach preparatory to marching inland and reporting to the Honorable Presidente, that they were very much exhausted, and much in need of food, and please to send him some. Of course that was the natural card to play to put Aguinaldo off his guard. The food came, and the bearers returned and casually reported to the Honorable Presidente that his honorable reinforcements would soon be along, much to the honorable joy—to make the thing a little Japanesque—of the president of the honorable republic. This incident has been since made the occasion of some criticism—that it was contrary to decency to accept Aguinaldo's food and then attack him afterwards. General Funston very properly replies in effect that the case would have been very different had he thrown himself on Aguinaldo's mercy, taken his food, and used treachery afterwards, but that his conduct was entirely correct, under the code of war, for the reason that should he and his command be captured while personating enemy's forces, Aguinaldo would have had a perfect right, under the rules of the game, to shoot them all as spies. He adds rather savagely, concerning "certain ladylike persons in the United States" who have censured his course in the matter, that he "would be *very much interested in seeing* the results of a surgical operation performed on the skull of a man who cannot readily see the radical difference between the two propositions," and that he doubts if a good quality of calf brains would be revealed by the operation.

At all events, the expedition was very much refreshed by the food and highly delighted at the proof, contained in the sending of it, that Aguinaldo did not suspect a ruse. But now came one of the many emergencies which had to be met by quick wit in the course of that memorable adventure. Aguinaldo sent word to leave the "prisoners" under a guard in one of the huts by the sea-shore, where there was one of the Aguinaldo retainers in charge, an old Tagalo. After a hurried, whispered conversation, "prisoner" Funston instructed "Commanding Officer" Placido to go ahead with his main column and then a little later send back a forged written order purporting to be from Aguinaldo, for the "prisoners" to come on also. This was shown to the old Tagalo, thus disarming suspicion on his part. But now came the "closest shave" they had. The column met a detachment from Aguinaldo's headquarters sent down with instructions to relieve the necessarily worn-out guard of the newly arrived "re-inforcements" that were supposed to be guarding the five prisoners at the beach, and let said guard come on up to headquarters with the rest of the "re-inforcements," the idea being to still leave the prisoners at the beach so they would not learn definitely as to the Aguinaldo whereabouts. Detaining the officer commanding this detachment for a moment or so on some pretext, the "Commanding Officer" of the "re-inforcements" whispered to a Maccabebe corporal to run back and tell General Funston and the rest of the "prisoners" to jump in the bushes and hide. This they did, lying within thirty feet of the detachment, as it passed them en route for the beach. Of course a fight would have meant considerable firing, and the quarry might hear it, take fright, and escape. Finally they reached Palanan, the "prisoners" quite far in the rear. Placido got safely into Aguinaldo's presence, followed at a short distance by the main body of his Maccabebes. Aguinaldo's life-guard of some fifty men, neatly uniformed, presented arms as Placido entered the insurgent headquarters building, and thereafter waited at attention outside. Then the worthy Placido entertained the honorable Presidente with a few cock-and-bull stories about the march across country, etc., made obediently to the President's order, keeping a weather eye out of the window all the time. As soon as the Maccabebes had come up and formed facing the Aguinaldo life-guard, Placido went to the window and ordered them to open fire. This they did, killing two of the insurgents and wounding their commanding officer. The rest fled, panic-stricken, by reason of the surprise. Then Placido, a very stout individual, grabbed Aguinaldo, who only weighs about 115 pounds, threw him down, and *sat on him*, until General Funston, the Hazzards, Mitchell, and Newton arrived. The orders were iron-clad that under no circumstances, if it could be avoided, was Aguinaldo to be killed. His signature to proclamations telling the people to quit the war was going to be needed too much. The party rested two days and then set out for the coast again, on March 25th, the day the *Vicksburg* had agreed to meet them. "At noon" says General Funston, "we again saw the Pacific, and far out on it a wisp of smoke—the *Vicksburg* coming in!" In due course they reached Manila Bay. The old palace of the Spanish captains-general, then occupied by our commanding general, is up the Pasig River, accessible from the bay by launch. By that method General Funston took his precious prisoner to the palace without the knowledge of a soul in the great city of Manila. He arrived before General MacArthur had gotten up. In a few minutes the General came out. "Where is Aguinaldo?" said he, dryly. He supposed General Funston simply had some details to tell, like the commanding officers of hundreds of other expeditions that had gone out before that on false scents in search of the illustrious but elusive Presidente. "Right here in this house," said General Funston. General MacArthur could hardly believe his ears. A few days later, General Funston walked into General MacArthur's office. The latter said; "Well, Funston, they do not seem to have thought much in Washington of your performance. I am afraid you have got into trouble." "At the same time he handed me," says General Funston in the *Scribner Magazine* article above mentioned, "a cablegram announcing my appointment as a brigadier-general in the regular army."

In his annual report for 1901,52 General MacArthur describes the capture of Aguinaldo as "the most momentous single event of the year," stating also that "Aguinaldo was the incarnation of the insurrection." This last statement explains why he was so anxious to capture him *alive*. If dead, he would be sure to get *re-incarnated* in the person of some able assistant of his entourage, thus insuring undisturbed continuance of the war. He was most graciously treated by General MacArthur during his stay as that distinguished soldier's "guest" at the Malacañan palace, from March 28th until April 20th. The word "guest" is placed in quotations because the host thought so much of him that he considered him worth many hundred times his weight in gold, and had him watched *night and day by a commissioned officer*. Everything that had been done by the Americans since November, 1899, was explained to him, and he was made to see that our purposes with regard to his people were not only benevolent but also inflexible; in other words that there was no altering our determination to make his people happy whether they were willing or not. Seeing this, Aguinaldo bowed to the inevitable. The programme explained to Aguinaldo is wittily described by a very bright Englishwoman as a plan "to have lots of American school teachers at once set to work to teach the Filipino English and at the same time keep plenty of American soldiers around to knock him on the head should he get a notion that he is ready for self-government before the Americans think he is"—a quaint scheme, she adds, "and one characteristic of the dauntlessness of American energy." To be brief, on April 19th, Aguinaldo took the oath of allegiance to the American Government, which all agree he has faithfully observed ever since, and issued a proclamation recommending abandonment of further resistance. This proclamation was at once published by General MacArthur and signalized by the immediate liberation of one thousand prisoners of war, on their likewise taking the oath of allegiance. In his proclamation Aguinaldo said, among other things:

The time has come, however, when they [the Filipino people] find their advance along this path [the path of their aspirations] impeded by an irresistible force. * * * Enough of blood, enough of tears and desolation.

He concludes by announcing his final unconditional submission to American sovereignty and advises others to do likewise.53

Soon after this General Tiño surrendered in General Young's district, and in another part of northern Luzon, General Mascardo, commanding the insurgent forces in the provinces of Bataan and Zambales, heretofore described as "the west wing of the great central plain," also surrendered. In the latter part of June, General Cailles, with whom we have already had occasion to become acquainted, in connection with Judge Taft's "Mafia on a large scale," also surrendered in Laguna Province. After that, there was never any more trouble in northern Luzon. But during the spring of 1901, the Commission had been very busy organizing the provinces of southern Luzon under civil government, thus cutting short the process of licking it into submission and substituting a process of loving it into that state through good salaries and otherwise—a policy which postponed the final permanent pacification of that ill-fated region for several years, as hereinafter more fully set forth.

The unconditional absoluteness with which Judge Taft acted from the beginning on the assumption that the Filipinos would make a distinction between civil and military rule, and that their objection to us was because we had first sent soldiers to rule them and not civilians, and that these objections would vanish before the benignant sunlight of a government by civilians, is one of the great tragedies of all history, considering the countless lives it eventually cost. As a matter of fact, the Filipino objection had little or no relation to the kind of clothes we wore, whether they were white duck or khaki. Their objection was to *us, i.e.*, to an alien yoke. However, to heal the bleeding wounds of war, the Filipinos were benevolently told to forget it, and a civil government was set up on July 4, 1901, pursuant to the amiable delusion indicated. That it has never yet proved a panacea, and why, will be developed in the next and subsequent chapters, but only in-so-far as such development throws light on the present situation—which it is the whole object of this book to do.

And now a few words by way of concluding the present chapter, as preliminary to the inauguration of a civil government, cannot be misconstrued, though they come from one who held office under it. I have certainly made clear that Judge Taft and his colleagues were as honest in their delusion about how popular they were with the Filipinos as many other public men who have been known to have hobbies, and my remarks must be understood as based on the comprehensive bird's-eye view which we have had of the whole situation from the outbreak of the war with Spain in 1898 to the end of June, 1901, as a summation of that situation. It is quite true that all contemporary history is as much affected by its environment as the writer of it is by his own limitations. But it certainly seems clear now that, in regard to the Philippine problem presented in 1898 by the decision to keep the islands, the American people were played upon by the politicians for the next few years thereafter, sometimes on the idea that the Filipino people were *not* a people but only a jumble of semi-civilized tribes incapable of any intelligent notion of what independence meant, and sometimes on the idea that while there was no denying that they *were* indeed a civilized, homogeneous, Christian people, yet the great majority of them did not want independence, and would prefer to be under a strong alien government. But the key-note to the McKinley policy from the beginning, his answer to the eager question of his own people, was that there was no real absence of the consent of the governed. In Senator Lodge's history of the war with Spain, written in 1899, there is a description of the long struggle for independence in Cuba, whose existence Spain denied year after year until we decided that patience had ceased to be a virtue, which description is so strikingly applicable to the situation in the Philippines during the first years of American rule that I cannot refrain from quoting it here:

And we were to go on pretending that the war was not there, and that we had answered the unsettled question, when we really had simply turned our heads aside and refused to look. And then when the troublesome matter had been so nicely laid to sleep, the result followed which is usual *when Congressmen and Presidents and nations are trying to make shams pass for realities.*"54

By the same high token the Philippine question will always remain "the unsettled question" until it is settled right. In other words, the American occupation of the Philippines, having been originally predicated on the idea that the Filipino people did not really want independence, a fiction which political expediency incident to government by parties inexorably compelled it to try to live up to thereafter, took the form, in 1901, of a civil government founded upon a benevolent lie, which expressed a hope, not a fact, a hopeless hope that can never be a fact. And that is what has been the matter with it ever since.

The papers 'id it 'andsome,
But you bet the army knows.

1Letter of July 22, 1898, by Duc d'Almodovar del Rio, Prime Minister of Spain, to President McKinley, suing for peace. *Senate Document 62*, pt. 1, 55th Congress, 3d Session, pp. 272–3.

2See *Congressional Record* of that date, p. 33.

3General Otis's appreciation of such "aid" was thus expressed in his cablegram to Washington of June 4, 1899: "Negotiations and conferences with insurgents cost soldiers' lives and prolong our difficulties." *Correspondence Relating to the War with Spain*, vol. ii., p. 1002.

4Address by Secretary of War Taft before the National Geographic Society at Washington, published in the official organ of that Society, *National Geographic Magazine* for August, 1905.

5Says General Chaffee in his annual report for 1902: "The intelligent element controlled the ignorant masses as perfectly as ever a captain controlled the men of his company."*War Department Report*, 1902, vol. ix., p. 191.

6*War Department Report*, 1900, vol. i., pt. 5, p. 61.

7August 29, 1898, to May 5, 1900.

8Especially independence.

9*Senate Document 331* (1902), pt. 1, page 50.

10A slander ignorantly repeated by the adverse report of the minority of the Insular Affairs Committee of the House, on the Jones Bill, introduced in March, 1912, proposing ultimate independence in 1921.

11 See *The Commoner*, April 27, 1906.

12 *Philippine Census*, vol. ii., p. 9.

13 These are the three main lines of cleavage, linguistically speaking. Nearly all the minor dialects are kin to some one of the principal three.

14 Peasant's hut, usually of bamboo, thatched with stout straw (*nipa*). It is the log cabin of the Philippines.

15 By way of protest against this kind of belittling of the army's work, General MacArthur says in his annual report (*War Dept. Rept.*, 1900, vol. i., pt. 5, p. 60), "Such a narrow statement of the case is unfair to the service," adding a handsome tribute, which might have come very graciously from the Commission had it felt so disposed, to "the endurance, fortitude, and valor" of his 70,000 men during the precise period while the Commission was filling the American papers with politically opportune nonsense about "Peace, peace," when there was no peace.

16 See Report of Secretary of War Root for 1900. *War Department Report*, 1900, vol. i., pt. 1, p. 80.

17 See *Report of Taft Philippine Commission of 1900*, p. 17.

18 *War Department Report*, 1900, vol. i., pt. 5, pp. 34–42.

19 *S. D. 435*, 56th Cong. 1st Sess.

20 *Report U. S. Philippine Commission*, November, 1900, p. 15.

21 General Lawton was killed in battle in the hour of victory at a point only about twelve miles out of Manila, in the winter preceding the spring of 1900 in which the Taft Commission left the United States for Manila.

22 This interview was indorsed as substantially correct by General MacArthur before the Senate Committee of 1902, Senator Culberson first reading it to him and then asking him if it quoted him correctly. See hearing on Philippine affairs, 1902, *Senate Document 331*, pt. 2, p. 1942.

23 *War Department Report*, 1901, vol. i., pt. 4, p. 88.

24 *Ibid.*, 1900, vol. i., pt. 5, p. 60.

25 November, 1899, to September, 1900, both inclusive.

26 *W. D. R.*, 1900, vol. i., pt. 5, p. 60.

27 Judge Taft had cabled Secretary of War Root on August 21, 1900, after his arrival in June: "Defining of political issues in United States reported here in full, gave hope to insurgent officers still in arms, * * * and *stayed surrenders* to await result of election." See *War Department Report*, 1901, vol. i., pt. 4, p. 80.

28 *War Department Report*, 1901, vol. i., pt. 4, p. 89.

29 See *Report of Taft Commission to Secretary of War*, dated November 30, 1900.

30 A sample of one of these death sentences that Cailles and all the rest of the insurgent generals were accustomed to issue against their "Copperheads" may be seen in General MacArthur's report for 1900. *War Department Report*, 1900, vol. i., pt. 5, p. 63.

31 *War Department Report*, 1901, vol. i., pt. 4, p. 90.

32 See Report of Secretary Root for 1902, p. 13.

33 Just how correct this was will be examined later.

34 "The people seem to be actuated by the idea that men are never nearer right than when going with their own kith and kin." *War Department Report*, 1900, vol. i., pt. 5, p. 61.

35 General MacArthur's Annual Report dated October 1, 1900. *War Department Report*, 1900, vol. i., pt. 5, pp. 61–2.

36General MacArthur's report which we are now quoting from, dated October 1, 1900, was forwarded by the ordinary course of mail, and even if it arrived before the day of the November election, the Secretary of War certainly did not at once place it before the public.

37Compare this MacArthur, October 1, 1900, statement with the Taft statements of the same situation between June and November, 1900, as expressed for instance in his November, 1900, report to the Secretary of War thus: "*A great majority of the people long for peace and are entirely willing to accept the establishment of a government under the supremacy of the United States.* They are, however, restrained by fear. * * * Without this, armed resistance to the United States authority would have long ago ceased. It is a Mafia on a very large scale." Report, Taft Commission, November 30, 1900, p. 17. This was before Judge Taft met Juan Cailles above mentioned and liked him well enough to make him governor of a province, in spite of his being an "assassin," in other words a Filipino general who had a few weak-kneed fellows shot for being too friendly with the Americans.

38Chapter XI., *ante*.

39See *War Department Report*, 1900, vol. i., pt. 5, pp. 65–6.

40As for my share as a soldier in that Philippine Insurrection, admitting, as I now do, that it was a tragedy of errors, the President of the United States would indeed be a very impotent Chief Executive if it were every American's duty to deliberate as a judge on the Bench before he decided to answer a president's call for volunteers in an emergency. I am not yet so highly educated as to find no inward response to the sentiment, "Right or wrong, my country." If this sentiment is not right, no republic can long survive, for the ultimate safety of republics must lie in volunteer soldiery.

41Page 93.

42*Correspondence Relating to the War with Spain*, vol. ii., p. 1211.

43*Correspondence Relating to the War with Spain*, vol. ii., p. 1222.

44*Ibid.*, vol. ii., p. 1223.

45*Ibid.*, p. 1226.

46*Ibid.*, p. 1237.

47See *Correspondence Relating to War with Spain*, vol. ii., p. 1239.

48Ten or twelve thousand.

49*Correspondence Relating to War with Spain*, vol. ii., p. 1249.

50See *Public Laws, U. S. Philippine Commission Division of Insular Affairs, War Department*, Washington, 1901, p. 181.

51See General Funston's article on "The Capture of Aguinaldo," which appeared in *Scribner's Magazine* for November, 1911.

52*War Department Report*, 1901, vol. i. pt. 4, p. 99.

53For a copy of this proclamation see *War Department Report*, 1901, vol. i., pt. 4, p. 100.

54*The War with Spain*, by H. C. Lodge, p. 20 .

Chapter XV. Governor Taft—1901–2

For they have healed the hurt of the daughter of my people slightly, saying—Peace, peace; when there is no peace. Jeremiah viii., 11.

On February 22, 1898, the American Consul at Manila, Mr. Williams, after he had been at that post for about a month, wrote the State Department, describing the Spanish methods of keeping from the world the outward and visible manifestations of the desire of the Filipino people to be free from their yoke thus:

Peace was proclaimed and, since my coming, festivities therefor were held; but there is no peace, and has been none for two years.

He adds:

Conditions here and in Cuba are practically alike. War exists, battles are of almost daily occurrence, etc.1

As will hereinafter appear, this is not far from a correct description of the conditions which prevailed successively in various provinces of the Philippines in gradually lessening degree for the six years next ensuing after the report of the Taft Commission of November 30, 1900, wherein they said:

A great majority of the people long for peace and are entirely willing to accept the establishment of a government under the supremacy of the United States.2

We have seen how from the date of the outbreak, February 4, 1899, to the date of his final departure from the islands for the United States on May 5, 1900, General Otis had diligently supplied the eager ear of Mr. McKinley with his "situation well in hand" and "insurrection about to collapse" telegrams, Secretary of War Alger having meantime been forced out of the cabinet—in part, at least—by a public opinion which indignantly believed that the real situation was being withheld. We have seen how, from soon after the arrival of the Taft Commission at Manila on June 3, 1900, until after the November elections of that year, the same eager presidential ear aforesaid was supplied with like material through the presumably innocent but opportunely deluded optimism of the Commission, as manifested in the above sample message; how the actual military situation as described by General MacArthur, the military commander at the time, was one of "desperate resistance by means of a general banding of the people in support of the guerrillas in the field,"3 he having wired the War Department on January 4, 1901, "Troops throughout the archipelago more active than at any time since November, 1899";4 and how this had been followed on July 4, 1901, by a civil government, the inauguration of which could by no possibility be construed as affirming to the people of the United States anything other than the existence of a state of peace.

We are to trace in this and subsequent chapters how, a short time after the civil government was instituted, the insurrection got its second wind; how a year later came another public declaration of peace, on July 4, 1902; and how this was followed by a long series of public disorders, combated by prosecutions for sedition and brigandage, until toward the end of 1906. The drama is quite an allegory— Uncle Sam wrestling with his guardian angel Consent-of-the-governed. He finally gets both the angel's shoulders on the mat, however, and so the two have lived at loggerheads in the Philippines ever since.

As soon as we had once blundered into the colonial business, the rock-bottom frankness with which we so dearly love to deal with one another, let carping Europe deny it as she will, was superseded by a systematic effort on the part of the statesmen responsible for the blunder to conceal it. It soon became clear to those on the inside that the sovereign American people had "bought a gold brick," that is to say, had made a grievous mistake and had *done wrong*. But as it is not expedient for courtiers to tell the sovereign he has done wrong, because "The king can do no wrong," thereafter all the courtiers,—*i. e.* persons desiring to control the "sovereign" while seeming to obey him—instead of risking loss of the "royal" favor by boldly telling the people they had done wrong and ought to mend the error of their ways, began to fill their ears and salve their conscience with mediæval doctrines about salvation of the heathen through governmental missions maintained by the joint agencies of Cross and Sword. For the foregoing and cognate reasons, Senator Lodge's description of Spain's last thirty years in Cuba fits our first six or seven in the Philippines, beginning in 1899 with the original Otis press censorship policy of "not letting anything go that will hurt the Administration," and coming on down to a certificate made in 1907 by the Philippine Commission for consumption in the United States, to the effect that a state of general and complete peace had prevailed throughout the islands for a stated period preceding the certificate, when, as a matter of fact, during the period covered by the certificate, an executive proclamation formally declaring a state of insurrection had issued, and the Supreme Court of the islands had upheld certain drastic executive action as legal *because* of the state of insurrection recognized by the proclamation.

The Taft civil government of the Philippines set up in 1901 was an attempt to answer the question which, during the crucial period of our country's history following the Spanish War, rang so persistently through the public utterances of both Grover Cleveland and Benjamin Harrison: "Mr. President, how are you going to square the subjugation of the Philippines with the freeing of Cuba?" Mr. McKinley's answer had been, in effect: "Never mind about that, Grover; you and Benjamin are back numbers. I will show you 'the latest thing' in the consent-of-the-governed line, a government *not* 'essentially popular,' it is true, nor indeed at all 'popular,' in fact very unpopular, but 'essentially popular *in form.*' You lads are not experts on the political trapeze." Accordingly, as Senator Lodge said concerning the dreary years of continuous public disorders in Cuba under Spain, which we finally put a stop to in 1898:

We were to go on pretending that the war was not there, etc.

Lack of frankness is usually due to weakness of one sort or another. The weakness of the Spanish colonial system lay in the impotent poverty of the home government and the graft tendencies of the colonial officials. The weakness of the American colonial system has always lain in the fundamental unfitness of republican governmental machinery for boldly advocating and honestly enforcing doctrines which deny frankly and as a matter of course that governments derive their just powers from the consent of the governed. There are so many people in a republic like ours who will always stand by this last proposition as righteous, and as being the chief bulwark of their own liberties, and so many who will always regard denial of that proposition as an insidious practice calculated ultimately to react on their own institutions, that no colonial government of conquered subject provinces eager for independence can ever have the sympathy and backing of all our people. Thus it is that to get home support for the policy, the supreme need of the colonial government is constant apology for its own existence, and constant effort to show that the subject people do not really want freedom to pursue happiness in their own way as badly as their orators say they do; that the oratory is mere "hot air"; and that the people really like alien domination better than they seem to.

Always in a mental attitude of self-defence against home criticism, in its official reports there is ever present with the Philippine insular government the tendency and temptation not to volunteer to the American people evidence within its possession calculated to awaken discussion as to the wisdom of its continuance. It thus usurps a legitimate function never intended to be delegated to the Executive, but reserved to the people. It thus makes itself the judge of how much the people at home shall know. The law of self-preservation prompts it not to take the American people into its confidence, at least not that portion of them who are opposed on principle to holding remote colonies impossible to defend in the event of war without a large standing army maintained for the purpose. There is always the apprehension that the value of apparently unfavorable evidence will not be wisely weighed by the people at home, because of unfamiliarity with insular conditions. This is by no means altogether vicious. It is a perfectly natural attitude and a good deal can be said in favor of it. But the real vice of it lies in the fact that your colonial government thus becomes not unlike the president of a certain naval board before which a case involving the commission of an officer of the navy was once tried. They had no competent official stenographer to take down all that transpired. The Navy Department was asked for one, but they referred it to the board. The president of the board knew very well that "the defence" wanted to show bias on his part. He exuded conscious rectitude and plainly resented any suggestion of bias. So a stenographer was refused and the case proceeded, the proceedings being recorded in long hand by a regular permanent employee of the board. Under such circumstances, there is so much which transpires that is absolutely irrelevant and immaterial, that the proceedings would be interminable if every little thing were recorded. Consequently, much that *was* material, including casual remarks of the president of the board clearly indicative of bias sufficient to disqualify any judge or juror on earth, failed of entry in the record. However, enough was gotten into the record to satisfy the President of the United States that the president of the board was not only not impartial, but very much prejudiced, and he reversed the action of the board. The case of that board is very much like the case of the Philippine Government. The case of the latter is, as it were, a case involving a question as to how long a guardianship ought to continue, and they simply fail and omit to have recorded in a form where it may be available to the reviewing authority, the American people, much that is material (on the idea of saving the reviewing authority labor and trouble), which they think the record ought not to be cumbered with, or the reviewing authority bothered with. This practice is due to a confident belief that the American people, being so far away, and being necessarily so wholly unacquainted with all the ins and outs of the situation in the Philippines, are not fitted to pass intelligently on the questions which continually confront the colonial government. This is not a mental attitude of insult to the intelligence of the people of the United States. It is simply a belief that they, the colonial officials, know much better than the American people can ever know, what is wisest, in each case, to be done in the premises. And there is much to be said in favor of this view, so far as details go. The fundamental error of it, however, lies in the assumption that the American people are forever committed to permanent retention of the Philippines, *i. e.*, permanent so far as any living human being is concerned—an assumption wholly unauthorized by any declaration of the law-making power of this government, and countenanced only by the oft-expressed hope of President Taft that that will be the policy some day declared, if any definite policy is ever declared. Thus it is that throughout the last twelve years those particular facts and events which (to me) seem most vitally relevant to the fundamental question in the case, viz., whether or not we should continue to persist in the original blunder of inaugurating and maintaining a—to all intents and purposes— permanent over-seas colonial government, have been withheld from the knowledge of the American public. The present policy of indefinite retention with undeclared intention is a mere makeshift to avoid a frank avowal of intention to retain the islands for all future time with which anybody living has any practical concern. Until it is substituted by a definite declaration by Congress similar to the one we made in the case of Cuba, and the present American Governor-General and his associates are substituted by men sent out to report back how soon they think the Filipinos may safely be trusted to attend to their own domestic concerns, all crucial facts and situations that might jeopardize the continuance of the present American régime in the Philippines will continue, as heretofore, to remain unmentioned in the official reports of the American authorities now out there. Until that is done, you will never hear the Filipino side of the case from anybody whose opinion you are willing to make the basis of governmental action. These remarks will, obviously from the nature of the case, be quite as true long after President Taft, the reader, and I are dead as they are now.

Mr. Taft would be very glad to have Congress declare frankly that it is the purpose of this Government to hold the Philippines permanently, *i. e.*, permanently so far as the word means continuance of the "uplift" treatment long after everybody now on the earth is beneath it. But because public opinion in the United

States is so much divided as to the wisdom of a policy of frankly avowed intention permanently to retain the islands, he prefers to leave the whole matter open and undetermined, so as to get the support both of those who think a definite programme of permanent retention righteous and those who think such a programme vicious. He wishes to please both sides of a moral issue, on the idea that, as the present policy is in his individual judgment best for all concerned, the end justifies the means. Yet, as the issue *is* a moral one, which concerns the cause of representative government throughout the world, and a strategic one which concerns the national defence, it should, in my judgment, no longer be dodged, but squarely met. You constantly hear President Taft talking quite out loud here at home, in his public utterances, about the great politico-missionary work we are doing in the Philippines by furnishing them with the most approved up-to-date methods for the pursuit of happiness, the avoidance of graft in government, the elimination of crimes of violence, in short the ideal way to minimize the ills that human governments are heir to, while every day and every dollar spent out there by Americans induced by him to go there, are time and money tensely arrayed against the ultimate independence he purports to favor. Give the Americans out there a square deal. Let them know whether we are going to keep the islands or whether we are not. Honesty is a far better policy than the present policy. The Americans in the islands, Mr. Taft's agents in the Philippines, talk no uncandid and misleading stuff about the Philippines being exclusively for the Filipinos. And they do considerable talking. They need looking after, if the present pious fiction is to be kept up at this end of the line. Nobody in the Philippines to-day, among the Americans, considers talk about independence as anything other than political buncombe very hampering to their work. Listen to this high official of the insular government, who writes in the *North American Review* for February, 1912:

The somewhat blatant note with which we at the beginning proclaimed our altruistic purposes in the Philippines has *died away into a whisper. To say much about it is to incur a charge of hypocrisy.* 5

The most important problem which confronted Mr. McKinley when he sent Judge Taft to the Philippines was how to so handle the supreme question of public order as to avoid any necessity of having to ask Congress later for more volunteers to replace those whose terms of enlistment would expire June 30, 1901. We have already reviewed the strenuous efforts of General MacArthur during the twelve months immediately following the arrival of the Taft Commission in June, 1900, to get rid of the shadow of this necessity by the date named, the regular army having been reorganized meantime and considerably increased by the Act of February 2, 1901. On March 22, 1901, while the Taft Commission was going around the islands with their Federal party folk, holding out the prospect of office to those who would quit insurging and come in and be good, General MacArthur reported progress to Secretary of War Root by cable as follows: "Hope report cessation of hostilities before June 30."6 His idea was to get a good military grip on the situation, if possible, by that time, and, as a corollary, of course, that the grip thus obtained should be diligently retained for a long time, not loosened, so that the disturbed conditions incident to many years of war might have a few years, at least, in which to settle. In his annual report dated July 4, 1901, the date of the inauguration of Judge Taft as "Civil Governor," he says, in regard to the imperative necessity for continuing the military grip by keeping on hand sufficient forces:

Anything in the immediate future calculated to impede the activity or reduce the efficiency of these instruments will not only be a menace to the present, but *put in jeopardy the entire future of American possibilities* in the archipelago.7

General MacArthur believed in keeping the islands permanently. His views were frankly imperialistic. He had no salve to offer to the conscience of pious thrift at home anxious to believe that the Filipinos were not bitterly opposed to our rule, and very much in favor of what was supposed to be a glittering opening for Trade Expansion. He was thoroughly imbued with the British colonial idea known as The White Man's Burden. On the other hand, Governor Taft firmly believed that kindness would cure the desire of the people for independence. The difference between these two gentlemen was fully ventilated afterward before the Senate Committee of 1902. A statement of General MacArthur's embodying the crux of this difference was read to Governor Taft by Senator Carmack, and the Governor's reply was:

We did not then agree with that statement, and we do not now agree with it.8

A little later, in the same connection, he said to the same Senate Committee, with the cheery tolerance of conflicting views which comes only from entire confidence in the soundness of one's own:

I have been called the Mark Tapley of this Philippine business.

There is no doubt about the fact that President Taft is an optimist. But while optimism is a very blessed thing in a sick-room or a financial panic, it is a very poor substitute for powder and lead in putting down an insurrection, or in weaning people from a desire for independence accentuated by a long war waged for that purpose, especially when your kindness must be accompanied by assurances to the objects of it that on account of a lack of sufficient intelligence they are not fit for the thing they want. It was upon a programme of this sort that Governor Taft entered upon the task of reconciling the Filipinos to American rule more than ten years ago. The impossibility of the task is of course obvious enough from the mere statement of it. The subsequent bitterness between him and the military authorities was quite carefully and very properly kept from the American public because it might get back to the Filipino public. The military folk knew that to go around the country setting up provincial and municipal governments, carrying a liberal pay-roll, with diligent contemporaneous circulation of the knowledge that anybody who would quit fighting would stand a good chance to get an office, would seem to many of the Filipinos a confession of weakness and fear, sure to cause trouble later. Many of them—of course it would be inappropriate to mention names—simply did not believe that Mr. Taft was honest in his absurd notion. They simply damned "politics" for meddling with war, and let it go at that. But the real epic pathos of the whole thing was that Mr. Taft was actually sincere. He believed that the majority of the Philippine people were for him and his policies. As late as 1905, he seems to have clung to this idea, according to various accounts by Senators Newlands, Dubois, and others, in magazine articles written after their return from a trip to the Philippines in that year in company with Mr. Taft, then Secretary of War. In fact so impressed were they with the general discontent out there, and yet so considerate of their good friend Mr. Taft's feelings in the matter and his confidence that the Filipinos loved benevolent alien domination, that one of them simply contented himself with the remark:

When we left the islands I do not believe there was a single member of our party who was not sorry we own them, except Secretary Taft himself.

Indeed it is not until 1907 that, we find Mr. Taft's paternal solicitude for his step-daughter, Miss Filipina, finally reconciling itself to the idea that while this generation seems to want Home Rule as irreconcilably as Ireland herself and "wont be happy 'til it gets it," yet inasmuch as Home Rule is not, in his judgment, good for every people, this generation is therefore a wicked and perverse generation, and hence the Filipinos must simply resign themselves to the idea of being happy in some other generation. This attitude was freely stated before the Millers' convention at St. Louis, May 30, 1907, the speech being reported in the *St. Louis Globe-Democrat* the next day. Said Mr. Taft on that occasion, after admitting that the Islands had been a tremendous financial drain on us:

If, then, we have not had material recompense, have we had it in the continuing gratitude of the people whom we have aided?

Answering this, in effect, though not in so many words, "Alas, no," he adds, with a sigh which is audible between the lines:

He who would measure his altruism by the thankfulness of those whom he aids, will not persist in good works.

Thus we see the Mark Tapley optimism of 1902 become in 1907 a species of solicitude which Dickens describes in *Bleak House* as "Telescopic Philanthropy," in the chapter by that title in which he introduces the famous Mrs. Jellyby, mother of a large and interesting family, "a lady of very remarkable strength of character, who devotes herself entirely to the public," who "has devoted herself to an extensive variety of public subjects, at various times, and is at present devoted to the subject of Africa, with a general view to the cultivation of the coffee berry—*and* the natives,"—to the woeful neglect of her own domestic concerns and her large and expensive family of children. Since 1907, Mr. Taft has frankly abandoned his early delusion about the consent-of-the-governed, and boldly takes the position, up to that time more or less evaded, that the consent of the governed is not at all essential to just government.

The apotheosis of Uncle Sam as Mrs. Jellyby is to be found in one of Mr. Taft's speeches wherein he declared that the present Philippine policy was "a plan for the spread of Christian civilization in the Orient."

Thus has it been that, under the reactionary influence of a colonial policy, this republic has followed its frank abandonment of the idea that all just government must derive its origin in the consent of the governed by a further abandonment of the idea that Church and State should be kept separate. I do not wish to make President Taft ridiculous, and could not if I would. Nor do I seek to belittle him in the eyes of his people,—for we *are* "his people," for the time being. No one can belittle him. He is too big a man to be belittled by anybody. Besides, he is, in many respects beyond all question, a truly great man. But he is not the only great man in history who has made egregious blunders. And there is no question that we are running there on the confines of Asia, in the Philippines, a superfluous governmental kindergarten whose sessions should be concluded, not suddenly, but without unnecessary delay. The two principal reasons for retaining the Filipinos as subjects, or "wards," or by whatever euphemism any one may prefer to designate the relation, are, first, that a Filipino government would not properly protect life and property, and second, that although they complain much at taxation without representation through tariff and other legislation placed or kept on the statute books of Congress through the influence and for the benefit of special interests in the United States, yet that such taxation without representation is not so grievous as to justify them in feeling as we did in 1776. Whether these reasons for retaining the Filipinos as subjects indefinitely are justified by the facts, must depend upon the facts. If they are not, the question will then arise, "Would a Filipino government be any worse for the Filipinos than the one we are keeping saddled on them over their protest?"

In his letter of instructions of April 7, 1900, to the Taft Commission, Mr. McKinley first quoted the noble concluding language with which the articles of capitulation of the city of Manila gave an immediate and supremely comforting sense of security to a city of some three hundred thousand people who had then been continuously in terror of their lives for three and one half months, thus:

This city, its inhabitants, * * * and its private property of all description * * * are placed under the special safeguard of the faith and honor of the American army;

and then added:

As high and sacred an obligation rests upon the Government of the United States to give protection for property and life * * * to all the people of the Philippine Islands. * * * I charge this commission to labor for the full performance of this obligation, which concerns the honor and conscience of their country.

How the premature setting up of the civil government of the Philippines in 1901 under pressure of political expediency, and the consequent withdrawal of the police protection of the army, was followed by a long series of disorders combated by prosecutions for sedition and brigandage, toward the end of which the writer broke down and left the Islands exclaiming inwardly, "I do not know the method of drawing an indictment against a whole people," will now be traced, not so much to show that the Philippine insular government has failed properly and competently to meet the most sacred obligations that can rest upon any government, but to show the inherent unfitness of a government based on the consent of the governed to run any other kind of a government.

There were five officers of the Philippine volunteer army of 1899–1901 appointed to the bench by Governor Taft in 1901. Their names and the method of their transition from the military to the civil *régime* are indicated by the following communication, a copy of which was furnished to each, as indicated in the endorsement which follows the signature of Judge Taft:

UNITED STATES PHILIPPINE COMMISSION

PRESIDENT'S OFFICE, MANILA , June 17, 1901.

Major-General ARTHUR MACARTHUR , U. S. A.,

Military Governor of the Philippine Islands, Manila.

    SIR:

I am directed by the commission to inform you that it has made the following appointments under the recent Judicial Act passed June 11, 1901:

You will observe that among our appointees are five army officers: Brigadier General James F. Smith, Lieutenant James H. Blount, Jr., 29th Infantry, Captain Adam C. Carson, 28th Infantry; Captain Warren H. Ickis, 36th Infantry; and Lieutenant George P. Whitsett, 32d Infantry.

It is suggested that it would be well for these officers to resign their positions in the United States military service to the end that they may accept the civil positions, take the oath of office, and immediately begin their new duties.

I have the honor to be, very respectfully,

Your obedient servant,

(*Signed*) WM. H. TAFT,

President.

Official extract copy respectfully furnished Lieutenant James H. Blount, Jr., 29th Infantry, U. S. Vols., Manila, P. I. Your resignation, if offered in compliance with above letter, will be accepted upon the date preferred.

By command of Major-General MacArthur:

(*Signed*) E. H. CROWDER

Lieutenant-Colonel and Judge Advocate, U. S. A. Secretary.

Military Secretary's Office,
June 18, 1901.

General Smith had come out as colonel of the 1st Californias, and had won his stars on the field of battle, as has already been described in an earlier chapter. He went from the army to the Supreme Bench—at Manila. The archipelago had been divided by the Taft Commission into fifteen judicial districts, containing three or four provinces each,—each district court to be a *nisi prius* or trial court. Judge Carson (Va.) went to the Hemp Peninsula District in the extreme south of Luzon, already described, and four years later to the Supreme Bench, where he still is. Judge Ickis (Ia.) went to Mindanao, and later died of the cholera down there. Judge Whitsett (Mo.) went to Jolo (the little group of islets near British North Borneo), but his wife died soon afterward, and he resigned and came home. The writer (Ga.) went to northern Luzon, to the First District hereinafter noticed.

Just here it may be remarked that the reader will need no long complicated description of the details of the organization of the new government, interspersed with unpronounceable names, if he will simply assume the view-point Governor Taft had in the beginning. Governor Taft simply analogized his situation to that of a governor of a State or Territory at home. His fifty provinces were to him fifty counties, twenty-five of them in the main island of Luzon, which, as heretofore stated, is about the size of Ohio or Cuba (forty odd thousand square miles), and contains half the population and over one-third the total land area of the archipelago. However, each of his provincial governors was liberally paid, and the authority of a governor of a province was, on a small scale, more like that of one of our own state chief executives than like the authority and functions of the chairman of the Board of County Commissioners of a county with us. For instance, the governorship of Cebu, with its 2000 square miles of territory and 650,000 inhabitants, was quite as big a job as the governorship of New Mexico, or some other one of our newer States.

So that the task on which Governor Taft entered July 4, 1901, was the governing of a potential ultimate federal union in miniature, containing nearly eight millions of people. One slight mistake I think he made was in providing that the governors of the provinces should be ex-officio sheriffs of the Courts of First Instance (of the fifteen several judicial districts aforesaid). This was to enable the Judges of First Instance to keep a weather eye on the provincial governors, the judiciary at first being largely American, and it being the programme to have native governors, some of them recently surrendered insurgent generals, as rapidly as practicable and advisable. The scheme was good business, but not tactful. It subtracted some wind from the gubernatorial sails to be a sheriff, a provincial governor under the Spanish *régime* having been quite a vice-regal potentate. But the judges were as careful to treat their native governors with the consideration the authority vested in them called for as Governor Taft himself would have been. So no substantial harm was done, and the real power in the provinces of questionable loyalty remained where it belonged, in American hands.

Just after Governor Taft's inauguration, the four newly appointed district judges just out of the army called on the governor. Judge Carson was the spokesman, though without pre-arrangement. He said: "Governor, we have called to pay our respects and say goodbye before going to the provinces. We have been acting under military orders so long, that while we are not here to get orders, we would like to have any parting suggestions that may occur to you." Governor Taft said: "Well, Gentlemen, all I can think of is to remind you that if what we have all heard is true the Spanish courts usually operated to the delay of justice, rather than to the dispensing of it. So just go ahead to your respective districts, and get to work, remembering that you are Americans." So we did. Of course none of us loaned ourselves for a moment to the amiable Taft fiction that "the great majority of the people are entirely willing to government under the supremacy of the United States." We had all had a share in the subjugation of the Islands as far as it had progressed at that time, and had seen the Filipinos fight—unskilfully and ineffectively, it is true (because they none of them understood the use of two sights on a rifle, and simply could not hit us much), but pluckily enough. We knew the Filipinos well, and our attitude was simply that of "Pharaoh and the Sergeant," in Kipling's ballad of the conquest of Egypt. However, we knew nothing of the Egyptians, except what we had learned in the Bible, gave no thought to whether our occupation was to be "temporary" like the British occupation of Egypt since 1882, or temporary like the American occupation of Cuba in 1898. That was a matter for the people of the United States to determine later. But somebody had to govern the Islands, and there we were, and there were the Islands. In the scheme of things some one had to do that part of the world's work, and, as the salaries were liberal, we went to the work, not concerning ourselves with amiable fictions of any kind. I think our attitude was really one of more intimately sympathetic understanding of the Filipinos than that of Governor Taft himself, because we had all known them longer, and all spoke their language, *i. e.*, the language of the educated and representative men (Spanish), and knew their ways, their foibles, and their many indisputably noble traits. But we did not start out to play the part of political wet-nurses. Our attitude was, if Mr. Filipino does not behave, we will make him.

Judge Carson and myself had one peculiar qualification for fidelity to the Taft policies for which we were entitled to no credit. We instinctively resented any suggestion comparing the Filipinos to negroes. We had many warm friends among the Filipinos, had shared their generous hospitality often, and in turn had extended them ours. Any such suggestion as that indicated implied that we had been doing something equivalent to eating, drinking, dancing, and chumming with negroes. And we resented such suggestions with an anger quite as cordial and intense as the canons of good taste and loyal friendship demanded. I really believe that the southern men in the Philippines have always gotten along better with the Filipinos than any other Americans out there, and for the reasons just suggested. Not only is the universal American willingness to treat the educated Asiatic as a human being endowed with certain unalienable rights going to redeem him from the down-trodden condition into which British and other European contempt for him has kept him, but the American from the South out there is a guarantee that he shall never be treated as if he were an African. The African is æons of time behind the Asiatic in development; the latter is æons ahead of us in the mere duration of his civilization. The Filipino has many of the virtues both of the European and the Asiatic. Christianity has made him the superior in many respects, of his neighbor and racial cousin, the Japanese. And Spanish civilization has produced among them many educated gentlemen whom it is an honor to call friend.

The five lawyers, who on ceasing to be volunteer officers became judges, had other incentives also to make the Taft Government a success. The possession of power is always pleasant. We knew the military folk were going to stand by and watch the civil government, and prophesy failure. This of course put us on our metal to impress upon the dictatorial gentry of the military profession, with didactic firmness, the fundamental importance to all American ideals that the military should be subordinate to the civil authority.

The First Judicial District to which the writer was first assigned comprised four provinces, Ilocos Norte, in the Ilocano country, the province situated at the extreme northwestern corner of Luzon, in the military district the conquest of which by General Young has already been fully described; and the three provinces of the Cagayan valley,9 overrun by Captain Batchelor on his remarkable march from the mountains to the sea in November, 1899, also already described. Here I remained for a year, and then came home on leave, desperately ill; being given, on returning to the Islands after my recovery, an assignment in one of the southern islands, hereinafter dealt with.

We volunteers were all commissioned as judges as of the 15th of June, though none of us I believe were mustered out until June 30th. The day after I was notified of my appointment as judge, as above set forth, desiring to enter upon my judicial emoluments, which were several times those I was receiving as a soldier, I removed the shoulder-straps and collar ornaments from my white duck suit, and went over and took the oath of office before the Chief Justice of the Islands. We had not yet been mustered out of the army, but as above stated, Governor Taft had suggested to General MacArthur that we resign without waiting for the day of muster out, so we could get to work that much sooner, and General MacArthur had notified us that if we cared to resign at once as suggested, he would cable our resignations to Washington. Immediately after qualifying before the Chief Justice, I left his office and on emerging from the courthouse hailed a *carromata*,10 but the driver said No, he would not carry me. I suggested in a very rudimentary way, in rather rudimentary Spanish suited to him, that he was a common carrier, and as such under a duty to transport me. He said his horse was tired. His horse did not look tired. He would not have thus casually toyed with veracity if I had had my shoulder-straps on. An *autoridad* (a representative of constituted authority) is to the masses of the Filipino people something which instinctively challenges their respect and obedience, more especially where the "authority" is firm and just. Respect for authority is their most conspicuous civic trait, and it is on this element in the lower ninety, on the intelligence and capacity to guide them of the upper ten, and on the ardent patriotism of both, that I predicate my difference with President Taft as to the capacity of the Filipino people for self-government. However, as I was to all appearances not an "authority," this ignorant man treated me as merely one of the Americans who, having invaded his country, apparently were not sure whether they were afraid of his people or not. Again I tried diplomacy, offering him an exorbitant fare. "Nothing doing." It was about siesta time, and he would not budge. Here then was the civil government proposition in a nutshell, to take the ignorant people and teach them their rights under theoretically free institutions, instead of letting their own people do it *in their own way*; to reason directly with such people as this *cochero* (hackman), to begin at the bottom of the social scale right on the jump, the idea being to fit them, the sacred (?) majority, to know their rights and "knowing dare maintain" them against the educated minority, as if the latter did not have a greater natural interest in their welfare than any stranger could possibly have. That I indulged all these reflections at the time I of course do not mean to say. The significance of the incident has of course deepened in the light of the subsequent years. At any rate, I did not succeed in budging that *cochero*. I walked home, forego the difference between the military and the judicial salary for the two weeks remaining before muster-out day, put my shoulder-straps back on, and kept them on until June 30, 1901.11

When I first landed on the China seacoast of the district I was to preside over, I was met by quite a reception committee of the leading men, who conducted me with great courtesy to the provincial capital. A little later the justices of the peace paid their respects. One of them came thirty miles to do so. The court-room was very long, and when I first spied this last man, he was at the other end of the room bowing very low. He would bow, then advance a few steps, then bow again, then resume the forward march toward me. I reminded myself of some ancient king, so profound were his obeisances. At first I thought to myself, "He bows too low, he must have been up to some devilment lately!" Experience showed me later that it was simply one of the ever-present manifestations of the respect of the Filipino for constituted authority. They positively love to show their respect for authority, just as a good soldier loves to show his respect for an officer. Here some American remarks: "Ah, but that is not good proof of capacity for self-government. They would not 'cuss out' the party in power enough." I answer: Who made you the judge to say that our particular form of government and our particular way of doing things is better for each and every other people under the sun than any they can devise for themselves? But there was of course another possible reason for the profundity of the obeisances of my judicial subordinate above mentioned. When I reached that province of Ilocos Norte in July, 1901, the people were in a state of submission that was simply abject. They had at first worked the *amigo* business on General Young, and treachery of that kind had been so inexorably followed by dire punishment, that every home in the country had its lesson. Yet that was the only way. The poor devils did not seem to know when they were licked. This is not maudlin sentiment. It is a protest against the cotemporary libel on Filipino patriotism about "the great majority" being "entirely willing" to accept our rule, and the cotemporary belittling of the work the army had to do to make them accept it.

I remained in charge of the First Judicial District for more than a year, and during that period tried few or no crimes of a political character, that is to say, indictments for sedition or the like—attempts to subvert the government. The district comprised a total population of about a half million people, more than one-eighth of the population of Luzon, and a total area of over 13,000 square miles, nearly one-third of all Luzon. But remember, this was in northern Luzon, where the work of pacification was lucidly completed by the army before the "peace-at-any-price" policy began. We will see what happened in my friend Judge Carson's district, and in the rest of southern Luzon later. The principal broad general fact I now recall, in connection with the administration of justice in the First Judicial District during the year or more I had it, is that the main volume of business on the court calendars was crimes of violence of a strictly non-political character due to lack of efficient police protection in the several communities, consequent on withdrawal of military garrisons. The country was in an unsettled state. The aftermath of war, lawless violence, was virulently present, and the presence of troops scattered through a province, under such circumstances, is a wonderful moral force to restrain lawlessness. However high the purpose, however kindly the motive, the setting up of a civil government in the Philippines at the time it was set up, when the country was far from ready for it, was a terrible mistake. Of course no one man in a given province or judicial district had a bird's-eye view of the whole situation and the whole panorama at the time, such as we can get at this distance, in retrospect. Of course it did not lie in human nature for the men responsible for the mistake to see it at first, and, the die once cast, they had to keep on, with intermittent resort to military help, the extent of which help was always minimized thereafter. To show how little the general state of the archipelago was understood by American provincial officials busy in a given part of it, and getting little or no news of the outside world, I remained in the First Judicial District from July, 1901, to August, 1902, and heard nothing of the great insurrection in southern Luzon, in Batangas, and the adjacent provinces, which raged during the winter of 1901–02, except a vague rumor that there was trouble down there. The Filipinos did, however. Of course for Mr. Root to be able to furnish in December, 1901, a report, as Secretary of War, to the President, for consumption by Congress and the people of this country, to the effect that his volunteer army had been mustered out on schedule time, June 30, 1901, and a "civil" government set up and in due operation, was a nice showing, calculated to sooth latent public discontent with wading through slaughter to over-seas dominion. Reports thereafter of disturbances could always be waived aside as merely local in character, and not serious. If it were stoutly asserted that everything was quiet all over the archipelago except in certain parts of certain localities, naming them, that sounded well, and as the public at home simply skipped the unpronounceable names, not caring much whether they represented molecules or hemispheres, all went well. For instance, most of the provinces of the archipelago were organized under "civil" government prior to the inauguration of Governor Taft, which occurred, July 4, 1901, and on July 17th, thereafter, Batangas, Cebu, and Bohol were restored to military control.12 I suppose the fact that Batangas, Cebu, and Bohol had been so restored was duly announced at the time in the Associated Press despatches from Manila. But what light did it throw on the situation? Who knew whether any one of these names represented a mountain lair, a country village, a remote islet, or a large and populous province? As a matter of fact, each was a province, and the total population of the three provinces was 1,180,655,13 and their total area 4651 square miles.14 The eminent gentlemen charged with the government of the Islands, once they committed themselves to their "civil" government, persisted always in treating the insurrection, as General Hancock's campaign speeches used to treat the tariff—as "a local issue." The true analogy, that of a house on fire, with the fire partly but not wholly under control, and momentarily subject to gusts of wind, never seems to have occurred to them. Here were provinces aggregating nearly twelve hundred thousand people, officially admitted to be still in insurrection within less than two weeks after the announcement of the inauguration of a civil government, which included them, with its implied assertion of a state of peace as to them.

If to the three provinces above named you add the province of Samar, later of dark and bloody fame, you have a fourth province as to which not only had there been no "civil" government organized on paper, but no claim yet made by any one that we had ever conquered it. We had been so busy in Luzon and elsewhere that we had not yet had time to bother very much with Samar. The area of Samar is 5276 square miles, and its population 266,237. (See the census tables already cited.) In their report dated October 15, 1901,15 you find the Commission admitting that "the insurrection still continues in Batangas, Samar, Cebu" and "parts of" Laguna and Tayabas provinces. Now the euphemistic limitation implied in the words "parts of" is quite negligible, for any serious purpose, since our troops kept the insurgents rather constantly on the move, and the population in all the "parts of" any province that was still holding out backed up the combatants morally and materially, with information as to our movements, supplies, etc., whenever the insurgent detachments, in the course of their peregrinations, happened to pass through those "parts." So, to make a recapitulation presenting the political situation admitted by the Commission to exist a little over three months after the inauguration of civil government, we have the insurrection still in progress as follows:

Province	Area (sq. m.)	Population
Batangas	1,201	257,715
Cebu	1,939	653,727
Bohol	1,511	269,223
Laguna	629	148,606

Province	*Area* (sq. m.)	*Population*
Tayabas	5,993	153,065
Samar	5,276	266,237
Total	16,549	1,748,573

According to his own official statements, it thus appears that on October 15th, after Governor Taft set up his "civil" government on the Fourth of July, throughout one-fifth of the territory and among one-fourth of the population insurrection was rampant. The total area of the archipelago, if Mohammedan Mindanao be excepted (for the reason that the Moros never had anything to do with the Filipinos and their insurrection against us), is about 80,000 square miles, having a total population of 7,000,000. So that, to restate the case, one-fifth of the house was still on fire, and one-fourth of the inmates were trying their best to keep the fire from being put out.

Just here I owe it to President Taft, under whose administration as governor I served as a judge, as well as to myself, to explain why I have so frequently put the word "civil" in quotations in referring to the civil government of the Philippines. Broadly speaking, if "civil" does not imply consent of the governed, it at least distinctly negatives the idea of a bleeding, prostrate, and deeply hostile people. And, in that the civil government of the Philippines founded in 1901 did so negative the actual conditions it was a kindly humbug. When you go around the country sending people to the penitentiary by scores for political crimes, and then get criticised afterwards for "subserviency" to the government you are thus serving, you get a trifle sensitive about such criticism. Now the core of the charges made in this country against the Philippine judiciary in the early days was that they were parties to a humbug, pliable servants of a government which was trying to produce at home an incorrect impression of substantial *absence of unwillingness* on the part of the governed. I am very sure that the five ex-officers of the volunteer army above named, who went from the army to the bench, never did, by act or word, lend themselves to the idea that there was any "consent" on the part of the governed. Those of us who had been in Cuba with General Wood had but a little while previously observed there a *civil régime* under a *military* name. We were now, in the Philippines, serving a *military régime* under a *civil* name. We had all of us doubtless—if there was an exception it is immaterial—served on military commissions. We therefore felt, without immodesty, that we could deal out to insurrectos and their political cousins, the brigands, more even-handed justice, as a *military commission of one*, than a board of several officers, booted, spurred, and travel-stained from some recent man-hunt. Turning, however, from the more inconspicuous objects of Professor Willis's attacks,[16] the American trial judges in the Philippines in the pioneer days, to the now wide-looming historic personage who was his real objective, I was asked at a public meeting in Boston, rather significantly, by one of the most eminent lawyers in this country, Mr. Moorfield Storey, formerly president of the American Bar Association, whether or not there had been attempts in the Philippines, while I was there, to make the judiciary subservient to the executive. My answer was, "No, the lawyers who have been in charge of the Philippine Government have never been guilty of any unprofessional conduct." But the distinguished Boston barrister above referred to has a nephew who is now and has been since 1909, Governor of the Philippines—and who, before he went out there was a representative of Big Business in Boston—Governor Forbes, and I have no idea that any judge who during that time has rendered any decision of importance he did not like has been promoted to the Supreme Bench of the Islands, though I know that under Governor Taft, Judge Carson unhesitatingly declared a certain act of the Commission null and void as being in conflict with an Act of Congress, and before the time-servers had gotten through wondering at his rashness, Mr. Taft had him put on the Supreme Bench of the Philippines17 because he liked that kind of a judge.

Having sown the wind by setting up his civil government too soon, let us now observe the whirlwind Governor Taft reaped within six months thereafter. Of course the civil and military folk were at daggers' points. That goes without saying. But their differences were decorously suppressed so that the Filipinos did not get hold of them. To that end, the situation was also diligently concealed in the United States. In his proclamation of July 4, 1902, you find President Roosevelt publicly smoothing the ruffled feathers of that rugged hero of many battles in two hemispheres, General Chaffee, and also commending Governor Taft, and telling them how harmoniously they had gotten along together to the credit of their common country. But in 1901, shortly after General Chaffee had relieved General MacArthur, you find the following cablegram:

EXECUTIVE MANSION, WASHINGTON,
October 8, 1901.

CHAFFEE, MANILA : I am deeply chagrined, to use the mildest possible term, over the trouble between yourself and Taft. I wish you to see him personally, and spare no effort to secure prompt and friendly agreement in regard to the differences between you. Have cabled him also. It is most unfortunate to have any action which produces friction and which may have a serious effect both in the Philippines *and here at home*. I trust implicitly that you and Taft will come to agreement.

THEODORE ROOSEVELT .18

The most important words of the above telegram are "and here at home." The "serious effect here at home" so earnestly deprecated was that the real issue between General Chaffee and Governor Taft might be ventilated by some Congressional Committee, and thus bring out the prematurity with which, to meet political exigencies, the civil government had been set up. The issue was that General Chaffee was recognizing the hostility of the people, and deprecating the withdrawal of the police protection of the army from districts in which there were many people who, though tired of keeping up the struggle, and willing to quit, were being harried by the die-in-the-last-ditch contingent. This would mean, ultimately, an examination, such as has already been made in this volume, of the evidence on which Governor Taft based his half-baked opinion of 1900 that "the great majority" were "entirely willing" to American sovereignty. It would also show up Mr. Root's nonsense about "the patient and unconsenting millions," so shamelessly flouted in the presidential campaign of 1900, and his pious Philippics against delivering said millions "into the hands of the assassin, Aguinaldo,"19 and would reveal the truth confessed by Secretary Root in a speech made to the cadets at West Point in July, 1902, after the trouble had blown over, in which, apropos of the valor and services of the army, he referred proudly to its having then just completed the suppression of "an insurrection of 7,000,000 people."

On September 28, 1901, just prior to President Roosevelt's above cablegram pouring oil on the troubled politico-military insular waters, a company of General Chaffee's command, Company C, of the 9th Infantry, had been taken off their guard and massacred at a place called Balangiga, in the island of Samar.20 This had made General Chaffee somewhat angry, and explains the subsequent dark and bloody drama of which General "Jake" Smith was the central figure, whereby Samar was made "a howling wilderness." But Governor Taft was filled with much more solicitude about the success of his civil government than he was about the obscure lives lost at Balangiga. Apropos of the Balangiga affair he was wearing the patience of the doughty Chaffee with remarks like this: "The people are friendly to the civil government," and suavely speaking of "the evidence which accumulates on every hand of the desire of the people at large for peace and protection by the civil government."21 The same Taft report goes on to deprecate "rigor in the treatment" of the situation and the "consequent revulsion in those feelings of friendship toward the Americans which have been growing stronger each day with the spread and development of the civil government."

General "Jake" Smith was sent to Samar shortly after the Balangiga massacre, and did indeed make the place a howling wilderness, with his famous "kill-and-burn" orders, instructions to "kill everything over ten years old" and so forth, and the army was in sympathy generally with most of what he did,—except, of course, the unspeakable "10 year old" part—piously exclaiming, as fallible human nature often will in such circumstances, "Vengeance is mine, saith the Lord." Now the civil government could have put a stop to all this if it had wanted to. It had the backing of President Roosevelt. But it quietly accepted the benefit of such "fear of God"—to use the army's rather sacrilegious expression about that Samar campaign—as the military arm put into the heart of the Filipino, and went on the even tenor of its way, still maintaining that the Filipinos must like us because the civil government was so benevolent,—as if the Filipinos drew any nice distinctions between Governor Taft and General Chaffee, or supposed the two did not represent one and the same government, the government of the United States. There was much investigation about that awful Samar campaign afterward. General Smith was court-martialed and partly whitewashed, at least not dismissed. At General Smith's court-martial, there was some dispute about the alleged orders to "kill and burn," to "kill everything over ten years old," etc. But the nature of the campaign may be inferred from General Smith's famous circular No. 6, which, issued on Christmas eve, 1901, advised his command, in effect, that he did not take much stock in the civil commission's confidence that the people really wanted peace; that he was "thoroughly convinced" that the wealthy people in the towns of his district were aiding the insurgents while pretending to be friendly and that he proposed to

adopt a policy that will create *in all the minds of all the people a burning desire for the war to cease*; a desire or longing *so intense, so personal, and so real* that it will *impel* them to devote themselves in real earnest to bringing about a *real state* of peace.22

During all his trial troubles, General Smith "took what was coming to him" without a murmur, and General Chaffee stuck to him as far as he could without assuming the primary responsibility for the fearful orders above alluded to. If, when General Smith went to Samar, his superior officer, General Chaffee, was in just the direly vengeful frame of mind he, General Smith, afterwards displayed, and prompted him to do, substantially, what he afterward did, which is by no means unlikely, General Smith never whimpered or put the blame on his chief. But a fearful lesson was given the Filipinos, and the civil government profited by it. General Chaffee was never really pressed on whether he did or did not prompt General Smith to do what he did; Governor Taft was never even criticised for not protesting; but with a flourish of presidential trumpets, General Smith was finally made "the goat," by being summarily placed on the retired list, and that closed the bloody Samar episode of 1901–02. I wonder General Smith has not gone and wept on General Miles's shoulder and like him become a member of the Anti-Imperialist League of Boston. Some of the best fighting men in the army say that as a soldier in battle General Smith is superb. At any rate he may find spiritual consolation in the following passage of the Scriptures which fits and describes his case:

But the goat, on which the lot fell to be the scapegoat, shall be presented alive before the Lord, to make an atonement with him, and to let him go for a scapegoat into the wilderness.23

In his Report for 1901 Governor Taft says that the four principal provinces, including Batangas, which gave trouble shortly after the civil government was set up in that year, and had to be returned to military control, were organized under civil rule "on the recommendation" of the then commanding general (MacArthur)24: It certainly seems unlikely that the haste to change from military rule to civil rule came on the motion of the military. If the Commission ever got, *in writing*, from General MacArthur, a "recommendation" that any provinces be placed under civil rule while still in insurrection, the text of the writing will show a mere soldiery acquiescence in the will of Mr. McKinley, the commander-in-chief. Parol contemporaneous evidence will show that General MacArthur told them, substantially, that they were "riding for a fall." In fact, whenever an insurrection would break out in a province after Governor Taft's inauguration as governor, the whole attitude of the army in the Philippines, from the commanding general down, was "I told you so." They did not say this where Governor Taft could hear it, but it was common knowledge that they were much addicted to damning "politics" as the cause of all the trouble.

Governor Taft's statement in his report for 1901, that the four principal provinces, above named, Batangas and the rest, were organized under civil rule "on the recommendation of General MacArthur," is fully explained in his testimony before the Senate Committee of 1902. From the various passages hereinbefore quoted from President McKinley's state papers concerning the Philippines, especially his messages to Congress, the political pressure Mr. McKinley was under from the beginning to make a show of "civil" government, thus emphasizing the alleged absence of any real substantial opposition to our rule by a seeming absence of necessity for the use of force, so as to palliate American repugnance to forcing a government upon an unwilling people, has been made clear. There were to be no "dark days of reconstruction." The Civil War in the United States from 1861 to 1865 was a love feast compared with our war in the Philippines. Yet the work of reconstruction in the Philippines was to be predicated on the theory of consent, so persistently urged by President McKinley before the American people from the beginning, viz., that the insurrection represented only a small faction of the people. We have seen how General MacArthur also had originally, in 1898, entertained this notion, and how by the time he took Malolos in March, 1899, he had gotten over this notion, and had—regretfully—recognized that "the whole people are loyal to Aguinaldo and the cause he represents." And now came Governor Taft, after fifteen months more of continuous fighting, to tell General MacArthur, on behalf of Mr. McKinley, that he, MacArthur, did not know what he was talking about, and that "the great majority" were for American rule. The representative men of my own State of Georgia welcomed the return of the State to military control in 1870. Most of them had been officers of the Confederate army. The Federal commander simply told them that if *they* could not restrain the lawless element of their own people, *he would*. By premature setting up of the Philippine civil government, the lawless element was allowed full swing. General MacArthur had been in the Civil War. He knew something about reconstruction. But here were the Taft Commission, with instructions from Mr. McKinley to the effect that civil government, government "essentially *popular* in form," was to be set up as fast as territory was conquered. It didn't make any difference about the government being "essentially popular" just so it was "essentially popular *in form*." To the Senate Committee of 1902, Governor Taft said:

General MacArthur and the Commission did differ as to where the power lay with respect to the organization of civil governments, as to *who should say what civil governments should be organized*, the Commission contending that, under the instructions, it was left to them, and General MacArthur thinking that everything was subject to military control ultimately, in view of the fact that the islands were *in a state of war*.25

Governor Taft then added that he and General MacArthur reached a *modus vivendi*. When a good soldier once finds out just what his commander-in-chief wants done, he will endeavor, in loyal good faith, to carry out the spirit of instructions, no matter how unwise they may seem to him. As soon as General

MacArthur saw what President McKinley wanted done, he proceeded to co-operate loyally with Governor Taft to carry out the plan. He well knew the country was not ready for civil government, but if Mr. McKinley was bent on crowding civil government forward as fast as territory was conquered, he would make his recommendations on that basis. In the matter of the utter folly of the prematurity with which the civil government was set up in the Philippines in 1901, and the terrible consequences to the hapless Filipinos, hereinafter described, which followed, by reason of the premature withdrawal of the police protection of the army and the sense of security its several garrisons radiated, from a country just recovering from some six years of war, General MacArthur's exemption from responsibility is shown by his reports for 1900 and 1901.26 The former has already been fully examined, and the original sharp differences between him and Governor Taft made clear. In the latter report dated July 4, 1901, the date of the Taft inauguration as Governor, and also, if I mistake not, the day of General MacArthur's final departure for the United States, the latter washes his hands of the kindly McKinley-Taft nonsense, born of political expediency, about there having never been any real fundamental or unanimous resistance, in no uncertain terms thus:

Anything in the immediate future calculated to impede the activity or reduce the efficiency of these instruments [our military forces,] will not only be a menace to the present, but *put in jeopardy the entire future of American possibilities in the archipelago.*27

No, President Taft can never make General MacArthur "the goat" for what General Bell had to do in Batangas Province in 1901–02 to make our "willing" subjects behave. Nor can the ultimate responsibility before the bar of history for the awful fact that, according to the United States Coast and Geodetic Survey Atlas of the Philippines of 1899, the population of Batangas Province was 312,192, and according to the American Census of the Philippines of 1903 it was 257,715,28 rest entirely on military shoulders. An attempt to place the responsibility for the prematurity of the civil government on General MacArthur was made by Honorable Henry C. Ide, who was of the Taft Commission of 1900, and later Governor General of the Islands, and is now Minister to Spain, in the *North American Review* for December, 1907. But Mr. Taft, a man of nobler mould, has at least maintained a decorous silence on the subject except when interrogated by Congress, and when so interrogated, his testimony, above quoted, if analyzed, places the responsibility where it honestly belongs. In 1900 the Taft Commission were not taking much military advice.

Batangas province was first taken under the wing of the peace-at-any-price policy by the Act of the Taft Commission of May 2, 1901, entitled "An Act Extending the Provisions of 'the Provincial Government Act'29 to the Province of Batangas." By the Act of the Commission of July 17, 1901, the provinces of Batangas, Cebu, and Bohol, were restored to military control. When the civil authorities turned those provinces back to military control, they well knew the frame of mind the military were in, and there is no escape from the proposition that they, in effect, said to the military: "Take them and chasten them; go as far as you like. After you are done with them, it will be time enough to pet them again. But for the present we mean business." General Bell was scathingly criticised on the floor of the United States Senate for what he did in Batangas in 1901–02, but by the time he took hold there it had become a case of "spare the rod and spoil the child." The substitution by the Commission of kindness, and a disposition to forget what the Filipinos could not forget, for firmness and the policy of making them submit unreservedly to the inevitable,—viz., abandonment of their dream of independence—had created among them a well-nigh ineradicable impression that, for some reason or other, whether due to disapproval in the United States of the so-called "imperial" policy or what not, we were afraid of them. General Bell's task in Batangas, therefore, was to eradicate this impression all over the archipelago by making an example of the Batangas people.

In General Chaffee's report for 1902,30 he prefaces his account of General Bell's operations in Batangas as follows:

The long-continued resistance in the province of Batangas and in certain parts of the bordering provinces of Tayabas, Laguna, and Cavite, had made it apparent to me and to others that the insurrectionary force keeping up the struggle there could exist and maintain itself only through the connivance and knowledge of practically all the inhabitants; that it received the active support of many who professed friendship for United States authority, etc.

This last was a thrust at Governor Taft's new-found Filipino friends and advisers, in whose lack of sympathy with the cause of their country the Governor so profoundly believed, but in whose continuing co-operation in the killing of his soldiers General Chaffee believed still more profoundly.

General Bell's famous operations on a large scale in Batangas began January 1, 1902. The great mistake of the Civil Commission, to which they adhered so long, was in supposing that when the respectable military element of the insurgents was pursued to capture or surrender, these last *could* and *would* thereafter control the situation. As a matter of fact, whether they could or not, they did not.

In his celebrated circular order dated Batangas, December 9, 1901, General Bell announced:

    To all Station Commanders:

A general conviction, which the brigade commander shares, appears to exist, that the insurrection in this brigade continues because the greater part of the people, especially the wealthy ones, *pretend* to desire, but do not in reality *want* peace; that when all *really want* peace, we can have it promptly. Under such circumstances, it is clearly indicated that a policy should be adopted that will, as soon as possible, make the people *want peace* and *want it badly.*

The only acceptable and convincing evidence of the real sentiments of either individuals or town councils should be such acts publicly performed as must *inevitably commit them irrevocably* to the side of Americans by arousing the animosity of the insurgent element. * * * No person should be given credit for loyalty simply because he takes the oath of allegiance, or secretly conveys to Americans worthless information and idle rumors which result in nothing. Those who *publicly* guide our troops to the camps of the enemy, who *publicly* identify insurgents, who *accompany troops in operations* against the enemy, who denounce and assist in arresting the secret enemies of the Government, who *publicly* obtain and bring *reliable* and *valuable* information to commanding officers, those in fact who *publicly* array themselves against the insurgents, and for Americans, should be trusted and given credit for loyalty, *but no others.* No person should be given credit for loyalty solely on account of having done nothing for or against us so far as known. Neutrality should not be tolerated. Every inhabitant of this brigade should be either active friend or be classed as enemy.

In his Circular Order No. 5, dated Batangas, December 13, 1901,31 General Bell announced that General Orders No. 100, Adjutant General's Office, 1863, approved and published by order of President Lincoln, for the government of the armies of the United States in the field, would thereafter be regarded as the guide of his subordinates in the conduct of the war. This order is familiar to all who have ever made any study of military law. Ordinarily, of course, a captured enemy is entitled to "the honors of war," *i. e.*, he must be held, housed, and fed, unless exchanged, until the close of the war. But where an enemy places himself by his conduct without the pale of the laws of war, *i. e.*, where he does not "play the game according to the rules," he may be killed on sight, like other outlaws.

Under General Orders No. 100, 1863, men and squads of men who, without commission, without being part or portion of the regularly organized hostile army, fight occasionally only, and with intermittent returns to their homes and avocations, and frequent assumption of the semblance of peaceful pursuits, divesting themselves of the character and appearance of soldiers; armed prowlers seeking to cut telegraph wires, destroy bridges and the like, etc., are not entitled to the protection of the laws of war and may be shot on sight. In other words, the game being one of life and death, you must take even chances with your opponent. General Bell's defenders on the floor of the Senate simply relied on General Orders No. 100. However, there is nothing about reconcentration in that order. We learned that from the Spaniards. In fact we never did succeed in bringing to terms the far Eastern colonies we bought from Spain, until we adopted her methods with regard to them. Another of the expedients adopted by General Bell in Batangas seems harsh, but it was used by Wellington in the latter end of the Napoleonic wars, and by the Germans in the latter end of the Franco-Prussian War. It was to promise the inhabitants of a given territory that whenever a telegraph wire or pole was cut the country within a stated radius thereof, including all human habitations, would be devastated. It is in General Bell's Circular Order No. 7 of December 15, 1901,32 that we find the genesis of the idea of basing tactics used by Weyler in Cuba on Mr. Lincoln's General Order 100. He there says:

Though Section 17, General Orders 100, authorizes the starving of unarmed hostile belligerents as well as armed ones, provided it leads to a speedier subjection of the enemy, it is considered neither justifiable nor desirable to permit any person to starve *who has come into towns under our control seeking protection.*

This order goes on to direct that all food supplies encountered be brought to the towns. Of course this does not mean supplies captured from the enemy's forces, which may lawfully be destroyed at once. To those not familiar with reconcentration tactics it should be explained that reconcentration means this: You notify, by proclamation and otherwise, all persons within a given area, that on and after a certain day they must all leave their homes and come within a certain prescribed zone or radius of which a named town is usually the centre, there to remain until further orders, and that all persons found outside that zone after the date named will be treated as public enemies. General Bell's order of December 20th, provided that rice found in the possession of families outside the protected zone should, if practicable, be moved with them to the town which was the centre of the zone, that that found apparently *cached* for enemy's use should be confiscated, and also destroyed if necessary.

Whenever it is found absolutely impossible to transport it [any food supply] to a point within the protected zone, it will be burned or otherwise destroyed. *These rules will apply to all food products.*

No person within the reconcentration zones was permitted to go outside thereof—cross the dead line—without a written pass. The Circular Order of December 23d, apparently solicitous lest subordinate commanders might become infected with the Taft belief in Filipino affection, directs that after January 1, 1902, all the municipal officials, members of the police force, etc., "who have not *fully complied* with their duty by *actively* aiding the Americans and rendering them *valuable* service," shall be *summarily thrown into prison.*33 Circular Order No. 19, issued on Christmas Eve, 1901, provided that,

in order to make the existing state of war and martial law *so inconvenient and unprofitable to the people that they will earnestly desire and work for* the re-establishment of peace and *civil government,* subordinate commanders might, under certain prescribed restrictions, put everybody they chose to work on the roads.34 This was an ingenious blow at the wealthy and soft-handed, intended to superinduce submission by humbling their pride. Note also the seeds of affection thus sown for the civil government under the reconstruction period which was to follow. In one of Dickens novels there occurs a law firm by the name of Spenlow and Jorkins. Mr. Spenlow was quite fond of considering himself, and of being considered by others, as tender-hearted. Mr. Jorkins did not mind. When the widow and the orphan would plead with Mr. Spenlow to stay the foreclosure of a mortgage, that benevolent soul would tell them, with a pained expression of infinite sympathy, that he would do all he could for them, but that they would have to see Mr. Jorkins, "who is a very exacting man," he would say. In the dual American politico-military régime in the Philippines of 1901–02, Governor Taft was the Mr. Spenlow, General Chaffee the Mr. Jorkins. But the former always seemed to harbor the amiable delusion that the Filipinos did not at all consider *the firm* as the movants in each proceeding against them, and that on the contrary they were sure to make a favorable contrast in their hearts between the kindness of Mr. Spenlow and the harshness of Mr. Jorkins. He seemed blind to the fact that the Filipinos, in considering what was done by *any* of us, spelled *us*—U. S.

General Bell's Circular Order No. 22, also a Christmas Eve product, re-iterates the usual purpose to make the people yearn for civil government, and the usual warning that none of them really and truly want the blessings of American domination and Benevolent Assimilation as they truly should, and adds:

To combat such a population, it is necessary to make the state of war as insupportable as possible; and there is no more efficacious way of accomplishing this than by *keeping the minds of the people in such a state of anxiety and apprehension that living under such conditions will soon become unbearable.* Little should be said. The less said the better. Let acts, not words, convey intentions.35

Under date of December 26, 1901, General Bell reports:

I am now assembling in the neighborhood of 2500 men, who will be used in columns of fifty each. I expect to accompany the command. * * * I take so large a command for the purpose of thoroughly searching *each ravine, valley, and mountain peak* for insurgents and for food, expecting to *destroy everything I find outside of town. All able-bodied men will be killed or captured.*

Such was the central idea animating the Bell Brigade that overran Batangas in 1902. The American soldier in officially sanctioned wrath is a thing so ugly and dangerous that it would take a Kipling to describe him. I have seen him in that mood, but to describe it is beyond me. Side by side with innumerable ambuscades incident to the nature of the field service as it then was, in which little affairs the soldier above mentioned had lost many a "bunkie," there had gone on for some time, under the McKinley-Taft peace-at-any-price policy, whose keynote was that no American should have a job a Filipino could fill, much appointing to municipal and other offices of Filipinos, many of whom had at once set to work to make their new offices useful to the cause of their country by systematic aid to the ambuscade business. With this and the Balangiga massacre ever in mind, the men of General Bell's brigade began their work in Batangas in a mood which quite made for fidelity in performance of orders to "make living unbearable" for the Filipino "by acts, not words." Also, the American soldier can sing, sometimes very badly, but often rather irrepressibly, until stopped by his officer. Also, whether justly or unjustly is beside the question, he considers a politician who pets the enemy in the midst of a war a hypocrite. So General Bell's 2500 men began that Batangas campaign on New Year's Day, 1902, giving preference, out of their repertoire, to a campaign song whose ominous chorus ran:

"He may be a brother of William H. Taft
But he ain't no friend of mine,"

and between songs they would say purringly to one another, "Remember Balangiga." *And their commanding officer was the very incarnation of this feeling.* So listen to the stride of his seven-league boots and the ring of his iron heel:

I expect to first clean out the wide Looboo Peninsula. I shall then move command to the vicinity of Lake Taal, and sweep the country westward to the ocean and south of Cavite, returning through Lipa. I shall *scour and clean up* the Lipa mountains. Swinging northward, the country in the vicinity of [here follows a long list of towns] will be *scoured*, ending at [a named mountain], which will then be *thoroughly searched and devastated*. Swinging back to the right, the same treatment will be given all the country of which [two named mountains] are the main peaks.

And so on *ad libitum*. General Bell's course in Batangas was commended in the annual report of his immediate superior, a very humane, as well as gallant, soldier, General Wheaton, as "a model in suppressing insurrections under like circumstances."36 The Batangas programme was approved by General Chaffee, the commanding general. In 1902 the United States Senate rang with indiscriminate denunciation of the Batangas severities and the Samar "kill and burn" orders. I tried in 1903, without success, to satisfy my distinguished and beloved fellow-townsman, Senator Bacon, that at the time it was adopted it had become a military necessity, which it had. The fact was that the McKinley-Taft policy of conciliation, intended to gild the rivets of alien domination and cure the desire for independence by coddling, had loaned aid and comfort to the enemy, by creating, among a people used theretofore solely to force as a governmental agency for making sovereignty respected, the pathetic notion that we were afraid of them, and might be weakening in respect to our declared programme of denying them independence. The Bell opinion of the Commission's confidence in Filipino gladness at its advent among them is sufficiently apparent in his orders to his troops. On May 23, 1902, Senator Bacon read in the Senate a letter from an officer of the army, a West Point graduate and a personal friend of the Senator's, whose name he withheld, but for whose veracity he vouched, which letter alluded to "a reconcentrado, pen with a dead line outside, beyond which everything living is shot"; spoke of "this corpse-carcass stench wafted in" (to where the letter-writer sat writing) as making it "slightly unpleasant here," and made your flesh crawl thus:

At nightfall clouds of vampire bats softly swirl out on their orgies over the dead.

This does not sound to me like Batangas and Bell. It sounds like Smith and Samar. There were about 100,000 people, all told, gathered in the reconcentrado camps in Batangas under General Bell,37 and they were handled as efficiently as General Funston handled matters after the San Francisco fire. There was no starvation in those camps. All the reconcentrados had to do was not to cross the dead line of the reconcentration zone, and to draw their rations, which were provided as religiously as any ordinary American who is not a fiend and has plenty of rice on hand for the purpose will give it to the hungry. The reconcentrado camps and the people in them were daily looked after by medical officers of the American army. General Bell's active campaigning began in Batangas January 1, 1902, Malvar surrendered April 16 thereafter, and Batangas was thoroughly purged of insurrectos and the like by July. During this period the total of insurgents killed was only 163, and wounded 209; and 3626 insurgents surrendered.38

The truth is General Bell's "bark" was much worse than his "bite." The inestimable value of what he did in Batangas in 1901–02 lay in convincing the Filipinos once and for all that we were not as impotent as the civil-government coddling had led them quite naturally, but very foolishly, to think we were. Reference was made above to the fact that the population of Batangas in 1899 was 312,192, and in 1903, 257,715. Those figures were inserted at the outset to make General Bell's "bark" sound louder, but now that we are considering his "bite"—how many lives his Batangas lesson to the Filipino people cost—another bit of testimony is tremendously relevant. On December 18, 1901, the Provincial Secretary of Batangas Province reported to Governor Taft that the mortality in Batangas due to war, pestilence, and famine "has reduced to a little over 200,000 the more than 300,000 inhabitants which in former years the province had."39 Considering that General Bell's 1901–'02 campaign in that ill-fated province cost outright but 163 killed,—how many of the 209 wounded recovered does not appear; they may have all recovered—the Bell programme in Batangas was indeed a very tender model, from the humanitarian stand-point, of civilizing with a Krag, a model of "suppressing insurrection under like circumstances." But it was never again followed. It had made too much noise at home. Senator Bacon's "corpse-carcass stench" from supposed reconcentrado pens and his "clouds of vampire bats softly swirling on their orgies over the dead," so vividly reminded our people of why they had driven Spain out of Cuba, that the Administration became apprehensive. Until the noise about the Batangas business, our people had been led by Governor Taft and President Roosevelt to believe that the Filipinos were most sobbingly in love with "a benign civil government" and had forgotten all about independence. It was obvious that a repetition of such a campaign in any other province might create in the public mind at home a disgust with the whole Philippine policy which would be heard at the polls in the next presidential election. So the Batangas affair made it certain that the army was not going to be ordered out again in the Philippines before said next presidential election, at least; whatever castigation might be deemed advisable thereafter.

It was intimated above that Senator Bacon's army friend's "clouds of vampire bats softly swirling" over the corpses of reconcentrados, were doing said swirling *not* over Batangas at all, but over Samar. Any man familiar with the lay of the land in the two provinces can see from the letter that it was written from Samar. Moreover, Colonel Wagner afterwards testified before the Senate Committee of 190240 that if there had been any great mortality in the reconcentration camps in Batangas, he would have known of it. He inspected practically all those Batangas camps. Nobody who was in the islands at the time doubts but what such conditions may have obtained in some places under General Smith in Samar, or believes for a moment that any such conditions would have been tolerated under General Bell. General Bell has that aversion to either causing or witnessing needless suffering, which you almost invariably find in men who are both constitutionally brave and temperamentally generous and considerate of others. But the moral sought to be pointed here is not that the Bell reconcentration in Batangas was as merciful as the Smith performances in Samar were hellish, but that, in all matters concerning the Philippines, the army, as in the case of Senator Bacon's friend, is gagged by operation of law, and its enforced silence is peculiarly an asset in the hands of the party in power seeking to continue in power, in a distant colonial enterprise. Senator Bacon withheld his friend's name, because for an army officer to tell the truth about the Philippines would be likely to get him into trouble with the President of the United States. The President, be it remembered, is also the leader of the political party to which he belongs. That is why the country has never been able to get any light from those who know the most about the Philippines and the wisdom or unwisdom of keeping them, viz., the army. In 1898 this republic was beguiled into abandonment of the faiths of the founders and started after a gold brick, thinking it was a Klondyke. Then and ever since, the most important and material witnesses concerning the wisdom or unwisdom of keeping the brick, viz., the army,—which best of all knows the rank folly of it—have been gagged by operation of law. All republics that have heretofore become monarchies, have become so through manipulation of the army by men in power seeking to continue in power. We should either resign our expensive kingship over the Philippines or get a king for the whole business, and be done with it. We have some ready-made coronet initials in T. R.41

"On June 23, 1902," says General Chaffee, in his report for that year,42 "by Act No. 421 of the Philippine Commission, so much of Act No. 173, of July 17, 1901, as transferred the province of Batangas to military control was revoked. Civil government was re-established in the province at 12 o'clock noon, July 4, 1902." The rest of the 1,748,573 people herein above mentioned as constituting the population of Batangas, Cebu, Bohol, Laguna, Tayabas, and Samar, were also in turn made to "want peace and want it badly," and on July 4, 1902, President Roosevelt issued his proclamation declaring that a state of general and complete peace existed. This is the famous proclamation in which he congratulated General Chaffee and the officers and men of his command on "a total of more than 2000 combats, great and small," most of them subsequent to the Taft roseate cablegrams of 1900, and the still more roseate reports of 1901 from the same source. The proclamation appeared in the Philippines as General Orders No. 66, Adjutant General's Office, Washington, dated July 4, 1902.43 It directed, in the body of it, that it be "read aloud at parade in every military post." It thanked the officers and enlisted men of the army in the Philippines, in the name of the President of the United States, for the courage and fortitude, the indomitable spirit and loyal devotion with which they had been fighting up to that time, alluded to the impliedly lamb-like or turn-the-other-cheek way in which they had been behaving (no special reference is made either to Batangas, Samar, or the water-cure), and closes with a bully Rooseveltian war-whoop about the "more than 2000 combats, great and small," above mentioned. It also referred to how, "*with admirable good temper* and loyalty to American ideals its (the army's) commanding generals have joined with the civilian agents of the government" in the work of superinducing allegiance to American sovereignty. This document is one of the most remarkable state papers of that most remarkable of men, ex-President Roosevelt, in its evidences of ability to mould powerful discordant elements to his will. It put everybody in a good humor. And yet, read at every military post, it served notice on the military that if they knew which side their bread was buttered on, they had better forget everything they knew tending to show the prematurity of the setting-up of the civil government, sheath all tomahawks and scalping knives they might have whetted and waiting for Governor Taft's exit from office, abstain from chatty letters to United States Senators telling tales out of school, such as the one Senator Bacon had read on the floor of the Senate (already noticed), and dutifully *perceive*, in the future, that the war was ended, as officially announced in the proclamation itself.

The report of the Philippine Commission for 1902, declares that the insurrection "as an organized attempt to subvert the authority of the United States" is over (p. 3). They then proceed, with evident sincerity, to describe the popularity of themselves and their policies with the same curious blindness you sometimes find in your Congressional district, in the type of man who thinks he could be elected to Congress "in a walk" if he should only announce his candidacy, when as a matter of fact, the great majority of the people of his district are, for some notorious reason connected with his past history among them,—say his war record—very much prejudiced against him. They repeat one of their favorite sentiments about the whole country—always except "as hereinafter excepted"—being now engaged in *enjoying* civil government. But they casually admit also that "much remains to be done" in suppressing lawlessness and disturbances, so as to perfect and accentuate said "enjoyment."

Let us see just what the state of the country was in this regard according to their own showing. They say:

The six years of war to which these islands have been subjected have naturally created a class of restless men utterly lacking in habits of industry, taught to live and prey upon the country for their support by the confiscation of food supplies as a war measure, and regarding the duties of a laborer as dull and impossible for one who has tasted the excitement of a guerrilla life. Even to the man anxious to return to agricultural pursuits, the conditions existing present no temptation. By the war and by the rinderpest, chiefly the latter, the carabaos, or water-buffaloes, *have been reduced to ten per cent. of their former number.*

Think of the condition of a country, *any* country, but especially one whose wealth is almost wholly agricultural, which has just had nine tenths of its plow animals absolutely swept off the face of the earth by war and its immediate consequences. The report proceeds:

The chief food of the common people of these islands is rice, and the carabao is the indispensable instrument of the people in the cultivation of rice,

adding also that the carabao is the chief means of transportation of the tobacco, hemp, and other crops to market, and that the few remaining carabaos, the ordinary price of which in normal Spanish times had been $10 was now $100. Then, after completing a faithful picture of supremely thorough desolation such as the Islands had never seen since they first rose out of the sea, certainly not during the sleepy, easy-going Spanish rule, they say: "The Filipino people of *the better* class have received the passage of the Philippine Act with great satisfaction"—meaning the Act of Congress of July 1, 1902, the Philippine Government Act. *Gott im Himmel!* What did the people care about paper constitutions concerning benevolent assimilation? What they were interested in was food and safety, not politics; food, raiment, shelter, and efficient police protection from the brigandage which immediately follows in the wake of all war, not details as to what we were going to do with the bleeding and prostrate body politic. But the Commission had started out to govern the Filipino people on a definite theory,—apparently on the idea that if Americans wore white duck and no brass buttons, in lieu of khaki and brass buttons, the Filipinos would at once forget the war and be happy with an exceeding great happiness. Now the real situation was this. The Islands had not yet been thoroughly beaten into submission. Northern Luzon had been conquered. The lake region of Southern Luzon had been conquered. The most important of the Visayan Islands had been conquered. But the extreme southern portion of Luzon, the enormously rich hemp peninsula already described in a former chapter, and the adjoining hemp island of Samar, were still seething with sedition which later broke out. All through the winter of 1900–01 General MacArthur had tried to get Mr. Root to let him close the hemp ports. But some powerful influence at Washington had prevented the grant of this permission. On January 9, 1901, General MacArthur had wired Mr. Root:

Hemp in southern Luzon in same relation to present struggle as cotton during rebellion.44

Nothing doing. General MacArthur must worry along with the "blockade-runners" as best he could, no matter how much hemp money might be poured into the insurgent coffers. So that in the latter part of 1902, although the more respectable of the insurgent leaders had then surrendered, even in the hemp country, the flames of public disorder, which had flickered for a spell after the Batangas lesson, broke out anew in the province of Albay, and in parts of Sorsogon, the two provinces of the hemp peninsula having the best sea-ports. The man at the head of this Albay insurrection was a sorry scamp of some shrewdness by the name of Simeon Ola, with whom I afterwards had an interesting and in some respects most amusing acquaintance. But that is another story. I have simply brought the whole archipelago abreast of the close of 1902, relatively to public order. In this way only may the insurrections in Albay and elsewhere in 1902–03, described in the chapter which follows, be understood in their relation to a comprehensive view of the American occupation from the beginning, and not be regarded as "a local issue" like General Hancock's tariff, having no general political significance. In this way only may those insurrections be understood in their true relation to the history of public order in the Islands. The Commission always represented all disturbances after 1902 as matters of mere banditti, such as have been chronic for generations in Calabria or the Transcaucasus, wholly distinct from, instead of being an inevitable political sequel of, the years of continuous warfare which had preceded. Their benevolent obsession was that the desire of the Philippine people for independence was wholly and happily eradicated.

1 Mr. Williams to Mr. Cridler, *Senate Document 62* (1898), p. 319.

2 See *First Report of Taft Philippine Commission to the Secretary of War*, p. 17.

3 General MacArthur's report for 1901, *War Department Report*, 1901, vol. i., pt. 4, p. 90.

4 *Correspondence Relating to the War with Spain*, vol. ii., p. 1241.

5 J. R. Arnold, of the Philippine Civil Service Board, in *North American Review*, for February, 1912.

6 *Correspondence Relating to War with Spain*, vol. ii., p. 1261.

7 *War Department Report*, 1901, vol. i., pt. 4, p. 98.

8 *Senate Document 331*, pt. 1, 57th Congress, 1st Session, 1902, p. 136.

9 Cagayan, Isabela, and Nueva Vizcaya.

10 A kind of two-wheeled buggy, the principal public vehicle of Manila.

11 As it turned out, I lost nothing in the end, because my resignation of my military commission was not acted on at Washington, and I only ceased to be an officer of the army by operation of law at the end of the fiscal year, June 30, 1901, as had been provided by the Act of Congress of March 2, 1899, organizing the twenty-five regiments for Philippine service.

12 See the Act of the U. S. Philippine Commission of July 17, 1901, entitled, "An act restoring the provinces of Batangas, Cebu, and Bohol, to the executive control of the military governor," in Public Laws, U. S. Philippine Commission, Division of Insular Affairs, War Department.

13 See *American Census of the Philippines*, vol. ii., p. 123.

14 *Ib.*, vol. i., p. 58.

15 *War Department Report*, 1901, vol. i., pt. 8, p. 7.

16 See pages 102 *et seq.* of *Our Philippine Problem* by H. Parker Willis, Professor of Economics and Politics in Washington and Lee University. New York, Henry Holt & Co., 1905.

17 Where he still is.

18 *Correspondence Relating to the War with Spain*, vol. ii., p. 1297.

19 The words quoted were used by Mr. Root in a speech delivered at Youngstown, Ohio, October 25, 1900.

20 Sixty-six men and three officers were surprised at breakfast and cut off from their guns by several hundred *bolo* men who had come into town as unarmed natives under pretence of attending a church fiesta. Forty-five men and officers were killed after a desperate resistance. Twenty-four only were able to escape. *War Department Report*, 1901, vol. i., pt. 8, p. 8.

21 Governor Taft's Report for 1901, *War Department Report*, 1901, vol. i., pt. 8, p. 8.

22 *War Department Report*, 1902, vol. ix., p. 208.

23 Leviticus xvi., 10.

24 *War Department Report*, 1901, vol. i., pt. 8, p. 12.

25 *Senate Document 331*, pt. 1, p. 86, 57th Congress, 1st Session (1902).

26 *War Department Report for 1900*, vol. i., pt. 5, p. 59 *et seq. Ibid.*, 1901, vol. i., pt. 4, p. 88 *et seq.*

27 *Report for 1901*, p. 98.

28 See *Philippine Census*, vol. ii, p. 123.

29The Provincial Government Act was an act passed February 6, 1901, outlining the general scheme of government for the several provinces, and indicating the various tempting official positions attaching thereto.

30*War Department Report*, 1902, vol. ix., p. 191.

31*Senate Document 331*, p. 1612 et seq.

32*Senate Document 331*, 1902, p. 1614.

33*S. D. 331*, 1902, p. 1622.

34*Ibid.*, p. 1623.

35*S. D. 331*, 1902, p. 1628.

36*War Department Report*, 1902, vol. ix., p. 221.

37Colonel Wagner's testimony before Senate Committee of 1902. *Senate Document 331*, pt. 3, p. 2873.

38*War Department Report*, 1902, vol. ix., p. 284.

39*Senate Document 331*, 1902, p. 887.

40*Senate Document 331*, pt. 3, p. 2878.

41Theodore *Rex*.

42*War Department Report*, 1902, vol. ix., p. 192.

43*Correspondence relating to the War with Spain*, vol. ii., pp. 1352–3.

44*Military Correspondence Relating to War with Spain*, vol. ii., p. 1244.

Chapter XVI. Governor Taft, 1903

Me miserable! Which way shall I fly?

Paradise Lost.

Throughout the last year of Governor Taft's administration in the Philippines, 1903, both he, and the peaceably inclined Filipinos in the disturbed districts, were between the devil and the deep sea. The military handling of the Batangas and Samar disorders of 1901–2 had precipitated in the United States Senate a storm of criticism, at the hands of Senator Bacon and others, which had reminded a public, already satiated with slaughtering a weaker Christian people they had never seen in the interest of supposed trade expansion, of "the days when Cicero pleaded the cause of Sicily against Verres, and when, before a senate which still retained some show of freedom, Tacitus thundered against the oppressor of Africa."1 He did not want to order out the military again if he could help it, and this relegated him to his native municipal police and constabulary, experimental outfits of doubtful loyalty,2 and, at best, wholly inadequate, as it afterwards turned out,3 for the maintenance of public order and for affording to the peaceably inclined people that sort of security for life and property, and that protection against semi-political as well as unmitigated brigandage, which would comport with the dignity of this nation. The better class of Filipinos, though not so enamored of American rule as Governor Taft fondly believed, had by 1903 about resigned themselves to the inevitable, and would have liked to see brigandage masquerading under the name of patriotism stopped by that sort of adequate police protection which was so obviously necessary in the disturbed and unsettled conditions naturally consequent upon many years of war, and which they of course realized could only be afforded by the strong arm of the American army.

But they knew that if the army were ordered out, the burden of proof as to their own loyalty would at once be shifted to them, by the strenuous agents of that strenuous institution. The result was a sort of reign of terror for nearly a year, in 1902–3, in the richest province of the whole archipelago, the hemp-producing province of Albay, at the southern end of Luzon, and also in portions of the province of Misamis. These conditions had begun in those provinces in 1902, and, not being promptly checked, because the army was held in leash and the constabulary were crude and inadequate, by 1903 brigandage therein was thriving like a garden of weeds. Super-solicitude concerning the possible effect of adequately vigorous governmental action in the Philippines on the fortunes of the Administration in charge of the Federal Government at Washington, an attitude not surprising in the colonial agents of that Administration, but which, as we have seen, had been from the beginning, as it must ever be, the curse of our colonial system, had rendered American sovereignty in the disturbed districts as humiliatingly impotent as senile decadence ever rendered Spain.

The average American citizen will admit that the average American statesman, even if he be not far-sighted, looks at least a year ahead, in matters where both his personal fortunes and those of the political party to which he belongs are intimately related to what he may be doing at the time. If in 1903 Governor Taft's administration of affairs in the Philippines was wholly uninfluenced by any possible effect it might have on President Roosevelt's chances for becoming an elected President in 1904, then he was a false friend and a very poor party man as well. Assuming that he was neither, let us examine his course regarding the disturbances of public order in the Philippines in that year, as related to the first and most sacred duty of every government, adequate protection for life and property.

In President McKinley's original instructions of April 7, 1900, to the Taft Commission, after quoting the final paragraph of the articles of capitulation of the city of Manila:

This city, its inhabitants * * * and its private property of all descriptions * * * are hereby placed under the special safeguard of the faith and honor of the American army;

the President had added:

As high and sacred an obligation rests upon the Government of the United States to give *protection for property and life* * * * *to all the people of the Philippine Islands.*

* * * *I charge this Commission to labor for the full performance of this obligation, which concerns the honor and conscience of their country.*

We will probably never again have a better man at the head of the Philippine Government than William H. Taft. We have no higher type of citizen in the republic to-day than the man now[4] at the head of it. In the *Outlook* of September 21, 1901, there appeared an article on the Philippines written in the summer previous by Vice-President Roosevelt, entitled "The First Civil Governor," which began as follows:

A year ago a man of wide acquaintance both with American public life and American public men[5] remarked that the first Governor of the Philippines ought to combine the qualities which would make a first-class President of the United States with the qualities which would make a first-class Chief Justice of the United States, and that the only man he knew who possessed all these qualities was Judge William H. Taft, of Ohio. The statement was entirely correct.

The writer subscribed then, and still subscribes, to the foregoing estimate of Mr. Taft, whether Colonel Roosevelt still does or not. Though I dissent most vigorously from more than one of President Taft's policies, and though this book is one long dissent from his chief pet policy, still it is to me an especial pleasure to do him honor where I may, not merely because he has greatly honored me in the past, but because my judgment approves the above estimate. Though as a party leader he is a very poor general, as Chief Magistrate of the nation he has certainly deserved and commanded the cordial esteem of the whole country, and the respectful regard of all mankind. With this admission freely made, if after reading what follows in this and the next chapter, and weighing the same in the light of all that has preceded, the reader does not decide that the writer, far from being animated by any intelligent high purpose, is merely a foolish person of the sounding-brass-and-tinkling-cymbal variety full of sound and fury signifying nothing, then he can reach but one other conclusion, viz., that colonization by a republic like ours, such as that we blundered into by purchasing the Philippines, is a case of a house divided against itself, a case of the soul of a nation at war with the better angels of its nature, a case where considerations of what may be demanded by home considerations of political expediency will always operate to the detriment of the Filipino people, and be the controlling factor in our government of them. And if I show that in the Philippines in 1903 Governor Taft failed properly to protect the lives and property of peaceably inclined people, as so sacredly enjoined in the language above quoted from President McKinley's original instructions to him, lest "the full performance of this obligation" might prejudice the presidential prospects of his friend, Mr. Roosevelt, and the success of the party to which they belonged, then I will have shown that for this republic to be in the colonizing business is an absolutely evil thing, and that any man who proposes any honorable way out of the conceded blunder of 1898, is entitled to a hearing at the hands of the American people, because it "concerns the honor and conscience of their country."

Having tried most of the cases which arose out of the public disorders in the Philippines in 1903, and knowing from what I thus learned, together with what I subsequently learned *which Mr. Taft knew then*, that the most serious of those disorders were very inadequately handled by native police, and constabulary, with much wholly unnecessary incidental sacrifice of life, in order to preserve the appearance of "civil" government and convey the impression of the state of peace the name implied, at a time when a reign of terror due to brigandage prevailed throughout wide and populous regions in whose soil lay the riches of agricultural plenty, while the United States Army looked on with a silent disgust which understood the reason, and a becoming subordination which regretfully bowed to that reason as one which must ever be the curse of colonization by a republic like ours, I know whereof I shall speak, and will therefore speak neither lightly nor unadvisedly, but soberly, charitably, and in the fear of God.

The insurrection in the Philippines against American authority which began with the outbreak of February 4, 1899, and whose last dying embers were not finally stamped out until 1906, systematic denials by optimist officialdom to the contrary notwithstanding, had three distinct stages:

(1) The original fighting in company, battalion, and regimental formation, with the ordinary wide-flung battle line; this having terminated pursuant to a preconcerted plan early in November, 1899.

(2) A period of guerrilla warfare maintained by the educated, patriotic, fighting generals, in a gradually decreasing number of provinces, until the summer of 1902.

(3) The final long drawn-out sputterings, which began to get serious in the fall of 1902, in provinces prematurely taken under the civil government, and stripped of adequate military protection before things had been given time to settle down in them to normal.

These last are the "gardens of weeds"—brigandage weeds—above mentioned. While the horticultural metaphor will help some, to really understand the case nothing so fits it as the more common illustration applied to grave public disorders having a common cause which likens such matters to a conflagration. The third and last stage through which the Philippine insurrection degenerated to final extinction is adequately and accurately described in the following extract from one of the military reports of 1902:

The surrender or capture of the respectable military element left the control of affairs and the remainder of the arms in the hands of a lot of persons, most of them ignorant, some criminal, and nearly all pertaining to a restless, irresponsible, unscrupulous class of people, whose principal ambition seems to be to live without work, and who have found it possible to so do under the guise of patriotism.6

Such was the problem which confronted Governor Taft in 1903 as to public order and protection of the peaceably inclined people, in the two main provinces hereinafter dealt with.

It is a great pity that in 1903 President Roosevelt could not have called in Secretary of War Root and sent for Senator Bacon, and those of the latter's colleagues whose philippics in the Senate of the year previous against Generals Jake Smith and J. Franklin Bell had reminded an aroused nation of the days of Cicero and Verres, Tacitus and Africa, etc., and had a frank talk with them somewhat after this fashion:

Gentlemen, Governor Taft has a hard job out there in the Philippines. There is a big insurrection going on in the province of Albay, which is the very richest province in the whole archipelago, a province as big as the State of Delaware,7 having a population of about a quarter of a million people, and he has, for police purposes, a crude outfit of native constabulary, officered mostly by ex-enlisted men of the mustered-out American volunteer regiments. The personnel of the officers may be weeded out later and made a fine body of men, but just at present there are a good many rather tough citizens among them. Moreover, as soon as the constabulary was gotten together they were at once set to work chasing little remnants of the insurgent army all over the archipelago. So as yet they are as undisciplined an outfit as you can well imagine, and have never had any opportunity to act together in any considerable command. Moreover, hardly any Filipinos have yet had a chance to learn much about how to shoot a rifle. Also, they know practically nothing about the interior economy of large commands, such as handling and distributing rations systematically for troops and for prisoners, or doing the same as to clothing, and nothing at all about medical care of the wounded, or the sick, or prisoners. So you can see that to handle this insurrection with such an outfit as this is sure to mean trouble of one sort or another. Wholly unauthorized overtures through officious natives, to the insurgent brigand chiefs, may, possibly, be made, promising them immunity, when they ought to be made an example of; and that will embarrass us in punishing them when we do finally get them, and be an encouragement to other cut-throats to do likewise in the future. Worst of all, you can see that if some five hundred or a thousand of these brigands, or insurgents, or whatever they are, suddenly surrender, the ordinary police accommodations for housing and feeding prisoners will be wholly inadequate; yet we will have to detain them all until our courts can sift them and see which are the mere dumb driven cattle and which are the mischievous fellows. Therefore, in case of such a surrender, the nature of this constabulary force, as I have already described it to you, makes it plain that its inadequacy to meet the serious conditions we are now confronted with may result in our having on our hands a series of little Andersonville prisons that will smell to heaven. The majority of the people of the province are really sick of the war. Their best men have all surrendered and come in. But there is an ignorant creature calling himself a general, by the name of Ola, who seems to have a great deal of influence with the lawless element that do not want to work. Ola has gathered together nearly a thousand malcontents, who obey him implicitly. He is terrorizing Albay province and the regions adjacent thereto, and as the constabulary are not adequate to patrol the whole province, the people do not know whether self-interest demands that they should side with Ola or with us. Clearly, therefore, this is a case for vigorous measures, if we all have a common concern for the national honor, for the maintenance of law and order in a territory we are supposed to be governing, and for the proper protection of life and property there. General Bell or somebody else ought to be sent there to comb that province just as Bell did Batangas. But we don't want any howl about it.

At this point of the supposed colloquy,—I say "colloquy," though tradition has it that most of President Roosevelt's "colloquys" with Senators were what Henry E. Davis, the Sidney Smith of Washington, calls "unilateral conversation"—one can imagine the senatorial Ciceros exchanging glances expressive of the unspoken thought: "The man certainly has his nerve with him. Does he think the Senate is an annex of the White House?" Then we can imagine President Roosevelt bending strenuously to his task with infinite tactfulness thus:

I put Jake Smith out of business, as you gentlemen all know, for his inhuman methods of avenging the Balangiga massacre in Samar, and I am just as much opposed to cruelty as any of you Senators can be. But Bell in Batangas is an altogether different case from Smith in Samar. All this about the odor of decomposing bodies wafted from reconcentration camps, and "clouds of vampire bats swirling out on their orgies over the dead," that Senator Bacon's army friend, whoever he may be, wrote the Senator, relates to Samar, and never did have any application to Bell's methods in Batangas. Bell did a clean job in a minimum of time and with a minimum sacrifice of life, and, while he did have those reconcentration camps in Batangas, he saw to it religiously that nobody starved, and that all those people received daily medical treatment.

For the correctness of the picture of conditions presented in the above hypothetical talk, I of course intend to be understood as vouching. If such a talk could have been had in 1903 by President Roosevelt with Senator Bacon and those of his colleagues who shared his views, the Albay situation might have been handled creditably. But the Administration was in no position to be frank with the Opposition. No Administration has ever yet during the last fourteen years been in a position to be frank with the Senate and the country concerning the situation at any given time in the Philippines, because at any given time there was always so much that it could not afford to re-open and explain. Mr. Root, for instance, might have been questioned too closely as to why, when Secretary of War, he had gone around the country in the fall of 1900 speaking for Mr. McKinley, and talking about *"the patient and unconsenting millions" so anxious to be rid of "Aguinaldo and his band of assassins,"* when at that very time his (Mr. Root's) generals in the Philippines were engaged in activities, the magnitude of which may be inferred from a telegram sent from Washington to General Wood at Havana, asking if he could possibly spare the 10th Infantry, and adding:

*Imperative that we have immediate use of every available company that we can lay our hands on for service in the Philippines,*8

although at West Point in 1902 he told the cadets how nobly the army had labored in putting down "an insurrection of 7,000,000 people." No, the Administration in 1903 simply could not afford to be frank concerning the situation in the Philippines. I need not recapitulate here any more of the long train of reasons why, because they have all been fully explained in the preceding chapters. Of course President Roosevelt had no such guilty knowledge of the facts as Mr. Root. He was not in constant daily contact with army officers at the War Department, familiar with the actual situation in the Philippines, as Mr. Root was. He was simply "sticking to Taft." Somewhere along about the time the military folk in the Philippines were scoffing at the unnecessary sacrifice of life incident to the lack of a strong government,

President Roosevelt had written his warm personal friend, Hon. George Curry, now a member of Congress from New Mexico, who had been a captain in his regiment before Santiago, was then an official of the civil government of the Philippines, and later Governor of New Mexico, by appointment of Mr. Roosevelt: "Stick to Taft, George" or words to that effect. Mr. Roosevelt's attitude was simply that of an intensely loyal friend of Mr. Taft who simply assumed that the Philippine Government was not going to tolerate impotence in the matter of protecting life and property. But everybody at both ends of the line was too deep in the mire of all the long and systematic withholding of facts from the American public which had been occurring ever since 1898, and which it has been the aim of the preceding chapters to illuminate by the light since becomingavailable in the published official records of the Government. Hence, in the hypothetical conference above supposed, President Roosevelt was in no position to take any high ground. He would have had to admit that the civil government of 1901 was set up too soon in order to stand by half-baked notions dished out in 1900 by the Taft Commission in aid of his own and Mr. McKinley's campaign for the Presidency and Vice-Presidency, respectively. In other words the truth about the Philippines from the beginning might, and probably would, have seriously jeopardized the Roosevelt presidential chances in 1904. So Governor Taft was left to his own resources in struggling with the problem of law and order in the Islands, intimately understanding the obvious bearing, just suggested, of what he might do out there, on the election of 1904. What then did Governor Taft do to meet the situation in 1903? Chronological order, as well as other considerations making for clearness, would suggest that I begin by telling what he did not do.

In May, 1903, I was sent to the province of Surigao to try some cases arising out of what has ever since been known in that out-of-the-way region as "the affair of March 23d" (1903). In his annual report for 1903, pages 29 and 30, in describing the Surigao affair, Governor Taft correctly states that a band of outlaws came into the town of Surigao on the day above named, killed Captain Clark, the officer in charge of the constabulary, took the constabulary's guns, while they were all away at their mid-day meal, scattered about the town, and departed. But Mr. Taft's report disposes of the whole incident in a most casual way. As a matter of fact the gist of it was that a heroic little band of Americans under Mr. Luther S. Kelly, the provincial treasurer, an old Indian scout of the Yellowstone country, hastily gathered the seven American women then in the town, one of them in a delicate condition, into the stone government house, and stood off those semi-civilized sensual brigands until reinforcements arrived. Governor Taft's failure adequately to present the gravity of the episode in his account of it does not argue well for the subsequent solicitude he might feel about other American women in other remote provinces which he was anxious to keep on his "pacified list," to say nothing of politically negligible native life therein.9 Nor does this report include any of the material facts showing the ineffectiveness of the rank and file of the constabulary to cope with the situation, or the general feeling of insecurity I found in the province as to how far the whole population might be in sympathy with the brigands. As a matter of fact, after that Surigao affair, Governor Taft had to turn the army loose in the province to go and get back and restore to his constabulary the seventy-five to one hundred stand-of-arms the brigands had so rudely and impolitely taken away from them, and I held court there for a month trying the people who were captured and brought in, with Colonel Meyer, of the 11th Infantry, one of the most thorough and able soldiers of the United States Army, and seven hundred soldiers of his regiment acting as deputy sheriffs, and yet all the time the province was under "civil" government, nominally. Colonel Meyer got the men who killed Clark, and, upon due and ample proof, I hung them, but Surigao was never taken for a day from the list of provinces enjoying "the peace and protection of a benign civil government." *The writ of habeas corpus was never suspended for a moment.*

In the report above quoted from, Governor Taft remarks that if the prompt steps he did take (he had already described the prompt sending of the military to the scene) had not been taken, "the trouble might have spread." But the Surigao affair seemed to teach the civil government nothing in the matter of subsequent protection of life, nor did it lessen their persistence in relying on their constabulary for due extension of such protection in time of need.

By June, 1903, another scheme was invented for avoiding calling on the military. When you are in a foreign country building a new government on the ruins of an old one, you naturally find out as much as you can about how the old one met its problems. The Spaniards had had the same problem in their day about not ordering out the military, because they did not have any military to order out. They were too poor to garrison the various provinces. They had long followed the plan, from time to time, of reconcentrating in the main towns of disturbed districts all the country population they could get to come in, and then acting on the assumption that all who did not come in were public enemies. This meant that when the country people came in, they simply looked out for themselves, while away from their homes, and farms, as best they could. Of course nobody at all looked after the farms, and nobody provided medical attention for the reconcentrados, or sanitary attention for the reconcentration camps. This general plan was formally sanctioned by the Commission, in so far as the following law sanctioned it. The law was enacted, June 1, 1903. It is section 6, of Act 781, which was an act dealing with all the constabulary problems, of which this was one. It read:

In provinces which are *infested to such an extent with ladrones or outlaws that the lives and property of residents in the outlying barrios10 are rendered wholly insecure by continued predatory raids—*

think of permitting a country to get into any such condition when you have an abundance of American troops on hand available to prevent it—

and such outlying barrios thus furnish to the ladrones or outlaws their sources of food supply, *and it is not possible with the available police forces constantly to provide protection to such barrios—*

there being all the time "available police forces," in the shape of regular troops, amply able to handle these unsettled conditions, which were the inevitable aftermath of lawlessness consequent on five or six years of guerrilla warfare—

it shall be within the power of the Governor-General, upon resolution of the Philippine Commission, to authorize the provincial governor to order that the residents of such outlying barrios be temporarily brought—

observe the length of time this may last is not limited—

within stated proximity to the *poblacion*, or larger barrios, of the municipality, there to remain until the necessity for such order ceases to exist.

To house and ration the reconcentrados, the following provision is made by the statute we are considering:

During such *temporary* residence, it shall be the duty of the provincial board, out of provincial funds, to furnish such sustenance and shelter as may be needed to prevent suffering among the residents of the barrios thus withdrawn.

The act also provides that during the course of the reconcentration, where the province does not happen to have the necessary ready cash, it may apply to the Commission, in distant Manila, for an appropriation to meet the emergency. What is to be done with those who starve during the temporary deficit, it does not say. If you must have reconcentration, to leave it to such agencies as the above, with the native police and constabulary as understudies, in lieu of availing yourself of the superb equipment of the American army, with all its facilities for handling great masses of people, as they did, for instance, after the San Francisco fire, is like preferring the Mulligan Guards to the Cold-stream Guards. Furthermore, there is no escape from the logic of the fact that reconcentration is essentially a war measure. The difference between what is lawful in war and what is lawful in peace is not a technical one. In war the innocent must often suffer with the guilty. In peace the theory at least is that only the guilty suffer. Hence it is that our Constitution is so jealous that in time of peace no man's life, liberty, or property, shall be taken from him without "due process of law," a provision which becomes inoperative in war times, being superseded by martial law. I know that the early question, "Does the Constitution follow the flag?" was answered by the Supreme Court of the United States in the negative as to the Philippines. But the Act of Congress of July 1, 1902, under which we were governing the Philippines in 1903, and still govern them, known as the Philippine Government Act, extended to the Islands all the provisions of the Bill of Rights of our Constitution except the right of jury trial and the individual right to go armed—"bear arms." It specifically said in section 5:

No law shall be enacted in said Islands which shall deprive any person of life, liberty, or property without due process of law.

It hardly needs argument to show that to bundle the rural population of a whole district out of house and home, and make them come to town to live indefinitely on such public charity as may drain through the itching fingers of impecunious town officials, abandoning meantime their growing crops, and the household effects they cannot bring with them, is depriving people of their property, and restraining them of their liberty, without due process of law. In fact, in 1905, in the case of Barcelon vs. Baker, vol. v., *Philippine Report*, page 116, during an insurrection in Batangas, to control which, the presidential election of 1904 being then safely over, the writ of habeas corpus had been suspended and martial law declared, the Supreme Court of the Philippines held that detention of people as reconcentrados under such circumstances "for the purpose of protecting them" was not an illegal restraint of their liberty, *because the ordinary law had been suspended.* This decision held it to be both the prerogative and the duty of the Governor-General to suspend the writ of habeas corpus when the public safety so required.

I refuse to believe for a moment that President Taft, the former wise and just judge, in whom is now vested by law the mighty power of filling vacancies on the highest court in this great country of ours, will seriously contend that that reconcentration law is not in direct violation of the above quoted section of the Act of Congress of July 1, 1902, for the government of the Philippines, and therefore null and void. The truth is, it was a piece of careless legislation, dealing with conditions that were essentially war conditions, under a government which was forever vowing that peace conditions existed, and determined not to admit the contrary. The civil government was like Lot's wife. It could not look back.

The Act of Congress of 1902 had made the usual provision permitting the governor to declare martial law in a given locality in his discretion. But the reconcentration law passed by the Philippine Commission was a way of avoiding the exercise of that authority, so as to keep up the appearance of peace in the provinces to which it might be applied, regardless of how many lives it might cost. In its last analysis the reconcentration law was at once an admission of a duty to order out the military and a declaration of intention to neglect that duty. I suppose the eminent gentlemen who enacted it justified it on the idea of teaching the natives how to maintain order themselves by letting them stew in the dregs of their own insurrection. Yet no one can read the Commission's own description of the widespread lawlessness which so long ran riot after the guerrilla warfare degenerated into brigandage, without seeing, from their own showing, how obvious was their duty to have waited, originally, until law and order were restored, by not interfering with the war itself until it was over, and by keeping the country properly garrisoned for a decorous and sufficient period after it *was* over, until something like real peace conditions should exist, on which to begin the work of post-bellum reconstruction. After all, it all gets us back to the original pernicious programme outlined in President McKinley's annual message to Congress of December, 1899, wherein was announced the intention to send out the Taft Commission, which message also announced, in effect, that it was Mr. McKinley's purpose to begin the work of reconstruction as fast as the patient and unconsenting millions "loyal to our rule" should be rescued from the clutch of the hated Tagals.

Recurring again to the reconcentration law itself, the moral quality of executive action putting it in operation was not unlike that which would attach should the Governor of Massachusetts, in lieu of ordering the state troops to the scene of great strike riots in half a dozen towns around Boston, issue a proclamation something like this:

The situation has grown so serious that your local police force, as you see, is wholly inadequate to cope with the situation. You will all, therefore, thrust your tooth-brushes, night-gowns, and a change of clothing, into the family grip, and assemble on the Boston Common and in the public gardens, there to remain until the necessity for this order ceases to exist, and we will there take the best care of you we can, as was done in the case of the San Francisco fire. As governor I am unwilling to order out the military.

If any lawyer on the Commission gave any thought at the time to the validity of the reconcentration law, in its relation to the "due process of law" clause of the Philippine Government Act, which none of them probably did, he must simply have justified the means by the benevolence of the end, on the idea that he knew so much better than Congress possibly could, the needs of the local situation. But if you read this law in the light of a knowledge of its practical operation, there is more suggestion between its lines of Senator Bacon's friend's "corpse-carcass stench" and "clouds of vampire bats softly swirling out on their orgies over the dead" than there is of benevolence. It really was unsportsmanlike for the Commission to have entrusted reconcentration to the native police and constabulary the native governors had, and it was wholly indefensible for them to take the liberty of violating an act of Congress in order to live up to their pet fiction about the war being "entirely over."

After the term of court at Surigao in the month of May, 1903, I was sent to Misamis province, where I remained until September, handling an insurrection down there. This province also was nominally in a state of peace, *i.e.*, there was no formal recognition of the existence of the insurrection by suspension of the writ of habeas corpus. Curiously enough, as I wrote Governor Taft afterwards, the Misamis crowd of disturbers of the peace were genuine *insurrectos*. Their movement was not so formidable as the Ola insurrection in Albay I dealt with later, but they were by no means unmitigated cut-throats. I have often wondered how they managed to be so respectable at that late date. They did not steal, as did most of the outlaws of 1903. Their avowed purpose was to subvert the existing government. The use of this word "insurrection" in connection with these various disturbances recalls a pertinent incident. In 1904 there was a vacancy on the Supreme Bench of the Islands. Some of my friends, members of the bar of my district, got up a petition to the then Governor-General setting forth in most partial terms my alleged qualifications for the place. Now in the Philippines, in the candor of informal social intercourse, all of us always called a spade a spade, *i.e.*, we called an insurrection an insurrection, instead of referring to the disturbance in the guarded and euphemistic terms which you find in all the official reports intended for home consumption. So in their petition, these gentlemen recited, among my other supposed qualifications, that I had held court in three different provinces "during insurrections in the same."

The Albay insurrection was the worst one I had to deal with during Governor Taft's administration as Governor of the Philippines. This was the insurrection headed by Simeon Ola. The first appearance of this man Ola in the official reports of the Philippine Government in connection with the Albay disturbances of 1902–3 is in the report of the colonel commanding the constabulary for the district which included Albay, Col. H. H. Bandholtz, dated June 30, 1903.11 This report contains a sort of diary of events for the year preceding the date of it. An entry for October 28, 1902, begins:

Early this month *negotiations* were opened with Simeon Ola, chief of the ladrones in this province, with a view of inducing him to surrender.

Think of this great government *negotiating* with the leader of a band of thieves who were openly and flagrantly defying its authority! The entry proceeds:

After many promises and conferences extending over a period of forty days, during which hostilities were suspended, Ola *broke off negotiations* and withdrew his entire force and *a large number of additional recruits that he had secured during the armistice.*

Before Ola finally surrendered he is supposed to have had a total command ranging at various times from a thousand to 1500 men. And I think Colonel Bandholtz must have had in the field opposed to him, first and last, at least an equal number of native forces. Ola also makes an official reappearance in the report of the Governor of Albay Province for 1904.12 It there appears that reconcentration was begun in Albay as part of the campaign against Ola and his forces, in March, 1903, and continued until the end of October of that year. Says this report of the Governor of Albay concerning reconcentration:

Naturally, the effect of this *unusual volume of persons* in a limited area was disease and suffering for want of food and ordinary living accommodations.

The Governor does not say how large the "unusual volume of persons" was that was herded into the reconcentration zones, nor does he furnish any mortality statistics. *Nobody kept any.* How much there was of the awful mortality and "clouds of vampire bats softly swirling out on their orgies over the dead," that Senator Bacon's army friend correspondent encountered in Samar does not affirmatively appear. The number of people affected by reconcentration in Albay and an adjacent province that caught the contagion of unrest and had to be given similar treatment, was about 300,000.13

In his report for 1903, in describing the Ola insurrection of 1902–3, Governor Taft says: "A reign of terror was inaugurated throughout the province." He then goes on to state that to meet it he applied the reconcentration tactics. In the same report he describes what is to my mind the most humiliating incident connected with the whole history of the American Government in the Philippines, viz., Vice-Governor Wright's visit to Albay in 1903, apparently in pursuance of the peace-at-any-price policy that the Manila Government was bent on. Governor Taft says of the civil government's dealings with His Excellency, the Honorable Simeon Ola, the chief of the brigands, that General Wright and Dr. Pardo de Tavera, a Filipino member of the Commission, went down to Albay and "talked to the people," the idea apparently being that those poor unarmed or ill-armed creatures should go after the brigands. This was to avoid ordering out the military, and summarily putting a stop to the reign of terror as became the dignity of this nation. I think these talks had something to do with the origin of the charge afterwards made that immunity was promised Ola and the men who finally did surrender with him. Of course General Wright made no such promises. But the idea got out in the province that the word was, "Get the guns," the inference being that if Ola and his people would come in and surrender their guns they would be lightly dealt with. In his book *Our Philippine Problem*, Professor Willis, at page 140, gives what purports to be an agreement signed by Colonel Bandholtz, dated September 22, 1903, whereby Bandholtz promises Ola immunity, and also promises a number of other things which are on their face rankly preposterous. Ola was much on the witness stand before me during that term of court, and, everything "came out in the wash." He was represented by competent, intelligent, and fearless Filipino counsel, and they did not suggest the existence of any such document. No proof of any offer of immunity was adduced before me. I think Ola simply finally decided to throw himself on the mercy of the government, on the idea that there would be more joy over the one sinner that repenteth than over the ninety and nine that are already saved. He was probably as much afraid that Governor Taft *would* order out the military as the wretched *pacificos* were that he would not. He immediately turned state's evidence against all the men under him of whose individual actings and doings he had any knowledge, the prosecuting attorney making, with my full approval, a promise to ask executive clemency as a reward. This was in keeping with the practice in like cases customary in all jurisdictions throughout the English-speaking world.

The magnitude of the Ola insurrection may be somewhat appreciated from the financial loss it occasioned. Says Governor Taft, in his report for 1903:

The Governor [of Albay] estimates that hemp production and sale have been interfered with to the extent of some ten to twelve millions of dollars Mexican [which is equivalent to five or six million dollars American money] .14

As the population of the province was about 250,000,15 a loss of $5,000,000 meant a loss of $20 per capita for the six months or so of reconcentration during which the farms were neglected. This would be equivalent to a loss of $1,800,000,000, in the same length of time to a country having a population of 90,000,000, which is the total population figure for the United States according to the Census of 1910.

It was in the latter part of October, 1903, I believe, that Ola finally surrendered with some five hundred or six hundred men. I was sent to Albay about the middle of November, to assist the regular judge of the district, Hon. Adam C. Carson, now one of the justices of the Supreme Court of the Philippines, in disposing of the case arising out of the Ola performances. Conditions at the time were also very much perturbed in various neighboring and other provinces, and the courts and constabulary were kept very busy.

An incident recurs to memory just here which illustrates the state of public order. But before relating it a decent respect to the opinions of the reader requires me to state my own attitude toward that whole situation at the time. I am perfectly clear in my own mind that as society stands at present, capital punishment is a necessary part of any sensible scheme for its protection. I have no compunction about hanging any man for the lawless taking of the life of another. We owe it to the community as a measure of protection to your life and mine and all others. So far as public order was concerned in the country now under consideration in 1903, the "civil" government was simply a well-meaning sham, a military government with a civil name to it. When the constabulary would get in the various brigands, cut-throats, etc., who might be terrorizing a given district, some of them masquerading as patriots, others not even doing that, the courts would try them. None of the judges cared anything about any particular brigand in any given case except to find out how many, if any, murders, rapes, arsons, etc., he had committed during the particular reign of terror of which he had been a part. Wherever specific murders were proven, the punishment would always be "a life for a life." And you have no idea how absolutely wanton some of the murders were, and how cruelly some of the young women, daughters of the farmers, were maltreated after they were carried off to the mountains. I would hate to try to guess how much more of this sort of thing would have had to occur in Albay in 1903 than did occur, to have moved Governor Taft to deprive Albay of "the protection of a benign civil government"—one of the pet expressions of contemporaneous official literature—and say the word to the army to take hold of the situation and give the people decent protection. But to come to the incident above broached. Shortly after I reached Albay, and set to work to hold Part II. of the district court, while my colleague, Judge Carson, held Part I. we had a call from a third judge, Judge Linebarger, of Chicago, who was on his way to some other perturbed region. I think that by that time, late in November, 1903, Governor Taft must have known he was soon to leave the Islands to become Secretary of War, and therefore was anxious to be able to make the best showing possible, in his farewell annual report as Governor, as to the "tranquillity" conditions. At any rate Judge Linebarger came to see us, for a few hours, his ship having touched en route at the port near the provincial capital of Albay. Judge Carson had had a gallows erected near the public square of the town, for the execution of some brigand he had convicted, whether it was for maltreating some poor farmer's daughter until she died, or burying an American alive, or what, I do not now recollect. But in going around the town some one suggested, as we passed this gallows, that we go up on it to get the view. So we went—the three of us. Then each looked at the other and all thought of the work ahead. Then Judge Carson smiled and dispelled the momentary sombreness by repeating with grim humor, an old Latin quotation he happened to remember from his college days at the University of Virginia: *Hæc olim meminisse juvabit* ("It will be pleasant to remember these things hereafter").

The Ola insurrection had continued from October, 1902, to October, 1903, without suspension of civil government. During that period the jail had been filled far beyond its reasonable capacity most of the time. It sometimes had contained many hundreds. As to the sanitary conditions, in passing the jail building one day in company with one of the provincial officials, he remarked to me, nonchalantly: "It's equivalent to a death sentence to put a man in that jail." I afterwards found out that this was no joke. During most of my visit to the province I was too busy holding court and separating the sheep from the goats, to think much of anything else. But toward the close of the term, after Christmas, after Governor Taft had left the Islands and gone home to be Secretary of War, an incident happened that produced a profound impression on me, suggested a new view-point, and started troubled doubts as to whether the whole Benevolent Assimilation business was not a mistake born of a union of avarice and piety in which avarice predominated—doubts which certain events of the following year, hereinafter related, converted in conviction that any decent kind of government of Filipinos by Filipinos would be better for all concerned than any government we could give them, hampered as we always will be by the ever-present necessity to argue that government against the consent of the governed is not altogether wrong, and that taxation without representation may be a blessing in disguise. The Yule-tide incident above alluded to was this. Most of the docket having been disposed of, and there being a lull between Christmas and New Year's day which afforded time for matters more or less perfunctory in their nature, the prosecuting attorney brought in rough drafts of two proposed orders for the court to sign. One was headed with a list of fifty-seven names, the other with a list of sixty-three names. Both orders recited that "the foregoing" persons had died in the jail—all but one between May 20 and Dec. 3. 1903 (roughly six and one-half months) as will appear from an examination of the dates of death—and concluded by directing that the indictments be quashed. The writer was only holding an extraordinary term of court there in Albay, and was about to leave the province to take charge of another district to which Governor Taft had assigned him before leaving the Islands. The newly appointed regular judge of the district, Judge Trent, now of the Philippine Supreme Court, was scheduled soon to arrive. Therefore the writer did not sign the proposed orders but kept them as legal curios. A correct translation of one of them appears below, followed by the list of names which headed the other (identical) order:

THE UNITED STATES OF AMERICA, PHILIPPINE ISLANDS, EIGHTH JUDICIAL DISTRICT

In the Court of First Instance of Albay

The United States against

Cornelio Rigorosa	died December	3, 1903
Fabian Basques	died September	25, 1903
Julian Nacion	died October	14, 1903
Francisco Rigorosa	died October	18, 1903
Anacleto Solano	died November	25, 1903
Valentin Cesillano	died November	6, 1903
Felix Sasutona	died September	26, 1903
Marcelo de los Santos	died June	3, 1903
Marcelo Patingo	died November	15, 1903
Julian Raynante	died September	7, 1903
Dionisio Carifiaga	died October	4, 1903
Felipe Navor	died September	17, 1903
Luis Nicol	died November	23, 1903
Balbino Nicol	died September	23, 1903
Damiano Nicol	died November	23, 1903
Leoncio Salbaburo	died November	20, 1903
Catalino Sideria	died July	25, 1903
Marcelo Ariola	died October	26, 1903
Francisco Cao	died November	26, 1903
Martin Olaguer	died November	13, 1903
Juan Neric	died November	16, 1903
Eufemio Bere	died November	21, 1903
Julian Sotero	died October	30, 1902
Juan Payadan	died September	10, 1903

Benedicto Milla	died July 30, 1903
Placido Porlage	died June 13, 1903
Gaudencio Oguita	died October 11, 1903
Alberto Cabrera	died September 8, 1903
Julian Payadan	died August 4, 1903
Eusebio Payadan	died August 10, 1903
Leonardo Rebusi	died November 2, 1903
Julian Riobaldis	died October 2, 1903
Victor Riobaldis	died October 23, 1903
Mauricio Balbin	died September 27, 1903
Tomas Rigador	died July 23, 1903
Miguel de los Santos	died July 28, 1903
Eustaquio Mapula	died November 18, 1903
Eugenio Lomibao	died November 1, 1903
Francisco Luna	died August 7, 1903
Gregorio Sierte	died October 31, 1903
Teodoro Patingo	died November 21, 1903
Teodorico Tua	died September 23, 1903
Ceferino Octia	died November 10, 1903
Graciona Pamplona	died September 12, 1903
Felipe Bonifacio	died November 26, 1903
Baltazer Bundi	died October 12, 1903
Julian Locot	died October 13, 1903
Francisco de Punta	died August 20, 1903
Pedro Madrid	died August 24, 1903
Felipe Pusiquit	died July 17, 1903

Rufo Mansalan	died July	14, 1903
Ignacio Titano	died June	20, 1903
Alfonso Locot	died June	29, 1903
Gil Locot	died May	23, 1903
Regino Bitarra	died September 7, 1903	
Bonifacio Bo	died August	2, 1903
Francisco de Belen	died September 29, 1903	

DECREE

The defendants above named, charged with divers crimes, having died in the provincial jail by reason of various ailments, upon various dates, according to official report of the jailer, it is

ORDERED BY THIS COURT, That the cases pending against the said deceased persons be, and the same are hereby, quashed, the costs to be charged against the government.

Judge of the Twelfth District acting in the Eighth.

ALBAY, December 28, 1903.

The foregoing order contains fifty-seven names. As already indicated, the second order was like the first. It contained the names of sixty-three other deceased prisoners, as follows, to wit:

Anacleto Avila	died September 2, 1903	
Gregorio Saquedo	died July	21, 1903
Francisco Almonte	died October	11, 1903
Faustino Sallao	died October	9, 1903
Leocadio Pena	died October	16, 1903
Juan Ranuco	died October	16, 1903
Esteban de Lima	died February	4, 1903
Estanislao Jacoba	died October	7, 1903

Macario Ordiales	died October	19, 1903
Laureano Ordiales	died October	27, 1903
Reimundo Narito	died October	4, 1903
Antonio Polvorido	died September	12, 1903
Norverto Melgar	died June	14, 1903
Bartolome Rico	died November	8, 1903
Simon Ordiales	died September	13, 1903
Candido Rosari	died September	29, 1903
Saturnino Vuelvo	died October	18, 1903
Vicente Belsaida	died May	26, 1903
Felix Canaria	died June	12, 1903
Pedro Cuya	died July	26, 1903
Evaristo Dias	died July	24, 1903
Felix Padre	died July	8, 1903
Alberto Mantes	died August	7, 1903
Joaquin Maamot	died September	5, 1903
Santiago Cacero	died May	28, 1903
Hilario Zalazar	died July	26, 1903
Tomas Odsinada	died October	1, 1903
Julian Oco	died October	4, 1903
Julian Lontac	died August	27, 1903
Ambrosio Rabosa	died September	19, 1903
Mariano Garcia	died September	12, 1903
Ramon Madrigalejo	died August	19, 1903
Albino Oyardo	died October	1, 1903
Felipe Rotarla	died September	29, 1903

Urbano Saralde	died October 5, 1903
Gil Mediavillo	died June 13, 1903
Egidio Mediavillo	died June 16, 1903
Mauricio Losano	died October 5, 1903
Bernabe Carenan	died September 27, 1903
Pedro Sagaysay	died September 29, 1903
Laureano Ibo	died August 5, 1903
Vicente Sanosing	died July 17, 1903
Francisco Morante	died June 10, 1903
Anatollo Sadullo	died September 16, 1903
Lucio Rebeza	died August 27, 1903
Eugenio Sanbuena	died August 13, 1903
Nicolas Oberos	died August 26, 1903
Eusebio Rambillo	died September 13, 1903
Tomas Rempillo	died August 19, 1903
Daniel Patasin	died August 19, 1903
Ignacio Bundi	died September 7, 1903
Juan Locot	died May 23, 1903
Zacarias David Padilla	died August 7, 1903
Juan Almazar	died September 12, 1903
Rufino Quipi	died June 13, 1903
Antonio Brio	died June 13, 1903
Timoteo Enciso	died September 12, 1903
Hilario Palaad	died August 28, 1903
Ventura Prades	died May 24, 1903
Alejandro Alevanto	died May 22, 1903

Rufino Pelicia	died May	20, 1903
Alejo Bruqueza	died July	19, 1903
Prudencio Estrada	died September 15, 1903	

These lists were printed in an article by the author which appeared in the *North American Review* for January 18, 1907, which article was reprinted by Hon. James L. Slayden, of Texas, in the *Congressional Record* for February 12, 1907. There can be little doubt that President Taft saw the article, and that if it had contained any inaccuracies they would long since have been noticed. So that in the Albay jail in 1903 we had a sort of Andersonville prison, or Black Hole of Calcutta, on a small scale.

If the military authorities had had charge of the Albay insurrection and of the prisoners in the Albay jail in 1903, it is safe to say that the great majority of those who died would have lived. But to have ordered out the troops would have been to abandon the official fiction that there was peace.

Of Ola's five or six hundred men, Judge Carson and I, assisted by the chief prosecuting attorney of the government, Hon. James Ross, turned several hundred loose. Another large batch were disposed of under a vagrancy law, which allowed us to put them to work on the roads of the provinces for not exceeding two years, usually six to twelve months. Most of the remainder, a few score, we tried under the sedition law, and sent to Bilibid, the central penitentiary at Manila, for terms commensurate with their individual conduct and deeds. The more serious cases were sent up for longer terms under the brigandage law. We indulged in no more maudlin sentiment about those precious scamps who had been degrading Filipino patriotism by occasionally invoking its name in the course of a long season of preying upon their respectable fellow-countrymen than Aguinaldo or Juan Cailles would have indulged. I am quite sure that either Aguinaldo or Juan Cailles would have made much shorter shrift of the whole bunch than Judge Carson and I did. It was only the men shown to have committed crimes usually punished capitally in this country that we sentenced to death—a dozen or more, all told. Ola was the star witness for the state. He held back nothing that would aid the prosecuting attorney to convict the men who had followed him for a year. He was given a sentence of thirty years (by Judge Carson), as a sort of expression of opinion of the most Christian attitude possible concerning his real deserts, but his services as state's evidence entitled him to immunity, and for that very good and sufficient reason Judge Carson, Prosecuting Attorney Ross, and myself so recommended to the Governor.

Ola could read and write after a fashion, though he was quite an ignorant man. But to show what his control must have been over the rank and file of his men, let one incident suffice. On the boat going up to Manila from Albay, after the term of court was over, Ola was aboard, en route for the penitentiary. But, as he was a prospective recipient of executive clemency, though the guards kept an eye on him, he was allowed the freedom of the ship. One night on the voyage up, the weather being extremely warm, I left my stateroom sometime after midnight, carrying blanket and pillow, and went back to the storm steering-gear at the stern of the ship, to spend the rest of the night more comfortably. Waking sometime afterward for some unassignable cause, I realized that the crown of another head was tangent to the crown of my own, and occupying part of my pillow. It was Ola, the chief of the brigands. I raised up, shook the intruder, and said: "Hello, Ola, what are you doing here?" He wakened slowly. He had no idea of any first-class passenger being back there, and had taken it for granted that I was one of the ship's crew, when he decided to share my pillow. As soon as he realized who I was, he sprang to his feet with profound and effusive apologies, and paced the deck until morning, perhaps thinking over the possible effect of the incident on my recommendation concerning himself.

After I had recovered the use of all my pillow I went back to sleep for a spell. About dawn I was wakened by some of the guards chattering. But I heard Ola, who had apparently been keeping watch over my august slumbers in the meantime, say in an imperious tone to the guards, *his keepers*, "Hush, the judge is sleeping." They looked at the brigand chief, and cowed, obeyed.

Ola was pardoned.

---

[1] Macaulay's *Trial of Hastings*.

[2] Says Gen. Henry T. Allen, commanding the Philippines constabulary, in his report for 1903 (*Report U. S. Philippine Commission*, 1903, pt. 3, p. 49), "For some time to come the number of troops (meaning American) to be kept here should be *a direct function of the number of guns put into the hands of natives*." He adds, "It is unwise to ignore the great moral effect of a strong armed force *above suspicion*."

[3] The constabulary force was about 5000. When disturbances in one province would become formidable, constabulary from provinces would be hurried thither, thus denuding the latter provinces of proper police protection.

[4] 1912.

[5] The reference is supposed to be to Mr. McKinley.

[6] *War Department Report*, 1902, vol. ix., p. 264.

[7] Delaware has 2050 square miles, Albay 1783.

[8] *Correspondence Relating to War with Spain*, vol. ii., p. 1249.

[9] President Roosevelt cabled Kelly, whom he had known in the West many years before, congratulating him on the results of his cool and determined fearlessness and presence of mind on that occasion, but elaboration on the Surigao affair was not part of the insular programme, which was one of irrepressible optimism as to the state of public order.

[10] Every province in the Philippines is divided into so many pueblos. Pueblo, in Spanish, means *town*. But the Spanish pueblo is more like a township. It does not mean a continuous stretch of residences and other buildings, but a given municipal area. Each pueblo is likewise subdivided into *barrios*, dotted usually with hamlets, and groups of houses.

[11] *Report U. S. Philippine Commission*, 1903, pt. 3, p. 92.

[12] *Report U. S. Philippine Commission*, 1903, pt. 1, p. 366.

[13] *Senate Document 170*, 58th Cong., 2d Sess., p. 16.

[14] *Report U. S. Philippine Commission*, 1903, pt. 1, p. 32.

[15] 240, 326, *Philippine Census*, 1903, vol. ii., p. 123.

Chapter XVII. Governor Taft, 1903 (*Continued*)

The Philippines for the Filipinos.

SPEECH OF GOVERNOR TAFT.

Just before Governor Taft left the Islands in 1903, he made a speech which made him immensely popular with the Filipinos and immensely unpopular with the Americans. The key-note of the speech was "The Philippines for the Filipinos." The Filipinos interpreted it to mean for them that ultimate independence was not so far in the dim distance of what is to happen after all the living are dead as to be a purely academic matter. And there was absolutely nothing in the speech to negative that idea, although he must have known how the great majority of the Filipinos would interpret the speech. On the other hand, the Americans in the Islands, popularity with whom was then and there a negligible factor, interpreted the speech, not inaccurately, to mean for them: "If you white men out here, not connected with the Government, you Americans, British, Germans and Spaniards, and the rest of you, do not like the way I am running this country, why, the boats have not quit running between here and your respective homes."[1] Then he came back to the United States and has ever since been urging American capital to go to the Philippines, all the time opposing any declaration by the law-making power of the Government which will let the American who goes out there know "where he is at," *i.e.*, whether we are or are not going to keep the Islands permanently, and how to formulate his earthly plans accordingly, though the educated Filipinos are concurrently permitted to clamor against American "exploitation," American rule, and Americans generally, and to keep alive among the masses of their people what they call "the spirit of liberty," and what the insular government calls the spirit of "irreconcilableness." Clearly, a policy which makes for race friction and race hatred is essentially soft-headed, not soft-hearted, and ought not to be permitted to continue. Yet it has been true for twelve years, as one of President Taft's admiring friends proudly boasted concerning him some time since:

One man virtually holds in his keeping the American conscience with the regard to the Philippines.[2]

This is true, and it is not as it should be. We should either stop the clamor, or stop the American capital and energy from going to the Islands. After an American goes out to the Islands, invests his money there, and casts his fortunes there, unless he is a renegade, he sticks to his own people out there. Then the Taft policy steps in and bullyrags him into what he calls "knuckling to the Filipinos," every time he shows any contumacious dissent from the Taft decision reversing the verdict of all racial history—which has been up to date, that wheresoever white men dwell in any considerable numbers in the same country with Asiatics or Africans, the white man will rule. Yet the American in the Philippines, once he is beguiled into going there, must bow to the Taft policies. He has taken his family to the Islands, and all his worldly interests are there. Yet he is living under a despotism, a benevolent despotism, it is true, so long as the non-office-holding American does not openly oppose the government's policies, but one which, however benevolent, is, so far as regards any brooking of opposition from any one outside the government hierarchy, as absolute as any of the other despotic governments of Asia. Though the Governor of the Philippines does not wear as much gilt braid as some of his fellow potentates on the mainland of Asia, still, in all executive matters he wields a power quite as immediate and substantial, in its operation on his subjects, as any of his royal colleagues. It never for a moment occurs either to the American Government official in the Philippines, or to the American citizen engaged in private business there who is in entire accord with the policies of the insular government and on terms of friendship with the officials, that the government under which he is living is any more of a despotism than the Government of the United States. The shoe never pinches the American citizen engaged in private business until he begins, for one reason or another, to be "at outs" with the insular government, and to have "opinions" which—American-like—he at once wants to express. If he permits himself to get thoroughly out of accord with the powers that be, the sooner he gets out of the Islands the better for him. This is the most notorious single fact in the present situation. There is no public opinion to help such a person, in any case where he differs with any specific act or policy of the insular government. The American colony is comparatively small, say between ten and twenty thousand all told, outside the army (which consists of ten or twelve thousand individuals living wholly apart from the rest of the community). The doctor who is known to have the patronage of high government officials is sure of professional success, and his wife is sure to receive the social recognition her husband's position in the community naturally commands; and this permits her to make auspicious entrance into the game of playing at precedence with her next neighbor called "society," so dear to the hearts of many otherwise sensible and estimable women—to say nothing of carpet knights, callow youths, cads, and aging gourmands. Also if the doctor and his lady have adult children, their opportunities to marry well are multiplied by the sunlight from the seats of the mighty. Thus the doctor and his wife are a standing lesson to the man "with convictions" that yearn for utterance, but who is also blessed with a discreet helpmate, more concerned in the general welfare and happiness of all the family than in seeing her husband's name in the paper. What is true of the doctor is also true of the lawyer known to be *persona grata* to the government. Again, the newspaper man in favor with the government is sure to get his share of the government advertising, according to a very liberal construction, and that insures his being able to command reportorial and editorial talent such as will sell his paper, and the consequent circulation is sure to get him the advertising patronage of the mercantile community, thus placing success for him on a solid, comfortable basis. Also, a contrary course will, slowly, maybe, but surely, freeze out any rash competitor. Consequently, the American in the Philippines is deprived of one of his most precious home pleasures, viz., letting off steam, in some opposition paper, about the real or imagined shortcomings of the men in charge of the government. For the reasonable expectancy of life of an opposition paper in Manila is pathetically brief. The hapless editor on the prosperous paper, whatever his talents, who happens to become afflicted with "views" which he airs in his editorial columns, is soon upbraided by his friends at his club as "getting cranky," and is told by the orthodox old-timers among them, "John, you've been out here too long. You better go home." If he does not change his tone, the receipts of the advertising department of his paper soon fall off, and his friend, the more tactful proprietor, who "knows how to get along with people," is not long in agreeing with the rest of his friends that he has "been out here too long." Again the successful merchant has too many interests at stake in which he needs the cordial friendship of the government to be able to afford to antagonize it. And so on, through every walk of life, the influence of the government permeates every nook and corner of the situation.

The average public man in the United States would not feel "nat'ral" unless intermittently bedewed with steam from the exhaust valve of the soul of some "outraged citizen," through the medium of the public press. But in the Philippines a public man occupying a conspicuous position with the government may be very generally detested and actually not know it.3 The American in the Philippines, with all his home connections severed, might as well send his family to the poor-house at once as to come out in a paper with an interview or speech,—even supposing any paper would publish it—which, copied by the papers back in the United States, would embarrass the National Administration's Philippine policy in any way. The same applies to talking too freely for the newspapers when home on a visit.

I think the foregoing makes sufficiently obvious the inherent impossibility of the American people ever knowing anything about current governmental mistakes in the Philippines, of which there must be some, in time for their judgment to have anything to do with shaping the course of the government out there for which they are responsible. And therefore it shows the inherent unfitness of their governmental machinery to govern the Filipinos so long as they do not change the home form of government to meet the needs of the colonial situation, by providing a method of invoking the public judgment on a single issue, as in the case of monarchical ministries, instead of lumping issues as we now do. It is certainly a shame that the fate and future of the Philippines are to-day dependent upon issues as wholly foreign to anything Philippine as is the price of cheese in Kamchatka or the price of wool in the United States. Whether the Filipinos are fit for self-government or not, under our present form of government we are certainly wholly unfit to govern them. In our government of the Filipinos, the nature of the case eliminates our most valuable governmental asset, to wit, that saving grace of public opinion which stops public men, none of whom are infallible, before they can accomplish irreparable mischief, through uncorrected faith in plans of questionable wisdom and righteousness to which their minds are made up.

To show how absolute was the executive and legislative power over 8,000,000 of people entrusted by the sole authority of President McKinley to Governor Taft—without consulting Congress, though afterwards the authority so conferred was ratified by Congress and descended from Governor Taft to his successor—an incident related to me in the freedom of social intercourse, and not in the least in confidence, by my late beloved friend Arthur W. Fergusson, long Executive Secretary to Governor Taft, will suffice. In 1901 the Commission had passed a law providing for the constitution of the Philippine judiciary,[4] according to which law an American, in order to be eligible to appointment as a Judge of First Instance (the ordinary trial court, or *nisi prius* court, of Anglo-Saxon jurisprudence) must be more than thirty years old, and must have practised law in the United States for a period of five years before appointed. In 1903 President Roosevelt wanted to make Hon. Beekman Winthrop (then under thirty years of age) now (1912), Assistant Secretary of the Navy, a Judge of First Instance. Governor Taft called Fergusson in and said: "Fergy, make me out a commission for Beekman Winthrop as a Judge of First Instance." Fergusson said: "You can't do it, Governor. It's against the law. He's not old enough." Winthrop was a graduate of the Harvard Law School. Governor Taft said humorously, "I can't eh? I'll show you. Send me a stenographer." A law was dictated[5] striking out thirty years and inserting twenty-five, and adding after the words "must have practised law for a period of five years" the words "or be a graduate of a reputable law school." Fergusson was then called in, and told to go down the hall, see the other commissioners,[6] and get them together, which he did, and the law was passed in a few minutes. Then Fergusson was sent for, and the Governor said, handing him the new "law"; "Now make out that commission." Even if Fergusson colored the incident up a bit, in the exercise of his inimitable artistic capacity to make *anything* interesting, his story was certainly substantially correct relatively to the absoluteness of the authority of the Governor, as will appear by reference to the two laws cited.

It is only fair to say that Winthrop made a very good judge. There used to be current in the Philippines a story that Governor Taft had said, in more or less humorous vein: "Gentlemen, I'm somewhat of an expert on judges. What you need in a judge is"—counting with the index finger of one hand on the fingers of the other—"firstly, integrity; secondly, courage; thirdly, common sense; and fourthly, he *must* know a *little* law." Winthrop's integrity, courage, and common sense were beyond all question. It could hardly have been otherwise. He came of a long line of sturdy and distinguished men, the first of whom had come over in the *Mayflower* days to the Massachusetts coast. And, he *did* know a *little* law. But the manner of his appointment is none the less illustrative of how much quicker, Governor Taft could make and publish a law than any of his fellow despots[7] over on the mainland of Asia, considering how slow-moving all *their* various grand viziers were, compared with Fergy, and his corps of stenographers.

Having now given, I hope, a more or less sympathetic insight into what absolute rulers our governors in the Philippines have been, in the very nature of the case, from the beginning, let us observe the change of tone of the government, after the reign of the first ended, and the reign of the second began.

---

[1] The speech referred to in the text was made at Manila in December, 1903, but the same "Philippines for the Filipinos" policy had already been proclaimed much earlier. The *Manila American* of February 28, 1903, reprints from the *Iloilo Times* of February 21, 1903, an account of Governor Taft's celebrated Iloilo speech of February 19, 1903, which was received with such profound chagrin by the American business community in the Islands. There had been much bad blood between the American colony at and about Iloilo and the native Americano-phobes. The following is from the Iloilo paper's account of Governor Taft's speech: "The Governor then gave some advice to foreigners and Americans, remarking that if they found fault with the way the government was being run here, they could leave the islands; that the government was being run for the Filipinos."

[2] James LeRoy in *The World's Work* for December, 1903.

3 A familiar instance of this will occur to any one acquainted with the situation in the Islands for any considerable part of the last ten years.

4 Act No. 136, U. S. Philippine Commission, passed June 11, 1901.

5 Act 1024, Philippine Commission, passed Oct. 10, 1903.

6 There were five members of the original Taft Commission, including President Taft.

7 I neither forget nor gainsay the generally benevolent character of his despotism; and having been a beneficiary of it myself I am therefore disposed to see much of wisdom in the way it was exercised.

Chapter XVIII. Governor Wright—1904

The blame of those ye better
The hate of those ye guard.

KIPLING'S *White Man's Burden.*

Governor Taft left the Philippines on or about December 23, 1903, to become Secretary of War in President Roosevelt's Cabinet, and shortly afterward Vice-Governor Luke E. Wright succeeded to the governorship. After the accession of Governor Wright, there was no more hammering it into the American business men having money invested in the Islands that the Filipino was their "little brown brother," for whom no sacrifice, however sublime, would be more than was expected. Governor Wright was quite unpopular with the Filipinos and immensely popular with the Americans and Europeans, because, soon after he came into power, he "let the cat out of the bag," by letting the Filipinos know plainly that they might just as well shut up talking about independence for the present, so far as he was advised and believed; in other words, that Governor Taft's "Philippines for the Filipinos" need not cause any specially billowy sighs of joy just yet, because it had no reference to any Filipinos now able to sigh, but only to unborn Filipinos who might sigh in some remote future generation; and that the slogan which had caused them all to want to sob simultaneously for joy on the broad chest of Governor Taft was merely a case of an amiable unwillingness to tell them an unpleasant truth, viz., that in his opinion they were wholly unfit for self-government—all of which, in effect, meant that Governor Taft had been merely "Keeping the word of promise to the ear and breaking it to the hope."

The Wright plain talk made the Filipinos one and all feel: "Alackaday! Our true friend has departed." But as Secretary of War Taft, after four years more of trying to please both sides, at home, at last frankly told the Filipinos when he went out to attend the opening of the first Philippine legislature, in 1907, practically just what Governor Wright had begun to tell them from the moment his predecessor had exchanged the parting tear with them on the water-front at Manila in 1903, the net result of the Wright policy of uncompromising honesty on the *present* political situation, may easily be guessed.

Governor Wright's method of repudiating the Taft straddle took for *its* key-note, in lieu of "The Philippines for the Filipinos," the slogan "An Equal Chance for All." What Governor Wright meant was merely that there would be no more browbeating of Americans to make them love their little brown brother as much as Governor Taft was supposed to love him, but that everybody would be treated absolutely alike and nobody coddled. However, the Filipinos of course knew that they could not compete with American wealth and energy, and so did the Americans in the islands. So what the Wright slogan, unquestionably fair as was its intent, inexorably meant to everybody concerned except the dignified, straightforward and candid propounder of it, was, in effect, the British "White Man's Burden" or Trust-for-Civilization theory, a theory whereunder the white man who wants some one else's land goes and takes it on the idea that he can put it to better use than the owner. Thus early did the original "jollying" Mr. Taft had given them become transparent to his little brown brother. Thus early did it become clear to the Filipinos that behind the mask of executive protestations that they shall some day have independence when fit for it, lurks a set determination industriously to earn for an indeterminate number of generations yet to come

The blame of those ye better
The hate of those ye guard.

This book has been written, up to this point, in vain, if the preceding chapters have not made clear how much political expediency, looking to the welfare of a party in power naturally seeking to continue in power, necessarily dominates Philippine affairs under American rule. We have observed under the microscope of history, made available by the official documents now accessible, the long battle between the political expediency germ and the independence bug which began in General Anderson's dealings with Aguinaldo and continued through General Merritt's and General Otis's *régimes*. We have seen General MacArthur's attempt at a wise surgical operation to excise the independence bug from the Philippine body politic—so that the expediency germ might die a natural death from having nothing to feed on. We have seen that operation interfered with by the Taft Commission during the presidential campaign of 1900, because the men in control of the republic could not ignore considerations of political expediency; and we saw the consequent premature setting up of the civil government in 1901, with all its dire consequences in the then as yet unconquered parts of the archipelago, southern Luzon, and some of the Visayan Islands. We have observed the effective though heroic local treatment administered to the Philippine body politic by General Bell in Batangas in 1901–2, with a view of killing off the independence bug there. We have seen the fierce struggle between some of the bug's belated spawn and the expediency germ's now more emboldened forces in Albay in the off year, 1903. We are now to take our fifth year's course in the colonial department of politico-entomological research, the presidential year 1904.

It was the way the Samar insurrection of 1904–5-6 was handled which finally convinced me that the Filipinos would not kill any more of each other in a hundred years than we have killed, or permitted to be killed, of them, in the fell process of Benevolent Assimilation.

American imperialism is not honest, like the British variety. American imperialism knows that Avarice was its father, and Piety its mother, and that it takes after its father more than it does after its mother. British imperialism frankly aims mostly to make *the survivors* of its policies happy, not the people it immediately operates on. American imperialism pretends to be ministering to the happiness of the living, and, though it realizes that it is not a success in that line, it resents identification with its British cousin, by sanctimonious reference to the alleged net good it is doing. Yet in its moments of frankness it says, with an air of infinite patience under base ingratitude, "Well, they will be happy in some other generation," and that therefore the number of people we *have* had or *may* have, to kill, or permit to be killed, in the process of Benevolent Assimilation, is wholly negligible. This is simply the old, old argument that the end justifies the means, the argument that has wrought more misery in the world than any other since time began.

When Judge Taft, General Wright, and their colleagues of the Taft Commission, came out to the Philippines in 1900, they came full of the McKinley convictions about a people whom neither they or Mr.

McKinley had ever seen, bound hand and foot by political necessity to square the freeing of Cuba with the subjugation of the Philippines. A perfectly natural evolution of this attitude resulted in the position they at once took on arriving in the Islands, viz., that to do for the Filipinos what we have done for the Cubans would mean a bloody welter of anarchy and chaos. And the presidential contest of 1900 was fought and won largely on that issue. After 1900, for all the gentlemen above referred to, the proposition was always *res adjudicata*. All protests by Filipinos to the contrary caused only resentment, and welded the authorities more and more hermetically to the correctness of the original proposition. Loyalty to the original ill-considered decision became impregnated, in their case, with a fervor not entirely unlike religious fanaticism, and belief in it became a matter of principle, justifying all they had done, and guiding all they might thereafter do. So that when General Wright "came to the throne" in our colonial empire, as Governor, and legatee of the McKinley-Taft Benevolent Assimilation policies, his attitude in all he did was thoroughly honest, and also thoroughly British. He honestly believed in the "bloody welter of anarchy and chaos" proposition, and was prepared, in any emergency that might arise, to follow his convictions in that regard whithersoever they might lead, without variableness or shadow of turning. Take him all in all, Governor Wright was about the best man occupying exalted station I ever knew personally, President Taft himself not excepted; although I still adhere to Colonel Roosevelt's opinion of 1901 concerning Mr. Taft, quoted in the chapter preceding this, from the *Outlook* of September 21, 1901, notwithstanding that in the contest for the Republican nomination for the presidency in 1912, the Colonel "recalled" that opinion. Seriously, a man may "combine the qualities which would make a first class President of the United States with the qualities which would make a first class Chief Justice of the United States" and still cut a sorry figure trying to fit a square peg into a round hole, or a scheme of government, the breath of whose life is public opinion, into the running of a remote colonial government, the breath of whose life is exemption from being interfered with by public opinion.

After the Albay insurrection of 1903 had been cleaned up, I took charge of the Twelfth Judicial District, having been appointed thereto by Governor Taft just before he left the islands to become Secretary of War. In those trying pioneer days they always seemed to give me the insurrections to sift out, but it was purely fortuitous. Whenever you ceased to be busy, prompt arrangements were made for you to get busy again. Judge Ide, the Minister of Justice, wasted no government money.

The Twelfth District consisted of the two island provinces of Samar and Leyte, two of the six Visayan Islands heretofore noticed as the only ones worth considering in a general view of the archipelago such as the student of world politics wants or needs. Leyte had a population of 388,922,[1] and an area of 3008 square miles.[2] Samar's population was 266,237, and its area, 5276 square miles, makes it the third largest island of the Philippine Archipelago. So that as Judge of the Twelfth District, consisting of two provinces, the Governor of each of which was *ex-officio* sheriff of the court for his province, I was, in a sense, a sort of shepherd of a political flock of some 650,000 people, whom I always thought of as a whole as "my" people.

Samar and Leyte are separated, where nearest together, by a most picturesque winding strait bordered with densely wooded hills. San Juanico Strait is much narrower than the inland sea of Japan at its narrowest point, and almost as beautiful. In fact, at its narrowest point it seems little more than a stone's throw in width. It is as pretty as the prettiest part of the Golden Horn. Leyte had been put under the Civil Government in 1901, and this premature interference with the military authorities in the midst of their efforts to pacify the island had had the usual result of postponing pacification, by filling local politicians, wholly unable to comprehend a government which *entreated* or *reasoned* with people to do things, with the notion that we were resorting to diplomacy in lieu of force because of fear of them. Leyte and Samar were strategically one for the insurgents, just as the provinces of the Lake district of Luzon, described in an earlier chapter, were, because they could flee by night from one province to another in small boats without detection, when hard pressed by the *Americano*. The main insurgent general in Samar, Lucban, had surrendered to General Grant in 1902, but the cheaper fellows stayed out much longer, preying upon those who preferred daily toil to cattle-stealing and throat-cutting as a means of livelihood, and continuing the political unrest intermittently in gradually diminishing degree, through 1903. By the spring of 1904, however, there still remained in Samar riffraff enough, the *jetsam* and *flotsam* of the insurrection—professional outlaws—to get up some trouble, so that, as brigand chiefs, they might resume the rôles of Robin Hood, Jesse James, *et al.* During the first half of that year the opportunity these worthies had been waiting for, while resting on their oars, developed. The crop of municipal officials resulting from the original McKinley plan of beginning the work of reconstruction *during*, instead of *after*, the war, and among the potential village Hampdens, instead of among the Cromwells, had resulted in some very rascally municipal officials who oppressed the poor, getting the hemp of the small farmer, when they would bring it to town, at their own prices—hemp being to Samar what cotton is to the South. From the lowland and upland farmers the ever-widening discontent spread to the hills, where dwelt a type of people constituting only a small fraction of the total population of the Islands—"half savage and half child"—but loving their hills, and wholly indisposed, of their own initiative, to start trouble, unless manipulated. Obviously, then, "the public mind" of Samar—those who know Samar will smile with me at the phrase, but it will do, for lack of a better—was likely soon to be in a generally inflammable condition. By July, 1904, the Robin Hoods, Jesse Jameses, *et al.*, touched the match to the material and a political conflagration started, apparently as unguided—save by the winds of impulse—and certainly as persistent, as a forest fire. Every native of the Philippine Islands, whether he be of the 7,000,000 Christians or of the 500,000 non-Christian tribes, is born with a highly developed social instinct either to command or to obey. The latter tendency is quite as common in the Philippines as the former is in the United States. Hence the Samar disturbances of 1904-5-6, though made up at the outset of raids and depredations by various roving bands of outlaws yielding allegiance only to their immediate chief, soon took on a very formidable military and political aspect.3 The roving bands would ask the peaceably inclined people our flag was supposed to be protecting, "Are you for us or for the Americans?" promptly chopping their heads off if they showed any lack of zeal in denouncing American municipal institutions and things American in general. Pursuant to Mr. McKinley's original scheme—concocted for a people he had never seen, under pressure of political necessity—to rig up in short order a government "essentially popular in form," a lot of most pitiable municipal governments had been let loose on the people, a part of our series of kindergarten lessons. The plan was as wise as it will be for the Japanese—some one please hold Captain Hobson while I finish the analogy—when they conquer the United States, to go to the Bowery and the Ghetto for mayors of all our cities. Thus by our pluperfect benevolence, we had contrived in Samar by 1904 to rouse the highland folk, or hill people, whom the Spaniards had always let alone, against the pacific agricultural lowland people and the dwellers in the coast villages. The latter, or such of them as did not join the hill folk for protection, we permitted to be mercilessly butchered by wholesale, from August to November, 1904, as hereinafter more fully set forth, because ordering out the army to protect them might have been construed at home to mean disturbances more serious and widespread than actually existed, and might therefore affect the presidential election in the United States by renewing the notion that the Administration had never been frank with the American people concerning conditions in the Philippines.

The annual report of the Philippine Commission for 1904 is dated November 1st, which was just a week before the presidential election day of that year. Their annual report for 1905 is dated November 1, 1905. In their report for 1904, the Commission deal with the general state of public order in the same roseate manner which, as we have seen, had made its first appearance during the political exigencies of 1900 in the language about "the great majority of the people" being "entirely willing" to benevolent alien domination in lieu of independence. When Rip Van Winkle was trying to quit drinking, he used to say after each drink: "Oh, we'll just let that pass." In their report for 1904, the Commission swallow the conditions in Samar with equal nonchalance. After stating that some (impliedly negligible) disturbances had occurred in Samar "two months since," they add that "the constabulary of the province took the field" against the bands of Pulajans, or outlaws, and that "as a result, they were soon broken up, and are being pursued and killed or captured" (p. 3). In their report dated November 1, 1905, by way of preface to an account of the extensive military operations inaugurated in Samar shortly after the presidential election of 1904, which operations had not only been in progress for nearly a year on the date of the 1905 report, but continued for more than a year thereafter, the Commission explain their 1904 nonchalance about Samar thus: "It was then believed that the constabulary forces had succeeded in checking the further progress of the outbreak" (p. 47).

Let us examine the facts on which they based this statement, since it meant that they believed that a duly reported epidemic of massacres of peaceably inclined people, over whom the American flag was floating as a symbol of protection to life and property, had stood effectually checked by November 1, 1904, the date of their report. And first, of the massacres themselves, their nature and extent.

The Samar massacres of 1904 began with what we all called down there "the outbreak of July 10th." In August, 1904, I went to Samar to handle the cases arising out of the disturbances there, assisted by the (native) Governor of the province, who, under the law already alluded to, was *ex-officio* sheriff of the court, and an army of deputy sheriffs, as it were, the constabulary, numbering several hundred. The outbreak of July 10th was always known afterwards as "the Tauiran affair." This Tauiran affair was a raid by an outlaw band on the *barrio* of Tauiran, one of the hamlets of the municipal jurisdiction of the township called Gandara, in the valley of the Gandara River, in north central Samar, wherein one hundred houses, the whole settlement, were burned, and twenty-one people killed. The term of court lasted from early in August until early in November. The day after the Tauiran affair, over on the other fork of the Gandara River, occurred what was called "the Cantaguic affair." Cantaguic was a hamlet or *barrio* about the size of Tauiran. The brigands killed the lieutenant of police of Cantaguic and some others, but they did not kill everybody in the place. Instead, after killing a few people, they went to the *tribunal* (town hall), seized the local *teniente*, or municipal representative of American authority, tied the American flag they found at the *tribunal* about the head of the *teniente*, turban fashion, poured kerosene oil on it, and took the *teniente* down stairs and out into the public square, where they lighted and burned the flag on his head, the chief of the band, one Juliano Caducoy by name, remarking to the onlookers that the act was intended as a lesson to those serving that flag. They then cut off the lips of the *teniente* so he could not eat (he of course died a little later), burned the *barrio* and carried off fifty of the inhabitants. Caducoy was captured some time afterward, and I sentenced him to be hanged. There was practically no dispute about the facts. After the Cantaguic affair, during the term of court mentioned, the provincial doctor, Dr. Cullen, an American who had been a captain doctor of volunteers, had occasion to run up to Manila. The doctor was a most accomplished gentleman, but he had a fondness for the grewsome in description equal to Edgar Allan Poe himself. After he came back he told me about having told the Governor-General of the Cantaguic affair, and repeated with an evident pleased consciousness of his ability to make his hearer's blood curdle, how the Governor had said to him slowly, "Doctor, that—is—*aw*ful!"

Blood seemed to whet the appetite for slaughter. The records of the August–November, 1904 term of the court of first instance of Samar show all the various *barrios* of the Gandara Valley in flames on successive days, after the affairs of July 10th and 11th. I do not speak from memory, but from documents contained in a large bundle of papers kept ever since, in memory of that incarnadined epoch. You find one *barrio* burned one day and another another day, until all the people of the Gandara Valley were made homeless. One of the constabulary officers, Lieutenant Bowers, a very gallant fellow, testified before me that from July 10th to the date of his testimony, which was on or about September 28th, some 50,000 people had been made homeless in Samar by the operations of the outlaws. I deem Lieutenant Bowers's estimate quite reasonable. His figures include only one-fifth of the population of an island which was in the throes of an all-pervading brigand uprising. The conservative nature of Lieutenant Bowers's estimate concerning the mischief that had already been wrought by the end of September, 1904, and was then gathering destructive potentiality like a forest or prairie fire, may be inferred from the contents of a memorandum appearing below, furnished me by a Spanish officer of the constabulary, a Lieutenant Calderon, who had been an officer of the Rural Guard in the Spanish days. It contains a list of fifty-three towns, villages, and hamlets (a *barrio* may be quite a village, sometimes even quite a town, though usually it is a hamlet) burned up to the date the memorandum was furnished me.

In order to a clear understanding of these Samar massacres and town-burnings of 1904, as well as for general geographical purposes, a few preliminary words of explanation will be appropriate just here. A province in the Philippines has heretofore been likened to a county with us. But in the largest provinces, the *subdivisions* of provinces called *municipalities* are more like counties; and each municipality is in turn subdivided into sections called *barrios*. A municipality (Spanish, *pueblo*) in the Philippines is not primarily a city or town, as we understand it,*i.e.*, a more or less continuous settlement of houses and lots more or less adjacent, but a specific area of territory, a township, as it were. This area or territory may be 5 × 10 square miles, or 10 × 20, or more, or less. For example, Samar's area is 5276 square miles. Yet it contained in 1904, and probably still contains, only twenty-five townships or municipalities all told, each municipality being subdivided in turn into*barrios*. Municipalities in the Philippines vary in size as much as counties do with us, and their total area accounts for and represents the total area of the province, just as the total area of the counties of a State represents with us the total area of the State. The seat of government of the municipality *always* bears the same name as the municipality itself, just as the county seat of a county usually, or frequently, bears the same name as the county, with us. Take for instance, the name of the first municipality or township in the list which appears below, Gandara. The municipality of Gandara might be described by analogy as the "county" of Gandara, the list of *barrios* burned as a list of towns and villages of the "county" of Gandara.

The municipality of Gandara included a watershed in north central Samar from which the Gandara River flowed in a southwesterly direction to the sea. Within this watershed, parallel 12½ north of the equator intersects the 125th meridian of longitude east of Greenwich. Northern Samar is a very rich hemp country, Catarman hemp being usually quoted higher than any hemp listed on the London market. If you stand at the highest point of the Gandara watershed you can see four streams flowing off north, northwest, northeast, and southwest to the sea. There are some half dozen streams having their source there. Brigands making their headquarters there could always, when hard pressed, get away in canoes toward the sea in almost any direction they wished. The following is Lieutenant Calderon's list:

RELACION POR MUNICIPIOS DE LOS BARRIOS QUEMADOS.

(List by Municipalities of the *Barrios* Burned.)

MUNICIPALITY OF GANDARA

Tauiran　　　July 10

Cantaguic	July 12
Cauilan	July 13
Erenas	July 16
Blanca Aurora	July 19
Bulao4	July 21
Pizarro	August 8
Cagibabago	August 8
Nueva	August 10
Hernandez	August 10
San Miguel	August 10
Buao	August 15
El Cano	August 17
San Enrique	August 20
San Luis	August 25

MUNICIPALITY OF CATBALOGAN

(Calderon's List of *Barrios* Burned, *continued*)

Malino	July 31
Silanga	August 9
Ginga	August 13
San Fernando	August 15
Maragadin	August 20
Talinga	August 21
Santa Cruz	August 22
Dap-dap	August 29
Palencia	August 31

Albalate   (date not given)

Villa Hermosa (date not given)

The above list of villages burned in the township of Catbalogan shows how bold the Pulajans had then grown. By that time they were committing depredations, robbery, murder, and town-burning, in all the various villages within the municipal jurisdiction of the township of Catbalogan, coming often within a few miles of the town proper of Catbalogan itself, the seat of the provincial government. In the attack on Silanga, which occurred August 9th, a number of people were killed. Silanga was but little more than an hour's walk from the court-house at Catbalogan. The Governor at once wired Manila as follows:

CATBALOGAN, SAMAR , Aug. 9, 1904.

EXECUTIVE SECRETARY , Manila:

The peaceably inclined people of the *barrios* near here are collecting here in large numbers, terrorized by Pulajans who are boldly roaming the country, burning *barrios* within seven or eight miles from Catbalogan. They kill men, women, and children without distinction. These Pulajans have fled from Gandara where they are being actively pursued by constabulary. All forces that could be spared have gone out. We have about thirty available fighting men here. *Pulajans liable at any time to enter Catbalogan.* We are in danger of some occurrence quite as serious as the Surigao affair.5 There are buildings here which I must protect at all hazards—Treasury, Provincial Jail with ninety-five prisoners, and commissary and ordnance stores of constabulary. We need at once at least three hundred men, scouts if possible, to handle situation, between here and Gandara. Pulajans undoubtedly have friends in Catbalogan. I suspect certain of the municipal authorities here. I estimate number of Pulajans now operating at about five hundred.

(*Signed*) FEITO , Governor.

On September 2d, the Provincial Governor of Samar sent to Manila the following telegram:

CATBALOGAN , Sept. 2, 1904.

CARPENTER , Actg. Ex. Secy., Palace, Manila:

Seven-thirty this evening simultaneous reports from north and south sides of town Pulajans approaching. They have not entered yet and may not, but have gathered Americans with wives and children in my house. Arms supplied. Treasury twenty-five thousand Conant.6 One hundred forty prisoners in jail. Only forty-seven constabulary here. If Pulajans enter much needless sacrifice life pacific citizens here. Feel sure Pulajans have friends in Catbalogan. Request company either scouts or soldiers from Calbayog stationed here, preferably former. Their presence guarantee stability.

(*Signed*) FEITO , Governor.

Of course Governor Feito did not call for the regular army of the United States. His job, poor devil, was to demonstrate as best he could that the military were not needed. He would at once have been suspected of trying to scuttle the ship of "benign civil government" if he had admitted that the regular army was needed. But to return to Calderon's list:

MUNICIPALITY OF CALBAYOG7

(Calderon's List of *Barrios* Burned, *continued*)

Ylo   August 17

Napuro August 17

Balud   August 17

MUNICIPALITY OF WRIGHT

(Calderon's List of *Barrios* Burned, *continued*)

Guinica-an July 25

Calapi   July 28

Bonga   August 4

Tutubigan August 19

Motiong   September 1

Lau-an   October 10

Sao Jose   (date not given)

A sample of the distressing communications I was getting as these massacres progressed is the notification of the Motiong affair of September 1st set forth below, which I give as a type of the methodical stoicism of those bloody times. Motiong was seven miles down the coast road from Catbalogan:

In the district of Motiong, municipality of Wright, province of Samar, Philippine Islands, September 1, 1904.

In the presence of the undersigned Peregrin Albano, member of the village council, there being also present the president of the Municipal Board of Health, Mr. Tomas San Pablo, and the principal men of the place, there has this day occurred the burial of the corpses, victims of the Pulajans, in the cemetery of this place, to wit: The officer of volunteers, Rafael Rosales, and the following volunteers, viz., Gualberto Gabane, Juan Pacle, Dionisio Daisno, Pedro Damtanan, Carmelo Lagbo; also the two women, Eustaquia Sapiten and Apolinaria N., also one unknown Pulajan. This in fulfilment of the official letter of instructions No. 136, from the office of the presidente of the town of Wright dated to-day. Said burial ceremonies were conducted by the Reverend Father Marcos Gomez, and were attended by the whole volunteer force of this place because of the death of their officer Rosales.

> TOMAS SAN PABLO,
> President of the Board of Health.
>
> PEREGRIN ALBANO,
> Councillor.

(*Illegible*)—— MORO, Captain of Volunteers.8

Fancy having documents like the foregoing handed you with ever-increasing regularity as you sauntered, morning after morning, from your bath to your coffee and rolls, preparatory to the daily sifting of incidents such as that which included the burning of the American flag on the head of the municipal representative of American authority already mentioned, and other like acts of poor misguided peasants stirred up by trifling scamps representing the dregs of insurrection. Motiong was not only within seven miles of the court-house at Catbalogan, but it was so near to Camp Bumpus, over in Leyte, where the 18th Infantry lay, that an order to them to move in the morning would have made life and property in all that brigand-harried region safe that night and continuously thereafter.

General Wm. H. Carter, Major-General U. S. A., well known to the American public as the able officer who, in 1911, commanded the United States forces mobilized on the Mexican border during the Mexican revolution of that year, that ousted President Diaz and seated President Madero, was in command at the time—the fall of 1904—of the military district of the Philippines which included Samar and Leyte. A word of request to him would have made life definitely safe in all the coast towns and their vicinity within two or three days after receipt of such a request.

Besides Gandara, Catbalogan, Calbayog, and Wright, Lieutenant Calderon's list included the trio of ill-fated municipalities set forth below, concluding with the illustrious name of Taft:

MUNICIPALITY OF CATUBIG

Poblacion   September 5

Tagabiran   August 11

San Vicente August —

Catubig was toward the north end of Samar. On the day of the burning and sacking of the *poblacion* of Catubig, September 5th, which was done by a force of several hundred Pulajans, the scouts and constabulary, so it was afterward reported, killed a hundred of the Catubig Pulajans in an engagement. If this report were correct, as is likely, it was the biggest single killing of natives since the early days of the insurrection.9But it did not in the least check the Pulajan insurrection, which simply swerved its fury from the Catubig region toward the coast (the Pacific coast), descending upon the towns, villages, and hamlets of the townships of Borongan and Taft, thus:

MUNICIPALITY OF BORONGAN

(Calderon's List of *Barrios* Burned, *continued*)

Sepa	Sept. 23
Lucsohong	Sept. 23
Maybocog	Sept. 23
Maydolong	Sept. 23
Soribao	Sept. 23
Bugas	Oct. 10
Punta Maria	Oct. 10
Canjauay	Oct. 11

MUNICIPALITY OF TAFT

(Calderon's List *continued*)

Del Remedio	Sept. 22
San Julian	Sept. 22
Nena	Sept. 22
Libas	Sept. 22
Pagbabangnan	Sept. 22
San Vicente	Sept. 21
Jinolaso	Oct. 3

Of the twenty-five pueblos or townships of Samar, the Calderon list only pretended to throw light on events in nine of them, those being the only ones from which definite news had then reached headquarters. But as a reign of terror prevailed all over Samar at the time, the rest may be imagined, though it can never be ascertained. Of these nine, the last two were:

MUNICIPALITY OF LLORENTE

Pagbabalancayan Sept. 23

MUNICIPALITY OF ORAS

Concepcion Sept. 23

Jipapad —

Now it feels just as uncomfortable to be boloed in Pagbabalancayan as it would in a place with a more pronounceable name, and the same is true of the comparatively mellifluous Jipapad. True, some of these places were mere hamlets of twenty to forty houses, but you may be sure there were five or six people, on an average, to each house. On the other hand, glance back again at the list of towns of the township of Taft that were sacked and burned, and consider that San Julian was about the size of the provincial capital, Catbalogan, and that Catbalogan, the town proper, contained a population of four thousand, though looked at from the amphitheatre of hills which surround it, Catbalogan does not look like such a very large group of houses. Filipino houses are usually full of people. It is easier to live that way than to build more houses.

After the Pulajan descent on Llorente, the people of Llorente all went off to the hills *to the Pulajans* for safety. They were not allowed to have firearms. This was forbidden by law, except on condition of making formal application for permission, getting it finally approved, and giving a bond, conditions which, in practical operation, made the prohibition all but absolute. The law was general for the whole archipelago. The theory of the law was that the inhabitants were under "the peace and protection of a benign civil government." The real reason of the law was that if the people were allowed to bear arms it was very uncertain which side they would use them on, our side or the other. But, by 1904, the lowland and coast people of Samar would have been glad enough to have stuck to us and gone out after the mountain robber bands had we armed them. Left unprotected, a feeling seemed to spread in many places that about the only thing to do to be safe was to depart from under the "protection" of the American flag and take to the hills and join, or seem to join, the uprising.

Toward the last of September, the provincial treasurer of Samar, an American, a Mr. Whittier, visited the east coast of Samar, including Taft. On October 5th, he stated before me as follows:

All the presidentes that I have talked with, and this man Hill,[10] said that they wanted some protection for their towns. Except at Borongan there are no guns in the hands of the municipal police.[11] This band near Taft was said to have nineteen guns, and they felt they could not *defend their towns with spears* against these guns. There were reported to be between 200 and 600 in operation on the coast at that time, and they felt that they could not defend their towns with the means at hand. I found at Taft that they had taken all the records of the municipality, and the money, and taken it over to an island away from the main coast, in order to protect their money and their records, and I understand the same thing was done at Llorente. At Oras they had practically decided to take the same step if it became necessary. All of the commercial houses on the east coast and a large number of people congregated at Borongan, which was safe on account of the protection of the constabulary; and the constabulary there were doing very good work, *doing everything they could with their small force*, and they (the presidentes) felt that if they had guns in the hands of the municipal police or if they had the constabulary to guard their towns, they could go out after these people themselves.

The importance of all this testimony, relatively to its forever sickening any one acquainted with it with colonization by a republic, is that a transcript of Mr. Whittier's statement of October 5th was placed in the hands of the Governor-General a few days later by Mr. Harvey, the Assistant Attorney-General, and yet this situation continued until shortly after the presidential election. Several years afterwards, in the *North American Review*, Judge Ide, who was Vice-Governor in 1904, after admitting that he was in constant consultation with the Governor-General all through that period (by way of showing his opportunities for knowing whereof he spoke), denied that the failure to order out the military to protect the people from massacre had any relation whatever to the presidential election then going on in the United States.

Mr. Whittier also stated before me that the total population of the municipality of Taft was 18,000, and that twenty-five men armed with guns in each of the four principal villages thereof that were burned would have prevented the destruction of those villages. So we did not protect the people, and we would not let them protect themselves. I do not select the pueblo of Taft on account of its distinguished name. "What's in a name?" The fate of Taft and its inhabitants was simply typical of the fate which descended upon scores of other places in "dark and bloody" Samar between the outbreak of July 10, 1904, and the presidential election of November 8th, of that year, and between those two dates the shadow of such a fate was over all the towns of the island on which it did not in fact descend. Mr. Whittier stated to me informally that at the time he was speaking of in the above formal statement, there were pending and had been pending for a long time (he seemed to think they must have been pigeon-holed) applications for permission to bear arms from fifteen different pueblos. After Mr. Whittier had finished his statement the Presidente of Taft made a like statement on the same day, October 5th. My retained copy shows that this official bore the ponderous name of Angel Custodio Crisologo. He declared a willingness to lead his people against the Pulajans if given guns, though the fervent soul *did* qualify this martial remark by adding, "If I am well enough," explaining that the presidential body was subject to rheumatism. Mr. Crisologo stated among other things that there had been eight hundred houses burned in the jurisdiction of Taft before he left the east coast for Catbalogan—about a week before. Like Mr. Whittier's, a copy of Mr. Crisologo's statement was delivered a few days later to the Governor-General in person by the Assistant Attorney-General, Mr. Harvey, who had been present when it was made and taken down.

This Mr. Harvey need not be, to the western hemisphere reader, a mere nebulous antipodal entity, as the Hon. Angel Custodio Crisologo might. He is a very live American, a very high-toned gentleman, and an excellent lawyer, and was at last accounts still with the insular government of the Philippine Islands, though in a higher capacity (Solicitor General) than he was at the date of the events herein narrated. There was very little congenial society in Catbalogan when Mr. Harvey came there to help dispose of the criminal docket, and his advent was to me a very welcome oasis in a desert of "the solitude of my own originality"—or lack of originality. On September 19th I had wired Vice-Governor Ide that there were 172 prisoners in the jail awaiting trial and "many more coming." Of course no justice of the peace would be trusted to pass on whether an alleged outlaw should or should not be held for trial. If he were secretly in sympathy with the discomfiture American authority in Samar was having, he might let the man go, no matter what the proof. Also he might seek to clear himself of all suspicion in each case by committing men against whom there was no proof, thus unnecessarily crowding an already fast filling provincial jail of limited dimensions, wherein beriberi12 was already making its dread appearance.

So the writ of habeas corpus remained unsuspended, thus making it possible to so state in later official certificates covering that period. But habeas corpus cut no more figure in the situation than it did at the battle of Gettysburg, or at the crossing of the Red Sea by the chosen people, or at the sinking of the *Titanic*. The constabulary would worry along with such force as they had in the island of Samar, only a few hundred, certainly nearer five hundred than one thousand. And, whenever they had a battle with the outlaws, if they themselves were not annihilated, which happened more than once, they would bring back prisoners in droves and put them in the jail, and I was expected to sift out how much proof they had, or claimed to have, of overt acts by persons not actually captured in action. Of course a race then began, a race against death, to see whether death or I would get to John Doe or Richard Roe first. And though I held court every day except Sunday from August to November 8th, sometimes getting in sixteen hours per day by supplementing a day's work with a night session, death would often beat me to some one man on the jail list whom I happened to have picked out to get to the next day. Men so picked out were men as to whom something I might have heard held out the hope of being able to dispose of their cases quickly by letting them loose,13 thus getting that much farther from the danger limit of crowding in the jail. Some of these would be specially picked out because reported sick. I kept track of the sick by visiting them myself when practicable, and talking to them. Of course many of them were brigands—-Pulajans—but some of them were the saddest looking, most abject little brigands that anybody ever saw. Of course you might catch some nasty disease from them, but nobody, somehow, ever seemed to have any apprehension on that score in the Philippines. This does not argue bravery at all. It is merely the listless stoicism that lurks in the climate. I recollect going to walk one afternoon, after adjourning court at 5 o'clock, saying to the prosecuting attorney before adjourning, "We will take up the case of Capence Coral in the morning; there does not seem, from what I can understand, to be enough proof to convict him of anything." Of course when you were dealing with hundreds of people, you did not have any nerve-racking hysterics about any one man. Leaving the court-house I passed by the hospital, where Capence had been transferred, pending the arrival of witnesses against him and the rest of the crowd captured with him. I asked the hospital steward how Capence was. The answer was he had died at 4:45—some twenty minutes before. Death had beat me to Capence. When I meet Capence he will know I did the best I could. I was under a great strain, a sort of writ of habeas corpus incarnate, the only thing remotely suggesting relief from unwarranted14 detention on the whole horizon of the situation. I was trying to do the best I could by the Constitution, in so far as the spirit of it had reached the Philippines. I broke down totally under the strain about November 8th, came home in the spring of the following year and remained an invalid for several years thereafter; and as a noted corporation lawyer once said after recovery from a similar illness, "I haven't had much *constitution* since, but have been living mostly under the by-laws."

American office-holding in the Philippines is not so popular with the Filipinos as to have moved them to any outburst of gratitude in the shape of an effort to create a pension system for Americans who lose their health in the government service out there. When they leave the Islands they become as one dead so far as the Philippine insular government is concerned. And *the men whose health is more or less permanently impaired by disability incurred in line of duty in the Philippines are not and will never be numerous or powerful enough back home to create any sentiment in favor of a pension system for former Philippine employees*, since the Philippine business is not a subject of much popular enthusiasm at best. So if I had not had private resources, the results of the Samar insurrection of 1904 would have left me also in the pitiable plight in which I have beheld so many of my repatriated former comrades of the Philippine service in the last seven years, to whom the heart of the more fortunate ex-Filipino indeed goes out in sympathy. But to return to the race to beat death to prisoners in that grim and memorable fall of 1904.

In September the crowded condition of the jail had begun to tell on the inmates. The constabulary force at Catbalogan was quite inadequate for the varied emergencies of the situation, there being, besides the town itself to protect, the provincial treasury to guard, the governor's office, the court-house, and the jail. Consequently the jail guard was too small. The jail buildings were in an enclosure a little larger than a baseball diamond, surrounded by high stone walls. But it was not safe to let the inmates sleep out in the enclosure at night. They had to be kept at night in the buildings. Any American who has visited the central penitentiary at Manila called Bilibid has seen a place almost as clean as a battleship. This is American work. But the Filipinos are not trained in sanitary matters, and all they know about handling large crowds of prisoners they learned from the Spaniards. The Governor was a native half-caste, a very excellent man, but free from that horror, which I think is an almost universal American trait, of seeing unnecessary and preventable sacrifice of human life, no matter whose the life. I inspected the jail as often as was practicable, and managed to keep down the death-rate below what it might have been, the prisoners being allowed to go out in the open court during the day. They also had such medical attention as was available. However, during the last five or six weeks of that term of court I would be pretty sure to find on my desk every two or three days, on opening court in the morning, a notice like this:

Carcel Provincial de Samar, I. F.
Oficina del Alcaide

CATBALOGAN, SAMAR, I. F.,
22 de Septiembre de 1904.

Hon. Sr. Juez de I^a Instancia de esta provincia,
CATBALOGAN, SAMAR, I. F.

SEÑOR :

Tengo el honor de poner en conocimiento de ese juzgado, que anoche entre 12 y 1 de ella, fallecio el procesado, Ramon Boroce, a consecuencia de la enfermedad de beriberi, que venia padeciendo.

Lo que tengo el honor de communicar a ese Juzgado para su superior conocimiento.

De U. muy respetuosamente,
GONZALO LUCERO ,

Alcaide de la Carcel Provincial.

which being interpreted means:

Provincial Jail of Samar, P. I.

CATBALOGAN, SAMAR, P. I.,
September 22, 1904.

His honor, the Judge of First Instance of this province,
CATBALOGAN, SAMAR, P. I.

SIR :

I have the honor to bring to the knowledge of the court that last night between 12 and 1 o'clock, the accused person Ramon Boroce died in consequence of the disease of beriberi from which he has been suffering; which fact I have the honor to communicate to the court for its superior knowledge.

Very respectfully,
>GONZALO LUCERO,

>Warden of the Provincial Jail.

Now a jail death-rate of only ten or twelve a month was not at all a bad record for an insurrection in a Philippine province. It would be rank demagoguery at this late date to be a party to anybody's getting excited about it. I was rather proud of it by comparison with the jail death-rate of the Albay insurrection of the year before, where 120 men had died in the jail in about six months. But it began to get on one's nerves to have to expect a *billet-doux* like the above on your desk at the opening of court each day, when the accused person had had no commitment trial and may have been wholly innocent. It all came back to the difference between war and peace, viz., that in war it is to be expected that many innocent persons will suffer, but that in peace only the guilty should suffer. Moreover, in war that admits it *is* war, your agents, your army, are better able to handle crowds of prisoners than native police and constabulary, and the percentage of innocent who suffer with the guilty in such war will be far less; whereas the contrary is true of war—waged by constabulary checked by courts—which pretends that a state of peace exists, *i.e.*, which pretends there is no need for declaring martial law and calling on your army.

It was this Samar insurrection which convinced me that waging war with courts and constabulary in lieu of the recognized method was, in its net results, the cruelest kind of war, and that the civil government of the Philippines was a failure, in so far as regarded Mr. McKinley's original injunction to the Taft Commission; where, after alluding to the articles of capitulation of the city of Manila to our forces, which concluded with the words:

> This city, its inhabitants * * * and its private property of all descriptions * * * are placed under the special safeguard of the faith and honor of the American Army,

he added:

> As high and sacred an obligation rests upon the Government of the United States to give protection for property and life * * * to all the people of the Philippine Islands. I charge this commission to labor for the full performance of this obligation, which concerns the honor and conscience of their country.

Commenting on this in his inaugural address as Governor of the Philippines, Governor Taft had said:

> May we not be recreant to the charge, which he truly says, concerns the honor and conscience of our country.

No matter who was to blame, here we were in Samar, with the 14th Infantry three hours away in one direction at Calbayog, doing nothing, and the 18th Infantry five hours away in another direction, at Tacloban, doing nothing, and a reign of terror going on in Samar, with the peaceably inclined people of the lowlands and coast towns appealing to us for protection and not getting it, sometimes crouching in abject terror without knowing which way to fly, sometimes taking to the hills and joining the outlaws as a measure of self-preservation. 'Twas pitiful, wondrous pitiful! I then and there decided that we ought to get out of the Philippines as soon as any decent sort of a native government could be set up, and that our republic was not adapted to colonization. In his *North American Review* article above cited, in denying that the unwillingness of the Manila government to order out the army in Samar in the fall of 1904 had anything to do with the possible effect so doing might have had on the presidential election, then in progress in the United States, Governor Ide rebuked me with patronizing self-righteousness thus: "Was Judge Blount opposed to kindness?" He means in giving the Filipinos, under such circumstances, the "protection of civil government," instead of ordering out the army. No, but I was opposed to using a saw, in lieu of a lancet, in excising the ulcers of that body politic at that time. In protesting that there was "nothing sinister" about the failure to use the troops, Judge Ide cunningly wonders whether my attitude was subsequently assumed after I left the Islands because of "proclivities as a Democrat," or whether it was merely due to "predilections in favor of military rule." Read Mr. McKinley's instructions to the Taft Commission, above quoted, that to protect life and property concerned the honor and conscience of their country, and consider if the Ide suggestion does not seem to hide its head and slink away in shame before the strong clear light of what was then a plain duty. As a matter of fact Judge Charles S. Lobinger, who is still with the Philippine judiciary, visited me en route to another point, during that Samar term of court, and he will recall, should he ever chance upon this book and this chapter, with what vehemence I said to him at the time, in effect, "Judge, we belong in the Western Hemisphere. We have no business out here permanently." If proclivities and predilections in favor of affording decent protection to the lives and property of defenceless people by properly garrisoning their towns constitutes lack of kindness, then the Ide rebuke was well taken.

These details are not related with Pickwickian gravity in order to acquaint the reader with *my* utterances as being important *per se*. But it *is*important to make clear to the reader, and he is entitled, in all frankness, to have it made clear by one who has now so long detained his attention on this great subject, to know just when "the light from heaven on the road to Damascus" broke upon this witness, and how and why he came to be in favor of Philippine independence, because the reasons which convinced him may seem good in the sight of the reader also. If the man who reads this book shall see that the man who wrote it was, in Samar in 1904, neither a Republican nor a Democrat, but simply an American in a far distant land, jealous of the honor of his country's flag in its capacity as a symbol of protection to those over whom it floated, then the work will not have been written in vain.

The presidentes or mayors of the various pueblos were in session at Catbalogan in semi-annual convention during the first few days of October, 1904, when the Assistant Attorney-General, Mr. Harvey, visited Catbalogan. Mr. Harvey and the writer had taken a number of long walks together in the suburbs of Catbalogan, though Major Dade, commanding the Samar constabulary, an officer of the regular army, had warned us it was not safe outside of town. We had talked over the situation fully. Besides all its other aspects, there were a number of American women in Catbalogan, an American lawyer's wife, the wife of the superintendent of schools, her sister, and others. It was not at all likely that the Pulajans would enter Catbalogan, but there was always the *possibility*, not to be wholly ignored, that some such episode as that of March 23d, of the preceding year, at Surigao, already described, might be repeated. As hereinbefore noted, on August 9th, the Pulajans had done some killing and burning at Silanga, less than ten miles north of Catbalogan and likewise at Motiong, less than ten miles south of Catbalogan, on September 1st, and on the evening of September 2d, about 7:30, there had been a false alarm caused by some native of Catbalogan running down the main street yelling, "Pulajans! Pulajans!" All of which did not tend to make you feel that your American women were quite as entirely safe from harm as they ought to be.

In the course of one of our walks Mr. Harvey and I had stopped on the mountain side overlooking Catbalogan, to catch our breath and take in the view of the town below and the sea beyond. I said to him, because I knew his mind also was on the one great need of the hour: "Yes sir, if President Roosevelt were here, and could see this situation as we do, he would order out the army and protect these defenceless people, no matter which way the chips might fly." Mr. Harvey agreed with me. He promised to go back to Manila and tell the authorities there so. After we came back to town, we were advised that the convention of presidentes desired to have Mr. Harvey favor them with an address. He said, "What shall I tell them?" I said, "Tell them that if they will do their duty by the American Government, the American Government will do its duty by them." He spoke Spanish fluently, made a good speech, and told them in effect just that thing. Then he went back to Manila, and shortly afterward wrote me the two letters which follow:

DEPARTMENT OF JUSTICE, PHILIPPINE ISLANDS,
OFFICE OF THE ASSISTANT ATTORNEY-GENERAL
FOR THE CONSTABULARY,

MANILA, P. I., October 15, 1904.

MY DEAR JUDGE: We arrived in Manila on Tuesday morning, the 11th instant, and I prepared my report and submitted it to the attorney-general on the 12th, in the meantime making a transcript of your summary and delivering a copy of same with other information to the attorney-general along with my report. After dictating the report and before delivering it I had a conversation with General Allen on the situation in Samar and told him what my recommendations would be. He agreed that rewards should be offered for the capture of Pablo Bulan, Antonio Anogar, and Pedro de la Cruz, but took issue on the other recommendations, and to my mind he takes a very extreme view; but I thought at the time and still think that he wanted to tone me down in my feelings in the matter. I think the real cause for his opposition is the effect that he fears an aggressive attitude might have on the presidential election. In other words, whatever they do aggressively might be misconstrued and made use of as political capital.

At Governor Wright's request I got the report from the attorney-general before it was sent up and went over to the Malacañan, and the governor read the report and read most of the data that I submitted with the report, including your summary, and while he did not say much what he did say convinced me that there would be something doing if it were not on the eve of election, and in my opinion there will be things doing in Samar within thirty days.

I inclose herewith a copy of your summary, and also a copy of my report to the attorney-general. On the 18th instant I received your telegram to hold the completion of your summary until receipt of a letter mailed by you that day. I telegraphed you in reply that my report and your summary were placed in the hands of the attorney-general on the 12th instant. If there is any additional data in your letter mailed on the 13th I will submit it to the proper authorities.

For the lack of time, I will close, and write more next time.

    Very truly yours,
        (*Signed*) GEO. R. HARVEY,
        Assistant Attorney-General.

DEPARTMENT OF JUSTICE, PHILIPPINE ISLANDS,
OFFICE OF THE ASSISTANT ATTORNEY-GENERAL,
FOR THE CONSTABULARY,

MANILA, P. I., October 19, 1904.

My dear Judge Blount : Since mailing my letter to you of last Saturday I have found the copies of your summary on the situation in Samar and inclose two herewith, in accordance with my promise.

This week we have received some good news from Samar with reference to important captures and killings of Pulajans. I am not in touch with what is going on with reference to Samar, and can give you no information along that line. As I remember, the governor told me the other day when I was talking with him that one more company of scouts will be sent down right away.

I sincerely hope the situation is improving, and that you are getting along rapidly in disposing of the large docket before you. If there is not a very great improvement in the situation by the 9th of November, I think there will be a considerable movement of troops in Samar within thirty days. For the good of the government, I hope the situation will improve materially before that time. I would like to see them put the troops there right now. I am of the opinion that it would not affect the election a half-dozen votes, and it might save two or three or a half-dozen massacres and the destruction of much property.

With best wishes for your success in your work, and with regards to Mr. Block, I am,

    Very truly yours,

    Geo. R. Harvey ,

    Assistant Attorney-General, Philippines Constabulary.
      To Hon. James H. Blount ,
      Judge of First Instance, Catbalogan, Samar, P. I.

These two letters may be found at p. 2532, *Congressional Record*, February 25, 1908, where they were the subject of remark in the House of Representatives by Hon. Thomas W. Hardwick of Georgia, apropos of Governor Ide's *North American Review* article of December, 1907.

A few weeks after the presidential election I saw Mr. Harvey in Manila. We naturally talked about Samar and his two letters to me. The troops had then been ordered out. He referred to his conference with the Governor-General and stated, "Yes, he told me that was the reason," meaning that the reason for not ordering out the troops was the one assigned in his (Harvey's) letter to me, viz., "Whatever we do aggressively might be misconstrued and made use of as political capital."

On October 18, 1904, there was received at Manila the following cablegram concerning the presidential campaign in the United States:

New York, 16th. Judge Parker, in addressing campaign clubs at Esopus the past week returned to the subject of the Philippines in the evident hope of making it a paramount issue of the campaign. He repeated his former declaration that the retention of the Philippines and the carrying out of the policy of the Republican Administration have cost six hundred and fifty millions of dollars and two hundred thousand lives. Secretary of War Taft, in addressing a mass meeting held in Baltimore, Saturday night, ridiculed Judge Parker's statement and characterized his figures as alarmist.

Of course Judge Parker's figures were rather high—of which more anon. He was not going to miss anything in the way of a chance of "getting a rise" out of the Administration, by understatement. But some statement from the Philippines at once became a supremely important desideratum, to counterbalance Judge Parker's over-statement, some optimism to meet the Parker pessimism. Encouraged by the public interest aroused by the figures furnished him, and the consequent apparent uneasiness it created in "the enemy's camp," Judge Parker soon had the whole Philippine group of islands going to "the demnition bow-wows." On October 20th, Secretary of War Taft cabled Governor Wright, then Governor-General of the Islands, a long telegram, quoting Judge Parker as having used, among other language descriptive of the beatitudes we had conferred on our little brown brother, the following: "The towns in many places in ruins, whole districts in the hands of ladrones."[15]

At that time the whole archipelago was absolutely quiet for the nonce, except Samar. Samar was the only island where Judge Parker's statement was true, and as to Samar, it was absolutely true. On October 23d Governor Wright wired Secretary of War Taft as follows:

There is nothing warranting the statement that towns are in ruins. It is not true that there are whole districts in the hands of ladrones. Life and property are as safe here as in the United States.[16]

This was followed by a perfectly true and correct picture of the peace and quiet which then prevailed for the time being everywhere throughout the archipelago, except in Samar, which dark and bloody isle was specifically excepted. Then followed a statement as to Samar, full of allusions as elaborately optimistic as any of the Taft cablegrams of 1900, to impliedly inconsiderable "prowling bands" of outlaws in Samar. Of course nobody at home knew the answer to this, so it silenced the Parker batteries, and the Samar massacres proceeded unchecked. Meanwhile the 14th Infantry at Calbayog, Samar, and the 18th Infantry, at Tacloban, Leyte, smiled with astute, if contemptuous, tolerance, at the self-inflicted impotence of a republic trying to make conquered subjects behave without colliding too violently with home sentiment against *having* conquered subjects; sang their favorite barrack room song,

He may be a brother of Wm. H. Taft,
But he ain't no friend of mine;

and continued to enjoy enforced leisure. They *did* chafe under the restraint, but it at least relieved them from the not altogether inspiring task of chasing Pulajans through jungles and along the slippery mire of precipitous mountain trails, and at the same time permitted the secondest second lieutenant among them to swear fierce *blasé* oaths, not wholly unjustified, about how much better he could run the Islands than they were being run.

On October 26th, I wired Governor Wright at Manila as follows:

Since my letter of October 6th, situation appears worse. Additional depredations both on east and west coast. Smith-Bell closing out.[17] Reliable American residing in Wright says that during week ending last Sunday thirteen families living along river Nacbac, *barrio* of Tutubigan, said pueblo, kidnapped by brigands and carried off to hills. This means some sixty people having farms along river, rice ready to be harvested. Seven of the eleven *barrios* of Wright have been burned.

BLOUNT.

When I sent that telegram of October 26th, the situation in the pueblo of Wright was typical of the reign of terror throughout the island. Wright could have been reached by the 18th Infantry (then over at Tacloban, in Leyte), and garrisoned on eight hours' notice. But I had little hope that the telegram would stir the 18th. The best man I had ever personally known well in high station was at the head of the government of the Islands, and as he was my friend, I sat down to think the situation out, determined, with the prejudice which is the privilege of friendship, to analyze his apparent apathy, and to conjecture *how many times* thirteen families "having farms along river, rice ready to be harvested" would have to be carried off to the hills by the brigands in order to move the 18th Infantry before the presidential election. Then I wondered just how many seconds it would have taken a British governor-general, backed by unanimous home sentiment concerning the wisdom of having colonies, to have acted, had a great British colonial mercantile house like Smith, Bell & Co. appealed to him for protection of its interests. And that brought me, there on "the tie-ribs of earth," as Kipling would phrase it, to the fundamentals of the problem. The British imperial idea of which Kipling is the voice and Benjamin Kidd the accompanist is based, superficially, upon a supposed necessity for the control of the tropics by non-tropical peoples, though fundamentally, it is an assertion of the right of any people to assume control of the land and destinies of another when they feel sure they can govern that other better than that other can govern itself. Is this proposition tenable, and if so, within what limits? Is it tenable to the point of total elimination of the people sought to be improved? If not, then how far? How far is incidental sacrifice of human life negligible in the working out of the broader problem of "the greatest good of the greatest number?" In his article in the *North American Review* for December, 1907, Governor Ide makes exhaustive answer to "the doctors who for some months past, in the columns of the *North American Review* and elsewhere, have published prescriptions for curing the ills of the Filipino people," including Senator Francis G. Newlands, Hon. William J. Bryan, and the writer. In the course of disposing of the quack last mentioned, Governor Ide gets on rather a high horse, asking, with much dignified indignation, "How many people in the United States would have known or cared whether the army was or was not ordered out in Samar in 1904?" I concede that the solicitude was a super-solicitude, as do the Harvey letters, but like them, I must recognize its reality. However, when Governor Ide reaches this rhapsody of conscious virtue: "It is inconceivable that the Commission could have been animated by the base and ignoble partisan prejudices thus charged against them," capping his climax by triumphantly pointing out that "Governor-General Wright was a life-long Democrat," he doth protest too much. For the angelic pinions he thus attaches to himself are at once rudely snapped by the reflection that a very short while after his article came out in the *North American Review* Governor Wright became Secretary of War in President Roosevelt's Cabinet, and a little later took the stump for Taft and Sherman, in 1908. Governor Wright did not stoop to deny or extenuate his share in the matter, and I honor him for it.18 But to stick to your own crowd and then deny afterwards that you did so—that is another story. However, let us brush aside such petty attempts to cloud the real issue, which is: How many people would Governor Wright and Vice-Governor Ide have permitted to be massacred by the Pulajans in Samar in 1904 before they would have ordered out the military prior to the presidential election? Let us consider the case, not with a view of clouding the issue, but of clearing it. The truth is, Governor Wright was very gravely concerned about the Samar situation from August to November, 1904. Of course it is due to him to make perfectly clear that he did not realize the gravity of that situation as vividly as those of us who were on the ground in Samar, four or five hundred miles away. But the information hereinbefore reviewed, conveyed to him by the Provincial Governor, by Mr. Harvey, the Assistant Attorney General sent to Samar for the express purpose of getting the Manila government in possession of the exact situation, and by myself, was certainly sufficient to make him "chargeable with notice" of all that happened thereafter, certainly chargeable with knowledge of all that had happened theretofore. Of course there was General Allen, the commander-in-chief of the constabulary, at Manila, presumably speaking well of his command—the right arm of the civil government—presumably giving industrious and tactful aid and comfort to the idea that the authorities could afford to worry along with the constabulary alone until after the presidential election. But that could not discount the actual facts reported from the afflicted province by the officials on the ground. General Allen, it should be noted, remained in Manila all this time. So that any Otis-like "situation-well-in-hand" bouquets he may have thrown at his subordinates in Samar, and the situation there generally, were mere political hothouse products, surer to be recognized as such by the shrewd kindliness of the truly considerable man at the head of the government than by most any one else he could hand them out to. That man knew, to all intents and purposes, in the great and noble heart of him, what was really going on in Samar. He knew that massacres had been occurring, and that they were likely to keep on occurring. In other words, he knew that *preventable* sacrifice of life of defenceless people was going on, and that he could put a stop to it any time he saw fit. The question he had to wrestle with was, should he stop it, knowing the "Hell fer Sartin" the Democratic orators in the United States would at once luridly describe as "broke loose" in the Philippines? I insist that there is no use for any holier-than-thou gentleman to become suffused with any glow of indignant conscious rectitude based on the premises we are considering. Better to look a little deeper, on the idea that you are observing your republic *in flagrante colonizatione*, with as good a man as you ever have had, or ever will have, among you, as the principal actor. Governor Wright's course was entirely right, *if the Philippine policy was right*. If his course was not right, it was not right because the Philippine policy is fundamentally wrong. Governor Wright of course believed that the Philippine policy was right. I myself did not come finally to believe it was wrong until it was revealed in all its rawness by the period now under discussion. Of course the Governor did not vividly realize that the American women in Catbalogan were not entirely safe. If he had, he would have rushed the troops there, politics or no politics. But native life was politically negligible. What difference would a few score, or even a few hundred, natives of Samar make, compared with that pandemonium of anarchy and bloodshed all over the archipelago which Messrs. Taft, Wright, and Ide had long been insisting would follow Philippine independence? Was the whole future of 8,000,000 of people to be jeopardized to save a few people in Samar? That was the moral question before the insular government, in its last analysis. And the government faced the proposition squarely, and answered it "No."

I will go farther than this. If I had believed, with Messrs. Taft, Wright, and Ide, that Philippine independence meant anarchy in the Islands, and the orthodox "bloody welter of chaos," I too might have hesitated to order out the troops on the eve of the election, and my hesitation, like theirs, might have continued until the election was safely over. So might yours, reader. Don't be so certain you would not. Practically absolute power, sure of its own benevolence, has temptations to withhold its confidence from the people that you wot not of. Don't condemn Governor Wright. Condemn the policy, and change your republic back to the course set by its founders. Give the Philippine people the independence they of right ought to have, instead of secretly hoping to unload them on somebody else, through the medium of your next great war.

The question of whether the troops should have been ordered out or not at the time above dealt with is by no means without two sides. On the "bloody welter" side, you have the well-known opinions of Messrs. Taft, Wright, and Ide. On the other side you have before you—for the moment—only my little opinion. So instead of having in Governor Wright a Bluebeard, you simply have a man of great personal probity and unflinching moral courage, following his convictions to their ultimate logical conclusion without shadow of turning, in the act of colonization. In other words, Mr. American, you see yourself, as others see you. So face the music and look at yourself. In your colony business, you are a house divided against itself, which cannot stand. On the other hand, I knew the Filipino people far more intimately than either Mr. Taft, Governor Wright, or Judge Ide. I spoke their language—which they did not. I had met them both in peace and in war—which they had not. I had held court for months at a time in various provinces of the archipelago from extreme northern Luzon to Mindanao—which they had not. I had met the

Filipinos in their homes for years on terms of free and informal intercourse impracticable for any governor-general. It was therefore perfectly natural that I should know them better than any of these eminent gentlemen. I was not prepared to be in a hurry about recommending myself out of office by assenting that our guardianship over the Filipinos should at once be terminated, but I knew there was nothing to the "bloody welter" proposition. The home life of the Filipino is too altogether a model of freedom from discord, pervaded as it is by parental, filial, and fraternal love, and their patriotism is too universal and genuine, to give the "bloody welter" bugaboo any standing in court.

But whosoever questions for one moment Governor Wright's high personal character, simply does not know the man. To do so, moreover, would fatally cloud the issue I have sought to make clear between his view of the duty of our government and my own. In his moods that reminded one of Lincoln, Governor Wright used to say: "Don't shoot the organist, he's doing the best he can." It is true that his answer to Judge Parker was not a full and frank statement of the case. But did it lie in American human nature, when your antagonist was recklessly over-stating the case in the heat of debate on the eve of a presidential election, to take him into your confidence and tell him all you knew, in simple trusting faith that he would thereafter quit exaggerating? To permit the dispute to boil down to the real issue, viz., how many lives it was permissible to abandon on the "greatest good to the greatest number" theory, would obviously jeopardize the existence of a government which the Governor of the Philippines naturally believed to be better for all concerned than any other. And there is your cul-de-sac. *Hinc illæ lachrymæ.*

We can point with pride to many things we have done in the Philippines, the public improvements,[19] the school system, the better sanitation, and a long list of other benefits conferred. But in the greatest thing we have done for them, we have builded wiser than we knew. "God moves in a mysterious way His wonders to perform." In fourteen years we have welded the Filipinos into one homogeneous political unit. In a most charming book, entitled *An Englishwoman in the Philippines*,[20] we can see our attempts to fit government by two political parties into over-seas colonization caricatured without sting until we really remind ourselves of a hippopotamus caressing a squirrel. In one passage the British sister describes our programme as one "to educate the Filipino for all he is worth, so that he may, in the course of time, be fit to govern himself *according to American methods*; but at the same time they have plenty of soldiers to knock him on the head if he shows signs of wanting his liberty before the Americans think he is fit for it"—"A quaint scheme," she naïvely adds, "and one full of the go-ahead originality of America."

The more we teach the Filipinos, the more intimately they will become acquainted, *in their own way*, with the history of the relations between our country and theirs from the beginning, including the taxation without representation, through Congressional legislation (hereinafter noticed) placed or kept on our statute-books by the hemp trust and other special interests in the United States. And they will learn all these things in the midst of a "growing gulf between the two peoples."[21]

In fourteen years we have made these unwilling subjects, whom we neither want nor need any more than they want or need us, a unit; a unit for Home Rule in preference to alien domination, it is true; but, nevertheless, a patriotic unit—one people—a potential body politic which can take a modest, but self-respecting place in the concert of free nations, with only a little more additional help from us.

In the handling of an insurrection in any given province with courts and constabulary during the first four or five years after the Taft government of the Philippines was founded, the function of a representative of the office of the Attorney-General, coming from Manila to help the local prosecuting attorney handle a large docket and a crowded jail, was by no means remotely analogous to that of a grand jury. He originated prosecutions, found "No Bill," etc. When Mr. Harvey came to Samar, he came direct to the court room, and I suspended the trial of the pending case, and, after greeting him, began an informal talk which was akin to the nature of a charge to a grand jury, putting him in possession of the general aspects of the uprising. He was a very just and kindly man, and entered into the spirit of the task. I elaborated on the class of cases where the defendant claimed, as most of them did, "Yes, I joined the band of brigands, but I was made to do so." It was also indictable to furnish supplies to the public enemy. This presented the class of cases where the brigands would swoop down on a town and demand rice, and not getting it, would sometimes kill the persons refusing it, and so intimidate the rest into finding rice for them. Also there was the class of cases where a man would claim to have been one of the inhabitants of an unprotected town who had gone off to the hills in a body, *for safety*, to propitiate the mountain people by becoming part of them. This sort of thing at one time threatened to become epidemic with all the coast towns. It did not, however. A *modus vivendi* of some sort, sometimes express, sometimes merely tacit, would be arranged between the coast people and the hill people. These *modus vivendi* arrangements enabled the coast people to obtain a certain degree of safety, in lieu of that we should have secured them but did not, by making the hill folk believe that the coast men were against us and for them. At one time the prosecuting attorney got hold of evidence sufficient to authorize the issuance of a warrant for the Presidente of Balangiga, the man supposed to have engineered the massacre of the 9th Infantry in September 1901. I authorized the issuance of the warrant for his arrest. But the native governor of the province, and also Major Dade, the American regular officer commanding the constabulary, satisfied me that we did not have force sufficient to protect Balangiga from the Pulajans, if we arrested the presidente, who, being *persona grata* to the Pulajans, was able to keep them from descending on his town. To arrest him would therefore mean, in their opinion, that the people of Balangiga would take to the hills for protection, and join the hill folk, or Pulajans, and if a town as large as Balangiga set any such example all the coast towns might follow it. So the supposed perpetrator of the 9th Infantry massacre was allowed to remain unmolested. The American court was impotent to enforce its processes.

In my mass of Philippine papers there is one containing a copy of my remarks to the Assistant Attorney-General on his arrival at Catbalogan, above referred to as analogous to a charge to a grand jury at home. It is dated Catbalogan, Samar, September 28, 1904, and is headed: "Remarks by the court upon the occasion of the arrival of Assistant Attorney-General Harvey, with regard to the recent disturbances in Samar, and the cases for brigandage and sedition growing out of the same." Certain parts of this *contemporary* document will doubtless give the reader a more vivid apprehension of the then situation than he can get from mere subsequent description. Of course the visiting representative of the Attorney-General's office was familiar in a general way with the manner of the handling of the Albay insurrection in the previous year, described in the chapter preceding this. In discussing the Samar situation the "remarks" of the court contain, among other things, this passage:

In the cases growing out of the Albay disturbances there were a great many people who strayed out to the mountains just like cattle. They did not know why or whither they went. As to those persons, Judge Carson, Mr. Ross, and myself were unanimous in the opinion that some of them could be indicted under the vagrancy law. There were others of a greater degree of guilt, but who did not appear to have been what you might call ordinary thieves, and we were all agreed to indict those under the sedition law, the limit of which is ten years and ten thousand dollars. Thus you do not force upon a Judge of First Instance the responsibility of sentencing a man to twenty years of his life for a connection with bandits which may be but little more than technical. Besides those two classes, there were in Albay of course the bandits proper, to whom the *bandolerismo* [brigandage] law was specially intended to apply. There cannot be any doubt about the fact that this *bandolerismo* law is one of the most stringent statutes that ever was on the statute-books of any country. It is very far from the purpose of this court to attempt to say what would be the wisest legislation, or to say that this is not the very best legislation, under the circumstances. *How we administer the several laws alluded to governing public order, will settle whether or not substantial justice is done.*

The men in the United States who in those days were slinging mud at the Philippine trial judges as being "subservient," wholly missed the core of the whole matter. In the provinces where so many heavy sentences were imposed, the real situation was that a state of war existed, and the judges believed, and I think correctly, that they were practically a military commission of one, and much more able to give a prisoner a square deal, tempering justice with mercy, than officers briefly gathered from the scenes of the fighting to act as a military commission. We tried those men with as little prejudice as if they had just come from the moon. Moreover, from the italicized concluding words of the above excerpt from my talk to the Assistant Attorney-General, it will be seen that the court had practically unlimited discretion in the matter of punishment, and was, in fact, about the only *court of criminal equity* in the annals of Anglo-Saxon jurisprudence.

In the last analysis, the righteousness or unrighteousness of a civil government in a country not yet entirely subjugated, depends on whether more innocent people suffer through completing the work of subjugation with constabulary whose "prisoners of war" are tried, to see what they may have done, if anything, by one-man courts, or whether more innocent people suffer through completing the work of subjugation as any other great power on earth but ourselves would have completed it, with an army, trying the prisoners by military commission. Unless you yourself were a traitor to your country, you considered as criminal attempts to subvert your government by cut-throats that no one of the respectable Filipinos, from Aguinaldo and Juan Cailles down, would have hesitated to have shot summarily. But you sought to make the punishment in each case fit the crime, by ascertaining as dispassionately as if the defendant were fresh from the moon, just what each accused man had himself done. Either Aguinaldo, or an American military commission would have had such people shot in bunches, as not entitled to be treated as prisoners of war. The trouble with the civil government did not lie in its judiciary, but in its constabulary. It was the physical handling of the crowds of prisoners by the constabulary, and their failure, because not numerous enough, to protect peaceably inclined people, which made it a fact that turning the situation over to the military would have meant less sacrifice of the innocent along with the guilty. It is much more merciful to kill a few hundred people, as a lesson to the rest, and let the rest go, with the clear understanding that if they insurrect again you will promptly kill a few hundred more, than to permit a reign of terror from one month to another and from one year to another, with all the untilled fields, famine, pestilence, and other disease this involves, merely in order to be able to invoke the blessing of the Doctor Lyman Abbots of the world on a supposedly benign "civil" government.

In all my sentences, and in all his indictments, Mr. Harvey and the writer sailed close to the wind, by holding only those responsible who had taken active parts in the sacking and burning of villages and the massacre of their inhabitants. I knew that sooner or later some officious prosecuting attorney of less noble mould than Harvey would ask me to convict some poor creature of brigandage for giving a little rice to the brigands, and my mind was made up to refuse to do so, and in so refusing to commit heresy once and for all by expressing my sentiments, in the decision, concerning the failure to give adequate protection to defenceless people, along the lines indicated in this chapter. No such case was in fact presented. I broke down under the strain of graver cases early in November and left Samar forever, bound for Manila.

Before I left, the whole island was seething with sedition. I was told by a credible American that the chief deputy sheriff of the court, an ex-insurgent officer, one of the "peace-at-any-price" policy appointees, had remarked among some of his own people where he did not expect the remark to be repeated: "I see no use persecuting our brethren in the hills." The municipal officials of the provincial capital, Catbalogan, were suspected by the native provincial governor, and the latter in turn was suspected by the Manila government. In fact the whole political atmosphere of the island had become full of rumor and suspicion as to who was *for* the government, and who was *against* the government. I left Samar, November 8th, which was the day of the presidential election of 1904, determined to try no more insurrections. By that time nearly everybody in the island was more or less guilty of sedition, and I did not know the method of drawing an indictment against a whole people.

1*Philippine Census*, vol. ii., p. 123.

2*Ib.*, vol. i., p. 58.

3Says Brigadier-General Wm. H. Carter, in his annual report for 1905 covering the Samar outbreak of 1904–5: "Whatever may have been the original cause of the outbreak, it was soon lost sight of when success had drawn a large proportion of the people away from their homes and fields. Except in the largest towns it became simply a question of joining the pulajans or being harried by them. *In the absence of proper protection* thousands joined in the movement." See *War Department Report*, 1905, vol. iii., p. 286.

4Bulao was situated on a high bluff on the left bank of a river called the Bangahon. The Pulajans entered before daybreak, on July 21st. There was a stiff fight at Bulao, also, between our native troops and the enemy on August 21st, but Calderon seems to have left it out of his list. See Gen. Wm. H. Carter's Report for 1905, *War Department Report*, 1905, vol. iii., p. 290. Capt. Cary Crockett, a descendant of David Crockett, commanded the constabulary, and though badly wounded himself, as were also half his command, he defeated a force of Pulajans greatly outnumbering his, killing forty-one of them. *Report U. S. Philippine Commission*, 1905, pt. 3, p. 90, Report of Col. Wallace C. Taylor. I think he was awarded a medal of honor for his work. He certainly earned it.

"Pulajan" means "red breeches," the uniform of the mountain clans, worn whenever they set out to give trouble.

5Of March 23d of the previous year, already described in a previous chapter, where Luther S. Kelly—"Yellowstone" Kelly—saved the American women by gathering them and a few men in the Government House and bluffing the brigands off.

6The "Conant" peso, named for the noted fiscal expert, Mr. Conant. It was worth fifty cents American money.

7The Fourteenth U. S. Infantry was stationed in garrison just outside the town proper of Calbayog, which was three hours by steam launch from the provincial capital, Catbalogan. But the depredations might have been carried to just outside the line of the military reservation, and the military folk would not have dared to make a move save on request first made by the Civil Government at Manila. In other words the above three villages were burned under their noses.

8One seems to get the stoicism better in the original, somehow, so I give the body of the original Spanish, as it came to me:

En el distrito de Motiong, municipio de Wright, provincia de Samar, Islas Filipinas, a primero de septiembre de mil novecientos quatro. Ante mi Peregrin Albano, consejal del mismo, y presente el Presidente de Sanidad Municipal, D. Tomas San Pablo y principales del mismo se procedio al enterramiento de los cadaveres victimas de los Pulajans en el sementerio de esta localidad el oficial de voluntarios, Rafael Rosales y otros voluntarios, Gualberto Gabane, Juan Pacle, Dionisio Daisno, Pedro Damtanan, Carmelo Lagbo, y particulares Eustaquia Sapiten y Apolinaria N: con otro tanto Pulajan desconocido; en conformidad de la carta oficial de la presidencia municipal de Wright de fecha de hoy registrada con el numero 136.

Del citado enterramiento ha sido asistido por el Reverendo Padre Marcos Gomez y acompanado por toda la fuerza voluntaria del mismo por la muerte del oficial Rosales.

9See *War Department Report*, 1905, vol. iii., p. 290.

10Hill was Whittier's deputy at Llorente.

11 Even if the municipal police had been like Cæsar's wife, they were like chaff before the wind in a Pulajan foray, though they were somewhat better if well led by some prominent and forceful man of the community in an expedition *after* Pulajans.

12 A disease of a dropsical variety, usually attacking the legs first, which easily becomes epidemic. It had been the cause of many of the 120 deaths in the Albay jail during the Ola insurrection. Ideal conditions for it are a steady diet of poor rice and lack of exercise.

13 It was not well to be too hasty. You might have the head of the whole uprising in custody, or one of his most important lieutenants, and find it out by the merest accident in the course of hearing a case against some apparently abject "private of the rear rank."

14 By unwarranted I mean without warrant. Nobody bothered much with warrants. The times were too strenuous.

15 See *New York Tribune*, Oct. 25, 1904.

16 *Ibid.*

17 Smith, Bell & Co. are an old British mercantile house, well known in Manila and Hong Kong.

18 *The North American Review* article by the writer, to which Judge Ide was replying, appeared in the issue of that magazine for January 18, 1907, and could hardly have escaped the attention of anybody concerned, having been given wide circulation; (1) by Mr. Andrew Carnegie through pamphlet reprints; (2) by Hon. Wm. J. Bryan, in his paper, the *Commoner*; (3) by Hon. James L. Slayden, M. C. of Texas, through reprinting in the *Congressional Record*.

19 Such as the breakwater at Manila, the road-building in various provinces, etc.—all, however, be it remembered, being paid for by the Filipino people, out of the insular revenues and assets.

20 By Mrs. Campbell Dauncey.

21 Words used by Governor-General James F. Smith, in an address at the Quill Club, Manila, January 25, 1909.

Chapter XIX. Governor Wright—1905

My heart is heavy with the fate of that unhappy people.

SPEECH OF HON. A. O. BACON IN U. S. SENATE. 1

Because the especially cordial relations which existed to the last between Governor Wright and myself2 are familiar to a number of very dear mutual friends, I deem it due both to them and to myself, in view of the contents of the preceding chapter, to state that I see no reason why, in writing a history of the American Occupation of the Philippines, I should omit or slur the facts which convinced me that that occupation ought to terminate as soon as practicable, and that any decent kind of a government of Filipinos by Filipinos would be better for all concerned than the McKinley-Taft programme of Benevolent Assimilation whereof Governor Wright was the legatee. By the thousand and one uncandid threads of that programme, slowly woven from 1898 to 1904, as indicated in the first sixteen chapters of this book, Governor Wright had found himself as hopelessly bound to concealment from the American people of the real situation in Samar in the fall of 1904, as a Gulliver in Lilliput.

When I finally left Samar and came to Manila, in November, 1904, I was not prepared to figure out how or how soon, the blunder we made by the purchase of the Philippine archipelago could be corrected. But my mental attitude toward the whole Philippine problem had undergone a complete change. In 1901 Governor Wright, then Vice-Governor, had written me: "You younger men out here, who have cast your fortunes with this country, are to be, in all likelihood, in the natural course of events, its future rulers." Up to 1903 I had clung to that idea with the devotion of what was really high and earnest purpose, untroubled with misgivings of any kind. In November, 1903, in Albay, Judge Carson and myself had talked over the long struggle of the civil government to walk without leaning on the military, and, with the readiness of one vested with authority to believe such authority wisely vested, and the readiness of a civilian lawyer to jealously guard the American home idea that the military should be subordinate to the civil authority, I had cordially agreed with a sentiment one day expressed by Judge Carson concerning Governor Taft about "the splendid moral fibre of the man," meaning in keeping the military from prancing out of the traces. After Governor Taft left the Islands to be Secretary of War (December 23, 1903), and while I was still in Albay, I had learned of the 120 men who had died in the Albay jail while awaiting trial, and thereafter something of the magnitude of the Ola insurrection there, and that had given me pause as to the practical benevolence of the operation of "a benign civil government." Then the Samar massacres of 1904, and the gory panorama I had there witnessed, had finally convinced me that a republic like ours is wholly unfitted to govern people against their consent. But I did not tell anybody in Manila all these things. I simply pondered them. Grover Cleveland was the only man in the world I would have liked to talk to just then freely and fully. And he was not about. "My heart was heavy with the fate of that unhappy people" as Senator Bacon had said in the Senate in 1902, after visiting the Islands in 1901. I did not condemn Governor Wright. I quite realized that I was "up against" about the largest ethical problem of world politics, one on which the nations are much divided, and that I was not infallible. I did not say to the Governor: "Governor, let's resign and go home and tell our people that this whole business is a mistake." Nor did I ever lose faith in Governor Wright personally. If I had, I might just as well have said: "After this, the deluge." I would simply have lost faith in human nature. I had not then, nor have I since, known a man of higher personal character. I had simply lost faith in Benevolent Assimilation, and begun to take the Filipino people seriously as a potential nation, probably better able to handle their own domestic problems than we will ever be able to handle them for them.

The day after I resigned, Mr. Justice Carson, of the Supreme Court, and Mr. Wilfley, the Attorney-General, came to call on me. My friends knew I was very much troubled over the Samar business. I was doing some grumbling, but without specifying, because to specify would mean that we all of us ought to give up the life careers we had planned for ourselves in the Islands. I knew the old familiar answer a grumbler was sure to get in the Philippines, viz., "Old man, you've been out here too long. You better go home." But I did a little more grumbling to my friends Judge Carson and Mr. Wilfley, during the course of their visit. They could both pretty well guess what was the matter. But Judge Carson and I had come out in 1899, and had served through the war together. He knew all about the Albay business, and somewhat of the Samar business. Wilfley had not come out until the civil government was founded in 1901. Mr. Wilfley said cheerily: "Oh, Blount, you are too conscientious." I shall never forget what happened then. Judge Carson said, with a ring of something like anger in his tone: "No, Wilfley, I'll be d—d if he is." Is it any wonder that ever since I have worn that man, as Hamlet would say, "in my heart's core"? Here was as brave and true an Irishman as ever gained distinction on battlefield or bench. *And he understood.* He did not say—which was the implication of Wilfley's tone—"Old man, you've been out here too long, and illness has made you peevish." He knew what was the matter. He knew that as trial judges he and I had not been small editions of Lord Jeffries, as some of our American critics had implied, BUT HE ALSO KNEW THAT THERE WAS NO METHOD OF DRAWING AN INDICTMENT AGAINST A WHOLE PEOPLE .

Possibly the intensity of my feelings on this great subject, then and ever since, hampers the power of clear expression. Therefore, a word more in attempt at elucidation. In 1898, Judge Carson and I, with many thousands of other young Americans, had trooped down to Cuba, in the wake of the impetuous Roosevelt, to free the inhabitants of that ill-fated island from Spanish rule, drive the Spaniards from the Western

Hemisphere, and put a stop to Spain's pious efforts "to spare the great island from the dangers of premature independence," as she always expressed her attitude toward Cuba. We had many of us been fired by the catchy Roosevelt utterance which did so much to bring on the Spanish War, viz., "The steps of the White House are *slippery with the blood of the Cuban reconcentrados*." Then in 1899, we had gone to the Philippines, and had ever since been engaged there in "sparing the Islands from the danger of premature independence," and the Samar massacres of 1904 were, to me, the apotheosis of the work. So that after November 8, 1904, I felt "The steps of the White House are *slippery with the blood of the people of my district*." It had all been done under the pious pretence that the Filipinos welcomed our rule—a pretence which had taken the form for six years of systematic asseveration that they did so welcome it. Yet it was not *true* that they, or any appreciable fraction of them, had ever welcomed our rule. *And it never will be true*. Surely no man can see in this book any scolding or unkindness. It is an attempt merely to bring home to my countrymen a *strategic* fact, a fact which it is folly to ignore. But to return to the thread of our story.

Four days after the presidential election of 1904, to wit, on November 12th, Governor Wright left Manila and went to Samar, including in his itinerary various others of the southern islands.3 Soon after their return, the seven hundred native troops in Samar were increased to nearly two thousand, and sixteen companies of regulars (say one hundred men to a company) were also thrown into Samar. It took until the end of 1906 to end the trouble. You cannot find in the reports of the civil authorities anything explaining their three or four weeks' stay in the Visayan Islands in November–December, 1904, that is not absolutely in accord with the original Taft obsession of 1900 about the popularity of the proposed alien "civil" government with its subjects. Governor Wright's description of the trip says: "The warm hospitality of the Filipino people made this trip of inspection a most agreeable one." As a matter of fact, on such occasions, the more disaffected a leader of the people was, the more he would seek, by "warm hospitality," "warm" oratory telling the visiting mighty what the visiting mighty longed to hear, parades, *fiestas*, etc., to divert suspicion of sedition from himself. The poor creatures had met General Young's cavalry column in northern Luzon in 1899 with their town bands, doing the only thing they knew of to do to "temper the wind to the shorn lamb"—*i.e.*, to temper it to their several communities—many of them doubtless expecting to be put to the sword by General Young's troopers, as the Cossacks did the Persians during the brief and sensational sojourn of that brilliant young administrator, Hon. W. Morgan Shuster, in Persia in 1911–12. I have no doubt that high on the list of those extending some of the "warm hospitality" above mentioned appeared the name of Don Jaime de Veyra. Yet in the summer of 1904 Don Jaime had gotten out of a sick bed to attend a convention called to send delegates to the Democratic National Convention in the United States that year,4 and also, in that same year, had run for Governor of Leyte on a platform the principal plank of which was *Carthago est delenda*—"Carthago" being *us*, the American *régime*. De Veyra was defeated that time, but ran again the next time and was elected. While the writer is not one of those who seek to show their "breadth of view" by gossiping with outsiders regarding what is peculiarly our own affair, still, the British view-point of the situation in the Visayan Islands, as conveyed by an Englishwoman whose husband was engaged in mercantile business there in 1904–5, and who therefore was certainly in a position to know the opinion of the little circle of British people at Cebu and Iloilo, may not be superfluous here. This lady, living then at Iloilo, wrote a series of letters to friends back home in England which she afterwards published in book form.5 In a letter dated Iloilo, January 22, 1905 (page 86), she says:

The Americans give out and write in their papers that the Philippine Islands are completely pacified, and that the Filipinos love Americans and their rule. This, doubtless with good motives, is complete and utter humbug, for the country is honeycombed with insurrection and plots; the fighting has never ceased; and the natives loathe the Americans and their theories, saying so openly in their native press and showing their dislike in every possible fashion. Their one idea is to be rid of the U. S. A. * * * and to be free of a burden of taxation which is heavier than any the Spaniards laid on them.

Also an Englishman who was in Samar in 1904–5, a Mr. Hyatt, who, with his brother, served with the American troops there in the bloody Pulajan uprising, afterwards wrote a book called the *Little Brown Brother*, wherein he fully corroborates Mrs. Dauncey's appreciation of the situation during that period.

In its blindness to the unanimity of Visayan discontent, as manifested in its report now under consideration, the civil government of the Philippines was not trying wilfully to deceive anybody. It was deceiving itself. It was obeying the law of its life, its existence having been originally predicated on the consent of a great free people to keep in subjection a weaker people eager to be also free, such consent having been obtained through diligent nursing of the original idea that the subject people were not in fact so eager, but were, on the contrary, in a mental attitude of tearful welcome toward the proffered protection of a strong power. In his report for 1905[6] General William H. Carter, commanding the Department of the Philippines which included Samar and the rest of the Visayan Islands, gives the key to the Commission's twenty-six-day stay in his district in the following part of said report:

Within a few days after the rendition of the annual report for last year[7] a serious outbreak occurred in the Gandara valley, Samar. *This was followed by disorders in all the other large islands of the department*, Negros, Panay, Cebu, and Leyte.

Nowhere in the civil government reports do you find the slightest recognition that these disorders had any relation to each other, or to the fundamental problem of public order, or any political significance whatsoever, each being treated as a purely local issue, the idea that the circumstance of Samar's having been thrown into pandemonium by the successes of the enemies of the American Government might have encouraged its enemies in the neighboring islands, never seeming to occur to the authors of the said reports. General Carter's report goes on to state that within five months after the Samar outbreak of July, 1904, seven hundred native troops had been put in the field in that turbulent island. In December, 1904, troops began to be poured into Samar, so that it was not long before the seven hundred native troops had become seventeen hundred or eighteen hundred, and, says General Carter, "in order to free them from garrison work in the towns, sixteen companies of the 12th and 14th Infantry were distributed about the disaffected coasts to enable the people who so desired to *come from their hiding places*"—whither they had gone because the American flag afforded them no protection—"and undertake the rebuilding of their burned homes." General Carter avoids touching on the civil government's (to him well-known) obsession about its popularity, a state of mind which could see no "political" significance in outbreaks of any kind. But he does use this very straightforward language about Samar:

Whatever may have been the original cause of the outbreak, it was soon lost sight of when success had drawn a large proportion of the people away from their homes and fields. * * * *Except in the largest towns it became simply a question of joining the Pulajans or being harried by them.* In the absence of proper protection thousands joined in the movement.

Early in 1905, Hon. George Curry, of New Mexico, who was an officer of Colonel Roosevelt's regiment in Cuba, and had gone out to the Philippines with a volunteer regiment in 1899, remaining with the civil Government after 1901, was made Governor of Samar. Governor Curry has since been Governor of the Territory of New Mexico, and is now (1912) a member of Congress from the recently admitted State of New Mexico. Governor Curry has told me since he was elected to Congress that it took him all of 1905 and most of 1906, aided by several thousand troops, native and regular, to put down that Samar outbreak. Yet a certificate signed March 28, 1907, by the Governor-General and his associates of the Philippine Commission states that "a condition of general and complete peace" had continued in the Islands for two years previous to the date of the certificate.8 We will come to this certificate in its chronological order later. How many and what sort of uprisings were blanketed in that "forget-it" certificate of 1907 is material to the question whether or not the National Administration has ever been or is now frank with the country about the universality of the desire of the Philippine people for independence and local self-government, and pertinent to the insistently recurring query: "Why should we make of the Philippines an American Ireland?" But inasmuch as, in addition to the Samar uprising which raged all through 1905, another insurrection occurred in that year, which was duly "forgotten" by said certificate, this last movement must now claim our attention.

The provinces which were the theatre of the outbreak last above mentioned were all near Manila. They were: Cavite, a province of 135,000 people almost at the gates of Manila; Batangas, a province of 257,000 inhabitants adjoining Cavite; and Laguna, a province of 150,000 people adjoining both. Some five hundred brigands headed by cut-throats claiming to be patriots were terrorizing whole districts. Far be it from me to lend any countenance to the idea that the leaders of this movement, Sakay, Felizardo, Montalon, and the rest of their gang, were entitled to any respect. But they certainly had a hold on the whole population akin to that of Robin Hood, Little John, and Friar Tuck. In refusing in 1907 to commute Sakay's death sentence after he was captured, tried, and convicted, Governor-General James P. Smith gives some gruesome details concerning the performance of that worthy, and his followers, yet in dealing with the nature and extent of the trouble they gave the Manila government he says they "assumed the convenient cloak of patriotism, and under the titles of 'Defenders of the Country' and 'Protectors of the People' proceeded to inaugurate a reign of terror, devastation, and ruin in three of the most beautiful provinces in the archipelago."9

It has already been made clear that, during the time of the insurrection against both the Spaniards and Americans, the *insurrecto* forces were maintained by voluntary contributions of the people. Major D. C. Shanks, Fourth U. S. Regular Infantry, who was Governor of Cavite Province in 1905, after calling attention to this fact, adds10:

When the insurrection was over a number of these leaders remained out and refused to surrender. Included among them were Felizardo and Montalon. The system of voluntary contributions, carried on during the *insurrecto* period, was continued after establishment of civil government.

Again Governor Shanks says, with more of frankness than diplomacy, considering that he was a provincial governor under the civil government:

The establishment of civil government of this province was premature and ill-advised. Records show the capture or surrender since establishment of civil government of *nearly 600 hostile firearms*.

One of the causes contributory to the Cavite-Batangas-Laguna insurrection is stated in the report of the Governor-General for 1905 thus:

In the autumn of 1904 it became necessary to withdraw a number of the constabulary from these provinces to assist in suppressing disorder which had broken out in the province of Samar.11

Another of the contributory causes is thus stated:

There was at the time [the fall of 1904] also considerable activity among the small group of irreconcilables in Manila, who began agitating for immediate independence, doubtless because of the supposed effect it would have on the presidential election in the United States, in which the Philippines was a large topic of discussion. Evidently this was regarded as a favorable time for a demonstration by Felizardo, Montalon, De Vega, Oruga, Sakay [etc]. *All these men had been officers of the Filipino army during the insurrection.*

Consider the benevolent casuistry necessary to include these fellows, and the tremendous following they could get up, and did get up, in Cavite, "the home of insurrection," and the adjacent provinces, in a certificate to "a condition of general and complete peace" alleged in the certificate to have prevailed for two years prior to March 28, 1907. To make a long story short, on January 31, 1905, a state of insurrection was declared to exist, the writ of habeas corpus was suspended in Cavite and Batangas, the regular army of the United States was ordered out, and reconcentration tactics resorted to, as provided by Section 6 of Act 781 of the Commission. This is the act already examined at length, intended to meet cases of impotency on the part of the insular government to protect life and property in any other way. Political timidity is conspicuously absent from the resolution of the Philippine Commission of January 31, 1905, formally recognizing a break in the peerless continuity of the "general and complete peace." It is virilely frank, the presidential election being then safely over.12 It concludes by authorizing the Governor-General to suspend the writ of habeas corpus and declare martial law, "the public safety requiring it." Then follows a proclamation of the same date and tenor, by the Governor-General.

It appears from the case cited in the foot-note that in the spring of 1905, one, Felix Barcelon, filed in the proper court a petition for the writ of habeas corpus, alleging that he was one of the reconcentrados corralled and "detained and restrained of his liberty at the town of Batangas, in the province of Batangas," by one of Colonel Baker's constabulary minions down there. The writ was denied by the lower court. In one part of the opinion of the Supreme Court in the case it is stated (p. 116) that the petitioner "has been detained for a long time * * * not for the commission of any crime and by due process of law, but apparently for the purpose of protecting him." The opinion of the court, delivered by Mr. Justice Johnson, very properly held that the detention was lawful *under the war power*, basing its decision on the authority conferred on the Governor-General of the Philippines by the Act of Congress of July 1, 1902, section 5 of which expressly authorizes the suspension of the writ of habeas corpus "when in cases of rebellion, insurrection, or invasion the public safety may require it." A long legal battle was fought, the court holding that the Executive Department of the Government is the one in which is vested the exclusive right to say when "a state of rebellion, insurrection, or invasion" exists, and that when it so formally declares, *that settles the fact that it does exist.* At page 98 of the volume above cited13 the court held, as to the above mentioned resolution of the Philippine Commission and the above mentioned executive order declaring a state of insurrection in Cavite and Batangas:

The conclusion set forth in the said resolution and the said executive order, as to the fact that there existed in the provinces of Cavite and Batangas open insurrection against the constituted authorities, was a conclusion entirely within the discretion of the legislative and executive branches of the Government, after an investigation of the facts.

Yet two years later the same "constituted authorities" certified to the President of the United States, in effect, as we shall see, that no open insurrection against the constituted authorities had occurred during the preceding two years. They do not in their certificate ignore Cavite and Batangas. They mention them by name, with a lot of whereases, explaining that after all they really believe that the majority of the people in the provinces aforesaid were not in sympathy with the uprising. However, after they get through with their whereases they face the music squarely, and certify to "the condition of general and complete peace." Of the "nigger in the woodpile" more anon.

Governor Wright was not a party to the certificate of 1907. He left the Islands on leave November 4, 1905. A speech made by him prior to his departure, as published in a Manila paper, indicates an expectation to return. He never did. In 1906 he was demoted to be Ambassador to Japan, a place of far less dignity, and far less salary, which he resigned after a year or so. Vice-Governor Ide acted as Governor-General until April 2, 1906, on which date he was formally inaugurated as Governor-General.

Just why Governor Wright did not go back to the Philippines as Governor, after his visit to the United States in 1905–6, does not appear. It would seem almost certain that if Secretary of War Taft had wanted President Roosevelt to send him back, he would have gone. Mr. Taft never did frankly tell the Filipinos until 1907 that they might just as well shut up talking about any independence that anybody living might hope to see. Governor Wright began to talk that way soon after Mr. Taft left the Islands. Possibly Governor Wright undeceived them too soon, and thereby made the Philippines more of a troublesome issue in the presidential campaign of 1904. President Roosevelt recognized the sterling worth of the man, by inviting him to succeed Mr. Taft as Secretary of War in 1908. But President Taft did not invite him to continue in that capacity after March 4, 1909. Gossip has it that when the incoming President Taft's letter to the outgoing President Roosevelt's last Secretary of War, Governor Wright, was handed to the addressee, and its conventional "hope to be able to avail myself of your services later in some other capacity" was read by him, the outgoing official quietly remarked: "Well, that is a little more round-about than the one Jimmie Garfield[14] got, but it's a dismissal just the same."

I have always thought that the reason Governor Wright did not go back to the Philippines as Governor after 1905 was that he did not continue to "jolly" the Filipinos, and abstain from ruthlessly crushing their hopes of seeing independence during their lifetime, as Mr. Taft did continuously during his stay out there. The inevitable tendency of the Wright frank talk was from the beginning to discredit the Taft pleasing and evasive nothings. Also, it was followed, as we have seen, by quite a crop of serious disturbances of public order, and somebody had to be "the goat."

---

[1]Delivered in 1902, after the Senator visited the Islands in 1901.

[2]The following is a copy of the letter accepting my resignation:

Office of the Civil Governor of the Philippine Islands,
January 25, 1905.

MY DEAR JUDGE BLOUNT :

I have to acknowledge the receipt of your communication of yesterday in which you tender your resignation as Judge of First Instance at large. I regret extremely that your ill-health has made this course imperative. Under all the circumstances, however, I am satisfied that you have acted wisely, as I have feared for some time that you would be unable to perform the duties pertaining to your office because of your physical condition. I, therefore, though with much regret accept your resignation.

At the same time I beg to express my appreciation of the faithful and efficient services you have rendered in the past. I hope very much that a rest and change of climate may have the effect of restoring you again to vigorous health, and I assure you that you carry with you my best wishes for your future prosperity and happiness.

Sincerely yours,
LUKE E. WRIGHT,
Civil Governor.

To the Honorable JAMES H. BLOUNT , Judge of First Instance at large, Manila, P. I.

3See annual report of the Governor-General for 1905, in *Report of the Philippine Commission for 1905*, pt. 1, p. 85.

4Which delegates were denied admission to the Convention on the ground that no American living in the Philippines could be in sympathy with the Democratic programme as to them.

5*An Englishwoman in the Philippines*, by Mrs. Campbell Dauncey.

6*War Department Report*, 1905, vol. iii., p. 285.

7Army reports are usually made right after the expiration of the American governmental fiscal year, June 30th.

8*Report, U. S. Philippine Commission*, 1907, pt. 1, p. 47.

9See *Report, U. S. Philippine Commission*, 1907, pt. 1, p. 38. He means Cavite, Batangas, and Laguna.

10*Report, U. S. Philippine Commission*, 1905, pt. 1, p. 212.

11*Report, U. S. Philippine Commission*, 1905, pt. 1, p. 52.

12For a copy of it, see the case of Barcelon *vs.* Baker, *Philippine Supreme Court Reports*, vol. v., p. 89.

13Volume v., *Philippine Reports*.

14Mr. Garfield was President Roosevelt's Secretary of the Interior.

Chapter XX. Governor Ide—1906

The Tariff is a local issue.

GENERAL W. S. HANCOCK.

After Governor Wright left the Islands finally on November 4, 1905, Vice-Governor Henry C. Ide acted as Governor-General until April 2, 1906, when he was duly inaugurated as such. He resigned and left the Islands finally in September thereafter.

All through 1905, Governor Curry, as Governor of Samar, which is the third largest island of the archipelago, wrestled with the Pulajan uprising there, aided, as has been stated in the previous chapter, by the native troops, scouts, and constabulary, and also by the regular army. But at the end of 1905 "the situation" was not yet "well in hand." Since his election to Congress in 1912, Governor Curry has told me that in 1905 many thousands of people of Samar participated actively as part of the enemy's force in the field during that period. By the spring of 1906 Governor Curry was getting a grip on the situation, and in the latter part of March of that year, some of the main outlaw chiefs agreed to surrender to him. The report of Colonel Wallace C. Taylor, commanding the constabulary of the Third District, which included Samar states1: "After several weeks of negotiating, during which time the camp of the Pulahanes was visited by Governor Curry, and the Pulahan officers visited the settlement at Magtaon"—a settlement in south central Samar—"an understanding was arrived at by which the Pulahanes were to surrender, March 24, 1906. Instead of surrendering as agreed, the Pulahanes, commanded by Nasario Aguilar, made a treacherous attack on the constabulary garrison on the day and hour appointed for the surrender." The constabulary numbered some fifty men, the pulajans about 130. After the pulajans opened fire they made a rush on the constabulary and a hand-to-hand fight ensued. Colonel Taylor's report continues:

After the first rush the fighting continued fiercely, and when the last of the pulahanes disappeared there remained but seven enlisted men of the constabulary able to fight. Seven more were lying about more or less seriously wounded and twenty-two were dead. Captain Jones received a bad spear thrust in the chest early in the fight, but fought on, regardless. Lieutenant Bowers received a gunshot wound through the left arm, which, however, did not put him out of the fight. Thirty-five dead pulahanes were found on the field and eight more have since been found some distance off. The number of wounded who escaped cannot be determined. The unarmed Americans present with Governor Curry escaped to the river and afterwards rejoined Captain Jones who armed them.

The explanation of this treachery, as given by Governor Curry, is curious and interesting. The outlaws had intended in good faith to surrender as a result of his negotiation with them, but at the last moment there arrived to witness the surrender certain native officials and other natives bitterly hated by the Pulajans and wholly mistrusted by them. Their arrival caused the outlaws to suspect treachery themselves and that was the cause of their change of plans. It was not until the end of the year 1906 that the various energetic campaigns which followed the Magtaon incident finally began to work more or less complete restoration of public order by gradual elimination of the enemy through killings, captures, and surrenders. An idea of the seriousness and magnitude of these operations may be gathered without going into the details, from the annual report for 1906 of General Henry T. Allen commanding the Philippines Constabulary. This report, dated August 31, 1906[2], states:

At present seventeen companies of scouts and four companies of American troops under Colonel Smith, 8th U. S. Infantry, are operating against the pulahanes, but with success that will be largely dependent upon time and attrition.

General Allen adds: "The entire 21st Regiment [of Infantry] is also in Samar." These facts are here given because they relate to the period covered by the certificate of the Philippine Commission of March 28, 1907, heretofore alluded to, and which will be more fully dealt with hereinafter, which stated that "a condition of general and complete peace" had prevailed throughout the archipelago for two years prior to March 28, 1907. Without a brief exposition of all these matters, it would be impossible to enable the reader to feel the pulse of the Filipino people as it stood at the time of the election of their assembly in 1907. The fact of our having been unable to discontinue Filipino-killing altogether for any considerable period from 1899 to the end of 1906 is too obviously relevant to the state of the public mind in 1907 to need elaboration.

The Report of the Philippine Commission for 1906[3] deals at some length with disturbances which occurred in the island of Leyte (area 3000 square miles, population nearly 400,000), beginning in the middle of June. It describes among other things a visit of Governor-General Ide to Tacloban, the capital of Leyte, made in consequence of said disturbances, and conferences held by him there with Major-General Wood, commanding all the United States forces in the Philippines, Brigadier-General Lee, commanding the Department of the Visayas (which included Leyte, headquarters, Iloilo), Colonel Borden, commanding the United States forces in the island of Leyte, Colonel Taylor, the chief of the constabulary of the District, etc. Certainly from this formidable gathering of notables, it is clear that there was about to take place in Leyte what our friends of the Lambs' Club in New York would call "An all star performance." Leyte was four to five hundred miles from Manila. Yet so serious was the disturbance that the highest military and civil representatives of the American Government in the archipelago deemed it necessary to meet in the island which was the scene of the trouble with a view of handling it. Yet in the

Report of the Philippine Commission for 1906 one finds the usual rotund rhetoric treating the disturbances as of no "political" significance—which was only another way of claiming that they were not serious. It is difficult to handle this aspect of the matter without imputing to the civil authorities intent to deceive, but to leave such an imputation unremoved would be to miss the whole significance of the matter. As has already been made clear, when Judge Taft, Judge Ide, and their colleagues of the Philippine Commission had left Washington for Manila in 1900 Mr. McKinley had assured them he had no doubt that the better element of the Philippine people, once they understood us, would welcome our rule. As soon as they set foot in the Philippine Islands they had at once begun to act upon the theory that there was no real fundamental opposition to us on the part of the people of the Philippines and had continued obstinately to act upon that theory ever since. Certainly the attitude of the civil government toward the disturbances in Leyte in 1906 is not surprising when the mind adverts for a moment to the panorama of the five more or less sanguinary years already fully described hereinbefore and then takes the following bird's-eye glance at the official reports for those years.

The Report of the Philippine Commission for 1900, (page 17) had said:

A great majority of the people long for peace and are entirely willing to accept the establishment of a government under the supremacy of the United States.

The Report of the Philippine Commission for 1901 (page 7) had said:

The collapse of the insurrection came in May.

The Report of the Philippine Commission for 1902 (page 3) had said:

The insurrection as an organized attempt to subvert the authority of the United States in these islands is entirely at an end,

referring farther on to "the whole Christian Philippine population" as "*enjoying* civil government." If the "enjoyment" thus described had been genuine, continued, profound, and sincere, it would have been another story. But the net attitude of the civil government toward the general health of the body politic, relatively to public order, reminds one of the cheerful gentleman who remarked of his invalid friend, "He seems to be 'enjoying' poor health."

The Report of the Philippine Commission for 1903 (page 25) says:

The conditions with respect to tranquillity in the islands have greatly improved during the last year.

The Report of the Philippine Commission for 1904 (page 1) says:

The great mass of the people, however, were domestic and peaceable.

The Report of the Philippine Commission for 1905 (part 1, page 59) says:

On the whole life and property have been as safe as in other civilized countries.

The Report of the Philippine Commission for 1906 (page 40) says:

Viewing the entire situation the islands are in a peaceable and orderly condition aside from——

various disorders which fill some ten pages of the report.

The inflexible attitude of the Commission from the beginning, of treating each successive disturbance of public order as a purely "local issue," after General Hancock's method with the tariff, is thus sufficiently apparent. They always refuse to see in successive outbreaks in various parts of the Islands any evidence of general and unanimous lack of appreciation for a benign alien civil government. Therefore it was of course clearly a foregone conclusion, in 1906, that Governor Ide, who had been in the Islands all these years, was going to be wholly unable to see anything in the disturbances in Leyte in the least tending to show that American rule was unpopular. And yet it was a matter of common knowledge all over the Visayan Islands that Jaime Veyra, then Governor of Leyte, elected by the people, was one of the most obnoxious anti-Americans in the archipelago. Both the army and constabulary were ordered out in Leyte and a good deal of fighting occurred before order was restored. The report of General Allen, commanding the constabulary for that year4 shows one engagement with the outlaws in Leyte participated in by the constabulary and the 21st Regular Infantry, in which the enemy numbered 450 and left forty-nine dead upon the field. All this period is covered by the certificate of general and complete peace of 1907, in the fall of which year a Philippine legislature was elected. And those of the membership of that body not in favor of Philippine independence were almost as few as the Socialist party in the American House of Representatives, which, I believe, consists of Representative Berger. True, the peace certificate does not ignore the Leyte outbreak. It "forgets and forgives it," so to speak, as we shall see.

Governor Ide left the Islands finally on September 20, 1906, having resigned. Why he should have resigned, it is difficult to say. Take it all in all, he made a splendid Governor-General, and ought to have been allowed to remain. He knew the Islands from Alpha to Omega and had been there six years. His going out of office to make way for still another Governor-General was wholly uncalled for. So far as the writer is informed, he was, when he left, still blessed with good health. He had filled a very considerable place in the history of his country most creditably. He had drawn up a fine code of laws for the Islands known as the Ide code. He had made a great minister of finance, successfully performing the perilous task of transferring the currency of the country from a silver basis to a gold basis, and in so doing had proven himself fully a match, in protecting the interests of the Government, for the wiley local financiers representing the Hong Kong and Shanghai Bank, the chartered bank of India, Australia, and China, and other institutions run by experienced men of more or less piratical tendencies. As Governor-General of the Islands, his justice, firmness, and courtliness of manner combined to produce an administration in keeping with the dignity of his great office. After returning to the United States, he remained in private life for a time, and was finally given a comparatively unimportant post as minister to a second-class country, Spain, which post he still occupies (in 1912).

When, fresh from the memory of the Samar massacres of 1904, I landed at Seattle, at the end of my last homeward-bound journey across the Pacific, in April, 1905, one of the "natives" of Seattle asked me: "Have those people over there ever got quiet yet?" The question itself seemed an answer to the orthodox official attitude at Manila, which had so long been elaborately denying, as to each successive local outbreak, that such outbreak bore any relation to the original insurrection, or was any wise illustrative of the general state of public feeling in the Islands. At the time the question was asked, the answer was, "Not entirely." Not until toward the end of 1906 did "Yes" become a correct answer to the question. In other words, there were no more serious outbreaks after 1906, nor was a state of general and complete peace ever finally established until then. Since 1906 there have been occasional despatches from Manila recounting small episodes of bloodshed, several of which have had quite a martial ring. These have related merely to the country of the Mohammedan Moros, who are as wholly apart from the main problem as the American Indian to-day is from our tariff and other like questions. The Moros are indeed what Kipling calls "half savage and half child." They never did have anything more to do with the Filipino insurrection against us than the American Indian had to do with the Civil War.

1*Report, U. S. Philippine Commission*, 1906, pt. 2, p. 255.

2See page 227, *Report of Philippine Commission*, 1906, pt. 2.

3*Report, Philippine Commission*, 1906, pt. 1, p. 37.

4See *Report of Philippine Commission*, 1906, pt. 2, p. 228.

Chapter XXI. Governor Smith—1907–9

Oh, but Honey, *dis* rabbit dess *'bleeged* ter climb *dis* tree.

UNCLE REMUS.

"On September 20, 1906," says the *Report of the Philippine Commission for 1907*,1 "the resignation of the Hon. Henry Clay Ide as Governor-General became effective, and on that date the Hon. James F. Smith was inaugurated as Governor-General of the Philippine Islands."

The year 1907 will be known most prominently to the future history of our Far Eastern possession as the year of the opening of the Philippine Assembly, which momentous event occurred on October 16th. But in the departments both of Politics and Psychology it should be known as the year of the Great Certificate. The Great Certificate was a certificate signed by certain eminent gentlemen on March 28, 1907, which made the preposterous affirmation that *a condition of general and complete peace* had prevailed throughout the archipelago, except among the non-Christian tribes, for the two years immediately preceding. Taken in its historic setting, that certificate can by no possibility escape responsibility, as "accessory after the fact" at least, to the pretence that a similar condition had prevailed ever since President Roosevelt's final war-whoop of July 4, 1902, published to the American troops in the Islands on the day named. That war-whoop, it will be remembered, was in the form of a presidential proclamation congratulating General Chaffee and "the gallant officers and men under his command" on some "two thousand combats, great and small," and declaring, in effect, that Benevolent Assimilation was at last triumphantly vindicated, and that opposition to American rule was at an end. The certificate of March 28, 1907, appears at pages 47–8 of the *Report of the Philippine Commission for 1907*, part 1. If we consider what is *now* going on in the Islands as "modern" history, and the days of the early fighting as "ancient" history, this certificate will serve as the connecting link between the two. It furnishes the key-note to all that had happened during the American occupation prior to 1907, and the key-note of all that has happened since. Therefore, though somewhat long, it is deemed indispensable to clearness to submit here in full the text of

THE GREAT CERTIFICATE OF 1907

Whereas the census of the Philippine Islands was completed and published on the twenty-seventh day of March, nineteen hundred and five, which said completion and publication of said census was, on the twenty-eighth day of

March, nineteen hundred and five, duly published and proclaimed to the people by the governor-general of the Philippine Islands with the announcement that the President of the United States would direct the Philippine Commission to call a general election for the choice of delegates to a popular assembly, *provided that a condition of general and complete peace with recognition of the authority of the United States should be certified by the Philippine Commission to have continued in the territory of the Philippine Islands for a period of two years after said completion and publication of said census*; and

Whereas since the completion and publication of said census there have been *no serious disturbances of the public order save and except* those caused by the noted outlaws and bandit chieftains, Felizardo and Montalon, and their followers in the provinces of Cavite and Batangas, and those caused in the provinces of Samar and Leyte by the non-Christian and fanatical pulahanes resident in the mountain districts of the said provinces and the barrios contiguous thereto; and

Whereas the overwhelming majority of the people of said provinces of Cavite, Batangas, Samar, and Leyte have not taken part in said disturbances and have not aided or abetted the lawless acts of said bandits and pulahanes; and

Whereas the great mass and body of the Filipino people have, during said period of two years, continued to be law-abiding, peaceful, and loyal to the United States, and have continued to recognize and do now recognize the authority and sovereignty of the United States in the territory of said Philippine Islands: Now, therefore, be it

Resolved by the Philippine Commission in formal session duly assembled, That it, said Philippine Commission, do certify, and it *does hereby certify*, to the President of the United States *that for a period of two years after the completion and publication of the census a condition of general and complete peace, with recognition of the authority of the United States, has continued to exist* and now exists in the territory of said Philippine Islands not inhabited by Moros or other non-Christian tribes; and be it further

Resolved by said Philippine Commission, That the President of the United States be requested, and is hereby requested, to direct said Philippine Commission to call a general election for the choice of delegates to a popular assembly of the people of said territory in the Philippine Islands, which assembly shall be known as the Philippine Assembly.

Let us examine these amiable liberties thus taken with the facts of history by men of irreproachable private character, briefly analyzing their action. Such an examination and analysis are indispensable to a clear understanding by a great free people whose proudest boast is love of fair play, of whether the Filipino people, or any appreciable fraction of them, have ever in the least consented, or do now in the least consent, to our rule, as the small minority among us interested in keeping the Islands, have systematically sought, all these years, to have this nation believe. As the above certificate of 1907 was the last hurdle that Benevolent Assimilation had to leap on the Benevolent Hypocrisy course over which we had to gallop in order to get from the freeing of Cuba to the subjugation of the Philippines, let us glance back for a moment at the first hurdle or two, leapt when Mr. Taft was in the Philippine saddle.

Judge Taft had said on November 30, 1900:

A great majority of the people long for peace and are entirely willing to accept the establishment of a government under the supremacy of the United States[2];

and, pursuant to that idea, he had set up his civil government on July 4, 1901. He never did thereafter admit that he was mistaken in his original theory, but kept on trying to fit the facts to his theory, hoping that after a while they *would* fit. He "clung to his policy of disinterested benevolence with a tenacity born of conviction," to borrow a phrase from Governor-General Smith's inaugural address of 1907. But in this same inaugural address of Governor Smith of 1907, you find, for the first time in all the Philippine state papers, a frank admission of the actual conditions under which the civil government of 1901 was in fact set up. Says he:

While the smoke of battle still hung over the hills and valleys of the Philippines and every town and barrio in the islands was smoking hot with rebellion, she [the United States] replaced the military with a civil regime and on the smouldering embers of insurrection planted civil government.3

That confession, made with the bluntness of a most gallant soldier, is as refreshing in its honesty as the Roosevelt war-whoop of 1902. There shall be no tiresome repetition here concerning the original withholding of the facts from the American people in 1898–9, but to place in juxtaposition Secretary of War Root's representations to the American public in the year last named, and the actual facts as stated *earlier in the same year* by General MacArthur, one of our best fighting generals, during the thick of the early fighting, in an interview already noticed in its proper chronological place, will forever fix the genesis of the original lack of frankness as to conditions in the Philippines which has naturally and inexorably made frankness as to those conditions impossible ever since. As late as October 7, 1899, Mr. Root—who had not then and has not since been in the Philippines—had said in Chicago, in a speech at a dinner of the Marquette Club:

Well, against whom are we fighting? Are we fighting the Philippine nation? No. There is none. There are hundreds of islands, inhabited by more than sixty tribes, speaking more than sixty different languages, and all but one are ready to accept American sovereignty.

As early as the beginning of April, 1899, just after the taking on March 31st of the first insurgent capital, Malolos, General MacArthur, who commanded our troops in the assault on that place, had said, in an interview with a newspaper man afterwards verified by the General before the Senate Committee of 1902 as substantially correct:

When I first started in against these rebels, I believed that Aguinaldo's troops represented only a faction. * * * *I did not like to believe that the whole population of Luzon * * * was opposed to us * * **. But after having come thus far, and having been brought much in contact with both*insurrectos* and *amigos,*4 *I have been reluctantly compelled to believe that the Filipino masses are loyal to Aguinaldo and the government which he heads.*5

The presidential election of 1900 had been fought out, in the midst of considerable bitterness, on the idea that the Root view was correct and the MacArthur view was altogether mistaken. So that after 1900, the McKinley Administration was irrevocably committed to the Root view.6The Philippine Government had, after 1900, diligently set to work to live up to the Root view, and to fit the facts to the Root view by prayer and hope, accompanied by asseveration. Hence in 1901 the alleged joyous sobs of welcome with which the Filipino people are, in effect, described in the report of the Philippine Commission for that year as having received the "benign" civil government, said sobs or other manifestations having spread, if the Commission's report is to be taken at its face value, "like wild-fire." Hence also the attempt of 1902 to minimize the insurrection of 1901–2, in Batangas and other provinces of southern Luzon, conducted by what Governor Luke E. Wright, in a speech delivered at Memphis in the latter part of 1902, called "the die-in-the-last-ditch contingent." Hence the quiet placing of the province of Surigao in the hands of the military in 1903 without suspension of the writ of habeas corpus, and the failure to order out the army in Albay in 1903 and in Samar in 1904. Hence also the prompt use of the army in Samar, Batangas, and Cavite in 1905, after the presidential election was safely over. Hence also the seething state of sedition which smouldered in the Visayan Islands in 1906, punctuated by the outbreak in Leyte of that year.

The psychologic processes by which the distinguished gentlemen who signed the Great Certificate of March 28, 1907, got their own consent to sign it make the most profoundly interesting study, relatively to the general welfare of the world, in all our Philippine experiments so far. They are the final flowering of the plant Political Expediency. They are the weeds of benevolent casuistry that become from time to time unavoidable in a colonial garden tended by a republic based on the consent of the governed and therefore by the law of its own life unfitted to run any other kind of a government frankly. These processes find their origin in the provisions of the Act of Congress of July 1, 1902, known as the Philippine Government Act. Three days after President Roosevelt approved the Act, he issued his proclamation of July 4, 1902, above noticed, declaring the insurrection at an end. Section 6 of that Act provided:

Whenever the existing insurrection in the Philippine Islands shall have ceased, and *a condition of general and complete peace shall have been established therein*, and the fact shall be certified to the President by the Philippine Commission, the President, upon being satisfied thereof, shall order a census of the Philippine Islands to be taken by said Philippine Commission.

This census was intended to be preliminary to granting the Filipinos a legislature of their own, but as a legislature full of *insurrectos* would of course stultify its American sponsors before all mankind, it was announced in effect, in publishing the census programme, that no legislature would be forthcoming if the Filipinos did not quit insurrecting, and remain "good" for two years. If they did remain good for two years after the census was finished, then they should have their legislature. During the lull of "general and complete" peace which, in the fall of 1902, followed the suppression of the Batangas insurrection of 1901–2, and preceded the Ola insurrection of 1902–3 in the hemp provinces of southern Luzon, the Commission made, on September 25, 1902, the certificate contemplated by the above Act of Congress, and the taking of the census was accordingly ordered by the President of the United States, Mr. Roosevelt, by a proclamation issued the same day.7 Section 7 of the aforesaid Act of Congress provided:

Two years after the completion and publication of the census, in case such condition of general and complete peace with recognition of the authority of the United States shall have continued in the territory of said islands *not inhabited by Moros or other non-Christian tribes*, and such facts shall have been certified to the President by the Philippine Commission, the President upon being satisfied thereof shall direct said Commission to call, and the Commission shall call, a general election for the choice of delegates to a popular assembly of the people of said territory in the Philippine Islands, which shall be known as the Philippine Assembly.

On March 27, 1905, the President of the United States was duly advised that the census had been completed, and on March 28th, the presidential proclamation promising the Filipinos a legislature two years later if in the meantime they did not insurrect any, was duly published at Manila. It is true that there is no Philippine state paper signed by anybody, either by the President of the United States, or the Governor-General of the Philippines, or any one else, certifying to a condition of "general and complete peace" between the certificate to that effect made by the Philippine Commission on September 25, 1902, above mentioned, which authorized commencing the census (and was justified by the facts), and the presidential promise of March 28, 1905, that if they would "be good" for two years more, they should have a legislature. But the whole manifest implication of the representations of fact sought to be conveyed by the action both of the Washington and the Manila authorities at the date of the presidential promise of March 28, 1905, is that a condition of general and complete peace had obtained ever since the last certificate to that effect, the certificate of September 25, 1902. Yet, as we saw in the chapter covering the last year of Governor Wright's administration, besides the Samar disturbances that lasted all through 1905, a big insurrection was actually in full swing in Cavite, Batangas, and Laguna provinces, on March 28, 1905, had then been in progress since before the first of the year, and continued until the latter part of 1905, the then Governor-General, Governor Wright, having, by proclamation issued January 31, 1905, declared Cavite and Batangas to be in a state of insurrection, ordered the military into those provinces, and suspended the writ of habeas corpus. President Roosevelt's proclamation of March 28, 1905, can by no possibility be construed as saying to the Filipinos anything other than substantially this: "You have not insurrected any since my proclamation of July 4, 1902. If you will be good two years *more*, you shall have a legislature." What then was the Philippine Commission to do at the end of those two years, peppered, as they had been, with most annoying outbreaks in various provinces not inhabited by "Moros or other non-Christian tribes." During the presidential campaign of 1904 the Commission had committed themselves, as we have seen, to the proposition that nothing serious was going on at that time in Samar. So how could they take frank official cognizance on paper of the reign of terror let loose there by their delay in ordering out the army until after the presidential election, a delay which, like a delay of fire-engines to arrive at the scene of a fire, had permitted the Samar outbreak to gain such headway that it took two years to finally put it down? Then there was the outbreak of 1906 in Leyte, described in the last chapter, as to which even the Commission had admitted in their annual report for that year8:

Possibly its [Leyte's] immediate vicinity to Samar has had to do with the disturbed conditions.

In other words, *possibly*, a fire *may* spread from one field of dry grass to another near by.

As to the Cavite-Batangas-Laguna insurrection of 1905, in an executive order dated September 28, 1907,9—noticed in a previous chapter, but too pertinent to be entirely omitted here—wherein are set forth the reasons for withholding executive clemency from the condemned leaders of that movement, Governor-General Smith describes in harrowing terms "a reign of terror, devastation, and ruin in three of the most beautiful provinces in the archipelago," wrought by the condemned men, who he says "assumed the cloak of patriotism, and under the titles of 'Defenders of the Country,' and 'Protectors of the People' proceeded to inaugurate" said reign of terror. These men were most of them former insurgent officers who had remained out after the respectable generals had all surrendered. This Cavite-Batangas-Laguna insurrection was *the very sort of thing which the conditional promise of a legislature made by Congress to the Filipino people* in Sections 6 and 7 of the Act of July 1, 1902—the Philippine Government Act—*had stipulated should not happen*. This is no mere *dictum* of my own. In the case of Barcelon against Baker, 5 *Philippine Reports*, pp. 87 *et seq.*, already very briefly noticed in a previous chapter, the Supreme Court of the Islands had, in effect, so held. Section 5 of the Act of Congress of July 1, 1902, had provided that if any state of affairs serious enough should arise, the Governor of the Philippines should have authority to suspend the writ of habeas corpus "when in cases of rebellion, insurrection, or invasion the public safety may require it." Sections 6 and 7 of the same Act had provided, on the other hand, that if a condition of general and complete peace should prevail for a stated period the Filipinos should have a legislature. In the case of Barcelon against Baker the Supreme Court held that the situation contemplated by Section 5 of the Act of Congress had arisen in the provinces of Cavite and Batangas. That, of course, automatically, so to speak, made the postponement of the Philippine Assembly a necessary logical sequence, under the provisions of Sections 6 and 7. These Sections 6 and 7 promised the Filipinos a legislature in the event the conditions contemplated by Section 5 should not arise. Barcelon, who was one of the (non-combatant) reconcentrados restrained of his liberty at Batangas, claimed that his detention as such reconcentrado by the defendant in the habeas corpus proceeding, the constabulary officer, Colonel Baker, was unlawful, in that, he being charged with no crime, such detention deprived him of his liberty without due process of law. The Philippine Commission, however, had declared, by virtue of the authority vested in it by Section 5 of the Act of Congress aforesaid, that a state of insurrection existed in Cavite and Batangas, and accordingly the Governor-General had suspended the writ of habeas corpus and declared martial law in those provinces. The Attorney-General representing the Philippine Commission before the court rested the Government's case on the proposition that the petitioner was not entitled to claim the ordinary "due process of law" because "open insurrection against the constituted authorities" existed in the provinces named. And the Supreme Court upheld his contention. In so holding, they say, among other things (page 93), in construing Section 5 of the Act of Congress we are considering:

Inasmuch as the President, or Governor-General with the approval of the Philippine Commission, can suspend the privilege of the writ of habeas corpus only under the conditions mentioned in the said statute, it becomes their duty to make an investigation of the existing conditions in the archipelago, *or any part thereof*, to ascertain whether there actually exists a state of rebellion, insurrection, or invasion, and that the public safety requires the suspension of the privilege of the writ of habeas corpus. When this investigation is concluded, and the President, or the Governor-General with the consent of the Philippine Commission, *declares that there exists these conditions*, and that the public safety requires the suspension of the privilege of the writ of habeas corpus, can the judicial department of the Government investigate the same facts and declare that no such conditions exist?

They answer "No!" The head note of the decision is as follows:

The privilege of the writ of habeas corpus may be suspended in the Philippine Islands in the case of rebellion, insurrection, and invasion, when the public safety requires it, by the President of the United States, or by the Governor-General of the Philippine Islands with the approval of the Philippine Commission.

Thus the Supreme Court of the Islands squarely held that *on the fourth day of August, 1905* (the day the writ of habeas corpus was made returnable), *open insurrection existed against the constituted authorities in the Islands*, in the provinces named, *and had existed since the Executive Proclamation of January 31st, previous, declaring a state of insurrection*, and on that ground denied the writ. Yet the Commission certified on March 28, 1907, that a state of general and complete peace as contemplated by the Act of Congress conditionally promising a legislature, had prevailed for the two years preceding. In other words the Philippine Commission declared a state of insurrection to exist in certain populous provinces, and was upheld by the Supreme Court of the Islands in so doing, and later certified to the continuance of a state of general and complete peace covering the same period.

All the uncandid things—uncandid in failure to take the American people into their confidence—that have been done by all the good men we have sent to the Philippines from the beginning, have been justified by those good men to their own consciences on the idea that, because the end in view was truly benevolent, therefore the end justified the means. As a matter of fact, American Benevolent Assimilation in the Philippines has, in its practical operation, worked more of misery and havoc, first through war, and since through legislation put or kept on the statute books by the influence of special interests in the United States with Congress, "than any which has darkened their unhappy past" to use one of Mr. McKinley's early expressions deprecating doing for the Philippines what we did for Cuba.10

But let us see just how much the Philippine Commission that signed the peace certificate of March 28, 1907, swallowed, and how they swallowed it. It will be observed that they sugar-coated their certificate with a lot of whereases. The first of these recites President Roosevelt's promise of March 28, 1905, that the Filipinos should have a legislature two years thereafter "provided that a condition of general and complete peace with recognition of the authority of the United States should be certified by the Philippine Commission to have continued in the territory of the Philippine Islands for a period of two years" after the proclamation. Whereas number two, it will be noted, goes on to state that there have been "no serious disturbances of public order save and except" those in Cavite, Batangas, Samar, and Leyte,[11] the magnitude of which has been fully described in previous chapters. Of the Cavite-Batangas insurrection, the only one they had previously formally admitted to bean insurrection, they say it was "caused by certain noted outlaws and bandit chieftains [naming them], and their followers." Obviously this was hardly sufficient to show that an insurrection they had once officially recognized as such was not in fact such at all. So in order to justify a statement that "a condition of general and complete peace" had continued in these two great provinces of Cavite and Batangas, which they had but shortly previously declared to be in a state of insurrection, and been upheld by the Supreme Court in so doing, they resort to the old Otis expedient of 1898–9, worked on the American people through Mr. McKinley to show absence of lack of consent-of-the-governed. This expedient, as we have seen in the earlier chapters of this book, consisted in vague use of the word "majority." It had stood Judge Taft in good stead in the campaign of 1900, because when he then said that "the great majority of the people" were "entirely willing" to accept American rule, there was no earthly way to disprove it in time for the verdict of the American people to be influenced by the unanimity of the Filipinos against a change of masters in lieu of independence. It was the only possible expedient for an American conscience, because every American naturally feels that unless he can, by some sort of sophistry, persuade himself that "the majority" of the people want a given thing, then the thing is a wrong thing to force upon them. So the ethical hurdle the Commission had to leap in order to sign the certificate of 1907 was cleared thus:

The overwhelming majority of the people of said provinces have not taken part in said disturbances and have not aided and abetted the lawless acts of said bandits.

As a matter of fact, the report of the American Governor of Cavite—and conditions were conceded to be identical in the two provinces of Cavite and Batangas—shows that the reason it was so hard to suppress the Cavite-Batangas troubles of 1905 was that the people would not help the authorities to apprehend the outlaws. No doubt the King of England would have signed a similar certificate as to the people of the shires and counties in which Robin Hood, Little John, and Friar Tuck, held high carnival. Of course I do not mean to libel the fair fame of that fine freebooter Robin Hood and his companions by placing the rascally leaders of the bands of outlaws now under consideration in the same jolly and respectable class with those beloved friends of the childhood of us all. But the Cavite-Batangas "patriots" of 1905 could never have given the authorities as much trouble as they did if the people had not at least taken secret joy in discomfiture of the American authorities. Until finally suppressed, all such movements as these always grew exactly as a snow-ball does if you roll it on snow. Says Governor Shanks, a Major of the 4th United States Infantry, who was Governor of Cavite, in 1905 in his report for that year,[12] in explaining the uprising under consideration, and the way it grew: "The Filipino likes to be on the winning side." Certainly this is not peculiar to the Filipino. Governor Shanks proceeds:

The prestige acquired (by the uprising) at San Pedro Tunasan, Paranaque, Taal, and San Francisco de Malabon had great weight in creating active sympathy for ladrone bands and leaders. Something was needed to counterbalance the effect of their combined successes, and the appearance of regular troops was just the thing needed.

This explains how "the overwhelming majority" of which the certificate of 1907 speaks was obtained in Cavite. It took six months to obtain said "majority" at that. I suppose the campaigning of the American regulars might be credited with obtaining the "majority," and the reconcentration of brother Baker of the constabulary might be accorded the additional credit of making the majority "overwhelming." If you have, as election tellers, so to speak, a soldier with a bayonet on one side, and a constabulary officer with a reconcentration camp back of him on the other, you can get an "overwhelming majority" for the continuance of American rule even in Cavite province.

Through men I commanded during the early campaigning, I have killed my share of Filipinos in the time of war; and after the civil government was set up I had occasion to hang a good many of them, under what seemed to me a necessary application of the old Mosaic law, "An eye for an eye, a tooth for a tooth, and a life for a life." But I thank God I have never been a party to the insufferable pretence that they, or any appreciable fraction of them, ever consented to our rule. This, however, is the whole theory of the Philippine Commission's certificate of March 28, 1907. It is curious how generously and supremely frank a brave soldier will get when he forgets to be a politician. In one of his state papers of 1907 Governor-General Smith[13] speaks of General Trias, who had been Lieutenant-General of the insurgent army in the days of the insurrection, and next in rank to Aguinaldo himself, as one "whose love of country had been tested on many a well fought field of honorable conflict." Contrast this tribute to the respectability of the original Philippine war for independence against us with the long list of stale falsehoods already reviewed in this volume, on the faith of which, in the presidential campaign of 1900, the American people were persuaded that to deny to the Filipinos what they had accorded to Cuba was righteous! The leaders of the Cavite-Batangas uprising of 1905 had been officers of the insurgent army, and that was the secret of their hold upon the people of those provinces. It is true that they must have been pretty sorry officers, and that they were *ladrones* (brigands). They were cruel and unmitigated scoundrels working for purely selfish and vainglorious ends. But it was the cloak of patriotism, however, infamously misused, that gained them such success as they attained in 1905. Says the American Governor of Cavite province in his annual report for 1906[14]:

The province should be most carefully watched. I am convinced that *ladrone leaders do not produce conditions*, but that *the conditions and attitude of the public produce ladrones*.

So much for the Cavite-Batangas hurdle. And now as to the Samar and Leyte hurdle.

The signers of the certificate of 1907 justify their certificate as to Samar and Leyte on a very ingenious theory. The Act of Congress of July 1, 1902, already cited, which had provided for the taking of a census preliminary to the call of an election for delegates to a legislature, had recognized the crude ethnological status of the Moros and other non-Christian tribes. These had never had anything whatever to do with the insurrection against us. Therefore in making the continuance of a state of general and complete peace for a prescribed period a condition precedent to granting the Filipinos a legislature, the Act of 1902 had limited that condition precedent to "the territory of said Islands not inhabited by Moros or other non-Christian tribes." In fact President Roosevelt's proclamation of September 25, 1902, already noticed, ordering the taking of the census on the theory that a state of general and complete peace then existed, explains that this theory is entirely consistent with trouble among the Moros and other non-Christian tribes because *they*, it says, quoting from a statement of the Philippine Commission previously made to the President, "never have taken any part in the insurrection." The Moros and other non-Christian tribes were, so to speak, in no sense assets of the Philippine insurrection. All the rest of the population was— that is, if there was anything in the veteran General MacArthur's grim jest of 1900, prompted by Governor Taft's half-baked opinion to the contrary, that "ethnological homogeneity" was the secret of the unanimity of the opposition we met, and that somehow people "*will* stick to their own kith and kin." When the Philippine Government Act of 1902 was drawn nobody pretended for a moment that there were any non-Christian tribes either in Samar or Leyte. The whole population of those Islands were valuable *assets* of the insurrection. If any one doubts it, let him ask the 9th Infantry. You will find in the Census of 1903 that there are no non-Christian tribes credited either to Samar or Leyte.[15] When the Philippine Government Act of 1902 was drafted, the exception about Moros and other non-Christian tribes was intended to except merely certain types of people as distinct from the great mass of the Philippine population as islands are from the sea. The fact is, no person connected with the Philippine Government *either before or after* the certificate under consideration, ever thought of classifying the ignorant country people of the uplands and hills of Samar or Leyte, as "non-Christian tribes." The Philippine Census of 1903 does not so classify them. The very volume of the *Report of the Philippine Commission for 1907* in which the certificate aforesaid appears, does not. In that volume,[16] the report of the Executive Secretary deals elaborately with the subject of non-Christian tribes. Professor Worcester of the Philippine Commission has for the last twelve years been the grand official digger-up of non-Christian tribes. He takes as much delight at the discovery of a new non-Christian tribe in some remote, newly penetrated mountain fastness, as the butterfly catcher with the proverbial blue goggles does in the capture of a new kind of butterfly. The Executive Secretary's report, out of deference to the professor, omits no single achievement of his with reference to his anthropological hobby. It treats, with an enthusiasm that would delight Mrs. Jellyby herself, of "the progress that was made during the fiscal year in the work of civilizing non-Christian tribes *scattered* throughout the archipelago." It gives an alphabetical list of all the provinces where there are non-Christian tribes, and, under the name of each province it gives notes as to the progress during the year with those tribes. *Neither Samar nor Leyte appear in that list of provinces.* So that the Samar "Pulajans," or "Red Breeches" fellows,—"fanatical" Pulajans, they are called in the certificate—were "non-Christian tribes" for peace certificate purposes only. One thing which makes it most difficult of all for me to understand how these gentlemen got their consent to sign that certificate is that each non-Christian tribe in the Philippines has a language of its own, whereas the country people of the uplands and mountains of Samar and Leyte who are labelled—or libelled—"non-Christian tribes" in the certificate of 1907, were no more different from the rest of the population of those islands than, for instance, the ignorant mountain people of Virginia or Kentucky are different, ethnologically, from the inhabitants of Richmond or Louisville. In his report for 1908,[17] Governor-General Smith himself makes this perfectly clear, where he describes the Samar Pulajan, or mountaineer, thus:

The Pulajan is not a robber or a thief by nature—quite the contrary. He is hard working, industrious, and even frugal. He had his little *late*[18] of hemp on the side of the mountain, and breaking out his *picul*[19] of hemp, he carried it hank by hank for miles and miles over almost impassable mountain trails to the nearest town or barrio. There he offered it for sale, and if he refused the price tendered, which was generally not more than half the value, he soon found himself arrested on a trumped-up charge, and unless he compromised by parting with his hemp he found himself, after paying his fine and lawyer's fees, without either hemp or money.

The non-Christian tribes, on the other hand, never have anything to do with the civilized people. The Act of Congress of 1902, therefore, had no sort of reference to the simple, ignorant, and ordinarily docile mountain folk who tilled the soil, revered the priests, paid their *cedula* or head tax like all the rest of the population of the Islands, and carried their agricultural products from season to season, their hemp and the like, to the coast towns to market. In other words, inclusion of the Samar "Pulajans," or "Red Breeches" brigade, and the Leyte bandits, in the peace certificate of 1907, as "non-Christian tribes" was an afterthought, having no foundation either in logic or fact. It was a part of Benevolent Assimilation. This is clearly apparent from President Roosevelt's message to Congress of December, 1905.[20] You do not find any buncombe about "non-Christian tribes" in that message. In there reviewing the Samar and other insurrections of 1905 in the Philippines, you find him dealing with the real root of the evil with perfect honesty, though adopting the view that *the Filipino people* were to blame therefor, because *we* had placed too much power in the hands of an ignorant electorate, which had elected rascally officials. "Cavite and Samar," he says, "are instances of reposing too much confidence in the self-governing power of a people." If we had let the Filipinos go ahead with their little republic in 1898, instead of destroying it as we did, they knew and would have utilized the true elements of strength they had, viz., a very considerable body of educated, patriotic men having the loyal confidence of the masses of the people. But we proceeded to ram down their throats a preconceived theory that *the only* road to self-government was for an alien people to step in and make the ignorant masses the *sine qua non*. Yet if there was one point on which Mr. McKinley had laid more stress than on any other, in his original instructions of April 7, 1900, to the Taft Commission, that point was the one consecrated in the following language of those instructions:

In all the forms of government and administrative provisions which they are authorized to prescribe, the commission should bear in mind that the government which they are establishing is designed *not for* * * * *the expression of our theoretical views*, etc.

Of course the ignorant electorate we perpetrated on Samar as an "expression of our theoretical views" proved that we had "gone too fast" in conferring self-government, or, to quote Mr. Roosevelt, had been "reposing too much confidence in the self-governing power of a people," if to begin with the rankest material for constructing a government that there was at hand was to offer a fair test of capacity for self-government. But President Roosevelt's message, above quoted, shows you that the "ignorant electorate" was merely an ignorant electorate, and not a non-Christian tribe, as the Philippine Commission later had the temerity to certify they were. Now the plain, unvarnished, benevolent truth is just this: The Commission knew that nobody in the United States, whether they were *for* retaining the Islands or *against* retaining them, had any desire to postpone granting a legislature to the Philippine people. So in their certificate they simply included everybody who had given trouble in Samar and Leyte as "non-Christian tribes." The only justification for this was that they had in fact acted in a most un-Christianlike manner,—*i.e.*, for people who devoutly murmur prayers to patron saints in good standing in the church calendar. In making their certificate, the Commission simply ignored the various uprisings of the preceding two years. They simply said, generously, "Oh, forget it." They knew nobody in the United States begrudged the Filipinos their conditionally promised legislature, or cared to postpone it. The leading Filipinos begged the authorities to "forget" the various disturbances that had occurred since the publication of the census, and there was a very general desire in the Islands to let bygones be bygones, wipe the slate, and begin again. Any other attitude would have meant that the legislature would have to be postponed. Then the opposition in the United States would want to know why, and by 1908 Philippine independence might become an issue again. In the eyes of the Commission, the end, being benevolent, justified stretching the language of the Act of 1902 as if it had been the blessed veil of charity itself—*i.e.*, the end justified the means. In fact it *did*—almost—justify the means. But not quite. The moral quality of the Great Certificate of 1907 was not as reprehensible as General Anderson's dealings with Aguinaldo, already described, which, like the certificate, were a necessary part of the benevolent hypocrisy of Benevolent Assimilation of an unconsenting people. Yet General Anderson is an honorable man. It was not as bad as General Greene's juggling Aguinaldo out of his trenches before Manila in a friendly way, and failing to give him a receipt for said trenches, as he had promised to do, because such a receipt would show co-operation and "might look too much like an alliance." This also was done on the idea that the end justified the means. Yet General Greene is an honorable man. The signers of the great peace certificate of 1907 are all honorable men. But they signed that certificate, just the same. "Judge not that ye be not judged." All I have to say is, I would not have signed that certificate. I would have said: "No, gentlemen, the end does *not* justify the means. The Philippine Assembly must be postponed, if we are going to deal frankly with Congress and the folks at home. The conditions Congress made precedent to the grant of an assembly have *not* been met, and we each and all of us know it. We owe more to our own country and to truth than we do to the Filipinos. The Act of Congress of 1902 did not vest in the Philippine Commission authority to pardon disturbances of public order. It imposed upon the Commission an implied duty to report such disturbances, fully and frankly. It is not true that there has been a continuing state of general and complete peace in these Islands for the last two years, and I for one will not certify that there has been."

The truth is, the attitude of the signers of the certificate was like that of Uncle Remus, when interrupted by the little boy in one of his stories. When Uncle Remus gets to the point in the rabbit story where the rabbit thrillingly escapes from the jaws of death, *i.e.*, from the jaws of the dogs, by climbing a tree, the rapt listener interrupts: "Why, Uncle Remus, a rabbit can't climb a tree." To which Uncle Remus replies, with a reassuring wave of the hand, "Oh, but Honey, *dis* rabbit dess *'bleeged* ter climb *dis* tree."

Should any of my good friends still in the Philippines feel disposed to censure such levity as the above, I can only say, as Kipling writes from England to his Anglo-Indian friends in a foreword to one of his books:

I have told these tales of our life
    For a sheltered people's mirth,
In jesting guise,—but ye are wise,
    And ye know what the jest is worth.

Moreover, my authority to speak frankly about these matters is also aptly stated by the same great poet thus:

I have eaten your bread and salt,
    I have drunk your water and wine,
The deaths ye died I have watched beside
    And the lives that ye led were mine.
Was there aught that I did not share
    In vigil or toil or ease,
One joy or woe that I did not know,
    Dear friends across the seas?

The above reflections are not placed before the reader to show him what a pity it is that the writer was not a member of the Philippine Commission at the time of their certificate of 1907, or to show what a fine thing for our common country it would be if he were made a member of that Commission now. He is, personally, as disinterested as if Manila were in the moon, for he cannot live in the tropics any more. The effect of a year or so of residence there upon white men invalided home for tropical dysentery and then returning to the Islands is like the effect of water upon a starched shirt. However, it is believed that the facts of official record collected in this chapter up to this point are a *demonstration* of this proposition, to wit: *What the Philippine Government needs more than anything else is that the minority party in the United States should be represented on the Commission.* By this I do not mean representation by what are called, under Republican Administrations, "White House" Democrats, nor what under a Democratic Administration, if one should ever occur, would probably be called "Copperhead Republicans." I mean the genuine article. A Democrat who has cast his fortunes with the Philippines is no longer a Democrat relatively to the Philippines, because the Democratic party wants to get rid of the Philippines and the Democrat in the Philippines of course does not. How absurd it is to talk about former Governors Wright and Smith, as "life-long Democrats," by way of preliminary to using their opinions as "admissions." In the law of evidence, an "admission" is a statement made against the interest of the party making it.

The first election for representatives in the Philippine Assembly was held on July 30, 1907, and on October 16th thereafter the Assembly was formally opened by Secretary of War, William H. Taft. The various "whereases" hereinabove reviewed, importing complete acquiescence in American rule since President Roosevelt's Proclamation of July 4, 1902, were first duly read, and then the Assembly was opened. Of course, no man could have been elected to the Assembly without at least pretending to be in favor of independence, and all but a corporal's guard of them were outspoken in favor of the proposition. As the present Governor-General Mr. Forbes, said, while Vice-Governor, in the *Atlantic Monthly* for February, 1909:

To deny the capacity of one's country for * * * self-government is essentially unpopular.

When he visited the Philippines to open their Assembly in 1907, Mr. Taft had said nothing definite and final on the question of promisingindependence since his departure from the Islands in 1903. His then benevolent unwillingness to tell them frankly he did not think they had sense enough to run a government of their own, and that they were unfit for self-government, has already been reviewed. For two years after 1903 Governor Wright had made them pine for the return of Mr. Taft. They longed to hear again some of the siren notes of the celebrated speech "the Philippines for the Filipinos." They had gotten very excited and very happy over that speech. Of course they would not have gotten very excited over independence supposed to be coming long after they should be dead and buried. During the two dark frank years of Governor Wright's *régime*, they had frequently been told that they were not fit for independence. So that when Secretary of War Taft had visited the Islands in 1905 they all had been on the *qui vive* for more statements vaguely implying an independence they might hope to live to see. During the visit of 1905 the time of the visiting Congressional party was consumed principally with tariff hearings, and comparatively little was said on the subject uppermost in the minds of all Filipinos. It is true that Mr. Taft said then *he* was of the opinion that it would take a generation or longer to get the country ready for self-government, but he said it in a tactful, kindly way, and did not forever crush their hopes. So when he went out to the Islands to open the assembly in 1907, the attitude of the whole people in expectation of some definite utterances on the question of a definite *promise* of independence at *some* future time, was just the attitude of an audience in a theatre as to which one affirms "you could hear a pin fall." In this regard Mr. Taft's utterances were as follows21:

I am aware that in view of the issues discussed at the election of this assembly I am expected to say something regarding the policy of the United States toward these islands. I cannot speak with the authority of one who may control that policy. The Philippine Islands are territory belonging to the United States, and by the Constitution, the branch of that government vested with the power and charged with the duty of making rules and regulations for their government is Congress. The policy to be pursued with respect to them is therefore ultimately for Congress to determine. * * * I have no authority to speak for Congress in respect to the ultimate disposition of the Islands.

After that there was some talk about "mutually beneficial trade relations" and "improvement of the people both industrially and in self-governing capacity." But with regard to the "process of political preparation of the Filipino people" for self-government the Secretary said that was a question no one could certainly answer; and so far as he was concerned he thought it would take "considerable longer than a generation." Somewhere in the early Philippine State papers there is a quotation used by Mr. Taft from Shakespeare about "Keeping the word of promise to the ear and breaking it to the hope." The Filipinos have eagerly read for the last twelve years every utterance of Mr. Taft's that they could get hold of. If any of those embryonic statesmen of the first Philippine Assembly, familiar with the various Taft utterances, had looked up the context of the Shakespearian quotation above alluded to, he would have found it to be as follows:

And be these juggling fiends no more believ'd,
That palter with us in a double sense:
That keep the word of promise to our ear
And break it to our hope.22

Since the announcement by Secretary of War Taft at the opening of the Philippine Assembly in October, 1907, of the policy of indefinite retention of the Islands with undeclared intention, the Filipinos have of course clearly understood that if they were ever to have independence they must look to Congress for it. But they know Congress is not interested in them and that they have no influence with it, and that the Hemp Trust, the Tobacco Trust, and the Sugar Trust, have. So that since 1907, both the American authorities in the Philippines and the Filipinos have settled down, the former suffused with benevolence— hardened however by paternalistic firmness, the latter stoically, to the programme of indefinite retention with undeclared intention. No conceivable programme could be devised more ingeniously calculated to engender race hatred. The Filipino newspapers call the present policy one of "permanent administration for inferior and incapable races." The Act of Congress of July 1, 1902, known as the Philippine Government Act, which is the "Constitution," so to speak, we have given the Filipinos, accords "liberty of the press" in the exact language of our own Constitution. The native press does not fail to use this liberty to the limit. Naturally the American press does not remain silent. So here are a pair of bellows ever fanning the charcoals of discontent. And the masses of the Filipino people read the Filipino papers. If they cannot read, their children can. In one of the reports of one of the American constabulary officials in the Philippines, there is an account of the influence of the native press too graphic to be otherwise than accurate. He says one can often see, in the country districts, a group of natives gathered about some village Hampden, listening to his reading the latest diatribe against the American Occupation. Never was there such folly in the annals of statesmanship. In their native papers, the race situation of course comes in for much comment. Now the most notorious and inflexible fact of that race situation is that the colonial Anglo-Saxon does not intermarry with "the yellow and brown" subject people, as the Latin colonizing races do. It would be an over-statement of the case to say that the Filipinos to-day had rather have the Spaniards back as their overlords instead of us. In 1898, they "tasted the sweets of liberty," to use an expression of one of their leaders, and I am perfectly sure that to-day the desire of all those people for a government of their own is so genuine and universal as that it amounts to a very hopeful positive factor in the equation of their capacity for self-government. But there is no doubt that many of the Filipinos after all have a very warm place in their hearts for the Spanish people. How could it be otherwise when so many of the Filipinos are sons and grandsons of Spaniards? Much of like and dislike in life's journey is determined pre-natally. On the other hand, the American women in the Philippines maintain an attitude toward the natives quite like that of their British sisters in Hong Kong toward the Chinese, and in Calcutta toward the natives there. The social status of an American woman who marries a native,—I myself have never heard of but one case—is like that of a Pacific coast girl who marries a Jap. This is merely the instinct of self-defence with which Nature provides the weaker sex, just as she provides the porcupine with quills. But look at the other side of the picture. When an American man marries a native woman, he thereafter finds himself more in touch with his native "in-laws" it is true, but correspondingly, and ever increasingly, out of touch with his former associations. This is not as it should be. But it is a most unpleasant and inexorable fact of the present situation. In an address delivered at the Quill Club in Manila on January 25, 1909, Governor Smith, after reciting the various beneficent designs contemplated by the government and the various public works consummated (at the expense of the people of the Islands) deplored, in spite of it all, what he termed "the growing gulf between the races." Said he:

An era of ill feeling has started between Americans and Filipinos, and, I hesitate to say it, race hatred.

Cherchez la femme! You find her, on the one hand, in the American woman whose attitude has been indicated, and you find her, on the other, in the refined and virtuous native woman, who finds her American husband's relations to his compatriots altered—queered—since his marriage to her, no matter how faithful a wife and mother she may be. This is the unspeakably cruel situation we have forced upon the Filipino people—whom I really learned to respect, and became much attached to, before I left the Islands—*and President Taft knows it as well as I do.* Yet he does not take the American people into his confidence. He simply worries along with the situation, wishing it would get better, but knowing it will get worse. That this situation is a permanent one is clearly shown by all the previous teachings of racial history. In his *Winning of the West*, written in 1889, speaking of the French settlers in the Ohio valley before 1776, and the cordial social relations of the dominant race with the natives—relations which have always obtained with all Latin races under like circumstances—Mr. Roosevelt says (vol. i., page 41):

They were not trammelled by the queer pride which makes a man of English stock unwilling to make a red-skinned woman his wife, though anxious enough to make her his concubine.

Men of English stock have changed but little in the matter of race instinct since 1776. If we had a definite policy, declared by Congress, promising independence, the American attitude in the Philippines toward the Filipinos would at once change, from the present impossible one, to our ordinary natural attitude of courtesy toward all foreigners, regardless of their color.

On May 7, 1909, the Honorable James F. Smith took his departure from the Philippine Islands forever and turned over the duties of his office to the Honorable W. Cameron Forbes, as Acting President of the Commission and Governor-General. As in the case of Governors Wright and Ide, so in that of Governor Smith, no reason is apparent why the Washington Government should have been willing to dispense with the services of the incumbent. This was peculiarly true in the case of General Smith. He was but fifty years of age when he left the Islands in 1909. He has rendered more different kinds of distinguished public service than any American who has ever been in the Philippine Islands from the time Dewey's guns first thundered out over Manila Bay down to this good hour. Going out with the first expedition in 1898 as Colonel of the 1st California Regiment, he distinguished himself on more than one battlefield in the early fighting and in recognition thereof was made a brigadier-general. Subsequent to this he became Military Governor of the island of Negros, that one of the six principal Visayan Islands which gave less trouble during the insurrection and after than any other—a circumstance doubtless not wholly unrelated to General Smith's wise and tactful administration there. Later on during the military *régime* he became Collector of Customs of the archipelago. The revenues from customs are the principal source of revenue of the Philippine Government and the sums of money handled are enormous. The customs service, moreover, in most countries, and especially in the Philippines, is more subject to the creeping in of graft than any other. General Smith's administration of this post was in keeping with everything else he did in the Islands. When the civil government was founded by Judge Taft in 1901, he was appointed one of the Justices of the Supreme Court and filled the duties of that office most creditably. Thence he was promoted to the Philippine Commission, which is, virtually, the cabinet of the Governor-General. Still later he became Vice-Governor, and finally Governor, serving as such from September, 1906, to May, 1909. Any other government on earth that has over-seas colonies and recognizes the supreme importance of a maximum of continuity of policy, would have kept Governor Smith as long as it could have possibly induced him to stay, just as the British kept Lord Cromer in Egypt. Governor Smith was succeeded by a young man from Boston, who had come out to the Islands four years before, and who, prior to that time, had never had any public service in the United States of any kind, had never been in the Philippine Islands, and probably had never seen a Filipino until he landed at Manila.

General Smith is now (1912) one of the Judges of the Court of Customs Appeals at Washington.

---

1 Pt. 1, p. 36.

2 *Report of Taft Philippine Commission for 1900*, p. 17.

3 See *Report of U. S. Philippine Commission*, 1907, pt. 1, p. 229.

4 *Amigo*, in Spanish, means friend. Every non-combatant Filipino with whom our people came in contact in the early days always claimed to be an "amigo," and never was, in any single instance.

5 See testimony of General MacArthur before the Senate Committee of 1902, *Senate Document 331*, 1902, p. 1942.

6 The adverse minority report on the pending Jones bill, which bill proposes ultimate Philippine independence in 1921, is full of the old insufferable drivel about "tribes," and of the rest of the Root views of 1900.

7 See *Report of U. S. Philippine Commission*, 1907, pt. 1, p. 211.

8 Part 1, p. 38.

9 *Report of Philippine Commission*, 1907, pt. 1, p. 37.

10 See President McKinley's annual message to Congress of December, 1899, *Congressional Record*, December 5, 1899, p. 34.

11 Provinces totalling about a million people.

12 *Report of U. S. Philippine Commission*, 1905, pt. 1, p. 211.

13 *Report of Philippine Commission*, 1907, pt. 1, p. 38.

14 *Ibid.*, 1906; pt. 1, p. 225.

15 To be absolutely accurate, there are 688 people classified as "wild" in the Census figures as to Samar, and 265,549 are put down as civilized; the total of population being 266,237. *All* the 388,922 people of Leyte are put down as civilized. See *Philippine Census*, Table of Population, vol. ii., p. 123.

16 *Report of Philippine Commission for 1907*, pt. 1, p. 195.

17 See *Report of Philippine Commission*, 1908, pt. 1, p. 62.

18 Tract. You speak of the small farmer's "*late* of hemp" in the Philippines as you do of his "patch of cotton" in the United States.

19 A *picul* is a bale of a given quantity—weight. "Breaking out a *picul* of hemp" is analogous, colloquially, to "picking a bale of cotton."

20 See *Congressional Record*, December 5, 1905, p. 103.

21 See *Report of Philippine Commission*, 1907, pt. 1, p. 215.

22 *Macbeth*, Act V., Sc. 8.

Chapter XXII. Governor Forbes—1909–1912

The trouble with this country to-day is that, under long domination by the protected interests, a partnership has grown up between them and the Government which the best men in the Republican party could not break up if they would.— WOODROW WILSON.

When Governor Forbes assumed the duties of Governor-General of the Philippines, some ten years after the ratification of the Treaty of Paris whereby we bought the Islands, he was the ninth supreme representative of American authority we had had there since the American occupation began. The following is the list:

(1) Gen. Thomas M. Anderson   June 30, 1898–July 25, 1898

(2) Gen. Wesley Merritt   July 25, 1898–Aug. 29, 1898

(3) Gen. Elwell S. Otis   Aug. 29, 1898–May 5, 1900

(4) Gen. Arthur MacArthur   May 5, 1900–July 4, 1901

(5) Hon. William H. Taft   July 4, 1901–Dec. 23, 1903

(6) Hon. Luke E. Wright   Dec. 23, 1903–Nov. 4, 1905

(7) Hon. Henry C. Ide   Nov. 4, 1905–Sept. 20, 1906

(8) Hon. James F. Smith   Sept. 20, 1906–May 7, 1909

(9) Hon. W. Cameron Forbes   May 7, 1909–1

No one of these distinguished gentlemen has ever had any authority to tell the Filipinos what we expect ultimately to do with them. They have not known themselves. Is not this distinctly unfair both to governors and governed?

Before Governor Forbes went to the Philippines he had been a largely successful business man. He is a man of the very highest personal character, and an indefatigable worker. He has done as well as the conditions of the problem permit. But he is always between Scylla and Charybdis. American capital in or contemplating investment in the Islands is continually pressing to be permitted to go ahead and develop the resources of the Islands. To keep the Islands from being exploited Congress early limited grants of land to a maximum too small to attract capital. So those who desire to build up the country, knowing they cannot get the law changed, are forever seeking to invent ways to get around the law. And, being firm in the orthodox Administration belief that discussion of ultimate independence is purely academic, *i.e.*, a matter of no concern to anybody now living, Governor Forbes is of course in sympathy with Americans who wish to develop the resources of the Islands. On the other hand, he knows that such a course will daily and hourly make ultimate independence more certain never to come. So do the Filipinos know this. Therefore they clamor ever louder and louder against all American attempts to repeal the anti-exploiting Acts of Congress by "liberal" interpretation. Many an American just here is sure to ask himself, "Why all this 'clamor'? Do we not give them good government? What just ground have they for complaint?" Yes, we do give them very good government, so far as the Manila end of the business is concerned, except that it is a far more expensive government than any people on the earth would be willing to impose on themselves. But their main staples are hemp, sugar, and tobacco, and we raise the last two in this country. Their sugar and tobacco were allowed free entry into the United States by the Paine Law of 1909 up to amounts limited in the law, but the Philippine people know very well that American sugar and tobacco interests will either dwarf the growth of their sugar and tobacco industries by refusing to allow the limit raised—the limit of amounts admitted free of duty—or else that our Sugar Trust and our Tobacco Trust will simply ultimately eliminate them by absorption, just as the Standard Oil Company used to do with small competitors. In this sort of prospect certainly even the dullest intellect must recognize just ground for fearing—nay for *plainly foreseeing*—practical industrial slavery through control by foreign2 corporations of economic conditions. So much for the two staples in which the Philippines may some day become competitors of ours. It took Mr. Taft nine years to persuade American sugar and tobacco that they would not be in any immediate danger by letting in a little Philippine sugar and tobacco free of duty. Then they consented. Not until then did they promise not to shout "Down with cheap Asiatic labor. We will not consent to compete with it." Their mental reservation was, of course, and is, "if the Philippine sugar and tobacco industries get too prosperous, we will either buy them, or cripple them by defeating their next attempt to get legislation increasing the amounts of Philippine sugar and tobacco admitted into the United States free of duty." And the Filipinos *know* that this is the fate that awaits two out of the three main sources of the wealth of their country. Their third source of wealth, their main staple, is the world-famous Manila hemp. This represents more than half the value of their total annual exports. And as to it, "practical industrial slavery through control by foreign corporations of economic conditions" is to-day not a *fear*, but a *fact*. The International Harvester Company has its agents at Manila. The said company or allied interests, or both, are large importers of Manila hemp. The reports of all the governors-general of the Philippines who have preceded Governor Forbes tell, year after year, of the millions "handed over" to American hemp importers through "the hemp joker" of the Act of Congress of 1902, hereinafter explained, in the chapter on Congressional Legislation (Chapter XXVI.). Why did these complaints—made with annual regularity up to Governor Forbes's accession—cease thereafter? You will find these complaints of his predecessors *transcribed* in the chapter mentioned, because if I had re-stated them you might suspect exaggeration. The "rake-off" of the American importers of Manila hemp for 1910 was nearly $750,000, as fully explained in Chapter XXVI.

Governor Forbes will be in this country when this book is issued. I think he owes it to the American people to explain why he does not continue the efforts of his predecessors to halt the depredations of the Hemp Trust. Why does he content himself in his last annual report with a mild allusion to the fact that the condition of the hemp industry is "not satisfactory"? I have said that Governor Forbes is a man of high character, and take pleasure in repeating that statement in this connection. The truth is we are running a political kindergarten for adults in the Philippines, and those responsible for the original blunder of taking them, and all their political heirs and assigns since, have sought to evade admitting and setting to work to rectify the blunder. Unmasked, this is what the policy of Benevolent Assimilation now is. They allege an end, and so justify all the ways and means. Benevolent Assimilation needs the support of the International Harvester Company and of all other Big Business interested directly or indirectly in Manila hemp. The end justifies the means. Hence the silence. Philippine gubernatorial reticence is always most reticent about that particular subject on which at the time the American people are most peculiarly entitled to information. As long as public order was the most pressing question, Philippine gubernatorial reticence selected that branch of our colonial problem either for especial silence or for superlatively casual allusion, as we have already seen. So now with the economic distresses. Frankness would obviously furnish too much good argument for winding up this Oriental receivership of ours. The Philippine Government will never tell its main current troubles until after they are over. But as the present trouble—the economic depredations of powerful special interests—must necessarily be fruitful of discontent which will crop out some day to remind us that as we sow so shall we reap, any one who helps expose the root of the trouble is doing a public service. No Congressman who in silence would permit Big Business to prey upon his constituents as Governor Forbes has, could long remain in office. Taxation without representation may amount to depredation, and yet never be corrected, when the powers that prey have the ear of the court, and the victims cannot get the ear of the American people. So the Hemp Trust continues to rob the Filipinos under the forms of law, and the Mohonk Conference continues to kiss Benevolent Assimilation on both cheeks. And Dr. Lyman Abbott periodically says Amen. I am not speaking disrespectfully of Dr. Abbott. I am deploring the lack of information of our people at home as to conditions in the Philippines.

It is a relief to turn from such matters to some of the real substantial good we have done out there to which Governor Forbes has heretofore publicly pointed with just pride. In an article in the *Atlantic Monthly* for February, 1909, Governor Forbes (then Vice-Governor) said, among other things:

We have completed the separation of Church and State, buying out from the religious orders their large agricultural properties, which are now administered by the government for the benefit of the tenants.

This statement I cannot too cordially endorse. It would be grossly unfair not to accord full measure of acclaim to Governor Taft for the way he worked out the problem of the Friar Lands. He has been attacked in some quarters in this regard, and most unjustly. Not being a Catholic, and all my people being Protestants, I have no fear of being suspected of special pleading in the matter. The working out of the Friar Land problem by Governor Taft in the Philippines was a splendid piece of constructive statesmanship. He was at his greatest and best in that very transaction. The Treaty of Paris had guaranteed that all vested rights should be respected, including those of ecclesiastical bodies. The friars had long owned the lands in question. There can be no particle of doubt on this point. The tenants on the land had all long ago attorned to them, father and son, from time out of mind, paying rent regularly. But by claiming jurisdiction over their tenants' souls also, and getting that jurisdiction effectively recognized, the thrifty friars used to raise the rent regularly, quieting incipient protest with threats of eternal punishment, or protracted stay in purgatory. The advent of our government let loose a revolt against the authority of the friars generally, and, their spiritual hold once loosened, this led the tenants to dispute the land titles of their spiritual shepherds, who were also their temporal landlords. Of course the titles had all been long recorded, and looked after by the best legal talent the country afforded. As long as you control the future of your tenant's soul, you can make him pay his last copeck for rent. But as soon as that control is lost, the man on whom the governing of the country thereafter devolves has a certain prospect of a great agrarian revolution on his hands, having in it many elements of substantial righteousness. Governor Taft's capacious mind, prompted by his strongest instinct, love of justice, conceived the idea of having the Philippine Government raise the money to buy the Friar Lands, by issuing bonds, and then buying the Friars out and re-selling the land to the tenants on long time, on the instalment plan, the instalments to be so graduated as to be equal to a moderate rental. Each tenant stayed right where he had been all the time, in possession of the tract he had always tilled, he and his father before him. To arrange all this it took an Act of Congress authorizing the bond issue, and a visit to Rome to arrange the bargain with the Pope. Some say His Holiness drove a hard bargain with Governor Taft, or to put it another way, that Governor Taft paid the Church people too much for the land. He did not. He may not have counted pennies with them, but the lands were worth what he paid for them. And the purchase protected the faith and honor of our government, as pledged by the Treaty of Paris, and at the same time prevented an agrarian revolution—which would have had a lot of elemental justice on its side.

Another of the good works we have done in the Philippines, to which Governor Forbes points in his magazine article above mentioned, is thus noted by him:

We have put the finances on a sound and sensible basis.

To this also I say Amen. The Forbes article then goes on to say that the government of the Islands is self-supporting. This is true, except the $14,000,000 a year it costs us to keep out there a garrison of 12,000 American troops (supplemented by certain native scouts—see chapter on "Cost of the Philippines," hereafter). This garrison is conceded to be a mere handful, sufficient merely, and intended merely—as a witty English woman has put it in a book on the Philippines—"to knock the Filipino on the head in case he wants his liberty before the Americans think he is fit for it." In other words, we only attempt to keep force enough there to quell any outbreak that might occur. So far as possible invasion by any foreign power is concerned, our $14,000,000 per annum is an absolutely dead loss. Brigadier-General Clarence Edwards, U. S. A., commanding the Bureau of Insular Affairs, said recently[3] before the Finance Committee of the Senate:

I would never think of the Philippines as a military problem for defence. If any nation wants them, it is merely a declaration of war.

What a shameful admission for a great nation to subscribe to, relatively to people it pretends to be protecting! The programme of the War Department is to abandon the Islands to their fate, for the time being at least, in our next war, letting them remain a football until the end of such war, when, as an independent republic they could, and would, rally as one man to the defence of their country against invasion, and would, with a little help from us, make life unbearable for an invading force. As things stand, we are just as impotent as Spain was out there in 1898, and it is utter folly to forget what happened then.

But to return to Governor Forbes's article and to a pleasanter feature of the situation. He says:

We have established schools throughout the archipelago, teaching upward of half a million children.

This also is true, and greatly to our credit. But as the American hemp trust mulcts the Philippine hemp output about a half million dollars a year (as above suggested, and later, in another chapter, more fully explained), it follows that each Filipino child pays the hemp trust a dollar a year for the privilege of going to school.

And now let us consider the most supremely important part of Governor Forbes's magazine article above quoted. The burden of the song of the adverse minority report on the pending Jones bill (looking to Philippine independence in 1921)[4] is that because there are certain "wild tribes" scattered throughout the archipelago, in the mountain fastnesses, therefore we should cling to the present policy of indefinite retention with undeclared intention until the wild tribes get civilized. Governor Forbes's article is an absolute, complete, and final answer to the misinformed nonsense of the minority report aforesaid. He says, apropos of public order:

It is now safe to travel everywhere throughout the Islands without carrying a weapon, excepting only in some of the remote parts of the mountains, where lurk bands of wild tribes who might possibly mistake the object of a visit, and in the southern part of the great island of Mindanao which is inhabited by intractable Moros.

The foregoing unmasks, in all its contemptible falsehood, the pretence that the presence of a few wild tribes in the Philippines is a reason for withholding independence from 7,000,000 of Christian people in order that a greedy little set of American importers of Manila hemp may fatten thereon. True, hemp is not edible, but it is convertible into edibles—and also into campaign funds. That the existence of these wild tribes—the dog-eating Igorrotes and other savages you saw exhibited at the St. Louis Exposition of 1903–4—constitute infinitely less reason for withholding independence from the Filipinos than the American Indian constituted in 1776 for withholding independence from us, will be sufficiently apparent from a glance at the following table, taken from the *American Census of the Islands of 1903* (vol. ii., p. 123):5

Island	Civilized	Wild	Total
Luzon	3,575,001	223,506	3,798,507
Panay	728,713	14,933	743,646
Cebu	592,247		592,247
Bohol	243,148		243,148
Negros	439,559	21,217	460,776
Leyte	357,641		357,641
Samar	222,002	688	222,690
Mindanao	246,694	252,940	499,634

I think the above table makes clear the enormity of the injustice I am now trying to crucify. Without stopping to use your pencil, you can see that Mindanao, the island where the "intractable Moros" Governor Forbes speaks of live, contains about a half million people. Half of these are civilized Christians, and the other half are the wild, crudely Mohammedan Moro tribes. Above Mindanao on the above list, you behold what practically *is* the Philippine archipelago (except Mindanao), viz., Luzon and the six main Visayan Islands. If you will turn back to pages 225 *et seq.*, especially to page 228, where the student of world politics was furnished with all he needs or will ever care to know about the geography of the Philippine Islands, you will there find all the rocks sticking out of the water and all the little daubs you see on the map eliminated from the equation as wholly unessential to a clear understanding of the problem of governing the Islands. That process of elimination left us Luzon and the six main Visayan Islands above, as constituting, for all practical governmental purposes all the Philippine archipelago except the Moro country, Mindanao (*i.e.*, parts of it), and its adjacent islets; Luzon and the Visayan Islands contain nearly 7,000,000 of people, and of these the wild tribes, as you can see by a glance at the above table, constitute less than 300,000, sprinkled in the pockets of their various mountain regions. Nearly all these 300,000 are quite tame, peaceable, and tractable, except, as Governor Forbes suggests, they "might possibly mistake the object of a visit." The half million "intractable Moros" of Mindanao, plus those in the adjacent islets, make up another 300,000. These last, it is true, will need policing for some time to come, but whether we do that policing by retaining Mindanao, or whether we let the Filipinos do it, is a detail that has no standing in court as a reason for continuing to deny independence to the 7,000,000 of people of Luzon and the Visayan Islands because they have some 300,000 backward people in the backwoods of their mountains. Yet see how the ingenuity of inspired ignorance states the case, by adding the 300,000 tame tribes of Luzon and the Visayas to the 300,000 fierce Moro savages away down in Mindanao, near Borneo, so as to get 600,000 "wild" people, and then alluding to the fact that so far only 200,000 Filipinos are qualified to vote. Says the report of the minority of the Committee on Insular Affairs on the pending Jones bill (proposing independence in 1921):

The wild and uncivilized inhabitants of the islands outnumber, 3 to 1, those who would be qualified to vote under the pending bill [the Jones bill].

You see the minority report is counting women and children, when it talks about the wild tribes, but not when it talks about voters. According to universally accepted general averages, among 7,500,000 people you should find 1,500,000 adult males. No one doubts that of these, by 1921, 500,000 will have become qualified voters. No one can deny that any such country having 500,000 qualified voters, the bulk of whom are good farmers, and the cream of whom are high-minded educated gentlemen, and all of whom are intensely patriotic, will be in good shape for promotion to independence. What wearies me about this whole matter is that the minority report above mentioned is permitted to get off such "rot," and the *New York Times*, the *Army and Navy Journal*, and others, to applaud it, while the Administration sits by, silent, and reaps the benefit of such stale, though not intentional, falsehoods, without attempting to correct them, so that our people may get at the real merits of the question. You see this silence inures to the benefit of the interests that have cornered the Manila hemp industry.

In the campaign of 1912 for the Republican nomination for the Presidency, there was much mutual recrimination between Colonel Roosevelt and Mr. Taft about which of them had been kindest to the International Harvester Company. It seems to me it is "up to" Governor Forbes, who in the Philippines has served under the present President and his predecessor also, to explain why he has abandoned the fight, so long waged by previous governors-general, to get what former Governor-General James F. Smith calls "the [hemp] joker" of the Act of Congress of 1902 concerning the Philippines, wiped from the statute books of this country.

1In June, 1912, Governor Forbes was still Governor-General.

2By "foreign" I mean, of course, American, *i.e.*, non-resident.

3Hearings on Sugar, April 5, 1912.

4Introduced in the House of Representatives by Hon. W. A. Jones, of Va., Chairman of the Committee on Insular Affairs of the House, in March, 1912.

5See also, in connection with this table, the folding map of the archipelago at the end of the book.

Chapter XXIII. "Non-Christian" Worcester

The cry of remote distress is ever faintly heard.

GIBBON'S *Decline and Fall of the Roman Empire.*

In the year 1911, the editor of one of the great metropolitan papers told me that President Taft told him that the Honorable Dean C. Worcester, the Secretary of the Interior of the Philippine Government, was "the most valuable man we have on the Philippine Commission." Certainly, reproduction of such an indorsement from so exalted a source shows a wish to be fair, in one who considers Professor Worcester the direst calamity that has befallen the Filipinos since the American occupation, neither war, pestilence, famine, reconcentration, nor tariff-wrought poverty excepted. During all my stay in the Philippines I never did have any official relations of any sort with the Professor, and only met him, casually, once, in 1901. The personal impression left from the meeting was distinctly that of an overbearing bully of the beggar-on-horseback type. Conscious of liability to error, and preferring that the reader should judge for himself, I give the main circumstances upon which this impression is based. Soon after the central insular government was set up, in 1901, Judge Taft and certain other members of the Philippine Commission, the Professor among the number, came into my judicial district to organize provincial governments. Their coming to each town where they stopped was telegraphed in advance, and before they reached the town where I then was holding court each one of the American colony of the town was designated by common consent to look after a fraction of the Taft party during their stay. The Professor fell to my lot. I always was unlucky. However, their stay was only a few hours. While they were there, I had occasion to observe that the Professor spoke Spanish quite well and so remarked to him. The well-bred reply was: "You'll find that I know a great many things you might not think I knew." Whether this was merely "The insolence of office" cropping out in a previously obscure young man suddenly elevated to high station, or whether it was an evidence of the Commissioner's idea of the relation of the Executive Department of a government to its Judiciary, is a question.1 At all events I think the incident gives an insight into the man not irrelevant to what is hereinafter submitted. I have met a number of other Americans since who had received impressions similar to my own. And the Professor's whole subsequent course in the Islands corroborates those impressions. I have never talked to any American in the Philippines who had a good word for him. Of course, Power, like Property, will always have friends. So that even Professor Worcester may have *some* friends, among his fellow-countrymen in those far-away Islands. But it has already been made clear in a former chapter how entirely possible it is for a man occupying high position in the government out there to be very generally and cordially disliked by his own countrymen there and actually not know it. Whether this is true of Professor Worcester, or not, as a general proposition it is quite possible. One thing is certain, namely, that he is very generally and very cordially detested by the Filipinos. That this detestation is perfectly natural under the circumstances, and entirely justifiable, and that it is a cruel injustice to those people, as well as a monumental piece of folly, to keep the Professor saddled upon them, it is now in order to show.

In Chapter VI (*ante*), we made the acquaintance of two young naval officers. Paymaster W. B. Wilcox and Naval Cadet L. R. Sargent, who, in the fall of 1898, while the fate of the Philippines hung in the balance at Paris, and peace still reigned in the Islands between us and the Filipinos, made a trip through the interior of Luzon, covering some six hundred miles, and afterwards furnished Admiral Dewey with a written report of their trip, which was later published as a Senate document. Professor Worcester's greatest value to President Taft, and also the thing out of which has grown, most unfortunately, what seems to be a very cordial mutual hatred between him and the Filipinos, is his activities in the matter of discovering, getting acquainted with, classifying, tabulating, enumerating, and otherwise preparing for salvation, the various non-Christian tribes. These tribes have already been briefly dealt with in Chapter XXI. (*ante*), apropos of that part of the Great Peace Certificate of 1907 which related to the "Moros and other non-Christian tribes"—uncivilized tribes which, being as distinct from the great mass of the Filipino people as islets from the sea, had had no more to do with the insurrection against us, than the Pawnees, Apaches, and Sioux Indians had to do with our Civil War of 1861–5. They were also dealt with, somewhat, in the chapter preceding this. Long before Professor Worcester was permanently inflicted upon the Filipino people, one of the young naval officers above mentioned, Mr. Sargent, published an article in the*Outlook* for September 2, 1899,2 based on this trip through the interior of Luzon, made by authority of Admiral Dewey the year before. In the course of his article Mr. Sargent says:

Some years ago, at an exposition held at Barcelona, Spain, a man and woman were exhibited as representative types of the inhabitants of Luzon. The man wore a loin cloth, and the woman a scanty skirt. It was evident that they belonged to the lowest plane of savagery.

He adds:

I think no deeper wound was ever inflicted upon the pride of the real Filipino people than that caused by this exhibition, the knowledge of which seems to have spread throughout the island. The man and woman, while actually natives of Luzon, were captives of a wild tribe of Igorrotes of the hills.

Professor Worcester was originally a professor of zoölogy, or something of that sort, in a western university. In the early nineties he had made a trip to the Philippines, confining himself then mostly to creeping things and quadrupeds—lizards, alligators, pythons, unusual wild beasts, and other forms of animal life of the kind much coveted as specimens by museums and universities. In 1899, just after the Spanish War, he got out a book on the Philippines, and as an American who had been in the Philippines was then a *rara avis*, it came to pass that the reptile-finder ultimately became a statesman. He was brought, possibly by conscious worth, to the notice of President McKinley, accompanied the Schurman Commission to the Islands, in 1899, and the Taft Commission in 1900, and finally evolved into his present eminence as Secretary of the Interior and official chief finder of non-Christian tribes for the Philippine Government.

The best known of the wild tribes in the Philippines are the Igorrotes, the dog-eating savages you saw at the St. Louis Exposition in 1903–4, the same Mr. Sargent speaks of in his article in the *Outlook*. Of course it was not a desire to misrepresent the situation, but only the enthusiasm of a zoölogist, anthropologically inclined, and accustomed to carry a kodak, which started the Professor to photographing the dog-eating Igorrotes and specimens of other non-Christian tribes soon after the Taft Commission reached the Philippines. But you cannot get far in the earlier reports of the Taft Commission, which was supposed to have been sent out to report back on the capacity of the Filipinos for self-government, without crossing the trail of the Professor's kodak—pictures of naked Igorrotes and the like. This, however innocent, must have been of distinct political value in 1900 and 1904 in causing the heart of the missionary vote in the United States to bleed for those "sixty different tribes having sixty different languages" of which Secretary Root's campaign speeches made so much. It must also have greatly awakened the philanthropic interest of exporters of cotton goods to learn of those poor "savage millions" wearing only a loin cloth, when they could be wearing yards of cotton cloth. By the time the St. Louis Exposition came off, in 1903–4, it was decided to have the various tribes represented there. So specimens were sent of the Igorrote tribe, the Tagalos, the Visayans, the Negrito tribe, and various other tribes. The Tagalos, the Visayans, etc., being ordinary Filipinos, did not prove money-makers. But it was great sport to watch the Igorrotes preparing their morning dog. So it was the "non-Christian tribes" that paid. It was they that were most advertised. It was the recollection of them that lingered longest with the visitor to the Exposition, and there was always in his mind thereafter an association of ideas between the Igorrotes and Filipino capacity for self-government generally. Many representative Filipinos visited the St. Louis Exposition, saw all this, and came home and told about it. One very excellent Filipino gentleman, a friend of mine, who was Governor of Samar during my administration of the district which included that island, sent me one day in October, 1904, a satirical note, enclosing a pamphlet he had just received called *Catalogue of Philippine Views at the St. Louis Exposition*. He knew I would understand, so he said in the note, that the pamphlet was sent "in order that you may learn something of certain tribes *still extant* in this country." Concerning all this, I can say of my own knowledge exactly what Naval Cadet

Sargent said concerning the lesser like indignity of the *one* Igorrote couple exhibited at Barcelona *while the Filipinos were asking representation in the Spanish Cortes, viz.*:

I think no deeper wound was ever inflicted upon the pride of the real Filipino people than that caused by this exhibition, the knowledge of which seems to have spread throughout the islands.

You see our Census of 1903 gave the population of the Philippines at about 7,600,000 of which 7,000,000 are put down as civilized Christians; and of the remaining 600,000, about half are the savage, or semi-civilized, crudely Mohammedan Moros, in Mindanao, and the adjacent islets down near Borneo. The other 300,000 or so uncivilized people scattered throughout the rest of the archipelago, the "non-Christian tribes," which dwell in the mountain fastnesses, remote from "the madding crowd," cut little more figure, if any, in the general political equation, than the American Indian does with us to-day. Take for instance the province of Nueva Vizcaya, in the heart of north central Luzon. That was one of the provinces of the First Judicial District I presided over in the Islands. I think Nueva Vizcaya is Professor Worcester's "brag" province, in the matter of non-Christian anthropological specimens, both regarding their number and their variety. Yet while I was there, though we knew those people were up in the hills, and that there were a good many of them, the civilized people all told us that the hill-tribes never bothered them. And on their advice I have ridden in safety, unarmed, at night, accompanied only by the court stenographer, over the main high-road running through the central plateau that constitutes the bulk of Nueva Vizcaya province, said plateau being surrounded by a great amphitheatre of hills, the habitat of the Worcester pets.

The non-Christian tribes in the Philippines have been more widely advertised in America than anything else connected with the Islands. That advertisement has done more harm to the cause of Philippine independence by depreciating American conceptions concerning Filipino capacity for self-government, than anything that could be devised even by the cruel ingenuity of studied mendacity. And Professor Worcester is the P. T. Barnum of the "non-Christian tribe" industry. The Filipinos, though unacquainted with the career of the famous menagerie proprietor *last* named, and his famous remark: "The American people love to be humbugged," understand the malign and far-reaching influence upon their future destiny of the work of Professor Worcester, and his services to the present Philippine policy of indefinite retention with undeclared intention, through humbugging the American people into the belief that the Islands must be retained until the three hundred thousand or so Negritos, Igorrotes, and other primitive wild peoples sprinkled throughout the archipelago are "reconstructed." Is it any wonder that the Filipinos do not love the Professor? To keep him saddled upon them as one of their rulers is as tactful as it would be to send Senator Tillman on a diplomatic mission to Liberia or Haiti.

Not long ago the famous magazine publisher Mr. S. S. McClure, who, I think, is trying to make his life one of large and genuine usefulness for good, said to me that if we gave the Filipinos self-government we would shortly have another Haiti or Santo Domingo on our hands. He must have seen some of Professor Worcester's pictures of Igorrotes and Negritos scattered through public documents related to the question of Filipino capacity for self-government. Mr. McClure has never, I believe, been in the Islands; and the cruelly unjust impression he had innocently received was precisely the impression systematically developed all these years through the Worcester kodak.

In February, 1911, there appeared an article in the *Sunset* magazine for that month entitled "The Philippines as I Saw them." The contributor of the article is no less a personage than the Honorable James F. Smith, former Governor-General of the Islands. At the top of the article one reads the legend "Illustrated by Photographs through the Courtesy of the Bureau of Insular Affairs." If you read this legend understandingly, you can, in so doing, hear the click of the Worcester kodak. General Smith's article is smeared all over with such pictures. One is merrily entitled "Eighteen Igorrot Fledglings Hatched by the American Bird of Freedom." Another is entitled "Subano Man and woman, Mindanao." Another is a picture of an Ifugao home in the province of Nueva Vizcaya, hereinabove mentioned. Ifugao is the name of one of the wild tribes, one of the results of Professor Worcester's anthropological excavations of the last few years. In front of the Ifugao home stands the master of the house, clothed in a breech-clout. Next in the menagerie in the article under consideration you find a group of Ifugao children, then a Bagobo of Mindanao, then some other specimen with a curious name, in which there is a woman naked from the waist up and a man in a loin-cloth. Then follows a picture of a Tingyan girl from Abra province. And, to cap the climax, among the last of these pictures you find a Filipino couple pounding rice. The rice pounders are ordinary Filipinos. The woman is decently dressed; the man is clothed only from the waist down, having divested himself of his upper garment, as is customary in order to work at hard labor more comfortably in hot weather. I do not so much blame General Smith for this libellous panorama of pictures, scattered though they are through an article by him on "The Philippines as I Saw them." He probably illustrated his article with what the Bureau of Insular Affairs sent him, without giving much thought to the matter. But the Bureau of Insular Affairs appears to neglect no occasion to parade the Philippine archipelago's sprinkling of non-Christian tribes before the American public, fully knowing that the hopes of the Filipinos for independence must depend upon impressions received by the American people concerning the degree of civilization they have reached.

For all these wanton indignities offered their pride and self-respect, the Filipinos well know they are primarily indebted to Professor Worcester and his non-Christian tribe bureau. The feud between the Professor and the Filipino people—the bad blood has been growing so long that the incident hereinafter related justifies its being called a feud—has been peculiarly embittered by the missionary aspect of the non-Christian industry. The great body of the Filipino people, the whole six or seven millions of them, are Catholics—most of them devout Catholics. Presumably, their desire for salvation by the method handed down by their forefathers would not be affected by a change from American political supervision to independence. Yet the darkest thing ahead of Philippine independence prospects is the Protestant missionary vote in the United States. Bishop Brent, Episcopal Bishop of the Philippines, one of the noblest and most saintly characters that ever lived, has devoted his life apparently to missionary work in the Philippines, having twice declined a nomination as Bishop of Washington (D.C.). The only field of endeavor open to Bishop Brent and his devoted little band of co-workers is the non-Christian tribes. It seems that the Catholic and Protestant ecclesiastical authorities in the Islands get along harmoniously, a kind of *modus vivendi* having been arranged between them, by which the Protestants are not to do any proselyting among the seven millions of Catholic Christians. So this field of endeavor is the one Professor Worcester has been industriously preparing during the last twelve years. Obviously, every time Professor Worcester digs up a new non-Christian tribe he increases the prospective harvest of the Protestants, thus corralling more missionary vote at home for permanent retention of the Philippines. Professor Worcester is quoted in a Manila paper as saying, "I am under no delusion as to what may be accomplished for the primitive wild people. It takes time to reconstruct them." This remark is supposed to have been made in a speech before the Young Men's Christian Association of Manila. Neither is Mr. Taft under any delusion as to how valuable is religious support for the idea of retaining the Philippines as a missionary field. The nature of the above allusion to Bishop Brent should certainly be sufficient to show that the writer yields to no one in affectionate reverence and respect for that rare and noble character. But neither Bishop Brent nor any one else can persuade him that it is wise to abandon the principle that Church and State should be separate, in order that our government may go into the missionary business. Since it has become apparent that the Philippines will not pay, the Administration has relied solely on missionary sentiment. In one of his public utterances Mr. Taft has said in effect, "The programme of the Republican party with regard to the Philippines is one which will make greatly for the spread of Christian civilization throughout the Orient."

The foregoing reflections are not intended to raise an issue as to the wisdom of foreign missions. They are simply intended to illustrate how it is possible and natural for President Taft to consider Professor Worcester "the most valuable man we have on the Philippine Commission." The Professor's menagerie is a vote-getter. Also, President Taft's whole Philippine policy being founded upon the theory that "the great majority" of the Filipino people are in favor of alien thraldom in lieu of independence, he tolerantly permits their editors to "let off steam" through clamor for independence. This privilege they do not fail to exercise to the limit. The attitude of the Insular Government permits the native press much latitude of "sauciness," in deference to the American idea about liberty of the press. In the exercise of this privilege during the last few years the native press has gone the limit. However, there was no way to stop them, on the principle to which we had committed ourselves. The thing was very mischievous, and became utterly intolerable. There was a native paper called *Renacimiento* (Renaissance). This paper was long permitted to say things more or less seditious in character which no self-respecting government should have tolerated. This was done pursuant to the original theory, obstinately adhered to up to date, that there was no real substantial unwillingness to American rule. Of course, if this were true, newspaper noise could do no harm. Therefore it was permitted to continue. Finally, however, like a boy "taking a dare," the *Renacimiento* published an article on Professor Worcester which intimately and sympathetically voiced the general yearning of the Filipino people to be rid of the Professor. In so doing, however, the hapless editor overstepped the limits of American license, and got into the toils of the law, by saying things about the Professor that rendered the editor liable to prosecution for criminal libel. The Professor promptly took advantage of this misstep, to the great joy of the authorities, who had been previously much goaded by independence clamor. The result was that the paper was put out of business and the editor was put in jail. No doubt the editor ought to have been put in jail, but his incarceration incidentally served to tone down Filipino clamor for independence. Subsequent to this *coup d'état*, the Professor did a little venting of feelings in his turn. He made a speech at the Y. M. C. A. on October 10, 1910, which was a highly unchristian speech to be gotten off in an edifice dedicated to the service of Christ. The Manila papers give only extracts from the speech, and I have never seen a copy of it. From the newspaper accounts, it seems that the Professor was determined to, and did, relieve his feelings about the Filipinos. The Manila*Cable-News* of October 11, 1910, quotes the Professor as referring to his pets, the non-Christian tribes, as "ancestral enemies of the Christians." Thus for the first time is developed an attitude of being champion of the uncivilized pagan remnant, left from prehistoric times, against the Christians of the Islands. The *Cable-News* also says that Professor Worcester "laughed at the idea that the Islands belonged to the *so-called civilized* people and held that if the archipelago belonged to any one it certainly belonged to its original owners the Negritos." This remark about the "*so-called civilized people*" was as tactful as if President Taft should address a meeting of colored people in a doubtful state and call them "niggers." Another of the Manila papers gives an account of the speech from which it appears that the burly Professor succeeded in amusing himself at least, if not his audience, by suggestions as to the superior fighting qualities of the Moros over the Filipinos, which suggestions were on the idea that the Moros would lick the Filipinos if we should leave the country. (The Moros number 300,000, the Filipinos nearly 7,000,000.) The Professor's remarks in this regard, according to the paper, were a distinct reflection upon the courage of the Filipinos generally as a people. The effect of Professor Worcester's speech before the Y. M. C. A. may be well imagined. However the facts of history do not leave the imagination unaided. The Philippine Assembly, representing the whole Filipino people, and desiring to express the unanimous feeling of those people with regard to the Worcester speech, unanimously passed, soon after the speech was delivered, a set of resolutions whereof the following is a translation:

Resolved that the regret of the Assembly be recorded for the language attributed to the Honorable Dean C. Worcester, Secretary of the Interior of the Philippine Government in a discourse before the Young Men's Christian Association, October 10, 1910. It is improper and censurable in a man who holds a public office and who has the confidence of the government. And as the statements made as facts are false, slanderous, and offensive to the Philippine people, their publication is a grave violation of the instructions given by President McKinley which required that public functionaries should respect the sensibilities, beliefs, and sentiments of the Philippine people, and should show them consideration. The words and the conduct of Mr. Worcester tend to sow distrust between the Americans and the Filipinos, whose aspirations and duties should not separate them but unite them in the pathway which leads to the progress and emancipation of the Philippine people. The influence of Mr. Worcester has caused injury to the feelings of the Filipinos, *encouraged race hatred, and tended to frustrate the task undertaken by men of real good will* to win the esteem, confidence, and respect of the Philippine people for the Americans.

Resolved further that this House desires that these facts should be communicated to the President of the United States through the Governor of the Philippines and the Secretary of War.

Presumably these resolutions were forwarded "to the President of the United States through the Governor of the Philippines and the Secretary of War." But apparently they were pigeonholed when they reached Washington. I stumbled on them in the Insular Affairs Committee of the House of Representatives whither they had landed through Mr. Slayden of Texas. The distinguished veteran Congressman from Texas, being known as an enemy of all wrong things, was appealed to by certain persons in the United States to bring the matter to the attention of Congress. He did so by presenting to the House of Representatives an American petition which embodied a copy of the resolutions of the Philippine Assembly.

It thus becomes apparent that one of Professor Worcester's principal elements of value is in bullying the Filipinos, and thereby smothering manifestations of a desire for independence, the existence of which desire is denied by President Taft's Administration. The more the Filipinos cry for independence the greater seems the sin of holding them in subjection. So that Professor Worcester is very valuable in silencing independence clamor and thereby creating an appearance of consent of the governed, when there is no consent of the governed whatsoever.

In describing the discontent in distant provinces under brutal pro-consuls, which contributed largely to the final disintegration of the Roman Empire, Gibbon says:

The cry of remote distress is ever faintly heard.

The total failure of the above temperate, dignified, and vibrant protest of the Philippine Assembly to reach the ears of the American people is but another reminder that history repeats itself.

---

[1] The greatest defect of the Philippine Government was in the beginning, and still is, that the Philippine Commission, which is the executive authority, controls the appointment and assignment of the trial judges, and also, largely, their chances for promotion to the Supreme Bench of the Islands. The Justices of the Supreme Court are appointed by the President of the United States, often on recommendation of the Commission, but thereafter they are absolutely independent. The trial judges ought also to be appointed by the President of the United States.

[2] Republished, *Congressional Record*, January 9, 1900, p. 715.

Chapter XXIV. The Philippine Civil Service

Is our Occupation of the Philippines to be temporary, like our occupation of Cuba after the Spanish War, or "temporary" like the British Occupation of Egypt since 1882? *The Unsettled Question.*

The policy to be pursued is for Congress to determine. I have no authority to speak for Congress in respect to the ultimate disposition of the Islands.

Secretary of War WM. H. TAFT to Philippine Assembly, 1907.

The Act of Congress of July 1, 1902, known as the Philippine Government Act, is entitled "An Act *temporarily* to provide" a government for the Philippine Islands. The young American who goes out to the Philippines to take a position with the Insular Government there has usually read his share of Kipling, and his imagination likes to analogize his prospective employment to the British Indian Civil Service. The latter, however, offers a career. But what does the former offer? Take the prospects of the rank and file, as set forth by Mr. J. R. Arnold, of the Executive Bureau of the Philippine Government, in an article published in the *North American Review* for February, 1912. Suppose a young man goes out to the Philippines at a salary of $1200. Mr. Arnold discusses fully and frankly the cost of living in the Islands, and how much higher board, lodging, etc., are out there than in the United States. He states that board and lodging will cost $15 to $20 a month more than here. So that, so far, a salary of $1200 in the Philippines would seem equivalent to a salary of say approximately $950 in the United States—say in Washington. Also he calls attention to the fact that the government will pay your way *out*, but you must get back the best way you can. He does not say so, but the walking is not good all the way from Manila to Washington. Seriously, according to the authority from whom we are quoting, it costs $225 to $300 to get back. So if you come back at the end of a three years' stay—you must contract to stay at least that long—you must have laid by, taking his maximum return fare as the more prudent figure to reckon on, one hundred dollars a year to buy your return ticket. Mr. Arnold does not say so, but it is a fact, that various little expenses *will* creep in that are sure to amount, even with the most rigidly frugal, to $50 per annum that you would never have spent in the United States. You are hardly respectable in the Philippines if you do not have a *muchacho*. *Muchacho*, in Spanish, means the same as *garçon* in French, or valet in English. But *muchachos* are as thick as cigarettes in the Philippines. And you can hire one for about $5 a month. To resolve not to have a *muchacho* in the Philippines would be like resolving at home never to have your shoes shined, or your clothes pressed. It would be contrary to the universal custom of the country, and would therefore be "impossible." You have not been long in the Philippines before you get tired of telling applicants for the position of *muchacho* that you do not want one, and, benumbed by the universal custom, you accept the last applicant. You *must* figure on a *muchacho* as one of your "fixed charges." Count then an extra $50 annual necessary expense that you would not have at home. If you do not succumb to the *muchacho* custom, you will get rid of the $50 in other ways fairly classifiable as necessary current expenses. Thus, if you take from your $1200, worth $950 in Manila, as above stated, the $100 per annum necessary to be laid by against your home-coming, and the other $50 last suggested, your salary of $1200 per annum in Manila becomes equivalent to one of $800 at home, so far as regards what you are likely to save by strict habits of economy. In other words, to figure how you are going to come out in the long run, if you go out as a $1200 man, while your social position will be precisely that of a man commanding the same salary in a government position in Washington, you must knock off a third of the $1200. This is not the way Mr. Arnold states the case exactly. I am simply taking his facts, supplemented by what little I have added, and stating them in a way which will perhaps illustrate the case better to some people. Mr. Arnold says you are apt to get up as high as $1500 and finally even to $1800 in three to five years.

Suppose you do have that luck. Still, if, as has been made plain above, you must consider $1200 in Manila as equal to only $800 in Washington (so far as regards what you are going to be able to save each year), by the same token you must consider $1500 in Manila as being equal to only $1000 in Washington, and $1800 as only $1200.

The utmost limit of achievement in the Philippine Government service, the only one of the higher positions not subject to political caprice, the only one regarded out there as a "life position"—and this excepts neither the Governorship of the Islands nor the Commissionerships—is the position of Justice of the Supreme Court. The salary is $10,000 per annum, American money. But there is not an American judge on that bench who would not be glad at any moment to accept a $5000 position as a United States District Judge at home. All of them whom I know are most happily married. But I believe their wives would quit them if they refused such an offer from the President of the United States, or else get so unhappy about it that they would accept and come home.

While we have now considered the case from bottom to top, we did not originally figure on the young American going out to the Philippines otherwise than single. In this behalf Mr. Arnold himself says:

I do not think it can be fairly called other than risky for an American to attempt to practise love in a cottage in the Philippines.

Says the late Arthur W. Fergusson—who gave his life to the Philippine Civil Service—in his annual report for 1905, as Executive Secretary:

The one great stumbling-block, and which no legislative body can eradicate, is the fact that very few Americans intend to make the Philippines their permanent home, or even stay here for any extended period. This is doubtless due to the location of the islands, their isolation from centres of civilization and culture, the enervating climate, lack of entertainment and desirable companionship, and distance from the homeland. *Every clerk*, no matter what his ideals or aspirations, *realizes after coming here that he must at some time in the future return to the United States and begin all over again.* After spending a year or more in the islands, the realization that the sooner the change is made the better, becomes more acute. This condition causes, doubtless, the class of men who are not adventurous or fond of visiting strange climes to think twice before accepting an appointment for service in these islands, and generally to remain away, and a great majority of those who do come here to leave the service again after a very short period of duty.1

Then Mr. Fergusson comes to the obvious but apparently unattainable remedy, which he says is

to make a Philippine appointment a permanent means of livelihood by providing an effective system of transfers to the Federal service after a reasonable period of service here. * * * Under the present regulations *influence must be brought to bear at Washington* in order that requisition may be made by the Chief of some bureau there for the services of a clerk desiring to transfer.

You see, if a Washington Bureau, say the Coast and Geodetic Survey, or the Geological Survey, sends a man out to the Islands, he is never for a moment separated from the Federal Civil Service or the Federal Government's pay-roll. The same is true of civilian employees of the army. But the man in the Insular Service, when he wants to get back home, is little better off than if he were in the employ of the Cuban Government, or the British Indian Government, or that of the Dutch East Indies. Mr. Fergusson also says:

It is believed to be useless to try to influence men to come out here unless there is something *permanent* offered to them at the expiration of a reasonable term of service. * * * *The average European is content to live and die "east of Suez"; the average American is not.* * * * I am firmly convinced that a *permanent* service under present conditions is entirely out of the question.

How can you have "a *permanent* service" unless you have a definite declared policy? Why not declare the purpose of our Government with the regard to the Islands?

In his annual report for 1906[2] Mr. Fergusson says:

Our relations to the islands are such that the education and specialization of a distinct body of high class men purposely for this service as is done in England for the Indian service, will probably be always a practical impossibility.

He then goes on to reiterate his annual plea for a law providing for transfer as *a matter of right, not of influence*, from the Philippine Civil Service to the Federal Civil Service in the United States, and tells of a very capable official of his bureau who got a chance during the year just closed to transfer from the Philippines to a $1400 government position in the United States, and was glad to get it, although $1400 was "considerably less than half what he received here." Mr. Fergusson quickly gives the key to all this in what he calls "the haunting fear of having to return to the States *in debilitated health and out of touch with existent conditions, only to face the necessity of seeking a new position.*" He adds:

That this is not a mere theory is proven by the number of army (civilian) employees who contentedly remain year after year.

In 1907, Mr. Fergusson reports on the same subject[3]: "Matters do not seem to be improving," and that the Director of the Insular Civil Service informs him that "during the fiscal year there were *five hundred voluntary separations from the service by Americans*, of whom one hundred were college graduates." He adds: "When *the expense of getting and bringing out new men, and of training them to their new work is considered*, the *wastefulness of the present system is evident.*"

You do not find any quotations from any of the Fergusson disclosures in Mr. Arnold's *North American Review* article. He would probably have lost his job, if he had quoted them. Yet the evils pointed out by Mr. Fergusson come from one permanent source, the uncertainty of the future of every American out there, due to the failure of Congress to declare the purpose of the Government.

On January 30, 1908, Arthur W. Fergusson died in the service of the Philippine Government. No general law putting that service on the basis he pleaded for to the day of his death has ever yet been passed. Since his death, his tactful successor appears to have abandoned further pleading, and concluded to worry along with the permanently lame conditions inherent in the uncertainty as to whether we are to keep the Islands permanently or not, rather than embarrass President Taft by discouraging young Americans from going to the Islands.

The report of the Governor-General of the Philippines for 1907, Governor Smith, says[4]:

American officials and employees have rarely made up their minds to cast their fortunes definitely with the Philippines or to make governmental service in the tropics a career. Many of those who in the beginning were so minded, due to ill health or the longing to return to friends or relatives, changed front and preferred to return to the home land, there to enjoy life at half the salary in the environment to which they were accustomed. * * * That which operates probably more than anything else to induce good men drawing good salaries to abandon the service * * * is the knowledge that they have nothing to look forward to when broken health or old age shall have rendered them valueless to the government.

If Congress should ever care to do anything to improve the Philippine Civil Service and the status of Americans entering the same, certainly the one supremely obvious thing to do is to make transfer back to the civil service in the United States after a term of duty in the Islands *a matter of right.*

1See *Report U. S. Philippine Commission*, 1905, pt. 1, p. 89 *et seq.*

2*Report Philippine Commission*, 1906, pt. 1, p. 99.

3*U. S. Philippine Commission Report*, 1907, pt. 1, p. 149.

4See *Report Philippine Commission for 1907*, pt. 1, p. 80.

Chapter XXV. Cost of the Philippines

If 't were well to do right, 't were better still if 't were more profitable.

Cynic Maxims.

General Otis's annual report for 1899,[1] dated August 31st, gives the number of Americans killed in battle in the Philippines, from the beginning of the American occupation to that date, as 380. This includes those wounded who afterwards died of such wounds. His report for 1900,[2] covering the period from his 1899 report to May 5, 1900, gives the number of Americans killed in battle from August 31, 1899, to May 1, 1900, as 258. General MacArthur succeeded General Otis in command of the American forces in the Philippines on May 5, 1900. General MacArthur's annual report for 1901,[3] gives the number of Americans killed in battle between May 5, 1900, and June 30, 1901, as 245. Thus the total number of Americans killed in battle up to the time the Civil Government was set up in 1901, was 883. The military reports do not always give the insurgents killed during the periods they cover. But on June 4, 1900, as we saw in a previous chapter, General MacArthur reported the number of Filipinos killed up to that time, so far as our records showed, to be something over 10,000. General MacArthur's report, above quoted, giving our killed for the period it covers (May 5, 1900, to June 30, 1901), at 245, gives the insurgent killed for the same period as 3854. If we add this 3854 to the 10,000 killed up to about where May merged into June in 1900, we have 13,854 Filipinos killed up to the time Judge Taft was inaugurated as Governor, in 1901. There was no record, of course, obtainable or attempted, by the Eighth Army Corps, of Filipinos who were wounded and not captured and who subsequently died. It is quite safe to assume that such fatalities must have swelled the enemy's list up to the time of the setting up of the Civil Government far above 16,000 killed. Thus, as has heretofore been stated, the ratio of the enemy's loss to our loss was, literally, at least 16 to 1, up to the time the civil government was set up. General MacArthur's report for 1900[4] would seem to bear out the above ratio. He there gives the number of our killed, from November 1, 1899, to September 1, 1900, including the wounded who afterwards died of such wounds, at 268, and the Filipinos killed, "as far as of record," 3227. While these last figures make our killed for the period they relate to, considerably over 200, and the enemy's killed but a very small figure over 3200, still, making allowances for the enemy's wounded that died afterwards, of which of course we have no record, the 16 to 1 ratio would seem to give a fairly accurate probable estimate of the relative loss of life.

These figures are explained by the facts, already noticed hereinbefore, that most of our people knew how to shoot and the Filipinos did not. The great part of their army were raw recruits who did not understand the use of two sights on a rifle, and frequently relied solely on the one at the muzzle, not even lifting up the sight near the lock which when not in use lies flat along the gun-barrel, with the result that they almost invariably got the range too high and shot over our heads.

Because the military reports overlap each other in many instances, it is not possible to state accurately how many men the Eighth Army Corps lost by disease, but our loss chargeable to this account was not far from our fatalities on the battlefield.5

It is not possible to even approximate the enemy's loss other than on the battlefield. The United States Coast and Geodetic Survey Philippine Atlas gives the table estimating the population of the various provinces of the Philippine archipelago prior to the American occupation. This estimate gives the population of Batangas province at 312,192. *The American Census of the Philippines of 1903* gives the population of Batangas province at 257,715.6 This would present a difference in the population of Batangas prior to 1898 and its population after the war of 54,477. The provincial secretary of Batangas province made a report to Governor Taft on December 18, 19017 on the condition of the province generally. This report, as it appears in the Senate Document, is a translation from the Spanish. The portion which relates to the reduction of the population of Batangas province reads as follows:

The mortality, caused no longer by the war, but by disease, such as malaria and dysentery, has reduced to a little over 200,000 the more than 300,000 inhabitants which in former years the province had.

Of course these appalling figures8 must be taken with a grain of salt. In the first place, the man who furnished them was merely reproducing the general impression of his neighbors as to the diminution of the population of the province. He does not pretend to be dealing with official statistics. On the other hand, all of the yearly reports of the various native provincial officers are, as a general rule, pathetically optimistic. They all seem to think it their duty to present a hopeful view of the situation. In fact if you read these reports one after the other, the various signers seem to vie with one another in optimism as if their tenure of office depended upon it. So that, balancing probabilities, it would seem unlikely that the provincial secretary of Batangas would have stated more than what he at least believed to represent actual conditions, and the results of the war. A comparison of the Atlas population tables above mentioned with the census tables of 1903 shows no very startling difference in the population of any of the other provinces of the archipelago before and after the war except Batangas. It is also notorious that Batangas suffered by the war more than any other province in the Philippine Islands. However, a glance at the table of population of the various provinces of the Census of 19039 shows you fifty provinces with a total of 7,635,426 people. While we will never know whether Batangas did or did not lose one hundred thousand as a result of the war and its consequences, still, if it did, the other forty-nine provinces above mentioned must have lost as many more, that is to say, must have lost another hundred thousand. So that while it is all a matter of surmise, with nothing more certain to go on than the foregoing, it would really seem by no means absurd to assume the Filipino loss of life, other than on the battlefield, caused by the war, and the famine, pestilence, and other disease consequent thereon, at not far from 200,000 people. In more than one province, the people died like flies, especially the women and children, as a result of conditions incident to and consequent upon the war. This will not seem an over-statement to men who have lived much among people that do not know much about how to take care of themselves in the midst of great calamities, people who *will* eat meat of animals carried off by disease, in time of famine; who *will* drink water contaminated by what may for euphony be called sewage; and who are unprovided with any save traditional home remedies against cholera, small-pox, etc.

As to the cost of the Philippines in money, it used to be said in the early days that we paid $20,000,000 for a $200,000,000 insurrection. Just what the Islands have cost us up to date in money it is utterly impossible to figure out with any degree of certainty, except that a safe minimum may be arrived at. Said the distinguished Congressman from Texas, Honorable James L. Slayden, in a speech which appears in the *Congressional Record* of February 25, 1908 (pp. 2532 *et seq.*):

On this point, and in reply to a resolution of the Senate in 1902, the Secretary of War reported that the cost of the army in the Philippines from June 30, 1898, to July 1, 1902, had been $169,853,512.00. To this let us add $114,515,643.00, the admitted cost of the army in the Philippines from May 1, 1902, to June 30, 1907, and we will have a grand total of $284,369,155.00. That does not take into account the additional cost of the navy.

Nor, be it noted, does it count the $20,000,000 we paid Spain for the Islands, which item, is, however included in another part of Mr. Slayden's speech.

The only other estimate of what the Islands have cost, made in the last few years, which seems to be specially worthy of consideration, is one which appeared in the *New York Evening Post* of March 6, 1907. This estimate was prepared by one of the best trained and most conservative newspaper men in the United States, Mr. Edward G. Lowry, then Washington correspondent of the *Evening Post*, and since 1911, its managing editor. The total which Mr. Lowry arrives at is $308,369,155, up to that time. There have been various absurd estimates made recklessly without knowledge, but Mr. Lowry's estimate is very carefully studied out, and presented in detail in the newspaper referred to. From the testimony of Mr. Slayden and Mr. Lowry, given as a result of their inquiries into the matter, it would thus seem that the Islands must have cost us by the end of 1907 something like $300,000,000. The Insular Government is now self-sustaining, except as to military affairs.

The cost per annum of the Philippine (native) scouts, of which there are 4000, is paid out of the United States Treasury, and amounts to $2,000,000 per annum.[10] The number of American troops in the islands for the last few years has been about 12,000. Those who are wedded to the present Philippine policy of indefinite retention with undeclared intention, insist that our military expenses in the Philippines, in respect to the regular army out there, are not fairly chargeable as a part of the current expenses of the Philippine occupation. This argument must be admitted to have some force as far as the navy is concerned, but as to the army it is clearly without merit. Under the Act of Congress reorganizing the army of the United States after the Spanish War, provision was made for a skeleton army of about 60,000 men capable of expansion to something like 100,000 in time of war. The method of expansion thus contemplated was to have companies of, say, for illustration, sixty men, in time of peace, which companies could be recruited up to a war footing of one hundred men, in time of war. The suggestion that the cost of the part of the regular army which we have to keep in the Philippines is not chargeable to the Philippines because those same troops would have to be somewhere in the United States if they were not where they are, is not well taken. If we did not need 12,000 men continually in the Philippines, the army could be at once reduced by that much without affecting its present organization. If we had no troops in the Philippines this would not mean the absolute elimination from the army of enough *regiments* to represent twelve thousand men. It would not eliminate any existing organization. It would simply mean contraction of the number of men in the several companies of the several regiments of the army toward a peace basis to the extent of a total of twelve thousand men, more or less. The War Department has long figured on the cost of an American soldier in the Philippines per annum including his pay, allowances, and transportation out and back, at $1000 per annum. The cost of 12,000 soldiers at $1000 per annum is $12,000,000, per annum. The conclusion would, therefore, seem inevitable that the extra military current expense chargeable to our occupation of the Philippines is $12,000,000, per annum, outside the Philippine scouts, or, a total of $14,000,000. Even if the Philippines have cost us $300,000,000, that is no reason why we should continue to run a kindergarten for adults out there, and let the Monroe Doctrine run to seed. "Something" *is not* "bound to turn up." The Philippine Islands will *not* prove a blessing in disguise. In every war with a nation having discontented colonial subjects, the enemy will always strike the colony first, and hope for aid from the inhabitants thereof.

Even if the Philippines *have* cost us $300,000,000, we are a nation of nearly 100,000,000 people. So they have cost us, all told, in the neighborhood of only about $3 a piece. And we subjugated them by mistake, after freeing a less capable people, the Cubans.

The Panama Canal is to be finished in 1913. This means a splendid, but free-for-all contest, for the trade of South America. In South America we will meet a tremendous pro-German sentiment, and a by no means inconsiderable anti-"Yankee" sentiment. The bigger Germany's army and navy grows, the more she will loom up as the one great menace to the peace of the world, and the one avowed enemy of the Monroe Doctrine. We need to build up a Pan-American *esprit de corps*, based on the instinct of self-defence. We *must* win the good will of South America, and we cannot do it so long as we insist, in another part of the world, upon the righteousness of the principle of one Christian people policing a weaker Christian people, ostensibly to keep them from having revolutions, and really in the hope of ultimate profit. To free the Filipinos should be the first step we take after the Panama Canal is completed toward getting ourselves foot-loose entirely, with a view of getting everything from the Canadian border to the Argentine wheat fields and beyond, solidly and sincerely *for* the Monroe Doctrine. In that direction lies our only sensible and reasonable hope that the canal will get for us the trade and friendship of South America. With such tremendous issues at stake, what does it matter to the richest nation on earth what the Philippines cost? What does it matter, anyhow, how much it costs to do right?

---

1 *War Department Report*, 1899, vol. i., pt. 4, p. 142.

2 *Ibid.*, pp. 559–560.

3 See *War Department Report*, 1901, vol. i., pt. 4, p. 98.

4 *War Department Report*, vol. i., pt. 5, p. 60.

5 From July 31, 1898, to May 24, 1900, we lost 1138 men by disease. See special report of the Surgeon-General of the Army, *Senate Document 426*, 56th Cong., 1st Sess. By the middle of 1900 our soldiers had pretty well learned how to take care of themselves in the tropics.

6 See vol. ii., p. 102.

7 See *Senate Document 331*, 1902, p. 887.

8 Appalling, because there are forty-nine other provinces besides Batangas.

9 Vol. ii., p. 123.

10 See page 78 of the special report of the Secretary of War Taft on the Philippines, January 23, 1908, transmitted by President Roosevelt to Congress, January 27, 1908, *Senate Document 200*, 60th Cong., 1st Sess.

Chapter XXVI. Congressional Legislation

Taxation without representation is good cause for revolt.

American Speech of 1776.

As a colony of Spain the Philippines enjoyed certain special privileges in the way of trade with the "mother country." When at the beginning of our military occupation in 1898 General Otis detailed an army officer to take charge of the Customs House, he continued for the time being the Spanish tariff laws concerning imports and exports. On September 17, 1901, the Philippine Commission passed a tariff act1 fixing the duties on imports into the Islands and also continuing to a considerable extent the system of duties on Philippine exports inherited from the Spanish régime. Among the products of the Philippine Islands on which the Act of September 17, 1901, imposed an export tax were the following:

Hemp, 75c. per 100 kilos2; sugar, 5c. per 100 kilos; manufactured tobacco, $1.50 per 100 kilos; raw tobacco, $1.50 down to 75c. per 100 kilos.3

On March 8, 1902, the United States Congress passed an Act, "temporarily to provide revenue for the Philippine Islands and for other purposes." The Act of 1902 re-enacted the Commission's tariff law for the Philippines of September 17, 1901, with one change, hereinafter to be discussed, as to its export tax features. As to the tariffs to be collected at our custom-houses on Philippine products shipped to the United States, the Act of 1902 reduced the rates fixed by the Dingley tariff to seventy-five per cent. of said rates. That was all Congress did in the way of lowering our tariff wall to Philippine products until 1909, when the Payne-Aldrich tariff bill became a law. This twenty-five per cent. reduction was no better than no reduction whatever would have been.

Governor Taft pleaded very earnestly with Congress, at the time of the passage of the Philippine Tariff Act of March 8, 1902, for a *substantial* reduction of the Dingley tariff rate on sugar and tobacco, so as to give his "constituents"—his Filipinos—something in lieu of the markets they had had under Spain. But our sugar and tobacco interests defeated his efforts, because they feared what they termed "competition with cheap Asiatic labor."

The Act of Congress of March 8, 1902, repealed the export duties imposed by the Act of the Philippine Commission of September 17, 1901, as to exports to the United States, *leaving unrepealed, however, the export duty on Philippine products shipped to foreign countries*. Section 2 of said Act of 1902 provided, as to exports from the Philippines to the United States, that the rates of duty upon products of the Philippine Archipelago coming into the United States, should be less any duty or tax levied, collected, and paid thereon (under the Act of the Philippine Commission of September 17, 1901, aforesaid) upon the shipment thereof from the Philippine Archipelago. This sounds liberal enough. It is, as far as it goes. But what those familiar with the hemp infamy of the Act of 1902 call "the joker" in it, is as follows:

All *articles*, the growth and product of the Philippine Islands, *admitted* into the ports of the United States *free of duty* under the provisions of this act, and coming directly from said islands to the United States, for use and consumption therein, shall be hereafter exempt from any export duties imposed in the Philippine Islands.

This also sounds liberal, on first reading, but its object was, and its effect has been, to enable the American Hemp Trust to corner and control the Manila hemp industry. *There is but one article of*

*Philippine export which any one in the United States is interested in, that was admitted into the United States free of duty under the Dingley Act.*4 *That article is hemp.* The object of the law was to favor Americans interested in exporting hemp from Manila to the United States as against Europeans exporting it to England and other foreign countries. This does not look, on its face, either unpatriotic or un-Christian. It is not unpatriotic or un-Christian, ordinarily, to favor your own people, as against their foreign competitors. The moral quality of such favoritism, however, must depend on who is to pay for it. Under the Act of 1902, the Manila authorities have always collected an export tax on hemp coming to the United States, just as they do on hemp going from Manila to foreign countries, exactly as if the law abolishing the export tax on hemp coming to the United States had never been passed. Later, on proof that the hemp was *in fact* carried to the United States and used and consumed therein, they refund the export tax. This is on the idea that they cannot tell where the hemp is *going to* until they know where it went to, nor where it is *going to be* "used and consumed" until they know where it *was in fact* finally "used and consumed." Of course the small farmer is in no position to follow his bale of hemp into the markets of the world and show, if it happens to go to the United States, that it did in fact go there and that it was there "used and consumed," and, finally obtaining the proof of this, submit it to the Manila Government and get his little export tax on his bale of hemp refunded. Only the big buyer's agents at Manila are in a position to do this. So the hemp crop is bought and moved under conditions which are the same as if *all* hemp were subject to an export tax. And only the big fish get the benefit. For instance, the International Harvester Company has its hemp buyers at Manila. And as to the part of the Philippine hemp crop it handles, it can, of course, follow the hemp to its ultimate consumption in the United States, make the proof, and get the refund.

The wealth of the Philippines is practically entirely agricultural. Neither mining nor manufactures cut any appreciable figure. Hemp, sugar, tobacco, and copra5 are the chief staples and main exports, and of the first of these Secretary of War Taft says in one of his reports:6

The chief export in value and quantity from the Philippines is Manila hemp, it amounting to between 60 and 65 per cent. of the total exports.

Let us see just how far, according to the annual reports of our own agents in the Philippines—those charged by us with governing them,—this piece of legislation gotten through by "special privilege" has depressed the Manila hemp industry, the chief source of wealth of the Islands. And before we even get to the main trouble, let us permit the Insular Government to "place on the screen," as a preliminary "view," a glance at what the instinct of self-preservation of American sugar and tobacco interests, fearing competition from "cheap Asiatic labor," have deemed it necessary to do to the Philippine sugar and tobacco industries, through the Dingley tariff. The annual report of the Philippine Commission for 1904, before it gets to the subject of hemp, draws a most gloomy picture of how we killed the markets for sugar and tobacco the Islands had under Spain, and gave them none instead. They speak of "the languishing state of these industries" (p. 26), and describe a state of affairs that sounds more like Egypt under Pharaoh than anything else, including a cattle disease that carried off ninety per cent. of the beasts of burden of the country, and wholesale destruction of crops by locusts.7 What they have to say of the annual tribute levied by the American Hemp Trust, through Congress, on the Manila hemp industry, should not be re-stated, but quoted. They say:8

We desire to call attention to the injustice effected upon the revenues of the islands by section 2 of the Act of Congress approved March 8, 1902, which provides that the Philippine Government shall refund all export duties imposed upon articles exported from the islands into and consumed in the United States. Under the provisions of this section there has been collected in the Philippine Islands, since its enactment down to the close of the fiscal year

1904, the sum of $1,060,460.20 United States currency, which is refundable. *These refundable duties are principally upon hemp exportations to the United States, and are in effect a gift of that amount to the manufacturers of the United States who use hemp in their operations.*

They add:

It is manifestly a discrimination in favor of our manufacturers as against those of foreign countries. No good reason is perceived why this *bounty to American manufacturers* should be extracted from the treasury of the Philippine Islands, and it is respectfully submitted that the law authorizing it should be repealed.

The annual report of the Philippine Commission for 1905, after the usual complaint about being made a political football by Benevolent Assimilation on the one side, and Louisiana and our sugar-beet States on the other, and the usual annual and true description of the consequent poverty, says concerning hemp:

We have several times in our reports called attention to the practical workings of that portion of the Act of Congress approved March 8, 1902, which provides for the refund of duties paid on articles exported from the Philippine Islands to the United States and consumed therein, and have as repeatedly recommended its repeal. *It is a direct burden upon the people of the Philippine Islands, because it takes from the insular treasury export duties collected from the people and gives them to manufacturers of hemp products in the United States.* These manufacturers were already prosperous before this bounty was given *them* and *it seems hardly consistent with our expressions of purpose to build up and develop the Philippine Islands when we are* thus enriching a few of our own people at their expense.[9]

By the end of the fiscal year 1905 (June 30), the American importers of Manila hemp—of whom the International Harvester Company and its allied interests are the most influential—had, under the operation of the rebate system based on the Act of 1902, milked the Philippine people to the tune of about $1,000,000. Says the Philippine Commission's annual report for 1905, immediately after the passage last above quoted:

The amount of duties refunded under this act to manufacturers in the United States during the three years ending June 30, 1905, is $1,057,251.12. Many of the departments of the government are much hampered in their operations because of the lack of funds, notably the bureau of education, and were the sum thus taken available for educational purposes, to say nothing of any other, the government would be enabled to give instruction to thousands of Filipino children whom they are now unable to reach and who must remain steeped in ignorance because of the lack of funds to provide such instruction.

Said the Manila Chamber of Commerce to the Taft Congressional party in August, 1905: "The country is in a state of financial collapse."[10]

Says the Philippine Commission's report for 1906 (pt. 1, p. 68):

The Commission has repeatedly called attention in its reports to the action of Congress providing for a refund of duties paid on articles exported from the Islands to the United States and consumed therein. The reasons that led the Commission heretofore to recommend the repeal of that provision are still operative. Since the passage of that act on March 8, 1902, the amount of duties collected and paid into the Philippine treasury and handed over to manufacturers in the United States down to June 30, 1906, is $1,471,208.47. *This money has been taken out of the poverty of the insular treasury to be delivered directly into the hands of manufacturers of cordage and other users of Philippine hemp in the United States for their enrichment.* The cordage interests are prosperous and do not need this help; the Philippine Islands are poor. Legislation which takes money directly from the Philippine treasury and passes it over to a particular industry in the United States is not founded on sound principles of political economy or of justice to the Filipinos. We renew our recommendation for the repeal of this provision.

You also find in the Commission's report for 1906 the usual annual protests against the Dingley tariff on Philippine sugar and tobacco. Said the Honorable Henry C. Ide in an article in the *New York Independent* for November 22, 1906, written shortly after he retired from the office of Governor-General of the Philippines and returned to the United States: "By annexation we killed the Spanish market for Philippine sugar and tobacco, and our tariff shuts these products from the United States market, and to-day both these [industries] are practically prostrated." In their annual report for 1907, the Philippine Commission say with regard to the American corner on Philippine hemp:11 "The price of hemp has fallen from an average of twenty pesos ($10 American money) per picul12 to thirteen pesos per picul." It thus appears that by judicious manipulation of the hemp market at Manila, through the leverage of the refund system, based on collection and subsequent refunding of the export tax on hemp coming to the United States, the Manila agents of the American hemp manufacturers had, as early as 1907, beat the price of hemp down to not far above half of what it had been formerly. To-day (1912) the Filipino hemp farmer gets for his hemp just one half what he got just ten years ago. During all this period of economic depression, the public utterances and State papers both of President Roosevelt and Mr. Taft are full of such preposterous stuff as the following:

No great civilized power has ever managed with such wisdom and disinterestedness the affairs of a people committed by the accident of war to its hands.13

This is what Mr. Roosevelt and Mr. Taft were *publicly pretending* to believe. But at practically the same time, during as dark a year, economically, as the American occupation has seen, 1907, let us see what they were privately admitting to their intimate friends.

In the *North American Review* for January 18, 1907, in an article contributed to that *Review* by the author of this volume, our treatment of the Philippine people, through our Congress, was briefly discussed. The article chanced to attract the attention of Mr. Andrew Carnegie, who gave a considerable sum of money to have it reprinted and distributed. Some correspondence followed between us, in the course of which Mr. Carnegie stated that he had been at the White House shortly before writing me, and described what happened as follows:

When at supper with the President [Mr. Roosevelt] recently, pointing to Judge Taft [then Secretary of War], who sat opposite, he [President Roosevelt] said: "Here are the two men in all the world most anxious to get out of the Philippines."

In another letter Mr. Carnegie described this same incident, this other letter's version of President Roosevelt's supper-table remark being:

Here are the two men in America most anxious to get rid of them [the Philippines].14

Now why all this public boasting about our "disinterestedness," when, if he had been a Filipino, Colonel Roosevelt would probably have hunted up all the American speeches of 1776 about taxation without representation, and played hide-and-seek with the public prosecutor at Manila, to see how far he could violate the sedition statute without getting in jail? And why this private admission to his friend Mr. Carnegie, which neither he nor Mr. Taft has ever publicly made? Why did he not send a message to Congress showing up the hemp rebate system? Simply because to do so would lose support for the Administration, would alienate powerful interests from the fatuous policy of Benevolent Assimilation bequeathed to Mr. Roosevelt by Mr. McKinley. His party was irrevocably committed to indefinite retention of the Islands. It was like Lot's wife. It could not turn back. So the protected and subsidized interests were permitted to continue to prey upon the Philippine people. Tariff evils were never President Roosevelt's specialty. Nor has war against intrenched privilege of any sort ever been Mr. Taft's specialty. Mr. Taft went out to the Philippines in 1907 to open the Philippine Assembly. In 1908 he came back and made a report to President Roosevelt which is as bland as his Winona declaration that the Payne-Aldrich bill is "the best tariff bill the Republican party ever passed." It makes the American reader's heart swell with pious pride at what he is doing for his "little brown brother," in the matter of vaccination, sewers, school-books, and the like. President Roosevelt sent this report to Congress, accompanied by a message, from which we have already quoted. In that same message he said:

I question whether there is a brighter page in the annals of international dealing between the strong and the weak than the page which tells of our doings in the Philippines.

Apparently, Messrs. Roosevelt and Taft thought, in 1907, that granting the Filipinos a little debating society solemnly called a legislative body, but wholly without any real power, was ample compensation for deserted tobacco and cane plantations and for the price of hemp being beat down below the cost of production by manipulation through an Act of Congress passed for the benefit of American hemp manufacturers. If we had had a Cleveland in the White House about that time, he would have written an essay on taxation without representation, with the hemp infamy of this Philippine Tariff Act of 1902 as a text, and sent it to Congress as a message demanding the repeal of the Act. But the good-will of the Hemp Trust is an asset for the policy of Benevolent Assimilation. The Filipino cannot vote, and the cordage manufacturer in the United States can. No conceivable state of economic desolation to which we might reduce the people of the Philippine Islands being other than a blessing in disguise compared with permitting them to attend to their own affairs after their own quaint and mutually considerate fashion, the Hemp Trust's rope, tied into a slip-knot by the Act of 1902, must not be removed from their throats. By judicious manipulation of sufficient hemp rope, you can corral much support for Benevolent Assimilation. Therefore, to this good hour, the substance of the hemp part of the Philippine Tariff Act of March 8, 1902, remains upon the statute books of the United States, to the shame of the nation.

At last, under the Payne tariff law of 1909, Mr. Taft's long and patient quiet work with Congressional committees prevailed upon Congress and the interests to admit Philippine sugar and tobacco to this country free of duty, up to amounts limited in the Act.15 Since then you find the reports of our American officials in the Philippines palpitating with gratitude to Congress. As a matter of fact all Congress had said to the Filipinos by its action may be summed up about thus: "The sugar and tobacco interests of this country have at last realized that such little of the sugar and tobacco you raise as may stray over to this side of the world will not be in the least likely to hurt them. Therefore they have graciously decided, in their benignity, to permit you to live, provided you do not get too prosperous." But this very same Payne bill continued the export tax features of the Act of 1902. Section 13 of the Payne bill is as follows:

Section 13. That upon the exportation to any foreign country from the Philippine Islands, or the shipment thereof to the United States or any of its possessions, of the following articles there shall be levied, collected, and paid thereon the following export duties: *Provided, however,* thatall articles the growth and product of the Philippine Islands coming directly from said islands, to the United States or any of its possessions for use and consumption therein shall be exempt from any export duties imposed in the Philippine Islands:

352. Abaca (hemp), gross weight, 100 kilos, 75 cents.

353. Sugar, gross weight, 100 kilos, 5 cents.

354. Copra, gross weight, 100 kilos, 10 cents.

355. Tobacco, gross weight:

(*a*) Manufactured or unmanufactured, except as otherwise provided, 100 kilos, $1.30.

(*b*) Stems, clippings, and other wastes of tobacco, 100 kilos, 50 cents.

Let us briefly glance at the net results of this law, and its predecessor, the Act of 1902, the export features of which it re-enacted. It is important that every fair-minded American who can possibly spare the time should take such a glance at what Congress has done to the Philippine hemp industry, because of the obvious bearing that such taxation without representation will probably have on the attitude of the Philippine people whenever we get into a war with a foreign power. Certainly the legislation Congress has perpetrated upon them, at the behest of special interests in the United States, has not soothed the original desire of those people to be free and independent.

At page 27 of the report of the Philippine Collector of Customs for 1910, a table is given showing the export duties subject to refund collected under the Act of Congress of March 8, 1902, and deposited in the Philippine treasury to the credit of the Insular Government at the end of each fiscal year (June 30), as follows:

1902 $ 71,064.69

1903 527,228.10

1904 462,433.83

1905 486,475.56

1906 433,991.79

1907 433,458.58

1908 370,513.36

1909 598,917.69

$3,384,083.60

The following table, taken from this same annual report of the Collector of Customs of the Philippines for 1910 (p. 22) shows the size (weight in kilograms), and value, of the annual Philippine hemp crop from

1899 to 1910, both inclusive. It gives in one set of columns the total exported to all countries, and in the other the part which comes to the United States:

	To All Countries.		To United States.	
	Kilos	Value	Kilos	Value
1899	59,840,368	$ 6,185,293	23,066,248	$ 2,436,169
1900	76,708,936	11,393,883	25,763,728	3,446,141
1901	112,215,168	14,453,110	18,157,952	2,402,867
1902	109,968,792	15,841,316	45,526,960	7,261,459
1903	132,241,594	21,701,575	71,654,416	12,314,312
1904	131,817,872	21,794,960	61,886,592	10,631,591
1905	130,621,024	22,146,241	73,351,136	12,954,515
1906	112,165,384	19,446,769	62,045,088	11,168,226
1907	114,701,320	21,085,081	58,388,504	11,326,864
1908	115,829,080	17,311,808	48,813,720	7,684,000
1909	149,991,866	15,883,577	79,210,362	8,534,288
1910	170,788,629	17,404,922	99,305,102	10,399,397

If you have the time and inclination, you can easily figure out the annual "rake-off" of the American hemp importers from the above table. For instance, take the last year, 1910: 99,305,102 kilos at 75 cents per 100 kilos is $744,788.26, which is more than 4% of $17,404,922, the total value of the hemp crop of the archipelago for that year. Add this $744,788.26 to the $3,384,183.60 shown by the above table of refundable duties collected from 1902 to 1909 inclusive, and you have over $4,000,000 rebates accruing to American importers of Manila hemp from 1902 to 1910 inclusive.

In his remarks on Section 13 of the Payne Law of 1909 (above set forth), in the House of Representatives, May 13, 1909,16 Hon. Oscar W. Underwood said, in part:

When you put a tax on your people for engaging in export trade, to that extent you lessen their ability to successfully meet their foreign competitor and reduce the territory in which they can successfully dispose of their surplus products abroad. Our forefathers in writing the Constitution of the United States, recognizing the false principle on which an export tax was based, put it in the fundamental law of our land that the United States Government should not lay export taxes. *If we enact this law, we write into the statute book for the Philippine Islands, legislation which is little short of barbarous, legislation that no government in the civilized world except Turkey, and Persia, and other second-class nations countenance to-day.*

But the hemp interests won out and the section was adopted. In an argument for the repeal of the export tax, delivered in the House of Representatives August 19, 1911, the Philippine delegate, Hon. Manuel L. Quezon, said:

There is one section in the Philippine tariff law, approved August 5, 1909, which is *seriously injuring the proper commercial development of the islands*.

Of course the earnestness with which Mr. Quezon pleaded his cause may be imagined from the circumstance that, as he says, he is continually advised by letters from his people, and verily believes that *if the export tax is not taken off soon the Philippine hemp industry will be entirely destroyed*, and the hemp farmers will have to take to raising something else in lieu of hemp, because the present prices hardly permit them to live. In the course of his speech Mr. Quezon offered the following truly eloquent and absolutely unanswerable argument:

Although it has been decided by the Supreme Court of the United States that the provisions of the Constitution are not in force in the Philippines, I have serious doubts as to whether said decision also meant that this Government has the power to enact laws for the islands which are expressly prohibited by the Constitution in the United States.

It is through the courtesy of Mr. Quezon that such light as I may have been able to throw on the subject has been obtained. He has shown me letters from the Philippine Chamber of Commerce at Manila and other commercial organizations prophesying ruin to the Manila hemp industry in the event the export tax should continue. One of these letters is addressed to the two Philippine Commissioners in Congress, Mr. Legarda and Mr. Quezon. It informs them of the hopes of the Filipinos at Manila that they, Messrs. Legarda and Quezon, may be successful in their campaign to get the law repealed and that many of them (the Filipinos at Manila) feel hopeful of results in that regard. Speaking for their fellow countrymen at Manila, they say, "The optimists are of the opinion that the matter being in such good hands as yours will be carried to a successful conclusion." Then they give the darker side of the picture thus:

But the representatives at this capital of the famous syndicate, the International Harvester Company, are of the opinion that we will be able to accomplish nothing, and theirs is an opinion to which great weight should be attached, because *the vast interests which that concern represents can set in motion powerful influences to keep the present law as it is*, since it concerns their interest to do so.

Mr. Quezon has also shown me a letter written to him, March 30, 1911, by his and my warm personal friend, Hon. James F. Smith, formerly Governor-General of the Philippines, now (1912) Judge of the Court of Customs Appeals at Washington, D. C., in which letter General Smith says, concerning the operation of that part of the export tax act of March 8, 1902 (continued by the Payne Tariff Law of 1909) by which American manufacturers are relieved from the payment of the export tax on Manila hemp:

In effect this really and truly amounts to the payment by the Philippine Government and the Filipino people of a large subsidy to American manufacturers of hemp. More than that, this concession to the American manufacturer, by enabling him to undersell his British competitor, gives him an undue control of the situation and has put him in a position, to some extent, to control prices for the raw product.

It seems to me that the American people had better look to their own liberties, when they remember that in the campaign for the Republican nomination in 1912, the Roosevelt Headquarters gave out that pending the Roosevelt dictation of Mr. Taft's nomination in 1908, the International Harvester Company furnished a floor of its Chicago building to the Taft people, this interesting fact being part of the leakage from the Roosevelt-Taft quarrel caused by the Roosevelt charge that Mr. Taft was unfit for re-election because he "meant well *feebly*"; and when it is recalled, on the other hand, that in the Roosevelt campaign of 1912 for the presidential nomination for a third term, Mr. George W. Perkins,[17] the very personification of undue corporation influence with the Government, assumed the rôle of Warwick for an ex-President who, when President, had repudiated the advice of his counsel, Governor Harmon, that a railroad company[18] be prosecuted for taking rebates*because the vice-president of the company was his personal friend.*[19] But let us return to the Philippine rebates, and their corner-stone, the export tax, Section 13 of the Payne-Aldrich Tariff.

In the case of Fairbanks *vs.* United States, 181 U. S. Supreme Court Reports, page 290, a case in which the court was asked to declare a certain Act of Congress unconstitutional and void, because it imposed what was virtually an export tax, the opinion of the court cites the absolute inhibition against such a tax imposed by our Federal Constitution, and says concerning the wise theory on which this fundamental tenet of our government rests:

The requirement of the Constitution is that exports should be free from any governmental burden.

The decision then goes on to elaborate on what it terms "that freedom from governmental burden in the matter of exports which it was the intention of our Constitution to protect and preserve." Finally, the court uses an expression which is certainly a stinging rebuke to any law-making power that permits the selfish greed of a little set of importers to get a law passed imposing for their special benefit a paralyzing export tax on the chief staple of a helpless colony:

The power to tax is the power to destroy.

But Mr. Quezon has no vote in Congress and his voice was not heard, at least not heeded.

The summation of the whole matter is this: Both the Philippine people and the American people are, and long have been, suffering from unjust taxation through laws for which special selfish financial interests in the United States, exercising grossly undue influence on governmental action, are responsible. Neither will ever get relief until the government of this nation is wrested from the control of the money-hogs and restored to the people. Until that is done, selfish greed will continue to sow sedition in the Philippines, and socialism in the United States.

---

[1] Act 230, U. S. Philippine Commission.

[2] For the convenience of readers who do not constantly use the metric system: A kilo is about 2.25 lbs.

[3] According to what part of archipelago grown.

[4] The Payne law of 1909 continued the export tax, etc.

[5] Dried cocoa-nut meat, used to make soaps and oils. I do not deal with copra because it nearly all goes to Europe, principally to Marseilles.

[6] *Senate Document 200*, 1908, Sixtieth Congress, First Session.

[7] I have myself seen a cloud of locusts three miles long.

8*Report*, U. S. Philippine Commission, 1904, pt. 1, pp. 26–7.

9*Report*, U. S. Philippine Commission, 1905, pt. 1, pp. 72–3.

10Senator Newlands, *North American Review*, December, 1905 . Senator Newlands was one of the party.

11Part 1, p. 99.

12137½ lbs.

13President Roosevelt's message to Congress of January 27, 1908, transmitting report of Secretary of War Taft on the Philippines.

14Before assuming to use these letters in this book, I sent them to Mr. Carnegie and asked his permission to so use them. He returned them to me with his consent entered on the back of one of them.

15300,000 tons of sugar, 150,000,000 cigars, etc.

16*Congressional Record*, May 13, 1909, p. 2009.

17Mr. Perkins is chairman of the Finance Committee of the International Harvester Company, a hundred million dollar corporation owning divers subsidiary companies which make twine and cordage. See MOODY'S MANUAL .

18The Atcheson, Topeka & Santa Fe.

19Paul Morton.

Chapter XXVII. The Rights of Man

The rights of man cannot be changed. It is the government which attempts to change them that must change.—
WEBSTER.

It was the homely common sense of Mr. Lincoln that first reminded us most vividly how like to the sins of an individual are those of a nation. To the Southern man who admires Mr. Lincoln as one of the great figures of all time, he seems like a great physician, who, with malice toward none and with charity for all, kept vigil for four years at the bedside of a sick nation through all the long agony of its efforts to throw off from its system the inherited curse of slavery. Of course, human slavery was a relic of barbarism. But in fixing the Rights of Man, the founders of the Republic actually overlooked the fact that a negro was a human being. So that, vast property rights having accrued pursuant to that mistake, the march of progress had to wipe them out, no matter whom it hurt financially. The enormity of the iniquity of human slavery did not dawn suddenly and exclusively upon William Lloyd Garrison. He is not the sole, original inventor and patentee of the idea. Lord Macaulay's father was doing the same sort of agitating in England about the same time. Westminster Abbey has its monument to the elder Macaulay, just as Commonwealth Avenue has its monument to the elder Garrison. Simultaneous like stirrings occurred elsewhere throughout Christendom. But, of course, in America, arguments for the emancipation of the slave first took root most readily in a thrifty section of our liberty-loving country which had nothing to lose by abolition.

John Quincy Adams once said that our government was "an experiment upon the heart of man." It is because this government of the people by the people for the people was a deliberate and thoughtful attempt upon the part of its founders to apply the Golden Rule as a doctrine of international and inter-individual law, that we believe our form of government is the last hope of mankind. It is, as we conceive it, the voice of humanity raised in protest against the proposition that might makes right. It is, as we conceive it, a government which entered the lists of the nations as the champion of the human mind, in the great struggle of Mind for the mastery over Matter, the world-old struggle between Good and Evil, Light and Darkness. Our government, like everything else, must follow the law of its being, or die. Its first great sin in violation of the Rights of Man was due to heredity. We inherited the institution of slavery, the governmental exception to the rule that all men are created with equal right to life, liberty, and the pursuit of happiness. This was a sin against human liberty, one of the "unalienable" Rights of Man, upon which the Republic purported to be built. The consequences of that sin are still with us; but, except for the occasional bloody-shirt waver, whose intellectual resources are not sufficient to provide him with a live issue, we are meeting those consequences, as a nation, bravely, and with the mutual forbearance born of the fact that none are wholly free from responsibility for present difficulties.

Our second great national sin was a yielding to the temptation of the environment which arose, unforeseen, after a splendid war waged for the Rights of Man against Spain in Cuba. The Philippine war was waged to subjugate the Filipino people, because Mr. McKinley believed it would be financially profitable to us to own the islands, and in the face of the fact that the only thing he knew officially about the Filipino people was that Admiral Dewey thought them superior to the Cubans and more capable of self-government. The war in the Philippines was, therefore, a war against the Rights of Man. Nowhere in any state paper has any American statesman, soldier, or sailor, had the temerity to invoke the name of God in connection with the retention of the Philippine Islands. Nowhere in any American state paper connected with the Philippines is there any reference to "a decent respect to the opinions of mankind." The sin of our Philippine policy is that it is a denial of the right of a people to pursue happiness *in their own way* instead of in *somebody else's* way. It is a denial of the very principles in maintenance of which we went to war against Spain to free Cuba, as we had previously gone to war against England to free ourselves.

Now the reason the nation blundered into taking the Philippines was that it believed the Filipinos to be, not a people, but a jumble of savage tribes. But the reason the men who controlled the action of the government at the time took the Philippines was because they believed they would pay. Nevertheless, there was a sufficient number of our fellow-citizens—controlled, some by altruistic motives and some by sordid motives—to cause the nation to follow the lead of those then in control. If the men then in control had taken the people into their confidence, the blunder would never have been made. If the correspondence between Mr. McKinley and the Paris Peace Commission in the fall of 1898, from which the injunction of secrecy was not removed until 1901, had been given out at the time, the treaty would never have been ratified except after some such declaration as to the Philippines as was made concerning Cuba, some reaffirmance of allegiance to faith in our cardinal tenet—the right of every people to pursue happiness in their own way, free from alien domination. The Bacon resolution of 1899, which was along this line, was defeated only by the deciding vote of the presiding officer, the Vice-President of the United States. The passage of that resolution would have prevented the Philippine Insurrection. Had it passed, the Filipinos would no more have had occasion to think of insurrection than the Cubans did. It was Mr. McKinley alone who decided to take the Philippines. Congress was not called together in extra session. The people were not consulted, except from the rear-end of an observation car.

Most people, whether they be lawyers or not, are more or less acquainted with the doctrine of what is called in law a "*bona fide* purchaser without notice." No man can claim to be a *bona fide* purchaser without notice, when he knows enough about the subject matter of his purchase to put him on reasonable notice of the existence of facts which, had he taken the trouble to verify them, would have caused him to halt and not purchase. The correspondence in 1898, made public in 1901, withheld by Mr. McKinley until after his second election in 1900, is sufficient to have made any honest man ask himself some such question as this: "After all, is it not quite possible that those people *can* run a decent government of their own? Admiral Dewey says they are superior to the Cubans." But Mr. McKinley did not pursue this inquiry, as it was his duty to do. He took the islands because he believed they would pay, knowing nothing in particular about the Filipinos, except what he had learned from Admiral Dewey's brief comment, yet hoping in spite of it that they would turn out sufficiently unfit for self-government for the event to vindicate the purchase. To demonstrate that the Filipinos were wholly unfit for the treatment accorded the Cubans was the only possible justification of the initial departure from the traditions of the Republic and from the principles which were its corner-stone. And he made the departure because the business "interests" of the country then believed—erroneously they all now admit—that it would pay. He decided to treat eternal principles as "worn-out formulæ." Senator Hoar once declined an invitation extended by his own city of Worcester, to deliver a eulogy on Mr. McKinley, because of his Philippine policy. True, he tempers the asperity of this action thus: "It was not because I was behind any other man in admiration or personal affection for that lofty and beautiful character. But * * * if a great Catholic prelate were to die, his eulogy should not be pronounced by a Protestant."[1] But all Senator Hoar's speeches against the McKinley Philippine policy were as emphatic as Luther's ninety-five theses. He was in possession at the time, along with the rest of the Senate, of the correspondence with the Paris Peace Commission made public after the presidential election of 1900.

Ever since Mr. McKinley took the Philippines, it has been the awkward but inexorable duty of the defenders of that good man's fame to deprecate Filipino capacity for self-government. President Taft's chief life-work since this century began has been to take care of his martyred predecessor's fame, by proving that Mr. McKinley guessed right in 1898 when he bought the Philippines and trusted to luck to be able to make out, in spite of what Admiral Dewey had said, a case sufficiently derogatory to Filipino intelligence to justify the purchase and subjugation of the islands at the very time we were freeing Cuba. Obviously, then, the more utterly unfit for self-government in the present or the near future Mr. Taft can make the Filipinos out, the nearer he gets to vindicating the memory of Mr. McKinley, that is, with men of his own, (Mr. Taft's) high character. He insists on treating as children a people who got up a well-armed army of thirty-odd thousand men in three or four months and held at bay, for two years and a half, some 125,000 husky American soldiers, over five times as many as it took to drive Spain from the Western hemisphere. Physical force is the basis of all government among men. If President Taft had anything of the soldier instinct of his immediate predecessor, he would not sniff demagoguery in the proposition that military efficiency is a better guaranty of capacity for self-government than all the school-books in the world, and that proven passionate willingness to die for freedom from alien domination is the best guaranty conceivable against internecine strife. It was a tremendous struggle with his own conscience that Mr. McKinley went through with before he decided to repudiate the principles on which we took Cuba in order, for a money consideration euphemistically called "trade expansion," to take the Philippines. He had advices before him at the time making it reasonably certain that this meant trouble with the Filipinos, i.e., bloodshed in the Philippines, the extent of which none could foresee, and about which he was of course apprehensive. In the matter of instructing our Paris Peace Commissioners to insist on Spain's ceding us the Philippines, Mr. McKinley took no moral ground tenable like a rock, such as truly great men take in great crises of their country's history. He did not attempt to lead the people. He simply decided that it would be a *popular* thing to do to take the islands. Fresh from a war entered upon to emancipate the Cubans from alien domination, he took a step which both Admiral Dewey and General Merritt warned him beforehand would probably mean war—to subjugate, against their will, a people superior to the Cubans. And in taking this step, he took into his confidence, neither the people who paid for the war, nor the soldiers who fought it. To deny that his motives were benevolent would be simply stupid. But he followed the mob which shouted from the rear-end of his observation car and repeated by cable to the Paris Peace Commission, what the mob yelled. Ever since the supposed Philippine Klondyke whispered in President McKinley's ear "Eat of the imperial fruits of a colonial policy," the archives of this government—the reports of the State, War, and Navy Departments, and the Congressional Documents—have reeked with the inevitable consequences of our fall from our high estate. No man can serve two masters. Philanthropy for pecuniary profit is a paradox. Duplicity ever follows deviation from principle. In our dealings in 1898 with Aguinaldo you find vacillation on the part of military commanders who personally did not know what fear was, and embarrassed hypocrisy in dealing with him on the part of men wearing the shoulder-straps of the American army, athwart the frankness of whose gaze no such shadow had ever fallen before. You find systematic concealment of our intentions in dealing with the insurgents, for fear they would insurge before the Treaty was signed, and thus cause such a revulsion of feeling in *our* country against the purchase of *theirs* as to defeat the ratification of the treaty. After that, you find a systematic minimizing of the opposition to our rule, reinforced by subtle depreciation of Filipino intelligence, and backed up by a "peace-at-any-price" policy, periodically punctuated by the horrors of war without its dignity. The denial of Filipino opposition to our rule, which opposition means merely a natural longing for freedom from alien rule, has gradually been abandoned. Nobody now clings to that stale fiction. Also, a long course of chastening, through reconcentration and kindred severities subsequent to the official announcement of a state of general peace, has at last gotten the situation as to public order well in hand. The only question for those who affect that "decent respect to the opinions of mankind" which the men of 1776 had in mind is, "Are the Filipinos a people?" President Taft was originally with Senator Hoar on the Philippine question. At least he was an "anti-expansionist." In all the heat of subsequent controversy he has never made bold to deny the general proposition of the unalienable right of every people to liberty and the pursuit of happiness in their own way. His position is that the Filipino people must be made an exception to the rule because they are not *a people*. This is the strongest I can state his proposition for him. It is very difficult to state even with apparent plausibility, anything which denies the right of every community of people to immunity from alien domination. The case must be an extreme one. The issue which the writer raises with the President's policy is that the Filipinos *are* a people.

I know of no graver responsibility that an American statesman can take upon himself before the bar of history than to deny the right of any given people to self-government. Certainly any man who denies that right at least assumes the burden of proof that they are unfit to attend to their own affairs. Mr. McKinley assumed it without pretending to know anything much about the Filipinos, the motive being that the Islands would be profitable to us. When Mr. Taft went to the Philippines in 1900, he went, not to investigate the correctness of Mr. McKinley's assumption, which was implied in the purchase, but to champion it; not to give advice concerning the righteousness of having taken over the Philippines, but to bolster up the policy. He assumed the burden of proof before he knew anything about the facts. The burden has been on him ever since. Any subordinate who helps him to bear that burden, finds favor in his eyes. But the burden is greater than he can bear. The proof fails. The proof shows that the Filipino people ought to be allowed to pursue happiness in their own way instead of being made to pursue it in Mr. Taft's way. Once you pretend that our true object in the Philippines is the "pursuit of happiness" for them, The Taft policy is condemned by the facts; and that is why I am opposed to it. The record shows this. He admits it. But he insists, with a sigh, that in some other generation they will be happy. Meantime, we are drifting toward our next war carrying in tow 8,000,000 of human beings who, if neutralized and let alone would not be disturbed by our next war, but whose destinies now must be dependent upon the outcome of such war, however little they may be concerned in the issues which bring it about.

The shifty opportunism which once actually held out to the Filipinos the hope of some day becoming a State of the United States of America, has long since lapsed into the silence of shame, because no American ever honestly believed that the American people would ever countenance any such preposterous proposition. And so a free republic based on representative government is face to face with the proposition of having a "crown colony" on its hands which wishes to be, and could soon be made fit to be, a free republic also.

If a federal republic cannot live half slave and half free, can it live with millions of the governed denied a voice in the federal government confessedly forever?

---

1 *Autobiography of Seventy Years*, vol. ii., p. 317.

Chapter XXVIII. The Road to Autonomy

Oh be ye not dismayed
Though ye stumbled and ye strayed.

KIPLING —*A Song of the English.*

He who points out a wrong without being prepared to suggest a remedy presumes upon the patience of his neighbor without good and sufficient cause. Up to this point the wrong has been unfolded, with such ability as was vouchsafed the narrator, "from Genesis to Revelations," so to speak; also his own attitude as an eye-witness, and its evolution from the Mosaic doctrine of an eye for an eye and a tooth for a tooth, to the more Christian doctrines of the New Testament. Let us now consider the remedy.

In the course of our travels with the army in the earlier chapters of this book, we first followed its northern advance, from Manila over the great central plain drained by the Rio Grande and crossed by the railroad connecting Manila Bay with Lingayen Gulf; its further advance from the northern borders of the plain over the mountains of Central Luzon; and its march from the central mountains to the northern sea, at the extreme northern end of the archipelago. We thus saw in detail the military conquest and occupation of that part of Luzon lying north of the Pasig River. Before leaving that part of the subject, the way the provinces thus occupied were grouped into military districts was indicated. Following the lines of the military occupation, it was shown that Northern Luzon was naturally and conveniently susceptible of division into four groups of provinces, which groups might ultimately be evolved into self-governing commonwealths—States of a Philippine Federal Union, as follows:

Name of State	Area (sq. m.)	Population
Ilocos[1]	6,500	650,000
Cagayan[2]	12,000	300,000
Pangasinan[3]	4,500	625,000
Pampamga[4]	5,000	650,000
Total	28,000	2,225,000

It will be remembered that after our narrative had followed the occupation of Northern Luzon by the American forces to practical completion, we turned to that part of Luzon lying south of Manila, and followed the military occupation as it was gradually extended from the Pasig River to the extreme point of Southern Luzon. Before closing the review of that military panorama, suggestions were made for an ultimate grouping of the provinces of Southern Luzon into two governmental units intended to be ultimately evolved into states. Those suggestions contemplated grouping the provinces of the lake region bordering on the Laguna de Bay and the adjacent provinces, into a territory designated for convenience as Cavite.5 This territory was to include all of Southern Luzon except the hemp peninsula, which lies to the south of the Lake country. It was also suggested in the same connection that the three provinces of the hemp peninsula might form a convenient ultimate State of Camarines. In other words, two states can be made out of Southern Luzon as follows:

Name of State	Area (sq. m.)	Population
Cavite	8,500	700,000
Camarines	7,000	600,000
Total	15,500	1,300,000

To recapitulate: All of Luzon except Manila and the vicinity can at once be divided into the six groups of provinces above mentioned—"territories," having what we are accustomed in the United States to call a "territorial form of government," and intended to be made states later. Luzon is about the size of Cuba (a little over 40,000 sq. miles), is twice as thickly populated (nearly 4,000,000 to Cuba's 2,000,000), and is not cursed with a negro question, as Cuba is.

The above totals, be it remembered, are only round numbers, but they get us "out of the woods" so to speak, and away from a lot of unpronounceable names. They show you how to handle Luzon as if it were about the size of Ohio—which it is. And, as has already been made clear in the earlier part of this volume, Luzon "*is*" the Philippines, in a very suggestive sense of the phrase, since it contains half the land area of the archipelago (outside of the Mohammedan island of Mindanao), and half the total population of the whole archipelago, besides being eight or ten times as large as any other island of the group except Mindanao; and it also contains the city which is the capital and chief port of the archipelago, and has been the seat of government for over three hundred years—Manila. And Manila is eight or ten times as large as any other town in the archipelago.

After the occupation of Luzon, General Otis's extension of our occupation to the Visayan islands was reviewed, and in that connection it was pointed out that each of the six largest of those islands to wit, Panay, Negros, Cebu, Leyte, Samar, Bohol, might be ultimately evolved into six states.6

The smaller islands lying between Luzon and Mindanao could easily be disposed of governmentally by being attached to the jurisdiction of one of the said six islands.

There is to-day no reason why a dozen Americans could not be at once appointed governors of the twelve prospective autonomous commonwealths above indicated, just as the President of the United States has in the past appointed governors for New Mexico, Arizona, and other territories of the United States which have subsequently been admitted to the Union. If the Congress of the United States should promise the Filipinos independence, to be granted as soon as American authority in the Islands should so recommend, the dozen territorial governments intended to be evolved into states of an ultimate federal union could soon be whipped into shape where they could take care of themselves to the extent that our state governments to-day take care of themselves. American representatives of American authority in the Islands, sent out to work out such a programme, might be instructed to watch these twelve territorial governments, granting to each the right to elect a governor in lieu of the appointed governor as soon as in their judgment a given territory was worthy of it. I have no doubt that such recommendations would follow successively as to all of said prospective states inside of four or five years. Whether this plan is wise or not, it certainly is not, as far as I am concerned, "half baked." Some five years ago, in the *North American Review*,[7] I suggested that Luzon could be so organized within less than ten years by American territorial governors selected for the work, naming the Honorable George Curry of New Mexico, formerly Governor of the territory of New Mexico, and now a member of Congress therefrom, as an ideal man to organize one such territory. It is true that there are not eleven other men as well qualified for the work as Governor Curry. In fact he is probably better qualified for the work than any man living. The language used as to Governor Curry in the *North American Review* article referred to was as follows:

If the inhabitants of these regions were told by a man whom they liked and would believe, as they would Curry, that they were to have autonomous governments like one of the Western Territories of the United States, at the very earliest possible moment, and urged to get ready for it, they could and would, under his guidance. We would get a co-operation from those people we do not now get and never will get, so long as we keep them in uncertainty as to what we are going to do with them. If next year we should formally disclaim intention to retain the islands permanently, and set to work to create autonomous Territories destined ultimately to be States of a Federated Philippine Republic, whenever fit, we would soon see the way out of this tangle, and behold the beginning of the end of it.

Whenever the twelve territorial governments should be gotten into smooth working order under elected native governors, the Philippine archipelago would then be *nearly* ready for independence, so far as its internal affairs are concerned. The danger of their being annexed on the first pretext by some one of the great land-grabbing powers should be met by our guaranteeing them their independence, as we do Cuba, until they could be protected by neutralization treaties, such as protect Belgium and Switzerland to-day, as explained in the chapter which follows this. Powers not specifically granted to the several states-in-embryo should of course, until the final grant of independence, be reserved to the central government at Manila. Manila and Rizal province would be available at almost any time as a thirteenth state. So that when the twelve states above suggested had shown themselves capable of local self-government, Manila and Rizal province might be added to make the final one of thirteen original states of a Philippine Republic.

Any American who has seen a Filipino *pueblo* transformed, as if by magic, from listless apathy to a state of buzzing and busy enthusiasm suggestive of a bee-hive, by preparations for some church *fiesta*, or for the coming of some dignitary from Manila, has seen something analogous to what would happen if the Filipino body politic should suddenly be electrified by a promise of independence under some such programme as the above. A generous rivalry would at once ensue all over the archipelago in each of the twelve prospective states. Each would seek to be the first to be recommended by American authority as ready for statehood. I do not believe the annals of national experience contain any analogy where every member of a given community has rallied to a common cause more completely than the whole Filipino people would rally to such a prospective programme of independence. The unanimity would be as absolute as the kind we saw among the American people at the outbreak of the Spanish War, when Congress one fine morning placed fifty millions of dollars at the disposal of President McKinley by a unanimous vote.

I especially invite attention to the fact that the above programme throws away nothing that has been done by us in the Islands in the last twelve years in the way of organization. It simply takes it and builds upon it. Congress should not attempt to work out the details from this end of the line. We should send men out there from here to work them out, with local co-operation from the leading Filipinos. Men animated by the idea of working out a programme under which *the living* may hope to see the independence of their country, should be sent out to take the place of the men now there who are irrevocably committed to the programme of indefinite retention with undeclared intention, which holds out no hope to the living. It is not wise to arrange the details of the programme by act of Congress without a year or two of study of the situation by such men *on the ground*. An act of Congress which goes into details before getting the recommendations of such men will inevitably set up a lot of straw men easy for the other side to knock down. All you need is a program, sanctioned by Congress, containing a promise of independence, and men sent out to the islands to work out the program. They would report back from time to time, and the Congress by whose authority they went out would have no hesitation in being guided by their recommendations. If unpatriotic greed for office among the Filipinos, or other opposition animated by evil motives, should block the game, your Americans so sent out would have to recommend the calling of a halt. This ever-present shadow in the background would in turn throw the shadow of ostracism over all demagogues.

Meantime the Filipinos should be given a Senate, or upper house, in which, the thirteen prospective "states" should be represented by two men, the bill therefor to be framed out there, and sent back here to Congress for approval. This would give them under the plan here suggested, as soon as the Americans sent out should so recommend, a Senate of twenty-six members. At present, if the native Assembly, or lower house, does not pass the annual appropriations necessary to run the government, the appropriation act of the preceding year again becomes law. At present, the upper house is the Philippine Commission. By withholding its consent, it can prevent any legislation whatsoever. So, at present, the Assembly is little more than a debating society. All questions as to appropriations, veto of legislation, and other details, in the event the Filipinos are given a Senate also, should be left to be fixed in the bill recommended by the men sent out to work out the program of promise.

On March 20, 1912, Honorable W. A. Jones, the distinguished veteran Congressman from Virginia, who is Chairman of the Committee on Insular Affairs, introduced in the House of Representatives a bill entitled "A bill to establish a qualified independence for the Philippines, and to fix the date when such qualified independence shall become absolute and complete." The greater part of what precedes this paragraph of this chapter was written prior to March 20, 1912. Mr. Jones's bill works out the details of the independence problem in a manner somewhat different from the plan I suggest, but that does not make me any the less heartily in favor of the principle which his bill embodies. The supreme virtue of the Jones bill is that it promises Independence at a fixed date, July 4, 1921. It ends the cruel uncertainty, so unjust to both the Filipinos and to the Americans in the Philippines, that is contained in the present program of indefinite retention with undeclared intention. Five years ago, in the *North American Review* for January 18, and June 21, 1907, the writer hereof expressed the belief that an earlier date was feasible, thus:

If three strong and able men, familiar with insular conditions, and still young enough to undertake the tasks were told by a President of the United States, by authority of the Congress, "Go out there and set up a respectable native government in ten years, and then come away," they could and would do it, and that government would be a success; and one of the greatest moral victories in the annals of free government would have been written by the gentlemen concerned upon the pages of their country's history.

As Mr. Jones's bill allows four years more of time, I believe it to be absolutely safe.

Governor Curry, the Congressman from New Mexico hereinabove mentioned, who spent eight years in the Philippines, agrees with the fundamental principle of the Jones bill, that as to making a definite promise of Independence within a few years, and does not consider 1921 too early.

Under the present law, the Philippine Assembly has some eighty members, each supposed to represent 90,000 people, more or less. This tallies, roughly, with the census total of population, which is 7,600,000.9 Under the existing law in the Philippines, the qualifications for voting are really of two kinds, though nominally of three kinds. There is a property qualification, and there is an educational qualification. In any case, in order to vote, the individual must be twenty-one years old, and must have lived for six months in the place where he offers to vote. The property qualification requires that the would-be voter own at least $250 worth of property, or pay a tax to the amount of $15. The explanation of how a man may not own $250 worth of property and yet pay $15 taxes is that under the old Spanish system, which we partially adopted, a man might pay such *cedula* or poll-tax as he preferred, according to a graduated scale, certain civic rights being accorded to those voluntarily paying the higher poll-tax which were denied to those paying less. The educational qualification requires the would-be voter to speak, read, and write either English or Spanish, or else to have held certain enumerated small municipal offices under the Spaniards—before the American occupation. Mr. Jones's bill proposes to add the speaking, reading, and writing of the native dialect of a given locality10 to the educational qualification. This would double, or perhaps triple, the electorate, and would, in my judgment, be wise. Thousands upon thousands of natives who only *speak* a little Spanish can both *speak, read, and write* their native Tagalo, Ilocano, or Visayan, as the case may be. The total of those qualified to vote for members of the Assembly in 1907 was only about 100,000. At a later election, that number was doubled. If there are 7,500,000 people in the archipelago, one fifth of these should represent the adult male population, say 1,500,000. Under Mr. Jones's bill, the electorate would probably increase to half a million long before the date he proposes for independence, July 4, 1921. But all such details as qualification for voting might, it seems to me, be left to people on the ground, their recommendations controlling. Under a promise of independence by 1921, a very fair electorate of at least one third, possibly one half, of the adult male population, could be built up. As the majority report on the Jones Bill, dated April 26, 1912, says:

For nearly ten years the average public-school enrolment has not been less than 500,000.11

I believe that the Moros should be left as they are for the present. The time for solving that problem has not yet been reached. Mr. Jones himself evidently bases his idea of allowing the Moro country representation in the Philippine Congress, or legislature provided by his bill, on the probability that enough Christian people will vote, down there, to make up an electorate that would not be "impossible," *i.e.*, absurd. For instance, he tells me that a great many people have moved into Mindanao from the northern islands for commercial reasons, and, if I recollect correctly, that Zamboanga, the most beautiful little port in Mindanao, which hardly had 10,000 people when I was there, now has possibly 50,000. But the Moro question need not stand in the way of setting up an independent government in the Philippines in 1921, as proposed by his bill. You have material for thirteen original states, representing a population of nearly seven million Christian people, in Luzon and the six main Visayan Islands. Why delay the creation of this republic on account of 250,000 semi-civilized, crudely Mohammedan Moros in Mindanao—a separate island lying off to the south of the proposed republic?12 A happy solution of the matter would be to send Mr. Jones out there as Governor-General and let him work out the problem on the ground. He has had a long and distinguished career in the public service, twenty-two years in Congress. His public record and speeches on the Philippine question from the beginning would make him to the Filipinos the very incarnation of a *bona fide* intention on our part to give them their independence at the earliest practical moment, that is, at some time which *the living* might hope to see. When Governor

Taft and Mr. Root drew the Philippine Government Act of 1902, the former had already been president of the Philippine Commission for two years, had been all over the archipelago, and knew it well. Suppose the Taft policy should be substituted by the more progressive Jones policy. Mr. Jones, or whoever is to change the policy, ought to have as much acquaintance with the subject, acquired on the ground, as Mr. Taft had when he formulated his policy of indefinite retention with undeclared intention. The nucleus of the Taft policy was stated by Governor Taft to the Senate Committee in 1902, as follows13:

My own judgment is that the best policy, if a policy is to be declared at all, is to declare the intention of the United States to hold the islands indefinitely, until the people shall show themselves fit for self-government, under a gradually increasing popular government, when their relation to the United States, either of statehood, or of quasi-independence, like the colony of Australia or Canada, can be declared after mutual conference.

The policy which Mr. Jones has favored for the last twelve years is almost as well known to the Filipinos as are the views of Mr. Taft himself.

In conclusion, the writer desires to say, with especial emphasis, that the suggestions outlining the plan which forms the bulk of this chapter are presented in a spirit of entire deference to the views of any one else who may have considered this great subject carefully, especially to the views of Mr. Jones, whose bill is so entirely right in principle. The one supreme need of the situation is a definite legislative declaration which shall make clear to all concerned—to the Filipino demagogue and the American grafter, as well as to the great body of the good people of both races out there—that the governing of a remote and alien people is to have no permanent place in the purposes of our national life; and that we do *bona fide* intend to give the Filipinos their independence at a date in the future which will interest *the living*, by extending to *the living* the hope to see the independence of their country. And the Jones Bill does that.

1P. 252, *ante*.

2P. 255.

3P. 258.

4Pp. 258–9.

5The name is immaterial, but the grouping is convenient and practicable, though not the only grouping practicable.

6*See* p. 267, *ante*.

7For June 21, 1907.

8In the article quoted from I named three men, adding "or any three men of like calibre." One of the three was Justice Adam C. Carson, of the Philippine Supreme Court, who has been a member of the Philippine Judiciary since the Taft Civil Government was founded in 1901. If this book has gained for me any character in the estimation of any reader who is or may hereafter be clothed with authority, I desire to say here, on the very highest public grounds, that, in my judgment, Judge Carson is the most considerable man we have out there now (1912)—a good man to have in an emergency. Though not as learned in the law as his colleague, Justice Johnson—who is quite the equal, as a jurist, of most of the Federal judges I know in the United States, Judge Carson is a man of great breadth of view, and is peculiarly endowed with capacity to handle men and situations effectively and patriotically.

9Says the census of the Philippines of 1903, vol. ii., p. 15: "The total population of the Philippine Archipelago on March 2, 1903, was 7,635,426. Of this number, 6,987,686 enjoyed a considerable degree of civilization, while the remainder, 647,740, consisted of wild people." By this same Census, the Moros are classified as uncivilized, and the population of the island on which they live,

Mindanao, is given at about 500,000 (499,634, vol. ii., p. 126), of which about half only (252,940) are Moros, the rest being civilized. The total of the uncivilized people of the archipelago, according to the Census, is 647,740 (vol. ii., p. 123), less than 400,000, leaving out the Moros.

10 Tagalo, Ilocano, and Visayan are the three main dialects that have been evolved into written language by the patience of the Spanish priests in the last couple of hundred years or so. Probably five sixths of the people of the archipelago speak some one of these three dialects. In fact they can hardly be called "dialects," for there are plenty of books—novels, plays, grammars, histories, dictionaries, etc.—written in Tagalo, Ilocano, or Visayan. Every educated Filipino of the well-to-do classes grows up speaking Spanish and the dialect of his native province, while the latter is the only language spoken by the less fortunate people of his neighborhood, the poorer classes.

11 This report is numbered Report 606, 62d Cong., 2d Sess., and accompanies H. R. 22143 (the Jones Bill).

12 According to the *American Census of the Philippines*, of 1903, the total population of Mindanao is 499,634 (see vol. ii., p. 126), of which 252,940 are Moros, and the rest civilized. In addition to said 252,940 Moros on Mindanao, the adjacent islets contain some 25,000 Moros.

13 See *Senate Document* 331, 1902, p. 339.

Chapter XXIX. The Way Out

Respect for the perpetual neutrality of Switzerland has now taken such lodgment in the conscience of Europe that its violation would inevitably provoke a storm of indignation.

M. DE MARTENS in the *Revue des Deux Mondes*.

On March 25, 1912, Honorable W. A. Jones, of Virginia, Chairman of the House Committee on Insular Affairs, introduced a resolution (*H. J. 278*) proposing the neutralization of the Philippines, to accompany his Philippine Independence Bill discussed in the preceding chapter. Such a resolution, accompanying such a bill, both introduced by one of the majority leaders in the House of Representatives, lifts the question of Philippine neutralization out of the region of the "academic," and brings it forward as a thing which must, sooner or later, command the serious consideration both of Congress and the country. There have been many such resolutions before that of Mr. Jones. But they are all the same in principle. All contemplate our guaranteeing the Filipinos their independence until the treaties they propose shall be consummated. In 1911, there were at least nine such resolutions proposing neutralization of the Philippines, introduced by the following named gentlemen, the first a Republican, the rest Democrats:

Mr. McCall, of Massachusetts; Mr. Cline, of Indiana; Mr. Sabath, of Illinois; Mr. Garner, of Texas; Mr. Peters, of Massachusetts; Mr. Martin, of Colorado; Mr. Burgess, of Texas; Mr. Oldfield, of Arkansas; and Mr. Ferris, of Oklahoma.

Because the neutralization plan to provide against the Philippines being annexed by some other Power in case we ever give them their independence would, if successfully worked out, reduce by that much the possible area of war, and be a distinct step in the direction of universal peace, it is certainly worthy of careful consideration by the enlightened judgment of the Congress and the world.

Mr. McCall is the father of the neutralization idea, so far as the House of Representatives is concerned, application of it to the Philippines having been first suggested at the Universal Peace Conference of 1904, by Mr. Erving Winslow, of Boston. Mr. McCall has been introducing his neutralization resolution at every Congress for a number of Congresses past.

The McCall Resolution (*H. J. Res. 107*) is the oldest, and perhaps the simplest, of the various pending resolutions for the neutralization of the Philippines, and is typical of all. It reads:

JOINT RESOLUTION

Declaring the purpose of the United States to recognize the independence of the Filipino people as soon as a stable government can be established, and requesting the President to open negotiations for the neutralization of the Philippine Islands.

Resolved by the Senate and House of Representatives of the United States of America in Congress assembled:

That in accordance with the principles upon which its government is founded and which were again asserted by it at the outbreak of the war with Spain, the United States declares that the Filipino people of right ought to be free and independent, and announces its purpose to recognize their independence as soon as a stable government, republican in form, can be established by them, and thereupon to transfer to such government all its rights in the Philippine Islands upon terms which shall be reasonable and just, and to leave the sovereignty and control of their country to the Filipino people.

Resolved, That the President of the United States be, and he hereby is, requested to open negotiations with such foreign Powers as in his opinion should be parties to the compact for the neutralization of the Philippine Islands by international agreement.

If the McCall Resolution, or any one of the kindred resolutions, were passed, and complied with by the President of the United States, and accepted by the other Powers, and the Filipinos were helped to organize territorial governments such as Arizona and New Mexico were before they became States, several such territories could form the nucleus about which to begin to build at once, as indicated in the chapter on "The Road to Autonomy." A number of such territories could be made at once as completely autonomous as the governments of the territories of Arizona and New Mexico were before their admission to our Union. With those examples to emulate, together with the tingling of the general blood that would follow a promise of independence and a national life of their own, similar territorial governments could be successively organized, as indicated in the preceding chapter, throughout the archipelago. These could, in less than ten years, be fitted for admission to a federal union of autonomous territories, with the string of our sovereignty still tied to it, and an American Governor-General still over the whole, as now. And when the last island knocked for admission and was admitted, the string could be cut, and the Federal Union of Territories admitted, through our good offices, to the sisterhood of nations, as an independent Philippine republic. They would not bother the rest of the world any more than Belgium and Switzerland do, which are likewise protected by neutralization.

The idea of international neutralization is not without pride of ancestry or hope of posterity. It was born out of the downfall of Napoleon I. The Treaty of Paris of 1815 declared that

the neutrality and inviolability of Switzerland, as well as its independence of outside influences, are in conformity with the true interests of European politics.

The Congress of Vienna, held afterwards in the same year, at which there were present, besides the various monarchs, such men as Wellington, Talleyrand, and Metternich, solemnly and finally reiterated that declaration. Would not "the neutrality and inviolability" of the Philippines be gladly acceded to by the great Powers as being "in conformity with the true interests of European politics," and Asiatic politics as well?

Says M. De Martens, in an article in the *Revue des Deux Mondes* for November 15, 1903:

Respect for the perpetual neutrality of Switzerland has now taken such lodgment in the conscience of the civilized nations of Europe that its violation would inevitably provoke a storm of indignation.

At present, the Philippines are a potential apple of discord thrown into the Balance of Power in the Pacific. The present policy of indefinite retention by us, with undeclared intention, leaves everybody guessing, including ourselves. Now is the accepted time, while the horizon of the future is absolutely cloudless, to ask Japan to sign a treaty agreeing not to annex the Philippine Islands after we give them their independence. By her answer she will show her hand. The overcrowded monarchies do not pretend any special scruples about annexing anything annexable. Germany very frankly insists that she became a great Power too late to get her rightful share of the earth's surface, and that she *must* expand somewhither. And only the virile menace of the Monroe Doctrine has so far stayed her heavy hand from seizing some portion of South America. But probably none of the Powers would object to converting the Philippines into permanently neutral territory, by the same kind of an agreement that protects Switzerland.

The Treaty of London of 1831, relative to Belgium and Holland, declares:

Within the limits indicated, Belgium shall form an independent and perpetually neutral state. She shall be required to observe this same neutrality toward all the other states.

The signatories to this treaty were Great Britain, France, Austria, Prussia, and Russia. Forty years after it was made, during the Franco-Prussian war, when Belgium's neutrality was threatened by manifestations of intention on the part both of France and of Prussia to occupy some of her territory, England served notice on both parties to the conflict that if either violated the territorial integrity of Belgium, she, England, would join forces with the other. And the treaty was observed. The specific way in which observance of it was compassed was this: Great Britain made representations to both France and Germany which resulted in two identical conventions, signed in August, 1870, at Paris and Berlin, whereby any act of aggression by either against Belgium was to be followed by England's joining forces with the other against the aggressor. So long as human nature does not change very materially, "the green-eyed monster" will remain a powerful factor in human affairs. The mutual jealousy of the Powers will always be the saving grace, in troubled times, of neutralization treaties signed in time of profound peace. If "Balance of Power" considerations in Europe have protected the Turkish Empire from annexation or dismemberment all these years, without a neutralization treaty, why will not the mutual jealousy of the Powers insure the signing and faithful observance of a treaty tending to preserve the Balance of Power in the Pacific? Who would object?

The Panama Canal is to be opened in 1913. We want South America to be a real friend to the Monroe Doctrine, which she certainly is not enthusiastic about now, and will never be while we remain wedded to the McKinley Doctrine of Benevolent Assimilation of unconsenting people—people anxious to develop, under God, along their own lines. In 1906, while Secretary of State of the United States, Mr. Root made a tour of South America. He told those people down there, at Rio Janeiro, by way of quieting their fears lest we may some day be moved to "improve" *their* condition also, through benevolent assimilation and vigorous application of the "uplift" treatment:

We wish for * * * no territory except our own. We deem the independence and equal rights of the smallest and weakest member of the family of nations entitled to as much respect as those of the greatest empire, and we deem the observance of that respect the chief guaranty of the weak against the oppression of the strong.

That Rio Janeiro speech of Mr. Root's is as noble a masterpiece of real eloquence, its setting and all considered, as any utterance of any statesman of modern times. Among other things, he said:

No student of our times can fail to see that not America alone but the whole civilized world is swinging away from its old governmental moorings and intrusting the fate of its civilization to the capacity of the popular mass to govern. By this pathway mankind is to travel, whithersoever it leads. *Upon the success of this, our great undertaking, the hope of humanity depends.*

As Secretary of War, "civilizing with a Krag," Mr. Root reminds one of Cortez and Pizarro. As Secretary of State, he permits us to believe that all the great men are not dead yet.

If, in making that Rio Janeiro speech, Mr. Root laid to his soul the flattering unction that the minds of his hearers did not revert dubiously to his previous grim missionary work in the Philippines, where the percentage of literacy is superior to that of more than one Latin-American republic, he is very much mistaken. If he is laboring under any such delusion, let him read a book written since then by a distinguished South American publicist, called *El Porvenir de La Americana Latina* ("The Future of Latin America"). If he does not read Spanish, he can divine the contents of the book from the cartoon which adorns the title-page. The cartoon represents the American eagle, flag in claw, standing on the map of North America, looking toward South America as if ready for flight, its beak bent over Panama, the shadow of its wings already darkening the northern portions of the sister continent to the south of us. To get the trade of South America, in the mighty struggle for commercial supremacy which is to follow the opening of the Panama Canal, we must win the confidence of South America. We will never do it until we do the right thing by the Filipinos. Concerning the Philippines, South America reflects that we annexed the first supposedly rich non-contiguous Spanish country we ever had a chance to annex that we had not previously solemnly vowed we would not annex. We must choose between the Monroe Doctrine of mutually respectful Fraternal Relation, which contemplates some twenty-one mutually trustful republics in the Western Hemisphere, all a unit against alien colonization here, and the McKinley Doctrine of grossly patronizing Benevolent Assimilation, which contemplates some 8,000,000 of people in the Eastern Hemisphere, all a unit against alien colonization there—a people, moreover, whose friendship we have cultivated with the Gatling gun and the gallows, and watered with tariff and other legislation enacted without knowledge and used without shame.

We should stop running a kindergarten for adults in Asia, and get back to the Monroe Doctrine. There are only two hemispheres to a sphere, and our manifest destiny lies in the Western one. We do not want the earth. Our mission as a nation is to conserve the republican form of government, and the consent-of-the-governed principle, and to promote the general peace of mankind by insuring it in our half of the earth. The first thing to do to set this country right again is to get rid of the Philippines, and give them a square deal, pursuant to the spirit of the neutralization resolutions now pending before Congress. All these resolutions contain the one supreme need of the hour, an honest declaration of intention. The longer we fight shy of that, the less likely we are ever to give the Filipinos their independence, and the deeper we get into the mire of mistaken philanthropy and covert exploitation.

We should resume our original programme of blazing out the path and making clear the way up which any nation of the earth may follow when it will. That path lies along the line of actually attempting as a nation a practical demonstration of the Power of Righteousness, or, in other words, the existence of an Omnipotent Omniscient Benevolent Good (whether you spell it with one *o* or with two is not important) shaping, guiding, and directing human affairs, such demonstration to be made through the concerted action of a self-governing people under a written Constitution based on equality of opportunity and the Golden Rule.

As a people we are very young yet. It is not yet written in the Book of Time how long this nation will survive. So far, our government is only an experiment. But, as John Quincy Adams once said, it and its Constitution are "an experiment upon the human heart," to see whether or not the Golden Rule will work in government among men.

ILLUSTRATIONS

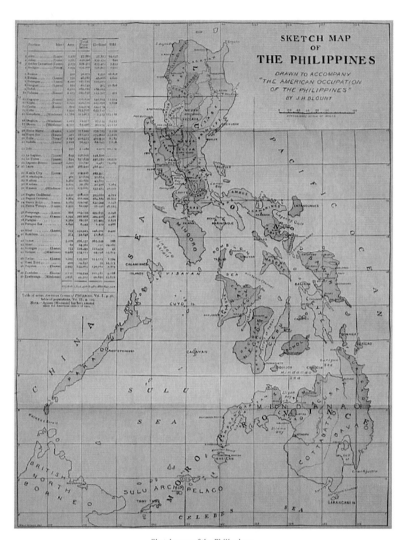

Sketch map of the Philippines.

The capture of Aguinaldo, March 22, 1901. The central fact of the American military occupation.

Manufactured by Amazon.ca
Acheson, AB

14010457R00168